A REFERENCE GRAMMAR OF THE ONONDAGA LANGUAGE

Hanni Woodbury

A Reference Grammar of the Onondaga Language

UNIVERSITY OF TORONTO PRESS

Toronto   Buffalo   London

© University of Toronto Press 2018
Toronto Buffalo London
www.utorontopress.com

ISBN   978-1-4875-0282-9

 Printed on acid-free paper.

Library and Archives Canada Cataloguing in Publication

Woodbury, Hanni, author
A reference grammar of the Onondaga language / Hanni Woodbury.

Includes bibliographical references and index.
ISBN 978-1-4875-0282-9 (cloth)

1. Onondaga language – Grammar. I. Title.

| PM2076.W66 2018 | 497'.55 | C2017-906365-0 |

All royalties from the sale of this work are paid to the Onondaga Nation Council of Chiefs and the Onondaga Language Program.

Financial support of this publication has been provided by the Government of Ontario through the Ontario Training and Adjustment Board (presently the Ministry of Training, Colleges and Universities).

University of Toronto Press acknowledges the financial assistance to its publishing program of the Canada Council for the Arts and the Ontario Arts Council, an agency of the Government of Ontario.

Canadä

This book is dedicated to the memory of Nora Carrier, Reg Henry, Harry Webster, and Gladys Williams. They have been so generous in giving their time, good cheer, and thoughtful attention to teach me their language by patiently answering my questions, telling me stories, helping me with translations and sharing their knowledge at every turn.

Contents

3 Parts of Speech

4 The Verb

6 Pro-forms

7 Syntactic Constructions

Figures and Tables

Acknowledgments

I thank the speakers whose memory is honored in the dedication to this volume and the students and teachers of the language classes who gave so much help with their insights into this amazing language.

I hope with this work to express my admiration for the speakers of Onondaga and for the students who with their efforts and enthusiasm in support of their language are learning to master its intricacies. By now many of the students have taken on the duties of teachers. Without them the language could not survive. I give special thanks to Percy Abrams and Jay Meacham for their generosity in sharing with me their knowledge, the language materials they created and collected, and the many ways they have helped me in my quest to document Onondaga, and I thank Jackie Bomberry for answering my many questions and thereby helping me to differentiate the two dialects of Onondaga. I am also grateful to Amos Key for connecting me with speakers of the Six Nations dialect of Onondaga.

I had the great good luck to be one of the late Floyd Lounsbury's students. His brilliant analysis of the Iroquoian languages and his meticulous approach to field-linguistics started us off with a wonderful foundation for pursuing our various quests. And I am so very indebted to my colleagues Clifford Abbott, Wallace Chafe, Michael Foster, Karin Michelson and Marianne Mithun for many years of illuminating discussions. I give special thanks to Karin Michelson for our long, stimulating conversations, for her sharing in depth her many interesting ideas about the Iroquoian languages, and her willingness to critique and discuss every part of this work in detail. I thank her also for sharing recordings she made with Sanford Schenandoah. I am also grateful for the extremely helpful comments and insightful suggestions made by two anonymous readers, most of which I followed and which greatly improved this work. I thank Jeff Good for planning and organizing the archive of my audio materials.

This work benefitted from Grant # B-6 *Onondaga Dictionary and Grammar*, co-sponsored by the Ontario Ministry of Training Colleges and Universities (formerly the Ontario Training and Adjustment Board - OTAB) and the Woodland Cultural Centre, Brantford, Ontario. The American Philosophical Society provided me with digitized recordings of the stories and incidents of daily life told by Lucenda George and Pat Johnson; the late Fred Lukoff recorded these and oversaw their initial translations.

Abbreviations

1	First person	EXT	Extent	O	Obstruent
2	Second person	F	Fricative	OPT	Optative
3	Third person	FACT	Factual	P	Patient
A	Agent	FCL	Facilitative	PL	Plural
ADD	Additive	FI	Feminine-indefinite	PNC	Punctual
AFF	Affirmative	FIL	Filler	POP	Populative
ALT	Alternative	FUT	Future	POSS	Possessive
AMT	Amount	FZ	Feminine-zoic	PRD	Predicator
ASP	Aspect	HAB	Habitual	PRES	Presentative
ASRT	Assertion	HBPST	Habitual past	PRG	Progressive
AUG	Augmentative	HRSY	Hearsay	PRON	Pronoun
AUTH	Authentic	HYP	Hypothetical	PRP	Purposive
BEN	Benefactive	ILL	Illustrative	PRPPST	Purposive past
C	Consonant	IMP	Imperative	PRT	Partitive
CHAR	Characterizer	IN	Inclusive	PST	Past
CIS	Cislocative	INCH	Inchoative	QNT	Quantifier
CMP	Complement	INDF	Indefinite	QUE	Question particle
CNJ	Conjunction	INST	Instrumental	R	Resonant
CNT	Continuative	INSTG	Instigative	REF	Reflexive
COIN	Coincident	INTR	Interrogative	REL	Relativizer
CON	Contrastive (prefix)	INTS	Intensifier	REP	Repetitive
CS	Causative	JN	Stem-joiner	REV	Reversative
CST	Customary	L	Laryngeal	RSN	Reason
CTR	Contrastive (particle)	LNK	Linking particle	RSTR	Restrictive
DEC	Decessive	LOC	Locative	SG	Singular
DEM	Demonstrative	M	Masculine	SIM	Similar
DGR	Degree	MAN	Manner	SRF	Semireflexive
DIM	Diminutive	MC	Main clause	STV	Stative
DIR	Direction	MLT	Multiplier	STV.PL	Stative plural
DIS	Dismissive	MOD	Modal	STV.PST	Stative past
DL	Dualic	N	Neuter	SUB	Subordinating
DSLC	Dislocative	NEG	Negative	SUFF	Suffix
DST	Distributive	NOM	Nominal; nominalizer	TAG	Question tag
DU	Dual number	NPF	Noun prefix	TMP	Temporal particle
EP	Epenthetic	NSF	Noun suffix	TRNS	Translocative
EVNT	Eventuative	NSG	Non-singular	TYP	Typicalizer
EX	Exclusive	NSP	Non-specific	V	Vowel
EXCL	Exclamation	NUM	Number	Z	Feminine-Zoic

A few of the pronominal prefixes have more than one denotation. When that is so, the identification appropriate to the particular example is supplied.

Symbols Used to Separate Morphemes and Morpheme Glosses in Interlinear Identifications

>	Separates agent from patient participants in transitive pronominal identifications
:	Placed between two segmentable prepronominal elements one of which occurs as a discontinuous morpheme
.	Separates words of multi-word glosses that identify a single morpheme
-	separates morphemes; separates morpheme glosses

Symbols Used to Identify Morphemes and Stem-Types

. (period)	Precedes citations of stems that must occur with a discontinuous prepronominal prefix in a given meaning, e.g., .a- + partitive 'be a size'
- (dash)	Precedes and follows morphemes or stems that consist of bound morpheme(s)
=	Marks off clitics

Symbols Used to Describe the Phonology and Rhythmic Structure

. (period)	Separates syllables from one another
· (raised dot)	Vowel length
´	Marks main stress
`	Marks secondary stress
-aʔ'	Example of a morpheme that attracts stress to the final syllable of a word
-'ʔs	Example of a morpheme that attracts main stress to the antepenultimate syllable of a word
σ	Syllable

Author, Source, and Speaker Abbreviations

CTL	*Concerning the League* (pp. 1-100 pronounced by the late Harry Webster; pp. 101-701 pronounced by Reg Henry). In Woodbury (1993) examples from *Concerning the League* are identified as W with page and line number.
EO	Eva Okun (Onondaga Nation)
GW	Gladys Williams (Six Nations)
H	J. N. B. Hewitt: Annual Reports of the Bureau of Ethnology, vol. 21 (citations with page numbers 143 - 220); Annual Reports of the Bureau of Ethnology, vol. 43 (citations with page numbers 612 - 791).
HW	Harry Webster (Onondaga Nation)
JM	Jay Meacham (Onondaga Nation)
LG	Lucenda George (Onondaga Nation)
NC	Nora Carrier (Six Nations)
PA	Percy Abrams (Onondaga Nation)
PJ	Pat Johnson (Onondaga Nation)
PS	Peter Skye (Six Nations)
RH	Reg Henry (Six Nations)
SS	Sanford Schenandoah (Onondaga Nation)

1 Introduction

1.1 Onondaga and the Iroquoian Family of Languages

The Iroquoian family of languages consists of a southern and a northern branch. The southern branch is composed of a single language, Cherokee, which is spoken in two dialects, an eastern one in North Carolina and a western one in Oklahoma. The northern and southern branches split approximately 3,500 to 3,800 years ago. Northern Iroquoian consisted of numerous languages, some of which are no longer spoken. The relationships among the Iroquoian languages are shown below:[1]

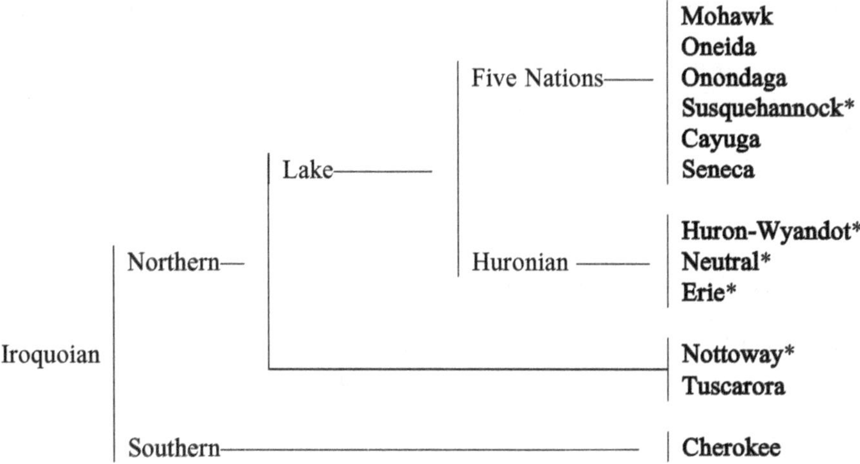

Figure 1.1 The Iroquoian family of languages

Onondaga is one of the six surviving languages belonging to the northern branch of the family. One of these, Tuscarora, is more distantly related to the other five than they are to one another. The Tuscarora migrated north from their original homeland in eastern North Carolina fairly recently, joining the northern groups in the early part of the eighteenth century following the Tuscarora Wars of 1711-1713. The remaining surviving nations were

---

[1] Asterisks mark languages that are no longer spoken. The names of languages are given in boldface. Names in regular type refer to language groupings. The figure is based on similar displays in Lounsbury (1978); Michelson (1988) and Mithun (1999).

the groups who formed the Iroquois Confederacy; their languages are grouped together as the Five Nations languages. Today's dialects of Onondaga exist in two locations: at Onondaga Nation which is located just south of Syracuse, New York and at Six Nations of the Grand River First Nations reserve, near Brantford, Ontario. At Onondaga Nation, currently, less than a dozen elderly persons are fluent speakers who grew up speaking Onondaga as a first language. The Sweetgrass First Nations Council reported that in 1994 there were 43 fluent speakers at Six Nations. However, successful language classes are set up in both communities with the aim of maintaining and revitalizing the language.

At contact, the hunting territories of the Five Nations groups extended from east to west in what is now upstate New York in the following order: the Mohawk, in the vicinity of the Mohawk River; the Oneida near Lake Oneida; the Onondaga in the area of present-day Onondaga County; the Cayuga in the vicinity of Lake Cayuga; and the Seneca in the area to the south of Rochester. The groups had formed a Confederacy and in doing so they likened their territory to a longhouse in which the Mohawk were thought of as the 'Keepers of the Eastern Door' of the Confederacy, and the Seneca were the 'Keepers of the Western Door'. Of the five languages spoken by these groups, roughly the ones most similar to one another are the ones that were geographically closest. Nevertheless, there is evidence that resemblances are due in part to more intense recontacts among the groups (Chafe and Foster 1981).

A number of events that took place in the recent history of the Onondaga people are known to have had an impact on their language:[2] The Onondaga usually lived in just two villages at any one time, one larger and one smaller. Because the Onondaga were the 'firekeepers' or 'wampum keepers' of the Confederacy, their large village also served as the meeting place of the Iroquois Confederacy Council. As was customary among all of the Iroquois peoples, the Onondaga moved their villages to new locations when the land surrounding a village became infertile from overuse, and when the supply of wood in its near surroundings became exhausted. These moves typically did not involve large distances. In 1681 the Onondaga lived in a village near present-day Jamesville, New York. Subsequently, and extending through much of the eighteenth century, they established settlements along Onondaga Creek and in the general area around Jamesville. During the Revolutionary War, the villages along Onondaga Creek were destroyed. In 1778 many Onondaga moved to Buffalo Creek where they joined a group of Seneca and Cayuga, leaving behind in Onondaga County only approximately 100 of their people. Meanwhile they reestablished the Confederacy in the new location.

Mithun (1980) and Chafe and Foster (1981:138-141) argue that it was during their time with the Seneca that Onondaga acquired certain phonological characteristics relating to the loss of the consonant r, a feature that modern Onondaga shares with Seneca and Cayuga. The council fire and the wampum records of the Confederacy remained at Buffalo Creek until 1847, after which they were returned to Onondaga. During a period beginning in 1788 and extending to 1822 all but 4,320 acres – the area of the present Onondaga Nation territory – was acquired by the State of New York.

In 1784, in a separate development, approximately 225 Onondaga from Buffalo Creek joined the Mohawk chief Joseph Brant, who led a group of approximately 1800 Iroquois loyalists from the several groups in New York State, to lands granted them along the Grand River, in Canada. Here a second, parallel, Confederacy was established. In 1841, Six Nations Reserve was formally established on a 20,000 acre tract to the south and east

---

[2] See Blau et al. (1978:491-499) and Weaver (1978:525-536).

of present-day Brantford, Ontario in exchange for the lands of the original grant. The reserve is the only one inhabited by members of all of the Six Nations (the Five Nations groups and the Tuscarora) and they reside there to this day. Since their separation from one another, the Six Nations and Onondaga Nation groups of Onondaga speakers have developed somewhat divergent dialects.

1.2 Linguistic Profile of Onondaga

Onondaga has a relatively small inventory of phonemes – seventeen in all – in addition to distinctive vowel length. There are seven vowels – five oral vowels and two nasal vowels – and eight consonants – three oral obstruents, three resonants, two laryngeal obstruents, and two internally complex consonants. Voicing is not distinctive. The prosodic system is interesting in that the principles that assign high pitch differ from the principles that assign stress such that high pitch frequently occurs on a syllable that precedes the syllable carrying primary stress in words of three or more syllables.

Onondaga is a non-configurational language (Hale 1983). It is polysynthetic and fusional. Except for certain linear order requirements within phrasal constituents, word order is governed by discourse considerations. The verbal morphology is extensive – more so than the nominal morphology – and there is very little formal syntax (Koenig & Michelson 2015a). The verb exhibits both inflectional and derivational morphology. The derivational morphology is, for the most part, non-productive. The morphological processes are not recursive, except for occasional examples of noun incorporation. Noun incorporation – a derivational process – is robust. It derives verbs from verbs. Many of the verb forms with incorporated nouns have become lexicalized[3] as nominals[4] and these constructions are used extensively to create new words for contemporary cultural items. Verbs can occur alone as complete clauses. This is because arguments of the verb are referenced morphologically within the verb. External nominals are optional.

Traditionally, Iroquoian languages have been analyzed as having three morphologically determined parts of speech: verbs, nouns, and particles. Koenig & Michelson (2010b) argue that kinship terms may be regarded as a fourth part of speech that has characteristics of both verbs and nouns. Verb stems form a much richer part of the lexicon than do either of the others. Morphological nouns are a closed class, as are particles. Verbs can be derived from verbs but not from nouns. There is only one process that derives a noun stem from a verb root. The ultimate source of particles frequently is a verb. Establishing the parts of speech – verb, noun, and particle – in terms of their morphological structure, overlooks recurring mismatches in discourse between morphological type and the grammatical functions each can perform.[5] As just one example, all three morphological types can function referentially, as entity expressions. In terms of the frequency of their occurrence as tokens in discourse, particles occur most frequently, next are morphological verbs, and least frequent are morphological nouns.

---

[3] Lexicalization is pervasive in the Iroquoian languages. The concept is used in this work to describe any combination of morphemes that is either semantically or morphologically non-compositional, such that its combined form or meaning cannot be predicted from the parts of which it is composed.

[4] The term *nominal* is used in this work as synonymous with the phrase *referring expression*.

[5] See Koenig & Michelson (2016 ms.) for an analysis of these distributional characteristics, which are present in all of the Five Nations languages.

4 Introduction

The Iroquoian languages are famed for their prolific pronominal prefix systems. Pronominal prefixes occur with all verb and noun forms. Onondaga has 59 pronominal prefixes that are divided into three series, grammatical agents, grammatical patients, and transitives. Their distribution is in part the result of verbal semantics and in part dependent on the aspectual system (Mithun 1991). Pronominal selection from the correct series is lexicalized for each verb and noun stem. The pronominal prefixes in each of the three series distinguish person (1st, 2nd, 3rd, inclusive, exclusive), number (singular, dual, plural), and gender (masculine, two feminine genders, and a non-animate (neuter) gender), although not all distinctions are available across the entire paradigm.

Onondaga is a head-marking language (Nichols 1986) as shown in (1) where the animate argument of the verb *waʔtho·yę́hdaʔ* 'he slams it'[6] is pronominally referenced on the verb, and where the possessor is marked pronominally on the possessive construction *hoʔsgwéhsaʔ* 'his tomahawk' that denotes the possession:

(1) Si · naʔ de·gáę́ʔ nę héʔ, tho <u>waʔthoyę̨hdáʔ</u> neʔ <u>hoʔsgwéhsaʔ</u> (HW07).
    si· naʔ degaęʔ   nę heʔ   tho   waʔ-t-<u>h</u>-oyęhd-aʔ
    LOC ASRT TMP   TMP REP   LOC   FACT-DL-<u>3M.SG.A</u>-slam.down-PNC
    every so often   again   there   he slammed it down

    neʔ   ho-aʔsgwehs-aʔ
    NOM   <u>3M.SG.P</u>-tomahawk-NSF
    the   his tomahawk
    Every so often, he slams down his tomahawk.

1.3 Previous Works on the Onondaga Language

There is a gratifying amount of early work on the Onondaga language. Two extensive dictionaries date from the 17th and 18th century, respectively, one – Shea (1860) – was compiled by an unidentified Jesuit Missionary[7] in the late 17th century and consists of 186 printed pages. Another, by the Moravian Missionary David Zeisberger (Horseford, 1887) consists of 253 printed pages. Zeisberger also compiled two vocabulary lists of Onondaga - – of 13 and 4 pages respectively – (Zeisberger 1887a), and a 45 page grammatical sketch (Zeisberger 1887-1888). Heckewelder (1820) reports that Zeisberger's dictionary was completed by the year 1760, and the grammatical sketch by 1780, but neither were published until over 100 years later. Horatio Hale's (1883) *The Iroquois Book of Rites* contains a version of the *Condolence Council* – a ritual held at the death of a chief to this day – consists of 52 pages of text in Onondaga with a translation. J.N.B. Hewitt's *Iroquoian Cosmology*, Parts 1 and 2 (1903, 1928) – contain two very long dictated texts with interlinear and free translations. The Onondaga version in the first of these is 80 pages long, the second is 372 pages. These are important works, much quoted in this volume as sources of in-context examples from speakers from speakers from the Six Nations Reserve who were either monolingual, or whose preferred language was Onondaga. Hewitt – his

---

[6] Citation- and in-context forms differ intonationally from one another as can be seen by the difference in intonational markers in the cited form and the form within the example (see sec. 2.7).

[7] The historian James Bradley (forthcoming) finds circumstantial evidence that the unknown author was the Jesuit Father Pierre-Joseph-Marie Chaumonot (b.1611-d.1693) who spent many years of his life in Huron and Iroquois country. He was said to speak both Huron and Onondaga fluently.

mother was a Tuscarora, and he himself learned to speak that language – had thorough training in language documentation, and was a meticulous scholar with an excellent ear. In addition to his published works in the Onondaga language, he produced a large trove of handwritten and typed manuscripts in Onondaga, all of which is archived in the Smithsonian Institution National Anthropological Archives (J.N.B. Hewitt Files) in Washington D.C. More recent works on Onondaga are Chafe (1970), a semantically based grammatical sketch of the Onondaga Nation dialect; Woodbury (1975) is a Ph.D. dissertation on Onondaga noun incorporation (Onondaga Nation dialect); Mithun & Woodbury, (eds.), (1980) is a collection of texts in each of the Northern Iroquoian languages with interlinear linguistic analysis and translation. Woodbury (1981) describes the reflexes of the loss of the phoneme *r in Onondaga. Michelson (1983) and (1988) are studies of accent in the Lake Iroquoian languages both of which include a description of the Onondaga accent system. Woodbury et al. (1992) is a 701 page word for word re-elicitation, with interlinear morpheme analysis and translation of an original manuscript containing the transcription of a very long account (525 ms. pages), dictated to Alexander Goldenweiser by Chief Arthur Gibson of Six Nations Reserve, that documents the formation of the Iroquoian Confederacy (Goldenweiser 1912). The text was not translated at the time of its transcription. The original of Goldenweiser's manuscript is located in the archives of the Canadian Museum of History (formerly the Canadian Museum of Civilization). The digitized re-elicitation and translation sessions that resulted in Woodbury et al. (1992) have been deposited in an archive of Onondaga audio materials at the University at Buffalo, in Amherst, NY. Woodbury (2003) is a comprehensive dictionary of the Onondaga language (both dialects) which should serve as a helpful companion to the present volume. Abrams (2006) is a Ph.D. dissertation on the pronominal prefix system of the Onondaga language. Barrie (2015) is a grammar focused mainly on the Six Nations dialect of Onondaga.

1.4 The Data: Resources, Their Uses, and Presentation

Because all speakers of Onondaga now use English as their primary language, I use, whenever possible, a textual approach to describe the language and hold elicited examples to a minimum. My hope is in this way to lessen any influence from English.

The data I have used are recorded (and digitized) materials as well as documentary sources. Because of the accuracy with which they convey phonological and prosodic information, the materials that have been recorded and subsequently digitized are used for the examples in this volume wherever possible. The data from speakers consist of stories and some elicited materials by the late Harry Webster (HW), the late Eva Okun (EO) – both speakers of the Onondaga Nation dialect – the late Nora Carrier (NC), the late Gladys Williams (GW), the late Reg Henry (RH), Jackie Bomberry (JB), the late Peter Skye (PS) and the late Isabel Burning (IB), all from Six Nations Reserve. When the examples are excerpts of stories, the story's number follows the speaker's initials, for example, (HW05) or (LG19). I recorded Onondaga materials beginning in the early 1970s until the late 1990s. Other elicited materials were recorded by Karin Michelson working in 1978 with the late Sanford Schenandoah of Onondaga Nation. All of the recorded materials are digitized and deposited in the archive of Onondaga materials The University at Buffalo. Additional audio data used in the present work consist of a large trove of stories told by two speakers of the Onondaga Nation dialect – 38 stories by the late Lucenda George (LG) and 17 stories by the late Pat Johnson (PJ), both speakers of the Onondaga Nation dialect – that were recorded by the late linguist Fred Lukoff in the years 1948-1950. Lukoff replayed many of the stories for the speakers and recorded their translations. These materials were provided to me in digitized form by the American Philosophical Society where the original recordings were deposited by Lukoff. I am responsible for their transcription and analysis.

The documentary sources date from 1889 when J.N.B. Hewitt began collecting his texts for the *Iroquoian Cosmology* until 1912 when Alexander Goldenweiser completed his work on the manuscript of *Concerning the League*.[8] I have transposed Hewitt's orthography to conform to the orthography used in this volume. Each example from the Hewitt texts is referenced by H – for Hewitt – and a page and line number, e.g., (H143.12). (Only the page and line numbers are referenced. There can be no confusion from which volume the excerpts are taken, because the page references in the 1921 volume run from 141 to 220 and the page references in the 1943 volume run from 612 to 791). Examples from Woodbury et al. (1992) are referenced as CTL – for *Concerning the League* – together with page and line references, e.g. (CTL468:5). I have transposed the phonemic orthography used in Woodbury et al. (1992) to the orthography used in this volume. While the texts for which we lack recorded versions are invaluable as sources for explicating the morphology, grammar, and discourse features of Onondaga – and this is the use they have been put to in this volume – they are less so as sources of phonological information. Hewitt (1921; 1943) and Woodbury et al. (1992) are comprised of dictated texts that were taken down in longhand. They differ *prosodically* from a story told in real time, because utterance-final and citation forms differ prosodically from utterance-medial forms. Thus, for the most part, each word in multi-word excerpts from these sources is typically pronounced as an utterance-final form. The fact that *Concerning the League* was re-elicited and recorded helped this to some extent, but nevertheless would not restore a genuine story telling performance. In addition, the careful reader will notice that examples from Hewitt's texts mark stress and vowel length inconsistently or sometimes not at all. Prosodic markings are reproduced in the examples as they are given by Hewitt for any possible information they may contain. Similarly, in the reconstituted text (examples marked CTL) the prosody is marked as it was given by speakers in the re-elicitation mode.[9] The result is that unlike the digitized sources, these sources may not conform to statements about Onondaga prosody that are made in Chapter 2, the phonology chapter. Sadly, this is one of the consequences of describing a highly endangered language. I have made an effort to alert the reader to these issues in footnotes.

Multi-word examples from texts are presented in a five line format. The first row presents an entire spoken utterance in Onondaga, and the last row is a free translation of the utterance. Between these two rows a word-by-word morpheme analysis is given. In the first line of this analysis words are segmented into component morphemes; in the second

---

[8] Hewitt (1921) was transcribed in 1889 with revisions in 1897, Hewitt (1943) was transcribed in 1900; the manuscript of Goldenweiser's text was completed in 1912, and re-elicited by me throughout the 1980's. Hewitt worked with the late Chief and Firekeeper John Buck at Six Nations on the work published in 1921, and with Chief John Arthur Gibson on the work published in 1943. Alexander Goldenweiser worked with Chief John Arthur Gibson. I worked with the late Harry Webster of Onondaga Nation (ms. pp 1 - 100) and the late Reg Henry of Six Nations (ms, pp. 101 - 525) on the re-elicitation of Goldenweiser's manuscript.

[9] See Woodbury et al. (1992:xv) where the process is described in detail.

line each morpheme is identified, and the third gives a word gloss. The first line of each of the examples is followed by the initials of the speaker and the numbered text that is the source of the example, e.g., (HW07) references Harry Webster's seventh story. *Single word examples* – these are often elicited – are presented in four lines: the first line is the Onondaga word, the second is a morpheme-by-morpheme analysis, the third identifies each morpheme, and the fourth glosses the word. The elicited examples for the most part are given without a source code.

The Onondaga Dictionary (Woodbury 2003) is a useful companion to this grammar, in that it provides the many inflectional and derivational possibilities for the stems that occur in the examples in the present volume. In the grammar, as in the dictionary, stems are cited either surrounded by hyphens (-), e.g., -*yẹthw*- 'plant' or they are preceded by a period (.) and followed by the name of a discontinuous prefix to show that the cited prefix is an obligatory part of the stem in a given meaning, e.g., .*aæhdast*- + dualic 'run something'.

Particles, a frequently occurring part of speech in Onondaga discourse, present a number of special problems of presentation. Because of Onondaga's prosodic patterns, multi-syllabic words are accented differently, depending on whether they occur utterance-internally, or utterance-finally. For simplicity's sake and to allow for ease in searching, particles are presented without prosodic markers, i.e., markers of stress and prosodic vowel length, in the morpheme segmentation line.[10] Because particles lack internal structure, they are presented as whole words in the morpheme segmentation line. Particles, especially particles with grammatical or discourse functions, are often difficult for speakers to gloss in a uniform way, so that for these the glosses may differ in different contexts.

---

[10] Where it is possible to determine that vowel length is phonemic, it is of course marked, even in the segmentation line.

2 The Sound System

2.1 Onondaga Sounds and the Symbols Used to Describe Them

Iroquoian linguists have often transcribed the Iroquoian languages phonemically using only nine consonant symbols, *t, k, s, n, r, y, w, ?, h,* and six vowel symbols, the oral vowels: *a, e, i, o* and two symbols for nasal vowels, which in Onondaga are ę, and ų. Onondaga has lost the Proto-Northern Iroquoian consonant **r*, and added an oral vowel *æ*. It would be entirely possible to write Onondaga using only 15 alphabetical symbols and the raised dot (·) indicating vowel length. With the remaining speakers in mind, a practical orthography is used in this book that is closely based on the orthographies used by speakers in the two dialect regions where Onondaga is spoken, except that it includes one or two necessary distinctions not represented in the practical orthographies, and it has simplified the symbols used for the two nasal vowels.

2.1.1 Vowels

There are five oral vowel phonemes in Onondaga:

Table 2.1: Oral vowels

Phoneme	Phone	Orthography	Example using the orthography
/i/	[i]	i	íhe? 'he is here'
/e/	[e]	e	hé?sgwa? 'he used to come around'
/æ/	[æ]	æ	hodǽ·gwęh 'he has claimed it'
/a/	[ɑ]	a	oyę́?gwa·? 'smoke'
	[a]		wa?ha·ę́? 'he put it in'
/o/	[o]	o	odékha? 'fire'

Oral vowels are pronounced with a raised velum and the breath exiting through the mouth. Table 2.1. shows the phonemic representation, the phonetic representation and the letters, or orthographic representation, for each oral vowel phoneme. These are followed by an example in the orthography used in this work in which the cited vowel is underlined. The phoneme /i/ occurs as a high front unrounded oral vowel; /e/ occurs as a mid front unrounded oral vowel; /æ/ occurs as a higher-low front unrounded oral vowel; /a/ occurs as a low back unrounded vowel before laryngeals, and as a low central unrounded vowel elsewhere; /o/ occurs as a mid back rounded vowel.

There are two nasal vowel phonemes in Onondaga: ę, a lower-mid front nasal vowel, and ų, a lower-high back somewhat rounded vowel. Nasal vowels are pronounced with a lowered velum and the breath exiting through the nose and the mouth.

Table 2.2: Nasal vowels

Phoneme	Phone	Orthography	Example
/ę/	[ẽ]	ę	oyę́ʔgwa·ʔ 'smoke'
/ų/	[ũ]	ų	odųyó·daʔ 'haystack'

2.1.2 Consonants

There are ten consonant phonemes in Onondaga which Iroquoianist generally arrange into four groups whose elements share distributional characteristics. The two plosives /t/ and /k/ and the fricative /s/ are grouped together as *oral obstruents*, /ts/ and /kw/ are *internally complex consonants*, the nasal consonant /n/ and the two glides /y/ and /w/ are grouped as *resonants*, and /h/ and /ʔ/ are *laryngeal obstruents*.

Table 2.3: Oral obstruents

Phoneme	Phone	Orthography	Example
/t/	[t]	t	tgųdidáʔshę·ʔ 'they have stopped'
	[d]	d	odékhaʔ 'fire'
/k/	[k]	k	eʔníkhųk 'she sews'
	[g]	g	gagáhæʔ 'glasses'
/s/	[s]	s	só·wæk 'duck'
	[dj]	j	dá·jyųh 'Come in!'
	[ʃ]	c	dewadekháhcyųs 'it comes apart' waʔwa·dæ·hwisdótcyaʔ 'it peeled off' wadyędakhwáʔtcis 'bench' ęhcyadųhsæ·yenáʔ 'you will get mail' ųtcisdodákhwaʔ 'lamp'

The plosives /t/ and /k/ are pronounced as voiceless unaspirated [t] and [k], before another obstruent; at the end of a word they are aspirated prepausally. There are some generational differences with regard to the pronunciation of the plosives when they occur before vowels and resonants: older speakers often have voiceless unaspirated [t] and [k] at the beginning of a word before a vowel or between a consonant and a vowel, whereas younger speakers have voiced [d] and [g] in these environments. All speakers have voiced [d] and [g] intervocalically. The phoneme /s/ occurs as the palatoalveolar affricate [dj] before /y/ or /i/ except when it is preceded or followed by a laryngeal; it occurs as a postalveolar fricative [ʃ] between a laryngeal and /y/, between /t / and the sequences /hi/ or /hy/ with loss of the h, between /h/ and the sequence /hy/ with loss of the second /h/, or between /t/ and /i/; /s/ occurs as [s] elsewhere.

Two internally complex consonants, /kw/ and /ts/ are a labiovelar consonant and an alveolar affricate, respectively. These two unitary consonants are phonetically indistinguishable from surface sequences with identical, but individuated, segments, i.e., /k/+/w/ and /t/+/s/, respectively. The internally complex consonants differ from their individuated twins in terms of their distribution as described in section 2.2. The internally complex segments are reflexes of Proto Northern Iroquoian */ts/ and */kw/ (Michelson 1988:55).

Table 2.4 Internally complex consonants

Phoneme	Phone	Orthography	Example
/kw/	[gw]	gw	hatgwí?tha? 'he moves'
/ts/	[dj]	j	ojísda? 'fire, ember'

The resonants /y/ and /w/ are high front and high back glides, respectively; /n/ is an alveolar nasal.

Table 2.5 Resonants

Phoneme	Phone	Orthography	Example
/y/	[y]	y	gayá·æ? 'bag'
/w/	[w]	w	owę́·na? 'word'
/n/	[n]	n	osnó·we? 'it's fast'

Onondaga, like Seneca, differs from the other Northern Iroquoian languages in having lost a fourth resonant *r in all environments.[1] The resonant occurs as /l/ or /r/ in the other languages. In Onondaga it was attested as /r/ in the seventeenth and eighteenth centuries (Shea 1860, Zeisberger 1887[1761]) this resonant has left numerous traces which will be discussed in section 2.3, below.

The laryngeal consonants /h/ and /?/ are a fricative and a stop, respectively. In the Iroquoian languages laryngeal consonants pattern like obstruents.

Table 2.6 Laryngeal obstruents

Phoneme	Phone	Orthography	Example
/h/	[h]	h	hwiks 'five'
/?/	[?]	?	ga?áhsæ·? 'basket'

2.2. Distribution of Phonemes

All the vowel phonemes listed in section 2.1.1 except /æ/ occur word-initially and word-finally. All the consonant phonemes listed in section 2.1.2 except the two internally complex consonant phonemes /kw/ and /ts/, the laryngeal obstruent /?/, and the resonant /y/ occur word-initially and all the consonants, except for the two internally complex phonemes /kw/ and /ts/ and the three resonants /y/, /w/, and /n/ occur word-finally. The internally complex consonants /kw/ and /ts/ can be distinguished synchronically from the otherwise identical sequences /k/+/w/ and /t/+/s/ in only two contexts: (i) at the

---

[1] Cayuga has lost *r in selected environments.

morpheme boundaries that require *e*-epenthesis with the latter, but not the former (section 2.6.2), and (ii) in contexts subject to the rule of second-syllable vowel length (section 2.7.4.3) which the internally complex consonants fail to condition without the presence of a second resonant. Thus it is impossible to establish their presence in other environments except by means of comparative evidence. Words ending in /h/ typically lose it utterance-medially except that some speakers retain word-final utterance-medial /h/ if the following word begins in /n/.[2] While underlying /ʔ/ does not occur word-initially, phonetic [ʔ] is added utterance-initially before a vowel and between two words the first of which ends in a vowel and the second begins in a vowel as in *degní é·git* [degní ʔé·git] 'two acres'. Words ending in a vowel are followed by a phonetic [h] prepausally.

2.2.1 Vowel Sequences

A maximum of two contiguous vowels occurs in the Onondaga word. Surface VV sequences are shown in Table 2.7.

Table 2.7 Surface VV sequences

	i	ų	e	o	ę	æ	a
i							
ų	ųi[3]					ųæ[4]	
e	ei				eę	eæ	
o	oi[5]					oæ[6]	
ę	ęi		ęe	ęo[7]		ęæ	
æ	æi		æe		æę	ææ	
a	ai	aų	ae	ao	aę	aæ	aa

Vowel sequences occur (i) within the prepronominal position of the verb where the sequence expresses the optative mode (section 3.2); (ii) at the boundary between certain pronominal prefix alternants and verb stems beginning in *o* or *ų*; (iii) at the boundary between a verb stem and certain aspect suffix alternants beginning in *o* and *ų*, and (iv) as a consequence of the loss of intervocalic **r*.[8] Many underlying vowel sequences beginning in *i, o, and ų* are modified by resonant insertions.

(1) <u>In the prepronominal position</u>: aųsahseʔnya·gęʔnhaʔ
    aų-sa-hse-ʔnyagę-ʔ-nhaʔ
    OPT-REP-2SG.A-escape-INCH-PNC
    you should escape

---

[2] Note that when word-final /h/ is deleted utterance-medially, there will be a *seeming* disparity between the first row of an excerpt – the representation of the spoken text – and the second row – the morpheme by morpheme analysis – where the word-final morpheme will be shown with the laryngeal.

[3] ON speakers who do not insert [w] after /o/ and /ų/.

[4] In J.N.B. Hewitt's transcriptions.

[5] ON speakers who do not insert [w] after /o/ and /ų/.

[6] In Hewitt transcriptions.

[7] In a single base /*atęRo/ where o has not fronted to /e/ due to loss of /*r/.

[8] The consequences of *r**-loss are disussed in section 2.3 below

(2) <u>Between pronominal prefix and verb stem</u>: ęshagá·ų?
     ę-shaga-ų-?
     FUT-3M.SG > 3-give-PNC
     he will give it to her/them

(3) <u>Between verb stem and aspect suffix</u>: gyená·ųs
     g-yena-ųs
     1SG.A-grab-HAB
     I grab (things)

(4) <u>Deletion of intervocalic *r</u>: wa?eihwahę́·ga?
     *wa?-e-rihw-ahę·g-a?
     FACT-3FI.A-matter-hear-PNC
     she heard the news

Vowel sequences may be pronounced as diphthongs forming a single syllable nucleus, or each vowel may be syllabified separately. The process of diphthongization is sensitive to the rules of prosodic vowel lengthening and stress placement (section 2.7 below).

2.2.1.1 Vowel Assimilation (Six Nations)

Many Six Nations speakers assimilate the *e* of the vowel sequences *eę*, and *eæ* to the following vowel with added length, pronouncing the sequences as *ę·*, and *æ·*, respectively.

(5) dwaga·dyę́ęhdih (ON) *or* dwaga·dyę́·hdih (6N)
       I was the first one

(6) ganęhagę́ædah (ON) *or* ganęhagǽ·dah (6N)
       white corn

A few Six Nations speakers also assimilate the vowel *e* of the sequence *ei* to the following vowel, pronouncing the sequence *i·*.

(7) gaya?dayeisdákhwa? (ON) / goya?dayi·sdákhwa? (6N)
       meeting house

2.2.2 Consonant Sequences

2.2.2.1 Surface Consonant Clusters

Consonant sequences of up to five consonant phonemes can occur in the Onondaga word. The following tables organize the information in terms of initial and medial position. Clusters occurring word-finally are listed at the end of the section.

Table 2.8 Word-initial /CC/ clusters

	/t/	/k/	/ts/[9]	/kw/[10]	/s/	/n/	/y/	/w/	/h/	/ʔ/
/t/		tk				tn	ty	tw	th	
/k/	kt					kn	ky	kw	kh	kʔ
/ts/							tsy			
/kw/										
/s/		sk	sts			sn	(sy)[11]	sw	sh	
/n/								nw	nh	
/y/										
/w/										
/h/		hk		hkw		hn	hy	hw		
/ʔ/										

Table 2.9 Word-medial /CC/ clusters

	/t/	/k/	/ts/	/kw/	/s/	/n/	/y/	/w/	/h/	/ʔ/
/t/	/tt/[12]	tk	tts	tkw	ts	tn	ty	tw	th	tʔ
k	kt		kts		ks	kn	ky	kw	kh	kʔ
ts							tsy			
kw									hkw	
s	st	sk				sn		sw	sh	sʔ
n							ny		nh	
y										
w										
h	ht	hk		hkw	hs	hn	hy	hw		
ʔ	ʔt	ʔk			ʔs	ʔn	ʔy	ʔw	ʔh	

Table 2.10 Word-initial /CCC/ clusters by initial CC[13]

	/t/	/k/	/ts/	/kw/	/s/	/n/	/y/	/w/	/h/	/ʔ/
/t/					tsy tsh					
/k/			ktsy							kʔn kʔw
/ts/										
/kw/										
/s/		skn sky skw								
/n/									nhw	

---

[9] /ts/ represents a single, internally complex consonant in this and all the following displays, except the last one, which deals with word-medial /CCCC/ clusters.

[10] /kw/ represents a single, internally complex consonant in this and all the following displays, except the last one, which deals with word-medial /CCCC/ clusters.

[11] The sequence /sy/ is realized as [djy].

[12] /tt/ is a permissible cluster at the boundary between the reflexive morpheme and a noun or verb root. Elsewhere this cluster is broken up by an epenethetic vowel.

[13] /y/ /w/ /h/ and /ʔ/ do not occur as first consonants in CCC clusters.

Table 2.11 Word-medial /CCC/ clusters by initial CC

	/t/	/k/	/ts/	/kw/	/s/	/n/	/y/	/w/	/h/	/ʔ/
/t/	tts		ttsy		tst tsk tsy tsh tsʔ				thn thy thw	tʔn tʔw
/k/			ktsy		kst ksh				khn khw	kʔn kʔw
/ts/	tts									
/kw/										
/s/	sty sth	skn sky skw				sny			shn shw	sʔn
/n/									nhw	
/y/										
/w/										
/h/	hty	hks hkw			hst hsk hskw hsts hsy hsh hsʔ	hny hnh				
/ʔ/	ʔtk ʔts ʔtn ʔty ʔtw ʔth	ʔkt ʔkn ʔky ʔkw ʔkh			ʔst ʔsk ʔsn ʔsw ʔsh ʔsʔ	 ʔny ʔnh			ʔhk ʔhn ʔhy	

Table 2.12 Word-medial /CCCC/ clusters by initial CCC

	/t/	/k/	/s/	/n/	/y/	/w/	/h/	/ʔ/
/ts/		tskw					tshy	
/tʔ/				tʔny				
/st/							sthw	
/ht/			htsy					
/hs/								hsʔn
/kʔ/				kʔny				
/ʔt/		ʔtkt ʔtkn ʔtky ʔtkw	ʔtst ʔtsy ʔtsh				ʔthn	
/ʔk/	ʔkth		ʔksh				ʔkhy ʔkhw	ʔkʔn ʔkʔy

Table 2.12 (Continued)

	/t/	/k/	/s/	/n/	/y/	/w/	/h/	/ʔ/
/ʔs/		ʔskw					ʔshk	
							ʔshy	
							ʔshw	
/ʔn/							ʔnhy	
							ʔnhw	

Other Consonant Clusters:
Word-initial /CCCC/ clusters: /tʔny/, /kʔny/
Word-medial /CCCCC/ clusters: /ʔtkts/, /ʔtskw/, /ʔtshy/
Word-final /CC/ clusters: /ʔk/, /ʔs/

2.2.2.2 Changes Involving /kk/ Clusters

The sequence /kk/ ([kk] and [kg]) is not permitted for most speakers in either dialect of Onondaga.[14] When the sequence arises across a morpheme-boundary /kk/ is replaced by /hk/. This is shown in (8a) and (8b); (8c) is an example where the source of the sequence /hk/ is original:

(8) a. ahgǫ́ʔshæ·ʔ
     ak-gǫʔshR-aʔ
     1SG.P-pillow-NSF
     my pillow

    b. hya tha·hgwé·nyaʔ
      hya   th-aa-k-gweny-aʔ
      NOT CONT-OPT-1SG.A-be.able-PNC
      I am not able to do it

    c. węda·déhgwaʔ
     w-ęd-ade-hgwaʔ
     NPF-day-exist-HABPST
     former days

Some speakers replace the sequence /kk/ by /hk/ across a *phrase-internal word-boundary*

(9) a. …jyadáh gahé·ʔ niyohsæ·gé… (LG01)
     jyadak   gáhe·ʔ   ni-y-ohsR-a-ge-h'
     NUM   NUM   PRT-3N/Z.SG.A-year-JN-amount.to-STV[15]
     (it is) seventeen years

---

[14] Seneca and Cayuga, which also do not permit *kk* sequences, insert an epenthetic *e* between the two consonants (Michelson 1988:25). Note that Onondaga resorts to this strategy when the *kk* sequence is followed by an oral obstruent.

[15] The pronominal prefix identifications 3N/Z.SG.A or 3N/Z.SG.P mark the use of the feminine-zoic singular prefix as a default prefix when a verb has only non-animate arguments. The use of the feminine-zoic in this function is described and justified in section 4.3.

b. ...jíh gaęhyá·gęt... (LG10)
    jik   ga-Ręhyagę-t-Ø
    DGR   3N/Z.SG.A-suffer.pain-CS-STV
    it's too much of a struggle.

However, if /kk/ is followed by an oral obstruent at the boundary between pronominal prefix and verb stem, then an epenthetic *e* is inserted between the two consonants.

(10) a. wa?gekdų́?
    wa?-g-e-kdų-?'
    FACT-1SG.A-EP-examine-PNC
    I examined it

   b. ęgeksoháe?
    ę-g-e-ks-ohae-?'
    FUT-1SG.A-EP-dish-wash-PNC
    I'll wash the dish

If /kk/ is preceded by a fricative, it is simplified:

(11) ahgwí a·sgę́hæ?s
    ahgwi aa-sk-gęhR-a?s-Ø
    don't   OPT-2SG > 1SG-belittle-BEN-IMP
    don't put me down!

2.2.2.3 Changes Involving Sequences with /h/

The sequence /hs/ becomes /s/ word-initially:

(12) sægé·was
    hs-Ragew-as
    2SG.A-wipe-HAB
    you wipe, you are wiping it

The sequence /hs/ becomes /sh/ after a plosive:

(13) wa?ksho·jyó·dę?
    wa?-k-hsojyod-ę?
    FACT-1SG.A-pile.up-PNC
    I piled it up
              cf. wa?hahsojyó·dę? *he piled it up*

The sequence /shs/ is simplified to /sh/ word-initially:

(14) sho·jyó·dęh
    s-hsojyod-ęh
    2SG.IMP-pile.up-IMP
    pile it up!

                cf. tshaʔ nęyawęhshę́·ʔ *the things that will happen*

The sequence /wh/ is not permitted in Onondaga.[16] Some speakers in both dialects drop the *w* and lengthen the vowel preceding the cluster, others, again in both dialects, replace the *w* by the nasal vowel *ų*:

(15) dwahsá·ha̱ʔ or dwahsáu̱haʔ
    d-w-ahsaw-haʔ
    CIS-3N/Z.SG.A-start-HAB
    it starts

The sequences /hth/ and /hkh/ do not occur in Onondaga; when /hth/ arises it is simplified to /th/. Hewitt (1903:177) spells the noun stem that contemporary speakers pronounce -gųkhoʔn- 'block of wood' as "-gųhkhoʔn-". There is otherwise no attestation of the underlying sequence *hkh* in the Onondaga Dictionary (Woodbury 2003). Forms with the first person singular agent pronominal prefix -*k*-, which would become -*h*- before another *k*, select the -*ke*- / -*ge*- alternant of the pronominal prefix for example dęgekháhcyaʔ [de-ge-khahcy-aʔ] 'I will divide it' [compare hypothetical and unacceptable *dęhkháhcyaʔ].

(16) ųhséthaʔ
    yų-ahseht-haʔ
    3FI.A-hide-HAB
    she hides it

The sequence /ht/ is simplified to /t/ word-finally:

(17) tshaʔ ní·yot
    tshaʔ   ni-yo-ht-Ø
    SUB   PART-3N/Z.SG.P-how.it.is-STV
    how it is

Interestingly, the sequence /hsh/, in which the remaining oral obstruent is surrounded by laryngeal fricatives, does occur in Onondaga:

(18) tshaʔdeganų́hshęh
    tshaʔ-de-ga-nųhs-hę-h
    COIN-DL-3N/Z.SG.A-house-be.in.the.middle-STV
    it is at the center of the house

The sequence obstruent + *h* + obstruent is simplified to obstruent + obstruent:[17]

---

[16] Cayuga, which also does not permit this cluster, breaks it up with an epenthetic *e* (Michelson 1988:25).

(19) a. kdá·gwas
     k-hdagw-as
     1SG.A-be.afraid.of-HAB
     I fear it

   b. otgwíʔdih
     yo-at-hgwiʔd-ih
     3N/Z.SG.P-SRF-move.something-STV
     it has moved

   c. hgwíʔthaʔ
     k-hgwiʔt-haʔ
     1SG.A-move.something-HAB
     I move things

In (19c), after simplification to *kgwiʔthaʔ*, the word-initial sequence *kg* is changed to *hg* by phonological rule changing /kk/ → /hk/.

2.2.2.4 Changes Involving Sequences with Resonants

The sequence /yi/ is not permissible. When it occurs preceded and followed by a consonant, the *y* is deleted and the sequence *yi* → *i*.

(20) <u>y-Deletion</u>: CyiC → CiC
   a. hadinoʔji·yóʔsgwaʔ[18]
     hadi-noʔjy-iyo-ʔs-gwaʔ
     3M.PL.A-tooth-be.good-STV.PL-HBPST
     they used to have good teeth

   c. ganaʔjíhnaʔ
     ga-naʔjy-i-h-naʔ
     3N/Z.SG.A-bucket-be.all.of.it-STV-PST
     the bucket had been full
            cf. ganáʔjyaʔ [ga-naʔjy-aʔ] *bucket*

The sequences /wo/ and /wų/ are not permissible in Onondaga. When they arise in derived contexts, the *w* is deleted and the sequences *wo* and *wų* become *o* or *ų*:

---

[17] Some obstruent + h + obstruent clusters are broken up with *e*-Epenthesis, but which process will occur is not predictable. Both pronunciations are acceptable to some speakers.

[18] Vowel length is due to antepenultimate vowel lengthening, a prosodic vowel lengthening rule (see sec. 2.7.4.2).

(21) <u>w-deletion</u>: CwųC → CųC; CwoC → CoC:
    a. ga?nahgó·da?
       ga-?nahgw-od-a?
       3N/Z.SG.A-barrel-be.upright-STV
       standing barrel

    b. dedyohyų<u>h</u>ogę́h
       de-d-yo-(i)hyhųh<u>w</u>-ogę-h'
       DL-CIS-3N/Z.SG.P-river-be.between-STV
       fork of the river

    c. deyeyo?g<u>ó</u>wanę?s
       de-ye-yo?g<u>w</u>-<u>o</u>wanę-?s
       DL-3FI.A-cheek-be.big-STV.PL
       she has big cheeks

     d. ekh<u>ų</u>nyátha?
       e-kh<u>w</u>-<u>ų</u>ni-at-ha?
       3FI.A-food-make-CS-HAB
       stove

    e. hęgohų́?
       h-ę-g-o-h<u>w</u>-<u>ų</u>-?'
       TRNS-FUT-1SG.A-be.in.water-CS-DSTR-PNC
       I will put several objects into water cf., *heyóhwih [he-y-o-hw-ih] it is in the water*

Following a vowel, the sequences /wo/ or /wų/ become /yo/ or /yų/, respectively:

(22) <u>Resonant substitution</u>: Vw + ųC → VyųC; Vw + oC → VyoC:
    a. nwa?oji?n<u>ų</u><u>y</u>ó?dę?
       n-wa?-o-ji?n<u>ų</u><u>w</u>-o?dę-?
       PRT-FACT-3N/Z.SG.P-worm-be.a.kind-PNC
       the kind of worm it was

    b. ęhakh<u>ų</u>y<u>ų́</u>·nyę?
       ę-hak-h<u>ų</u><u>w</u>-<u>ų</u>ny-ę-?
       FUT-3M.SG > 1SG-boat-make-BEN-PNC
       he will make me a boat

    c. wa?shago?noyodáhcya?
       wa?-shago-?no<u>w</u>-<u>o</u>dahcy-a?
       FACT-3M.SG > 3-carapace-reveal-PNC
       he revealed her [secrets]
                cf. ga?nowá?geh [ga-?now-a?-ge] *on the carapace, hunchback*

Similarly, stems beginning in /o/ or /ų/ select the *y* alternant of the non-animate agent pronominal prefix [from underlying *w*]:

(23) deyó·gęh
    de-y-ogę-h
    DL-3N/Z.SG.A-be.between-STV
    it is between [things]

A second case of resonant substitution resulted from the replacement of intervocalic *r* in the sequences *irV*, *u̧rV*, and *orV*, where homorganic y was substituted for *r* when it occurred after *i*, and *w* was substituted for *r* when it occurred after *o* or *u̧*.[19]

(24) <u>Intervocalic resonant substitution with *r-loss*</u>:
    a. wa?hewiyǽkhwa?
      *wa?-he-wiR-a-khw-a?
      FACT-1SG > 3M.SG-baby-JN-take-PNC
      I took a baby from him

    b. wa?gyu̧wædáhcya?
      *wa?-g-yu̧r-ada-hcy-a?
      FACT-1SG.A-gut-be.in-REV-PNC
      I gutted it

    c. ó·wæ?
      *o-r-a?
      NPF-wind-NSF
      wind

Some speakers insert *y* in *erV sequences, most do not.

(25) ohé·<u>y</u>æ? or ohé·æ?
    *o-her-a?
    NPF-cornsalk-NSF
    cornstalk

2.3 Changes Resulting from the Loss of Northern Iroquoian *r

Onondaga, like Seneca, has lost the Northern Iroquoian resonant *r in all environments as was pointed out above. In addition, it experienced the partial loss of the resonant /*w/ in a single environment (section 2.4). The loss of the resonant *r in Onondaga occurred in at least two stages (Woodbury 1981). The exact timing of the first – partial – loss of the resonant is unknown, but we do know that it occurred before the anonymous author of the French-Onondaga Dictionary (Shea 1860) compiled that dictionary in the later part of the seventeenth century. These early changes are discussed in section 2.3.4; the more pervasive changes brought about in the second stage of *r-loss are discussed in the present section.

---

[19] Resonant substitution in the sequence *orV* when neither vowel is stressed is quite variable, and much more common in the Six Nations than the Onondaga Nation dialect.

By the 1790s Onondaga had lost the resonant consonant *r in all environments.[20] The loss, once completed, resulted in the addition of a vowel into the sound system (section 2.3.1), and phonological changes of vowel quality (section 2.3.2) and vowel length (section 2.3.3) in certain environments.

2.3.1 The New Vowel

The second-stage loss of *r resulted in the introduction of the low front oral vowel phoneme /æ/. Consequently, contemporary Onondaga has one more vowel than did Old Onondaga. Table 2.13 compares the inventory of Old Onondaga vowels with the vowels of contemporary Onondaga:

Table 2.13: Inventory of Old and New Onondaga vowel phonemes.

Old Onondaga	New Onondaga
a	a
–	æ
e	e
ę	ę
o	o
ų	ų

2.3.2 Changes in Vowel Quality: Vowel Fronting

The changes in vowel quality occurred in sequences where *r was followed by a back vowel. The changes of vowel quality are shown in Table 2.14:

Table 2.14: Vowel changes associated with the loss of *r

Old Onondaga	New Onondaga
ra	æ(·)
ro	e(·)
rų	ę(·)

Table 2.14 shows that the Old Onondaga sequence *ra is pronounced æ in modern Onondaga. Similarly, Old Onondaga ro and rų are pronounced e and ę, respectively. These vowels are lengthened in environments specified in section 2.3.3. Together the changes in vowel quality are referred to as vowel fronting. Thus if a morpheme ends in *r and combines with a following element beginning in the vowels a, o, or ų, these vowels will be pronounced æ, e, or ę instead. This is illustrated in the following examples:

---

[20] The former presence of r in Onondaga is attested in Shea (1860), Zeisberger (1887[1761], 1887a, 1887-88). See Mithun (1980), Michelson (1986) for an account of *r-loss in Onondaga, and Chafe and Foster (1981) for an account of *r-loss in Cayuga, Seneca, and Onondaga.

(26) <u>Vowel fronting:</u> [21]

    a. waʔhaʔwáhæ·dat
       waʔ-ha-ʔwahR-<u>a</u>dat-Ø
       FACT-3M.SG.A-meat-pass-PNC
       he passed [the] meat

    b. waʔhaʔwáhe·k
       waʔ-ha-ʔwahR-<u>o</u>-k
       FACT-3M.SG.A-meat-put.in.water-PNC
       he boiled [the] meat

    c. waʔhaʔwahę́·da·k
       waʔ-ha-ʔwahR-ųdaR-k
       FACT-3M.SG.A-meat-put.into.container-PNC
       he put meat into a container

In (26a) *-ʔwahR-* is followed by *-adat-*. The R of *-ʔwahR-* disappears and the *a* of *-adat-* is fronted to *æ*, thus combined the two are pronounced *-ʔwahæ·dat-* (lengthening of *æ* is also a reflex of old Onondaga *r* and is discussed in the next section). Similarly, in (26b) and (26c) *-ʔwahR-* is followed by verb roots beginning in *o* and *ų*, respectively, and these are fronted to *e* and *ę*, with loss of the R.

2.3.3 Changes in Vowel Length: Compensatory Lengthening

Vowel length has numerous sources in Onondaga. Some of these are phonological, such as those occasioned by the loss of **r* discussed here, and the loss of **w* when it occurred before another resonant (section 2.4). Other sources of vowel length are prosodic (section 2.7.4). In addition to the change in vowel quality discussed in section 2.3.2, the loss of **r* in certain environments resulted in vowel length. Thus, when **r* occurred between a consonant and a vowel, i.e., **CrV*, or between a vowel and a consonant, i.e., **VrC*, then the vowel is lengthened in modern Onondaga. The following examples show both of these processes:

---

[21] <u>On the notation used to represent **r* in the morpheme segmentation line:</u> The former presence of historical **r* is marked as *R* in the morpheme segmentation line when it occurs at the beginning or end of a morpheme, but with the modern reflexes of R-loss if it occurs morpheme internally. The system is an adaptation of that originated by Michelson (1986). The reason for using the symbol *R* at the edge of morpheme segments but not morpheme internally is that it is at the morpheme boundaries that multiple reflexes of the lost consonant can occur. For example, *-Rik-* 'bite into something' and *-ʔwahR-* 'meat' are examples with **r* occurring morpheme initially and morpheme finally, and for each of them the modern reflex will differ depending on what precedes it, in the first of these, and what follows it, in the second. Morpheme internally the *modern* reflexes of historical **r* are shown, because the phonological environment of the lost consonant remains constant there and thus the reflex will never change. For example, the base meaning 'stir' was historically **.awęrye-* +dualic, with **r* occurring morpheme internally. In the segmentation line this base is cited as *.awę·ye-* +dualic with the constant modern reflex of morpheme internal **r* shown as vowel length.

24 The Sound System

(27) <u>Compensatory lengthening:</u> [22]
    a. waʔhehnų́·dę·ʔ
      waʔ-he-hnųdR-ę̀ʔ
      FACT-1SG > 3M.SG-follow-PNC
      I followed him

    b. gathnáʔtsho·s
      g-at-hnaʔtshoR-s
      1SG.A-SRF-wear.pants-HAB
      I wear pants

The following minimal pair shows that vowel length that is due to **r*-loss is phonemic:

(28) <u>Vowel length due to **r*-loss is phonemic:</u>
    a. hęgnęhę́·hwaʔ
      h-ę-g-nęhR-ęhw-aʔ
      TRNS-FUT-1SG.A-crowd-take-PNC
      I'll lead the group

    b. hęgnęhę́hwaʔ
      h-ę-g-nęh-ęhw-aʔ
      TRNS-FUT-1SG.A-EP-corn-take-PNC
      I'll take corn [along]

In some sequences where **r* is preceded by the laryngeals *h* or *ʔ*, there is no length. For example:

(29) <u>Unpredictable absence of compensatory lengthening with laryngeals:</u>
    a. haʔgęhę́thaʔ
      h-aʔgęhR-ęt-haʔ
      3M.SG.A-dust-push.down-HAB
      he dusts

---

[22] For simplicity's sake, and following the usage of Iroquoianists, I use *compensatory lengthening* to describe both of these processes, although Hayes (1989: 297) finds, in an extensive comparative study of compensatory lengthening within a moraic theory of phonology, that the process does not compensate for segments lost from onset positions of syllables in the languages considered by him. He analyses Onondaga's change from CrV → CV· as a case of vowel coalescence (ibid., 282-3) which retraces actual historical changes involving an intermediate stage with epenthetic *e.* Thus in the intermediate stage *CrV → *CerV; *CerV → CeV with loss of the **r.* Finally the two vowels coalesced, producing CV·. There is no historical evidence for an intermediate stage with an epenthetic vowel to break up the consonant cluster in the sequence *VrC which became V·C. That case, in which a consonant following a vowel is lost, according to Hayes' survey, is a classic case of compensatory lengthning. The loss of **r* in sequences consisting of *VrV did not produce vowel length, and this, also, is common cross-linguistically. (See Woodbury 1981 for an examination of historical documents before the loss of the resonant *r).

b. ohgíʔæʔ
   o-ahgiʔR-aʔ
   NPF-rag-NSF
   rag

In others there *is* vowel length with preceding *h* or *ʔ*.

(30) <u>Vowel length with contiguous laryngeals</u>:
   a. hya deʔhahę́·khaʔ < *deʔhahrųkhaʔ
      hya   deʔ-h-ahę·k-haʔ
      NEG   NEG-3M.SG.A-hear-HAB
      he doesn't listen

   b. gado·yáhę·k
      g-ado·y-ahę·-k < *gadoryahrųk
      1SG.A-move-DST-HAB
      I'm moving around

These differences appear to be a feature of specific lexical items, which are so marked.[23]

2.3.4 Changes Resulting from the First Stage of *r-Loss

The earliest stage of *r-loss, in which the sequence *ara was changed to *aa* → *a·*, affected certain noun and verb roots that ended in the sequence *ar when they were combined with a following morpheme beginning in *a*, but did not affect others. The loss is attested in Shea (1860) and Zeisberger (1887[1761], 1887a, 1887-1888), and appears to show that the resonant was unstable at that time. However, when taking into account the modern development of vowel fronting discussed in section 2.3.2, it seems probable that rather than showing instability, the older dictionaries show that there were two classes of stems containing the *ara sequence, only one of which underwent the change to *aa*. The modern reflex of this stage of loss has become lexicalized as a property of the affected roots and is learned by speakers along with such a root's meaning.[24]

In modern Onondaga, the affected roots are impervious to the rule of vowel fronting when it comes to a following *a*; hence the sequences *aro and *arų are realized as *ae* and *aę* respectively (by the second-stage vowel-fronting rule discussed in section 2.3.2) as expected, but the sequence *ara is realized as *a·* (from *aa*) without vowel fronting. An example of a noun root of this type is *-hesgaR-* 'arrow':

(31) <u>An *ara noun root</u>:
   a. gahésga·ʔ
      ga-hesgaR-aʔ
      NPF-arrow-NSF
      arrow

---

[23] Chafe (1970:76) noted this peculiarity as well.

[24] Attempts to explain the difference between the classes phonologically can be found in Woodbury (1981:114-7), and Michelson (1988:176). However, none of the explanations account for all or even most of the data.

   b. waʔgahesga<u>é</u>ʔnhaʔ
      waʔ-ga-hesga<u>R</u>-<u>o</u>ʔ-nhaʔ
      FACT-3N/Z.SG.A-arrow-fall.into.water-PNC
      an arrow fell into the water

   c. hehohesgá<u>e</u>·dyeʔs
      he-ho-hesga<u>R</u>-ų dy-eʔs
      TRNS-3M.SG.P-arrow-throw-HAB
      he is throwing arrows

The first stage of **r*-loss affected both nouns and verbs. An example of an **ar + a* verb is
.gweʔdaR- + dualic 'scratch something', which belongs to the H1 conjugation class that
takes the habitual aspect allomorph *-ųs*, the stative allomorph *-ųh*, and the punctual
allomorph *-aʔ*:

(32) <u>An *ara verb root</u>:
   a. dehagwéʔda<u>e</u>s
      de-ha-gweʔda<u>R</u>-ųs
      DL-3M.SG.A-scratch-HAB
      he scratches it

   b. dehųwagwéʔda<u>e</u>h
      de-hųwa-gweʔda<u>R</u>-ųh
      DL-3 > 3M.SG-scratch-STV
      someone has scratched him

   c. waʔthagwéʔda·<u>ʔ</u>
      waʔ-t-ha-gweʔda<u>R</u>-aʔ
      FACT-DL-3M.SG.A-scratch-PNC
      he scratched it

Eventually, during the second stage of **r*-loss (described in 2.3.1 to 2.3.3), the remaining
lexical roots ending in **ar* also lost the **r*, but with these roots all back vowels following
**r*, <u>including</u> *a*, were fronted,. A root belonging to this second set is *-aʔaR-* 'veil, netting':

(33) <u>A late-stage *ara root that undergoes a-fronting</u>:
   a. oʔá·æʔ
      o-aʔaR-aʔ
      NPF-veil-NSF
      veil, netting

   b. godaʔáewih
      go-ad-aʔaR-oR-ih
      3FI.P-SRF-veil-cover.st-STV
      she is wearing a veil

c. goda?aẹníh
   go-ad-a?aR-ụni-h'
   3FI.P-SRF-netting-make-STV
   she has made lace

Tables 2.15 and 2.16 list noun and verb roots ending in **ar* that have lost the resonant but do not front a following *a*.[25]

Table 2.15 Noun roots affected by the earliest stage of *r-loss

Noun Root	Gloss	Noun Root	Gloss
-adẹhaR-	*sun*	-na?ahgaR-	*shore, bank*
-adụnaR-	*ladder, steps*	-na?gaR-	*horn, antler*
-ashaR/shaR-	*handle, strap*	-nụdaR-	*thick soup, cracked corn soup*
-a?shaR-	*knife*	-nụhsodaR-	*supernatural illness*
-RæhgwaR-	*sun, moon*	-nụ?waR-	*head*
-RẹdaR-	*magic power*	-nyadaR-	*lake*
-RẹgaR-	*branch, brush*	-sdaR-	*rain*
-RẹwaR-	*needle, wire*	-sgohaR-	*branch, brush*
-gụ?nhwaR-	*fur, fuzz*	-sgụdaR-	*inner layer of bark*
-hdegaR-	*rib*	-shegwaR-	*spear, fork*
-hesgaR-	*arrow*	-shwẹ?gaR-	*board, flooring*
-hna?gaR-	*protrusion*	-sohgwaR-	*lip*
-hụgaR-	*elm, hickory*	-tkwẹhdaR-	*red*
-hụ?gwaR-	*throat, windpipe*	-wẹyụhgaR-	*inch*
-hwẹ?gaR-	*stick*	-yẹ?gwaR-	*smoke*
-jihgohaR-	*pin*	-yụhgaR-	*thumb*
-ji?tgwaR-	*bile, yellow*	-?nowaR-	*turtle*
-jyụtgaR-	*hook*	-?nyụgwaR-	*pricker bush*
-nagaR-	*pole*		

Table 2.16 Verb stems affected by the earliest stage of *r-loss

Verb base	Gloss	Verb base	Gloss
-[R]-/-aR-	*put in, incorporate*	-haR-	*hang up, suspend*
-N-aR-[26]	*apply put on*	-hẹdadẹhdaR-	*be a flatland*
.adaR- + cislocative	*ingest*	-hẹhji?daR-	*singe someone's hair, trick someone*
-adahsụdaR-	*get dark, shadowed*	-hnhohwaR-	*close a door*
.adæ·hdi?tshẹ·daR + dualic	*put on socks*	.hsihaR- + dualic	*be tight, be stuck*
.adæ·?negaR- + dualic	*burst, explode*	-hsiyehaR-	*thread a needle*
.adetgwẹ?da?negaR- + dualic	*reveal a secret*	-hwisdaR-	*iron something, press something*
.adethaR- + dualic	*get talked about*	.RihodaR- + dualic	*oppose, be undecided*
-adethe?tshæR-	*powder oneself*	-RihwaR-	*have something to say*
-adẹ·hohaR-	*sit on the top of a tree, perch on a tree*	-jikhe?daR-	*salt something*

---

[25] In the Onondaga Dictionary (Woodbury 2003) these are referred to as R1 verbs and nouns.

[26] The notation -N- indicates the the verb form that follows the second dash requires an incorporated noun. This notation is also used in the Onondaga Dictionary (Woodbury 2003).

Table 2.16 (Continued)

Verb base	Gloss	Verb base	Gloss
-adidaR-	*board, get in*	-jisdanohgwaR-/ -jisdęnohgwaR-	*be a star, be a spot*
-adi·ʔsdaR-	*vocalize*	-jiʔdaR-	*cause someone to cry constantly, put tears on someone*
-adnųhgaR-	*cut one's hair*	-naʔnawęhsehaR-	*tip with lead*
.adodaR- +dualic	*tangle*	-nedodaR-	*ascend a hill*
.adohdaR- +dualic	*clean up, clear out one's place*	-neʔwaR-	*feel horrified*
.adųdaR- +dualic	*condition, pattern*	-nęyųdaR-	*load a gun*
-adųhwęjyadethaR-	*be an earthquake*	-nųhgaR-	*cut someone's hair*
.adwęnųdaR- +cis or trans	*make a telephone call.*	-odaR-	*hook on, get snagged*
-adyaʔdaR-	*join a group*	-ogaR-	*knock down*
-adyaʔdadęhdaR-	*lie down*	-ohaR-	*put on top of, put on the tip of*
-at-N-aR-	*apply something for oneself*	.ohdaR- +dualic	*clean something, clear something out*
-at-N-aR-	*emit*	-sdaR-	*have scales*
-at-N-awethaR-	*go into, insert itself*	-thaR-	*speak, talk*
-atgęhdaR-	*get scraped*	.thaR- +dualic	*converse, talk*
-athwisdęʔda·R-	*be a spendthrift, waste ones money*	-theʔtshæR-	*flour something*
-at-N-ųdaR-	*get into, put into for oneself*	-ųdaR-/ -yaʔdųdaR-	*put in a container*
-awethaR-	*insert, put between*	-węnohaR-	*act boisterously*
-aʔęnaR-	*bewitch*	-wihsadęhdaR-	*ice up*
-aʔgaR-	*become dark*	-wihsa·thaR-	*spread butter*
.aʔgaR- +cislocative	*become faint*	-yaʔdaR-	*picture something, join a group*
.aʔgaR- +dualic	*become dark, be night*	-yaʔdohdaR-	*eliminate someone from a game*
.RæʔnegaR-/.ʔnegaR- +dualic	*burst something*	.yędaR- +dualic and repetitive	*resemble*
-RæʔwisdagęhtaR-	*peel*	-yęhsæ·dęhdaR-	*lay a carpet*
-dęhdaR-	*spread out, lay out*	-ʔdųhgwaR-/ -dųhgwaR-	*have a fever*
-ęʔdaR-/-ęʔda·w-	*burn something*	.ʔnigųhaR- +dualic	*bother someone*
-ęʔnigųhæR-	*observe*	-ʔnigųhgwęhdaR-	*be in mourning*
-gęhdaR-	*scrape something*	.ʔnisgwęhdaR-/.ęʔnisg węhdaR-	*lie on one's stomach, lie upside down*
-gohaeʔtshæR-	*soap something*	-ʔnųhdaR-	*bury*
-gųʔtshehaR-	*weigh*	.ʔwashaR- +dualic	*be an earring*
.gweʔdaR- +dualic	*scratch*		

2.3.5 *r-Initial Stems Pattern Like Consonant-Initial Stems

Stems beginning with *r select pronominal prefixes from the consonant-stem series (section 4.3) even though historical *r is no longer pronounced. Thus, the stem -Ret- 'gather something, collect something' selects the *ha-* alternant of the masculine agent prefix that occurs with consonant stems, rather than the *h-* alternant that occurs with *e*-stems, as in the following example:

(34) a. <u>*r-initial stem</u>: háets
     ha-Ret-s
     3M.SG.A-gather-HAB
     he gathers

   b. <u>*e*-initial stem</u>: íthe?s
     i-t-h-e-?s
     EP-CIS-3M.SG.A-walk-HAB
     he's around there

Verb stems beginning in *r are treated as consonant-initial stems with respect to stem-joiner *a* insertion (section 2.6.3), following the rule that incorporated nouns ending in a consonant and verbs beginning in a consonant must be separated by the joiner vowel:

(35) a. <u>C + *rV sequence</u>: ęgahyáehga?
     ę-g-ahy-<u>a</u>-Rehg[27]-a?
     FUT-1SG.A-berry-JN-gather-PNC
     I will gather berries

   b. <u>C + V sequence</u>: niyohsojyés (LG20)
     ni-yo-hsojy-es-Ø´
     PRT-3N/Z.SG.P-pile-be.long-STV
     how high the pile is

Finally, *r-initial stems are sensitive to the rule of *e*-epenthesis (section 2.6.2). At the boundary between a pronominal prefix or a reflexive morpheme and a lexical morpheme beginning in *r such stems select a conditioned allomorph of the pronominal or reflexive that includes epenthetic *e*, on condition that they begin in certain combinations of two consonants (including *r) as in (36a) and (36b). Without *r as one of the resonants the same sequence lacks the epenthetic *e* (37a) and (37b):

(36) <u>With epenthesis</u>: C + CC → CeCC
   a. <u>Pronominal allomorph with epenthetic *e*</u>: wa?gé·yo?
     wa?-ge-Ryo-?
     1.SG.A-kill-PNC
     I killed it

---

[27] -*Rehg*- is the alternant of suppletive -*Ret-/-Rehw-/-Rehg*- 'gather' selected by the punctual aspect.

    b. <u>Semireflexive allomorph with epenthetic *e*</u>: hadé·yos
      h-ade̲-Ryo-s
      3M.SG.A-SRF-kill-HAB
      he fights; he is a fighter

(37) <u>Without epenthesis</u>: C + C → CC
    a. <u>Pronominal allomorph without epenthetic *e*</u>: waʔgyená?
      waʔ-g-yena-ʔ´
      FACT-1SG.A-grab-PNC
      I grabbed it

    b. <u>Semireflexive allomorph without epenthetic *e*</u>: a·hų·dyenawásda?
      aa-hų-ad-yenaw-asd-aʔ
      OPT-3M.PL.A-SRF-grab-CS-PNC
      they would hang onto it

2.4 Loss of **w* before *y* or **r*

A second historical source of vowel length in Onondaga is due to the loss of the resonant **w* whenever it occurred before another resonant. The modern reflex of the loss is vowel length preceding the resonant sequence.[28] For example:

(38) ga·yęnędáʔih
    ga-Wyęn-ędaʔ-ih
    3N/Z.SG.A-task-complete-STV
    it was completed [by someone]

When the two resonants **wy* occurred immediately following an obstruent consonant, a conditioned allomorph of the pronominal prefix that includes epenthetic *e* is selected. In modern Onondaga the epenthetic *e* occurs as a long vowel due to compensatory lengthening in (39):

(39) age·yęnę·dáʔih
    age̲-Wyęn-ędaʔ-ih
    1SG.P-task-complete-STV
    I have finished it

The resonant **w* was also lost when it occurred before **r* with, sometimes, dramatic results as in (40):

---

[28] Because the reflex of vowel lengthening is identical to that involving **r*, comparative evidence is required for which of the resonants is involved. In this case the Oneida base *-wyʌnʌtaʔ-* 'get something ready' corresponds to Onondaga example (38) and (39).

(40) hya de?sga·ǽ·dah
    hya de?-s-ga-WR-ada-h
    NEG NEG-REP-3N/Z.SG.A-wind-be.in-STV
    there's no longer air in it

In contemporary Onondaga both segments expressing the noun root *-WR-* 'wind' have disappeared. Their former presence is marked only by the two reflexes of vowel length and the change of vowel color in the following morpheme. Thus *a* → *æ* before the two resonants; **w* is lost; *-ada-* → *-æda-* with loss of **r*.

2.5 Non-Automatic Morphophonemic Alternations

2.5.1 Word-Initial and Prepronominal-Pronominal Prefix Boundaries[29]

2.5.1.1 Change of the sequences *wa? + wa* or *a + wa* to *ų*

The morphophonemic rule *(w)a(?) + wa* → *ų* (where + represents the morpheme boundary between prepronominal and pronominal prefixes) is optional in Onondaga.[30] The second *wa* sequence of this rule must be fully contained in the pronominal prefix position of the verb, which means that the rule applies only to the first person patient pronominal prefix alternants *-wag(e)-/-wak-*.[31]

(41) a. ųgnó·węʔ
    waʔ-wag-nowę-ʔ
    FACT-1SG.P-fail.to.do-PNC
    I failed, I couldn't do it

    b. hya thaųgéʔse·k
       hya th-aa-wage-ʔse·-k
       NEG CON-OPT-1SG.P-drag-PNC
       I wouldn't drive

    c. ųgadeʔnyę́·dęʔ...
       waʔ-wag-adeʔnyędę-ʔ
       FACT-1SG.P-try-PNC
       I was tested

    d. dųgadęhsæ·yę́hdaʔ
       d-a-wag-adęhsæ·yęhd-aʔ
       CIS-FACT-1SG.P-smell.an.odor-PNC
       I smelled an odor passing by

---

[29] See Table 4.48 which lists all combinations of prepronominal prefixes.

[30] This rule is observed more frequently by Onondaga Nation speakers than by Six Nations speakers. But even speakers who observe it seem to have no particular preference either way.

[31] This is true for all but one speaker I know about (LG) for whom the domain of the rule extends to the stem. For example: dųdyéęhdaʔ [da-w-adyeęhd-aʔ] 'it happened first' (LG23).

In older texts there is a special alternant *-ųgw-* of this portmanteau segment which occurs before stems beginning in *a*:

(42) ųgwa·dæ·ʔshwahetgę́hdę̨ʔ (CTL51.5)
     waʔ-wag-adæ·ʔshw-ahetgę-hd-ę-ʔ
     FACT-1SG.P-luck-be.bad-CS-BEN-PNC
     I'm having bad luck

   2.5.1.2 Vowel Raising

The factual prepronominal prefix alone or in combination with the coincident, contrastive, or partitive prepronominal prefix, i.e., *waʔ-, tshaʔ-,* or *tha(ʔ)-, nwaʔ-* is changed to *weʔ-,*[32] *tsheʔ-, the(ʔ)-,* or *nweʔ-,* respectively, if it is followed by one of the following set of pronominal prefixes: (i) second person singular patient; (ii) second person singular imperative; (iii) second person dual or plural; (iv) first person inclusive dual or plural agent as in (43a-d). A factual prefix that occurs with certain combinations of prepronominals also undergoes vowel raising in that environment as in (43e):

(43) a. we̲ʔsahdędyų̨há·dyeʔ
        weʔ-sa-ahdędyų-h-adye-ʔ
        FACT-2SG.P-travel-STV-PRG-PNC
        you are traveling along

     b. tshe̲ʔdwadųwi·shę́ʔ
        tsh-eʔ-dw-adųwishę-ʔ'
        COIN-FACT-1IN.PL.A-rest-PNC
        while we (incl.) rested

     c. Dyę́haʔ gwaʔ ęhsgwenyaʔ hya the̲sawęnohdah... (H621.2)
        dyę́haʔ gwaʔ   ę-hs-gweny-aʔ   hya the-sa-węnohd-ah
        HYP   RESTR FUT-2SG.A-can.do-PNC   NEG CON-2SG.P-vocalize-IMP
        if   just   you can do it   you shouldn't make a sound
        If you're able not to make a sound...

     d. ...neʔtho nweʔdwagwenyaʔ... (H634.10)[33]
        neʔtho   n-weʔ-dwa-gweny-aʔ
        MAN   PRT-FACT-1IN.PL.A-can.do-PNC
        how   thus we could do it
        ...how we were able to do it...

---

[32] The Onondaga factual prefix *weʔ-* after vowel raising differs from cognate forms in the other Five Nations languages, where it is *we-* and, in Seneca, *-e-*. Lounsbury, in Oneida, assigns the *e* of *we-* to the pronominal prefix (1953:68). Chafe notes that in Proto-Northern-Iroquoian the factual was **w* and the **e* was part of the pronominal prefix. Seneca lost **w* from **we-* leaving *e-* which was reanalyzed as factual (2015:29). Karin Michelson suggests (p.c.) that in Onondaga, *e* was also reanalyzed as factual and the glottal has been extended from the *waʔ-* factual to form *weʔ-*.

[33] Hewitt did not mark accent and vowel length in the excerpts cited in example (43).

e. ... tsha? nigé nhwe?dwa?shędá?nha?... (CTL324.6)
   tsha?   nigę   n-h-we?-dwa-?shęda?-nha?
   SUB   EXT   PRT-TRNS-FACT-1IN.PL.A-leave.off-PNC
   that   extent we left off there
   ...the extent of our accomplishments...

Similarly, the final vowel of prepronominal prefixes ending in *a* is raised to *e* if it is followed by one of the same set of pronominal prefixes.

(44) a. a<u>e</u>sni·hų́·di?
     ae-sni-Rihw-ųdi-?
     OPT-2DU-matter-throw-PNC
     you two should leave word

   b. dų<u>se</u>jyóhda·k
     d-ųse-jy-ohdaR-k
     DL-REP:FACT-2PL-clean.something-PNC
     you all cleared it out

   c. s<u>e</u>sahdę́·dyah
     se-s-ahdędy-ah
     REP:FACT-2SG.IMP-leave-IMP
     go home!

   d. dų<u>de</u>dwadę́sda?
     d-ųda-dwa-dęsd-a?
     DL-CIS:FACT-1IN.PL.A-jump.up-PNC
     we all suddenly jumped up

2.5.1.3 i-Insertion

The vowel *i* is inserted between a prepronominal prefix that ends in the repetitive or cislocative and one of the following pronominal prefixes: (i) second person singular patient; (ii) second person singular imperative; (iii) second person dual or plural; (iv) first person inclusive dual or plural agent.

(45) a. ęj<u>i</u>·dyathó·ya?
     ę-s-dy-athoy-a?
     FUT-REP-1IN.DU.A-tell-PNC
     we two will repeat it

   b. ęd<u>i</u>·dwadiyę́·dę?
     ę-d-dw-adiyęd-ę?
     FUT-CIS-1IN.PL.A-pull-PNC
     we will pull it

   c. waʔdiswahwáhnhaʔ
     waʔ-t-swa-hwahnh-aʔ
     FACT-DL-2PL-form.a.circle-PNC
     you all formed a circle

   d. diswaná·ge·ʔ
     d-swa-nage·-ʔ
     CIS-2PL-reside-STV
     you all live there

2.5.1.4 Dissimilation

The consonant cluster /s/ + /hs/ composed of the repetitive prepronominal prefix -*s*- and the second person singular agent prefix -*hs*- is changed to *tsh* by some speakers:

(46) ętshadathe·wáhdaʔ
    ę-s-hs-adathe·wahd-aʔ
    FUT-REP-2SG.A-repent-PNC
    you will repent

The consonant cluster s + s composed of the repetitive prepronominal prefix -*s*- and pronominal prefix beginning in *s* is changed to *ts*:

(47) ętshagonátgaʔk
    ę-s-shagon-atgaʔk-Ø
    FUT-REP-3M.NSG > 3-release-PNC
    they will release them

2.5.1.5 Glide Deletion

With some exceptions (see below) glides of pronominal prefixes are deleted word-initially and after a prepronominal prefix ending in *ʔ*:

(48) a. ohésgaeʔ
      (y)o-hesgaR-o-ʔ
      3N/Z.SG.P-arrow-immerse.in.water-STV
      an arrow is immersed in water

   b. waʔagotgá·yaʔk
      waʔ-(y)ago-atga·yaʔk-Ø
      FACT-3FI.P-get.paid-PNC
      she got paid

The initial segment *ya* is deleted word-initially from the feminine-indefinite patient prefix -*yago*- (pronominal prefix #22) and the interactive prefix -*yagodi*- (pronominal prefix #44) :

(49) a. godahųhsá·deʔ
   (ya)go-adahųhsad-eʔ
   3FI.P-be.listening-STV
   she is listening

   b. godíkdųk
   (ya)godi-kdų-k
   3FZ.NSG > 3NSG-examine-HAB
   they tell their fortunes

The initial segment *w* of the first person patient pronominal prefix is deleted word-initially:

(50) agadó·dih
   wag-adodi-h
   1SG.P-grow.up-STV
   I'm a grown up

Many speakers in both communities drop the w- alternant of prefix #9 word-initially with nouns:[34]

(51) ade·yóhsæ·ʔ
   w-ade·yo-hsR-aʔ
   NPF-fight-NOM-NSF
   warfare

2.5.2 The Boundary between Pronominal Prefix and Stem[35]

2.5.2.1 Vowel Sequences

Vowel sequences that occur at the boundary between pronominal prefixes and stems are subject to a variety of patterns that depend on stem-initial elements. Stems are classified as *c*-initial (consonant-initial), *a*-initial, *e*-initial, *ę*-initial, *i*-initial, *o*-initial, and *ų*-initial. These initial elements select different pronominal prefix alternants. Furthermore, the initial element is either left intact, deleted, or the two elements coalesce. For example, stem-initial *i* is deleted when it is joined to pronominal prefixes ending in *o* or *ų* as in (52a), it is retained when it is joined to pronominal prefixes ending in a consonant as in (52b), and when a pronominal prefix ending in *a* combines with stem-initial *i*, the two vowels coalesce, becoming *ę* as in (52c):[36]

---

[34] Prefix #9 is retained word-initially with verbs by all speakers.

[35] See Tables 4.7 and 4.8 showing the pronominal prefixes of both Onondaga dialects.

[36] A very few stems beginning in *i* are exceptions to this rule. For example, the suppletive alternant, -*ihę*- 'say' retains the sequence as in *waʔaihę́·ʔ* 'she said'; and the stem -*ihey*- 'die' retains the sequence *ai* with pronominal prefix #11 – *waʔaihé·yaʔ* [waʔ-a-ihey-aʔ] 'she died', but has the vowels coalesce with other pronominals, e.g., *waʔhęhé·yaʔ* [waʔ-ha-ihey-aʔ] 'he died'.

(52) a. <u>Stem-initial vowel element is deleted</u>: hegųhnų́ks
  he-gų-(i)hnųk-s'
  TRNS-1SG > 2SG-fetch-HAB
  I am fetching you

  b. <u>Stem-initial vowel element is retained</u>: hegihnų́ks
  he-g-ihnųk-s'
  TRNS-1SG.A-fetch-HAB
  I fetched it

  c. <u>The two vowels coalesce</u>: hųsahųwę́hnųk
  h-ųsa-hųwa-ihnųk-Ø
  TRNS-REP:FACT-3 > 3M.SG-fetch-PNC
  she/they brought him back

Table 2.17 shows all of the combination that are subject to these changes.

Table 2.17: Stem-initial modifications[37]

Pronominal ending	Stem-initial element	Modification
o- e.g., -yo-	-a e.g., -awę·ye- 'stir'	a is deleted deyagowę·yéh 'she is stirring it'
ų- e.g., -yų-	-a e.g., -awę́·ye- 'stir'	a is deleted dęyųwę́·ye? 'she will stir it'
ę- e.g., -yę-	-e e.g., -e- 'walk'	e is deleted ę́·yę? 'she will be walking'
o- e.g., -ho-	-ę e.g., -ęnihdyę- 'have around one's neck'	ę is deleted honíhdyę? 'he has it around his neck'
ų- e.g., -hų-	-ę e. g., -ęni·hę- 'cease, quit'	ę is deleted wa?hųni·hę́? 'they quit'
a- e.g., -hųwa-	-i e.g., -ihnųk- 'fetch'	a and i coalesce to ę hųsahųwę́hnųk she brought him back'
e- e.g. -he-	-i e.g., -idagR- 'lay someone down'	i is deleted wa?hedá·gę? 'I laid him down'
ę- e.g., -gę-	-i e.g., -idęR- 'take pity on, help out'	i is deleted gędé·ih 'it is helping'
i- e.g., -yakhi-	-i e.g., -idagR- 'lay someone down'	i is deleted ęyakhidá·gę? 'we will lay them down'
o- e.g., -shago-	-i e.g., -idagR- 'lay someone down'	i is deleted ęshagodá·gę? 'he will lay them down'

---

[37] The table design is modeled on one devised by Michelson & Doxstator 2002:15.

2.5.2.2 Sequences with Resonants

If the sequences /wo/ and /wų/ arise at the boundary between a pronominal prefix and a
stem, i.e. when a pronominal prefix ends in *w* and a stem begins in *o* or *ų,* the sequences
become *yo* or *yų* even when it is preceded by a consonant (compare the automatic
phonological rule in section **2.2.3.4** above):

(53) a. sg<u>y</u>ohae?séh
     sg<u>w</u>-<u>o</u>hae-?se-h'
     2PL < 1PL-wash-BEN-STV
     you (pl) have washed it for us

   b. jyųg<u>y</u>ųhwęjyadáshų?
     s-yųg<u>w</u>-ųhwęjy-ada-shų?
     REP-1PL.P-nation-be.one-PL
     each of our nations, one at a time

2.5.3 The Boundary between Stem and Aspect Suffix

/y/ alternates with /i/ before an aspect morpheme beginning in a consonant:

(54) a. wa?dye·dé·n<u>i</u>? *she changed it, she exchanged it*
     wa?-d-ye-den<u>y</u>-?
     FACT-DL-3FI.A-change-PNC
     she changed it
          cf. dekdé·nyųs [de-k-deny-ųs] *I make changes*
   b. hohsę·n<u>í</u>h
     ho-hsę·n<u>i</u>-h´
     3M.SG.P-make-STV
     he has made it
          cf. wa?gehsę·nya? [wa?-ge-hsę·ny-a?] *I made it*

   c. agekhųníhna?
     age-khw-ųni-h´-na?
     1SG.P-meal-make-STV-PST
     I had cooked a meal
          cf. gekhų·nyáha? [ge-khw-ųny-aha?] *I cook*

In the habitual aspect the sequence *hgw* + *ha?* is replaced by *khwa?.*

(55) a. hadega?dá<u>khwa?</u>
     ha-adega?d-a<u>hgw</u>-ha?
     3M.SG.A-light.a.fire-INST-HAB
     he lights fires with it
          cf. wadega?dáhgwih *it was used to light [the] fire*

   b. hųwaihwanowę́khwaʔ
     hųwa-Rihw-a-nowęhgw-haʔ
     3 > 3M.SG-matter-JN-respect-HAB
     they treat him respectfully
             cf. waʔha·gi·hwanowę́hgwaʔ *he treated me respectfully*

   c. degayaʔdákhwaʔ
     de-ga-yaʔd-a-hgw-haʔ
     DL-3FZ.SG.A-body-JN-pick.up-HAB
     hawk [literally: it picks up bodies]
             cf. dehóhgwęh *he has picked it up*

2.6 Epenthesis

Onondaga has three processes that insert epenthetic vowels. Each of these are inherited from similar historical processes that are played out somewhat differently in each of the modern languages: (i) a prothetic *i-* prefixes that vowel to single syllable words; (ii) an epenthetic *e* breaks up impermissible consonant clusters at certain morpheme boundaries; and (iii) the stem-joiner *a* intervenes between an incorporated noun ending in a consonant and a verb beginning in a consonant as well as between verb stems and derivational and aspectual suffixes under similar conditions. The next three sections describe each of these in detail.

2.6.1 Prothetic i-

An empty syllable consisting of an *i-* is added to the beginning of inflected words that contain only one vowel at the stage when the rule applies. Prothetic *i-* was already present in Proto Northern Iroquoian. It may have been added to a word in order to provide a syllable to receive regular penultimate stress. The pattern is continued in Onondaga with a variation that is due to Onondaga's stress placement rules. Regular examples with stressed *i-* are:[38]

(56) ígeks
    i-ge-k-s
    EP-1SG.A-eat-HAB
    I eat it

(57) íheʔ
    i-ha-e-ʔ
    EP-3M.SG.A-walk-PRP
    he is walking

In one-syllable words whose aspect suffix attracts stress to the final syllable there are two patterns, (i) prothetic *i-*, though present, remains unstressed, and (ii) prothetic *i-* is absent. The latter forms often vary with forms that have the unstressed *i-* as in (58):

---

[38] Note that while open, stressed penults are regularly lengthened in Onondaga, prothetic *i-* cannot undergo lengthening.

(58) <u>With unstressed prothetic i-:</u>
    tho ijyę̂h
    tho   i-s-yę-h´
    there   EP-2SG.IMP-place-IMP
    Put it down there!

(59) <u>Single-syllable word without prothetic *i-*:</u>
    ų́s   *or*   iyų́s
    (y)-ų̨s-Ø´   i-y-ų̨s-Ø´
    3N/Z.SG.A-be.long-STV   EP-3N/Z.SG.A-be.long-STV
    It is long.

Certain morphemes and aspect suffixes move stress to the antepenult. In this situation prothetic i- is prefixed to the resulting two-syllable words and then stressed, thus performing its original function of providing a place for the word stress:

(60) íkhawaʔ
    i-k-haw-´aʔ
    EP-1SG.A-hold-STV[39]
    I am holding it

Exceptions to these patterns are the following forms consisting of two syllables – types of stems usually not eligible for the prothetic *i*. For these an unstressed prothetic *i-* has become lexicalized:

(61) <u>Two syllable words with unstressed prothetic i-:</u>
    a. iyų́·dų̨k[40]
       i-yų-adų̨-k
       EP-3FI.A-say-HAB
       she says, they say

    b. tho igá·yę̨ʔ
       tho   i-ga-yę-ʔ
       there   EP-3N/Z.SG.A-place-STV
       that's where it is

    c. nę nų́ ikhǽ·haʔ
       nę   nų́   i-k-hR-ahaʔ
       there   place   EP-1SG.A-put.on.top.of-HAB
       I am putting it up here

---

[39] Note that in words that are utterance-medial – these are generally stressed on the final syllable – stress moves away from prothetic *i-*, as in ikhawá? ihsá·węh *I'm holding [what] belongs to you.*

[40] This example suggests that prothetic *i* with two syllable examples may have originated with the new iambic stress pattern – one in which even-numbered syllables tend to be stressed – that followed the loss of **r* in Onondaga. The prothetic syllable is lacking in cognate forms of the time before **r-loss*, e.g., *nètho ne jõnto* 'they say' as documented in Zeisberger (1887[1761]:65).

2.6.2 e-Epenthesis

A vowel *e* is inserted to break up impermissible consonant clusters at the morpheme boundary between a pronominal prefix and a stem, and at the boundary between a reflexive morpheme and a lexical morpheme. Consonant clusters broken up by epenthetic *e* are formed when a morpheme ending in an oral obstruent is followed by a morpheme beginning with a cluster of two or more consonants. Of these, formations in which the second morpheme begins in any three or more consonants are always separated by epenthetic *e* from the preceding morpheme that ends in an oral obstruent. If the second morpheme begins in a two consonant cluster, then epenthetic *e* is inserted if such a cluster consists of (i) two oral obstruents, (ii) an oral obstruent and a laryngeal, (iii) an oral obstruent (other than the internally complex consonant /ts/) and a resonant, (iv) two resonants (including **r* and **w*), (v) any resonant (including**r*) and a laryngeal, (vi) a laryngeal and an oral obstruent,[41] (vii) two laryngeals, (viii) a fricative and a laryngeal.

(62) <u>Clusters of three or more consonants preceded by epenthetic *e*</u>:
    a. gehnya?sagų́·wah
       g-e-hnya?s-agųwa
       1SG.A-EP-throat-LOC
       my throat

    b. ageksdę?áh
       ag-e-ksdę?ah'
       1SG.P-EP-be.an.old.person
       I am old

    c. ęhsadadehsę́·nyę?
       ę-hs-adad-e-hsę·ny[42]-ę-?
       FUT-2SG.A-REF-EP-make-BEN-PNC
       you will make it for yourself

    d. agé·jyę?
       ag-e-jyę-?[43]
       1SG.P-EP-dish-NSF
       my dish

    e. dewa·géhgwęh
       de-wag-e-hgw-ęh
       DL-1SG.P-EP-pick.up-STV
       I have picked it up

---

[41] Some lexical roots simplify an obstruent + *h* + obstruent cluster by deleting *h*.

[42] The stem -hsę·ny- is etymologically -hsRųny-.

[43] Recall that the written symbol *j* represents underlying /ts/. These two segments contrast with the internally complex consonant (also written *j*) which functions as a single segment, and which does not take the epenthetic *e* in comparable environments, e.g. *dewatjisdó·gwa?s* [de-w-<u>at-jisd</u>-ogw-a?s] 'sparks, scattered lights'.

(63) Environment (i): O + OO → O + e + OO
    a. wa?gekdų́?
       wa?-g-e-kdų-?'
       FACT-1SG.A-EP-examine-PNC
       I examined it

    b. hadetgítha?
       ha-ad-e-tgiht[44]-ha?
       3M.SG.A-SRF-EP-get.something.dirty-HAB
       he gets dirty

    c. ęwadésda?
       ę-w-ad-e-sd-a?
       FUT-3N/Z.SG.A-SRF-EP-use.something-PNC
       it will get used

    d. hadesgatgwá?tha?
       ha-adesgatgwa?t[45]-ha?
       3M.SG.A-entertain-HAB
       he entertains

(64) Environment (ii): O + OL → O + e + OL
    a. wa?hųdekhų́·nya?
       wa?-hų-ad-e-khw-ųny-a?
       FACT-3M.PL.A-SRF-EP-meal-make-PNC
       they ate a meal

    b. ųdethé?tshæ·s
       yų-ad-e-the?tshR-aR-s
       3FI.A-SRF-EP-flour-apply-HAB
       she powders herself

(65) Environment (iii): O + OR → O + e + OR
    a. wa?gé·gwa?
       wa?-g-e-gw-a?
       FACT-1SG.A-EP-pick-PNC
       I picked it

    b. gé·dye?
       g-e-dye-?
       1SG.A-EP-fly-PRP
       I am flying

---

[44] The sequence *hth* is simplified to *th*

[45] The base -*adesgatgwa?t*- is composed of -*at*- semireflexive, epenthetic *e*, a verb root -*sgatgw*- which occurs only with derivational suffixes, and -*?t*-.

(66) <u>Environment (iv): O + RR → O + e + RR</u>
    a. ad<u>e</u>·yóhsæ·ʔ
       w-ad-e-Ryo-hsR-aʔ
       NPF-SRF-EP-kill.someone-NOM-NSF
       warfare

    b. ųgwad<u>e</u>·yęnędáʔih
       yųgw-ad-e-Wyęnędaʔ-ih
       1PL.P-SRF-EP-finish.a.task-STV
       we all have finished

    c. dewad<u>e</u>nyá·yaʔks
       de-w-ad-e-nyaR-yaʔk-s
       DL-3N/Z.SG.A-SRF-EP-neck-break.st.off-HAB
       violet

(67) <u>Environment (v): O + RL → O + e + RL</u>
    a. ęhs<u>é</u>ʔoʔ
       ę-hs-e-Rʔo-ʔ
       FUT-2SG.A-EP-chop.into-PNC
       you will chop into it

    b. g<u>e</u>nhęhá·khwaʔ
       g-e-nhęh-aR-hgw-haʔ[46]
       1SG.A-EP-urine-put.in-INST-HAB
       my bladder

(68) <u>Environment (vi): O + LO → O + e + LO</u>
    a. hųdad<u>é</u>ʔgęʔ
       hų-adad-e-ʔgęʔ
       3M.PL.A-REF-EP-younger.sibling
       they are moiety brothers

    b. ag<u>e</u>hdé·ga·ʔ
       ag-e-hdegaR-ʔ
       1SG.P-EP-rib-NSF
       my rib

(69) <u>Environment (vii): O + LL → O + e + LL</u>
    a. ag<u>e</u>ʔhó·wih
       ag-e-ʔhoR-ih[47]
       1SG.P-EP-cover-STV
       I've covered it

---

[46] The sequence *hgw-haʔ* is pronounced *khwaʔ*.
[47] *w* is inserted between *o* and a following vowel.

   b. hode̲ʔhó·wih
      ho-ad-e-ʔhoR-ih
      3M.SG.P-SRF-EP-cover-STV
      he has covered up

(70) <u>Environment (viii): O + FL → O + e + FL</u>
    ohwakdagí·ʔ gade̲shesdų·nyáhaʔ
    ohwakdagi·ʔ   g-ad-e-shesd-ųny-haʔ
    maple syrup   1SG.A-SRF-EP-sticky.substance-make-HAB
    I make [myself] maple syrup

Note that in Onondaga, unlike the other Northern Iroquoian languages, epenthetic *e* can accept main stress in open syllables as can be seen in some of the examples given above.[48] Also, with one exception epenthetic *e* can undergo prosodic vowel lengthening rules. The exception is antepenultimate vowel lengthening (sec. 2.7.4.2).

2.6.3 The Stem-joiner -a-

An epenthetic vowel *a* is, with a few exceptions, inserted at the morpheme boundaries between (i) an incorporated noun root and a verb root, (ii) between a verb root and a derivational suffix, (iii) between derivational suffixes, and (iv) between a noun and a following noun suffix, if joining the two morphemes results in a consonant cluster of two or more elements. The exceptions occur where the absence of a stem-joiner has become lexicalized. The stem-joiner *a* accepts main stress and prosodic lengthening rules other than antepenultimate lengthening.[49]

(71) <u>Joiner at the boundary between an incorporated noun and a verb root:</u>
    a. hoyehdá·yęʔ
       ho-yęhd-a-yę-ʔ
       3M.SG.P-pocket-JN-place-STV
       he has a pocket

    b. hahná·æs
       ha-hn-a-Ræ-s
       3M.SG.A-oil-JN-apply-HAB
       he greases it

Note that the verb root in (71b) begins in **r* and is treated as consonant-initial (section 2.3.5), so that the boundary is marked with a stem-joiner.

---

[48] Other NI languages can accept stress on epenthetic vowels in closed, but not open syllables (Michelson 1981; 1989).

[49] The joiners separating the derivational suffixes from verb stems and from each other, and morphological nouns from noun suffixes are not marked as separate morphemes in the sections following the present one. The reason for this is that Onondaga has in many cases no reliable way – as do the other Five Nations languages – to determine synchronically which occurrences of *a* in these environments are joiners and which are a part of aspect, derivational, and noun suffixes. The joiner will continue to be marked off by dashes between noun stem and verb stem.

44 The Sound System

(72) <u>Joiner at the boundary between a verb root and a derivational suffix is:</u>
    waʔgyadegáʔdaʔ
    waʔ-gy-adeg-a-ʔd-aʔ
    FACT-3FZ.DU.A-burn-JN-CS-PNC
    they burned it

(73) <u>Joiner between derivational suffixes:</u>
    dęsheyadųhwaęhęhgwáʔdę?
    d-ę-shey-adųhwaęhę-hgw-a-ʔd-ę-ʔ
    DL-FUT-2SG > 3-get.worried-INST-JN-CS-BEN-PNC
    you will cause her to worry

(74) <u>Joiner between a noun root and a noun suffix:</u>
    ga·hagṹ·wah
    ga-Rh-a-gųwa
    NPF-forest-JN-LOC
    in the forest

2.7 Prosody

The discussion in this section deals with accent patterns at the level of the word; it touches only lightly on larger discourse units. Sections 2.7.1 - 2.7.3 discuss preliminary matters: 2.7.1 provides historical background of the accent patterns as far as these can be known from comparisons with the extant Northern Iroquoian languages and from historical sources; 2.7.2 deals with the expression of accent; and 2.7.3 describes characteristics of the Onondaga syllable. Section 2.7.4 concerns the processes – various vowel lengthening rules – that affect the rhythmic patterns of the language. These sections provide the preliminaries to sections 2.7.5 which describes the rhythmic patterns of the language in terms of the metrical structures that organize them; section 2.7.6 which compares accent patterns utterance-internal with utterance-final units, and section 2.7.7 which deals with how pitch aligns with the rhythmic patterns of the language.

2.7.1 Historical Background

In Proto-Northern Iroquoian (PNI), main stress fell on the penultimate syllable, which, if it was an open syllable, was lengthened. This was true, unless an open penult contained the stem-joiner *a* (sec. 2.6.3), in which case main stress moved one syllable to the left (Chafe 1977a, Michelson 1988). Onondaga has inherited the pattern of stressing the penult and generalized it, so that an open penultimate containing the stem-joiner also accepts main stress. The process of lengthening vowels in open penults has also been inherited. However, the definition of what constitutes an open syllable has been broadened from a syllable that is followed by a single non-laryngeal consonant, to also include syllables that are followed by a CC cluster consisting of (i) an obstruent followed by a resonant, or (ii) two resonants (section 2.7.4.1). This, more recent definition, is used in applying the inherited pattern of lengthening open penults as well as other prosodic vowel lengthening processes in contemporary Onondaga.

Zeisberger's dictionary (Zeisberger 1887) and grammatical sketch (Zeisberger 1887-8), while published in the late nineteenth century, was actually written in the years from 1750 to 1761 predating the loss of the resonant *r* (Heckewelder 1820). His works document that by then the stem-joiner had already accepted main stress in open syllables where the other Northern Iroquoian languages did not, as shown, among others, in the entry for *ganatáje* 'town; Ort, Stadt' (1887:203), where the stressed *a* is the stem-joiner (contemporary Onondaga: *gana·dá·yę?* 'village, town'). While Zeisberger frequently marked stress with acute or grave accent,[50] he noted vowel length only very sporadically, marking it, when he did, with the circumflex.[51] Zeisberger's dictionary and grammar, as well as a dictionary dating from the 17th century by an unknown author (Shea 1860), show that Onondaga at that time inserted an epenthetic *e* to break up unacceptable consonant clusters, much as contemporary Onondaga does (sec. 2.6.2), but with a more extensive distribution at the earlier stage.[52] Zeisberger also documents that main stress on epenthetic *e* was *not* yet permitted, so that when the penultimate syllable contained an epenthetic *e*, stress moved to the antepenult, for example: *gahúchsera* 'chest; Kasten' (Zeisberger 1887[1761]:36) where *e* in the penultimate syllable is epenthetic (contemporary *gahų́hsæ·?* 'box'). Comparison of the modern and early forms shows that the epenthetic *e* that in Zeisberger's day broke up consonant clusters consisting of an oral obstruent and *r* in this environment, exists now only in the modern reflex of vowel length. As can be seen in the examples, it has disappeared together with the *r in contemporary Onondaga. Of interest, though, is that main stress is aligned with the same morpheme at both stages of the language. How and whether secondary stress was expressed in PNI is unknown at this time.

2.7.2. Accent[53]

Within the Onondaga word, some syllables are longer than others, some are louder than others, and some are pronounced with higher pitch than others. This is in part due to the rhythmic structure of the word. *Stress* is used here to designate the realization of the abstract notion of *accent* in terms of pitch, intensity, and duration. The basic rhythm of an Onondaga word is such that in addition to one syllable – typically the penult – receiving main stress, there are others that receive secondary stress, and yet others that remain unstressed. The acoustic manifestation of main stress is falling or – less frequently – level,

---

[50] An example with grave accent is *yehàwi* 'bring' (1887-8:37) contemporary *ehá·wi?* 'she is carrying it along'. There is no consistent difference in modern Onondaga that corresponds to Zeisberger's use of the acute vs. grave accent marks, so that the distinction Zeisberger is marking is unknown.

[51] *gathŏnte* 'I hear' (contemporary *agathų́de?* 'I am hearing, listening') which contrasts with *gathondéchqua* [no gloss in Z] which lacks length in the second syllable (1887-8:37) as it does in the contemporary version *agathų́déhgwa?* 'I used to hear'. An entry on p.12 of the dictionary (1887) shows *wathŭdahqua* 'approved; approbiert, gebilligt' showing, possibly, that the rule of antepenult lengthening (sec. 2.7.4.2) existed at that time. (Contemporary speakers use a different term to express the concept of approval).

[52] *e*-Epenthesis, occurs in Seneca, Cayuga, Mohawk and Oneida, but with different distributions. The process is not reconstructable for Proto-Lake-Iroquoian (Michelson 1988).

[53] Onondaga prosody is also reviewed in Chafe (1977a); Michelson (1988:90ff); Woodbury, et al. (1992: 715ff). Note that Hewitt did not mark vowel length consistently and sometimes not at all, so that examples citing Hewitt do not show vowel length reliably.

or rise/fall pitch, an increase in vowel length, and an increase in intensity.[54] Secondary stress is heard as a rhythmic beat[55] - coursing through the word from left to right until it meets the syllable with main stress (see sec. 2.7.5).

Where in a given word main stress docks depends on the location of the word in an utterance. There are three patterns here called (i) *utterance-final* intonation, which occurs at the end of an utterance or in a citation form; (ii) *phrase-final* intonation which occurs utterance-medially at the end of a phrasal unit; and (iii) *word-level* intonation which occurs elsewhere. *Utterance-final* intonation is marked by penultimate main stress with a steep decline of pitch in the ultima, is followed by a substantial pause and a pitch reset at the beginning of a new utterance. In the examples, utterance-final intonation is followed by a period. As noted, citation forms are also pronounced with utterance-final intonation. As in utterance-final intonation, main stress docks on the penultimate syllable in *phrase-final* intonation, but with only a minimal pitch decline in the ultima, and the phrase is followed either immediately by another word or phrase or after a less pronounced pause than the utterance-final pause. Phrase-final intonation is not followed with a pitch reset when a speaker resumes the utterance. In examples where this pattern occurs, a comma follows the intonational phrase. Finally, when *word-level* intonation occurs, main stress docks on the final syllable of a word that is immediately followed by another word without pause. Differences between utterance-final and word-level intonation are detailed in section 2.7.6.

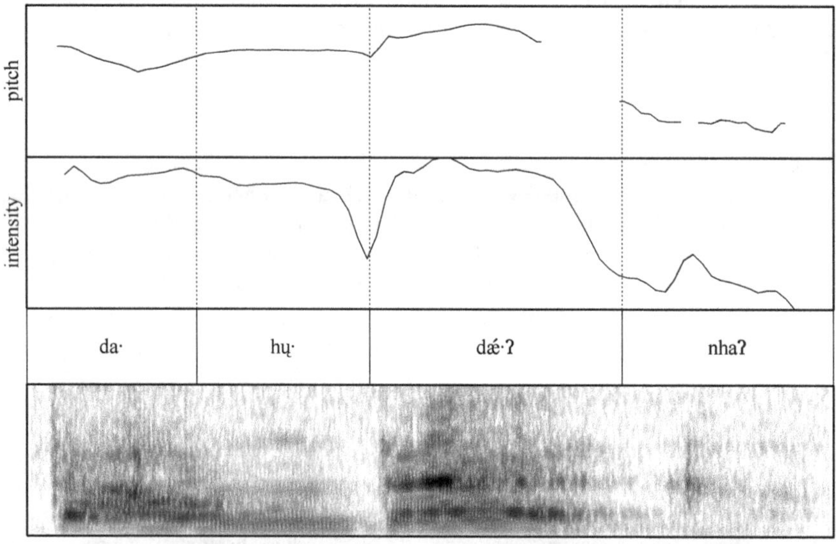

Figure 2.1 Utterance- and phrase-final intonation: *dahų·dǽ·ʔnhaʔ* 'for them to meet up'

---

[54] In earlier work (1992, 2002), relying on perceptual impressions, I equated prominence with the property of loudness (intensity). As it turns out, this property, by itself, is an unreliable indicator of prominence.

[55] This *rhythmic beat* will be shown in section 2.7.5.2 to consist of a rhythmic patterning of iambic feet which consist of a light followed by a heavy syllable.

The description in this and the immediately following sections is of utterance-final stress patterns. Representations using *Praat* (Boersma & Weenink 2015) show the acoustic manifestations of main stress which, as noted above, occurs on the penult. Figs. 2.1 to 2.3 show falling or level pitch contours on the penult. In all three of the traces below there is a noticeable decrease in pitch and intensity on the final syllable. In Figure 2.1, a representation of a citation form of the word *dahy·dǽʔnhaʔ* 'for them to meet up', the pitch contour falls off sharply by the time it reaches the ultima. Pitch peak and the initial descent of the pitch contour both occur in the penultimate syllable.

The distribution of main stress and high pitch (F_0) are not identical in Onondaga. A characteristic of Onondaga, that distinguishes it from the other Five Nations Iroquoian languages, is that the syllable containing the pitch peak *precedes* the syllable receiving main stress in more than half of documented utterance-final forms.[56] The pitch traces in Figures 2.2 and 2.3 illustrate variations on that pattern: In Fig. 2.2 – a trace of the citation form of the word *agenyʔkhwéʔæʔ* 'my hair' – the peak occurs in the antepenult with main stress occurring on the rise/fall contour of the penult. (Note that the length of the final syllable as shown in Fig. 2.2 is due to the fact that the final glottal stop was released). Fig. 2.3 shows a pattern that can occur in longer words: In the trace of the citation form of the seven syllable word *honathwisdani·yǫ́·daʔ* 'they've got bells hanging' the F_0 reaches its peak three syllables to the left of the penult, is followed by a more or less level contour, and eventually descends on the lengthened penult.

Together the pitch traces show that the location of peak F_0 is not a defining feature of main stress in Onondaga, but rather, that it is acoustically manifested by a combination of features that includes pitch contours, vowel length, intensity, and a sharp contrast in the expression of these features between the penult and the ultima. In a sense, then, there are two pitch events: one relating to the location of peak F_0, and another relating to marking accent. Hence, much like in Oneida, peak F_0 is not where the most relevant pitch event is realized.[57] (The alignment of pitch and stress is discussed in section 2.7.7).

---

[56] The acoustic manifestation of stress in Seneca (Chafe 1967, 1988; Melinger 2002), and Cayuga (Dyck 1997), is high pitch (f_0). In Oneida stress is manifested as a *rise* in f_0. Peak f_0 usually occurs one mora to the right of the mora that has the rise; that means that if the stressed syllable is a long vowel then the rise and the peak are in the same sylllable, but if it is a short vowel then the peak is on the mora of the following syllable (Grimm 1997).

[57] I am grateful to Karin Michelson for noticing the similarity and for suggesting this formulation.

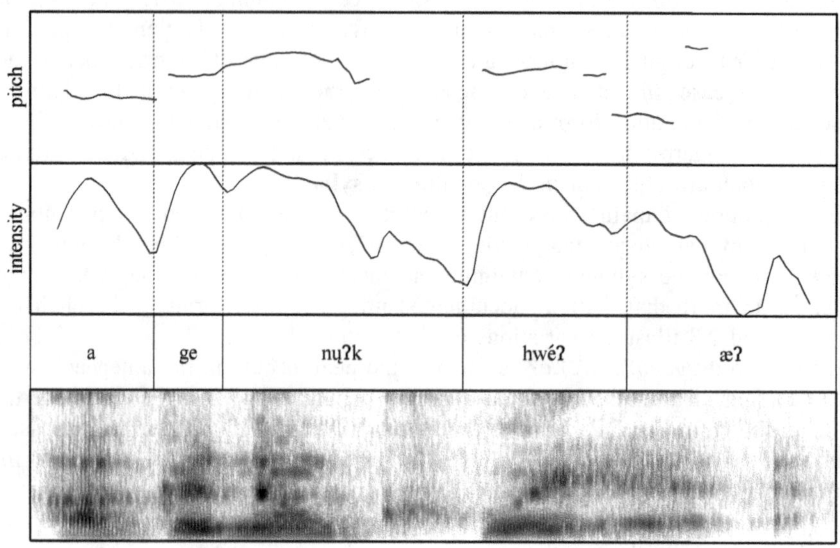

Figure 2.2 Pitch/intensity trace of *agenų?khwé?æ?* 'my hair'

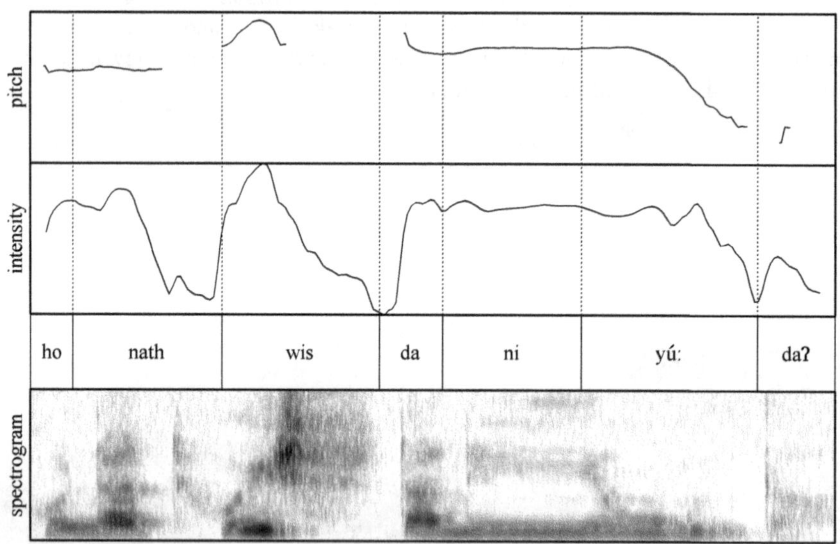

Figure 2.3 Pitch/intensity trace of *honathwisdani·yų́·da?* 'they've got bells hanging'

2.7.3 Syllable Shape and Syllable Weight

The stress bearing unit of a word is the syllable (Hayes 1995). The syllable is a unit that is internally structured into two elements, the *onset* (consisting of any initial consonantal segments) and the *rhyme* (consisting of a *nucleus* (the vocalic segment) and a *coda* (one or more consonantal segments)). In Onondaga, *main* stress is distributed by *position* of the syllable in the word, i.e., it docks invariably on the penult. The distribution of syllables receiving *secondary* stress, on the contrary, depends on a classification of syllables in terms of the rhythmic system, which invokes *syllable-weight* as a criterion. Heavy syllables attract secondary stress. Syllable-weight is a property of the syllable's rhyme and is determined by counting *morae*: heavy syllables are *bimoraic*, light syllables are *monomoraic*. In Onondaga, light syllables are CV; heavy syllables are CV·, CVV (diphthongs), or CVC(C). A cross-cutting classification of syllables divides them into *open* and *closed* syllables. An open syllable is one that is followed by (i) a single, non-laryngeal consonant, i.e. (C)V.CV, or (ii) a consonant cluster consisting of either an oral obstruent followed by a resonant, i.e., (C)V.CR, or of two resonants, i.e. (C)V.RR. With some exceptions discussed in the next paragraphs, two or more obstruents, i.e., (C)VC.C, or a single intervocalic laryngeal consonant, i.e., (C)VL.V close a syllable. The differences between the two ways of classifying syllables is displayed in the following array:

Rhythmic Structure		Vowel Lengthening Processes	
Light	Heavy	Open	Closed
(C)V	(C)V·	(C)V.CV	(C)VC.CV
	(C)VV	(C)V.CRV	(C)VL.V
	(C)VC(C)	(C)V.RRV	

   Prosodic vowel-lengthening rules[58] are sensitive to the criterion of *openness* in the Iroquoian languages. Syllable *weight,* as mentioned above, functions to mark the *rhythmic structure* of the word. Since vowel lengthening rules affect the weight of a syllable, the two criteria of weight and openness become mingled in Onondaga. These topics are taken up in the next paragraphs.

Syllabification Algorithms[59]

VV sequences are syllabified as (C)V.V(C) unless they are diphthongized. Diphthongs and long vowels form a single syllable nucleus, and are parsed as. (C)VV(C). [diphthong] and .(C)V·(C). [long vowel], respectively.

---

[58] All of these are vowel lengthening rules except for compensatory lengthening which is due to the loss of **r* (sec. 2.3.3).

[59] Syllable boundaries are marked with a period (.); word boundaries are marked with the pound sign (#); parentheses surround optional elements; V stands for any vowel; C stands for any consonant; L stands for a laryngeal consonant.

(75) <u>Syllabification of VV sequences</u>:
    a. (C)V.V(C) (disyllabic): waʔ.<u>ha</u>.ǽʔ.thę̣ʔ *he climbed*
    b. .(C)VV(C). (diphthong): <u>haæ</u>.gé·.was *he is wiping it*
    c. .(C)V·(C). (long vowel): waʔ.ha.dih.<u>ne·</u>.gíh.æʔ *they drank*

Sequences consisting of VLV – i.e., VʔV or VhV – are syllabified as (C)V.LV, except
that for the determination of two prosodic vowel lengthening rules, penultimate and
antepenultimate vowel lengthening, the sequences are syllabified as (C)VL.V. The
(C)VL.V syllabification is an inherited pattern; it blocks prosodic lengthening of a vowel
that is followed by a laryngeal in vowel lengthening environments, i.e., the penultimate or
an even antepenultimate (sections 2.7.4.1 and 2.7.4.2).[60] The effect is shown in (76) where
the *a* and *b* examples syllabify with the inherited algorithm for the purpose of determining
vowel lengthening rules (here the criterion is whether the syllable is open or closed)
(section 2.7.4), and the *c* and *d* examples syllabify with the algorithm that applies in
relation to stress assignment rules (here the criterion is whether the syllables are heavy or
light) (section 2.7.5). This means that laryngeals add a mora to the syllable with the
inherited algorithm, but are weightless in terms of the newly introduced algorithm.
Syllabification depends on the location of a cluster within the syllable or word as indicated
in Table 2.18..

(76) <u>Syllabification of VLV sequences</u>:
    a. (C)VL.V(C) syllabification (inherited algorithm): ni.ya.go.yaʔ.da.wę̣́ʔ.ih *the*
       way it happened to her
    b. (C)VL.V(C) syllabification (inherited algorithm): ę.g<u>ę</u>h.é·.yaʔ *she will die*
    c. (C)V.LV(C) syllabification: ę.<u>ha</u>.da.ʔę.no.jyę́h.daʔ *he will pry it out with a*
    d. (C)V.LV(C) syllabification: sa.<u>ha</u>.geʔ.sgo·.gwáʔ.neʔ *he came to pull me back*
       out of the water[61]

Table 2.18 Syllabification of medial C-clusters

Heterosyllabic	Tautosyllabic in onset position
obstruent + obstruent obstruent + fricative obstruent + laryngeal	oral obstruent + resonant
fricative + *n* or *w*	
resonant + laryngeal	resonant + resonant
laryngeal + obstruent laryngeal + fricative laryngeal + resonant laryngeal + laryngeal	

---

[60] The inherited algorithm is shared with Mohawk and Oneida (Michelson 1988:64,75), Cayuga
(Dyck 1997:4-5), and Seneca (Melinger 2002:289) which all require parsing intervocalic laryngeals
into coda- rather than onset-position for certain purposes involving accent assignment. Michelson
(ibid., 93) has observed that laryngeals close a syllable in Onondaga. Compare Chafe's (1970:76)
suggestion that examples like (76a) where there is no vowel lengthening be analyzed as having
underlying geminate *h* and *ʔ*.

[61] Vowel length in the fourth syllable of this example is due to the rule of antepenultimate vowel
lengthening (sec. 2.7.4.2)

The first column – *heterosyllabic* CC-clusters – lists CC-clusters that divide into the coda of one syllable and the onset of the following syllable. The second column – *tautosyllabic* CC-clusters – lists CC-clusters that occur together in the onset position. Much like the examples in (76) illustrating the syllabification of laryngeals, Table 2.18 shows that an obstruent adds a mora to a syllable if it is followed by another obstruent, i.e., (C)VC.C, but is weightless if it is followed by a resonant (including *r), i.e., (C)V(·).CR.

(77) <u>Syllabification of heterosyllabic CC clusters</u>:
        a. de.yųt.<u>ga</u>.hék.hwaʔ *glasses* [obstruent + obstruent]
        b. ų.de<u>k.sa</u>ʔ.dų·.nyáh.aʔ *she is being childish* [obstruent + fricative]
        c. waʔ.ge<u>k.hų</u>·.nyaʔ *I cooked* [obstruent + laryngeal]
        d. da<u>k.ʔ</u>áh.sęʔ *spider* [obstruent + laryngeal]
        e. waʔ.ga.nų.nyo.wá<u>n.ha</u>ʔ *they came to have a great dance* [resonant + laryngeal]
        f. ni.ya.go.ya<u>ʔ.da</u>.węʔ.ih *the way it happened to her* [laryngeal + obstruent]
        g. ho<u>h.sé</u><u>h.di</u>h *he has hidden it* [laryngeal + fricative; laryngeal + obstruent]
        h. ho.naæ<u>ʔ.sé</u>s.hę·ʔ *they are members of the opposite moiety* [laryngeal
           + fricative]
        i. waʔ.khèi<u>h.wí</u>hs.ʔas *I promised her* [laryngeal + resonant]
        j. wa<u>ʔ.ha</u>·dí·gęʔ *they saw it* [laryngeal + laryngeal]

(78) <u>Syllabification of tautosyllabic CC clusters</u>:
        a. waʔ.ha·.<u>gni</u>.yų́·.dęʔ *he hung it on me* [obstruent + resonant]
        b. ę.he·.<u>sni</u>.no.węk.hwák *you will be kind to him* [obstruent + resonant]
        c. des.hot.dé·.<u>nyų</u>h *he's changed back again* [resonant + resonant]

All medial CCC-clusters are syllabified as C.CC; medial CCCC-clusters syllabify as CC.CC.

2.7.4 Stress and Vowel Lengthening Processes

Onondaga has a mixed system of main stress placement: (i) *morphological* and (ii) *positional*. Secondary stress is assigned by rhythmic rules (sec. 2.7.5).

(i) The <u>*morphological* system of main stress assignment</u> consists of (a) certain grammatical morphemes attract main stress to the antepenult as in (79) (i.e., certain aspect morphemes, the stative plural, certain alternants of the benefactive suffix, etc.) and (b) grammatical morphemes that attract primary stress to the ultima as in (80) (i.e., mainly certain aspect morpheme alternants, the diminutive clitic, etc.). Because the patterning is morphologically determined, it is marked in the dictionary entry for that class of morpheme and is mentioned here only to explain examples that occur later in this volume and show main stress in other than the penultimate syllable.

(79) <u>Morphological stress on the antepenult</u>:
        a. swęh.níʔ.da.dah *one month*
        b. ha.di.gó.wa.nęʔs *their chiefs*

(80) <u>Morphological stress on the ultima</u>:
      a. de.ya.go.wę·.yéh *she is stirring it*
      b. wa.ʔų·.dyę́ʔ *she sat down*
      c. hak.saʔ.áh *boy*

There is some variation among speakers involving mainly the *-h* stative aspect suffix of the A conjugation class, and the *-k* habitual aspect suffix of the B4 conjugation class.

(81) <u>Variation among speakers</u>:
      a. ho.na.dųn.hų.níh or ho.na.dųn.hų́·.nih *toddlers*
      b. gyaʔ.da·s.dah.ę́·k or gyaʔ.da·s.dáh.ę·k *I draw pictures*

(ii) <u>The *positional* system of main stress assignment</u> aligns main stress regularly with the penultimate syllable of a word as noted above and shown in words from two to nine syllables in length in (82). Main stress is assigned by a syllable's position in the word rather than the rhythmic system - it docks on the penultimate whether that syllable is open or closed, heavy or light, or even or odd:

(82) <u>Main stress on the penult</u>:
      a. <u>gę́ʔ</u>.dę·ʔ *she lives there*
      b. hoh.<u>séh</u>.dih *he has hidden it*
      c. o.nę.<u>hóh</u>.gwaʔ corn soup
      d. ho.daʔ.dits.<u>hé·</u>.daʔ *he has a cane*
      e. dę.jih.sa.yah.<u>yáʔ</u>.kdę? *it will take you across again*
      f. waʔ.hų.wa.yaʔ.dah.<u>ní·h</u>.daʔ *they propped him up*
      g. a.ga.deʔ.nhaeʔt.shæ.ni.<u>yų́·</u>.daʔ *I've got rope hanging*
      h. de.wa.ga.doʔ.ji.neh.dah.<u>nų́h</u>.naʔ *I went skating*

<u>The interaction of vowel lengthening rules with stress placement</u>: Recall that vowel length has a number of sources that are due either to history (i.e., compensatory lengthening due to the loss of **r*) or to the prosodic structure of the language. Vowel length that is the consequence of **r*-loss is contrastive; it can occur in any syllable of a word, and regardless of where the word occurs in the utterance (medially or finally). On the contrary, prosodically conditioned vowel length (with one exception that is discussed in section 2.7.6) only affects certain syllables of words that occur utterance-finally and in citation forms. The placement of prosodic stress is sensitive to vowel length whatever its source; all syllables with long vowels are heavy and therefore attract secondary stress, as noted. Vowel length from **r* has been discussed in sections 2.3.3-2.3.4. The following three sections deal with prosodic vowel lengthening rules. These rules affect (i) the penult (ii) the antepenult, and (iii) the second syllable of a word, under conditions that are listed in section 2.7.4.1 to 2.7.4.3. When more than one contrastive or prosodic lengthening process affects the same syllable, no extra vowel length is produced. Whichever process applies second, is presumably blocked.

2.7.4.1 Penultimate Vowel Lengthening

If the penultimate is *open* (as defined in sec. 2.7.3) it is lengthened, unless it has already undergone an earlier lengthening process. Thus V → V· before (i) a single non-laryngeal consonant, (ii) an oral obstruent followed by a resonant (including *r), (iii) one or more resonant consonants, or (iv) the palatoalveolar affricate /ts/ (phonetically [dj], orthographic *j*) alone or (v) followed by the resonant y.

Penultimate vowel lengthening (PN):
(83) (C)V_σ → (C)V·_σ /___ σ#
    Condition: The vowel is in an open syllable.

Open syllable environments:
a.	Environment (i):	o.dé·.gẹh *it is burnt*
b.	Environment (ii):	o.da.dų.ni.há·.dyeʔ *it is starting to grow*
c.	Environment (iii):	o.gá·.yųh *it is old;* waʔ.gek.hų́·.nyaʔ *I cooked*
d.	Environment (iv):	o.hyá·.jih *blueberry, huckleberry*
e.	Environment (v):	o.gá·.jyẹʔ *dish, pan*

The examples in (83) show, crucially, that PN affects both even and odd syllables. In contrast, Antepenultimate Vowel Lengthening (section 2.7.4.2) and Second Syllable vowel lengthening (section 2.7.4.3) are restricted to even numbered syllables and to a narrowed set of conditioning environments. Note that the rule of penultimate vowel lengthening has the effect of causing *every* penultimate syllable that is not already so to become heavy.

2.7.4.2 Antepenultimate Vowel Lengthening

Lengthening of the antepenultimate vowel occurs if it is in an open syllable, is in an even syllable counting from the beginning of the word *and* the antepenult is followed by a penultimate syllable of the form (i) (C)V·, or (ii) .(C)VL.[62] If the vowel of the antepenult is the stem-joiner *a* or epenthetic *e*, antepenultimate lengthening is blocked. For this rule openness of the *antepenult* is defined more narrowly than for the rule of penultimate lengthening, such that an open antepenult is one that is followed by a (i) single non-laryngeal consonant, (ii) by a consonant cluster consisting of an oral obstruent followed by a resonant, or (iii) by one or two resonant consonants.

Antepenultimate vowel lengthening (APL):
(84)   (C)V_σ → (C)V·_σ /___ σσ#
    Condition: The antepenult is an even, open syllable and followed by an open, lengthened penult or a penult closed with a laryngeal obstruent.

a.	Environment (i):	waʔ.ha·.dí·.gẹʔ *they saw it*
b.	Environment (ii):	waʔ.ha.dẹh.ni·.nų́h.e·ʔ *he is on his way to sell (it)*
		dak.he·.yáʔ.dų̨ʔ *I handed it [an animal] to her*

---

[62] Note syllables of the form (C)VL are a subtype of the heavy (bimoraic) syllables (C)VC that function to mark rhythmic patterns.

Cf. oh.sų.dát.gi? *stormy night* in which the penult is closed with oral obstruents, and wa?.ga.nų.nyo.wán.ha? *it got to be a great dance* in which a resonant + laryngeal cluster close the penult, thus preventing antepenultimate vowel lengthening in both examples.

c. Environment (iii):   ga.da·.di·.hų·.nyę́·.nik[63] *I teach myself*

For many speakers initial consonant clusters change the syllable count.[64]

(85) Effect of initial consonant cluster on antepenult vowel lengthening:
    a. even antepenult without length: dyo.hų.dó·.da? *a tree stands there*
        cf. o.hų·.dó·.da? *a standing tree*
    b. lengthening in odd antepenult: dyowæ?nę·dá·gih *it is stuck on here*
        cf. owæ?nędá·gih 'it is stuck to it'

Note that except for the shift in syllable count produced by initial consonant clusters, the 'even syllable' requirement limits antepenultimate vowel lengthening to words consisting of even numbers of syllables and excludes words with fewer than four syllables. The corollary is that in words with initial clusters antepenultimate lengthening can only occur in words with odd numbers of syllables and excludes words with less than five syllable.

Speaker variation occurs insofar as speakers ignore a condition, or add one. For some speakers antepenult vowel lengthening is blocked when the vowel of the penult is short and followed by an *h* or *?* as in (86a); for some speakers antepenult length is blocked in words where the vowel to be lengthened precedes resonants that replace **r* as in (86b and c).[65]

(86) Speaker variation:
    a. wa?.tho.níh.nyę? *vs.* wa?.tho·.níh.nyę? *he acted crazy*
    b. gų.di.yǽ·.gwas *vs.* gų.di·.yǽ·.gwas [< *gų.di.ra.gwas] *they choose*
    c. hoh.sų.wǽ·.dih *vs.* hoh.sų·.wǽ·.dih [< *hoh.sų.ra.dih] *he has shot [a gun]*

2.7.4.3 Second Syllable Vowel Lengthening

In words of four or more syllables, the vowel of the second syllable of a word is lengthened if it is followed by a consonant sequence consisting of (i) an oral obstruent followed by a resonant (including former **r* and **w*) or (ii) by two resonants (including **r*

---

[63] Length in the second syllable is due to 2nd syllable vowel lengthening (2.7.4.3); length in the third syllable is compensatory (due to the loss of *r).

[64] The effect may be due to the fact that, speakers insert a short transitional vowel between an initial oral obstruent followed by a resonant, so that (85a), for example, is pronouced [diyohųdó·da?] by most speakers, thus changing the syllable count. Similarly, the initial consonant cluster of tganiyų́·da? 'it's hanging there' is pronounced [thganiyų́·da?] with a substantial voiceless segment inserted between the two initial stops and, perhaps, a similar effect on syllable count. Compare tganiyų́·da? 'it's hanging there' with ga.ni·yų́·.da? 'it is hitched on' without initial CC cluster and with antepenult lengthening in the (even) second syllable.

[65] Compare Chafe (1970:77) who reported on the effect of initial consonant clusters on syllable count but apparently encountered no variation among speakers.

and *w).[66] Second syllable vowel lengthening does not apply to the internally complex single segments /ts/ and /gw/ (which are written *j* and *gw*, respectively) as can be seen in (88e and f) unless the internally complex vowel is followed by a resonant (88g). Second syllable vowel lengthening also applies to epenthetic vowels for most speakers as shown in (89b) where the lengthened *e* is epenthetic:

Second Syllable Vowel Lengthening (SSL):
(87) (C)V$_\sigma$ → (C)V·$_\sigma$ /#σ___
    <u>Condition</u>: If followed by a cluster consisting of an oral obstruent + resonant or by two resonants.

(88) <u>Second syllable vowel length, environment (i)</u>:
    a. a.ga·dyétshæʔ *my seed*
    b. ga.da·.di·h.wíh.sʔę.nik (< *gada̲d̲r̲ihwihsʔęnik) *I am making plans*
    c. ę.he·.sni.no.węk.hwák *you will be kind to him*
    d. ę.ya·.gwa.da.hųh.si.yós.daʔ *we will listen*
    e. no lengthening with internally complex /ts/: ęd.wa̲.j̲is.dų·.nyaʔ *we lit a fire*
    f. no lengthening with internally complex /gw/: waʔhagwáthwaʔ *he dropped in*
    g. lengthening with internally complex /ts/ + resonant: ęj.ye̲·.j̲yęʔ.dáʔ.nhaʔ *she will begin to get healed.*

(89) <u>Second syllable vowel length, environment (ii)</u>:
    a. o.nų·.nyá·.gaks *it makes noise*
    b. ho.de·.yęs.dáh.nųh (< *hode̲w̲yęsdahnųh) *he went to study*
    c. oh.na·.ya.hęʔ.ih (< *ohna̲r̲yahęʔih) *the oil has come to a boil*
    d. a.ge·.nya.ę̇·.daʔ *I have a neck, my neck*

2.7.5 Footing and the Distribution of Primary and Secondary Stress

Languages like Onondaga, whose prosodic systems are based on stress (as against tone) organize stress patterns into rhythmic structures generating syllables of greater or lesser prominence within words and utterance-level constituents (Hayes 1995, Liberman 1975, Liberman & Prince 1977 and the sources cited there). Two major rhythmic patterns occur: one in which even-numbered syllables are stressed – *iambic* patterning – and one in which odd-numbered syllables are stressed – *trochaic* patterning. Hayes (ibid.) posits that human languages organize this patterning into metrical structures the smallest of which is the *foot*, a prosodic constituent containing no more than two syllables. He argues that there are three basic patterns of footing, (i) iambs, (ii) syllabic trochees, and (iii) moraic trochees. Of these, iambs and moraic trochees are sensitive to syllable weight, whereas syllabic trochees are not. Trochaic feet have a default stress pattern that is strong-weak, and iambic systems have a default stress pattern that is weak-strong. Typically, heavy syllables attract stress. While the default alternating stress patterns underlie the system, numerous processes –

---

[66] Note that in three syllable words, second syllable length is indistinguishable from penult length, since the conditioning environment for penultimate length includes that of second syllable length; in four syllable words second syllable length is indistinguishable from antepenultimate length unless the vowel in the antepenult is followed by a single, non-laryngeal consonant or the penult is followed by a consonant cluster that does not begin in a laryngeal as in (88a).

such as the vowel lengthening rules discussed above or residues from earlier systems – can interfere with them in various ways.

Although the rhythmic pattern of PNI is unknown, there are indications, that Onondaga may have moved from an earlier trochaic pattern to one that is iambic. The earlier trochaic system is suggested by Onondaga's very regular pattern of locating main stress on the penultimate syllable of a word and by its rule of open penultimate lengthening (section 2.7.4.1). The development of an iambic pattern is suggested in the main by the presence of rhythmic vowel lengthening rules that privilege even numbered syllables – i.e., Second Syllable Lengthening and Antepenultimate Lengthening in even syllables (sections 2.7.4.2-3).

2.7.5.1 The Choice of a Foot Type

Recall that main stress (marked as ´) regularly aligns with the penultimate syllable of a content word. Secondary stress (marked as `) occurs on one or more syllables to the left of main stress. Unlike main stress which is conditioned by the *location* of the stressed syllable (if a syllable is penultimate, it receives main stress whether it's light or heavy), the distribution of secondary stress is conditioned by the rhythmic structure of the language, which is sensitive to the number and weight (=morae count) of the syllables that go to make up the word. As mentioned above, Onondaga has an iambic rhythmic pattern – one in which a metrically weak syllable is followed by a metrically strong syllable.

Iambic footing permits two types of feet (Hayes 1995:71ff): (i) a bisyllabic foot, consisting of an initial light (single mora) syllable that occupies the metrically weak position, followed by a second syllable that occupies the the metrically strong position, but that, weight-wise, can consist of either a light (single mora) or a heavy (two morae) syllable;[67] or (ii) a monosyllabic foot consisting of a single heavy syllable. The other logically possible option – a single light syllabled foot – is prohibited in Onondaga. This is so, because there are no content words in the language consisting of a single light syllable.[68] Footing proceeds from left to right. Taken together, these characteristics mean that secondary stress docks on all heavy syllables and on the second of two contiguous light syllables that occupy the same foot. In addition, Onondaga requires an extrametricality rule which permits a final syllable to be impervious to footing.[69]

Demonstrating the available iambic foot types in a single word is example (90)[70] in which the word *wa?gany̨nyowánha?* has an initial foot consisting of a single heavy

---

[67] Of these two "maximal" foot types, a foot consisting of a light followed by a heavy syllable is the "canonical" iambic foot (Hayes 1995:86).

[68] Hayes (1995:86-89) discusses the relevance of minimal word requirements to the prohibition on "degenerate" feet.

[69] Extrametricality rules are common in the languages of the world. They "designate a particular prosodic constituent as invisible for purposes of rule application" (Hayes 1995:57) as long as the constituent is peripheral on the left or, more commonly, the right edge of the word. In Onondaga the constituent is the final syllable of a word. The need for Onondaga's extrametricality rule has its source in the inherited pattern of penultimate main stress.

[70] Feet are surrounded by parentheses (), syllables within the foot are marked off by a period, extrametrical constituents are surrounded by angled brackets < >, square brackets [] surround the joiner vowel.

syllable, a second foot consisting of two light syllables, a third foot consisting of a light syllable followed by a heavy second syllable, and, finally, an extrametrical ultima.[71]

(90) <u>Iambic foot types:</u> (wàʔ)(ga.nừ)(nyo.wán) < haʔ >   *they had a great dance*

Example (91) lists a variety of footed words ranging from two to nine syllables:

(91) <u>Iambic footing with words containing from two to nine syllables</u>
a.	(hgá·) < yaʔks >	*I pay*
b.	(hòh)(séh) < dih >	*he has hidden it*
c.	(o)(hǽ·h) < gwaʔ >	*bread*
d.	(wàʔ)(ha.géts) < gwaʔ >	*he raised it*
e.	(o.nè)(nòh)(gw[á]·) < gi·ʔ >	*potato soup*
f.	(ę.gừ)(yę̀ʔ)(gw[à]h)(ní·) < nụʔs >	*I will buy tobacco from you*
g.	(de.yà)(go.yàʔ)(do.wéh) < dih >	*she is considering it*
h.	(wàʔ)(sha.gòʔ)(sè·h)(d[a].nì)(háh) < dęʔ >	*he loaned her a car*
k.	(de.wa)(ga.dòʔ)(ji.nèh)(dàh)(nụ́h) < naʔ >	*I went skating*

á The examples show that (i) <u>main stress</u> can dock on both even and odd syllables counting from the beginning of a word; (ii) the stressed penultimate can occur in a foot consisting of a single metrically strong syllable, as in (91a, b, c, e, f, h and k), or as the second syllable of a foot that consists of a metrically weak syllable followed by a metrically strong one, as in (91 d and g); (iii) main stress can dock on a penult that contains the stem-joiner vowel (91e).[72]

Similarly, the examples show that <u>secondary stress</u> (i) can align with both even and odd syllables counting from the beginning of the word; (ii) can dock on a foot consisting of a single metrically strong syllable as in (91b); on the second syllable of a foot that consists of a light followed by a heavy syllable as in (91g and h); or on the second syllable of a foot that consists of a light followed by a light syllable as in (91e and f); and (iii) that secondary stress can occur on the stem-joiner as in example (91f).

2.7.5.2 Sequencing of Diachronic Developments

It is possible that, because of its effect on syllable weight and syllable count,[73] the staged loss of *r may have had a role in the shift from an early trochaic to the present iambic system. If so, the new system represents the outcome of integrating two radically different rhythmic patterns. Describing the resulting stress pattern is the task attempted in this section.

As pointed out above, heavy syllables attract secondary stress, and vowel lengthening processes – both contrastive and prosodic – can change originally light syllables to ones that are heavy. The loss of *r affects syllable weight in various ways and breaks down to a

---

[71] Metrically strong positions are the second syllable of a disyllabic foot, or the single position comprising a foot on its own.

[72] Recall that in the other Five Nations Iroquoian languages open penults containing the stem-joiner is skipped for the purpose of determining accent placement in open syllables.

[73] The earliest stage of *r-loss affected syllable count (sec. 2.3.4).

set of rules that must be carefully sequenced. For example, intervocalic *r-deletion does not apply to all *VrV sequences: recall that the resonant in the sequences *irV, *ųrV, and *orV is replaced by y or w, respectively (sec. 2.2.3.4 example (24)). Since the substituted resonants are retained in the modern language, resonant substitution must precede intervocalic *r-deletion. Also, for most speakers VV sequences are diphthongized under certain conditions (Table 2.19 below). When these are not met, the two retained vowels continue as nuclei of separate syllables; when they are met, the two vowels are diphthongized to form the nucleus of a single heavy syllable. Diphthongization thus affects both syllable weight and the odd-even count of syllables in the word, and the latter conditions antepenultimate and second-syllable vowel lengthening rules; thus diphthongization must be in place after intervocalic *r-deletion and before footing and stress assignment. Thus in (92a) the first vowel of the sequence is in the penultimate syllable and has been lengthened by the rule of penultimate vowel lengthening. In (92b) the second vowel of the sequence is in the penult but the syllable is closed so that penultimate lengthening doesn't apply. In (92c) neither of the VV segments resulting from *r-loss (and vowel-fronting) have been lengthened by either contrastive or rhythmic lengthening processes. In the latter two examples the two vowels are diphthongized, and function as a single syllable nucleus.

(92) a. wà?hagų̀?tshehá·ę? < *wa?.ha.gų?t.she.<u>ha</u>.rę? *he weighed it*
  b. wà?hadagwáihcya? < *wa?.ha.da.gwa.<u>rih</u>.cya? *he straightened it*
  c. gas.hwę?.<u>gaę</u>.nyáh.a? < *gas.hwę?.<u>ga.rų</u>.nya.ha? *sawmill*

The set of rules affecting the weight and even/odd status of syllables, together with their ordering, is set out in Table 2.19. It is assumed that Rules 1-6 which govern segmental processes, are in place before the prosodic lengthening processes apply. Finally, as noted, there are no extra-long vowels in Onondaga, so that once a vowel has been lengthened, no other lengthening rules apply.

Table 2.19 Ordered rules affecting syllable weight and the even-odd status of a syllable

1	Intervocalic resonant substitution (2.2.3.4; 2.5.2.2):	*irV→ iyV; ųrV→ ųwV; orV→ owV
2	Intervocalic *r-deletion (2.3):	*VrV → VV
3	Compensatory Vowel lengthening 1 (2.3.3):	*CrV → CV· (variably applied in laryngeal environments)
4	Compensatory Vowel lengthening 2 (2.3.3):	*VrC → V·C
5	*r-Deletion 2:	*r → Ø (deletes remaining *r)
6	Penult vowel length (2.7.4.1):	$(C)V_\sigma \rightarrow (C)V·_\sigma$ /___ σ# <u>Condition</u>: The vowel is in an open syllable.
7	Diphthongization (many speakers) (2.7.3):	V.V(·)→ .VV(·). in words of 4 or more syllables;[74] <u>Condition</u>: The first vowel has not been lengthened by prior vowel lengthening rules.

---

[74] A few speakers apply the rule to words of three syllables as well.

Table 2.19 (Continued)

8	Second syllable vowel lengthening (2.7.4.3):	$(C)V_\sigma \rightarrow (C)V\cdot_\sigma$ /#σ___ Condition: If followed by a cluster consisting of (i) an oral obstruent + resonant or (ii) by two resonants
9	Antepenultimate vowel lengthening (2.7.4.2):	$(C)V_\sigma \rightarrow (C)V\cdot_\sigma$ /___ σσ# Condition: If in an even, open syllable and followed by (i) an open, lengthened penult, or (ii) a penult closed with a laryngeal obstruent. Excluded are antepenultimate syllables containing the stem-joiner *a*.

2.7.5.3 Foot Construction

As has been pointed out, penultimate stress is regular and is assigned not by the rhythmic rules of the language, but in terms of a syllable's position – penult or not penult (sec. 2.7.3). Furthermore, accented open penults are lengthened by Penultimate Vowel Lengthening with the two rules presumably applying in that sequence.

Using the metrical framework of Hayes (1995), the rules listed in (93a-c) attempt to integrate Main Stress Assignment into a rhythmic account of the distribution of main and secondary stress:

(93)   a. Foot Construction: Form iambs from left to right
                                           Degenerate feet are prohibited
                                           Footing is persistent

       b. Final Syllable Extrametricality: σ → <σ> /_____]$_{word}$
                                           (renders final syllable invisible for footing)

       c. Word Layer Construction: End Rule Right
                                           (places main stress on final visible syllable)

The following derivations illustrate footing and the rules of Main stress assignment (94) and Penultimate Vowel Lengthening (95) (where applicable) for (96a) *waʔhagétsgwaʔ* 'he picked up one end', (96b) *deyųshęthwáheʔ* 'she's crying as she goes' and (97a) *dyohsojyó·daʔ* 'it is piled up there, upright pile', and (97b) *ęganaʔjyó·dak* 'it will be boiling'.

(94) Main Stress Assignment: $(C)V(V)(C)_\sigma \rightarrow (C)V(V)(C)_\sigma$ /___σ#
     (End rule right)

(95) Penultimate Vowel Lengthening: $(C)V_\sigma \rightarrow (C)V\cdot_\sigma$ /___ σ#
     Condition: The vowel is in an open syllable.

(96) <u>With closed penults</u>: Iambic footing and primary and secondary stress assignment
a. waʔ.ha.géts.gwaʔ   b. de.yųs.hęt.hwáh.eʔ   segmental rules + main
                                                          stress

    (wàʔ)(ha.géts) < gwaʔ >   (de.yųs)(hęt)(hwáh) < eʔ >   iambic footing, syllable
                                                          extrametricality, secondary
                                                          stress assignment

(97) <u>With open penults</u>: Penultimate vowel lengthening, iambic footing, stress assignment

a. dyoh.so.jyó.daʔ   b. ę.ga.naʔ.jyó.dak   segmental rules + main stress

(dyòh)(so.jyó) < daʔ >   (ę.gá)(nàʔ) jyó < dak >   iambic footing, syllable extrametricality, secondary stress assignment

(dyòh)(so.jyó·) < daʔ >   (ę.gà)(nàʔ) jyó· < dak >   penult vowel lengthening

                             (ę.ga)(nàʔ)(jyó·) < dak >   iambic footing (2nd round)

Note that in (97b), because of Onondaga's prohibition on constructing degenerate feet (single syllable light feet), the fourth syllable is left stray after the first round of iambic footing. The rule of penult vowel lengthening remedies that situation.

As shown in Table 2.19, there are two 'iambic' lengthening rules (rules that strengthen even-numbered syllables). Derivations with the first of these, Second Syllable Lengthening (98) are shown in (99a-b) for the words *aga·dyaʔdanósdih* 'I'm cooling down' and *waʔha·gniyų́·dę́ʔ* 'he hung it on me' and *deho·nyę́·daih* 'sparrow'.

(98) Second Syllable Vowel lengthening: (C)V$_\sigma$ → (C)V·$_\sigma$ /#σ___
Condition: If followed by a cluster consisting of (i) an oral obstruent + resonant or (ii) by two resonants.

(99) <u>Deriving Second Syllable Vowel Lengthening</u>

a. a.ga.dyaʔ.da.nós.dih   b. waʔ.ha.gni.yų́.dęʔ   segmental rules + main stress
                                 c. de.ho·.nyę́.daih

                                 (wàʔ)(ha.gnì) yų́ < dęʔ >   syllable extrametricality, iambic footing
(a.gà)(dyàʔ)(da.nós) < dih >   (de.hò) nyę́ < daih >

                                 (wàʔ)(ha.gnì) yų́· < dęʔ >   penult vowel lengthening
                                 (de.hò) nyę́· < daih >

                                 (wàʔ)(ha.gnì)(yų́·) < dęʔ >   iambic footing (2nd round)
                                 de.ho)(nyę́·) < daih >

(a.gà·)(dyàʔ)(da.nós) < dih >   (wàʔ)(hà·)(gnì)(yų́·) < dęʔ >   second syllable vowel lengthening, iambic footing
                                 (de.ho·)(nyę́·) < daih >

Second Syllable Vowel Lengthening changes a light (CV) syllable into a heavy (CV·) syllable. Note that in (99a and c) the second syllable was metrically strong to begin with; in (99b) the second syllable began as metrically weak and is made strong due to the rule application. In (99a and c) Second Syllable Vowel Lengthening strengthens the metrically strong syllable of the first foot, and may serve as clash avoidance with the stressed syllable to its right (see Michelson 1988).[75] In (99b) the function of Second Syllable Lengthening is limited to promoting iambicity.

The other iambic lengthening rule is Antepenultimate Lengthening which lengthens vowels in even, open syllables as given in (100):

(100) Antepenultimate Vowel Lengthening: $(C)V_\sigma \rightarrow (C)V{\cdot}_\sigma$ /___ σσ#
    Condition: If in an even, open syllable and followed by (i) an open, lengthened
    penult, or (ii) a penult closed with a laryngeal obstruent. Excluded are
    antepenultimate syllables containing the stem-joiner *a*.

Examples (101a-b) derive *waʔha·dí·gęʔ* 'they saw it', and *hodadahdę·dyéhdih* 'he's pushing himself':

(101) <u>Deriving Antepenultimate Vowel Lengthening</u>

a. waʔ.ha.dí.gęʔ	b. ho.da.dah.dę.dyéh.dih	segmental rules + main stress
(wàʔ)(ha.dí)<gęʔ>	(ho.dà)(dàh)(dę.dyéh)<dih>	syllable extrametricality, iambic footing, stress assignment
(wàʔ)(ha.dí·)<gęʔ>		penultimate vowel lengthening
(wàʔ)(hà·)(dí·)<gęʔ>	(ho.dà)(dàh)(dę̀·)(dyéh)<dih>	antepenult vowel lengthening, iambic footing

Antepenultimate Vowel Lengthening strengthens metrically weak syllables in both (101a) and (101b). Again, one of the rule's functions is, presumably, clash avoidance.

2.7.6 Comparing Word-Level with Utterance-Final Accent Patterns.

As noted in section 2.7.2 accent rules differ depending on whether a word is followed by another word without a pause, or whether it is followed by a pause between phrasal units in discourse. Comparing figures 2.4 and 2.5, the main difference in the two patterns is that word-level accent occurs on the ultima,[76] whereas utterance-final accent is on the penult.

---

[75] Clash is a situation in which contiguous syllables are stressed. Lengthened vowels serve to lengthen the interval between contiguous stressed syllables by inserting a mora between the two syllables.

[76] Accent on the ultima in phrase-medial forms is very frequent but not completely regular in discourse. Certain final morphemes do not take accent, which then moves to the antepenult. This is also documented in Chafe (1970:73). In addition, a number of particles do not accept accent unless they are a part of particle clusters. The pattern also gets disrupted by fluency issues (serching for words, rephrasings, etc). Recall also that text examples from earlier published sources either do not record accent at all or do so unreliably because they are the result of word for word dictations which

In addition, word-level pronunciation of content words, although it exhibits all the contrastive lengthening processes, lacks all but one of the prosodic lengthening processes discussed above. Figures 2.4 and 2.5 show typical differences in pitch, intensity, and rhythmic lengthening patterns of two matched content words. Note that while there is a sharp drop in both pitch and intensity in the final syllable of the utterance-final pattern (Fig. 2.4), both pitch and intensity rise sharply in the ultima of the utterance-medial form (Fig. 2.5) before falling at the very end of the syllable. Secondly, the penultimate lengthening rule shows clearly in the utterance-final stress pattern, but is absent in the in the word-level stress pattern.

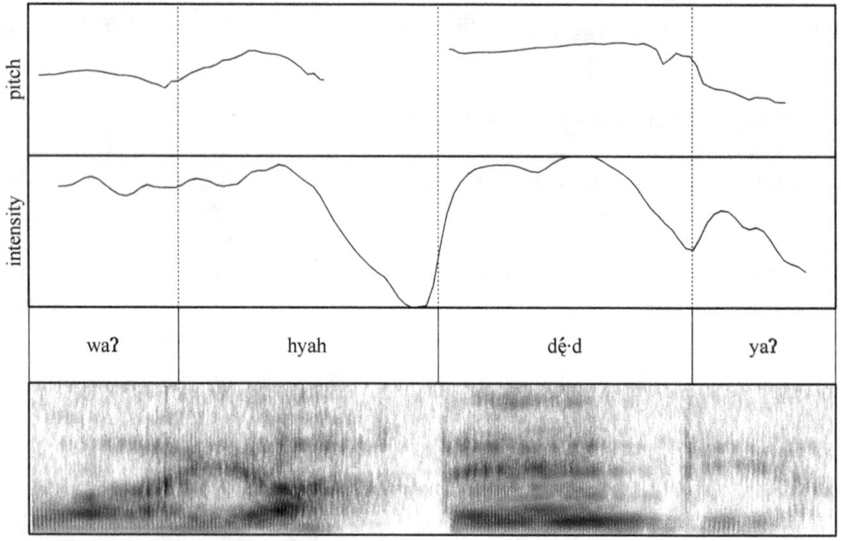

Figure 2.4 Utterance-final stress pattern: *wàʔhyàhdę́·dyaʔ* 'they two departed'

results in phrase-final patterns on each word. In this work, examples from those sources are used only when accent is not at issue.

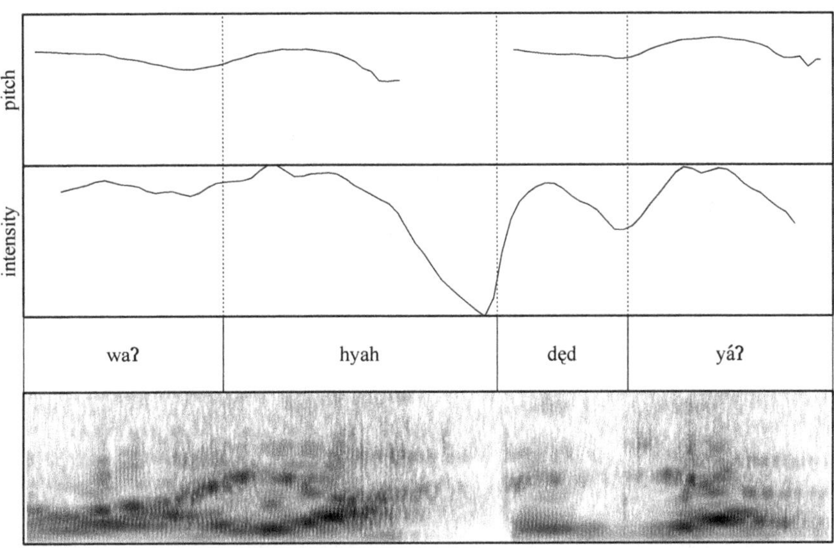

Figure 2.5 Word-level stress pattern: *wàʔhyàhdẹdyáʔ* 'they two departed'

Examples in (102) of non-final expressions demonstrate that the contrastive processes relating to the loss of **r* which affect syllable weight and position remain in place with utterance-medial pronunciations:

(102) a. <u>Intervocalic **r*-deletion</u> (with diphthongization): waʔgaæʔthẹ̀ʔ *she climbed up*
   (< *waʔgaraʔthẹʔ)
   b. <u>Compensatory Lengthening 1</u>: tshaʔ nigànagé·ʔ *where she lives*
   (< *niganagreʔ)
   c. <u>Compensatory Lengthening 2</u>: hụdè·yós *[they are] fighters*
   (< *hụderyos)

With one exception – Second Syllable Vowel Lengthening (104) – prosodic vowel lengthening rules do not occur with word-level pronunciations (103):

(103) a. <u>Penultimate Vowel Lengthening is absent</u>: wàʔhyàhdẹdyáʔ *they two departed*
         Compare utterance-final wàʔhyàhdẹ́·dyaʔ
   b. <u>Antepenultimate Vowel Lengthening is absent</u>: wàʔthadàʔnháʔ *he stopped*
      Compare utterance-final wàʔthà·dáʔnhaʔ

Puzzlingly, Second-syllable Vowel Lengthening, which appears in every other respect to be a prosodic lengthening rule, remains in place with word-level pronunciations:

(104) wàʔhà·dnụdaẹnyáʔ *he made himself soup*
      Compare utterance-final waʔhà·dnụdáẹ·nyaʔ

2.7.7 Pitch

Recall that main stress and peak F_0 frequently do not occur on the same syllable of content words. When the two occur on different syllables, peak F_0 always occurs earlier in the word than does main stress. The data examined for pitch-stress alignments in utterance-final words show that pitch occurred to the left of main stress in words of four or more syllables 56% of the time. Specifically, peak F_0 occurred on the penult in 44% of examples, on the antepenult in 36%, and in a syllable to the left of the antepenult in 20% of examples. Main stress meanwhile occurred invariably on the penult in all examples. In words of two or three syllables, high pitch always is aligned with main stress on the penult, unless the final syllable is marked for lexical stress. In addition, longer words can occur with more than one tonal contour, sometimes with peaks that are nearly equivalent in height (i.e., within 4 Hz).[77]

2.7.7.1 Previous Work

A number of attempts have been made to account for Onondaga's unusual prosodic patterns: Chafe (1977a:173-5) and Michelson (1988:91-2) compare and contrast the Onondaga pattern with that of the other Five Nations Iroquoian languages. Chafe (1977a) hypothesizes that the occurrence of peak F_0 to the left of main stress is a retention of an earlier PNI pattern in which epenthetic vowels were skipped in determining accent placement. Thus, as noted in section 2.7.1 above, historically, if the vowel of an open penult was the stem-joiner, main stress moved to the antepenult. Similarly, both Mohawk and Oneida have retained rules that do not count open penults with epenthetic vowels for the purpose of main stress placement, but instead, stress the antepenult. By extension, Chafe hypothesizes for Onondaga, that syllables with epenthetic vowels are counted for the determination of penultimate accent, but not for determining the syllable bearing high pitch. This solution accounts for examples with peak F_0 on the antepenult when the penult contains an epenthetic vowel, but not for the many examples in which the vowel of the penult is not epenthetic. Nor does it account for many of the examples in which high pitch and main stress occur together on the penult.

Lehnert-LeHouillier (2006) investigated – and subsequently ruled out – a possible explanation of Onondaga's dissimilar distribution of pitch and stress as a phonetic manifestation that is due to a mismatch between the phonetic property of *alignment* – the timing of a given F_0 event with respect to the segmental string – and the phonological property that defines the abstract domain – the syllable – with which the event is *associated*. Thus she hypothesized that the F_0 peak associated with a certain syllable may surface prior to that syllable. While these mismatches did occur in her data, their number was not statistically significant.

Prince (1983:84ff and see also Hayes (1995:225)), argues that the Iroquoian languages have a strong tonal component, analyzing the languages with an independent tonal level of representation that interacts with the metrical structure. Prince postulates an Iroquoian word melody of LHL (level-high-level) and a PNI "pitch-accent rule" which accents all penults with a tonal H together with a rule of backward H-spread that would have been "generalized so that H-tone spreads to any stressed syllable that immediately precedes the

---

[77] Peak F_0 was measured within vowel spans.

accent, regardless of whether it is pretonically lengthened" (ibid., p.86). It is from this kind of a system that he postulates Onondaga would have developed its pattern of separating pitch from stress. However, lacking sufficient data, neither Prince, nor Hayes after him, were able to sketch in the particulars they envisioned.

2.7.7.2 The Data

The data used for the account presented below were examined acoustically using Praat (Boersma & Weenink 2015). They were from female and male speakers of the Onondaga Nation dialect. Approximately a quarter of the examples have their source in stories told by two male speakers (Harry Webster and Pat Johnson) and two female speakers (Lucenda George and Eva Okun); the rest are elicited data from two male speakers, (Harry Webster and Sanford Schenandoah).[78] All the data were collected during a period spanning the 1950s to the 1980s, with sporadic work in the period since then. However, the elicited data are *post hoc*, in that the elicitation sessions were not conducted with the intention of examining prosodic patterns. Lacking also are perceptual data that would show the degree to which speakers are sensitive to the tonal properties of their language.[79] Not infrequently it is difficult to decide which syllable is meant to carry the peak because the F_0 measurements between the two most prominent syllables are extremely close (within 3 Hz). Furthermore, there are some inconsistencies in the data, in that for each of the speakers, a few of the elicited examples were pronounced – when repeated – with the pitch peak on a different syllable.[80]

Given these weaknesses of the data, the discussion that follows falls short of predicting the location of peak F_0 reliably, so it does not solve the question of whether the phenomena are in free variation or lexical. However, there are enough apparent consistencies for it to seem worthwhile to list them, given that at this time it is probably no longer possible to elicit experimental data in the field.

2.7.7.3 Determining the Location of Peak F_0

<u>Pitch and the metrical structure</u>: Several properties of the syllable that are relevant for determining *stress* patterns are wideley shared by the extant Iroquoian languages. Among these are (i) the location of the stress-bearing syllable within the word; (ii) its metric strength within the foot; (iii) its weight; (iv) the alternating count, i.e. a syllable's odd or even status counting from the left; (v) its status with respect to closure. For the purpose of locating high pitch in *Onondaga*, these characteristics line up as follows: The syllable with peak F_0

---

[78] Sanford Schenandoah is a speaker who worked with Karin Michelson in 1978. She was kind enough to share digitized versions of her audio tapes with me. Pat Johnson and Lucenda George were speakers whose stories were recorded by Fred Lukoff in the years between 1948-1950, and whose digitized audio materials were provided by the American Philosophical Society. All other materials are the result of my own fieldwork.

[79] This is an important shortcoming in the light of research (e.g. Pierrehumbert 1979) comparing the complex interaction of the perception of fundamental frequencies in speech data with instrumental realities.

[80] Chafe (1977a:174), who also found inconsistencies within and between speakers, speculates that these may be signs of variability indicating linguistic change.

    i. is always non-peripheral
    ii. is always metrically strong
    iii. is *nearly* always bimoraic (i.e., 97% of the data)
    iv. can be even or odd counting from the left
    v. can be open or closed

Thus non-peripherality and metrical strength are the constant surface characteristics of the syllable marked by peak F_0; syllable weight is nearly constant; and a syllable's position and structure are both variable. Peak F_0 can and does occur on the penult, the antepenult, and either of the two syllables preceding the antepenult. Examples with high pitch on the penult or antepenult far outnumber examples with high pitch to the left of the antepenult.[81]

<u>Peak F_0 Assignment by Metrical Strength and Non-peripherality</u>: Examples of words ranging from four to seven syllables, each with the peak first on the penult and next on the antepenult, are listed in (105). (Syllables with peak F_0 are underlined):[82]

(105)   a. 4σ: (diòh)(so.<u>jió·</u>) < da? > *there's a pile there*
        b. 4σ: (a.<u>gè·</u>)(nų́h) < dų? > *I know*
        c. 5σ: (ęh)(sì·h)(wa.<u>gwé·</u>) < nya? > *you will accomplish it*
        d. 5σ: (ų̀k)(?ni.<u>gų̀h</u>)(ę́h) < a? > *I forgot*
        e. 6σ: (àk)(?ni.gų̀h)(æ.<u>hét</u>) < gę?s > *I'm sad*
        f. 6σ: (hę.jià)(gò?)(<u>nhè?t</u>)(shę́·) < di? > *she'll throw the ball again*
        g. 7σ: (wa?.hò?)(ni.gų̀h)(æ.<u>géts</u>) < gwa? > *he encouraged him*
        h. 7σ: (da.wà?)(gè·)(wa.<u>nèh</u>)(á·) < die? > *there's a big snow coming*

In (105) peak F_0 occurs on the antepenult if it is metrically strong and on the penult if the antepenult is metrically weak. Syllable count is apparently irrelevant: both even and odd penults, and even and odd, antepenults carry peak F_0 in (105). Stated provisionally, the pitch assignment rule is as in (106):

(106) Assign peak F_0 to the antepenult if it is metrically strong. Otherwise, assign
      peak F_0 to the penult.

But the rule fails to account for a number of examples in which both the penult and antepenult are metrically strong and peak F_0 occurs in the penult, as well as examples in which F_0 occurs to the left of the antepenult. Some of these can be explained in systematic ways, as listed in (i) through (iii):

---

[81] High pitch on the syllable just preceding the antepenult only occurs in some words of five or more syllables; high pitch on the syllable to the left of that only occurs in some words of six or more syllables.

[82] <u>A Note on Syllabification</u>: The *y* of CyV sequences are vocalized and syllabified as CV.V and diphthongized as .CVV. where C is any consonant and VV is a diphthong. *Y*-vocalization corresponds to contemporary pronunciations of such sequences. It is perhaps telling that early scholars (Zeisberger, Hewitt) spell CyV sequences with an *i*. Vocalization is significant, because it changes a moraically light CCV syllable to a heavy CVV syllable, which in turn affects weight-sensitive footing.

(i) _Effect of Early Footing_:

a. _Syllables that are metrically weak at initial footing_: Compare (107a and b) both with metrically strong antepenults: only the (a) example conforms to the pitch assignment rule as stated in (106).

(107)   a. (wà?)(hà·)(dé?) < gwa? > _he fled_
      b. (ho.nì·)(dá?) < wih > _they are sleeping_

The difference between them is their starting foot structure, that is, the initial foot structure before adjustments that are a consequence of prosodic vowel lengthening rules:

wa?.ha.de?.gwa?	syllabification
wa?.ha.dé? < gwa? >	extrametricality, main stress
→ (wà?)(ha.dé?) < gwa? >	iambic footing, secondary stress
(wà?)(ha.dé?) < gwa? >	pitch assignment
(wà?)(hà·)(dé?) < gwa? >	antepenult lengthening, adjust footing

ho.ni.da?.wih	syllabification
ho.ni.dá?. < wih >	extrametricality, main stress
→ (ho.nì)(dá?) < wih >	iambic footing, secondary stress
(ho.nì)(dá?) < wih >	pitch assignment
(ho.nì·)(dá?) < wih >	antepenult lengthening

The examples suggest that pitch assignment takes place early on in the derivation, at a point when the antepenult in (107a) is metrically weak in contrast to the antepenult in (107b).

b. _Syllables that are stray at initial footing_:[83] The data on the effect of stray syllables are inconsistent, although most of the time stray syllables are avoided. In (108a) peak F_0 occurs on the antepenult, avoiding the originally stray syllable; in (108b) the peak is on the originally stray syllable:

(108)   a. (ga.nì·)(yǘ·) < da? > _it's hitched on_
      Initial footing: (ga.ni) yų́ < da? >

      b. (ę.hà·)(ę́·) < da·k > _he will put air in it_
      Initial footing: (ę.ha) ę́ < da·k >

---

[83] Recall that stray syllables, occur due to Onondaga's prohibition against constructing degenerate feet, i.e., single syllable light feet.

(ii) *Avoiding the stem-joiner a:*

For the most part, a metrically strong syllable containing the stem-joiner *a* does not take high pitch, but there is some variability in how this constraint plays out.[84] (109) is an example of a word that was pronounced twice by the same speaker, once as in (a) with the peak on the penult, and once as in (b) where the peak moves to the metrically heavy syllable immediately preceding the rejected antepenult, so that the syllable containing the stem-joiner is avoided in both cases.[85] Apparently the two versions are equally acceptable.

(109) a. (wà?)(hụ.wa)(yà?)(d[a]h)(ní·h) < da? > *they propped him up*
    b. (wà?)(hụ.wa)(yà?)(d[a]h)(ní·h) < da? > *they propped him up*

Which of these two strategies is chosen, depends to some extent on the length of the word, so that in words with four syllables with the penult containing the stem-joiner together with the constraint against placing high pitch on a peripheral syllable, there is little choice. In (110a) the only metrically strong syllable (at initial footing) is the antepenult; in (110b) the penult is the only metrically strong syllable, and it contains the joiner vowel. If nothing else, (110b) suggests that metric strength is more highly valued than avoiding the joiner:

(110) a. (ho.nụ̀h)(s[á]·) < yẹ? > *he has a house*
      Initial footing: (ho.nụh) sá < yẹ? >
    b. (òh)(nè·)(g[á]·) < gi·? > *soup*
      Initial footing: (oh)(ne.gá) < gi·? >

In longer words, the strategy used in (109b) is more often preferred over the one used in (109a), but both occur. Examples in (111) consist of five and six syllables, respectively, and both have metrically strong penults that are bypassed in terms of peak F_0 placement. In (111a) the metrically weak antepenult contains the joiner vowel, and high pitch docks on the immediately preceding metrically heavy syllable. In (111b) the stem-joiner is in the metrically strong antepenult and again, high pitch occurs on the metrically strong syllable immediately preceding the antepenult.

(111) a. (gà·)(yò?)(d[a].ná·) < ge·? > *the game [animals] are plentiful*
    b. (gàh)(sa.hè?)(d[a]h)(í·h) < wih > *the beans were spilled*

Examples (112a and b) have six syllables, and in both peak F_0 occurs in the metrically strong penult:[86]

---

[84] The stem-joiner plays an important role in all of the extant Iroquoian languages. For example, as noted above, open syllables containing the stem-joiner, are skipped in counting syllables for the purpose of stress placement in the extant languages *except* Onondaga. Recall also that in Onondaga syllables containing the joiner, if even-numbered, are exempt from the rule of Antepenultimate Vowel Lengthening.

[85] The stem-joiner is surrounded by square brackets.

[86] Surprisingly, the fact that, at initial footing, the penults in both words were stray seems to have no bearing on their ability to bear the pitch peak.

(112) a. (wà?)(hàh)(niụ̀h)(s[a]t)(<u>shę́·</u>) < ni? >   *he found squash*
       Initial footing: (wa?)(hah)(niụh)(s[a]t) shę́ < ni? >
   b. (wà?)(ha.nụ̀h)(s[a]h)(<u>ní·</u>) < nụ? >   *he bought a house*
       Initial footing: (wa?)(ha.nụh)(s[a]h) ní < nụ? >

An example where both the penult and the antepenult contain stem-joiner vowels, and the pitch peak occurs on the next metrically strong syllable to the left is (113):

(113) (ę.hà)(da.dià?)(d[a].<u>gèh</u>)(nh[à]?)(d[á]h) < gwa? > *he will help himself with it*
    Initial footing: (ę.ha)(da.dia?)(d[a].geh)(nh[a]?)(d[á]h) < gwa? >

In summary, the examples in (109) - (113) suggest that if the antepenult contains the joiner vowel, peak F_0 occurs on either the metrically heavy penult, or on the metrically heavy syllable immediately preceding the antepenult, with a preference of the former over the latter choice.

<u>Anomalous data</u>: But data on avoiding the stem-joiner are not entirely consistent. (114) lists examples where peak F_0 occurred in the syllable *containing* the joiner vowel. In light of the discussion above, one would wrongly predict that peak F_0 should occur in either the penult or the pre-antepenult in (114);

<u>Peak F_0 on the antepenult containing the joiner vowel</u>
(114) (ę.yè)(nęh)([<u>à</u>]t)(hé?) < da? > *she will pound corn*
    Initial footing: (ę.ye)(nęh)([a]t)(hé?) < da? >

and given that the antepenult is weak in (115), the prediction would be that peak F_0 should occur in the pre-antepenult in order to avoid the joiner vowel.

<u>Peak F_0 on the penult containing the joiner vowel</u>
(115) (a.gàę)(do.<u>d[á]·</u>) < gwęk > *for a tree to be uprooted*
    Initial footing: (a.gaę)(do.dá) < gwęk >

In (116) both the penult and the syllable immediately preceding the antepenult contain joiner vowels; the antepenult is metrically strong, the other syllable with the joiner is metrically weak. Surprisingly, instead of docking on the intervening metrically strong antepenult, peak F_0 skips to the next metrically strong syllable (two syllables to the left of the antepenult):

<u>Peak F_0 on second syllable to the left of the antepenult</u>
(116) (gò?)(ni.<u>gụ̀</u>)(h[æ].yę̀·)(d[á]?) < ih > *she understands*
    Initial footing: (go?)(ni.gụ)(h[æ].yę)(d[á]?) < ih >

  (iii) *Avoiding epenthetic e:*

An epenthetic *e* is inserted between morphemes at the boundaries between the pronominal prefix and the lexical root or between the reflexives and the root (section 2.6.2). This occurs with high frequency in the second syllable of verbs. Hence the fact that syllables with epenthetic *e* do not take peak F_0 can be most easily demonstrated with words of four syllables as in (117) (epenthetic *e* is surrounded with curly brackets in the following example). Note that although the antepenultimate syllable containing the epenthetic vowel is metrically strong, peak F_0 occurs on the penult, not on the antepenult as predicted by the rule as stated in (106):

(117) (wà?)(g{è}k)(hű·) < nia? > *I cooked*

In the light of (i) - (iii) above (and ignoring the anomalous data), the pitch assignment rule as stated in (106) can be revised as in (118):

(118) <u>Revised Pitch assignment rule</u>: Assign peak F_0 to the antepenult if it is metrically strong. Otherwise, assign peak F_0 to the penult.
   <u>Conditions</u>: (i) Avoid syllables that are weak at initial footing;
      (ii) avoid syllables containing the stem-joiner *a* and epenthetic *e*.

3 Parts of Speech

3.1 The Word: Verbs, Nouns, and Particles

3.1.1 Identifying the Word

In the Onondaga lexicon, there is no lexeme that denotes the concept *word* specifically: -wẹn- is a morpheme glossed 'word', 'language', or 'voice' by speakers. Minimally inflected, it occurs, as the noun *owẹ́·naʔ*. Incorporated into a verb it often means 'language', as in *gadwẹnodákhwaʔ* 'my language', or 'voice' as in *howẹnadét* 'his voice is strong'. Nonetheless, there is phonological and grammatical evidence for 'wordness', and speakers themselves feel no hesitation about accepting such an entity. First, speakers can identify separate words by repeating an utterance one word at a time with pauses between words; and they do not pause within words. Second, while speakers can provide the meaning of an inflected word, they are typically unable to identify the meanings of single bound morphemes unless they have been trained to do so. In addition, inflected verbs can occur as well-formed utterances in isolation, whereas bound morphemes cannot. Words, moreover, can occur in different positions of identical utterances with the same literal – if not discourse – meaning, i.e., *waʔhagẹ́ʔ honụhsá·yẹʔ* vs. *honụhsayẹ́ʔ waʔhá·gẹʔ* both mean literally 'he saw his house'. Bound morphemes fail this test. Morphophonological clues are: (i) Verbs and nouns with a pronominal prefix beginning in *y* word-medially, drop that *y* (and sometimes the sequence *ya*) word-initially: *eyéthwas* [ye-yẹthw-as] 'she plants', cf. *ẹyeyẹ́thwaʔ* [ẹ-ye-yẹthw-as] 'she will plant'; and (ii) morphophonological alternations, and suppletion occur within the domain of the word but not outside of it.[1] Two metrical clues are: (i) Except for a few single syllable particles, each word contains a single main accent; and (ii) main stress typically occurs on the final syllable of utterance-medial words and on the penultimate syllable of utterance-final words (sec. 2.7).[2]

---

[1] The single exception to this statement is the phonological rule that changes the cluster *kk* to *hk* for Onondaga Nation speakers (see section 2.2.3.2). This rule also functions across word boundaries for some speakers.

[2] This list fails to resolve the issue of whether a small number of particles, treated in this work as single words, e.g., *néʔtho* 'there' and *sų́·gaʔ* 'somebody' consist, actually, of two particles *neʔ* 'nominalizer' plus *tho* 'there', and *sų́* 'who' plus *gaʔ* indefinite particle, respectively. All four of these also occur alone in other contexts.

3.1.2 Parts of Speech

In Onondaga three parts of speech – nouns, verbs, and particles – can be identified on the basis of their internal structure. Nouns and verbs – the latter include adverbial and adjectival expressions – are morphologically complex; particles lack internal structure. Verbs and nouns can be distinguished from one another on the basis of the kinds of affixes they take. Lexical roots are lexically specified as noun roots or verb roots. For example, *-nųhs-* 'house' is a noun root; *-adawę-* 'swim' is a verb root.[3] *Héʔtgę* 'above' and *nę́gę* 'this' are particles. With very minor exceptions they accept no affixes.

Cross linguistically, parts of speech are often divided into two subsidiary classes: open classes (usually comprised of content words), which are continually in flux in the sense that their membership constantly increases or decreases, and closed classes (mostly comprised of function words) which remain relatively stable over time. In many languages nouns, verbs, adjectives, and adverbs are examples of open classes; pronouns, articles, demonstratives, i.e., words that form sets, are examples of closed classes. The open classes are typically much larger and more diverse than the closed classes.

The Northern Iroquoian languages, differ from this description. In these languages only words based on verb roots or stems form an open class, and they are much more frequent in discourse than are words based on noun roots or stems. As Koenig & Michelson (2013) point out, this is due, in part, to the morphology of nouns and verbs: verb roots productively derive verb stems while only a single morphological process derives noun stems from verb stems. There are no processes that derive nouns or verbs from nouns. In the Northern Iroquoian languages, nominal functions such as reference, are not limited to words that are morphological nouns; they can be performed as well by words that are morphological verbs or particles.[4] Not infrequently, expressions based on verb stems are lexicalized as referring expressions (section 5.3).

Contemporary Iroquoianists generally follow Lounsbury (1953) and subsequently (Chafe 1967) in analyzing the words with complex morphological structures in terms of position classes and that is the approach adopted in this grammar.[5] An analysis in terms of position classes postulates that every Onondaga verb or noun is composed of one or more lexical elements, surrounded by various classes of affixes, which must occur in specific positions in relation to the lexical element(s) and in relation to one another. The position classes differ, depending on whether the word is a verb (sec. 3.2) or a noun (sec. 3.3). The least elaborated set of affixes is a small group of clitics with diverse meanings whose attachment is not specific to a particular lexical class although clitics occur much more frequently with nouns than with verbs or particles. Clitics are attached to fully inflected words. They are discussed in section 3.5.

This chapter introduces the basic morphological characteristics of the three morphologically defined parts of speech. Chapters 4 through 7 will treat each of their

---

[3] See Mithun (2000) and Koenig & Michelson (2013) for exhaustive accounts of the differences between nouns and verbs in the Northern Iroquoian languages.

[4] Koenig & Michelson (2016) address the difficulties for a part-of-speech classification presented by these overlapping distributions.

[5] But see Chafe (1970) where he uses a generative semantics approach to analyze Onondaga word structure.

inflectional and derivational characteristics in depth. Chapter 7, the final chapter of this grammar, deals with the elements of syntactic constructions.

3.2 The Structure of the Verb

A verb consists, minimally, of a *pronominal prefix* that specifies the participants in the situation, a morphologically simple or complex *stem* which expresses a situation or state, and an *aspect suffix* that indicates how the situation expressed by the verb stem proceeds through time. (A set of prepronominal prefixes may or may not mark additional modal and adverbial meanings.)

Table 3.1 Position classes within the verb

Prepronominal Prefix	Pronominal Prefix	Verb Stem	Aspect suffix

Of the four position classes shown in Table 3.1, only the *verb stem* may be hierarchically organized, the elements comprising the three other classes each are linearly ordered in relation to one another.

<u>The prepronominal prefix</u>: A prepronominal prefix may or may not be a discontinuous but obligatory part of a verb stem in a given meaning. Thus the verb stem meaning 'assemble, connect' requires the dualic prepronominal prefix in that meaning. (Recall that the citation forms of stems that require a prepronominal prefix are cited here and in the Onondaga Dictionary (Woodbury 2003) with a preceding period (.), rather than the usual hyphen (-), together with the name of the prepronominal, e.g., .khahʉ- + dualic 'assemble, connect'. This is done to distinguish stems with obligatory prepronominals from ones with prepronominals that are optional.) Prepronominal prefixes are discussed in section 4.7.

<u>The pronominal prefix</u>: Table 3.1 shows that to the left of the nucleus of the verb – the *verb stem* – is the pronominal prefix. This prefix must occur in every well formed verb. It identifies the core participant(s) of the verb – the agent and/or patient – in terms of person, number, and gender. There are three series of pronominal prefixes, the agent series, the patient series, and the transitive series (section 4.3). The choice between transitive or non-transitive pronominal depends in part on the number and animacy of the participants. The choice between agent and patient pronominal depends in part on the aspect inflection. However, because the choice is not fully predictable, it must be lexically specified for every verb. The pronominal prefix system is discussed in section 4.3.

<u>The verb stem</u>: The nucleus of the verb – the verb stem – consists, minimally, of a verb root, for example -*yẹthw*- 'plant' as shown in (1). The stem can be expanded to include one or more of the following: reflexives and an incorporated noun root or stem between the pronominal prefix and the verb root, and one or more of a number of root suffixes between the verb root and the aspect position (see below). The reflexives and the root suffixes are derivational and are, largely, lexically determined. Chafe (1967), Abrams (2006), and Koenig & Michelson (2016) distinguish between two morphological constituents of the verb, the *verb base* and the *verb stem*, such that the verb base is the constituent between the pronominal prefix and the aspect suffix, and the verb stem is the constituent that consists of the verb base and the aspect suffix. The reason for this is that in the Northern Iroquoian languages, including Onondaga, it is the aspect suffix that selects the form of an *active* verb's pronominal prefix and determines the presence or absence of modal

prepronominal prefixes. In this work, *stem* is used in its more standard sense to refer to the constituent that is subject to inflectional processes, i.e., the constituent, simple or complex, that in the Northern Iroquoian verb is located between the pronominal prefix and the aspect suffix. When the term needs to be used in the special sense where it includes the aspect suffix, this will be made clear in the text of this work.[6] The verb stem is discussed in section 4.8.

The aspect suffix: To the right of the verb stem is the aspect suffix position. This position is filled in every well-formed Onondaga verb. The three basic aspect categories, the habitual, the stative, and the punctual, differ in how they represent a situation as it proceeds through time (section 4.2). Aspect distinguishes between situations that endure over a stretch of time and those that take place at one point in time. The former are marked by the habitual and stative aspect suffixes, the latter are marked by the punctual aspect suffix. A second perspective that is reflected in the category of aspect differentiates among situations in terms of duration. It classifies situations into dynamic, evolving processes, which are signaled by the habitual aspect, as opposed to more homogeneous, unchanging states of affairs, which are signaled by the stative aspect. A shorthand way to think of the situations described by the three aspects is that the habitual identifies a process, the stative identifies a state, and the punctual identifies an event. Note that the habitual and the punctual aspects take agent pronominals, whereas the stative aspect takes a patient pronominal. These differences are exemplified in (1):

(1)   a. hayę́thwas
           ha-yęthw-as
           3M.SG.A-plant-HAB
           he plants (it)

      b. hoyę́thwih
           ho-yęthw-ih
           3M.SG.P-plant-STV
           he has planted (it)

      c. waʔhayę́thwaʔ
           waʔ-ha-yęthw-aʔ
           FACT-3M.SG.A-plant-PNC
           he planted (it)

The aspect position can be expanded to accommodate a set of suffixes whose function it is to increase the range of aspectual meanings for some of the verb classes (section 4.6). For example, verbs inflected with durative aspects – the habitual and stative – can be marked as enduring situations in the future, the past, or at some indefinite time (aspect is discussed in sections 4.5 and 4.6.). Examples are:

---

[6] The notion *base* is not used as a technical term in this grammar, to avoid confusion with its special use in the Onondaga Dictionary (Woodbury 2003:3-4). Chafe (2015) uses *base* for the constituent named *stem* in the present work.

(2) a. hayęthwásgwaʔ
     ha-yęthw-as-<u>gwaʔ</u>
     3M.SG.A-plant-HAB-HBPST
     he used to plant

   b. ęhayęthwáhsek
     ę-ha-yęthw-ahs-<u>ek</u>-Ø
     FUT-3M.SG.A-plant-HAB-CNT-PNC
     he will be planting

   c. hoyęthwíhnaʔ
     ho-yęthw-ih-naʔ
     3M.SG.P-plant-STV-STVPST
     he had planted it

Table 3.2 shows the resources for expanding the verb stem.

Table 3.2 The expanded verb stem

Verb Stem			
Reflexives	Noun Stem	Verb Root	Root Suffixes

<u>The reflexive prefixes</u> – the *reflexive* and the *semireflexive* – affect the number and kind of arguments. Both affixes derive a new verb stem from the original one. The reflexive prefix indicates that the action of the verb is performed by the actor on himself, or, when combined with the dualic prepronominal prefix it has the effect of a reciprocal, i.e., two participants or two sets of participants acting on each other (section 4.8.4). Examples of the two are:

(3) a. ęhadátgę?
     ę-ha-<u>adat</u>-gę-ʔ
     FUT-3M.SG.A-REF-see-PNC
     he will see himself

   b. dęhųdátgę?
     <u>d</u>-ę-hų-<u>adat</u>-gę-ʔ
     DL-FUT-3M.PL.A-REF-see-PNC
     they see each other; they meet each other

The semireflexive, as Iroquoianists call it (after Lounsbury), detransitivises a verb or modifies the meaning of the verb root in a number of ways including, frequently, a meaning in which the actor undertakes an activity that affects himself or his interests in some more remote way than is the case with the reflexive (section 4.8.4.1). For example:

      <u>Plain stem</u>   <u>Stem with semireflexive</u>
(4) a. tho waʔe·yę?   tho waʔų·dyę?
     tho   waʔ-e-yę-ʔ'   tho waʔ-ų-<u>ad</u>-yę-ʔ'
     LOC   3FI.A-set.down-PNC   LOC FACT-3FI.A-<u>SRF</u>-set.down-PNC
     she set it down there   *she sat down there*

b. waʔhayẹ́thwaʔ   waʔha·dyẹ́thwaʔ
  waʔ-ha-yẹthw-aʔ   waʔ-h-ad-yẹthw-aʔ
  FACT-3M.SG.A-plant-PNC   FACT-3M.SG.A-SRF-plant-PNC
  he planted (it)   *he did his planting*

<u>The noun stem position</u>: This position, located between the reflexive and the verb root may be filled by a second lexical element, a noun root or noun stem. Such a stem, which is *incorporated* into a verb stem, typically identifies the object that undergoes the action described by the verb root. Most noun roots that denote non-animate entities can be incorporated. Noun incorporation is derivational. The resulting form is a verb (section 4.8.3). An example of a verb with an incorporated noun *root* is:

(5) hanẹhayẹ́thwas
    ha-<u>nẹh</u>-a-yẹthw-as
    3M.SG.A-corn-JN[7]-plant-HAB
    he plants corn; he corn-plants

An example of a verb with an incorporated *derived noun stem*, consisting of a verb root and a nominalizer, is:

(6) waʔagathowæhsí·nyụʔs
    waʔ-ag-<u>athowæ-hsR</u>-inyụ-ʔs-Ø
    FACT-1SG.P-feel.cold-NOM-arrive-BEN-PNC
    I caught a cold; I cold-caught

An example of an hierarchically organized verb stem with an incorporated derived noun stem that includes an aspect suffix *-a·dyẹdakhwaʔ* [-adyẹd-a-hkw-haʔ] 'seat'[8] that is nominalized with a nominalizer morpheme – in this case *-(a)tshR-* – and subsequently incorporated into a second verb stem *-od-* 'set up':

(7) Thohgé ó·nẹ waʔha·dyẹdakhwaʔtshé·dẹʔ (CTL80.7).
    thohge   onẹ   waʔ-h-adyẹd-hgw-haʔ-atshR-od-ẹʔ
    TMP   TMP   FACT-3M.SG.A-sit.down-INST-HAB-NOM-set-up-PNC
    Then he set up a seat.

<u>The root suffix position</u>: To the right of the verb root there is a position that may be occupied by numerous root suffixes (section 4.8.5) which derive a new verb stem from the original one. Three suffixes – the *causative, benefactive,* and *instrumental* – affect the number and kind of argument; other root suffixes with diverse functions are the *inchoative, ambulative, dislocative, distributive, and reversative.* Some of these can combine with one another. Examples of a verb root with a benefactive suffix (8a), a causative suffix (8b) and a causative plus distributive suffix combination (8c) are:

---

[7] Recall that an incorporated noun and the verb that incorporates it are separated by the joiner vowel *a* if the noun ends in a consonant and the verb begins in a consonant.

[8] Literally, '[it is] used for sitting down'.

(8) a. wa?kheyóhae?s
        wa?-khey-ohae-?s-Ø
        MODAL-1SG>3-wash-BEN-PNC
        I washed it for her

     b. honadegá?dih
        hon-adeg-a?d-ih
        3M.NSG.P-burn-CS-PNC
        they lit a fire [literally: they caused it to burn]

     c. wa?thahsiha·hdahę·?
        wa?-t-ha-hsíhaR-hd-ahę·-?'
        FACT-DL-3M.SG.A-plug.up-CS-DST-PNC
        he caused several of them to get plugged up [e.g., gaps or holes]

An example of a suffix that changes verb class membership is the dislocative, which changes an active verb to a motion verb with consequences, among other things, for the aspectual categories available to it (section 4.5):

(9) a. wa?tshagodæ·hdáhne?
        wa?-t-shago-adæ·hd-ahne-?
        FACT-DL-3M.SG>3-meet-DSLC-PRP
        he is going [somewhere] to meet her

     b. wa?tshagodǽ·hda?
        wa?-t-shago-adæ·hd-a?
        FACT-DL-3M.SG>3-meet-PNC
        he met her

The prepronominal prefix position: Onondaga verbs can, and often must, specify additional kinds of meanings. This is done at the very beginning of the verb by affixes in the prepronominal position:

Table 3.3 The prepronominal position

Prepronominal	Pronominal	Verb Stem	Aspect

In that position, occur up to eleven prefixes, alone and in combination. They specify categories of modality, a category in the Northern Iroquoian languages that combines tense and modal meanings. Other prepronominals express adverbial meanings having to do with situational and temporal aspects of the speech event (sections 4.2 and 4.7). Verbs inflected with the punctual aspect require, as noted above, modal prepronominal prefixes and a fair number of verbs require a particular adverbial prepronominal as a part of the basic meaning of the verb stem. But prepronominal prefixes can also be used optionally as a way to expand the basic meaning of a verb stem. Examples of verbs with a modal (10a) and an adverbial (10b) prepronominal prefix are:

(10) a. a·hayę́thwaʔ
    <u>aa</u>-ha-yęthw-aʔ
    OPT-3M.SG.A-plant-PNC
    he should plant (it)

   b. shodaʔgái·deʔ
    <u>s</u>-ho-adaʔdaide-ʔ
    REP-3M.SG.P-be.healthy-STV
    he has recovered, he is healthy again
      cf. without the repetitive: hodaʔgái·deʔ *he's healthy, he feels good*

3.3 The Structure of the Noun

A morphological noun consists, minimally, of a noun root/stem, a noun prefix, and a noun suffix. The morphological constituent labeled *noun stem* in the table below can consist of a noun root or a derived noun stem consisting of a verb root followed by a nominalizer.

Table 3.4 The minimal noun

Noun prefix	Noun Stem	Noun suffix

Prefixes that occur with nouns are a subset of the pronominal prefixes occurring with verbs. They are formally identical to the two intransitive series that occur with verbs. But though the forms are identical, their functions differ depending on whether they occur with a noun or a verb. The basic noun prefix identifies the constituent as a noun; the possessive prefix identifies the possessor of the entity denoted by the noun. Noun prefixes do not mark semantic case, as do the verbal pronominal prefixes.

<u>The basic noun prefix</u> (NPF): Nouns whose referents are non-animate entities are prefixed with noun prefixes that are formally identical to the verbal neuter/zoic singular agent (*ga-/gę-/w-/Ø-*) or patient (*o-/aw-/a-*) pronominal prefixes (section 5.2.1), but function in this context to mark the stem as a noun. The selection of prefix alternants is determined by the initial segment of the noun stem (see Table 4.9 for the distribution of alternants). The prefixes occur as *ga-* or *o-* with consonant-initial stems:

(11) a. ganáʔjyaʔ
    ga-naʔjy-aʔ
    NPF-bucket-NSF
    bucket

   b. gahésga·ʔ
    ga-hesgaR-aʔ
    NPF-arrow-NSF
    arrow

(12) a. onę́haʔ
    o-nęh-aʔ
    NPF-corn-NSF
    corn

b. oyę́ʔgwaʔ
   o-yęʔgw-aʔ
   NPF-tobacco-NSF
   tobacco

Though up to a point the choice of *ga-* or *o-* prefix is semantically motivated –
man-made objects tend to take the *ga-*prefix from the agent series of pronominal prefixes
as in examples (11a and b), and natural objects tend to take the *o-*prefix from the patient
series as in examples (12a and b) – the choice is not fully predictable and is lexically
specified.

Examples (13a and b) consist of a noun prefix, a noun stem that is composed of a verb
root plus nominalizer, and a noun suffix.

(13) a. adyaʔdawı́ʔtshæ·ʔ[9]
        Ø-adyaʔdawiʔt-shR-aʔ
        NPF-get.dressed-NOM-NSF
        garment, clothes

     b. gahyadų́hsæ·ʔ
        ga-hyadų-hsR-aʔ
        NPF-write-NOM-NSF
        book, paper, magazine

<u>Marking a noun for possession</u> (sec. 5.2.1.2): To mark a noun for possession, a
pronominal prefix from the agent or patient series of verbal pronominal prefixes
referencing the possessor is used.[10] Whether an agent or patient prefix is chosen depends
on whether the possessed entity is alienable or inalienable. Inalienable entities are most
body part nouns and some kin terms, all others are alienably possessed.

(14) a. Alienable possession:
        hohų́·waʔ
        ho-hųw-aʔ
        3M.SG.P-boat-NSF
        his boat

     b. Inalienable possession:
        khų́ʔgwáʔge
        k-hųʔgw-aʔ=ge
        1SG.A-throat-NSF=LOC[11]
        (on) my throat

---

[9] Most derived nouns drop the *w-* allomorph of the *ga-* noun prefix that occurs with non animate
noun stems beginning in *a, e,* or *ę.*

[10] In Oneida and Mohawk possessive prefixes are formally distinguishable from agent and patient
prefixes. This is not the case in Onondaga.

[11] The locative clitic must be added to most body part nouns.

The noun suffix: The simple noun suffix is realized as *-(a)ʔ* or *-(a)h, or less frequently - iʔ.* [12] The distribution of the alternants is lexically specified, but *-(a)ʔ* far outnumbers the other alternants, and *-iʔ* occurs with certain body part nouns and with *-ihs-* 'wall, ceiling'.[13] The simple noun suffix can be replaced by the *internal* locative suffix *-(a)gųwa* 'in, under,' which derives a location expression from a simple noun.

(15) a. gaihsęhdagų́·wa
    ga-Rihsę·hd-agųwa
    NPF-dream-LOC
    in a dream

   b. ohgiʔægų́·wa
    o-ahgiʔR-agųwa
    NPF-rag-LOC
    under the rags

Nouns denoting animate entities (sec. 5.2.1.1): The structure of nouns denoting animate entities (humans, large animals) is variable. They take animate pronominals from either the agent or patient series, depending on which is lexically assigned to the stem. Often it is difficult to isolate the stem from the suffix. The stems in (16) are always entity expressions; examples like those in (17) are stative verbs with denotations that are situations or entities; and examples in (18) are nouns derived from verb stems:

(16) a. ų́·gweh
    (y)-ųgweh
    NPF-person:SUFF
    person

   b. agų́·gweh
    ag-ųgweh
    3FI.A-person:SUFF
    woman

(17) a. haʔshę́·nih
    h-aʔshęnih
    3M.SG.A-be.a.white.person:SUFF
    he is a white man; white man

   b. hoksdęʔá
    ho-ksdęʔ = á
    3M.SG.P-be.an.old.person.or.animal = DIM
    he is old; old man/animal

---

[12] The parentheses indicate morpheme alternants such that an alternant with *a* follows a stem ending in a consonant and an alternant without the *a* follows a stem ending in a vowel.

[13] Here the *-iʔ-* alternant is used to change meaning: gęhsaʔ 'wall'; gę́hsiʔ 'ceiling'. (Jay Meacham p.c.)

(18) a. godųniʔá
    go-adųni-ʔ = á
    3FI.P-grow-NSF = DIM
    baby girl

  b. hadihnháʔtshæʔ
    hadi-hnhaʔ-tshR-aʔ
    3M.PL.A-hire-NOM-NSF
    hired persons

As noted above, numerous bases referring to entities are, structurally, verbs. Verbal nouns are discussed in section 5.3.

3.4 Particles

Particles are a closed class. They are by definition monomorphemic. They cannot be analyzed into smaller components although some particles are recognizable as reduced forms of verbs that have, with time, become lexicalized in this reduced form. As a class, particles are particularly prolific in Onondaga. Not counting a sizable group of particles that denote entities, there are approximately 185 particles with a variety of functions in addition to a fair number of particle clusters that have been lexicalized as unitary constituents. Particles can be divided into four categories: (i) pro-forms, (ii) adverbials, (iii) particles with grammatical functions, and (iv) particles with discourse-pragmatic functions.

Pro-forms function to identify and keep track of participants and consist of personal pronouns (sec. 6.2), interrogative pronouns (sec. 6.3), indefinite expressions (sec. 6.4), and demonstrative particles (sec. 6.5). Adverbials typically function to describe details of temporal and locational settings (sec. 7.6). Examples of particularly common grammatical particles are the assertion particle *naʔ*, the nominal particle *neʔ*, the subordinating particle *tshaʔ*, and a number of interrogative particles. Particles (bold type) compared to nouns and verbs occur prolifically.

(19) **Onę díʔ hyaʔ yágę̣ʔ gá·ʔ gwaʔ nigę̣ nę̣gę̣** nhwahéʔ oyáʔ dyenagé·ʔ **tho nų́,**
    nhwaʔhoyaʔdę́hawaʔ (HW05).

onę	díʔ	hyaʔ	yagę̣ʔ	ga·ʔ	gwaʔ	nigę̣	nę̣gę̣
TMP	LNK	MOD	HRSY	INDF	RSTR	EXT	DEM
now	moreover	indeed	they say	about	just	up to	this

n-h-waʔ-h-e-ʔ	o-oya-ʔ	d-ye-nage·-ʔ	tho nų
PRT-TRNS-FACT-3M.SG.A-walk-PNC	3N/Z.SG.A-different-STV	CIS-3FI.A-live-STV	LOC LOC
he went there	it is different	they live there	at the place

n-h-waʔ-ho-yaʔd-ęhaw-aʔ
PRT-TRNS-FACT-3M.SG > 3M.SG-body-take-PNC
he took him there

So they say at this point he went to a different place where someone lived, [and] that's where he took [the dog].

Although particles are internally unstructured, there are selected affixes and clitics that can be added to some of them. An example of the former is the locative particle í·nų *far*. To negate this, it is possible to prefix the negative verbal prefix *deʔ-*:

(20) hya deʔí·nų
  hya deʔ-inų
  NEG NEG-LOC
  it isn't far

The demonstrative particle *nę́·gę* 'this' and the first and second person independent pronouns *iʔ* 'I/we' and *is* 'you (pl)' can take the diminutive clitic = (h)á:

(21) a. nęgęhá
   nęgę = há
   DEM = DIM
   this alone, this specific one

  b. iʔá
   iʔ = á
   PRON = DIM
   I/we only, I/we specifically

As noted, certain particles can occur together as single units or as elements that modify each other's meanings. In (22), for example, the animate interrogative *sų́* 'who' is modified by the indefinite particle *ga·ʔ* to express the indefinite meaning 'somebody' (the particle hya *not* functions together with the verbal prefix *deʔ-* to negate the verb):

(22) hya sų gá·ʔ deʔthoyų́h (CTL178.5)
  hya sų ga·ʔ deʔ-t-ho-yų-h'
  NEG INTR INDF NEG-DL-3M.SG.P-arrive-STV
  not someone he hasn't arrived
  No one has arrived

3.5 Cliticization

Clitics are a small group of affixes which attach to the right of fully inflected words.[14] They are not specific to particular lexical classes. Although they occur more commonly attached to nouns, many of them can also attach to verbs, and even particles, as is exemplified in examples (21a and b) above and (23c) below. To mark these characteristics of clitics, their connection to fully inflected words is symbolized with an equal sign (=) rather than the dash (-) that separates morphemes. The following set of examples shows the pluralizer clitic = shų́ʔ(a) attached to nominal, verbal, and particle forms, respectively:

---

[14] A rare example showed up in a story in which the hearsay particle *yágęʔ* 'it is said' actually intervenes between a noun form and a clitic: *Onę yágęʔ nęgę́ neʔ <u>osháisdaʔ</u> yágęʔ = goná waʔgęhę́·ʔ...* 'then they say this huge, they say, snake said...' (HW07). Without this rhetorical device the cliticized noun is *oshaisdaʔgó·na* 'huge snake'.

(23) a. Nayéʔ gwaʔ tho neʔ gaʔdátshæ·ʔ néʔtho wá·dah[15] neʔ <u>akhesgá·ʔshų̄ʔ</u> (CTL192.6-7).

naye?	gwa?	tho	ne?	ga-?datshR-a?	ne?tho	w-ada-h		ne?
ASRT	RSTR	LOC	NOM	NPF-quiver-NSF	LOC	3N/Z.SG.A-be.in-STV		NOM
it's	just	there	the	quiver	there	it is in it		the

ak-hesgaR-a? = shų?
1SG.P-arrow-NSF = PL
my arrows
My arrows are in the quiver.

b. ...nędyéʔ tshaʔ <u>niyodekdehinéshų̄ʔ</u>... (CTL317.2)

n-ę-d-yę-e-?		tsha?	ni-yo-ade-kdehR-ine-Ø = shų?
PART-FUT-CIS-3FI.A-come-PRP		SUB	PART-3N/Z.SG.P-SRF-root-lead-STV = PL
they will come		that	thus the roots of the trees lead them

...they will come [from various directions] as the roots of the trees lead them.

c. Nayéʔ neʔ dę̄hadawę́·yeʔ neʔ ę· <u>nųwéshų̄ʔ</u> ... (CTL24.7-8)

naye?	ne?	d-ę-ha-ad-awę-ye-?	ne?	ę·	nųwe = shų?
ASRT	NOM	DL-FUT-3M.SG.A-SRF-stir-PNC	NOM	DIR	LOC = PL
it's	the	they will travel	the	other direction	places

They will travel to other locations...

In all there are nine clitics as shown in Table 3.5, each with numerous functions. In addition to the general meanings indicated in the fourth column of Table 3.5, there are many instances in which meanings of forms with clitics have become lexicalized so that their combined meanings, though related to the components of the form, are not in fact, predictable. For example:

(24) a. ahsųhekháʔ
Ø-ahsųhe-Ø = khá?
3N/Z.SG.A-be.dark-STV = CHAR
nocturnal, by night

b. oyę̄ʔgwaʔų́·we
o-yę?gw-a? = ųwe
NPF-tobacco-NSF = AUTH
native tobacco

Several of the clitics can occur together. When they do, it is in a given order.

(25) a. <u>Authentic plus locative:</u>
ųgwehųwéhne
(y)-ųgweh = ųwe = hne
NPF-person:SUFF = AUTH = LOC
on the reserve; on the reservation

---

[15] Utterance-final prosody of utterance-medial words and the presence of word-final *h* utterance-medially is because the source of the excerpt is a dictated text (see sec. 1.3).

b. <u>Authentic plus characterizer</u>:
ųgwehųwekhá?
(y)-ųgweh = ųwe = khá?
NPF-person:SUFF = AUTH = CHAR
Indian language

c. <u>Diminutive plus locative</u>:
nigęhyųhwa?áhne
ni-ga-ihyųhw-a? = á = hne
PART-NPF-river-NSF = DIM = LOC
at the small river

d. <u>Locative and plural</u>:
ųgwe·yahnéshų?
ųgw-e·yah = ne = shų?
1PL.P-heart = LOC = PL
our hearts

e. <u>Locative and characterizer</u>:
enųda?gegá?
e-nųd-a? = ge = ga·?
3FI.A-hill-NSF = LOC = CHAR
Onondaga woman

f. <u>Locative and populative</u>:
hadihwisda?gehé·nų?
hadi-hwisd-a? = ge = he·nų?
3M.PL.A-metal-NSF = LOC = POP
iron workers

g. <u>Plural and augmentative</u>:
ohsųdagųwashų?gowá·neh
o-ahsųd-agųwa = shų? = gowanę
NPF-be.dark-LOC = PL = AUG
in large dark places

h. <u>Plural and decessive</u>:
ganųhsahse?shų?géhæ?
ga-nųhs-ahse-? = shų? = gęhæ?
3N/Z.SG.A-house-new-STV = PL = DEC
formerly new houses; abandoned houses

Table 3.5 lists the clitics and summarizes their functions:

Table 3.5 The clitics

Name	Form	Function / Distribution
(External) Locative	= ge / = (h)ne	Adds the meaning *on, at* to nominals; focus with pronoun referents; obligatory with possessed body part nouns; nominalizes *season-* and *direction*-verbs
Plural	= shų? / = shų?á	Occurs with plural referents of nominals (with = shų? plural referents are all alike; with = shų?á plural referents differ from one another); in counting expressions; in phrases with *amount*-particles; = shų?á adds *approximate* meaning to numbers; = shų? adds distributive *each* and *at a time* meanings to counting stems.
Augmentative	= gona / = gowanę	With nominal: referent is large for its kind. With verb: indicates increased effort or effect.
Diminutive	= á / = há	Referent is small or young; adds exclusivity meanings *only, even, at least;* with verbs: adds the meaning *only, barely, really* depending on verb; diminishes particle meanings.
Decessive	= gęhæ?	Referent is deceased, broken down, or abandoned: *the former, the late;* with time verbs: indicates times past; nominalizes verbs with incorporated nouns.
Populative	= he·nų?	Adds the meaning *people of* to place names.
Authentic	= ųwe	Adds the meaning *authentic, real, and really.*
Characterizer	= khá? / = há?	Adds the meaning *characterized by, the way of.*
Repeater	= ?é / = é	With repetitive prefix disambiguates the meaning *again* from the meaning *back.*

4 The Verb

4.1 Introduction

The verb is the nucleus of Onondaga utterances. It is the most morphologically complex of the word classes, and unlike nouns and particles, it can function syntactically as a complete clause. Table 4.1 is a skeleton outline of the structure of the verb together with its four major position classes: (i) prepronominal prefixes, (ii) pronominal prefixes, (iii) verb stem, and (iv) aspect suffixes. Each of these position classes will be expanded as the description proceeds in the following sections. The division into position classes is based on how the classes combine, and how the elements within each class are related to one another. This approach to the Iroquoian verb's analysis was developed by Lounsbury (1953:17-22) and has been followed in most subsequent work by Iroquoianists.

Table 4.1 The Onondaga verb

Inflect./Deriv.	Inflectional	Derivational	Lexical		Derivational	Inflectional	
Prepronominal and Modal Prefixes	Pronominal Prefixes	Reflexives	Noun Root or Stem	Verb Root	Root Suffixes	Basic Aspect Suffixes	Expanded Aspect Suffixes
			Verb Stem				

The description of the verb will proceed by working from the simplest to the most elaborate structures, rather than by discussing the parts of the verb from left to right. The pronominal prefix and the aspect suffix together with a verb stem make up the obligatory parts of the minimal verb. Section 4.2 deals with the inflectional categories of *aspect* and *mode* and their uses. In section 4.3, we examine the three series of pronominal prefixes that identify the core participants of the verb and describe how pronominal selection interacts with the major verb classes and their aspectual inflections. In section 4.4 we step back and consider Onondaga verb classes, investigating specifically how aspect and situation-types interact in the language. A set of verbs involving non-directional motion are in a class by themselves in terms of the aspect and mode categories they take, and these are discussed separately in section 4.5. In section 4.6 we examine the expanded aspect-mode categories. In section 4.7 we look at the non-modal prepronominal prefixes, which for the most part consist of adverbial modifiers to the meanings of the verb stems. Finally, in section 4.8 we describe the different types of stem-derivations available to the language.

4.2 Aspect and Mode

4.2.1 The Basic Aspect Categories

Aspect is concerned with the temporal organization of situations as these are described by the verbs of a language. It gives information about how a situation unfolds through time and how this unfolding is described from various perspectives. Aspect is expressed lexically as well as grammatically: *lexical aspect* concerns aspectual meanings that are inherent in the semantic structure of a language's complement of verbs, so that these can be classified into verbs describing basically dynamic situations: actions like *hit, sing, etc.*, processes like *burn, grow*, etc., and basically stative situations, like *happy, old, etc*; and within these, states that are inherent, like *new, green*, and resultant states that are the consequence of an activity, like *clean, successful*, in addition to many other subcategories to these larger divisions.[1] *Grammatical aspect* classifies the verbs of a language into a much smaller set of categories that are sensitive to specific rule-sets. In Onondaga these rules specify whether in a given situation a verb signals completion vs. an enduring situation, whether an activity is repetitive, habitual, punctual (a single event), or progressive (internally structured); whether the focus is on the inception or the termination of a situation; etc. Grammatical aspect is primarily signaled morphologically in Onondaga, by means of suffixes to the verb stem. Lexical and grammatical aspect interact in complex ways, which we attempt to describe in this and the sections to follow.

In Onondaga, the category of aspect is entwined with that of *mood*. Mood signals whether the situation that is reported is real, in the sense that it has actually taken place, or whether it is unreal, or *irrealis*, perhaps off in the future sometime, hypothetical, or otherwise in doubt. *Tense*, which is only weakly developed in Onondaga, is expressed by the modal categories (4.2.1.3; 4.6.2 and 4.6.3).

Onondaga has three, morphologically marked, basic aspects: the *habitual*, the *stative*, and the *punctual*.[2] Two of the three main aspects, the habitual and the stative are *durative*, that is, they express situations in terms of their endurance over time; one of the basic aspects, the punctual, primarily expresses an action or event as a single complete event. A second perspective differentiates among situations that have duration, classifying them into dynamic, evolving processes (habitual aspect) as against more homogeneous, unchanging states of affairs (stative aspect). A shorthand way to think of the situations described in terms of the three aspects is that the habitual identifies a situation as a *process*, the stative identifies it as a *state*, and the punctual identifies it as an *event*.

---

[1] Chafe (1970:9) classifies Onondaga verb roots as states, actions, processes, and action-processes on lexical semantic grounds and then subclassifies them according to aspect and pronominal prefix selection.

[2] These names for the aspect categories are currently in use by many Iroquoian linguists (e.g., Chafe 2015, Foster (1982), Froman, et al. 2002; Michelson & Doxtator 2002; Rudes 1999) and for Onondaga it continues the usage in Woodbury (1992 and 2003). Mithun, in most recent works calls the punctual *perfective*, more in line with current non-Iroquoianist linguistic naming-practice of aspects with the punctual's characteristics. In earlier work on Onondaga, Chafe (1970:16) introduced *iterative* for the habitual, and *descriptive* for the stative. Lounsbury (1953) describing Oneida, used *serial* for the habitual, and *perfective* for the stative. Abbott (2000; 2006), also on Oneida, stays with Lounsbury's terminology.

durative	habitual: *process*
	stative: *state*
non-durative	punctual: *event*

Another perspective, which overlaps with these distinctions, divides Onondaga verbs in terms of the aspect categories they can take: (i) *active* verbs can be inflected with the habitual, the stative, and the punctual, and (ii) *stative* verbs may be inflected with only one aspect – the stative.[3]

<u>Pronominal selection</u>: Every Onondaga verb must have a pronominal prefix, which references the verb's argument(s). As has been noted, there are three series of pronominal prefixes, an *agent* series, a *patient* series, and a series of *transitive* prefixes. Agent or patient prefixes occur when there is a single *animate* argument; transitive prefixes occur when there are two *animate* arguments. There is no pronominal prefix that references *non-animate* arguments. Verbs with only non-animate (neuter) arguments take the feminine-zoic singular pronominal as a default prefix as described in Koenig & Michelson (2012) and below in section 4.3.[4]

The choice of pronominal prefix from one or another of the series is lexically specified for each verb. *However* the choice of agent or patient prefix for active verbs that are lexically specified to take agent prefixes is aspectually conditioned, such that with the exception of a small group of verbs that take agent prefixes in all three aspects (sec. 4.4.3.1), an active verb will take agent prefixes with the habitual and the punctual aspects as in (1a and c), and patient prefixes with the stative aspect as in (1b).

The basic aspect suffixes are attached directly to the verb stem. In addition to the three basic aspects, a fourth category, the *imperative,* not actually a type of aspect, occurs in the basic aspect position (section 4.2.1.4). Modal prefixes co-occur with the punctual (1c), and are marked in the very beginning of the verb in the prepronominal position. The positions of the modal, and aspect affixes within the verb are shown in Table 4.2:

Table 4.2 Location of the modal and aspect affixes

Modal Prefixes	Pronominal Prefixes	Verb Stem	Aspect Suffixes

<u>An active verb inflected with the three basic aspects:</u>
(1) a. Inflected with the habitual aspect: hųhdę́·dyųs
    <u>hų</u>-ahdędyų-<u>s</u>
    3M.PL.A-leave-<u>HAB</u>
    they leave

    b. Inflected with the stative aspect: honahdędyų́h
    <u>hon</u>-ahdędyų-<u>h'</u>
    3M.NSG.P-run-<u>STV</u>
    they have gone

---

[3] In the Onondaga dictionary (Woodbury 2003) every active verb is marked v.a. and every stative verb is marked v.s.

[4] In this work the default pronominal prefix and its alternants are marked 3N/Z.SG in the morpheme identification line of examples whenever it references a single non-animate (neuter) argument; it is marked 3FZ.SG when it references an animate argument.

c. Inflected with the punctual aspect: waʔhų̄hdę́·dyaʔ

waʔ-hų-ahdędy-aʔ
<u>FACT</u>-<u>3M.PL.A</u>-leave-<u>PNC</u>
they went

Table 4.3 Aspect conjugation classes of active and stative verbs

Class	Habitual	Stative	Punctual	Imperative
A1	-(a)haʔ[5]	-h(')/Ø[6]	-(a)ʔ/-Ø[7]	-(a)h/Ø
A2	-(a)s			
A3	-k			
A4	-heʔ			
B1	-haʔ	-ʔ	-ʔ´	-h
B2	-s			
B3			-k	-k
B4	-k		-ʔ´	-h
C1	-(a)haʔ[8]	-aʔ	-ęʔ	-ęh
C2	-as		-aʔ	-ah
D1	-haʔ	-eʔ	-aʔ	-ah
D2	-as			
E1	-haʔ	-ih	-(a)ʔ/-Ø[9]	-(a)h/-Ø
E2	-as			
E3				
E4	-s		-nhaʔ	-nhah
E5			-k	-k
F1	-s	-hwih	-k/-Ø[10]	-k
G1	-(a)haʔ[11]	-ęh	-aʔ	-ah
G2	-(a)s			
H1	-ųs	-ųh	-(a)ʔ[12]	-(a)h
H2	-eʔs			

Table 4.3 lists the aspect conjugation classes of active and stative verbs.[13] The aspect suffixes have numerous alternants, and although their choice is in part phonologically conditioned by stem-finals, they are not fully predictable; they are lexically assigned as sets

---

[5] Stems whose habitual alternant ends in a vowel or *t* take habitual -haʔ; -ahaʔ occurs elsewhere.

[6] Stative stems ending in *t* take the Ø alternant; -h occurs elsewhere.

[7] Stems whose punctual alternant ends in a vowel take the punctual -ʔ; the alternant -Ø occurs with numerous stems whose punctual alternant ends in *t, k, s,* or *ʔ*; -aʔ occurs elsewhere.

[8] Stems whose habitual alternants end in *t* take -haʔ; -ahaʔ occurs elsewhere.

[9] Stems whose punctual alternant ends in a vowel, or a *VR* sequence take the punctual -ʔ; the -Ø alternant occurs with numerous stems ending in *t, k, s,* or *ʔ*; -aʔ occurs elsewhere.

[10] Stems whose punctual aspect alternant ends in *k,* takes the -Ø alternant; the -k alternant occurs elsewhere.

[11] Stems whose habitual alternant ends in *t, k,* the sequence *VR,* or the cluster *hgw* take the -haʔ alternant; -ahaʔ occurs elsewhere.

[12] Stems whose punctual alternant ends in a vowel, take the -ʔ alternant; the -aʔ alternant occurs elsewhere.

[13] Column three of Table 4.3 lists the aspect class of stative verbs. Imperative suffixes are listed in column 5. They replace punctual aspect suffixes in imperative forms (section 4.2.1.4).

to each verb and learned with it by speakers.[14] Active verbs are inflected with three aspects: the habitual, the stative, and the punctual. Stative verbs occur in only one of the aspects, the stative. Conjugation classes are established on the basis of the set of aspect suffixes a given verb takes.

4.2.1.1 The Habitual Aspect[15]

The forms of the habitual aspect suffix are displayed in Table 4.3 together with their membership in aspect classes. Words inflected with the habitual describe an action or event, typically taking place in the present, that is either (i) an instantaneous event, (ii) a continuous activity, (iii) a repetitive or iterative activity, or (iv) a habitual activity without reference to time. The exact effect of the habitual aspect is a consequence of the meaning of the particular verb and its pragmatic context.

In (2) the aspectual meaning of *godi·hwá·ʔsek* 'someone gets blamed' is present-instantaneous. In the story, a family's chicks have disappeared, and they blame their son's cat, Clyde (a female cat):

(2) Náʔ go·ʔ, godi·hwá·ʔsek, neʔ Clyde (NC01).
    naʔ   go·ʔ   go-ad-Rihw-aR-ʔse-k   neʔ   Clyde
    ASRT   CTR   3FI.P-SRF-matter-put.in-BEN-HAB   NOM   NAME
    it's   however she gets blamed   the   Clyde
    Clyde, however, gets blamed.

In (3) the aspectual meaning of *hųwanų́hweʔs* 'he likes him' is present-continuous:

(3) Ihswáʔ hųwanų́hweʔs, neʔ hohsó·dah (NC01).
    ihswaʔ   hųwa-nųhweʔ-s   neʔ   ho-hsodah
    QNT   3M.SG > 3M.SG-like-HAB   NOM   3M.SG.P-grandfather
    a lot   he likes him   the   his grandfather
    He likes his grandfather a lot.

In (4) the aspectual meaning of *hodinasgwahdų́·nik* 'they keep losing their chicks' is present-repetitive:

(4) Nę́·gę ų́hgęʔ hodinasgwahdų·ník neʔ nigųnaʔsʔá gítgit (NC01).
    nęgę ųhgęʔ   hodi-nasgw-ahdų-ni-k   neʔ   ni-gųn-aʔsʔa-h   gitgit
    DEM TMP   3M.NSG.P-pet-lose-BEN-HAB   NOM   PRT-3FZ.PL.A-small-STV   NOUN
    at this time they keep losing their pets   the   they are small   chicken
    At this time, they keep losing their little chicks.

In (5) the habitual inflection of *hųde·yós* 'they fight, they are fighters' marks a habitual activity without reference to time.

---

[14] There is some amount of speaker variation regarding aspect assignment.

[15] The habitual aspect has also been called the *serial* (Lounsbury 1953; Abbott 2000), and the *iterative* (Chafe 1967; 1970).

(5) Gaʔt khę́ oyá? ga? gwa? nų́· thadiná·ge·?, hųde·yós da·hų·dǽ·?nha?. (HW07)

ga?t khę	(y)-oya?		ga?	gwa?	nų	t-hadi-nage·-?
HYP QUE	3N/Z.SG.A-different-STV		INDF	RSTR	LOC	CIS-3M.PL.A-live-STV
maybe	it is different		somebody	just	place	they live there

hų-ade-Ryo-s	d-aa-hų-adR-a?-nha?
3M.PL.A-SRF-kill-HAB	DL-OPT-3M.PL.A-meet-INCH-PNC
they fight/are fighters	they may meet up

Perhaps strangers live in the vicinity, they may even meet up with <u>fighters</u>.

Finally, a verb inflected with the habitual aspect can be ambiguous between two possible interpretations – the *generic-habitual* one as in (5) and the *present-continuous* meaning as in (3) – if it belongs to the class of *consequential* verbs (Chafe 1980). Consequential verbs are ones whose actions 'produce a new state of affairs' (Chafe 1996:560) whereas non-consequential verbs do not. The verb *-hninų-* 'buy' describes a consequential activity, inflected with the habitual, *hahnı́·nųk,* it has two possible interpretations, a generic-habitual one without reference to time, 'he buys, he's a buyer', or a present-continuous meaning 'he's buying'. This is not the case with the verb *-ade·yo-* 'fight' which is classified, in Onondaga, as non-consequential. Inflected with the habitual, *hųdé·yos,* has only the generic-habitual interpretation 'they fight, they are fighters'. In order to express the present-continuous meaning, this verb, and others of its class, must be inflected with the stative aspect *hona·de·yóh* 'they are fighting' (section 4.4.2, which deals with consequentiality).

4.2.1.2 The Stative Aspect[16]

The forms of the stative aspect suffix are displayed in Table 4.3 together with their membership in aspect classes. As Lounsbury (Lounsbury 1953:85) put it, the stative expresses either *given* or *resultant states.* Thus active verbs inflected with the stative express states that are the result of an action, whereas verbs that occur only in the stative aspect tend to express *given* states. Chafe (1970:16) characterizes active verbs that have been inflected with the stative as "dynamic state[s]" in which there is a condition of verbing going on. Some verbs that occur only in the stative aspect – basically stative verbs – describe a state, such as *be new, be good,* etc., concepts that are often expressed by adjectives in English, but which are expressed with stative verbs in Onondaga (see Chafe 2012a for Seneca). These are states that we think of as unchanging over time. The basically stative verbs, expressing given, more enduring states are exemplified in (6-12).

---

[16] The stative aspect has also been called the *perfective* (Lounsbury 1953) and the *descriptive* (Chafe 1967; 1970).

(i) <u>Given states</u>:

(6) Ųnís?i ahsų́ tciyohnegiyó ne? gahnegáę·nyų?, wa?hahnegihǽ? ná? ne? osgęnųdų́? (NC02).

ųnis?i	ahsų	<u>tci-yo-hneg-iyo-h'</u>		ne?	ga-hneg-aR-ųnyų-?
TMP	REP	COIN-3N/Z.SG.P-liquid-be.good-STV		NOM	3N/Z.SG.A-liquid-be.in-DST-STV
long time	again	when the water is good		the	water is in various locations

wa?-ha-hnegihR-a?		na?	ne?	osgęnųdų́?.
FACT-3M.SG.A-drink-PNC		ASRT	NOM	NOUN
he drank		it's	the	deer

A long time ago, when the waters everywhere were clear, a deer was drinking.

(7) Naye? ne? tsha? niya·wę́?ih[17] ne? oihwagá·yųh (CTL1.2).

naye?	ne?	tsha?	ni-yaw-ę?-ih		ne?	<u>o-Rihw-a-gayų-h</u>
ASRT	NOM	SUB	PRT-3N/Z.SG.P-happen-STV		NOM	3N/Z.SG.P-matter-JN-be.old-STV
it's	the	that	thus it happened		the	it's an old matter

That's what happened in ancient times.

Other basically stative verbs, like *-adyehwad-* 'be wakeful' in (8), and *-ęnųhdų-* 'know' in (9), describe a kind of steady-state experience:

(8) Ne? ó·nę tshųgi·hó·da?s né?tho nwa?oníshe? thiwagadyéhwada? hyá de?wa·gí·daks (CTL112.7-8).

ne? onę	tshųg-Rihw-od-a?s-Ø		ne?tho
NOM TMP	COIN:FACT:1SG.P-matter-stand-BEN-PNC		LOC
then	as I got the message		there

n-wa?-o-nishe-?		thi-wag-ad-yehwad-a?	hya
PRT-FACT-3N/Z.SG.P-long.time-STV		CON-1SG.P-SRF-be.awake-STV	NEG
it is a long time		I've been really wakeful	not

de?-wag-idak-s
NEG-1SG.P-sleep-HAB
I'm not sleeping

For a long time now, since receiving the message, I've been excessively wakeful – I've not been sleeping.

(9) Jyęnųhdų? khęh gaę nų nidisnenų, gaę ohni? nų hęjisné? ne? hwędų gwa? ne? onę́ hęjijyahdędya? (H641.7).[18]

<u>jy-ęnųhdų-?</u>	khę	gaę	nų	ni-di-sn-e-nų		gaę	ohni?	nų
2DU-know-STV	QUE	INTR	LOC	PRT-CIS-2DU-come-STV		INTR	ADD	LOC
do you know?		where	place	you have come from there		where	also	place

---

[17] Utterance-final prosody and the presence of word-final h utterance-medially is because the source of the excerpt is a dictated text (see sec. 1.3).

[18] Hewitt did not mark stress and vowel length in this excerpt.

```
h-ę-ji-sn-e-?                    ne?   hwędų  gwa?  ne?  onę
TRNS-FUT-REP-2DU-go-PRP          NOM   INTR   REST  NOM  TMP
you will go there                the   when   just  the  now

h-ę-ji-jy-ahdędy-a?
TRNS-FUT-REP-2DU-leave-PNC
you two will return home
```
Do you to <u>know</u> where you've come from and where you'll go when you return home?

A basically stative verb with a range of meanings, in part a property concept in part a kind of steady-state, depending on whether its referents are human, animal, or non-animate, is *-nage·-*, which means 'be plentiful' (of animals or non-animates), and 'be present, live or dwell somewhere' (of humans). This verb, in all its meanings, takes only the stative aspect and indicates that there is no change over time, no indication of a beginning or an end:

(10) Tho gna·gé·? thogę ganųhsá·yę?.
```
    tho   g-nage·-?          thogę   ga-nųhs-a-yę-?
    LOC   1SG.A-reside-STV   DEM     3N/Z.SG.A-house-JN-place-STV
```
I live there in that house

(11) gaihwaná·ge·?
```
    ga-Rihw-a-nage·-?
    3N/Z.SG.A-matter-JN-plentiful-STV
```
[there is] lots of news or gossip

(12) Dogęs ni?á ga·yo?danage·? tsha? nųwe hege?sgwa? (H671.8-9).[19]
```
    dogęs   ne?   i?=á         ga-Ryo?d-a-nage·-?                tsha?  nųwe
    MOD     NOM   PRON=DIM     3N/Z.SG.A-animal-JN-plentiful-STV SUB    LOC
    truly   the   I alone      there are lots of animals         that   place

    he-g-e-?s-gwa?
    TRNS-1SG.A-go-HAB-HBPST
    I was there
```
Truly, I alone was at a place where there were lots of animals.

(ii) <u>Resultant states</u>:

A *resultant state* is a state that is the consequence of some activity or event. Active verbs inflected for the stative aspect often express resultant states. With some verbs, this inflection signals completion similar in meaning to the perfect in English. In Onondaga resultant states are frequently expressed as the consequence of an activity that was completed in the past: an activity was performed, and now there exists the state of having performed the action. For example:

---

[19] Hewitt did not mark stress and prosodic vowel length in this excerpt.

94 The Verb

(a) <u>Completive resultant states:</u>

(13) tho nę honadeʔse·hdayęʔ néʔtho (EO01).
    tho   nę   hon-ade-ʔse·hd-a-yę-ʔ   neʔtho
    DEM LOC   3M.NSG.P-SRF-vehicle-JN-place-STV LOC
    that here they have parked their car   there
    They'd parked their car right there.

(14) waʔtha·dáʔnhaʔ tshaʔ dewahsę·nųh[20] tshaʔ nų goyaʔdayéiʔ (CTL36.8).
    waʔ-t-ha-d-aʔ-nhaʔ   tshaʔ   de-w-ahsęnų-h
    FACT-DL-3M.SG.A-stand.up-INCH-PNC SUB   DL-3N/Z.SG.A-be.the.middle-STV
    he stood up   that   it is the middle

    tshaʔ   nų   go-yaʔd-a-yei-ʔ
    SUB   LOC   3FI.P-body-JN-be.complete-STV
    that   place they have assembled
    He stood up in the center of the place where they had assembled.

(15) Tshaʔ niyogęhnhanóh naʔ nęgęha, hya gwas deʔodiyanę·ʔsé neʔ Clifford hoyęthwáhųʔ (LG02).
    tshaʔ   ni-yo-gęhnh-a-no-h   naʔ   nęgę = há   hya   gwas
    SUB   PRT-3N/Z.SG.P-sumer-JN-cold-STV   ASRT DEM = DIM NEG   INTS
    that   it's a cold summer   it's   this particular not   very

    deʔ-odi-yanę·-ʔse-h'   neʔ   Clifford   ho-yęthw-ahų-ʔ
    NEG-3FZ.NSG.P-good-BEN-STV   NOM   NAME   3M.SG.P-plant-DST-STV
    it wasn't good for them   the   Clifford   he has planted [it]
    This summer has been cool; it's not been good for Clifford's garden.

Example (13) expresses a situation in which men have parked their car, and now they are in the state that results from having parked their car: hence the patient pronominal prefix. Similarly, in (14) people are now in the state of having assembled to hear someone speak. In (15) the discussion is about Clifford's garden, literally *[the things] he has planted*.

Another group of active verbs, such as *sit, watch, cough,* or *do* and verbs describing weather-events are interpreted as present-continuative (i.e., an imperfective) in the stative:

(b) <u>Present-continuative resultant states:</u>

(16) tho getgodáʔ dekhegahǽ·ʔ tshaʔ nihonadyé·ęh (EO01).
    tho   ge-tgod-aʔ[21]   de-khe-gahR-aʔ   tshaʔ ni-hon-ad-yeR-ęh
    LOC   1SG.A-sit-STV DL-1SG > 3-watch-STV SUB   PRT-3M.NSG.P-SRF-do-STV
    there I'm sitting   I'm watching them   that   so they do it
    I'm sitting there, watching what they're doing.

---

[20] Utterance-final prosody and the presence of word-final *h* word-medially is because the source of the excerpt is a dictated text (see sec. 1.3).

[21] The verb -tgod- is one of a group of verbs that takes agent prefixes in all three aspects (section 4.4.3.1).

(17) Sthwihá osdáę·dyųh.
    sthwiha   o-sdaR-ųdy-h
    QNT   3N/Z.SG.P-rain-throw.away-STV
    It's raining a little.

Verbs like *sit, watch, cough,* and *do,* and weather-words like *rain, snow,* are *non-consequential* and verbs like *park* and *leave,* and *cut* are *consequential* (sections 4.2.1.1, and 4.4.2). The dimension of consequentiality affects both their habitual and stative interpretations in predictable ways.

In summary, verbs inflected with the stative can express *given* or *resultant* states. Given states express qualities of persons or objects; or they can express states of affairs of various kinds. Resultant states are typically active verbs inflected with the stative aspect. These are interpreted as either ongoing or completed, depending on the particular verb so inflected.

4.2.1.3   The Punctual Aspect and Marking Mood

The forms of the punctual aspect suffix are displayed in Table 4.3 above together with their membership in aspect classes. The punctual aspect describes a unitary occurrence; it takes a perspective from outside the situation, describing it as an entire event that takes place at a certain point in time rather than as a process developing through time, as does the habitual, or as a static situation, as does the stative.

A verb inflected with the punctual aspect always occurs with one of three modal prepronominal prefixes: the *factual,* the *future,* or the *optative.* The forms of these prefixes are given in Table 4.4:

Table 4.4 The modal prepronominal prefixes

Factual	wa?-, we?-, ų-, -a-, ų-a-, -a?-
Future	ę-
Optative	aa-, ae-, aų-, ųų-a-/aų-a-

The alternants *we?-* and *ae-* of the factual and the optative, respectively, occur with second person dual or plural pronominal prefixes, any second person patient, or the first person dual or plural inclusive pronominal prefixes. The alternants *ų-* and *aų-* of the factual and optative, respectively, occur, optionally, to replace the sequences *wa?+wa-* or *a+wa-* (section 2.5.1.1).[22] The factual alternant *-a-* occurs in combinations of the factual and the cislocative prepronominal prefix, and the factual and the repetitive prepronominal prefix; the alternant *-a?-* occurs when the factual combines with the contrastive prepronominal; the discontinuous factual alternant *ų-a-* occurs when the factual combines with the dualic and repetitive, dualic and cislocative, or the translocative and repetitive prepronominals. The optative alternants *aa-, ae-,* and *aų-* are realized as *a·, ae·-,* and *aų·-,* although the length is often lost in fast speech. The discontinuous optative alternant *ųų-a-/aų-a-* occurs when the optative combines with the non-modal prepronominals listed for the discontinuous factual alternant *ų-a-,* above. The alternants *wa?-* and *aa-* occur

---

[22] The replacement while optional in Onondaga, is obligatory in the other Northern Iroquoian languages.

elsewhere The future prepronominal prefix occurs in the single form ę-. (See Table 4.48 for all possible combinations of modal and non-modal prepronominal prefixes).

The meanings of the prefixes are modal, that is, they signal the speaker's certainty with regard to the factuality of the situation described in his/her statement. The factual signals that the speaker thinks of the event expressed in the clause as a known fact; that he/she is sure it has taken place in the past or is taking place contemporaneously with the speech event, that it may have been witnessed by the speaker or he/she has it on good authority. The future and optative signal potential events: the future signals that an event will likely occur, and the optative signals various degrees of uncertainty; it is used to mark hypotheticals, wishes, hopes, possibility, obligation, and permission. The optative often occurs with, and is required by, matrix verbs that establish the nature of the modality that is being expressed: epistemic (degree of certainty or commitment by speaker), deontic (permission, obligation, moral desirability), or dynamic (ability) (section 7.9). There is a strong tendency for the modal prefixes to do double duty to establish location in time, such that the factual has a tendency to line up with the past, the future and optative with future or potential events.

4.2.1.3.1 The Punctual Aspect with the Factual Mode

The form of the factual is wa?-, we?-, ų-, -a-, -a?-, ų-a- (Table 4.4). The factual is often glossed in the simple past or as a contemporaneous event. The factual is used, in the first place, to establish facts. In (18) the speaker is holding out an item that she had lost:

(18) Nę hagwá wa?getshę́·ni?.

    nę   hagwa   wa?-ge-tshęni-?

    PRES DIR   FACT-1SG.A-find-PNC

    Here it is, I found it.

In (19) a boy's father has given him permission to keep his pet:

(19) Onę́ sgę́·nų?, sahęnųhdų́·nyų? (NC01).

    onę   sgęnų?   s-a-h-ęnųhdų-nyų-?

    TMP   peaceful REP-FACT-3M.SG.A-think-DST-PNC

    Now he is happy again [literally: he is thinking peacefully again].

The events in (18) and (19) are presented as facts that took place in the (recent) past or in the present. The factual is also used in *speech acts* and with *performative* verbs. In (20) the chief is giving two messengers instructions to extend an invitation to someone in another camp:

(20) Thohgé ęsnihę́·? ne? hauhwá?ge, "Onę wa?gninętshadi·yę́·dę? né?tho hęhsé? hahsęnowá·nę thonųhsá·yę?" (CTL185.4-6).

    thohge ę-sn-ihę·-?'   ne? ha-ųhw-a?=ge   onę

    TMP   FUT-2DU-say-PNC NOM 3M.SG.P-self-NSF=LOC TMP

    then   you two will say the   to him, himself   now

wa?-gni-nẹtsh-adiyẹd-ẹ?   ne?tho   h-ẹ-hs-e-?   ha-hsẹn-owan-ẹ
FACT-1DU.EX > 2SG-arm-pull-PNC   LOC   TRNS-FUT-2SG.A-go-PRP   3M.SG.A-name-large-STV
we two invite you   there   you will go there   chief

t-ho-nụhs-a-yẹ-?
CIS-3M.SG.P-house-JN-place-STV
where he has his house

Then you two will say to him, "Now we (two) invite you to go there to the chief's house."

In (21) the messengers have delivered their invitation and their interlocutor gives his answer:

(21) Onẹ di? wa?gyená? né?tho hẹgé? tsha? nú·we tganakdá·gwẹh (CTL186.5-6).

onẹ   di?   wa?-g-yena-?'   ne?tho   h-ẹ-g-e-?   tsha?   nụwe
TMP   LNK   FACT-1SG.A-accept-PNC   LOC   TRNS-FUT-1SG.A-go-PRP   SUB   LOC
now   moreover   I am accepting   there   I will go there   that   place

t-ga-nakd-a-gw-ẹh
CIS-3N/Z.SG.A-space-JN-choose-STV
a space was chosen

So now I accept; I will go to the chosen location.

In both examples the speech acts, *wa?gninẹtshadi·yẹ́·dẹ?* 'we invite you' and *wa?gyená?* 'I accept' are inflected with the punctual aspect in the factual mode.

A third use of the factual is with *weather verbs*. These too are inflected with the punctual in the factual mode, but rather than indicating a past event, this construction expresses the *onset* of a weather-event:

(22) Tshụdawẹnúhda? wa?osdáẹ·di?.

tsh-ụda-w-ẹnụhd-a?   wa?-o-sdaR-ụdi-?
COIN-CIS:FACT-3N/Z.SG.A-sudden-PNC   FACT-3N/Z.SG.P-rain-throw.away-PNC
it is sudden   it began to rain

Suddenly, it began to rain.

(23) Wa?wa?gæ·nawẹ́? ne? ga·hagụ́·wah (LG03).

wa?-w-a?gR-a-nawe-?   ne?   ga-Rh-agụwa
FACT-3N/Z.SG.A-snow-JN-melt-PNC   NOM   NPF-forest-LOC
snow began to melt   the   in the forest

The snow began to melt in the forest.

4.2.1.3.2 The Punctual Aspect with the Future Mode

The future modal occurs in only a single form: *ẹ-* (Table 4.4). Inflected with the future, the punctual aspect expresses the speaker's expectation that the action or event described by the verb will take place at some future time.

(24) Naʔ gę́s neʔ nę· ųgwę·nų́hdų?, tshaʔ niga·hawíʔ dę́theʔ, ęshá·yųʔ (HW02).

na?	gęs	ne? nę	ųgw-ęnųhdų-?	tsha?	ni-ga-hawi-?
ASRT	REP	NOM TMP	1PL.P-know-STV	SUB	PRT-3N/Z.SG.A-carry-STV
it's	usually	that's when	we know	that	it is time

d-ę-t-h-e-?	ę-s-ha-yų-?
DL-FUT-CIS-3M.SG.A-come-PNC	FUT-REP-3M.SG.A-arrive-PNC
he will come back	he will arrive home

Usually, we know when it's time for him to get back home.

In (24) the children have a *moderately certain expectation* that it's time at this point for their father to return home from work.

The more specifically the activity of the verb is described, the more certainty is signaled by the future mode. In (25) the bread is right there, ready for the eating:

(25) …ękhǽ·hgwak, neʔ sano·háʔ gothǽhgų́·daʔ (NC01).

ę-k-hæhgw-a-k-Ø	ne?	sa-noha?	go-at-hæhgw-ųd-a?
FUT-1SG.A-bread-JN-eat-PNC	NOM	3FZ.SG > 2-mother	3FI.P-SRF-bread-put.in.oven-STV
I will eat bread	the	your mother	she has baked bread

I will eat the bread your mother has baked.

But the future mode carries a note of contingency. To remove that sense of contingency, speakers add the contrastive connective particle *go·ʔ* 'however, but, actually', as in (26-28):

(26) Owæs gó·ʔ ęsgųyaʔdagéhnhaʔ (HW07).

owæs	go·?	ę-s-gų-ya?d-a-gehnh-a?
MOD	CTR	FUT-REP-1SG > 2SG-body-JN-help-PNC
for sure	however	I will help you

But for sure, I'll keep helping you.

(27) Ęgeʔsé·ʔ go·ʔ thó·gęh.

ę-ge-?se-?	go·?	thogę
FUT-1SG.A-drag-PNC	CTR	DEM
I will I will drag it	however	that

But for sure, I'll drag that [thing].

(28) Nę gó·ʔ ętgahsá·węʔ.

nę	go·?	ę-t-g-ahsaw-ę?
TMP	CTR	FUT-CIS-1SG.A-start-PNC
now	however	I will start

But I'm starting right now

Speakers also use verbs inflected with the future mode to describe customary activities. In (29) the narrator, having listed the ingredients of a recipe, told how these are customarily dealt with:

(29) Naʔ thogę dęyų·wę·yéʔ, ęyejikhe·ʔdá·k oʔ gwas sí nigę thogę, ganaʔjyodáʔ nęh, ęyedahgwáʔ nę nęwá·dųʔ ę́·yek (LG01).

naʔ	thogę	d-ę-yų-awę·ye-ʔ	ę-ye-jikheʔd-aR-k	oʔ	gwas	si	nigę
ASRT	DEM	CIS-FUT-3FI.A-stir-PNC	FUT-3FI.A-salt-put.in-PNC	ADD	INTNS	LOC	EXT
it's	that	one will stir it	one will put in salt	also	very	far	extent

thogę	ga-naʔjy-od-aʔ	onę	ę-ye-d-ahgw-aʔ	onę
DEM	3N/Z.SG.A-kettle-stand.up-STV	TMP	FUT-3FI.A-be.in-REV-PNC	TMP
that	it is boiling	now	one will take it out	now

n-ę-w-adų-ʔ	ę-ye-k-Ø
PRT-FUT-3N/Z.SG.A-become-PNC	FUT-3FI.A-eat-PNC
it will get ready	they will eat.

They will stir that; they will salt it too; it's boiling hard [and] when it's ready, they will take it out and eat it.

4.2.1.3.3 The Punctual Aspect with the Optative Mode

The form of the optative is aa-, ae-, aų-/ aų-a-/ųų-a- (Table 4.4). Verbs inflected with the optative express uncertainty that the activity described by the verb reflects a real event. They occur as predicates expressing contingency, duty, obligation, or possibility. The optative is also used to express politeness. The verb in (30) expresses obligation:

(30) Naʔ néʔ tho hae·dwatgwiʔthák tshaʔ nų thęʔdę́·ʔ neʔ hoyaʔdado·gęhdí Shųgwade·yęnóʔkdaʔ (HW06).

naʔ	neʔ	tho	h-ae·-dw-atgwiʔt-ha-k-Ø	tshaʔ	nų
ASRT	NOM	LOC	TRNS-OPT-1IN.PL.A-move-HAB-CNT-PNC	SUB	LOC
that	the	there	we should move there	that	place

t-hę-iʔdę·-ʔ	neʔ	ho-yaʔd-dogę-hd-ih
CIS-3M.SG.A-dwell-STV	NOM	3M.SG.P-body-be.a.certain-CS-STV
he lives	the	he is sacred

shųgw-ade-Wyęn-oʔkd-aʔ
3M.SG > 1PL-SRF-task-finish-STV
Creator

We should move towards the place where the sacred one dwells, the Creator.

The verb in (31) expresses uncertainty or possibility:

(31) Shayáʔdada yágęʔ ihádųk, "gaʔt séʔ naʔ ųse·dyákdaʔ" (HW07).

s-ha-yaʔd-a-d-ah	yagęʔ	i-h-adų-k	gaʔt	seʔ	naʔ
REP-3M.SG.A-body-JN-be.one-STV	HRSY	EP-3M.SG.A-say-HAB	HYP	MOD	ASRT
one person	they say	he says	if	actually	it's

ų-se-dy-akd-aʔ
OPT-REP-1IN.DU.A-be.near-PNC
you and I might go back

One of [the men] says, "maybe we could go back [where we came from]."

Note that in (31) the verb inflected with the optative is preceded by conditional particles. Example (32) is a true conditional utterance:

(32) Dyę gwá? ahsehék dęhsadųgóhda?, tho nęhcyé·æ?, wádę? ęgųyathó·yę? (HW07).

    dyę gwa?   aa-hs-eR-he?-k   d-ę-hs-ad-ųgohd-a?

    HYP   OPT-2SG.A-want-HAB-CNT   DL-FUT-2SG.A-SRF-pass.through-PNC

    if   you may want   you will survive

    tho   n-ę-hs-yeR-a?   wadę?   ę-gųy-atho·y-ę-?

    MAN   PART-FUT-2SG.A-do-PNC   INTR   FUT-1SG > 2SG-tell-BEN-PNC

    thus   how you will do it   what   I will tell you

    If you want to survive, you will do what I tell you.

The three optatives in (33) mark the utterance – a proposal of marriage – as a polite, and likely tentative, request:

(33) Ahsathųdat khę ne? i? agęk ayųgninyákhe? (H635.22-636.1).[23]

    aa-hs-athųd-at-Ø   khę ne? i?   aa-ga-i-k-Ø

    OPT-2SG.A-hear-CS-PNC QUE   NOM PRON OPT-3N/Z.SG.A-be,exist-CNT-PNC

    would you listen?   the   I   it may be

    aa-yųgni-nyak-he?-Ø

    OPT-1DU.P-marry-INCH-PNC

    we two should get married

    Would you agree [that] you and I should get married?

The optative shows up in conjunction with verbs that express propositional attitudes such as *know, want, etc.*, and that require optatives in argument clauses (section 7.4.) When optatives occur in dependent clauses, it is the matrix verb that establishes the modality of the event. The matrix verb *-eR-* 'want' requires that a dependent verb is inflected with one of the two irrealis modal prefixes, the future or the optative. In (34) the dependent verb *-adęnasgų-* 'give away one's pet' is inflected with the optative:

(34) Do gá·? nwa?wa·dyét?a? gęs hehé? a·hadęnásgų? (HW05).

    do ga?   n-wa?-w-adyet?-a?   gęs   h-eR-he?

    INTR IND PRT-FACT-3N/Z.SG.A-times-PNC CST   3M.SG.A-want-HAB

    some   thus many times   habitually he wants

    aa-h-adę-nasgw-ų-?

    OPT-3M.SG.A-SRF-pet-give-PNC

    he might give away his pet

    He frequently wanted to give away his pet.

In (35) the verb *-ade?nyędę-* 'try' occurs with a dependent verb in the optative:

---

[23] Hewitt did not mark stress and prosodic vowel length in this excerpt.

(35) Waʔhadeʔnyę́·dę́ʔ, da·háæhdat, dagayenáʔ neʔ honáʔga·ʔ, tshaʔ ohųdų́·nyųʔ (NC02).

waʔ-h-adeʔnyędę-ʔ	d-aa-h-aæhdat-Ø	d-a-ga-yena-ʔ'	neʔ
FACT-3M.SG.A-try-PNC	DL-OPT-3M.SG.A-run-PNC	CIS-FACT-3N/Z.SG.A-catch-PNC	NOM
he tried	he should run	it's catching it	the

ho-naʔgaR-aʔ	tshaʔ	o-hųd-ųnyų-ʔ
3M.SG.P-antler-NSF	SUB	3N/Z.SG.P-be.a.shrub-DST-STV
his antler	at	shrubs

He tried to run, [but] his antlers got caught in the shrubs.

In (36) a chief is asking his people to guess a dream he has had. Here the verb *-gweny-* 'be able to do something' requires that -Rihwaʔsæ·gw- 'answer' is inflected with the optative.

(36) Dyęhaʔ gwaʔ giʔshę is swagwenyų aeswaihwaʔsægwaʔ tshaʔ nigayéhaʔ neʔ akʔnigųhæʔ (H617:20-21).[24]

dyęhaʔ	gwaʔ	giʔshę	is	swa-gweny-ų	ae-swa-Rihwaʔsæ·gw-aʔ	tshaʔ
HYP	RSTR	ALT	PRON	2PL-be.able-STV	OPT-2PL-answer-PNC	SUB
if	just	alternatively	you	you are able to	you could answer	that

ni-ga-yeR-haʔ	neʔ	ag-ʔnigųhR-aʔ
PRT-3N/Z.SG.A-do-HAB	NOM	1SG.P-mind-NSF
how it does it	the	my mind

Alternatively, you might be able to answer what [it is] that is agitating my mind.

4.2.1.4 The Imperatives

4.2.1.4.1 The Simple Imperative

The imperative is not usually considered an aspect category, however in the Iroquoian languages, as was pointed out above, the imperative suffix occurs in the same position of the verb as the aspect suffixes, and Iroquoianists generally treat it in that context. The forms of the imperative suffix are *-h, -ah-, -ęh, -nhah, -k, -Ø* (Table 4.3). The alternants ending in *h* simply replace the *ʔ* of the punctual aspect suffixes. The *-k* and *-Ø* alternants are the same as the punctual alternants. The distribution is identical to the distribution described for punctual alternants in Table 4.3. The meaning of the imperative includes the hortative (let's...).

In its simplest form, the imperative verb takes the imperative suffix and agent pronominal prefixes. (The imperative alternant of the second person singular agent pronominal prefix is s-, rather than (-h)s-).

(37) sęni·hę́h!

    s-ęni·hę-h'
    2SG.IMP-stop-IMP
    Stop!

---

[24] Hewitt did not mark stress and vowel length in this excerpt except as shown.

The imperative occurs with all three persons and numbers:

(38) a. <u>First person</u>: gade?nyę́·dęh!
    g-ade?nyędę-h
    1SG.A-try-IMP
    Let me try!

    b. <u>Second person</u>: sna?jyódęh!
    s-na?jy-od-ęh
    2SG.IMP-bucket-stand-IMP
    Boil it!

    c. <u>Third person</u>: hathų·gá·ya?k!
    h-at-hųgaR-ya?k-Ø
    3M.SG.A-SRF-draft.somebody-IMP
    Let him volunteer!

(39) a. <u>Singular</u>: desáæhdat!
    de-s-aæhdat-Ø
    DL-2SG.IMP-run-IMP
    Run!

    b. <u>Dual</u>: jyadéhs?ah!
    sy-ade-hs?-ah
    2DU-SRF-finish-IMP
    Get ready, <u>you two</u>! Prepare!

    c. <u>Plural</u>: <u>sw</u>adé·hgah!
    sw-ad-Rehg-ah
    2PL-SRF-collect-IMP
    <u>You all</u>, assemble!

The Imperative occurs with semantically intransitive, transitive and ditransitive verbs:

(40) a. <u>Intransitive</u>: desatga·hadé·nih!
    de-s-atga·hadeni-h
    DL-2SG.IMP-turn.around-IMP
    Turn around!

    b. <u>Transitive</u>: sheyatshohgwaęnyų́h!
    shey-at-hsohgw-aR-ųnyų-h'
    2SG > 3-SRF-lip-put.on-DST-IMP
    Kiss her!

    c. <u>Ditransitive</u>: shehǽ·s!
    she-hR-as-Ø'
    2SG > 3-put.on-BEN-IMP
    Cover her! [Literally, you put it on her]

While the simple imperative forms do not take modal prefixes, there are a few exceptions. Imperatives between speaker and addressee, take the factual prepronominal prefix together with the cislocative prepronominal prefix (section 4.7.2) which indicates motion toward a point of reference:

(41) 2nd Person > 1st Person Imperatives with the factual and cislocative:
    dasgathó·yęh!
    d-a-sg-atho·y-ę-h
    CIS-FACT-2SG > 1SG-tell-BEN-IMP
    Tell me!
        Without factual: hes-atho·y-ę-h [2SG > 3M.SG-tell-BEN-IMP] *Tell him!*

With examples in which the speaker commands the addressee to do something involving the speaker as in (41), the cislocative is used to indicate the direction of the action from the point of view of the speaker.[25] Speakers also accept a reduced form of pronominal marking, so that both (41) with the transitive pronominal prefix -sg- 'you to me', and (42) with the prefix -g- 'I', marking only the speaker, are acceptable forms.[26] Example (42) strings together two imperatives; it is a saying used by story-tellers:

(42) dagi·dę· dagyę?gwanú·dah!
    d-a-g-idęR-h   d-a-g-yę?gw-a-nųd-ah
    CIS-FACT-1SG.A-pity-IMP   CIS-FACT-1SG.A-tobacco-JN-share-IMP
    Take pity on me, give me tobacco!

A few verbs that lexically require certain non-modal prepronominal prefixes (section 4.7), combine these with the factual in the imperative as did (41) and (42) above. It is difficult to find an explanation for the presence of factuals here, since the non-modal prefixes can occur without modals in other environments. In any event, examples are:

(43) Imperatives with non-modal prepronominal prefixes and the factual:
    a. hwa?hejíhnųk
       h-wa?-hes-ihnųk-Ø
       TRNS-FACT-2SG > 3M.SG-fetch-IMP
       Fetch him!

    b. dájyųh!
       d-a-j-yų-h
       CIS-FACT-2SG.IMP-enter-IMP
       Come in!

---

[25] A possible alternative analysis of the 2 > 1 imperatives is to set up a *dasg* / *dag* alternant of the 2nd person singular to 1st person singular pronominal prefix (#53 Tables 4.7 and 4.8) for imperatives. This is the approach taken by Mithun for Mohawk (p.c.). Lounsbury (1953:56(3)) likewise analyzes *ta* of Oneida as an alternant.

[26] A speaker of the Onondaga Nation dialect, noting that both are equally acceptable, felt that the *dag-* forms were older than the *dasg-* forms (p.c. Jay Meacham, reporting on his aunt, the late Eva Okun's response).

   c. sayetcihnyóhah!
      s-a-yetci-hnyo-h-ah
      REP-FACT-2NSG > 3-ferry.across-DSLC-IMP
      Go to ferry them back!

The verb in (a) requires a locative prepronominal prefix, depending on the direction of the action. Here the translocative marks an action away from the speaker; in (b) the speaker is located inside the space being entered, and marks the action towards himself with the cislocative prepronominal prefix; in (c) the repetitive prepronominal prefix reverses the action of the verb.

4.2.1.4.2 The Continuative Imperative

Imperative forms tend to occur with active verbs, because commands and suggestions imply that the speaker assumes the addressee is able to control the action expressed by the verb. But in Onondaga, it is possible to inflect stative forms of active verbs and a few verbs that occur only in the stative aspect for stative and habitual versions of the imperative. To do so, the continuative morpheme *-k* is suffixed to the verb (section 4.6.3). The meaning of such commands is that the action expressed by the verb is to be continued. In (44) and (45)[27] the (a) examples are with the *stative continuative*, and the (b) examples are with the *habitual continuative*. They are like the simple imperative in that they lack modal prefixes, but they differ in requiring continuative morphology:

(44)   a. Sade·yę́sdik ne? ųgwehųwekhá?!
       s-ade·yęsd-i-k-Ø   ne?   (y)-ųgweh = ųwe = kha?
       2SG.IMP-study-STV-CNT-IMP   NOM   NPF-person:SUFF = AUTH = CHAR
       Keep studying the Indian language!

      b. Sade·yę́sthak ne? ųgwehųwekhá?!
       s-ade·yęst-ha-k-Ø   ne?   (y)-ųgweh = ųwe = kha?
       2SG.IMP-study-HAB-CNT-IMP   NOM   NPF-person:SUFF = AUTH = CHAR
       Keep studying the Indian language [at regular intervals]!
             cf. <u>the simple imperative</u>: ha? di? sade·yę́sdah *Go on, study!*

(45)   a. Sadų?tgę́k ohahadá?geh!
       s-adų?tg-ę-k-Ø   o-ahahad-a? = ge
       2SG.IMP-move.aside-STV-CNT-IMP   NPF-road-NSF = LOC
       Keep out of the road!

      b. Sadų?tgehsek ohahadá?geh!
       s-adų?tg-e-hs-e-k-Ø   o-ahahad-a? = ge
       2SG.IMP-move.aside-EP-HAB-CNT-IMP   NPF-road-NSF = LOC
       Keep out of the road!
             cf. <u>the simple imperative</u>: sadų?tgah *get out of the way!*

---

[27] The examples in (44-5) were relayed to me by Jay Meacham who elicited them from his aunt, the late Eva Okun.

Examples with stative only verbs with the imperative are:

(46)   a. Etciyathų́·dek! (CTL689.2)
           etciy-athųde-k-Ø
           2NSG > 3-hear-CNT-IMP
           Keep listening to them!

        b. ísdak
           i-s-d-ak-Ø
           EP-2SG.IMP-stand-CNT-IMP
           Keep standing!

        c. sʔnigųhǽ·k
           s-ʔnigųhR-aR-k-Ø
           2SG.IMP-mind-put.in-CNT-IMP
           Be on the watch for it!

        d. sadaʔgái·dek
           s-adaʔgaid-e-k-Ø
           2SG.IMP-be.healthy-EP-CNT-IMP
           Stay healthy!

Examples (a-c) are basically stative verbs, but they belong to a group of statives that take agent pronominal prefixes, ones that describe states in which the experiencer exercises some degree of control (section 4.4.3.3). However, that is not the case with (d), which amounts to a wish rather than a command.

4.2.1.4.3 The Negative Imperative

A sentence in which a participant is commanded *not* to do something requires the negative imperative particle *áhgwih* 'don't [do it]' followed by a verb specifying the action. For the same reason that the verb in a simple imperative expression is typically active, the verb in a negative imperative expressions is chosen in terms of the expectation that the participant is able to control the event. The verb modified by *áhgwih* can be formed in one of four ways: (i) with the simple imperative as in (47); (ii) with either the future or the optative prepronominal prefix and the imperative suffix as in (48a and b); (iii) with the future or optative prepronominal prefix and the punctual suffix as in (49) and (50); and (iv) inherently repetitive verbs can take the habitual with the negative imperative as in (51). Of these alternatives (i) is considered the more peremptory form of the negative command:

(47) <u>Simple negative imperative</u>:
        ahgwí satshę́hah!
        ahgwi   s-atshęh-ah
        NEG   2SG.IMP-get.scared-IMP
        Don't get scared!

(48) a. <u>Negative imperative with future prepronominal prefix and imperative suffix:</u>
    ahgwi tho hęhséh!
    ahgwi   tho   h-ę-hs-e-h
    NEG   LOC   TRNS-FUT-2SG.A-go-IMP
    Don't go there!

    b. <u>Negative imperative with optative prepronominal prefix and imperative suffix:</u>
    ahgwíh a·hcyęthwah!
    ahgwi   aa-hs-yęthw-ah
    NEG   OPT-2SG.A-plant-IMP
    You shouldn't plant!

(49)   <u>Negative imperative with future prepronominal prefix and punctual suffix:</u>
    ahgwí ęhsę·ni·hę́? sayó?de?!
    ahgwi   ę-hs-ęni·hę-?'   sa-yo?de-?
    NEG   FUT-2SG.A-cease-PNC   2SG.P-work-STV
    Don't quit working!

Example (49) has a complex predicate, part of which is inflected with the punctual aspect. Here *ahgwíh* modifies *ęhsę·ni·hę́?* 'you will quit'; *-yo?de-* 'work' is a stative verb that is lexically marked to take patient prefixes (section 4.4.3.3):

(50)   <u>Negative imperative with optative mode and punctual suffix:</u>
    Ahgwí hwę́·dų ne? ís ha?dehcyá?di[28] da·hsadadya?dowéhda?... (CTL699.5-6)
    ahgwi   hwędų   ne?   is   ha?-de-hs-ya?d-i-h
    NEG   INTR   NOM PRON TRNS-DL-2SG.A-body-be.the.only-STV
    don't   when   the   you   you are the only one

    d-aa-hs-adad-ya?dowehd-a?
    CIS-OPT-2SG.A-REFL-think.about-PNC
    you should think about yourself
    Don't ever think of just yourself...!

Note that the negative imperative *áhgwih* and the verb it modifies need not occur side by side, as in (48a) where a locative particle that modifies the same verb intervenes, and as in (50) where *áhgwih* modifies a verb that has been extraposed to the end of the clause.

(51) <u>Negative imperative, with an inherently repetitive verb, and habitual suffix:</u>
    ahgwí desaæhsę́thwas
    ahgwi   de-s-aæhsęthw-as
    NEG   DL-2SG.IMP-kick-HAB
    Don't kick!

Like simple imperatives, negative imperatives can occur with semantically intransitive, transitive, and ditransitive verbs (52) and with pronominal prefixes in all three persons and numbers (53):

---

[28] Utterance-final prosody in utterance-medial forms is because the source of the excerpt is a dictated text (see sec. 1.3).

(52) a. <u>With an intransitive verb:</u>
    ahgwí sadá·dyah.
    ahgwi   s-adady-ah
    NEG   2SG.IMP-talk-IMP
    Don't talk!

  b. <u>With a transitive verb:</u>
    ahgwí ęhyá·gęh
    ahgwi   ę-hya-gę-h
    NEG   FUT-3M.SG > 2SG-see-IMP
    Don't let him see you!

  c. <u>With a ditransitive verb:</u>
    ahgwí ęthésųh[29]
    ahgwi   ę-t-hes-ų-h
    NEG   FUT-CIS-2SG > 3M.SG-give-IMP
    Don't give it to him!

(53) a. <u>With 1st person plural pronominal prefix *-yųgwa-*:</u>
    Áhgwi ųsayųgwaʔnigų·hęhaʔ neʔ tshaʔ nigaihoʔdęh neʔ ó·nę ode·yęnędáʔih
    (CTL63.7-8).
    ahgwi   ųsa-yųgwa-ʔnigų·hęh-aʔ   neʔ   tshaʔ   ni-ga-Rihw-oʔdę-h'
    NEG   OPT:REP-1PL.P-forget-PNC   NOM   SUB   PART-3N/Z.SG.A-matter-kind-STV
    don't   we should forget   the   that   the kind of matter it is

    neʔ   onę   o-ade-Wyęn-ędaʔ-ih
    NOM   TMP   3N/Z.SG.P-SRF-task-finish-STV
    the   now   [the] task has been completed
    We should not forget what the message is, [which] has now been completed.

  b. <u>With second person dual pronominal prefix sni-:</u>
    Ahgwí ęsniʔnigųhæhetgéʔnhaʔ ó·nę waʔdi·dwadekháhsyaʔ (CTL57.7).
    ahgwi   ę-sni-ʔnigųhR-ahetgę-ʔ-nhaʔ   onę   waʔ-di-dw-ade-khahcy-aʔ
    NEG   FUT-2DL-mind-be.bad-INCH-PNC   TMP   FACT-DL-3IN.PL.A-SRF-divide-PNC
    don't   you two will get unhappy   now   we all are separating
    Don't get unhappy you two, now [that] we are separating!

  c. <u>With 3d person masculine singular pronominal prefix *h(a)-*:</u>
    Ahgwí ęhatdó·gah!
    ahgwi   ę-h-atdog-ah
    NEG   FUT-3M.SG.A-notice-IMP
    He shouldn't notice!

Interestingly, the negative imperative can also occur in non-peremptory contexts as in
(54) and (55). In (54), an excerpt from an adventure story, two young men are camping

---

[29] Eva Okun via Jay Meacham, personal communication.

overnight, and before going to sleep, they build a fire to keep away lurking animals. Here *ahgwi* occurs in a 'reason' clause with a hypothetical agent:

(54) Naʔ neʔ <u>áhgwi</u> díʔ sdę̨ʔ, <u>ahodiʔnya·æʔnháʔ</u> neʔ ode·yoʔdatgíʔ ga·yoʔdaná·ge·ʔ (HW07).

naʔ	neʔ	ahgwi	diʔ	sdęʔ	aa-hodi-ʔnya·æʔ-nhaʔ	neʔ
ASRT	NOM	NEG	LNK	INDF	OPT-3M.NSG.P-molest-PNC	NOM
it's	the	don't	moreover	something	for it to molest them	the

o-ade-Ryoʔd-a-tgi-ʔ	ga-Ryoʔd-a-nage·-ʔ
3N/Z.SG.P-SRF-animal-JN-wild-STV	3N/Z.SG.A-animal-JN-be.plentiful-STV
wild beast(s)	lots of animals

[They do this] so that the plentiful wild beasts <u>shouldn't molest them</u>.

In (*55*), an excerpt from a text by J. N. B. Hewitt, *ahgwi* modifies a verb with a non-animate referent, also hardly compatible with a command. In the story, two mythical beings, a father and a son, prepare to protect the world from the work caused by the evil twin. The father instructs the son to, among other things, clear various dangerous objects from the ground. Then he says:

(55) <u>Áhgwi</u> sdęʔ <u>ęyodadę́k</u> neʔ hehdáʔge agayę́dak (H730.14).[30]

ahgwi	sdęʔ	ę-yo-adadęR-Ø-k-Ø	neʔ	hehd-aʔ=ge
NEG	INDF	FUT-3N/Z.SG.P-be.left.over-STV-CONT-PNC	NOM	dirt-NSF=LOC
do not	anything	it will remain	the	on the ground

aa-ga-yęd-a-k-Ø
OPT-3N/Z.SG.A-be.lying-STV-CNT-PNC
it should be lying

Do not let any be left lying on the ground (free translation by Hewitt) [literally, *nothing should remain lying on the ground*].

4.3 The Pronominal Prefix System

All of the Northern Iroquoian languages have extremely elaborate pronominal prefix systems. Although the systems are not identical, there are very large areas of overlap among the languages. As it happens, the pronominal system is one of the areas in which the two dialects of Onondaga diverge in minor ways (see below).[31]

Pronominal prefixes are a requirement of every verb; they identify the core participant(s) of the action, event, or state described by the verb. The position of the pronominal prefix within the verb is just to the left of the verb stem as shown in Table 4.5:

Table 4.5 Location of the pronominal prefix

Modal Prefixes	Pronominal Prefixes	Verb Stem	Aspect Suffixes

---

[30] Hewitt did not mark vowel length in this excerpt; stress is supplied as marked by Hewitt.

[31] Abrams (2006) is the most detailed study to date of the Onondaga Nation pronominal prefix system. It was written with the student of Onondaga as a second language in mind, and represents a unique and valuable approach to its analysis, both formally and substantively. It, and materials based on it, is used extensively as a teaching tool at Onondaga language classes.

As noted, Onondaga pronominal prefixes occur in three series: the *transitive* series which references two animate arguments, and two intransitive series, termed the *agent* and the *patient* series by Iroquoianists, which (with certain exceptions, see section 4.3.1) reference (i) a single animate argument or (ii) a single animate argument and a non-animate argument (neuter).

There is no pronominal morpheme or morpheme partial that marks non-animates. In the presence of an animate argument, any non-animate semantic argument remains morphologically unmarked. A verb with *only* non-animate arguments, like *ęwá·dyaʔk* 'it will break off' takes the feminine-zoic singular morpheme as a default prefix. In the examples, this default use is marked with the identification *3N/Z.SG.A* 'third person neuter or zoic singular agent' or *3N/Z.SG.P* 'third person neuter or zoic singular patient'.[32]

Onondaga pronominal prefixes distinguish four major semantic categories: (i) *three persons*: first person, second person, and third person; (ii) *four genders*: masculine, non-animate and two feminine gender categories – feminine-indefinite and feminine-zoic; (iii) *four numbers*: singular, dual, plural (3 or more), and non-singular (2 or more); and (iv) *two roles*: agent and patient. Many of the distinctions expressed within these categories are neutralized when they co-occur (see Tables 4.7 and 4.8 and discussion below). All of the categories require explanation:

Person: The first and second person pronominals distinguish two speech act participants, I, the *speaker*, and you, the *addressee*. The third person identifies a person who is not addressed, or who is entirely absent from the speech act. In addition to these three person categories, Onondaga marks a distinction of *inclusive* vs. *exclusive* in the first persons dual and plural, which is used by the speaker to specifically include or exclude the addressee. Thus Onondaga speakers have four different pronominals for the category *we* of English. These are (i) I, the speaker, and you, the addressee; (ii) I, the speaker, and he or she, a bystander or a person absent from the scene, who is not the addressee; (iii) I, the speaker, and several of you, who are addressees; and (iv) I, the speaker, and a group of persons, excluding addressee(s), who may be present or not. Of these (i) and (iii) are *the first person inclusive*, that is, they include the addressee(s); and (ii) and (iv) are *the first person exclusive*, that is, they exclude the addressee(s). The inclusive-exclusive distinction is limited to the agent series of intransitive prefixes, and transitive prefixes in which the first person dual and/or plural occur as agent of the interaction.

Table 4.6 Inclusive and exclusive pronominal prefixes

1st person singular	I
1st person dual inclusive	I and you
1st person dual exclusive	I and he or she
1st person plural inclusive	I and you all
1st person plural exclusive	I and they all

---

[32] Note that in all my previous work the morphemes that referenced *only* non-animate arguments and their alternants were identified as *NA* 'neuter agent' and *NP* 'neuter patient', respectively. The new terminology recognizes Jean-Pierre Koenig and Karin Michelson's insights recently spelled out by them in a series of works all of which are listed in the *References* section of this work.

<u>Gender</u>: Gender is distinguished in the third person only. Onondaga has two feminine genders, *feminine-indefinite* and *feminine-zoic*.[33] The uses of these two feminine genders have shifted somewhat in the last fifty or so years as described above. The *feminine-indefinite* is now used to identify a female of any age, in addition to a person or persons whose gender is either not known or irrelevant in a given context. Its feminine meaning is *she singular,* its indefinite meaning is a bit like the indefinite pronoun *one, they* in English, or German *man*, which may reference females as well as males. The feminine-indefinite is often glossed *someone* in order to conserve space. When it is used as an indefinite pronoun, it is not only the gender that is indefinite, but also the number.

Until fairly recently – for just a few speakers this usage was still in effect at Onondaga Nation in the 1970s and can be found in older texts – the *feminine-zoic singular* identified either an adult female, a large-sized animal (e.g. cats, dogs, cows, etc., but not mice and toads), and mythic creatures, in contrast to the indefinite, which was used to refer to a female child and to an adult women in a more 'delicate' way.[34] In texts dating from the 1950s the feminine-zoic singular is still used to identify a woman who is disliked for some reason (a gypsy fortune-teller who had been harassing the speaker, is an example), and for objects with moving parts (e.g., machines, water). Contemporary speakers no longer use the feminine-zoic singular to reference a woman except in a group of kinship terms that mark the difference in age between two members of a relationship.[35] Apart from that, it is now considered rude to use the zoic singular to reference a woman. However, the feminine-zoic singular is still used to refer to an animal or a mythic creature. Note that the feminine-zoic category is still used freely in non-singular contexts where it does not contrast with the feminine-indefinite (see the discussion of 'number', below).

The *masculine* prefix references a male in the singular; in the non-singular – the dual or plural – it references two males or a male and a female, or three or more males, or three or more mixed groups of males and females, respectively.

Non-animates are a special case in Onondaga and in Iroquoian generally. As can be seen in Tables 4.7 and 4.8, pronominal prefixes #9 and #20 both merge the categories *neuter* and *feminine-zoic singular*. Koenig & Michelson (2012:188) argue that instead of analyzing neuter and feminine-zoic singular as separate categories, non-animate (neuter) should be understood as a semantic gender that is realized by the feminine-zoic singular pronominal prefixes as a default. The default category is used because all verbs are required to include a pronominal prefix and there is no separate prefix that references non-animates. Some of the evidence supporting this approach is that (i) semantically dyadic verbs with an animate and a non-animate argument, for example -*yęthw*- 'plant,' take pronominal prefixes from the intransitive rather than the transitive series; and (ii) verbs with non-animate participants take the neuter/feminine-zoic *singular* pronominal even when the verb has a plural argument.

<u>Number</u>: The four number categories – singular, dual, plural, and non-singular – are distinguished in some but not all persons and roles. First and second persons distinguish singular, dual, and plural in both intransitive series. In the third person, number is expressed variously depending on gender and role. The feminine-indefinite in all series is singular in the feminine interpretation and unmarked for number in the indefinite

---

[33] The term zoic to describe one of the feminine genders was used by J.N.B. Hewitt (1903:140) and later adopted by Floyd Lounsbury (1953) and his students and others thereafter.

[34] Harry Webster, p.c.

[35] See Abrams (2006:17n8; 85); see also sec. 5.4 below.

interpretation. The feminine-zoic distinguishes singular, dual, and plural (3 or more) in the agent series. In the patient series of intransitive prefixes feminine-zoic distinguishes singular (no longer in use except as noted) and non-singular (2 or more), the dual and plural being merged into one non-singular category. Number does not apply to non-animates, since they are always realized by the feminine-zoic *singular* prefix as a default. The masculine prefixes distinguish singular, dual, and plural (3 or more) in the agent series; in the patient series singular is distinguished from the non-singular (2 or more), the dual and plural being merged. In the transitive series the number and gender distinctions are even more drastically neutralized as will be seen below.

Role: Role is distinguished for first and third person pronominals in all numbers, and for second person pronominals in the singular only. A peculiarity of the system is that for the second persons dual and plural, the agent and patient categories are merged. A general observation about the intransitive series of prefixes is that the agent series incorporates more distinctions of person, gender, and number, than does the patient series.

The complete tables of the two systems together with alternants and their distributions appear as Tables 4.7 (Onondaga Nation Pronominal Prefixes) and 4.8 (Six Nations Pronominal Prefixes).[36] The pronominal prefixes are numbered from 1 to 59. The heavily framed areas mark intransitive prefixes. Prefixes 1 - 15 in the vertical framed column are agent prefixes. Prefixes 16 - 24 in the horizontal framed row are patient prefixes. Prefixes 25 to 59 are transitive. The first column to the left of the tables lists the person and number of agent categories. The first row across the top of the tables lists the person and number of patient categories. Transitive prefixes are identified at the intersection of agent and patient categories in the unframed portions of the tables. Each cell lists the alternants of a prefix together with the conditions of the alternations in terms of preceding and following environments.

Conditions of Alternation:
Alternations conditioned by preceding environments are indicated as follows:

(-y)	Parenthesized initial segments of pronominal prefixes preceded by a dash do not occur word-initially.
((-y)a)go- or ((-y)a)godi-	Indicates that prefixes 22 and 24 occur as *go-* and *godi-* word-initially; as *-ago-* and *-agodi-* word-medially after *ʔ*; and as *-yago-* and *-yagodi-* elsewhere.

Alternations conditioned by following environments, are indicated by superscripts or subscripts to the right of each alternant as follows:

c	with consonant-initial stems including stems beginning in *r.
cc	indicates a stem that begins in two consonants
y	with y-initial stems
k	with stems beginning in *k or g*
aeçiou̧	with vowel-initial stems as indicated
v	with any vowel-initial stem
(a)	Parentheses enclosing a superscripted vowel, indicate that the stem-initial vowel is deleted.
Imp	The subscript *Imp* accompanies the imperative alternant of the second person singular agent.

---

[36] The tables are modeled after one devised by Floyd Lounsbury (1953) for Oneida.

Table 4.7 Pronominal prefixes: Onondaga Nation

A \ P	1 singular	1 dual	1 plural	2 singular	2 dual	2 plural
1 singular				^{53}gų$^{c(i)}$ gųy ^{aeçoų}		
1 + 3 dual (exclusive)					^{54}gni^c gn^{eioų} gy^{aę}	
1 + 3 plural (exclusive)						^{55}gwa^c gwę$^{(i)}$ gw^{aeę} gy^o
1 + 2 dual (inclusive)						
1 + 2 plural (inclusive)						
2 singular	^{56}sk^c sge^{cc} sg^{vr}					
2 dual		^{57}sgni^c sgn^{eioų} sgy^{aę}				
2 plural			^{58}sgwa^c sgwę$^{(i)}$ sgw^{aeę} sgy^{oų}			
No Agent	^{16}(-w)ak^c[ų]k^c (-w)ag^{vr} [ų]gw^a (-w)ah^{kg} (-w)age^{cc}	^{7}(-y)ųgni^c (y)ųgn^{eioų} (-y)ųgy^{aę}	^{8}(-y)ųgwa^c (y)ųgwę$^{(i)}$ (-y)ųgw^{aeę} (-y)ųgy^{oų}	^{19}sa^c sę$^{(i)}$ s^{aeçoų} sa$_{imp}$	^{7a}sni^c sn^{eioų} jy^{aę}	^{8}swa^c swę$^{(i)}$ sw^{aeę} jy^{oų}
Neuter						
3Fem-Zoic sg						
3 Masc singular	^{34}hak^c hag^{vr} hah ^{kg} hage^{cc}	^{35}shųgni^c shųgn^{eioų} shųgy^{aę}	^{36}shųgwa^c shųgwę$^{(i)}$ shųgw^{aeę} shųgy^{oų}	^{37}hya^c hyę$^{(i)}$ hy^{aeę} hyay^{oų}	^{31a}hesni^c hesn^{eio} hejy^{aę}	^{32a}heswa^c heswę$^{(i)}$ hesw^{aeę} hejy^{oų}
3 Fem singular / Indefinite	^{46}(-y)ųk^c (-y)ųg^{vr} (-y)ųh^{kg} (-y)ųge^{cc} (-y)ųgw$^{(a)c}$	^{48}(y)ųkhi$^{c(i)}$ (y)ųkhiy^{aeų}		^{49}(-y)esa^c (-y)esę$^{(i)}$ (-y)es^{aeę} (-y)esay^{oų}	^{43a}(-y)etci$^{c(i)}$ (-y)etciy^{aeçoų}	
3 Fem-Zoic dual						
3 Fem-Zoic plural						
3 Masculine dual	^{47}hųk^c hųg^v hųh^{kg} hųge^{cc}					
3 Masculine plural						

Table 4.7 (continued)

No Patient	Neuter	3FZ singular	3 singular — Masculine	3 singular — Feminine-Indefinite	3 non-singular — Feminine-zoic	3 non-singular — Masculine
^{1}k ^{c} g^{vr} h^{kg} ge^{cc}			^{25}he$^{c(i)}$ hey^{aeęou}	^{39}khe$^{c(i)}$ khey^{aeęou}		
^{2}(-y)agni^{c} (-y)agn^{eiou} (-y)agy^{aę}			^{26}shagni^{c} shagn^{eiou} shagy^{aę}	^{40}(-y)akhi$^{c(i)}$ (-y)akhiy^{aeęou}		
^{3}(-y)agwa^{c} (-y)agwę$^{(i)}$ (-y)agw^{aeę} (-y)agy^{ou}			^{27}shagwa^{c} shagwę$^{(i)}$ shagw^{aeę} shagy^{ou}			
^{4}dni^{c} dn^{eiou} dy^{aę}			^{28}shedni^{c} shedn^{eiou} shedy^{aę}	^{41}(-y)ethi$^{c(i)}$ (y-)ethiy^{aeęou}		
^{5}dwa^{c} dwę$^{(i)}$ dw^{aeę} dy^{ou}			^{29}shedwa^{c} shedwę$^{(i)}$ shedw^{aeę} shedy^{ou}			
^{6}(-h)s (-h)se^{cc} j/-hc^{y} s$_{Imp}$			^{30}hes^{cv} hese^{cc} hej^{y}	^{42}she$^{c(i)}$ shey^{aeęou}		
^{7}sni^{c} sn^{eiou} jy^{aę}			^{31}hesni^{c} hesn^{eiou} hejy^{aę}	^{43}(-y)etci$^{c(i)}$ (-y)etciy^{aeęou}		
^{8}swa^{c} swę$^{(i)}$ sw^{aeę} jy^{ou}			^{32}heswa^{c} heswę$^{(i)}$ hesw^{aeę} hejy^{ou}			
^{9}ga^{c} gę$^{(i)}$ w^{aeę} (-y)^{ou} (-y)a^{ou}	^{20}(y)o(w)$^{c(a)(i)(ę)}$ (-y)aw^{eę}		^{21}ho(w)$^{c(a)(i)(ę)}$ haw^{eę} ha^{ou}	^{22}((-y)a)go(w)$^{c(a)(i)(ę)}$ ((-y)a)gaw^{eę} ((-y)a)ga^{ou}	^{23}(-y)odi^{c} (-y)on^{v}	^{24}hodi^{c} hon^{v}
^{10}ha^{c} hę$^{(i)}$ h^{aeęou} hR^{aęu}				^{38}shago(w)$^{c(a)(i)(ę)}$ shagaw^{eę} shaga^{ou}		
^{11}(-y)e$^{c(i)}$ (-y)a^{i} (-y)ę$^{(e)}$ (-y)ų(w)$^{(a)(ę)}$ (-y)ag^{eęoųa}		^{50}gųwa^{c} gųwę$^{(i)}$ gųw^{aeę} gųway^{ou}	^{33}hųwa^{c} hųwę$^{(i)}$ hųw^{aeę} hųy^{ou}	^{59}(-y)ųdat^{c} (-y)ųdad^{vr} (-y)ųdade^{cc}	^{51}gųwadi^{c} gųwan^{v}	^{52}hųwadi^{c} hųwa/ęn^{v} hųwadiy^{v}
^{12}gni^{c} gy^{aę} gn(w)^{eiou}				^{44}((-y)a)godi^{c} ((-y)a)gon^{v}		
^{13}gųdi^{c} gų(w)$^{(a)}$ gųn ^{eęiou}						
^{14}hni^{c} hn^{eiou} hy^{aę}				^{45}shagodi^{c} shagon^{v}		
^{15}hadi^{c} hęn^{eiou} hų(w)$^{(a)(ę)}$						

Table 4.8 Pronominal prefixes: Six Nations

A \ P	1 singular	1 dual	1 plural	2 singular	2 dual	2 plural
1 singular				[53] guų^c(i) guy^aeçoų		
1 + 3 dual (exclusive)					[54] gni^c gn^eioų gy^aç	
1 + 3 plural (exclusive)						[55] gwa^c gwę^(i) gw^aeç gy^o
1 + 2 dual (inclusive)						
1 + 2 plural (inclusive)						
2 singular	[56] sk^c sge^cc sg^vr					
2 dual		[57] sgni^c sgn^eioų sgy^aç				
2 plural			[58] sgwa^c sgwę^(i) sgw^aeç sgy^oų			
No Agent Neuter 3F-Zoic sg	[16] (-w)ak^c [ų]k^c (-w)ag^vr [ų]gw^a (-w)ah^kg (-w)age^cc	[17] (-y)ųgni^c (-y)ųgn^eioų (-y)ųgy^aę	[18] (y)ųgwa^c (y-)ųgwę^(i) (-y)ųgw^aeę (-y)ųgy^oų	[19] sa^c sę^(i) s^aeçoų sa_imp	[7a] sni^c sn^eioų jy^aę	[8a] swa^c swę^(i) sw^aeę jy^oų
3 Masc singular	[34] hak^c hag^vr hah^kg hage^cc	[35] shųgni^c shųgn^eioų shųgy^aę	[36] shųgwa^c shųgwę^(i) shųgw^aeę shųgy^oų	[37] hya^c hyę^(i) hy^aeę hyay^oų	[31a] shesni^c shesn^eio shejy^aę	[32a] sheswa^c sheswę^(i) shesw^aeę shejy^oų
3 Fem singular / Indefinite	[46] (-y)ųk^c (-y)ųg^vr (-y)ųh^kg (-y)ųge^cc	[48] (y)ųkhi^c(i) (y)ųkhiy^aeų		[49] (-y)esa^c (-y)esę^(i) (-y)es^aeę (-y)esay^oų	[43a] (-y)etci^c(i) (-y)etciy^aeçoų	
3 Fem-Zoic dual						
3 Fem-Zoic plural						
3 Masc dual	[47] hųk^c hųg^v					
3 Masc plural	hųh^kg hųge^cc					

Table 4.8 (continued)

| No | 3F-Zoic | N/Z | 3 singular | | 3 non-singular | |
Patient	singular		Masc	Fem-Indef	Fem-Zoic	Masculine
^{1}k^{c} g^{vr} h^{kg} ge^{cc}			^{25}he$^{c(i)}$ hey^{aeęoų}	^{39}khe$^{c(i)}$ khey^{aeęoų}		
^{2}(-y)agni^{c} (-y)agn^{eioų} (-y)agy^{aę}			^{26}shagni^{c} shagn^{eioų} shagy^{aę}	^{40}(-y)akhi$^{c(i)}$ (-y)akhiy^{aeęoų}		
^{3}(-y)agwa^{c} (-y)agwę$^{(i)}$ (-y)agw^{aeę} (-y)agy^{oų}			^{27}shagwa^{c} shagwę$^{(i)}$ shagw^{aeę} shagy^{oų}			
^{4}dni^{c} dn^{eioų} dy^{aę}			^{28}shedni^{c} shedn^{eioų} shedy^{aę}	^{41}(-y)ethi$^{c(i)}$ (y-)ethiy^{aeęoų}		
^{5}dwa^{c} dwę$^{(i)}$ dw^{aeę} dy^{oų}			^{29}shedwa^{c} shedwę$^{(i)}$ shedw^{aeę} shedy^{oų}			
^{6}(-h)s (-h)se^{cc} j/-hc^{y} s$_{Imp}$			^{30}hes^{cv} hese^{cc} hej^{y}	^{42}she$^{c(i)}$ shey^{aeęoų}		
^{7}sni^{c} sn^{eioų} jy^{aę}			^{31}shesni^{c} shesn^{eioų} shejy^{aę}	^{43}(-y)etci$^{c(i)}$ (-y)etciy^{aeęoų}		
^{8}swa^{c} swę$^{(i)}$ sw^{aeę} jy^{oų}			^{32}sheswa^{c} sheswę$^{(i)}$ shesw^{aeę} shejy^{oų}			
	^{20}(y)o(w)$^{c(a)(i)(ę)}$ (-y)aw^{eę} (-y)a^{oų}		^{21}ho(w)$^{c(a)(i)(ę)}$ haw^{eę} ha^{oų}	^{22}((y)a)go(w)$^{c(a)(i)(ę)}$ ((-y)a)gaw^{eę} ((-y)a)ga^{oų}	^{23}(-y)odi^{c} (-y)on^{v}	^{24}hodi^{c} hon^{v}
^{9}ga^{c} ge$^{(i)}$ w^{aeę} (-y) ^{oų}						
^{10}ha^{c} hę$^{(i)}$ h^{aeęoų} hR^{aęų}		^{50}gųwa^{c} gųwę$^{(i)}$ gųw^{aeę} gųway^{oų}	^{33}hųwa^{c} hųwę$^{(i)}$ hųw^{aeę} hųy^{oų}	^{8}shago(w)$^{c(a)(i)(ę)}$ shagaw^{eę} shaga^{oų}		^{52}hųwadi^{c} hųwan^{v} hųwęn^{v} hųwadiy^{v}
^{11}(-y)e$^{c(i)}$ (-y)a^{i} (-y)ę$^{(e)}$ (-y)ų(w)$^{(a)(ę)}$ (-y)ag^{eęoųa}		^{51}gųwadi^{c} gųwan^{v}		^{59}(-y)ųdat^{c} (-y)ųdad^{vr} (-y)ųdade^{cc}		
^{12}gni^{c} gy^{aę} gn(w)^{eioų}			^{52a}hųwadi^{c} hųwan^{v} hųwęn^{v} hųwadiy^{v}	^{44}((-y)a)godi^{c} ((-y)a)gon^{v}		
^{13}gųdi^{c} gų(w)$^{(a)}$ gųn ^{eęioų}						
^{14}hni^{c} hn^{eioų} hy^{aę}				^{45}shagodi^{c} shagon^{v}		
^{15}hadi^{c} hęn^{eioų}						

Tables 4.7 and 4.8 above chart the pronominal systems of the two dialects, showing every prefix type together with all conditioned alternants.

The second set of prefix alternations, are due in large part to a variety of morphophonemic patterns that affect stem-initial elements in Onondaga (sec. 2.5.2). Table 4.9 lists the modifications resulting from combining specific pronominal prefix ending elements with stem-initial elements.[37]

Table 4.9: Stem-initial modifications

Pronominal prefix ending	Stem-initial element	Modification of stem-initial element
o- e.g., -yo-	-a e.g., -awę·ye- 'stir'	a is deleted deyagowę·yéh 'she is stirring it'
ų- e.g., -yų-	-a e.g., -awę·ye- 'stir'	a is deleted dęyųwę́·ye? 'she will stir it'
ę- e.g., -yę-	e- e.g., -e- 'walk'	e is deleted ę·yę? 'she will be walking'
o- e.g., -ho-	ę- e.g., -ęnihdyę- 'have around one's neck'	ę is deleted honíhdyę? 'he has it around his neck'
ų- e.g., -hų-	-ę e. g., -ęni·hę- 'cease, quit'	ę is deleted wa?hų·ni·hę́? 'they quit'
a- e.g., -hųwa-	-i e.g., -ihnųk- 'fetch'	a and i coalesce to ę hųsahųwę́hnųk 'be brought him back'
e- e.g. -he-	-i e.g., -idagR- 'lay someone down'	i is deleted wa?hedá·gę·? 'I laid him down'
ę- e.g., -gę-	-i e.g., -idęR- 'take pity on, help out'	i is deleted gędé·ih 'it is helping'
i- e.g., -yakhi-	-i e.g., -idagR- 'lay someone down'	i is deleted ęyakhidá·gę·? 'we will lay them down'
o- e.g., -shago-	-i e.g., -idagR- 'lay someone down'	i is deleted ęshagodá·gę·? 'he will lay them down'

---

[37] Note that in the morpheme analysis of examples in this work the stem is cited in its underlying form for ease of recognition.

<u>A Note on Terminology</u>: The terms *transitive* and *intransitive* as applied to pronominal prefixes must be understood only at the morphological level of analysis. As was pointed out, transitive prefixes reference two animate arguments morphologically, and intransitive prefixes reference a single animate or a single non-animate argument morphologically. As noted, a non-animate *semantic* argument is not expressed in the pronominal prefix *unless it is the only* argument in which case the feminine-zoic singular is used as a default prefix as explained above. Thus, it is important to distinguish between a verb's *semantic* arguments and its *morphological* arguments, i.e., the ones that are referenced by the pronominal prefix. This is because an 'intransitive' pronominal can occur with two types of verbs, a semantically *monadic* verb, i.e., a verb that denotes a one-place predicate as in (56a), as well as a verb that is semantically *dyadic*, i.e. a verb that denotes a two-place predicate one of whose arguments is non-animate, as in (56b):

(56) a. dehá·da?s
       de-<u>ha</u>-da?-s
       DL-3M.SG.A-stand.up-HAB
       he stands up

     b. há·ya?ks
       <u>ha</u>-ya?k-s
       3M.SG.A-cut.off-HAB
       he cuts it off

Note in (56b) the activity requires two participants, one being non-animate. The non-animate participant is not referenced morphologically: the identical intransitive pronominal prefix, *ha-* occurs in both examples. Henceforth the two uses will be terminologically distinguished in order to keep the two levels of analysis distinct. In short, both (56a and b) are *morphologically intransitive*, but in (56a) the verb is *semantically monadic* and in (56b) the verb is *semantically dyadic*.[38]

A similar situation exists with the transitive series of pronominal prefixes. The transitive prefixes are structurally portemanteau-like in that they are mostly not segmentable into component morphs.[39] In their basic function they identify two animate semantic arguments. But the identical transitive pronominal, for example *-hųwa(y)-*, may be used with a dyadic (57a) as well as a triadic (57b) verb stem:

(57) a. <u>with a dyadic stem</u>: wa?hųwayę́hda?
       wa?-hųwa-yęhd-a?
       FACT-3 > 3M.SG-hit-PNC
       they hit him

---

[38] Although this characteristic of the Iroquoian pronominal systems has been clearly recognized by Iroquoianists since the beginning, not all discussions, including my own, have used terms that keep the two levels of analysis distinct. I follow here the usage introduced by Koenig & Michelson in their numerous papers whose argument hinges on maintaining the distinction, see especially (2012 and 2015a).

[39] But see Lounsbury (1953:61ff., especially Table 7) who did make the attempt to segment Oneida transitive pronominals.

b. <u>with a triadic stem</u>: waʔhųwá·yų?

    waʔ-hųway-ų-ʔ
    FACT-3 > 3M.SG-give-PNC
    they gave it to him

Furthermore, certain verb stems can express either dyadic or triadic meanings depending on whether they occur with an intransitive or a transitive pronominal. As it happens, the verb stem *-hninų-* has two meanings with different participant structures, the *dyadic* 'buy something' and the *triadic* 'buy something from someone'. It can occur with an intransitive pronominal prefix in the meaning 'buy something':

(58) Wadę́? shní·nųk?

    wadę? s-hninų-k
    INTR   2SG.A-buy-HAB
    What are you buying?

The same verb stem can occur with a transitive pronominal prefix in the meaning 'buy something from someone', in which the semantic *agent* argument and the semantic *source* argument, both of which are animate, are referenced by the pronominal prefix *-shago-* 'he acts on her'. The non-animate semantic theme 'it' is not referenced in either of the pronominals of (58) or (59):

(59) waʔshagohní·nų?

    waʔ-shago-hninų-ʔ
    FACT-3M.SG > 3-buy-PNC
    he bought it from her

The verb *-hninų-* is dyadic but morphologically intransitive in (58) and triadic but morphologically transitive in (59). (See also section 4.4).

4.3.1 The Intransitive Pronominal Prefixes

There are two series of intransitive prefixes, as noted – the *agent* series and the *patient* series. The notions *agent* and *patient* should be understood broadly. Prototypical agents are in general active, instigating participants, participants who are apt to be in control and act voluntarily; prototypical patients are generally the affected participants, the ones undergoing change, and less likely to be in control (see e.g., Mithun (1991) especially p. 538ff). Non-animate arguments are far more likely to turn up as patients than as agents since they often lack the agentive characteristics outlined above. Despite these semantic characteristics, the distribution of intransitive agent and patient prefixes is only partially predictable. It is also motivated by lexical, grammatical and situational factors, a combination that often obscures the underlying semantics. The factors involved in the distribution are discussed at length in section 4.4.3, below. The present discussion seeks to facilitate familiarity with the meanings and forms of the pronominals.

The agent series is typically used with stems that describe an action or event in which the participant identified by the prefix carries out the action and exercises control as instigator as shown in examples (56) and (57) above; agent prefixes also occur with stems describing attitudes, the more active forms of perception, intellectual activities, etc. as in (60):

(60) a. gnų́hwe?s *I like it*
    b. gyę·déih *I know, I have an inkling*
    c. wa?ę́·gę? *she saw it*
    d. hathų́·dats *he listens, he pays attention*
    e. ęwadagęhé·ya? *it (an animal) will slow down*

Pronominals from the patient series typically are used with a verb that describes a situation or state in which the single participant is not in control, is the affected one, the undergoer. It is also used for involuntary activities and for the less active forms of perception as in (61a-d). In addition, there is a *grammatical* requirement that selects for patient prefixes: when an active verb is inflected with the stative aspect, active pronominals are regularly replaced by stative pronominals as in (61e-g):

(61) a. hó?se·?s *he rides [in a vehicle], it drags him*
    b. dewakhų́·ya?ks *I'm choking*
    c. agathų́·de? *I hear, I am hearing it*
    d. deyagogohędų́s *she is ill, she is shaking from her illness*
    e. odahséhdih *it has disappeared*
    f. hoyę́thwih *he has planted it*
    g. dewagęna?sgwáhgwęh *I have jumped up*

In the Onondaga Nation dialect (but not the Six Nations dialect) there are a number of exceptions to the statement that intransitive prefixes can reference only a single animate argument. All are examples of syncretism, where a single morpheme expresses two separate meanings: (i) pronominal prefix <u>21</u> -*ho*- and its alternants can reference either a singular intransitive third person masculine patient 'him' (3M.SG.P), or transitive 'he > him' a singular third person masculine agent acting on a singular third person masculine patient (3M.SG > 3M.SG) as in (62a);[40] (ii) with dyadic verbs that can describe an interaction between two animate participants the 'intransitive' patient prefixes <u>16-24</u> all have glossing alternants with transitive meanings where the feminine-zoic singular acts as agent. This usage is preserved in texts dated up to the mid twentieth century and in the contemporary kinship terminology; its description is included here for that reason. An example with the intransitive first person singular patient pronominal -*wag(e)*- and the dyadic stem -*kdų*- 'examine, observe' is given in (62b). (iii) With dyadic verbs that require an animate patient, the agent prefixes <u>1-15</u> all have glossing alternants with transitive meanings in which the feminine-zoic singular participates as the patient. However, in this situation the patient can only by an animal or a mythical creature. An example is (62c):

(62) a. hothų́·de? *he hears* (ON)(6N); *he hears him* (ON)
    b. wa?wagekdų́? *she examined me* (ON)
    c. wa?há·yo? *he has killed her* (an animal).[41]

---

[40] In the 6N dialect the transitive reference is included in pronoun <u>33</u> -*hųwa*- 'third person > him'.

[41] Had the patient of this verb been a human being, the speaker would have used transitive prefix # 38 *wa?shagó·yo?* 'he killed her (a human being)'.

Tables 4.10 through 4.21 present the intransitive prefix series with different consonant- and vowel-initial stems to show the different pronominal alternants in context. The tables use verbs that have a single animate participant. Table 4.22 and 4.23 present the intransitive series with the verb stem *-gę-* 'see', which can occur with two animate participants in the ON dialect.

The numbers in the first column of Tables 4.7 and 4.8 correspond to the prefix numbers, the second column presents the prefix alternant selected by the stem. As noted above, the ON and 6N dialects differ in how these prefixes are understood because of a difference (i) in the interpretation of prefix 21 (*-ho-* and its alternants), and (ii) because of the older usage that included the 'feminine' interpretation of the feminine-zoic singular prefix 9 (*-ga-* and its alternants) which could until approximately the middle of the 20th century refer to a grown woman as well as to an animal. At present, its reference to animates is confined to animals except for kinship terms (sec. 5.4). The glosses used – following Lounsbury's (1953) notation – are *it, IT, and she* where lower case *it* refers to a non-animate entity, *IT* in small caps refers to an animal, and *she* or *her* refers to a grown woman. Glosses that are starred (*) are not presently in use.

Table 4.10 Agent pronominal prefixes with consonant-initial verb stem: *-yęthw-* 'plant'

#	Alternant	Example	Gloss
1	g-	gyęthwas	*I plant (it)*
2	(a)gni-	gniyęthwas/agniyęthwas	*we (du ex) plant (it)*
3	(a)gwa-	gwayęthwas/agwayęthwas	*we (pl ex) plant (it)*
4	dni-	dniyęthwas	*we (du in) plant (it)*
5	dwa-	dwayęthwas	*we (pl in) plant (it)*
6	(h)c-	cyęthwas	*you (sg) plant (it)*
7	sni-	sniyęthwas	*you (du) plant (it)*
8	swa-	swayęthwas	*you (pl) plant (it)*
9	ga-	gayęthwas	*it/*she plants (it)*
10	ha-	hayęthwas	*he plants (it)*
11	e-	eyęthwas	*she/someone plants (it)*
12	gni-	gniyęthwas	*they (FZ du) plant (it)*
13	gudi-	gudiyęthwas	*they (FZ pl) plant (it)*
14	hni-	hniyęthwas	*they (M du) plant (it)*
15	hadi-	hadiyęthwas	*they (M pl) plant (it)*

Table 4.11 Patient pronominal prefixes with consonant-initial verb stem: *-yęthw-* 'plant'

#	Alternant	Example	Gloss
16	ag-	agyęthwih	*I have planted (it)*
17	ugni-	ugniyęthwih	*we (du) have planted (it)*
18	ugwa-	ugwayęthwih	*we (pl) have planted (it)*
19	sa-	sayęthwih	*you (sg) have planted (it)*
7a	sni-	sniyęthwih	*you (du) have planted (it)*
8a	swa-	swayęthwih	*you (pl) have planted (it)*
20	o-	oyęthwih	*it is planted/*she has planted (it)*
21	ho-	hoyęthwih	*he has planted (it)*
22	go-	goyęthwih	*she/someone has planted (it)*
23	odi-	odiyęthwih	*they (FZ nsg) have planted (it)*
24	hodi-	hodiyęthwih	*they (M nsg) have planted (it)*

Table 4.12 **Agent** pronominal prefixes with *R-initial verb stem: *-Rægew-* 'wipe'

#	Alternant	Example	Gloss
1	g-	gæ·gé·gwas	*I wipe (it)*
2	(a)gni-	gniyægé·was/agniyægé·was	*we (du ex) wipe (it)*
3	(a)gwa-	gwaægé·was/agwaægé·was	*we (pl ex) wipe (it)*
4	dni-	dniyægé·was	*we (du in) wipe (it)*
5	dwa-	dwaægé·was	*we (pl in) (it)*
6	s-	sægé·was	*you (sg) wipe (it)*
7	sni-	sniyægé·was	*you (du) wipe (it)*
8	swa-	swaægé·was	*you (pl) wipe (it)*
9	ga-	gaægé·was	**she wipes (it)*
10	ha-	haægé·was	*he wipes (it)*
11	e-	eægé·was	*she/someone (FI) wipes (it)*
12	gni-	gniyægé·was	*they (FZ du) wipe (it)*
13	gųdi-	gųdiyægé·was	*they (FZ pl) wipe (it)*
14	hni-	hniyægé·was	*they (M du) wipe (it)*
15	hadi-	hadiyægé·was	*they (M pl) wipe (it)*

Table 4.13 Patient pronominal prefixes with *R-initial verb stem:
-Rægew- 'wipe'

#	Alternant	Example	Gloss
16	ag-	agæ·gé·węh	*I have wiped (it)*
17	ųgni-	ųgniyægé·węh	*we (du) have wiped (it)*
18	ųgwa-	ųgwaægé·węh	*we (pl) have wiped (it)*
19	sa-	saægé·węh	*you (sg) have wiped (it)*
7a	sni-	sniyægé·węh	*you (du) have wiped (it)*
8a	swa-	swaægé·węh	*you (pl) have wiped (it)*
20	o-	oægé·węh/owægé·węh	*it is wiped; *she has wiped it*
21	ho-	hoægé·węh/howægé·węh	*he has wiped (it)*
22	(a)go-	goægé·węh/agowægé·węh	*she/someone has wiped (it)*
23	odi-	odiyægé·węh	*they (FZ nsg) have wiped (it)*
24	hodi-	hodiyægé·węh	*they (M nsg) have wiped (it)*

Table 4.14 Agent pronominal prefixes with a-initial verb stem:
-aæhdat- 'run'

#	Alternant	Example	Gloss
1	-g-	degáæhdats	*I run; I am a runner*
2	-yagy-	deyagyáæhdats	*we (du ex) run*
3	-yagw-	deyagwáædats	*we (pl ex) run*
4	-dy-	dedyáæhdats	*we (du in) run*
5	-dw-	dedwáæhdats	*we (incl) run*
6	-hs-	dehsáæhdats	*you (sg) run*
7	-jy-	dejyáæhdats	*you (du) run*
8	-sw-	deswáæhdats	*you (pl) run*
9	-w-	dewáæhdats	*it/IT/*she runs*
10	-h-	deháæhdats	*he runs*
11	-yų-	deyúæhdats/deyúwæhdats	*she/someone runs*
12	-gy-	degyáæhdats	*they (FZ du) run*
13	-gų-	degúæhdats/degúwæhdats	*they (FZ pl) run*

Table 4.14 (Continued)

#	Alternant	Example	Gloss
14	-hy-	dehyáæhdats	*they (M du) run*
15	-hų-	dehųæhdats/dehúwæhdats	*they (M pl) run*

Table 4.15 Patient pronominal prefixes with a-initial verb stem:
-aæhdat- 'run':

#	Alternant	Example	Gloss
16	-wag-	dewagaæhdá·dih	*I am running*
17	-yųgy-	deyųgyaæhdá·dih	*we (du) are running*
18	-yųgw-	deyųgwaæhdá·dih	*we (pl) are running*
19	-s-	desaæhdá·dih	*you (sg) are running*
7a	-jy-	dejyáæhdá·dih	*you (du) are running*
8a	-sw-	deswaæhdá·dih	*you (pl) are running*
20	-yo-	deyoæhdá·dih/deyowæhdá·dih	*it/IT/*she is running*
21	-ho-	dehoæhdá·dih/dehowæhdá·dih	*he is running*
22	-yago-	deyagoæhdá·dih/deyagowæhdá·dih	*she/someone is running*
23	-yon-	deyonaæhdá·dih	*they (FZ nsg) are running*
24	-hon-	dehonaæhdá·dih	*they (M nsg) are running*

Table 4.16 Agent pronominal prefixes with e-initial verb stem:[42]
-ehsag-/-ehsak- 'look for'

#	Alternant	Example	Gloss
1	-g-	ęgéhsak	*I will look for it*
2	-yagn-	ęyagnéhsak	*we (du) (excl) will look for it*
3	-yagw-	ęyagwéhsak	*we (pl) (excl) will look for it*
4	-dn-	ędnéhsak	*we (du) (incl) will look for it*
5	-dw-	ędwéhsak	*we (pl) (incl) will look for it*
6	-hse	ęhséhsak	*you (sg) will look for it*
7	-sn-	ęsnéhsak	*you (du) will look for it*
8	-sw-	ęswéhsak	*you (pl) will look for it*
9	-w-	ęwéhsak	*IT/*she will look for it*
10	-h-	ęhéhsak	*he will look for it*
11	-yag-/-yę-	ęyagéhsak/ęyéhsak	*she/someone will look for it*
12	-gn-	ęgnéhsak	*they (FZ du) will look for it*
13	-gųn-	ęgųnéhsak	*they (FZ pl) will look for it*
14	-hn-	ęhnéhsak	*they (M du) will look for it*
15	-hęn-	ęhęnéhsak	*they (M pl) will look for it*

Table 4.17 Patient pronominal prefixes with e-initial verb stem:
-ehsag-/-ehsak- 'look for'

#	Alternant	Example	Gloss
16	-ag-	agehsá·gih	*I am looking for it*
17	-ųgn-	ųgnehsá·gih	*we (du) are looking for it*

---

[42] e- and ę-initial stems select the same prefix alternants

Table 4.17 (Continued)

#	Alternant	Example	Gloss
18	-ųgw-	ųgwehsá·gih	*we (pl) are looking for it*
19	-s-	sehsá·gih	*you (sg) are looking for it*
7a	-sn-	snehsá·gih	*you (du) are looking for it*
8a	-sw-	swehsá·gih	*you (pl) are looking for it*
20	-aw-	awehsá·gih	*IT/*she is looking for it*
21	-haw-	hawehsá·gih	*he is looking for it*
22	-gaw-	gawehsá·gih	*she/someone is looking for it*
23	-on-	onehsá·gih	*they (FZ nsg) are looking for it*
24	-hon-	honehsá·gih	*they (M nsg) are looking for it*

Table 4.18a Agent pronominal prefixes with i-initial verb stem:
-idagæ?- 'fall down'

#	Alternant	Example	Gloss
1	-g-	ęgidagǽ?nha?	*I will fall down*
2	-yagn-	ęyagnidagǽ?nha?	*we (du) (excl) will fall down*
3	-yagwę-	ęyagwędagǽ?nha?	*we (pl) (excl) will fall down*
4	-dn-	ędnidagǽ?nha?	*we (du) (incl) will fall down*
5	-dwę-	ędwędagǽ?nha?	*we (pl) (incl) will fall down*
6	-hs-	ęhsidagǽ?nha?	*you (sg) will fall down*
7	-sn-	ęsnidagǽ?nha?	*you (du) will fall down*
8	-swę-	ęswędagǽ?nha?	*you (pl) will fall down*
9	-gę-	ęgędagǽ?nha?	*it/IT/*she will fall down*
10	-hę-	ęhędagǽ?nha?	*he will fall down*
11	-ye-	ęyedagǽ?nha?	*she/someone will fall down*
12	-gn-	ęgnidagǽ?nha?	*they (FZ du) will fall down*
13	-gųn-	ęgųnidagǽ?nha?	*they (FZ pl) will fall down*
14	-hn-	ęhnidagǽ?nha?	*they (M du) will fall down*
15	-hęn-	ęhęnidagǽ?nha?	*they (M pl) will fall down*

Table 4.18b Agent pronominal prefixes with irregular i$_2$-Initial verb stem:
-ihę·- 'say'

#	Alternant	Example	Gloss
1	-g-	ęgihę́·?	*I will say (it)*
2	-yagn-	ęyagnihę́·?	*we (du ex) will say (it)*
3	-yagwę-	ęyagwęhę́·?	*we (pl ex) will say (it)*
4	-dn-	ędnihę́·?	*we (du in) will say (it)*
5	-dwę-	ędwęhę·?	*we (pl in) will say (it)*
6	-hs-	ęhsihę́·?	*you (sg) will say (it)*
7	-sn-	ęsnihę́·?	*you (du) will say (it)*
8	-swę-	ęswęhę́·?	*you (pl) will say (it)*
9	-gę-	ęgęhę·?[43]	**she will say (it)*
10	-hę-	ęhęhę́·?	*he will say (it)*

---

[43] No longer in use.

Table 4.18b (Continued)

#	Alternant	Example	Gloss
11	-ya-[44]	ẹyahẹ́·ʔ	*she/someone will say (it)*
12	-gn-	ẹgnihẹ́·ʔ	*they (FZ du) will say (it)*
13	-gụn-	ẹgụnihẹ́·ʔ	*they (FZ pl) will say (it)*
14	-hn-	ẹhnihẹ́·ʔ	*they (M du) will say (it)*
15	-hẹn-	ẹhẹnihẹ́·ʔ	*they (M pl) will say (it)*

Table 4.19 Patient pronominal prefixes with i-initial verb stem:
-idaʔk- 'sleep, be sleepy'

#	Alternant	Example	Gloss
16	-ag-	agí·daʔks	*I am sleepy*
17	-ụgn-	ụgní·daʔks	*we (du) are sleepy*
18	-ụgwẹ-	ụgwẹ́·daʔks	*we (pl) are sleepy*
19	-s-	sẹ́·daʔks	*you (sg) are sleepy*
7a	-sn-	sní·daʔks	*you (du) are sleepy*
8a	-swẹ-	swẹ́·daʔks	*you (pl) are sleepy*
20	-o-	ó·daʔks	IT /*she is sleepy
21	-ho-	hó·daʔks	*he is sleepy*
22	-go-	gó·daʔks	*she/someone is sleepy*
23	-on-	oní·daʔks	*they (FZ nsg) are sleepy*
24	-hon-	honí·daʔks	*they (M nsg) are sleepy*

Table 4.20 Agent pronominal prefixes with o-initial verb stem:[45] *-ohae-* 'wash'

#	Alternant	Example	Gloss
1	-g-	ẹgoháeʔ	*I will wash it*
2	-yagn-	ẹyagnoháeʔ	*we (du) (excl) will wash it*
3	-yagy-	ẹyagyoháeʔ	*we (pl) (excl) will wash it*
4	-dn-	ẹdnoháeʔ	*we (du) (incl) wash it*
5	-dy-	ẹdyoháeʔ	*we (incl) will wash it*
6	-hs-	ẹhsoháeʔ	*you (sg) will wash it*
7	-sn-	ẹsnoháeʔ	*you (du) will wash it*
8	-jy-	ẹjyoháeʔ	*you (pl) will wash it*
9	-y-	ẹyoháeʔ	**she will wash it*
10	-h-	ẹhoháeʔ	*he will wash it*
11	-yag-	ẹyagoháeʔ	*she/someone will wash it*
12	-gn-	ẹgnoháeʔ	*they (FZ du) (women/animals) will wash it*
13	-gụn-	ẹgụnoháeʔ	*they (FZ pl) (women/animals) will wash it*
14	-hn-	ẹhnoháeʔ	*they (M du) will wash it*
15	-hẹn-	ẹhẹnoháeʔ	*they (M pl) will wash it*

---

[44] The irregular verb *-ihey-/-ẹhey-* 'die' differs from *-ihẹ-* 'say' in pronominal selection only in so far as pronominal prefix <u>11</u> does not cause the initial *i* of the stem to delete, thus: ẹyaihé·ya? [ẹ-ya-ihey-a?] 'she will die'.
[45] o- and ụ-initial stems select the same prefix alternants

Table 4.21 Patient pronominal prefixes with o-initial verb stem:
-ohae- 'wash'

#	Alternant	Example	Gloss
16	-ag-	agoháeh	*I have washed it*
17	-ųgn-	ųgnoháeh	*we (du) have washed it*
18	-ųgy-	ųgyoháeh	*we (pl) have washed it*
19	-s-	soháeh	*you (sg) have washed it*
7a	-sn-	snoháeh	*you (du) have washed it*
8a	-jy-	jyoháeh	*you (pl) have washed it*
20	-a-	aoháeh	**she has washed it*
21	-ha-	haoháeh	*he has washed it*
22	-ga-	gaoháeh	*she/someone has washed it*
23	-on-	onoháeh	*they (FZ) have washed it*
24	-hon-	honoháeh	*they (M) have washed it*

Tables 4.22 and 4.23 present the intransitive series with the consonant-initial dyadic verb stem *-gę-* 'see', a verb that can describe an interaction between two animate participants.

Table 4.22 Agent pronominal prefixes: two animate participants: *-gę-* 'see'

#	Alternant	Example	Gloss
1	-h-	wá?hgę?	*I saw it/*IT (ON)* *I saw it (6N)*
2	-agni-	wa?a·gní·gę?	*we (du) (excl) saw it/*IT (ON)* *we (du) (excl) saw it (6N)*
3	-agwa-	wa?a·gwá·gę?	*we (pl) (excl) it/*IT(ON)* *we (pl) (excl) saw it (6N)*
4	-dni-	we?dní·gę?	*we (du) (incl) saw it/*IT (ON)* *we (du) (incl) saw it (6N)*
5	-dwa-	we?dwá·gę?	*we (pl) (incl) saw it/*IT (ON)* *we (pl) (incl) saw it (6N)*
6	-s-	wá?sgę?	*you (sg) saw it/*IT (ON)* *you (sg) saw it (6N)*
7	-sni-	we?sní·gę?	*you (du) saw it/*IT (ON)* *you (du) saw it (6N)*
8	-swa-	we?swá·gę?	*you (pl) saw it/*IT (ON)* *you (pl) saw it (6N)*
9	-ga-	wa?gá·gę?	*IT/*she saw it (ON)* *IT saw it (6N)*
10	-ha-	wa?há·gę?	*he saw it/*IT (ON)* *he saw it (6N)*
11	-e-	wa?é·gę?	*she /someone saw it*
12	-gni-	wa?gní·gę?	*they (FZ du) saw it*
13	-gųdi-	wa?gųdí·gę?	*they (FZ pl) saw it*
14	-hni-	wa?hní·gę?	*they (M du) saw it*
15	-hadi-	wa?hadí·gę?	*they (M pl) saw it*

Table 4.23 Patient pronominal prefixes: two animate participants: -gę- 'see'

#	Alternant	Example	Gloss
16	-wah-/ -wak-	ų́hgę? / ų́kgę? / wa?wáhgę? / wa?wakgę?[46]	*IT/*she saw me (ON)
17	-ųgni-	wa?ųgní·gę?	*IT/*she saw us (du)
18	-ųgwa-	wa?ųgwá·gę?	*IT/*she saw us (pl)
19	-sa-	we?sá·gę?	*IT/*she saw you (sg)
7a	-si-	we?sní·gę?	*IT/*she saw you (du)
8a	-swa-	we?swá·gę?	*IT/*she saw you (pl)
20	-o-	wa?ó·gę?	*IT/*she saw it /*her
21[47]	-ho-	wa?hó·gę?	he /*IT/*she saw him (ON)
22	-ago-	wa?agó·gę?	*IT/*she saw her
23	-odi-	wa?odí·gę?	*IT/*she saw them (FZ nsg)
24	-hodi-	wa?hodí·gę?	*IT/*she saw them (M nsg)

4.3.2 The Transitive Pronominal Prefixes

The transitive prefixes identify two animate arguments of a verb, one as agent and the other as patient in the sense discussed above. Representative examples are given in (63):

(63) (a) shųgwáhnha?s *he hires us; our boss*
     (b) wa?gų?se·hdahní·nų? *I bought a car from you*
     (c) wa?shagohwísdų? *he gave her money.*
     (d) hekheyadęnyehdí hwa?esęhnų́k *I sent them to summon you* (CTL97.8).
     (e) wa?hųwahyadų́hsę·? *they gave him a summons.*

To detail the distinctions referenced by the transitive pronominal prefixes, it is helpful to divide Tables 4.7 and 4.8 into quadrants. The distribution (though not all meanings) in three of the quadrants are identical for both dialects, the two dialects differ in the fourth quadrant. Thus the sub-tables illustrating the quadrants will be numbered *Table 4.7a/4.8a, 4.7b/4.8b, 4.7c/4.8c,* and where they differ *4.7d* and *4.8d* They will be limited to consonant-stem alternants for the sake of clarity. The upper left quadrant, Table 4.7a/4.8a deals with interaction between first and second persons, that is, (i) first persons as agents and second persons as patients, and (ii) second persons as agents and first persons as patients. The upper right quadrant, Table 4.7b/4.8b, deals with interactions between first and second persons as agents and third persons as patients. The lower left hand quadrant, Table 4.7c/4.8c, deals with third persons as agents and first and second persons as patients. The lower right hand quadrant, Tables 4.7d and 4.8d, deals with third persons as agents and third persons as patients.

The transitive prefixes with first person agents acting on second person patients and second person agents acting on first person patients are modeled in Table 4.7a/4.8a. Recall that the first column to the left of the tables lists the person and number of agent categories. The first row across the top of the tables lists the person and number of patient

---

[46] The variants containing either *hg* or *kg* sequences document speaker variation in both dialects. The shorter forms are optional variants of the longer forms.

[47] Prefix 21 is also listed in Table 4.27.

categories. Transitive prefixes are identified at the intersection of agent and patient categories in the unshaded portions of the tables.

Table 4.7a/4.8a Transitive prefixes: first and second person interactions

A \ P	1 singular	1 dual	1 plural	2 singular	2 dual	2 plural
1 singular				[53] gų		
1 + 3 dual					[54] gni	
1 + 3 plural						[55] gwa
1 + 2 dual						
1 + 2 plural						
2 singular	[56] sk/sg					
2 dual		[57] sgni				
2 plural			[58] sgwa			

Note the absence of first person and first person inclusive acting on first person(s), and second person(s) acting on second person(s). For those arrays of participants Onondaga speakers use a reflexive constructions. Prefix 53 expresses a first person agent acting on a second person patient. Prefixes 54 and 55 are ambiguous, and this is indicated by the fact that they occupy more than one cell. The space occupied by prefix 54 shows that either the agent, the patient, or both may be dual; the space occupied by prefix 55 shows that either the agent, the patient, or both may be plural. Prefix 56 expresses a second person agent acting on a first person patient; prefixes 57 and 58 are ambiguous in that prefix 57 expresses that either agent, patient, or both may be dual and prefix 58 expresses that either agent, patient, or both may be plural. Table 4.24 presents this information with pronominal alternants for consonant-initial stems:

Table 4.24 Transitive prefixes for consonant-initial stems:
1st and 2nd person participants: -gę- 'see'

#	Alternant	Example	Gloss
53	-gų-	ęgú·gę?	I will see you (sg)
54	-gni-	ęgní·gę?	I / we (du ex) will see you (sg) / you (du)
55	-gwa-	ęgwá·gę?	I / we (pl ex) will see you (sg) / you (pl)
56	-sge-	ęsgé·gę?	you (sg) will see me
57	-gni-	ęsgní·gę?	you (sg) /you (du) will see me / us (du ex)
58	-sgwa-	ęsgwá·gę?	you (sg) / you (pl) will see me / us (pl ex)

The upper right hand quadrant of Tables 4.7 and 4.8 models transitive pronominal prefixes that express first and second person agent participants acting upon third person patient participants. The quadrant is reproduced here as Table 4.7b/4.8b.

Table 4.7b/4.8b Transitive prefixes: first and second person agents acting on third person patients

P A	3 singular		3 non-singular	
	Masculine	Fem-Indefinite	FZ nsg	M nsg
1 singular	[25]he	[39]khe		
1 + 3 dual	[26]shagni	[40](-y)akhi		
1 + 3 plural	[27]shagwa			
1 + 2 dual	[28]shedni	[41](-y)ethi		
1 + 2 plural	[29]shedwa			
2 singular	[30]hes	[42]she		
2 dual	[31](s)hesni	[43](-y)etci		
2 plural	[32](s)heswa			

Table 4.7b/4.8b shows that the transitive prefixes in which the patient is masculine singular incorporate all of the distinctions of person, number, and inclusion present for the agent series. This is not the case for prefixes that have the feminine-indefinite singular and the feminine-zoic and masculine non-singular categories as patient. Feminine-indefinite singular, feminine-zoic and masculine non-singular merge into a general third person category when they are expressed as patients. All dual and plural distinctions for first and second person agents are neutralized into non-singular. Pronouns 31 -(s)hesni- and 32 -(s)heswa- have two forms, with and without an initial *s*. This is an ON and 6N dialect divergence. In addition, pronouns 31, 32, and 43 (-y)etci- you (nsg) acts on third persons merge the role distinctions, so that the same forms are used for the reversal of these roles. This fact is marked in Tables 4.7 and 4.8 by listing the prefixes twice as 31 and 31a, 32 and 32a, and 43 and 43a. The doubles marked with *a* show up in the lower left quadrant of the tables (see Table 4.7c/4.8c). Table 4.25 presents this information with pronominal alternants for consonant-initial stems.

Table 4.25 Transitive prefixes for consonant-initial stems: 1st and 2nd persons as agents, third persons as patients: *-gę-* 'see'

#	Alternant	Example	Gloss
25	-he-	ęhé·gę?	I will see him
26	-shagni-	ęshagní·gę?	we (du ex) will see him
27	-shagwa-	ęshagwá·gę?	we (pl ex) will see him
28	-shedni-	ęshední·gę?	we (du in) will see him
29	-shedwa-	ęshedwá·gę?	we (pl in) will see him
30	-hes-	ęhesgę?	you (sg) will see him
31	-hesni- -shesni-	ęhesní·gę? (ON) ęshesní·gę? (6N)	you (du) will see him
32	-heswa- -sheswa-	ęheswá·gę? (ON) ęsheswá·gę? (6N)	you (pl) will see him
39	-khe-	ękhé·gę?	I will see somebody/her/them
40	-yakhi-	ęyakhí·gę?	we (nsg ex) will see somebody/her/them
41	-yethi-	ęyethí·gę?	we (sg in) will see somebody/her/them
42	-she-	ęshé·gę?	you (sg) will see somebody/her/them
43	-yetci-	ęyetcí·gę?	you (nsg) will see somebody/her/them

The lower left quadrant of Tables 4.7 and 4.8 models transitive pronominal prefixes that express interactions between third persons as agents acting on first and second persons as patients. This quadrant is reproduced as Table 4.7c/4.8c.

Table 4.7c/4.8c Transitive prefixes: 3rd person agents acting on 1st and 2nd person patients.

A \ P	1 singular	1 dual	1 plural	2 singular	2 dual	2 plural
Masculine singular	[34]hak/hah	[35]shųgni	[36]shųgwa	[37]hya	[31a]hesni	[32a]heswa
Feminine-Indefinite singular	[46](-y)ųk/ (-y)ųh	[48](-y)ųkhi		[49](-y)esa	[43a](-y)etci	
Feminine-Zoic dual						
Feminine-Zoic pl						
Masculine dual	[47]hųk/ hųh					
Masculine plural						

Prefixes expressing the interactions of masculine agents with first and second persons as patients, distinguish all the available number categories. There are numerous merges for feminine-indefinite, feminine-zoic non-singular and masculine non-singular as agents. Thus feminine-indefinite singular, feminine-zoic dual, and feminine-zoic plural merge into a feminine category that neutralizes the feminine-indefinite / feminine-zoic and the number distinctions, when the first person singular is patient. Masculine dual and plural merge into non-singular with a first person singular patient. All except the masculine singular merge into a generalized third person category as agent with first person plural as patient. All first and second person patient duals and plurals merge into non-singulars with the third person generalized agent. Table 4.26 presents this information with pronominal alternants for consonant-initial stems.

Table 4.26 Transitive prefixes for consonant-initial stems: 3rd persons as agents, 1st and 2nd persons as patients: -gę- 'see'

#	Alternant	Example	Gloss
34	-hah-	ęháhgę?	he will see me
35	-shųgni	ęshųgní·gę?	he will see us (du)
36	-shųgwa-	ęshųgwá·gę?	he will see us (pl)
37	-hya-	ęhyá·gę?	he will see you (sg)
31a	-hesni- -shesni-	ęhesní·gę? (ON) ęshesní·gę? (6N)	he will see you (du)
32a	-heswa- -sheswa-	ęheswá·gę? (ON) ęsheswá·gę? (6N)	he will see you (pl)
46	-yųh-	ęyų́hgę?	somebody/she/they (FI/FZ nsg) will see me
47	-hųh-	ęhų́hgę?	they (M nsg) will see me

Table 4.26 (Continued)

#	Alternant	Example	Gloss
48	-yųkhi-	ęyųkhí·gę?	somebody/she/they (FI/FZ nsg/M nsg) will see us (nsg)
49	-yesa-	ęyesá·gę?	somebody/she/they (FI/FZ nsg/M nsg) will see you (sg)
43a	-yetci-	ęyetcí·gę?	somebody/she/they (FI/FZ nsg/M nsg) will see you (nsg)

The lower right quadrant of Tables 4.7 and 4.8 models transitive pronominal prefixes that express interactions between third persons as agents acting on third persons as patients. This is the single area[48] in which there is a structural difference between the two dialects of Onondaga. The quadrant is reproduced as Table 4.7d for the ON dialect and Table 4.8d for the 6N dialect.

Table 4.7d Transitive prefixes: 3rd person agents acting on 3rd person patients, ON dialect.

A \ P	Feminine-Zoic	3 singular Masculine	3 singular Fem-Indefinite	3 non-singular FZ nsg	3 non-singular M nsg
Masculine singular	[10]ha	[21]ho	[38] shago		
Feminine- Indefinite singular	[50]gųwa	[33]hųwa	[59](-y)ųdat	[51]gųwadi	[52]hųwadi
Feminine-Zoic dual			[44]((-y)a)godi		
Feminine-Zoic plural					
Masculine dual			[45]shagodi		
Masculine plural					

Table 4.8d Transitive prefixes: 3rd person agents acting on 3rd person patients, 6N dialect.

A \ P	Feminine-Zoic	3 singular Masculine	3 singular Fem-Indefinite	3 non-singular FZ nsg	3 non-singular M nsg
Masculine singular	[50]gųwa	[33]hųwa	[38]shago		[52]hųwadi
Feminine-Indefinite	[51]gųwadi		[59](-y)ųdat		
Feminine-Zoic dual		[52a]hųwadi	[44]((-y)a)godi		
Feminine-Zoic plural					
Masculine dual			[45]shagodi		
Masculine plural					

The structural differences between the two tables occur in the masculine singular as patient and feminine-zoic as patient columns. In Table 4.7d, representing the ON dialect, the space occupied by the third person singular masculine patient prefix -ho- extends into the space of the transitive prefixes, so that -ho- and its alternants can in that dialect refer transitively to a third person singular masculine agent acting on a third person singular masculine patient (he > him) in addition to its intransitive meanings. In the 6N dialect, -ho- is strictly intransitive, and -hųwa- is always transitive. Pronominal 52, -hųwadi-, divides into two spaces as shown in Table 4.8d; one of them has third person non-singular masculine or feminine-zoic agents acting on the third person masculine

---

[48] It is interesting to see that the 6N dialect distribution of pronominals in this quadrant is very similar to the third person acting on third person distribution of the Cayuga pronominal system (Froman et al., 2002).

singular (they > him), the second has third person singular (masculine or feminine-indefinite) acting on third person non-singular (he/she/someone > them males). The semantic spaces of the remaining pronominals accommodate to these changes as shown in Table 4.7d,[49] Prefix 38 *-shago-* masculine singular acting on feminine-indefinite, and zoic and masculine non-singular, merges all numbers in the feminine genders and all genders in the non-singular; it is the mirror image of *-hųwa-* in the ON dialect. In the 6N dialect the meaning of *-shago-* is narrower: masculine singular agent acting on feminine-indefinite or feminine-zoic non-singular (he > she/someone/they female). Table 4.27 presents this information with pronominal alternants for consonant-initial stems.

Table 4.27 Transitive prefixes for consonant-initial stems: 3rd persons as agents, 3rd persons as patients: *-gę-* 'see'

#	Alternant	Example	Gloss
21[50]	-ho-	waʔhó·gęʔ	he /*she /it (Z) / saw him (ON) it (animal) saw him (6N)
33	-hųwa-	ęhųwá·gęʔ	somebody/she/they will see him (ON) he/somebody/she will see him (6N)
38	-shago-	ęshagó·gęʔ	he will see somebody/her/them (M/FZ nsg) (ON) he will see somebody/her/them (FZ) (6N)
44	-yagodi-	ęyagodí·gęʔ	they (FZ nsg) will see somebody/her/them
45	-shagodi-	ęshagodí·gęʔ	they (masculine, nsg) will see somebody/her/them
50	-gųwa-	ęgųwá·gęʔ	somebody/she/they will see *her/it (FZ) (ON) he will see her/it (6N)
51	-gųwadi-	ęgųwadí·gęʔ	somebody/she/they will see them (FZ nsg) (ON) she/they (FZ) will see her/it (6N)
52	-hųwadi-	ęhųwadí·gęʔ	somebody/she/they will see them (M nsg) (ON) (i) they (FZ/M) will see him (ii) he/she/someone will see them (M nsg) (6N)
59	-yųdat-	ęyųdátgęʔ	somebody/she will see somebody/her (ON) somebody/she will see somebody/her/them (FZ nsg) (6N)

4.4 How Aspect, Pronominal Selection, and Situation-Type Intersect

4.4.1 The Major Verb Classes

The aspect system of Onondaga distinguishes between two major classes of the verb and one subsidiary class. The major classes are: (i) the basically *active* verb, which can be inflected with all three of the aspects, the habitual, the stative, and the punctual; and (ii) the basically *stative* verb, which can be inflected with just one aspect, the stative. A third – subsidiary – class is a type of active verb, the manner-of-motion verb,[51] which can be inflected with the three basic aspects like the class of active verbs, and a fourth aspect –

---

[49] The division of pronominal 52 into two spaces in the 6N dialect was not understood at the time the Onondaga Dictionary (Woodbury 2003) was compiled.

[50] Prefix 21 is also listed in Table 4.23.

[51] This group of verbs was first identified and described by Karin Michelson in 1993 for Oneida, in a presentation at the Conference on Iroquoian Research and subsequently in Michelson (1995); she introduced the label 'manner-of-motion verb' for these verb forms. The term is used in this work to describe a group of verbs in Onondaga with similar characteristics.

the *purposive* – that is restricted to manner-of-motion verbs. Approximately 70% of all verbs are basically active, 20% are basically stative, and 10% are manner-of-motion verbs.[52] The discussion in this section concerns the verbs in each of the two major classes. Apart from illustrating the four aspects of manner-of-motion verbs in this section, they are discussed separately in section 4.5.

An active verb inflected with all three aspects is *-dogęsd-/-dogęst-* 'fix something'. Note that while the habitual and the punctual aspect inflections take pronominal prefixes from the agent series, in this case the first person singular agent prefix *k-* as in (64a and c), but when inflected with the stative aspect it takes pronominal prefixes from the stative series, in this case the first person singular patient *ak-* as in (64b).

(64) a. kdogęstha?
     k-dogęst-ha?
     1SG.A-fix.something-HAB
     I am fixing it, I am a fixer

   b. akdogęsdih
     ak-dogęsd-ih
     1SG.P-fix.something-STV
     I have fixed it

   c. ęgdogęsda?
     ę-k-dogęsd-a?
     FUT-1SG.A-fix.something-PNC
     I will fix it

Stative verbs select lexically for agent or patient pronominals. The stative verb stem *-asgų?shų-* 'be barefoot' takes patient prefixes, in (65a) the first person singular patient prefix *ag-*; the stem *.gahR-* + dualic takes agent prefixes, in (65b) the first person agent alternant *h-*:

(65) a. agasgų́?shų?
     ag-asgų?shų-?
     1SG.P-barefoot-STV
     I am barefoot

   b. dehgáhæ·?
     de-h-gahR-a?
     DL-1SG.A-watch.sthg,observe.sthg-STV
     I'm watching

A manner-of-motion verb, in contrast to active and stative verbs, is inflected with four different aspects, the *purposive* aspect, in addition to the three aspects of active verbs as in (66a-d). The form of the purposive aspect is *-(e)?*. The purposive aspect takes agent pronominals, as do the habitual and the punctual. The stative of manner-of-motion verbs takes patient pronominals.

---

[52] The data that form the basis for this calculation are from the Ononaga Dictionary (Woodbury 2003).

(66) a. ehyákhe?
    e-ahyakh-e?
    3FI.A-go/come.to.pick.berries-PRP
    she's coming to pick berries, she's here to pick berries

  b. hahyákhe?s
    ha-ahyakh-e?s
    3M.SG.A- go/come.to.pick.berries-HAB
    he goes to pick berries (now and then)

  c. hohyákhųh
    ho-ahyakh-ųh
    3M.SG.P- go/come.to.pick.berries-STV
    he has gone to pick berries

  d. wa?gahyákha?
    wa?-g-ahyakh-a?
    FACT-1.SG.A- go/come.to.pick.berries-PNC
    I went to pick berries

The grammatical distinction underlying the division into active and stative verbs is strongly motivated by the meanings of the verbs, but because of processes of lexicalization it is not entirely predictable into which grammatical category a given verb will belong. Nevertheless, it is largely true that basically active verbs are in general the ones which describe dynamic actions and processes; that basically stative verbs tend to describe inherent or acquired characteristics of persons and things, and states of affairs of all kinds. Manner-of-motion verbs describe different ways of moving around. We will say here, as indicated above, that a verb is active if it is inflected with the three basic aspects; that a verb is stative, if it can only be inflected with the stative aspect; and that an active verb is a manner-of-motion verb if it takes the purposive aspect in addition to the three basic aspects (section 4.5).

4.4.2 Consequentiality and the Active Verb[53]

Active verbs fall into two *semantic* classes, based on whether or not they are thought to describe activities that have meaningful consequences. Consequential verbs describe actions which, when completed, have a more or less concrete result. Thus -ahdų- 'disappear' has the concrete result of some object or person becoming absent or invisible, whereas -ade·yo- 'fight', at least in the Onondaga universe, is an activity without much consequence. The distinction affects how speakers interpret the *aspectual meanings* of active verbs when they are inflected with the two *durative* aspects, the *habitual* and the *stative*. As was discussed above (section 4.2.1.1), words in the habitual aspect express an action or event, often taking place in the present, that is either a continuous activity in the present, or a repetitive-habitual activity without reference to

---

[53] The discussion in this section is based on Wallace Chafe's (1970; 1980) recognition that speakers of the Northern Iroquoian languages make distinctions based on this dimension.

time. And we have also seen that active verbs inflected with the stative aspect can have either 'perfective' (completed action) or 'imperfective' (ongoing action) meanings (section 4.2.1.2). Thus, the two durative aspects can express three kinds of temporal organization: habitual action, ongoing action, or completed action. The habitual aspect never expresses completed action, and the stative aspect never expresses habitual activity, but both of the durative aspects can express ongoing action, i.e., imperfective meanings. Chafe hypothesized that in Onondaga (1970:17-18) and in the closely related language, Seneca (1980:561), the semantic dimension that determines which aspect will express the ongoing action for a given verb is one he calls *consequentiality*: Consequential verbs express ongoing action when inflected with the habitual aspect; non-consequential verbs express it when inflected with the stative. Table 4.28 shows the distribution of aspectual meanings of the two durative aspects for both kinds of verbs.

Table 4.28 Aspectual meanings of consequential and non-consequential verbs[54]

	Habitual action	Continuous action	Completed action
Consequential	habitual aspect: kʔníkhųk *I sew/am a seamstress*	habitual aspect: kʔníkhųk *I'm sewing (it)*	stative aspect: akʔníkhų? *I've sewn (it)*
Non-Consequential	habitual aspect: gatcí·dok *I swing* (on a swing)/*am a swinger*	stative aspect: agatcí·dok *I'm swinging*	(does not occur)

<u>Consequential verbs</u>, in Onondaga, tend to be inherently *telic*, that is, involving accomplishments of various sorts. For example:

-dogęst-	*fix something*
-yęthw-	*plant*
-a- / -awi- / -ų- / -yų-	*give something to someone*
.adnųhgi·st- + dualic	*curl one's hair*
adody- / -adodyag-	*grow up*
.adogwat-/.adogwahd- + dualic	*spread something around*
-adų- / -ę- / -ihę·-	*say*
.adųgot-/.adųgohd- + dualic	*pass through, graduate*
-adųnhet-	*come to life*
-adwędet- / -adwędehd-	*share, lend*
.adwęnųdaR- + cislocative or translocative	*make a telephone call*
.Rihwaʔsæ·gw- + dualic	*answer a question*
-ʔagw-	*shoot an arrow*
-adodahcy-	*appear, reveal one's presence*
-hninų-	*buy, buy from*
-ahsehdęni-/-ahsehdę-	*hide something from someone*

<u>Non-consequential verbs</u> tend to be inherently *atelic*, involving every-day activities without successive stages and without specific outcomes. For example:

.aæhdat- + dualic	*run*
-naʔjyot-	*boil, cook*
-ashet-	*count*

---

[54] The table is adapted from Chafe (1980:561 Table 4).

adadadyę?se-/.adadadyę?s- + dualic	*play ball*
-adiwatk- / -watg-	*fool around*
.adiyęthwat-/.adiyęthwahd- + cislocative	*jerk, yank*
-adi·?sdaR-	*vocalize, mumble*
.adų·daikt- + dualic	*snicker*
-adyage-	*urinate*
-adųwishę- / -adųwishęd-	*rest*
-adųnhahR-	*rejoice*
.ahjyaR- + dualic	*push, shove*
-asgehnh-	*have a conflict*
-he·t-/-he·d-	*smoke tobacco*
-hnhohwa?e-/-hnhohwa?egw-	*knock on a door*

Some verbs can have both <u>consequential and non-consequential</u> interpretations, depending on their meanings in context. For example:

.adiyęt- + dualic or cislocative	*stretch something* or *pull something*
-adųhehsę·-	*pray, worry*
-khųnyęni- / -khųnyę-	*cook for someone*
.adyeR-/.adyR- + partitive	*do or act a certain way*
-ahdędyų-/-ahdędy-/-ahdędye-	*leave, roam about, travel*
.atga·hadeny- + dualic	*turn around*
-adyanowæt-	*run fast*

4.4.3 Pronominal Prefix Selection in the Major Verb Classes

The unusually complex system governing pronominal prefix selection in the Iroquoian languages has preoccupied scholars of these languages for many years. Early treatments, in which the pronominal prefixes were analyzed as subject and object markers, are by Boas (1909), Barbeau (1915), Lounsbury (1953) for Oneida, and Chafe (1967) for Seneca. These authors explained the distribution largely in terms of aspect. Chafe (1970) was the first to identify the system as one of agent and patient rather than subject and object marking. He analyzed the distribution of pronominal prefixes in terms of how aspect intersected with situation types and certain semantic properties of verbs. Mithun (1991) and Michelson (1991), responding to a marked cross-linguistic interest in what became known as 'split intransitive systems', greatly expanded the exploration of the underlying verbal semantics in their effort to facilitate greater understanding (and predictability) of the distribution. While their investigations were decidedly helpful in this regard, it became clear to both that the solutions they found are predictive only up to a point, due to long lasting processes of lexicalization and grammaticalization. The discussion in this section, while heavily influenced by the works cited here, is confined to the situation that obtains in Onondaga.

4.4.3.1 The Basically Active Verb

Pronominal prefix selection for basically active verbs occurs in four patterns, as shown in Table 4.29. The first three patterns occur with monadic verbs or with dyadic verbs with a single animate argument; these classes of verbs are treated, morphologically, as intransitives. The fourth pattern occurs with *polyadic* (i.e. dyadic or triadic) verbs when they occur with two animate arguments. These classes of verbs are treated, morphologically, as transitive (section 4.3: <u>A Note on Terminology</u>).

Table 4.29 Pronominal selection in active verbs

	Habitual and Punctual Aspects	Stative Aspect
1	agent pronominals	patient pronominals
2	patient pronominals	patient pronominals
3	agent pronominals	agent pronominals
4	transitive pronominals	transitive pronominals

The majority of active verbs in Onondaga (75%) take pattern 1 (and 4 if they occur with two animate arguments); 13% of active verbs take pattern 2 (and pattern 4 if they occur with two animate arguments); 2% take pattern 3 (and pattern 4 if they occur with two animate arguments); 10% of active verbs take pattern 4, transitive pronominals only.[55]

<u>Pattern 1 and pattern 4</u>: Active verbs that take pronominal prefixes according to pattern 1 are (i) monadic, like *-et-/-ehd-* 'tread, walk'; or (ii) verbs that are semantically dyadic, like *-yẹthw-* 'plant; plant something', but have only one animate argument. Both of these select pattern 1 like dyadic *.awẹ·ye-* + dualic 'stir (something)' in (67):

(67) a. Agent pronominal in the habitual aspect
Monadic: hétha?
            h-et-ha?
            3M.SG.A-walk-HAB
            he walks

Dyadic: deyụ·wẹ́·yek
            de-yụ-awẹ·ye-k
            DL-3FI.A-stir-HAB
            she stirs; she stirs it

   b. Patient pronominal in the stative aspect
Monadic: hawéhdih
            haw-ehd-ih
            3M.SG.P-walk-STV
            he has walked

Dyadic: deyagowẹ·yéh
            de-yago-awẹ·ye-h'
            DL-3FI.P-stir-STV
            she is stirring; she is stirring it

   c. Agent pronominal in the punctual aspect
Monadic: ẹhéhda?
            ẹ-h-ehd-a?
            FUT-3M.SG.A-walk-PNC
            he will walk

---

[55] The source for the data is the Onondaga Dictionary (Woodbury 2003).

Dyadic: dęyǫ·wę́·yeʔ
d-ę-yǫ-awę́ye-k
DL-FUT-**3FI.A**-stir-PNC
she will stir; she will stir it

<u>Active monadic verbs with non-animate participants</u>: Active monadic verbs that describe certain processes undergone by non-animate participants and take non-animate prefixes, like the verb *-Ri-* 'get done, ripen' also follow pattern 1. In the following set of examples the verb incorporates the noun root *-ahy-* 'fruit, berry', but that does not affect pronominal selection:

(68) a.   Agent pronominal in the habitual aspect
wahyá·is
w-ahy-a-Ri-s
3N/Z.SG.A-fruit.berry-JN-ripen-HAB
[the] fruit is ripening, [the] berries are ripening

      b.   Patient pronominal in the stative aspect
ohyá·ih
o-ahy-a-Ri-h
3N/Z.SG.P-fruit.berry-JN-ripen-STV
[the] fruit is ripe, the berries are ripe

      c.   Agent pronominal in the punctual aspect
waʔwahyá·ik
waʔ-w-ahy-a-Ri-k
<u>FACT-**3N/Z.SG.A**</u>-fruit.berry-JN-ripen-PNC
[the] fruit ripened; the berries ripened

As noted, some active, dyadic verbs can select pattern 1 as well as pattern 4. Such verbs are marked, morphologically, as intransitive (69a-c) or transitive (69d) depending on whether the second argument is animate or not. A verb of this kind is *-atgathw-* 'look at':

(69) a. Agent pronominal in the habitual aspect
hatgáthwas
h-atgathw-as
3M.SG.A-look.at-HAB
he's looking at it

     b. Patient pronominal in the stative aspect
hotgáthwih
ho-atgathw-ih
3M.SG.P-look.at-STV
he has seen it

c. Agent pronominal in the punctual aspect
    waʔhatgáthwaʔ
    waʔ-h-atgathw-aʔ
    FACT-3M.SG.A-look.at-PNC
    he looked at it

d. Transitive pronominal with two animate arguments in all aspects
    waʔhųwatgáthwaʔ
    waʔ-hųw-atgathw-aʔ
    FACT-3 > 3M.SG-look.at-PNC
    she/someone/they looked at him [ON]; *he/she/someone looked at him* [6N]

Pattern 2 and pattern 4 : Another group of verbs takes the second pattern, that is, stative prefixes in all aspects. They are (i) monadic verbs, which take pattern 2 only, like -*adek-/adeg-* 'burn', (ii) dyadic verbs with non-animate agents and animate patients, like -*hsadę-* 'ride on an animal' [literally: [it] carries someone on [its] back].or (iii) dyadic verbs, which can take both patterns 2 and 4, -*ady-/-adi-/-adye-/-ųdy-/-ųdi-* 'abandon, throw something away', .a·haʔ- +repetitive 'remember something'. Some of these verbs describe activities that are non-volitional, so that it seems natural that they take patient prefixes, but others are volitional. The patterns have become lexicalized and must be learned together with each verb.

(70)   a.   Patient pronominal in the habitual aspect
Monadic: odékhaʔ
    o-adek-haʔ
    3N/Z.SG.P-burn-HAB
    it burns; fire

Dyadic with non-animate/zoic agent: hohsá·dęs
    ho-hsadę-s
    3M.SG.P-ride-HAB
    he rides [literally: it carries him on its back]

Dyadic: agá·dyeʔs
    ag-ady-eʔs
    1SG.P-throw.away-HAB
    I'm throwing [things] out

b.   Patient pronominal in the stative aspect
Monadic: odé·gęh
    o-adeg-ęh
    3N/Z.SG.P-burn-STV
    it is burnt

Dyadic with non-animate/zoic agent: hohsá·dęh
    ho-hsadę-h
    3M.SG.P-ride-STV
    he has been riding

Dyadic: agá·dyųh
            ag-ady-ųh
            1SG.P-throw.away-STV
            I've thrown it out; I give up

    c.   Patient pronominal in the punctual aspect
Monadic: waʔo·dé·gaʔ
            waʔ-o-adeg-aʔ
            FACT-3N/Z.SG.P-burn-PNC
            it burned

Dyadic with non-animate/zoic agent: waʔhohsá·dę̌ʔ
            waʔ-ho-hsadę-ʔ
            FACT-3M.SG.P-ride-PNC
            he rode

Dyadic: waʔagá·diʔ
            waʔ-ag-adi-ʔ
            FACT-1SG.P-throw.away-PNC
            I threw it away

    d.   Transitive pronominal with two animate arguments in all aspects
          hųwayaʔdų́·dyųh
          hųwa-yaʔd[56]-ųdy-ųh
          3 > 3M.SG-body-throw.away-STV
          she/they have abandoned him [ON]; *he/she abandoned him* [6N]

<u>Pattern 3 and pattern 4</u>: A third group of verbs selects agent prefixes in all of the three basic aspects. These are even rarer than those following the second pattern. Examples are *-adatshęnaR-* 'sign one's name', *-atga·hadų-* 'roll, roll over [as when sitting in a tire]'; *.ęniʔdo-* + dualic 'fart'; *-ʔnigųhe·t-/-ʔnigųhed-* 'worry, keep thinking about', among others. An example is *-gųhgw-* 'hit, punch':

(71) a.   Agent pronominal in the habitual aspect
            hagų́hkhwaʔ[57]
            ha-gųhgw-haʔ
            3M.SG.A-hit,punch -HAB
            he hits, he punches

      b.   Agent pronominal in the stative aspect
            hagų́hgwęh
            ha-gųhgw-ęh
            3M.SG.A-hit,punch-STV
            he has hit it, he has punched it

---

[56] This verb is one of a group that involves physical contact. Such verbs must incorporate -yaʔd-, a noun root, when they occur with transitive pronominal prefixes (see section 4.8.3.8).

[57] Recall that the sequence *hgw-haʔ* is pronounced *khwaʔ* (see sec. 2.5.3)

c. Agent pronominal in the punctual aspect
wa?hagų́hgwa?
wa?-ha-gųhgw-a?
FACT-3M.SG.A-hit,punch-PNC
he hit it, he punched it

d. Transitive pronominal with two animate arguments in all aspects
wa?hyagų́hgwa?
wa?-hya-gųhgw-a?
FACT-3M.SG > 2SG-hit,punch-PNC
he hit you, he punched you

<u>Pattern 4 exclusively</u>: Finally, there are a fair number of active polyadic verbs whose meanings entail two animate arguments. These always select transitive prefixes, for example, *.adya?dadų-* + dualic 'surround someone, protect someone', *-ahset-/-ahsed-* 'rob someone', *.a?sha·?est-/a?sha·?esd-* + dualic 'stab someone'. A good many of these verbs are based on derived stems that include the benefactive suffix (section 4.8.5.1), as in (72):

(72) a. khenadahę́·?sek
khe-nadahR-ę?se-k
1SG.A > 3-visit-BEN-HAB
I visit her/them regularly

b. Hya de?shagonadahę·?séh
hya de?-shago-nadahR-ę?se-h'
NEG NEG-3M.SG > 3-visit-BEN-STV
He didn't visit her/them.

c. Is gwá? ęgųnadáhę·?s
is gwa? ę-gų-nadahR-ę?s-Ø
PRON REST FUT-1SG > 2SG-visit-BEN-PNC
It's you I'm going to visit

4.4.3.2 Agent Neuters in the Stative Aspect of Active Verbs

A special, passive-like, use of the stative aspect of active polyadic verbs is one in which the verb stem takes agent prefix #9 and a stative aspect suffix. The construction implies the action of an agent but suppresses the agent's identity.[58] The construction appears in numerous contexts where the identity of the agent is unknown, of no importance, or easily recoverable from the linguistic or non-linguistic context, or suppressed as a rhetorical device. In this construction the patient pronominal referencing the semantic agent in the stative aspect as in (73a) is replaced by a agent pronominal #9 that references the semantic patient as in (73b).

---

[58] Chafe (1970:18) refers to the construction as "actions without agents"; Michelson (1991:127-129) observes that the inflection is used by speakers of Oneida as a discourse strategy either because the identity of the agent is unknown or unimportant, or because the speaker does not want to identify the agent.

(73) a. honi·yų́·daʔ
    ho-niyųd-aʔ
    3M.SG.P-hang.something.up-STV
    he has hung it

   b. gani·yų́·daʔ
    ga-niyųd-aʔ
    3N/Z.SG.A-hang.something.up-STV
    it was hung [by someone]

Examples in various contexts are (74) to (77). The excerpt in (74), tells about a man, now deceased, who in order to keep the rightful heir from finding his money, had hidden it behind pictures and other objects that "had been hung on the wall [by someone]." Here the identity of the person who had originally hung up the pictures was irrelevant:

(74) Hohséhdi nęgę neʔ he·naʔgę̨hǽ·ʔ, tshaʔ <u>ganiyųdú·nyųʔ</u> gųdiyaʔdáe·niyųʔ, nę héʔ naʔ
    néʔ ųtgathwáthaʔ oʔ naʔdéyų go·ʔ tshaʔ nú· negę gę̨hsáʔge <u>ganiyųdú·nyųʔ,</u> tho
    hohsehdí ohwísdaʔ, do gá·ʔ nigahų̨hsǽ·géh (LG17).

ho-ahsehd-ih	nęgę	neʔ	he·naʔ = gę̨hæʔ	tshaʔ	ga-niyųd-ųnyų-ʔ
3M.SG.P-hide-STV	DEM	NOM	spouse = DEC	SUB	3N/Z.SG.A-hang.up-DST-<u>STV</u>
he has hidden it	this	the	deceased spouse	where	it has been hung up

gųdi-yaʔd-aR-ų-nyų-ʔ		nę	heʔ	naʔ	neʔ	ų-atgathw-at-haʔ
3FZ.PL.A-body-put.in-DST-DST-STV		LOC	REP	ASRT	NOM	3FI.A-look.at-CS-HAB
their pictures		here	again	it's	the	mirror

oʔ	naʔ-de-y-ų-h		go·ʔ	tshaʔ	nų	nęgę
ADD	PART-DL-3N/Z.SG.A-be.an.amount-STV		CTR	SUB	LOC	DEM
also	it is a number of [them]		however	that	place	this

gę-ihs-aʔ = ge	ga-niyųd-ųnyų-ʔ	tho	ho-ahsehd-ih	o-hwisd-aʔ
NPF-wall-NSF = LOC	<u>3N/Z.SG.A-hang.up-DST-STV</u>	LOC	3M.P-hide-STV	NPF-money-NSF
on the wall	it had been hung up	there	he has hidden it	money

do gá·ʔ	ni-ga-hų̨hsR-a-ge-h'
QNT	PART-3N/Z.SG.A-box-JN-amount.to-STV
several	a number of thousands

It seemed that this deceased husband, had hidden thousands of dollars [behind] where the pictures and mirrors and a number of other things <u>had been hung up</u> on the wall.

In excerpt (75), the speaker had suggested a way of solving a problem, but no one had paid attention to what she said. *Who* had ignored her suggestion – the white man in charge of the project – was identified earlier in the narration, and thus recoverable from context:

(75) ...naʔ ya go·ʔ hyaʔ niʔá seʔ <u>deʔgasdá?</u> nwadę̨·ʔ waʔgihę̨·ʔ, neʔ agę̨hyų̨hwagwaihcyų́k...
    (LG04).

naʔ	hya	go·ʔ	hyaʔ	neʔ	iʔ = á	seʔ	deʔ-ga-sd-aʔ
ASRT	NEG	CTR	MOD	NOM	PRN = DIM	MOD	NEG-<u>3N/Z.SG.A</u>-use-<u>STV</u>
it's	not	however	indeed	the	I alone	actually	it isn't used [by them]

142 The Verb

nwadę́?   wa?-g-ihę́·-?'   ne?   aa-ga-ihyų̨hw-gwaihcy-ų̨-k'
INTR   FACT-1SG.A-say-PNC   NOM   OPT-3N/Z.SG.A-river-straighten.out-STV-CONT
what   I said   the   river should get straightened

...but what I said [=my suggestion], that the river should be straightened, wasn't used...

In (76) the identity of the agent is unknown:

(76) Wa?hodi?nigų̨hæyę̨dá?nha? hohsæ·?á o?ę́·na? <u>degayá?khų̨?</u> niwa·gwa?s?á
     <u>gaha?dadáhgwę̨h</u> (CTL145.4-5).

wa?-hodi-?nigų̨hR-a-yę̨d-a?-nha?   hohsR-a?-áh   o-a?ę̨n-a?
FACT-3M.NSG.P-mind-JN-have-INCH-PNC   basswood-NSF-DIM   NPF-stick-NSF
they came to have thoughts   small basswood objects   stick

de-<u>ga</u>-ya?k-hų̨-<u>?</u>   ni-w-agwa-?s = ?á   <u>ga</u>-ha?d-ada-hgw-ę̨h
DL-<u>3N/Z.SG.A</u>-cut.up-DST-<u>STV</u>   PRT-NPF-small-PL = DIM   3N/Z.SG.A-pulp-be.in-REV-STV
it had been cut into pieces   small ones   pulp had been removed

They are trying to understand [the meaning of] the small basswood sticks which had been broken into short lengths and cored.

In (77) the identity of the agent is suspected but not known for certain. The protagonist suspects the man he is watching of cannibalism. He looks down the chimney of the man's cottage to check for evidence, and this is what he sees:

(77) Onę́ wa?hatgathwá? ganų̨hsgų́·wa wa?há·gę̨? <u>ga·yę̨nę̨dá?i</u> dega?wahæhi·hdíh
     ohso·jyó·da? (CTL79.6-7).

onę̨   wa?-h-atgathw-a?   ga-nų̨hs-agų̨wa   wa?-ha-gę̨-?
TMP   FACT-3M.SG.A-look.at-PNC   NPF-house-LOC   FACT-3M.SG.A-see-PNC
then   he looked   into the house   he saw it

<u>ga</u>-yę̨n-ę̨da?-<u>ih</u>   de-<u>ga</u>-?wahR-a-hi·-hd-<u>ih</u>   o-hsojy-od-a?
3N/Z.SG.A-task-complete-<u>STV</u>   DL-<u>3N/Z.SG.A</u>-meat-JN-spill-CS-<u>STV</u>   3N/Z.SG.A-pile-set.up-STV
the task had been completed   meat has been chopped up   it is piled up

Then he looked into the house [and] saw the flesh had been chopped [into pieces] and piled up.

A fair number of active verb stems take both the non-animate patient and the non-animate agent forms with the stative aspect. In the following set (a) implies a human agency whereas (b) carries no such implication:

(78) a.   gaę̨dá·yę̨?
           ga-Rę̨d-a-yę̨-?
           3N/Z.SG.A-tree-JN-lay.down-STV
           (it is a) felled tree [literally: tree lying]

    b.   o?gǽ·yę̨?
           o-a?gaR-a-yę̨-?
           3N/Z.SG.P-snow-JN-lay.down-STV
           (there is) snow on the ground [literally: snow lying]

4.4.3.3 The Basically Stative Verb

It is important to keep in mind how pronominal selection with basically stative verbs differs from that of the *stative inflection* of basically active verbs. For basically active verbs, pronominal selection is overwhelmingly grammatical: an active participant is morphologically expressed as a patient when an active verb is inflected with the stative aspect. For basically stative verbs, agent or patient pronominal selection is lexico-semantically determined. Basically stative verbs, as was pointed out above, occur only in the stative aspect. Approximately 55% of basically stative verbs take patient prefixes, and 45% take agent prefixes. Although the choice of agent or patient pronominal prefixes for specific verb stems is lexicalized, semantic motivation is often recognizable in particular cases. The semantics, to a large extent, involve features of control, volition, and affectedness, such that verbs that express states in which a participant exercises control and or volition tend to take agent prefixes, and verbs that express involuntary states or affectedness on the part of a participant tend to take patient prefixes. An overlapping broad generalization that holds in many cases is that the verb selects agent prefixes when a state is permanent (an inherent state) and patient prefixes when a state is transitory (a resultant state). Michelson (1991:130ff., for Oneida) and Mithun (1991:531ff., for Mohawk and Northern Iroquoian in general) present particularly thoroughgoing accounts of the semantics of stative verbs in relation to pronominal selection.

The verbs in the following examples describe qualities and attributes of core participants, notions that are generally glossed with adjectives in English. A basically stative verb that describes an inherent state and selects agent prefixes is *-ahetgę-* 'be bad, be evil':

(79)   a.   wahétgę?
           w-ahetgę-?
           3N/Z.SG.A-bad-STV
           it is bad, it is evil

       b.   agųgwe?dahétgę?
           ag-ųgwe?d-ahetgę-?
           3FI.A-person-bad-STV
           they (indef) are evil people

A basically stative verb that expresses a transitory state and selects patient prefixes is *-a?daihę- / -ya?dadaihę-* 'be hot':[59]

(80)   a.   o?dáihęh
           o-a?daih-ęh
           3N/Z.SG.P-hot-STV
           it is hot

---

[59] The verb stem -a?daih-/-ya?d-a-daih- *be hot*, must incorporate the noun root *-ya?d-* 'body' with animate participants. In addition, the form of the verb root is different, depending on whether or not a noun is incorporated. These effects are discussed in section 4.8.3.8.

  b. agya?dadáihęh
    ag-ya?d-a-daih-ęh
    1SG.P-body-JN-hot-STV
    I'm hot

In (81) a stative verb that takes agent prefixes, *-hwishe-* 'be strong', and a stative verb that takes patient prefixes, *-he?dę-* 'be soft, gentle', are used in the same utterance; both incorporate the noun root *-węn-* 'word, voice':

(81) Onę ęthawęnitgę?nha? nayé? ne? <u>owęnahé?dę</u> ęhásda? hya tha·yoyanę·?khé? dyęhá?
  gwa? nayé? gi?shę ne? <u>gawęnahwíshe?</u> a·hásda? nayé? sé? ne? e?nigụhgwęhda?
  (CTL536.1-4).

onę	ę-t-ha-węn-itgę-?-nha?		naye?	ne?
TMP	FUT-CIS-3M.SG.A-word-emerge-INCH-PNC		ASRT	NOM
then	he will begin to speak		it's	the

<u>o-węn-a-he?dę-h</u>	ę-ha-sd-a?	hya
3N/Z.SG.P-word-JN-be.gentle-STV	FUT-3M.SG.A-use-PNC	NEG
it is a gentle word	he will use it	not

th-aa-yo-yanR-ę?khe?-Ø	dyęha?	gwa?	naye?	gi?shę	ne?
CON-OPT-3N/Z.SG.P-good-INCH-PNC	HYP	RSTR	ASRT	ALT	NOM
it may not turn out well	if		it's	alternatively	the

<u>ga-węn-a-hwishe-?</u>	aa-ha-sd-a?	naye?	se?	ne?
3N/Z.SG.A-word-JN-be.strong-STV	OPT-3M.SG.A-use-PNC	ASRT	MOD	NOM
it is a strong word	he might use it	it's	actually	the

e-?nigụhR-gwęhdaR-a?
3FI.A-mind-be.upside.down-STV
they are grieving
Then he will begin to speak, using gentle words, [for] it would not be fitting if,
he would use strong words when they are grieving.

Basically stative verbs that encode dynamic states also differ in whether they take agent or patient prefixes. Thus *-awę-* 'own' in (82a) takes patient prefixes, *-nage·-* 'live, dwell' in (82b) takes agent prefixes; and in (82c) *-adesnoR-* 'do quickly' takes patient prefixes, and *-yas-* 'be named' takes agent prefixes:

(82) a. Í? <u>agá·węh</u>, ne? gahyadụ́hsæ·?.

	i?	ag-awę-ęh	ne?	gahyadụhsR-a?
	PRON	1SG.P-own-STV	NOM	NPF-book-NSF

    I own the book

  b. Tho <u>gna·gé·?</u> thogę ganụhsá·yę?.

	tho	g-nage·-?	thogę	ga-nụhs-a-yę-?
	LOC	1SG.A-live-STV	DEM	3N/Z.SG.A-house-JN-lie-STV

    I live in that house

c. <u>Godesnówe? di? Gahędéhsųk eyajih</u> (H170.11).[60]

   go-ade-snoRe-?   di?   Gahędehsųk   e-yas-ih

   3FI.P-SRF-be.fast-STV   LNK   NAME   3FI.A-be.named-STV

   she's [growing] fast   moreover   Gahędehsųk   she is called

   Indeed, Gahędéhsųk is growing rapidly.[61]

4.4.3.4 Stative Verbs with Incorporated Nouns

As noted, pronominal prefixes are obligatory with every noun and verb and the forms of nominal and verbal prefixes are identical in Onondag.[62] While the forms of the pronominals are identical, they differ functionally. With verbs, pronominal prefixes code for person, number, gender, and role. With nouns the pronominal prefixes code for person, number, gender, and possession, but not role. When not incorporated, morphological nouns take pronominal prefixes from the agent and patient series, but not from the transitive series. The agent and patient categories are lexically assigned (section 5.2.1). When a verb incorporates a noun it only incorporates the noun stem, omitting the noun's pronominal prefix; the resulting construction is a verb (section 4.8.3) and pronominals from the agent or patient series are selected by the verb in the manner discussed above.

Typically, noun incorporation has no impact on a verb's pronominal prefix selection (sec. 4.8.3). For example, the stative-only verb stem *-a?daihę-/-daihę-* 'be hot' takes patient prefixes without incorporation:

(83) o?dáihęh

   o-a?daihę-h

   3N/Z.SG.P-be.hot-STV

   it is hot

The noun stem *-khw-* 'food' takes agent prefixes:

(84) gákhwa?

   ga-khw-a?

   NPF-food-NSF

   food

When *-khw-* is incorporated into *-daihę-*, the incorporating form of the verb stem, the prefix is selected by the verb, and the resulting construction is a verb:

(85) okhwadáihęh

   o-khw-a-daihę-h

   3N/Z.SG.P-food-JN-be.hot-STV

   the food is hot, (it is a) hot meal

---

[60] Hewitt did not mark vowel length in this excerpt; stress as marked by Hewitt.

[61] The meaning 'grow rapidly' is lexicalized and probably results from combining the semireflexive with the verb root *-snoRe-* 'be fast, be rapid'. One of the functions of the semireflexive is to derive stems that closely involve the core-participant or his or her possessions. The functions of the semireflexive are discussed in section (4.8.4.1).

[62] The only difference is that the non-animate agent pronominal prefix *w-* that occurs with *a-* and *ę-*stems is often dropped word-initially by nouns, but not by verbs.

However, there are a number of stative-only verbs, some that describe property concepts, some with positional meanings, some with quantity meanings, and a few color terms, where the lexically assigned prefix category of the noun governs prefix selection if it occurs with non-animate pronominal prefixes. With a few exceptions, the stative verbs with this characteristic take agent pronominal prefixes when there is no noun incorporation. The stative verb *-(g)owaŋ-* 'be large', which without incorporation takes agent prefixes, serves as an example showing that the category assignment varies with the incorporated noun rather than holding constant as in examples (83-85). Example (86) is without incorporation:

(86) Onę waʔhadí·gęʔ <u>gagowanę́</u> ga·yoʔáh (CTL168.4).
    onę   waʔ-hadi-gę-ʔ   <u>ga-gowanę-h</u>[63]   ga-Ryoʔá
    TMP   FACT-3M.PL.A-see-PNC   3N/Z.SG.A-large-STV   NPF-bird
    then   they saw it   it is large   bird
    Then they saw a large bird.

In (87) the noun stem *-doʔd-* 'wave', which occurs independently as *odóʔdaʔ* with a patient prefix, is incorporated. The resulting construction takes a patient prefix:

(87) Ogųdá·dyeʔ waʔgaædát gahwísheʔ <u>odoʔdówanęʔs</u> (CTL225.1).
    ogųdadyeʔ   waʔ-ga-R-a-d-at-Ø   ga-hwishe-ʔ
    TMP   FACT-3N/Z.SG.A-wind-JN-stand-CS-PNC   3N/Z.SG.A-strong-STV
    immediately   wind arose   it is strong

    o-doʔd-owanę-'ʔs
    NPF-wave-big-PL
    big waves
    Immediately, a strong wind arose [and] large waves.

Compare example (88). Here the noun stem *-idyohgw-* 'crowd, group', which occurs independently as *gędyóhgwaʔ* with an agent prefix, is incorporated and the resulting construction takes an agent pronominal prefix:

(88) ó·nę waʔha·ǽʔthęʔ thó hwaʔha·dyęʔ gaęhagęhyá·daʔ <u>gędyohgowá·nę</u> deyegáhæ·ʔ
    eihwa·gwaihcyųs ó·nęh waʔha·díʔoʔ tshaʔ gǽ·heʔ (CTL118.5-7).
    onę   waʔ-ha-Ræthę-ʔ   tho   h-waʔ-h-adyę-ʔ
    TMP   FACT-3M.SG.A-climb-PNC   LOC   TRNS-FACT-3M.SG.A-sit.down-PNC
    then   he climbed   there he sat down there

    ga-Ręh-gęhyad-aʔ   ga-idyohgw-owanę-h   de-ye-gahR-aʔ
    3N/Z.SG.A-tree-elevate-STV   3N/Z.SG.A-crowd-be.large-STV   DL-3FI.A-be.watching-STV
    high up in the tree   big crowd   they are watching

---

[63] Words ending in /h/ typically lose it utterance-medially except that some speakers retain word-final utterance-medial /h/ if the following word begins in /n/.

e-Rihw-a-gwaihcy-ųs	onę	waʔ-hadi-Rʔo-ʔ	tshaʔ	g-Ræhe-ʔ
3FI.A-matter-JN-enlighten-HAB	TMP	FACT-3M.PL.A-chop-PNC	SUB	NPF-tree-NSF
they witness it	then	they chop into it	that	growing tree

Then he climbed up [and] sat down on top of the tree, a large crowd watching, witnessing as they chopped into the living tree.

Mithun & Corbett (1999) and Mithun (2001) suggest that verbs whose incorporated forms acquire the pronominal prefixes of their incorporated nouns, are undergoing lexicalization processes that are changing them from verbs to nominals. They refer to this process as "headedness reversal". The extended examples above, show that the constructions are functioning as referring expressions in context, although they are identifiable as verbal constructions morphologically. Other stative-only verb stems with this characteristic, although not all with equal consistency, are:

Qualities:

-adagwęhd- / -gwęhd-	*be wide*
.agwaha- +partitive	*be short*
-ahse-	*be new, be young*
.aʔa-/.aʔsʔa-/.uʔu-/.uʔsʔu- +partitive	*be small*
-det-	*be vigorous, be strong, be lively*
-dęs-/-dęj-	*be thick, be thickset, have thickness*
-gęR-	*be scarce, be limited*
-N-gweniyo-[64]	*be the main one, be the principal one*
-N-iyo-	*be good, be nice*
ųs/-ųj-/-es-/-ej-/-eji-/-is-	*be long*
.N-oʔdę- +partitive	*be a kind of, look like a kind of.*

Positions:

-akd-	*be nearby, be beside.*
-awęhd-	*be with, be added to.*
-N-hę-	*be the middle of something*

Quantities:

.d-/.yaʔdad- +coincident and factual mode	*be the same.*
.N-d-/.yaʔdad- +repetitive	*be one.*
-Ręnyų-	*be in various locations, be in*
.N-ge- +translocative and dualic	*be every, be all.*
.N-ge- +dualic	*be two.*
.N-ge- +partitive	*be a number of [greater than two].*
-gweg-/-gwek-	*be all*

Colors:

-N-gęæda- / -N-gæ·da-	*be white, be light [colored]*
-hų?ji-/-ji-	*be black, be dark [colored]*

---

[64] -N- marks the fact that a verb so marked must incorporate a noun.

A second characteristic of these verbs, first noted by Michelson (1991) describing the situation in Oneida, is that with animate pronominal prefixes, the entity referenced by the incorporated noun is understood as possessed, and that the selection of agent or patient pronominal prefixes depends on whether the incorporated noun is alienably or inalienably possessed. *Alienably possessed* entities are entities that denote objects that can be taken or given away, or that are impermanent in some way, *inalienably possessed* entities, typically, are body parts or blood relatives. Examples with -iyo- incorporating the inalienably possessed -gųhs- 'face' (89) and the alienably possessed -yoʔdęhsR- 'work' (90) are:

(89) Onę héʔ sahatgáthwaʔ ganaʔjya·gų́·wa waʔhó·gęʔ neʔ hę́·gweh dethagáhæ·ʔ
     hoyaʔda·yę́sdih <u>hagųhsiyóh</u> (CTL82.3-5).

onę	heʔ	s-a-h-atgathw-aʔ		ga-naʔjy-agųwa
TMP	REP	REP-FACT-3M.SG.A-look-PNC		3N/Z.SG.A-bucket-LOC
then	again	he looked again		into the bucket

waʔ-ho-gę-ʔ		neʔ	hR-ųgweh	de-t-ha-gahR-aʔ
FACT-3M.SG > 3M.SG-see-PNC		NOM	3M.SG.A-person:SUFF	DL-CIS-3M.SG.A-watch-STV
he saw him		the	man	he is watching

ho-yaʔd-a-yęsd-ih	ha-gųhs-iyo-h'
3M.SG.P-body-JN-look.nice-STV	3M.SG.A-face-be.good-STV
he is nice looking	he has a nice face

Then he looked into the bucket again [and] saw [the reflection of] the man watching him; he is nice looking and has a nice face.

(90) ...dyęhaʔ gwaʔ neʔ ęgahnehdó·dęʔ thaihwayé·iʔ <u>hoyoʔdęhsi·yóh</u> ... hegagųdáhgwih
     hoihwayę·dáhgwih (CTL470.6-8).

dyęhaʔ	gwaʔ	neʔ	ę-ga-hnehd-od-ęʔ	...
HYP	REST	NOM	FUT-3N/Z.SG.A-pine-stand-PNC	
if	just	the	it will be a pine tree chief	

t-ha-Rihw-a-ye·i-ʔ	ho-yoʔdę-hsR-iyo-h'[65]	he-ga-gųdahgw-ih
CIS-3M.SG.A-matter-JN-right-STV	3M.SG.P-work-NOM-good-STV	TRNS-3N/Z.SG.A-continue-STV
he is righteous	his work is good	it will continue

...if the one who will be made Pine Tree [Chief] is righteous [and] his work is good... his duties will become permanent.

This second characteristic – possession – attributed to the verbs listed above is shared by five positional verbs. These, over and beyond their function as possessives, classify the entities described by the incorporated noun in terms of shape and manner of attachment. Two of the verbs, -N-ade- and -ada-, are stative only and three -od-, -ųd-, and -yę-, are active verbs with possessive meanings when they are inflected with the stative aspect and incorporate a noun. The verbs are:

-N-ade-   have unattached; be large unmovable or shapeless objects
-ada-   have inside; be contained objects

---

[65] Words ending in /h/ typically lose it utterance-medially except that some speakers retain word-final utterance-medial /h/ if the following word begins in /n/.

-od-	have rooted, have sticking up; be standing or growing objects
-ųd-	have dangling; be objects with a secondary attachment to an intervening object
-yę-	have lying in a neutral position; be extended entities, all others

Except for *-yę-* which is the possessive verb for most entities that aren't otherwise classified, the key to pronominal selection by the positional verbs is that (i) *inalienably possessed controllable entities* (e.g., arm, leg) select agent prefixes; (ii) *inalienably possessed non-controllable* entities (e.g., hair, heart) select patient prefixes; (iii) alienably possessed entities select patient prefixes. The exception is *-yę-* which takes patient pronominals with all possessive constructions, regardless of alienability.

Table 4.30 summarizes the discussion above listing each of the positional verbs with an inalienably (a) and an (b) alienably possessed incorporated noun.

Table 4.30 Pronominal selection with positional verbs

Verb	Noun	Construction	Prefix
-N-ade-	-ya?d- *body*	(a) gya?dá·de? *I have a body*	agent
	-hwajiR- *family*	(b) akhwajiyǽ·de? *I have a family*	patient
-ada-	-gahR- *eye*	(a) dehgáhæda *I have eyes [inside]*	agent
	-Rihw- *matter*	(b) agí·hwada *I have an idea [inside]*	patient
-od-	-hųhd- *ear*	(a) khųhdó·da? *I have ears [sticking up]*	agent
	-hųd- *wood, underbrush*	(b) akhųdo·da? *I have a sapling growing*	patient
-ųd-	-nętsh- *arms*	(a) gnętshų́·da? *I have arms [dangling]*	agent
	-nųhs- *house*	(b) agnųhsų́·da? *I have added to my house*	patient
-yę-	-?nųhs- *nose*	(a) ak?nųhsá·yę? *I have a nose*	patient
	-nųhs- *house*	(b) agnųhsá·yę? *I have a house*	patient

4.5 The Aspect-Mode Categories of Manner-of-Motion Verbs

4.5.1 Identifying Manner-of-Motion Verbs.[66]

Manner-of-Motion verbs are a subset of a group of mostly active verbs with distinctive characteristics that Abbott (1981) identifies as *motion verbs.* He defines these as verbs that involve "movements of a whole individual or object in a consistent direction (p. 51)." He subdivides this group into numerous others in terms of how the locative prepronominal prefixes (section 4.7.2 below) differentially impact the meaning and distribution of these verbs. Michelson (1995) adopts Abbott's definition of motion verbs and subdivides them

---

[66] This group of verbs was first identified and named 'manner-of-motion' verbs by Karin Michelson in a series of papers delivered at the Conference on Iroquoian Research in 1992 and 1993 and is further analyzed in an unpublished paper dated 1995 entitled 'Aspect Inflections of Oneida Manner-Of-Motion Verbs'. In Michelson & Doxtater (2002:19) the set of verbs is identified as "motion verbs," as they are also in the Onondaga Dictionary (Woodbury 2003). Michelson's discussions describe the phenomenon in Oneida. Despite a great deal of overlap, the equivalent Onondaga group of verbs patterns somewhat differently. However, the analysis in this work owes much to Michelson's insights.

into two semantic classes that can be differentiated, in addition, in terms of their aspectual morphology. The two classes are (1) *directional motion verbs* "whose lexical meaning involves a path with a natural endpoint or starting point" (ibid., p.21) and (2) *manner-of-motion verbs* "whose lexical meaning involves the manner in which motion, or locomotion, is carried out" but whose meaning does not include directional components (ibid.).[67] Examples of directional motion verbs are '*depart, arrive, ascend, descend*', etc. Examples of manner-of-motion verbs are '*walk, run, slither*', etc. Directional motion verbs thus are verbs that have a point of reference – source or goal – that determines the directional meaning; manner-of-motion verbs lack this reference point. Manner-of-motion verbs involve movement in a consistent direction, but lack, unless further modified, a point of reference and thus are non-directional. They describe the kind of motion involved in an activity.

Table 4.31 Motion verbs

Motion Verbs	
+Point of Reference	Directional Motion Verbs
-Point of Reference	Manner-Of-Motion Verbs

Unlike directional motion verbs which are inflected with three aspects, manner-of-motion verbs take four: the basic three – habitual, stative, and punctual – and, in addition, an aspect that we shall call the *purposive*.[68] Manner-of-motion verbs select pronominal prefixes like active verbs using pattern 1 in the basic three aspects (Table 4.29); when inflected with the purposive, they select agent prefixes as shown in Table 4.32.[69] Manner-of-motion verbs select aspect morphemes from conjugation classes H2 and H3 as shown in Table 4.33.

Table 4.32 Pronominal selection in manner-of-motion verbs

Aspect	Pronominal Choice
Purposive	agent
Habitual	agent
Punctual	agent
Stative	patient

---

[67]Manner-of-motion verbs can and often are, prefixed with the translocative or the cislocative prefix, thereby modifying the verb root's meaning by indicating the direction in which the activity takes place.

[68] The term was first used by Lounsbury (1951:83) as a name for a derivational suffix. Chafe (1970:19) introduced 'purposive' for the aspectual function described in this section, and it was so used by Michelson (1995) and Woodbury (1993 and 2003). Michelson & Doxtater (2002:22) use 'intentive' in order not to conflict with Lounsbury's terminology. More recently both Abbott and Michelson are calling the fourth aspect the 'present' (Michelson p.c.). Chafe in his account of the purposive (1970:41-42; see also p. 22) confines his discussion of the purposive aspect to what are called *derived* manner-of-motion verbs in this volume (section 4.5.3).

[69] Exceptions to this statement, to be discussed in section 4.5.3.2, are progressive manner-of-motion verbs.

Table 4.33 Aspect conjugation classes of motion verbs

Class	Purposive	Habitual	Stative	Punctual
H2	-ʔ/-eʔ[70]	-ʔs/-eʔs[71]	-nųh/-ųh/-ęh[72]	-ʔ/-Ø/-aʔ[73]
H3				-k

4.5.2 Inherent Manner-of-Motion Verbs

The number of *inherently* manner-of-motion verb stems is small and several are lexically related (Table 4.34). But there are some extremely productive ways to derive manner-of-motion verbs (discussed in section 4.5.3), so in all the group of Onondaga verb stems taking four aspects is rather large. Table 4.34 lists the inherent manner-of-motion verbs.[74]

Table 4.34 Inherent manner-of-motion verbs

-adeʔs(e·)-	*crawl, drag oneself*
-adakhe-/-yaʔdadakhe-	*ride in a vehicle*
.adųtgwine-/.adųtgwi- + dualic	*crawl, creep*
-adyaʔdawin(e)-	*slither*
-adyaʔdiʔs(e)·-	*drag oneself*
.ahdahgwiʔs(e)·- + cislocative	*shuffle*
-ahyakh-	*go berry-picking*
-athahidakhe-	*walk on a path, follow a path*
-athahin(e)-	*walk along a path, be the course of a road*
-athawi-	*have a reason, have an intention*
.athawi-/.at-N-ęhawi- + partitive	*time passing*
.awin(e)- + cislocative	*glide, move*
-Ræde-	*climb*
-dakhe-/-idakhe-	run
-dye-/-idye-/-ųdye-	fly (through the air), paddle or run a boat
-e-	walk, be somewhere

---

[70] Stems whose purposive alternant ends in a vowel take the *-ʔ* alternant; the *-eʔ* alternant occurs elsewhere.

[71] Stems whose habitual alternant ends in a vowel take the *-ʔs* alternant; the *-eʔs* alternant occurs elsewhere.

[72] Stems whose stative alternant ends in a vowel take the *-nųh* alternant; stems ending in R, take the *-ęh* alternant, the *-ųh* alternant occurs elsewhere. The *n* of the *-nųh* alternant, apparently stems historically from a root suffix Chafe (1967:23) calls the "directive morpheme" and which occurs in Seneca with the three basic aspects. The morpheme is also clearly present in Tuscarora, where Mithun (2002) refers to it as the "directional applicative". Since it occurs only in the stative in Onondaga, and because it does not require the presence of the translocative prefix as it does in Seneca and Tuscarora, I analyze it from a synchronic perspective as a part of the stative aspect morpheme, as does Michelson (1995) for Oneida where the situation is similar to that in Onondaga.

[73] Stems whose punctual alternant ends in a vowel take the *-ʔ* alternant; stems ending in *k, t,* or *s* take the *-Ø* alternant; the *-aʔ* alternant occurs elsewhere.

[74] A number of the verbs listed in the table are multi-morphemic stems composed of an inherent manner-of-motion verb and a reflexive morpheme and/or an incorporated noun. The data are from the Onondaga Dictionary (Woodbury 2003) and represent what has been collected from fieldwork and texts over many years.

Table 4.34 (Continued)

.ẹnaʔsgṵdy- / .ẹnaʔsgṵdi- +dualic	leap, skip along, jump around.
-hawi-/-ẹhawi-/-yaʔdẹhawi-	carry along
-hẹd-/-hẹt-	walk ahead, lead, be in front
-hs-	ride somewhere on an animal
-hs(e)·-	chase something, follow something
-nadahR-	visit
-nẹtcin(e)-/-nẹtci-	lead by the arm, take by the hand
-shaine-/-shai-	lead by the reins
-yanẹhawi-/-yanẹha-/-yanẹhw-	follow, track something
-ʔs(e)·-/-iʔs(e)·-/-yaʔdiʔs(e)·-	drag, ride in a vehicle

Example (91) shows the four basic aspect inflections of the manner-of-motion verb *-hs(e)·-* 'chase or follow someone':

(91) a. <u>Habitual</u>
  shagóhse·ʔs
  shago-hse·-ʔs
  3M.SG > 3-follow-HAB
  he follows her/them around

  b. <u>Stative</u>
  shagohsẹ·h
  shago-hsR-ṵh
  3M.SG > 3-follow-STV
  he has followed her/them around

  c. <u>Punctual</u>
  waʔshagohsé·k
  waʔ-shago-hse·-k
  FACT-3M.SG > 3-follow-PNC
  he followed her/them

  d. <u>Purposive</u>
  shagóhse·ʔ
  shago-hse·-ʔ
  3M.SG > 3-follow-PRP
  he is following her/them [right here, right now]

The meanings contributed by the aspect suffixes to inherent manner-of-motion verbs differ in nuance from their meanings with other active verbs. The habitual suffix, which with other active verbs describes habitual or repetitive action, adds the meaning that the activity is distributed in space when it combines with manner-of-motion verbs. Speakers often gloss distributed located action by adding the word *around*. In (92) *tshaʔ nṵwe ídyẹʔs* means, literally, 'where she walks around', but in this context is glossed as 'where she lives'.

(92) <u>Habitual action distributed in space:</u>
> Onę háhsaʔ néʔtho nhųsahéʔ tsháʔ nų́we <u>ídyeʔs</u> néʔ hohsó·dah (H725.11).[75]

onę	hahsaʔ	neʔtho	n-h-ųsa-h-e-ʔ		tshaʔ	nųwe
TMP	TMP	LOC	PRT-TRNS-REP:FACT-3M.SG.A-walk-PRP		SUB	LOC
now	immediately	there	he went back		that	place

i-d-yę-e-ʔs		neʔ	ho-hsodah
EP-CIS-3FI.A-walk-HAB		NOM	3FZ.SG > 3M.SG-grandparent
she walks around there		the	his grandmother

He immediately went to the place where his grandmother lives.

(93) <u>Repetitive action distributed in space:</u>
> Nahgųdahgwahnéʔ <u>gųdí·dyeʔs,</u> onųhsagahę́·daʔ

(o-ʔ)nahgųd-ahgw-ahn-eʔ	gųdi-dye-ʔs	o-nųhs-a-gahęd-aʔ
(3N/Z.SG.P)-sting-INST-DIS-PRP	3FZ.PL.A-fly-HAB	3N/Z.SG.P-house-JN-make.a.hole-NSF
bee(s)	they are flying around	window

Bees are flying around the window.

The stative aspect of inherent manner-of-motion verbs describes completed action or a state of affairs.

(94) a. <u>Completed action:</u>
> Nayéʔ saho·háʔnhaʔ nayéʔ <u>thonętcinų́</u> neʔ onę́haʔ gahę·dákdaʔ (CTL328.7-8).

naye?	s-a-ho-a·ha?-nha?		naye?	t-ho-nętsh-in-ųh
ASRT	REP-FACT-3M.SG.P-remember-PNC		ASRT	CIS-3M.SG.P-arm-lead-STV
it's	he remembered		it's	it has lead him here

neʔ	o-nęh-aʔ	ga-hęd-akd-aʔ
NOM	NPF-corn-NSF	3N/Z.SG.A-field-be.near-STV
the	corn	near the field

He remembered what had lead him here to near the cornfield.

b. <u>State of affairs:</u>
> Onę óhniʔ ęgahdę́·dyaʔ néʔtho nhęgéʔ naʔdeyoyahyáʔgih neʔ ade·yóhsæ·ʔ ohá·deʔ
> neʔ haʔdewatshóthwas dęʔseʔ tgaæhgwítgęʔs <u>nheyothahinų́</u> ena·gé·nųʔ
> haʔdeyagaųhwęjyagéh (CTL89.7-90.3).

onę	ohniʔ	ę-g-ahdędy-aʔ	neʔtho	n-h-ę-g-e-ʔ
TMP	ADD	FUT-1SG.A-leave-PNC	LOC	PRT-TRNS-FUT-1SG.A-go-PRP
now	also	I will leave	there	I will go there

naʔ-de-yo-yahyaʔg-ih		neʔ	Ø-ade·yo-hsR-aʔ	o-hade-ʔ	neʔ
PART-DL-3N/Z.SG.P-cross.over-STV		NOM	NPF-fight-NOM-NSF	NPF-path-NSF	NOM
where it crosses over		the	war	path	the

haʔ-de-w-atshothw-as		dęʔseʔ	t-ga-Rahgw-itgę-ʔ-s
TRNS-DL-3N/Z.SG.A-sun.settting-HAB		CNJ	CIS-3N/Z.SG.A-sun-spill-INCH-HAB
west		and	sun rises

<u>n-he-yo-at-hah-inu̧-h</u>
PRT-TRNS-3N/Z.SG.P-SRF-road-lead-STV
where the road leads

e-nage·-nyu̧-ʔ
3FI.A-live-DST-STV
settlements

haʔ-de-yaga-u̧hwęjy-a-ge-h'
TRNS-DL-3FI.P-earth-JN-amount.to-STV
every nation

I also will depart now, I will go to the place where the warpath crosses over the water from west to east, <u>the path that leads</u> to settlements of all of the nations.

Recall that the punctual aspect requires the presence of modal prefixes, and that these express both modal and temporal meanings in active verbs (4.2.1.3). This is also the case when modals co-occur with manner-of-motion verbs that are inflected with the punctual aspect, as in the next set of examples:

(95) a. With punctual and factual:
Thohgé ó·nę gędyohgwáʔge óhniʔ neʔ hadíkdu̧k gagwé·gi waʔthu̧·wǽ·hdat
<u>waʔhadihsé·k</u> (CTL169.1-2).

thohge	onę	ga-idyohgw-aʔ-ge	ohniʔ	neʔ	hadi-kdu̧-k	ga-gweg-ih
TMP	TMP	NPF-crowd-NSF-LOC	ADD	NOM	3M.PL.A-examine-HAB	3N/Z.SG.A-all-STV
then	now	at the crowd	also	the	they examine it	it is all

waʔ-t-hu̧-aæhdat-Ø   waʔ-hadi-hse·-k'
FACT-DL-3M.PL.A-run-PNC   FACT-3M.PL.A-follow/chase-PNC
they ran   they chased it

Then the crowd and also the spectators all ran chasing after [the bird].

b. With punctual and future: Su̧ nwahoʔdęʔ ęhahęt (H640.7)[76]

su̧	nwahoʔdęʔ	ę-ha-hęt-Ø'
INTR	INTR	FUT-3M.SG.A-take.the.lead-PNC
who	what	he will take the lead

Who will take the lead?

c. With punctual and optative:
Hyá hu̧ tʔagathu̧dat néʔ ís <u>háshawaʔ</u> neʔ onú̧waʔ swáʔjik híhyaʔ oyędet
sʔnigu̧háʔthaʔ náyeʔ néʔ desʔnigu̧hǽʔshæ·ʔ (H747.15-17).[77]

hya	hu̧	deʔ-aa-g-athud-at-Ø	neʔ	is	h-aa-s-haw-aʔ
NEG	MOD	NEG-OPT-1SG.A-hear-CS-STV	NOM	PRON	TRNS-OPT-2SG.A-carry-PNC
not	maybe	I shouldn't agree	the	you	you may carry it there

neʔ	o-nu̧ʔwaR-ʔ	swaʔjik	hihyaʔ	o-yędeR-t-Ø	s-ʔnigu̧·haʔt-ha?	nayeʔ
NOM	NPF-head-NSF	DGR	MOD	3N/Z.SG.P-know-CS-STV	2SG.A-cheat-HAB	ASRT
the	head	too	indeed	it is noticeable	you cheat	it's

---

[76] Hewitt did not mark stress in this excerpt.
[77] Stress and vowel length as provided by Hewitt.

ne? de-s-?nigµhR-a?shR-a?
NOM DL-2SG.A-mind-layer.sthg-STV
the you are duplicitous
I should probably not agree to you carrying the head because it is noticeable,
indeed, that you cheat and deceive.

As noted, the purposive aspect selects pronominal prefixes from the agent series (unless there are two animate arguments). The meaning conveyed by the purposive is one of *immediate presence in time and space*, or, as Michelson characterizes it, as "immediacy and localness" (1995:35). Manner-of-motion verbs inflected with the purposive occur in descriptions of ongoing events. In addition they occur frequently in juxtaposed dependent clauses, especially as internally headed relative clauses:

(96) a. <u>Purposive aspect in a description of ongoing events</u>:
    Onę né?tho <u>hadidakhenµdyé?</u>[78] <u>hadíhse·?</u> ne? ga·yo?á wa?tshagodiya?dahí·hda? ne?
    Hayęhwátha? shagóhawah[79] wa?agonµ́hya?k (CTL137.7-8).

onę	ne?tho	hadi-dakhe-nµ-adye-?	hadi-hse·-?	ne?	ga-Ryo = ?á
TMP	LOC	3M.PL.A-run-STV-PRG-PRP	3M.PL.A-chase-PRP	NOM	NPF-animal = DIM
now	there	they are running along	they are chasing it	the	bird

wa?-t-shagodi-ya?d-a-hi·hd-a?		ne?	Hayęhwatha?	shago-hawah
FACT-DL-3M > 3FI-body-JN-smash-PNC		NOM	NAME	3M.SG > 3-child
they smashed her		the	Hayęhwatha?	his daughter

wa?-ago-nµhya?k-Ø
FACT-3FI.P-hurt-PNC
she got hurt

Then <u>they are running along</u>, <u>chasing</u> the bird, [and] they smashed into
Hayęhwatha?'s daughter, injuring her.

  b. <u>Internally headed relative clause with purposive aspect</u>:[80]
    Gwas yágę? nę gę́s wa?dwákda?, nęgę́ hehonahdµ́h <u>ne?</u> hohsé·? nęgę́ ne?
    shayá?dadah, nę hothµ·dé? dayohsµwæ·gáehæ? (HW07).

gwas	yagę?	nę	gęs	wa?-t-w-akd-a?		nęgę
INTNS	HRSY	TMP	CST	FACT-DL-3FZ.SG.A-get.close-PNC		DEM
very	they say	now	repeatedly	she got close		this

he-hon-ahdµ-h'		ne?	ho-hse·-?		nęgę	ne?
TRNS-3M.NSG.P-disappear-STV		NOM	3FZ.SG > 3M.SG-chase-PRP		DEM	NOM
they have disappeared		the	she is chasing him		this	the

s-ha-ya?d-a-d-'ah		nę	ho-athµd-e?
REP-3M.SG.A-body-JN-be.one-STV		TMP	3M.SG.P-hear-STV
one man		now	he hears it

---

[78] *hadidakhenµdyé?* 'they are running along' is a derived manner-of-motion verb.

[79] The failure to delete word final *h* is because the source of the excerpt is a dictated text (see sec. 1.3).

[80] Internally headed relative clauses are described in section (7.5.1).

de-yo-hsųR-a-gaehR-aʔ
DL-3N/Z.SG.P-gun-JN-noise-STV
a gun makes a noise
She kept getting closer, this one, [and] when they had disappeared, the [one] she's chasing hears a gun shot.

The purposive aspect also occurs with modal prefixes, although the paradigms are often defective; that is, the purposive does not occur together with each of the modalities for each verb. The factual occurs with a fair amount of frequency, the future somewhat less so, and the optative, while not difficult to elicit, rarely shows up in narratives.

Recall that the modals in active verbs inflected with the punctual aspect mark both modal and temporal dimensions. When manner-of-motion verbs are inflected with the purposive, the modals signal *modality to the exclusion of temporality*. The time perspective of the purposive aspect, as was indicated above, is the narrative present. When a manner-of-motion verb co-occurs with a modal prefix and the purposive, the inflection is referred to as the *modal purposive* in this work, following the usage in the Onondaga Dictionary (Woodbury 2003). In the following example the verb *-hse·-* 'chase or follow someone' is shown with the three modalities:

(97) a. Modal purposive with factual:
    waʔháhse·ʔ
    waʔ-ha-hse·-ʔ
    FACT-3M.SG.A- follow/chase-PRP
    he is chasing it [here and now]

   b. Modal purposive with future:
    ęháhse·ʔ
    ę-ha-hse·-ʔ
    FUT-3M.SG.A- follow/chase-PRP
    presumably, he is chasing it

   c. Modal purposive with optative:
    a·háhse·ʔ
    aa-ha-hse·-ʔ
    OPT-3M.SG.A-follow/chase-PRP
    he may/could be chasing it

Examples of the modal purposive occurring in discourse are:

(98) a. Modal purposive with factual:
    Waʔhatdogáʔ nęgę tshaʔ daga·ǽ·deʔ (HW07).

waʔ-h-atdog-aʔ		nęgę	tshaʔ	d-a-ga-Rǽde-ʔ
FACT-3M.SG.A-notice-PNC		DEM	SUB	CIS-FACT-3N/Z.SG.A-climb.up-PRP
he notices it		thi	that	she is climbing up [towards him]

    He noticed that she is climbing up [the tree towards where he is perched]

b. Modal purposive with future:
   Tho nų́· <u>nhęhsdakhé?</u> nęgę́ nheyothahinų́h... (HW07)

tho	nų	n-h-ę-hs-dakhe-?	nęgę	n-he-yo-at-hah-in-ų
LOC	LOC	PRT-TRNS-FUT-2SG.A-run-PRP	DEM	PRT-TRNS-3N/Z.SG.P-SRF-path-lead-STV
there	place	presumably, you'll be running	this	the path leads there

Presumably, you'll be running to where[ever] the path leads [you]...

4.5.3 Derived Manner-of-Motion Verbs

Like non-derived manner-of-motion verbs, derived manner-of-motion verbs occur in the habitual, stative, punctual, and purposive aspects. The Iroquoian languages have developed two ways of deriving manner-of-motion verbs. The first method (section 4.5.3.1) derives manner-of-motion verbs by suffixing the dislocative or the ambulative suffix to an active verb stem and inflecting it for aspect like a manner-of motion verb. The second method (section 4.5.3.2) derives manner-of-motion verbs from fully inflected stative verbs by adding the progressive morpheme and re-inflecting it as a manner-of-motion verb.

4.5.3.1 Dislocative and Ambulative Manner-of-Motion Verbs

The dislocative alternants are *-(a)h-*, *-(a)hR-*, *-(a)hn-*, *-(a)hs-*, *-hsR-*, *-(a)?n-*.[81] The ambulative morpheme has two alternants, *-(a)h- and -(a)hn-*, that are formally identical to two of the dislocative alternants. The parenthesized *a* is a joiner vowel that intervenes when combining the suffix with an adjacent morpheme would result in a cluster of two or more consonants. The dislocative and the ambulative differ in meaning: the dislocative adds the meaning that performing the action described by the verb involves going somewhere else. The ambulative adds the meaning that the actor is performing the action described by the verb while he is walking.[82]

Table 4.35 identifies the location of the root suffixes within the Onondaga verb stem. The discussion here is limited to the root suffixes that derive manner-of-motion verbs. The set of root suffixes other than these is discussed in section 4.8.5 below, and that section also deals with how the dislocative and ambulative combine with non-motion suffixes.

Table 4.35 Position of root suffixes within the verb

The Verb						
Prefixes	Pronominal	Reflexive	Noun Root	Verb Root	Root Suffixes	Aspect

Pronominal selection and aspectual conjugation classes of manner-of-motion verbs that have been derived with the dislocative and ambulative suffixes are identical to those described in Tables 4.32 and 4.33 for inherent manner-of-motion verbs. Thus pronominal

---

[81] The dislocative is identical in function to the morpheme called *purposive* (Lounsbury 1953), *transient* (Chafe 1967), and *andative* (Chafe 1996).

[82] Because the two morphemes have alternants that are formally alike, and because they both derive manner-of-motion verbs, one is tempted to group them together as one and the same, but there is at least one verb, *-atgathw-* 'look at' that takes both the dislocative and the ambulative with the predicted difference in meaning: together with the dislocative *-hn-* it means 'go [somewhere] to look at asomething'; together with the ambulative *-h-* it means 'look as one goes'.

selection is according to pattern 1; their aspectual conjugation classes are patterns H2 an H3 (see Table 4.3).

The aspectual meanings of the derived manner-of-motion verbs differ marginally from those of the inherent manner-of-motion verbs in line with the fact that the meanings of the verb stems are modified by the meanings of the dislocative/ambulative suffixes. Mainly, there is a clearer sense of intention, purpose, or the expectation of engaging in the activity in forms inflected with the purposive aspect. A dislocative manner-of-motion verb inflected with its four basic aspects is *-aædath-* 'go somewhere to run':

(99) a. <u>Habitual aspect</u>: dehaæhdathe?s
     de-h-aæhdat-h-e?s
     DL-3M.SG.A-run-DSLC-HAB
     he goes around to run [e.g., to participate in different races]

   b. <u>Stative aspect</u>: dewagaæhdáthųh
     de-wag-aæhdat-h-ųh
     DL-1.SG.P-run-DSLC-STV
     he has gone [somewhere] to run

   c. <u>Punctual aspect</u>: wa?thaæhdátha?
     wa?-t-h-aæhdat-h-a?
     FACT-DL-3M.SG.A-run-DSLC-PNC
     he went [somewhere] to run

   d. <u>Purposive aspect</u>: dehaæhdáthe?
     de-h-aæhdat-h-e?
     DL-3M.SG.A-run-DSLC-PRP
     he is here [intending] to run

An ambulative manner-of-motion verb is *.ahsęthwah-* + dualic 'cry as you go':[83]

(100) a. <u>Habitual aspect</u>: deyųshęthwáhe?s (H146.12)
      de-yų-ashęthw-ah-?s
      DL-3FI.A-cry-AMB-HAB
      she goes about weeping

    b. <u>Purposive aspect</u>: degashęthwahé? tshųdá·ge?
      de-g-ashęthw-ah-e?   tshų-d-a-g-e-?
      DL-1SG.A-cry-AMB-PRP   COIN-CIS-FACT-1SG.A-walk-PRP
      I am crying as I go   while I come
      I'm crying as I'm coming

The purposive can occur plain as in (99d) and (100b) above, or with modal prefixes, as in (101). The modals lose the temporal component of their meaning in the purposive aspect, just as they did when they combined with inherent manner-of-motion verbs. Together with the dislocative, they signal, instead, the modal dimensions associated with

---

[83] Ambulative manner-of-motion verbs seem to inflect only for two aspects: the habitual and the purposive.

the prefixes.[84] In addition, the purposive aspect is strongly associated with the current locality of the speaker, but the combination of the factual with the purposive has the agent typically moving away from the narrative location.[85]

(101) a. <u>Modal purposive with factual prefix:</u>
wa?thaæhdáthe?
wa?-t-h-aæhdat-h-e?
FACT-DL-3M.SG.A-run-DSLC-PRP
[right now] he is going [intending] to run [e.g., in the Brantford marathon]

b. <u>Modal purposive with future prefix:</u>
dǫhaæhdáthe?
d-ǫ-h-aæhdat-h-e?
DL-FUT-3M.SG.A-run-DSLC-PRP
he will [presumably] be here [intending] to run

c. <u>Modal purposive with optative prefix:</u>
da·haæhdáthe?
d-aa-h-aæhdat-h-e?
DL-OPT-3M.SG.A-run-DSLC-PRP
he should be here [intending] to run

The next example from a text contains a dislocative and an ambulative verb; both are modal purposives with factual prefixes:

(102) <u>Dislocative and ambulative purposives with the factual:</u>
Desawęnawęhǽ·t ne? ga·hodǫ́·nyǫ? <u>dawawęhæ·sdahę́·hne?</u> degahęhwá·nyǫ?
<u>dahsatgathwáhe?</u> ne?tho hadiyanáę·nyǫ? ne? ųgwahsodashę·dáhgwa?
(CTL593.8-594.6).

de-sa-węn-awęhR-at-Ø	ne?	ga-Rh-od-ųnyǫ-?
DL-2SG.P-voice-move.across-CS-STV	NOM	3N/Z.SG.A-forest-stand-DST-STV
your voice is moving across	the	forests

d-a-w-awęhR-asd-ahę-<u>hn</u>-e?		de-ga-hęhw-anyų-?
CIS-FACT-3N/Z.SG.A-move.across-CS-DST-DSLC-PRP		DL-3N/Z.SG.A-put.across-DST-STV
it is coming, moving across		barriers

d-a-hs-atgathw-<u>ah</u>-e?	ne?tho	hadi-yan-aR-ųnyų-?	ne?
CIS-FACT-2SG.A-look.at-<u>AMB</u>-PRP	LOC	3M.PL.A-track-be.in-DST-STV	NOM
you are looking at it as you come	there	their tracks are in it	the

---

[84] Although most of the verbs derived with the dislocative take the factual prefix, not all take the future prefix and while it is usually possible to elicit the optative prefix, this combination hasn't been attested in texts.

[85] Mithun (p.c June 2003) hypothesizes that what appears to be the factual prefix is a reanalysis of a prefix that is historically the translocative, remnants of which can still be found in Seneca and Tuscarora.

    ųgwa-hsodah-shR-ųd-ahgwaʔ
    1PL.P-be.grandparent-NOM-have.attached-HBPST
    our ancestors
    Your voice is sounding from over the forest, it is moving across barriers, [and] you
    are seeing traces of our ancestors as you go.

The dislocative and purposive also combine with a number of verbs that describe experiences rather than activities. In this context the purposive aspect expresses the expectation that the participant is about to experience the event in the immediate future, rather than his or her purpose or intention to do so. This sense is expressed in the following example from a story about an earlier time when people are only just discovering the existence of illness and of death. A man is ill, and when his mother asks what seems to be the matter, he replies, saying:

(103) <u>The dislocative and purposive in combination with an experiencer verb:</u>
    Agenóhaʔ ónęh ęgųyathóyęʔ ná·yeʔ neʔ níʔa <u>giheyų́hseʔ</u>. (H144.5-6)[86]

age-nohaʔ	onę	ę-gųy-atho·y-ę-ʔ		nayeʔ	neʔ	iʔ = á
1SG.P-mother	TMP	FUT-1SG > 2SG-tell-BEN-PNC		ASRT	NOM	I = DIM
Mother	now	I will tell you		it's	the	I, alone

    g-iheyų-<u>hsR</u>-eʔ
    1SG.A-die-DSLC-PRP
    I am about to die
    Mother, I will tell you that as to me, I am about to die.

Similarly, in the following example a mother notices that her daughter is pregnant, that she *has the expectation* of bearing a child:

(104) Ónę dawahsá·węʔ waʔųtdó·gaʔ neʔ goksdęʔá oyę́·det neʔ gohá·wah[87]
    goksaʔdayę·dáʔshe·ʔ (CTL3.3-4).

onę	d-a-w-ahsaw-ęʔ		waʔ-ų-atdog-aʔ		neʔ	go-ksdęʔah
TMP	CIS-FACT-3N/Z.SG.A-begin-PNC		FACT-3FI.A-notice-PNC		NOM	3FI.P-old.person
now	it began		she noticed		the	old lady

o-yęde·t-Ø		neʔ	go-hawah		go-ksaʔd-a-yęd-<u>ahs</u>-eʔ
3N/Z.SG.P-be-noticeable-STV		NOM	3FZ.SG > 3FI-have.a.child		3FI.P-child-JN-have-DSLC-PRP
it is noticeable		the	her daughter		she is expecting a child

    Then the old lady began to notice that her daughter is expecting a child.

4.5.3.2 Progressive Manner-of-Motion Verbs

The progressive suffix occurs post-aspectually and is suffixed to active verbs inflected with the stative, and to some basically stative verbs. The suffix derives a manner-of-motion verb

---

[86] Stress and vowel length as provided by Hewitt.

[87] Utterance-final prosody and the presence of word-final *h* utterance-medially is because the source of the excerpt is a dictated text (see sec. 1.3).

that is itself suffixed with an aspect suffix. In Onondaga progressive manner-of-motion verbs apparently take only the habitual and purposive aspects.[88]

Table 4.36 Position of the progressive suffix within the derived verb

Prefixes	Pronominal	Reflexive	Noun Root	Verb Root	Root Suffixes	Aspect	Progressive	Aspect

The form of the progressive suffix is *-(a)dye-*, where *-adye-* occurs after stative aspect suffixes ending in *h,* and *-dye-* occurs after stative aspect suffixes ending in *ʔ* with loss of the glottal stop. Selected stems that take the stative aspect suffix *-(n)ųh* are lexicalized with the *-dye-* alternant with loss of *h.*[89] Stems that take the *-Ø* alternant of the stative aspect suffix, replace the *-Ø* alternant with *-ih-* before the progressive.[90]

Table 4.37 Combining the stative aspect with the progressive

ih-adye-	> -ihadye-
hwih-adye-	> -hwihadye-
h-adye-	> -hadye-
ęh-adye-	> -ęhadye-
ųh-adye-	> -ųhadye-
nųh-adye-	> -nųhadye- / -nųdye-
aʔ-adye-	> -adye-
ʔ-adye	> -adye- / -dye-
eʔ-adye	> -edye- / -ehadye-

Since the progressive suffix is added to a fully inflected stative verb, pronominal selection has been completed during the earlier derivation. Thus progressive manner-of-motion verbs occur with patient pronominal prefixes, unless the progressive suffix has combined with a verb stem that selects agent prefixes in the stative aspect. The aspect conjugation classes selected by the progressive stem are those of manner-of-motion verbs, H2 and H3 (Tables 4.3 and 4.33).

The meaning added by the progressive morpheme is that the action or situation described by the verb is distributed over time, occurring as part of a process which, although it often relates to motion, need not do so. Speakers often convey the meaning of the progressive in English glosses with the word 'along'. A sample of derived meanings is: *be paddling along* (from 'paddle'), *be growing large* (from 'be large'), *be making a noise right along* ('from be loud'), *be drying out* (from 'be dry'), etc. The process is extremely productive: the progressive combines with inherently active and inherently stative verbs of all varieties, deriving manner-of-motion verbs from any one of these.

---

[88] This is not the case in Oneida, where this suffix also takes the punctual according to Michelson (1995:38).

[89] An example is the stem *-dakhe-* 'run' which derives *-dakhe- + -nųh- + -dye- > -dakhenųdye-* 'run along'.

[90] An example is the stem *.hd- +* partitive 'the way it is': *tshaʔ níˑyot* [ni-yo-t-Ø] (where *hd >t* word-finally by regular rule) 'the way it is' derives *tshaʔ niyohdihadyeʔ* [ni-yo-hd-ih-adye-ʔ] 'the way it continues on'.

(i) Deriving progressive manner-of-motion verbs from inherently active verbs:

(105) a. <u>Progressive and habitual</u>:
   dehowæhdadihá·dye?s (w replaces *r by regular rule sec. 2.2.2.4)
   de-ho-aæhdad-ih-adye-?s
   DL-3M.SG.P-run-STV-PRG-HAB
   he is running along

b. <u>Progressive and purposive</u>:
   tsha? niyotgẹisdihá·dye?
   tsha?   ni-yo-at-gẹisd-ih-adye-?
   SUB   PRT-3N/Z.SG.P-REF-move.something-STV-PRG-PRP
   as it is moving along

c. <u>Progressive and modal purposive</u>:
   ẹgųdidye·nų́·dye?
   ẹ-gųdi-dye-nų(h)-dye-?
   FUT-3FZ.PL.A-fly-STV-PRG-PRP
   they will be flying along

(ii) Deriving progressive manner-of-motion verbs from inherently stative verbs:

(106). a. <u>Progressive and habitual</u>:
   degųgahǽ·dye?s
   de-gų-gahæ-(?)-dye-?s
   DL-1SG > 2SG-watch-STV-PRG-HAB
   I have my eye on you; I'm watching you right along

b. <u>Progressive and purposive</u>:
   onẹhathẹhá·dye?
   o-nẹh-a-thẹ-h-adye-?
   3N/Z.SG.P-corn-JN-be.dry-STV-PRG-PRP
   the corn is drying out

c. <u>Progressive and modal purposive</u>:
   ẹyoihwadá·dye?
   ẹ-yo-Rihw-a-d-a(?)-dye-?
   FUT-3N/Z.SG.P-matter-JN-be.standing-STV-PRG-PRP
   the matter will continue on, it will be the custom

4.6 The Expanded Aspect Categories

The Onondaga verb allows for suffixes that add number and tense categories to fully inflected verbs. These make it possible to pluralize certain stative (4.6.1) and continuative (4.6.4) forms and to inflect habitual and stative forms for the past (4.6.2), future, and optative (4.6.3). Iroquoianists refer to these as *expanded aspects*. The expanded aspect categories are marked with suffixes that are attached to the right of habitual or stative aspect suffixes. Table 4.38 shows their position within the verb.

Table 4.38 Position of the expanded aspect suffixes within the verb

The Verb							
Prepronominal Prefixes	Pronominal Prefixes	Reflexive	Noun Root	Verb Root	Root Suffixes	Aspect Suffixes	Expanded Aspects

Table 4.39 expands the rightmost position of Table 4.38, the expanded aspect position, within the verb:

Table 4.39 Expanded aspect positions

Aspect suffix	Expanded Aspect Suffixes
Habitual	+ continuative -k + habitual past -gwa?
Stative	+ stative plural -?s + continuative -k; + continuative plural -s + stative past -na?
Purposive	+ purposive past -ena?

4.6.1 The Stative Plural

The form of the stative plural suffix is *-?s*. It is added to fully inflected, basically stative verbs – often property concepts – and to the occasional active verb when it is inflected with the stative. Stative aspect suffixes ending in *h* or in *?* lose those segments when they combine with the stative plural. The stative plural is not particularly productive; it appears to be lexicalized as an available way to pluralize the patients of certain verbs or to distribute their activities over time and place. Typically, verbs inflected with the stative plural function syntactically as nominals:

(107) a. hona·dó·di?s
       hon-adodi-(h)-?s
       3M.NSG.P-grow-STV-STVPL
       grown-ups
            cf. hona·dó·dih *they are growing*

   b. oná?no?s
       o-na?no-(h)-?s
       3N/Z.SG.P-be.cold-STV-STVPL
       cold objects
            cf. ona?nóh *it is cold*

   c. ne? hya de?etciyędę́·i?s (CTL28.1)
       ne?   hya   de?-etci-yędeR-i(h)-?s
       NOM   NEG   NEG-2NSG > 3-know-STV-STVPL
       the ones you (non-singular) don't know
            cf. etciyędé·ih *you know them*

Verbs taking the stative plural often incorporate nouns:

(108) a. honųhsanó?s
        ho-nųhs-a-no[91]-(h)-?s
        3M.SG.P-house-JN-be.cold-STV-STVPL
        his cold houses

   b. hadiksa?dí·yo?s
        hadi-ksa?d-iyo-(h)-?s
        3M.PL.A-child-be.good-STV-STVPL
        nice children

   c. ne? tsha? nigaiho?dę́?s
        ne?   tsha?   ni-ga-Rihw-o?dę-(h)-?s'
        NOM   SUB   PRT-3N/Z.SG.A-matter-be.a.kind-STV-STVPL
        the kinds of matters/messages

Stative plural forms can be inflected with the habitual past (section 4.6.2.1):

(109) a. ne? tsha? nigaiho?dę́?sgwa?
        ne?   tsha?   ni-ga-Rihw-o?dę-(h)-?s-gwa?
        NOM   SUB   PRT-3N/Z.SG.A-matter-be.a.kind-STV-STVPL-HBPST
        the former kinds of messages

   b. honųhsanó?sgwa?
        ho-nųhs-a-no-(h)-?s-gwa?
        3M.SG.P-house-JN-be.cold-STV-STVPL-HBPST
        his formerly cold houses

   c. ga?se·hdiyó?sgwa?
        ga-?se·hd-iyo-(h)-?s-gwa?
        3N/Z.SG.A-vehicle-be.good-STV-STVPL-HBPST
        the formerly good cars

Uses of the stative plural are shown in the following narrative excerpts. In (110) representatives of the several Iroquoian nations have assembled to create the framework of the Confederacy. As a first task, each nation is given a name:

(110) Onę hí·hya? we?dwa·yę·nędá?nha? ne? <u>niyų·gwahsęnó?dę?s</u> ne? tsha?
     we?dwahwajiyæ·dá·dye? (CTL221.3-5).
       onę   hihya?   we?-dwa-yę·n-ęda?-nha?   ne?   ni-yųgwa-hsęn-o?dę-(h)-?s
       TMP   MOD   FACT-1IN.PL.A-task-finish-PNC   NOM   PRT-1PL.P-name-kind-STV-STVPL
       now   indeed   we finished the task   the   our names

       ne?   tsha?   we?-dwa-hwajiR-a-d-a(?)-adye-?
       NOM   SUB   FACT-1IN.PL.A-family-JN-stand-STV-PRG-PRP
       the   that   our ongoing family
       Now, indeed, we have finished the task of [giving] our names to the enduring
     families [nations].

---

[91] *-no-* is the incorporating alternant of the verb stem *-na?no-* 'be cold'.

Example (111) describes the mystical power of the protagonist who by a single command can raise the wind and the waves.

(111) Oné wa?thohéehda? wa?hęhę·?, "áhsµ khę nę́·" ogµdá·dye? wa?gaædát gahwíshe? odo?dówanę?s oné wa?honi?dahdę́ha? ne? hadiya?dadákhe? gahµwagµ́·wa (CTL224.8-225.2).

oné	wa?-t-ho-hęehd-a?	wa?-ha-(i)hę·-?	ahsµ khę	nę
TMP	FACT-DL-3M.SG.P-holler-PNC	FACT-3M.SG.A-say-PNC	TMP QUE	TMP
now	he hollered	he said	is it time?	now

ogudadye?	wa?-ga-R-t-at-Ø	ga-hwishe-?
TMP	FACT-3N/Z.SG.A-wind-stand-cs-PNC	3N/Z.SG.A-be.strong-STV
immediately	the wind arose	it is strong

o-do?d-owanę-(h)-'?s	oné	wa?-hon-i?dahdę-h-a?	ne?
3N/Z.SG.P-wave-big-STV-STVPL	TMP	FACT-3M.NSG.P-be.frightened-INCH-STV-PNC	NOM
big waves	now	they got frightened	the

hadi-ya?d-a-dakhe-?	ga-hµw-agµwa
3M.PL.A-body-JN-run-PRP	NPF-boat-LOC
they're in it running	in the boat

When he hollered, saying, "Is it time yet?", immediately a strong wind arose, [with] big waves, [and] then they got frightened as they sped along in their boat.

4.6.2 Adding the Past Tense to Active, Stative, and Manner-of-Motion Verbs

One series of expansions adds past tense suffixes to verbs inflected with the habitual and stative aspects with meanings indicating that the action or state has happened in the past. They are (i) the *habitual past,* which attaches to verbs inflected with either the habitual or the stative; (ii) the *stative past* which attaches to verbs inflected with the stative; (iii) and the *purposive past* which attaches to verbs inflected with the purposive. In addition, stative past forms can take an optative prepronominal prefix, resulting in (iv) the *optative past* inflection. That series of expansions is discussed in sections 4.6.2.1-4.6.2.4. A second series adds the continuative *-k-* to habitual or stative stems, deriving new verb stems that are inflected with the imperative or the punctual aspects. They take future or optative prepronominal prefixes. That series is discussed in sections 4.6.3.1-4.6.3.4 below.

4.6.2.1 The Habitual Past

The form of the habitual past is *-gwa?*. It attaches to alternants of the habitual aspect suffix with morphophonological changes as shown in Table 4.40:

Table 4.40 Habitual and habitual past combinations

Habitual	Habitual Past	Combined
-ha?-	gwa?-	> -hahgwa?
-aha?-	gwa?-	> -ahahgwa?
-?s-	gwa?-	> -?sgwa?

Table 4.40 (Continued)

Habitual	Habitual Past	Combined
-eʔs-	gwaʔ-	>-eʔsgwaʔ
-s-	gwaʔ-	>-sgwaʔ
-as-	gwaʔ-	>-asgwaʔ
-k-	gwaʔ-	>-hgwaʔ

The meaning of the habitual past is that an activity used to be performed in the past but not in the present. Verbs inflected with the habitual past select pronominal prefixes in accordance with the base form. Thus active verbs inflected with the habitual past take agent prefixes unless the suffix is attached to a verb that is lexically specified to take patient prefixes in all three aspects:

(112) With a verb that takes agent prefixes in the habitual and punctual aspects and patient prefixes in the stative aspect:
    degadęháhgwaʔ
    de-ga-dę-haʔ-gwaʔ
    DL-3N/Z.SG.A-fly-HAB-HBPST
    it used to fly

(113) With a verb that takes patient prefixes in all three aspects:
    dethohsiʔdyáʔksgwaʔ
    de-t-ho-ahsiʔd-yaʔk-s-gwaʔ
    DL-CIS-3M.SG.P-foot-break-HAB-HBPST
    he used to trip

When the habitual past occurs with a verb that expresses repetitive action the meaning is that a repetitive activity used to take place in the past:

(114) gadawęháhgwaʔ
    g-adawę-haʔ-gwaʔ
    1SG.A-swim-HAB-HBPST
    I used to swim

The habitual past also attaches to alternants of the stative aspect suffix with morphophonological changes as shown in Table 4.41:

Table 4.41 Stative and habitual past combinations

Stative	Habitual Past	Combined
-aʔ-	gwaʔ-	>-ahgwaʔ
-ʔ-	gwaʔ-	>-hgwaʔ
-eʔ-	gwaʔ-	>-ehgwaʔ
-h-	gwaʔ-	>-hgwaʔ

The meaning of such a form is that a state or quality persisted over time in the past but not in the present. When the habitual past follows a stative aspect suffix, the form takes patient prefixes with active verbs inflected with the stative. (This is so unless the suffix is attached to a verb that is lexically specified to take agent prefixes in all three aspects):

(115) hohgwishędáhgwaʔ
    ho-ahgwishęd-aʔ-gwaʔ
    3M.SG.P-try.hard-STV-HBPST
    he used to try hard

With 'resultant state' expressions (see sec. 4.2.1.2) the sense is that the state not only has ended, but that it has reverted to the initial state:

(116) akʔnikhų́hgwaʔ
    ak-ʔnikhų-ʔ-gwaʔ
    1SG.P-sew-STV-HBPST
    I had it sewn [but it came apart again]

When an inherently stative verb that takes patient prefixes is inflected with the habitual past, it selects pronominal prefixes in accordance with the base form.

(117) agathųdéhgwaʔ
    ag-athųde-h-gwaʔ
    1SG.P-hear-STV-HBPST
    I used to hear (it)

When an inherently stative verb that takes agent prefixes is inflected with the habitual past, it selects pronominal prefixes in accordance with the base form:

(118) haʔnigųhǽ·hgwaʔ
    ha-ʔnigųhR-aR-h-gwaʔ
    3M.SG.A-mind-put.in-STV-HBPST
    he was waiting

The contrast in meaning between attaching the habitual past to a verb inflected with the habitual or stative aspects shows clearly in the following set of examples using the verb stem *-adę·not-/-adę·nod-* 'sing':

(119) a. hadę·notháhgwaʔ
       h-ad-Ręn-ot-haʔ-gwaʔ
       3M.SG.A-SRF-song-stand.up-HAB-HBPST
       he used to sing regularly; he used to be a singer

    b. hodę·nodáhgwaʔ
       ho-ad-Ręn-od-aʔ-gwaʔ
       3M.SG.P-SRF-song-stand.up-STV-HBPST
       he used to be singing

Finally, the habitual past attaches to non-derived (120a) and derived (120b) manner-of-motion verbs inflected with the habitual with agent pronominal prefixes:

(120) a. hadakhé?sgwa?
      ha-dakhe-?s-gwa?
      3M.SG.A-run-HAB-HBPST
      he used to run around

    b. hadowæthé?sgwa?
      h-adowæt-h-e?s-gwa?
      3M.SG.A-hunt-DSLC-HAB-HBPST
      he used to go around hunting

In example (121) the habitual past occurs with both a stative and an active stem. Here the habitual past is used to describe conditions before the creation of the Great Law of the Iroquois Nations. The choice of habitual past signals that things have changed since then:

(121) Nayé? ne? tsha? niya·wé?ih ne? oihwagá·yu? nayé? ne? <u>odi·hwadéhgwa?</u> ne? ade·yóhsæ·? <u>deyudada?wethwásgwa?</u> ne? tsha?deyu·gwehú·we ne? tsha? honuhwejya·dé·nyu? (CTL1.2-4).

naye?	ne?	tsha?	ni-yaw-e?-ih		ne?	o-Rihw-a-gayu-?
ASRT	NOM	SUB	PRT-3N/Z.SG.P-happen-STV		NOM	3N/Z.SG.P-matter-JN-old-STV
it's	the	that	how it happened		the	in olden times

naye?	ne?	o-ad-Rihw-ade-h-gwa?		ne?	w-ade-Ryo-hsR-a?
ASRT	NOM	3N/Z.SG.P-SRF-matter-exist-STV-HBPST		NOM	NPF-SRF-kill-NOM-NSF
it's	the	it used to exist		the	warfare

de-yu-adad-a?wethw-as-gwa?	ne?	tsha?-de-y-ugweh = uwe	ne?	tsha?
DL-FI.A-REF-slaughter-HAB-HBPST	NOM	COIN-DL-NPF-person:SUFF = AUTH	NOM	SUB
they used to kill one another	the	the same Indians	the	that

hon-uhwejy-ade-nyu-?
3M.NSG.P-nation-exist-DST-STV
they are several nations

This is what happened in ancient times: there <u>used to be</u> warfare, <u>and they used to kill one another</u>, the Indians of the several nations.

4.6.2.2 The Stative Past

The stative past suffix is *-na?*. It attaches to alternants of the stative aspect suffix with morphophonological changes as shown in Table 4.42:

Table 4.42 Stative and stative past combinations

Stative	Stative Past	Combined
-?-	-na?	> -hna?
-a?-	-na?	> -ahna?
-h-	-na?	> -hna?
-ih-	-na?	> -ihna?
-hwih-	-na?	> -hwihna?
-uh-	-na?	> -uhna?
-nuh-	-na?	> -nuhna?
-eh-	-na?	> -ehna?

The stative past can combine with inherently active, stative, or manner-of-motion verbs. The meaning of the stative past is completive. For consequential verbs (Table 4.28) the event appears to be set further in the past than the plain stative:

(122) <u>The stative past with a consequential verb</u>:
    ak?nikhų́hna?
    ak-?nikhų-h-na?
    1SG.P-sew-STV-STVPST
    I had sewn it
        cf. ak?níkhų? *I have sewn it*

With non-consequential verbs the stative past is completive as against the plain stative which describes an ongoing state:

(123) <u>The stative past with a non-consequential verb</u>:
    hodowædíhna?
    ho-adowæd-ih-na?
    3M.SG.P-hunt-STV-STVPST
    he had been hunting; he was hunting
        cf. hodo·wǽ·dih *he is hunting*

Just like verbs inflected with the habitual past, verbs inflected with the stative past select agent or patient pronominal prefixes in accordance with the base form as in (124)-(126).

(124) <u>The stative past with an inherently stative stem that selects agent prefixes</u>:
    haya·jíhna?
    ha-yas-ih-na?
    3M.SG.A-be.named-STV-STVPST
    it had been his name
        cf. hayá·jih *(it is) his name*

(125) <u>The stative past with an inherently stative verb that takes patient pronominal prefixes</u>:
    tsha? niwa·gyo?dęhse?dę́hna?
    tsha? ni-wag-yo?dę-hsR-o?dę-h'-na?
    SUB   PRT-1SG.P-work-NOM-be.a.kind-STV-STVPST
    the kind of work I had been doing

(126) <u>The stative past with a manner-of-motion verb</u>:
    hohyakhų́hna?
    ho-ahyakh-ųh-na?
    3M.SG.P-go.to.pick.berries-STV-STVPST
    he had gone to pick berries

In narratives, stative past forms are used to clearly distinguish a time line in the past from the narrative present. In the following excerpt, two men had been sent by their chief to search out other friendly encampments. Now they are asked to report back about their task:

(127) Thohge ó·nęh waʔhęhę́·ʔ "oné ęsgwathó·yęʔ nwahóʔdę nwaʔawę́haʔ neʔ
jyahdędyúhnaʔ sniyę́ʔgwaihsakhúhnaʔ" (CTL207.3-5).

thohge	oné	waʔ-hę-hę-ʔ		oné	ę-sgw-atho·y-ę-ʔ		nwahoʔdę?
TMP	TMP	FACT-3M.SG.A-say-PNC		TMP	FUT-2PL > 1PL-tell-BEN-PNC		INTR
thereafter		he said		now	you will tell us		what

n-waʔ-aw-ęh-aʔ		neʔ	jy-ahdędyų-h-naʔ
PRT-FACT-3N/Z.SG.P-happen-PNC		NOM	2DU-depart-STV-PST
it happened		the	you two had departed

sni-yęʔgwaR-ihsak-h-ųh-naʔ
2DU-smoke-search-DSLC-STV-PST
you two went to search for smoke

Then he said, "So now you shall tell us what has happened [since] you left to look for smoke."

4.6.2.3 The Optative Past

The optative prepronominal prefix (section 4.2.1.3.3) may be added to stative past forms (section 4.6.2.2) to express past irrealis meanings. Inherently active, stative, and manner-of-motion verbs can all be inflected with the optative past.

(128) <u>Active verb inflected with optative past:</u>
a·wa·gyoʔdęʔíhnaʔ
aa-wag-yodęʔ-ih-naʔ
OPT-1SG.P-work-STV-STVPST
I might/would have worked; had I worked

(129) <u>Inherently stative verb inflected with optative past:</u>
a·yagawe·ʔíhnaʔ
aa-yagaw-eR-ʔ-ih-naʔ
OPT-3FI.P-think-INCH-STV-STVPST
she might/would have wondered; had she wondered

(130) <u>Manner-of-motion verb inflected with optative past:</u>
a·hodowæthúhnaʔ
aa-ho-adowæt-h-ųh-naʔ
OPT-3M.SG.P-hunt-DSLC-STV-STVPST
he might/would have gone hunting; had he gone hunting

In narratives, optative past forms are often embedded in hypothetical constructions:

(131) Dyę́ gwaʔ <u>da·wagatgahdųnyųhwíhnaʔ</u>, akhé·gęʔ giʔshę́ naʔ (GW).

dyę	gwaʔ	d-aa-wag-atgahd-ųnyų-hwih-naʔ	aa-khe-gę-ʔ		giʔshę		naʔ
HYP	REST	DL-OPT-1SG.P-look-DST-STV-PST	OPT-1SG > 3-see-PNC		ALT		ASRT
if	just	I would have looked around	I would see her		alternatively		it's

Had I looked around, I would have seen her.

(132) Tsha? ó? tsha? niyót tsha? sahųwa?nyagę́hda? ne? <u>aho·yohná?</u> gwa?yę?á
wa?ho·ya?dagehnhá? tsha? gáyę? ne? gwás tgá·e? (HW07).

tsha?	o?	tsha?	ni-yo-hd-Ø		tsha?
SUB	ADD	SUB	PRT-3N/Z.SG.P-how.it.is-STV		SUB
that	also	that	how it is		that

s-a-hųwa-?nyagęhd-a?		ne?	aa-ho-Ryo-h'-na?
REP-FACT-3 > 3M.SG-cause.to.escape-PNC		NOM	OPT-3M.SG. > 3M.SG-kill-STV-STVPST
someone helped him escape		the	he might have killed him

gwa?yę?á	wa?-ho-ya?dagehnh-a?	tsha?	gayę?	ne?	gwas	tgae?
NOUN	FACT-3M.SG > 3M.SG-help-PNC	SUB	REL	NOM	INT	DGR
rabbit	he helped him	the one		the	very	smallest

*[He] also [told them] how it was that he was helped to escape from the one who
<u>might</u> have killed him, by rabbit, the very smallest one.*

4.6.2.4 Purposive Past

The form of the purposive past suffix is *-(e)na?*. It replaces the purposive suffix *-(e)?* in
manner-of-motion verbs. Verbs inflected with the purposive past select agent pronominal
prefixes unless a verb is lexically specified to select patient prefixes. The meaning of the
purposive past with non-derived manner-of-motion verbs is an ongoing activity that takes
place in the past.

(133) haya?dadakhé·na?
    ha-ya?dadakhe-na?
    3M.SG.A-ride.in.a.vehicle-PRPPST
    he had been riding in it

(134) shagohsé·na?
    shago-hse·-na?
    3M.SG > 3-chase-PRPPST
    he had been chasing her/them

The meaning of the purposive past with derived manner-of-motion verbs is a past
intention to perform the action described by the verb. There is an implication that the
action was intended but not necessarily realized.

(135) hadowæthé·na?
    h-adowæt-h-ena?
    3M.SG.A-hunt-DSLC-PRPPST
    he had come to hunt; he had intended to hunt

(136) e?nikhųhné·na?
    e-?nikhų-hn-ena?
    3FI.A-sew-DSLC-PRPPST
    she was going to sew; she had intended to sew

With some semantically *dyadic* but morphologically intransitive manner-of-motion verbs as in (137), replacing the agent prefix with a patient prefix can produce a meaning change (at least in translation). The basic meaning of the manner-of-motion verb *-ʔse·-* is 'drag something'. In this basic meaning the purposive past takes agent prefixes as in (137a). But a second meaning, 'ride in a vehicle' literally '[it] drags someone' is understood with a reversal of semantic participants as in (137b).

(137) a. haʔsé·naʔ
        ha-ʔse·-naʔ
        3M.SG.A-drag.something-PRPPST
        he had been dragging it

    b. hoʔsé·naʔ
        ho-ʔse·-naʔ
        3M.SG.P-drag.someone-PRPPST
        he had been riding [in a vehicle] [literally: it had been dragging him]

An example of the purposive past occurred in a narrative where a manner-of-motion verb inflected with the purposive past was derived by means of the progressive suffix (see section 4.5.3.1). In the story, a grandmother is talking to one of her grandsons:

(138) Satgathwah nigayaʔdoʔdęh neʔ ha·yohadyenaʔ (H671.5).[92]
      s-atgathw-ah   ni-ga-yaʔd-oʔdę-h'   neʔ   ha-Ryo-h-adye-naʔ
      2SG.IMP-look-IMP   PRT-3N/Z.SG.A-body-kind-STV   NOM   3M.SG.A-kill-STV-PRG-PRPPST
      look!   the kind of body   the   he had gone along killing it[93]
      Look at the kind of animal he [the brother] had come along and killed.

4.6.3 Expanded Aspect Categories with the Continuative -k

Verbs inflected with the two durative basic aspects, the habitual and the stative, may be suffixed with the continuative suffix *-(e)k* to derive a new verb stem that is inflected with the punctual aspect or the imperative both of which require modal prefixes. See Tables 4.38 and 4.39 above for the location of the continuative in the verb. The continuative makes it possible to express future action or irrealis situations in the durative aspects.

Combining habitual and stative aspect alternants with continuative *-(e)k* results in certain morphophonological modifications as shown in Tables 4.43 an 4.44:

Table 4.43 Habitual and continuative combinations

Habitual	+ Continuative[94]	Combined
-haʔ		> -hak
-ahaʔ	-k	> -ahak
-heʔ		> -hek

---

[92] Hewitt did not mark stress in this excerpt. Phonetic final *h* in non-prepausal forms are present in Hewitt's transcription because this is a dictated text.

[93] Hewitt's word gloss is "he brought it back killed".

[94] The *e* of the continuative alternant *ek* is epenthetic.

Table 4.43 (Continued)

Habitual	+ Continuative[95]	Combined
-s		> -hsek[96]/-sek[97] / -shek[98]
-as		> -ahsek
-us	-ek	> -ųhsek
-eʔs		> -eʔsek
-ʔs		> -ʔsek
-k		> -hek

Table 4.44 Stative and continuative combinations

Stative	+ Continuative	Combined
-h		> -k
-ʔ		> -k
-aʔ		> -ak
-eʔ		> -ek
-ih	-k	> -ik
-hwih		> -hwik
-ęh		> -ęk
-ųh		> -ųk
-nųh		> -nųk

The new stem is inflected with the punctual aspect or with the imperative. The continuative imperative forms have been described above in section 4.2.1.4.2 together with other imperative inflections. The punctual forms of the continuative are described in sections 4.6.3.1-4. The punctual continuatives take future or optative prepronominal prefixes, resulting in four stem types: (i) the future habitual, (ii) the optative habitual, (iii) the future stative, and (iv) the optative stative. The form of the punctual aspect alternant that follows the continuative is -Ø.

4.6.3.1 The Future Habitual

The future habitual adds future prefixes to continuative habitual forms of basically active and of manner-of-motion verbs. The future habitual takes agent pronominal prefixes unless it occurs with a verb that is lexically specified to take patient prefixes in all aspects. The future habitual inflection expresses a future activity that is ongoing or habitual:

(139) <u>The future habitual with basically active verbs</u>:
    a. ęgatho·yáhak
       ę-g-atho·y-ahaʔ-k-Ø
       FUT-1SG.A-tell-HAB-CNT-PNC
       I will keep telling (it)

---

[95] The *e* of the continuative alternant *ek* is epenthetic.

[96] With stems ending in a vowel.

[97] With stems ending in *h* or *ʔ*.

[98] With stems ending in a stop consonant.

   b. ęgųdodyáhsek
     ę-gų-adody-as-ek-Ø
     FUT-3FZ.PL.A-grow-HAB-CNT-PNC
     they will keep growing

   c. ęhahdędyų́hsek
     ę-h-ahdędyų-s-ek-Ø
     FUT-3M.SG.A-move.on-HAB-CNT-PNC
     he will be leaving now and then

   d. ęhųwakhųnyęnihék
     ę-hųwa-khw-ųny-ęni-k-ek-Ø
     FUT-3 > 3M.SG-food-make-BEN-HAB-CNT-PNC
     she will be his cook [literally: she will habitually be making food for him]

With basic or derived manner-of-motion verbs (section 4.5 above) the habitual meaning of such verbs – habitual or repetitive action distributed in space – is retained but cast into the future.

(140) <u>The future habitual with non-derived manner-of-motion verbs</u>:
   a. ękhawíʔsek
     ę-k-hawi-ʔs-ek-Ø
     FUT-1SG.A-carry.along-HAB-CNT-PNC
     I will be carrying it around

   b. dęgęnaʔsgų·dyéʔsek
     d-ę-g-ęnaʔsgųdy-eʔs-ek-Ø
     DL-FUT-1SG.A-jump.around-HAB-CNT-PNC
     I will be jumping [rope]

(141) <u>The future habitual with derived manner-of-motion verbs</u>:
   a. ęhadowæthéʔsek
     ę-h-adowæt-h-eʔs-ek-Ø
     FUT-3M.SG.A-hunt-DSLC-HAB-CNT-PNC
     he will go hunting around

   b. ęhehsakhéʔsek
     ę-h-ehsak-h-eʔs-ek-Ø
     FUT-3M.SG.A-search-DSLC-HAB-CNT-PNC
     he will be going there to search [around]

In narratives, the future habitual occurs in forecasts of future events and prescriptions for action. In the following sequence more peaceful times are predicted after the formation of the Iroquoian Confederacy, a time when the different nations can meet to arrive at decisions on important issues:

(142) Onę óhniʔ ęwá·dụʔ <u>ęyagoyaʔdayéihsek</u> (CTL39.4-5).

onę	ohniʔ	ę-w-adụ-ʔ	ę-yago-yaʔdayei-s-ek-Ø
TMP	ADD	FUT-3N/Z.SG.A-become-PNC	FUT-3FI.P-assemble-HAB-CNT-PNC
then	also	it will become [possible]	they will keep assembling

Then it will become possible for them to keep assembling.

The following is a stretch of prescriptive text in which the culture hero – the good twin – introduces humans to the cultural staple of corn together with its preparation. The excerpt contains a future stative and a future habitual, side by side:

(143) Thóhge ónęh onụhgwęʔyáʔgeh jyonę́hada waʔhahnyodágwaʔ, néʔtho hwaʔhók,
     waʔhęhę́ʔ, "Neʔtho ụ́gweh <u>nęye·yęnoʔdę́k nęyeyéhak</u> néʔ ęyekhụ́nyaʔ neʔ
     ęyụdekhụ́nyaʔ" (H192.9-11).[99]

thohge	onę	o-nụhgwęʔy-aʔ-ge	s-yo-nęh-a-d-ah
TMP	TMP	NPF-corncob-NSF-LOC	REP-3N/Z.SG.P-corn-JN-be.one-STV
then	now	on the corncob	one corn

waʔ-ha-hnod-agw-aʔ		neʔtho	h-waʔ-h-o-k
FACT-3M.SG.A-set.up-REV-PNC		LOC	TRNS-FACT-3M.SG.A-put.in.water-PNC
he picked it		there	he put it in water

waʔ-hę-ihę·-ʔʼ	neʔtho	(y)-ụgweh	n-ę-ye-Wyęn-oʔdę-ʔ-k-Ø
FACT-3M.SG.A-say-PNC	MAN	NPF-human:SUFF	PRT-FUT-3FI.A-task-kind.of-STV-CNT-PNC
he said	thus	humans	the kind of task one will be continuing

<u>n-ę-ye-yeR-haʔ-k-Ø</u>	neʔ	ę-ye-khw-ụny-aʔ	neʔ
PRT-FUT-3FI.A-do-HAB-CNT-PNC	NOM	FUT-3FI.A-food-make-PNC	NOM
the way one will keep doing it	the	one will cook	the

ę-yụ-ade-khw-ụny-aʔ
FUT-3FI.A-SRF-food-make-PNC
one will eat

He plucked a single grain of corn from the corncob, put it in the water, and said, "That is the way humans shall prepare their food for eating."

4.6.3.2 The Optative Habitual

The optative habitual adds optative prefixes to continuative habitual forms of basically active and manner-of-motion verbs. Like the future habitual, the optative habitual takes agent pronominal prefixes unless it occurs with a verb that is lexically specified to take patient prefixes in all aspect. Habitual aspect suffixes combine with the continuative as shown in Table 4.43. Optative habituals occur in irrealis contexts, adding meanings of uncertainty, possibility, obligation, or admonition to habitual and ongoing activity. The meaning of particular occurrences depends on the context or the presence of other modifiers.

---

[99] Stress as marked by Hewitt. He did not mark vowel length in this example.

(144) <u>The optative habitual with basically active verbs</u>:
    a. a·hayęthwáhsek
       aa-ha-yęthw-as-ek-Ø
       OPT-3M.SG.A-plant-HAB-CNT-PNC
       he might/could/should be planting

    b. a·yodékhak
       aa-yo-adek-haʔ-k-Ø
       OPT-3N/Z.SG.P-burn-HAB-CNT-PNC
       it might/could/should be burning

    c. naʔ ayųdųhék
       naʔ   aa-yų-adų-k-ek-Ø
       ASRT   OPT-3FI.A-say-HAB-CONT-PNC
       this is what she would be saying

As with the future habitual inflection, the habitual meaning of the stems – i.e., habitual or repetitive action distributed in space – is retained, but it is cast into the optative mode. The first two examples are with non-derived manner-of-motion verbs.

(145) <u>The optative habitual with non-derived manner-of-motion verbs</u>:
    a. a·hahsé·ʔsek
       aa-shago-hse·-ʔs-ek-Ø
       OPT-3M.SG > 3-chase-HAB-CNT-PNC
       he might/could/should be chasing them around

    b. <u>a·hnéʔsek</u> neʔ dehyadęhnų́·dæ·ʔ
       aa-hn-e-ʔs-e-k-Ø   neʔ   de-hy-adę-hnųdR-aʔ
       OPT-3M.DU.A-walk-HAB-CNT-PNC   NOM   DL-3M.DU.A-SRF-follow.behind-NSF
       they might/could/should be around   the   two brothers
       the two brothers could be around together

(146) <u>The optative habitual with derived manner-of-motion verbs</u>:
    a. a·hadowæthéʔsek
       aa-h-adowæt-h-eʔs-ek-Ø
       OPT-3M.SG.A-hunt-DSLC-HAB-CNT-PNC
       he might/could/should be hunting around

    b. a·hadadyéʔsek
       aa-ha-d-adye-eʔs-ek-Ø
       OPT-3M.SG.A-stand-PRG-HAB-CNT-PNC
       he might/could/should be standing around

An example from a narrative, in which the optative habitual occurs in a conditional construction is:

(147) Dyę gwá? <u>ahsehék</u> dęhsadųgóhda?, tho nęhcyé·æ?, wádę? ęgųyathó·yę? (HW07).

dyę	gwa?	<u>aa-hs-eR-he?-k-Ø</u>		d-ę-hs-adųgohd-a?		tho
HYP	RST	OPT-2SG.A-want-HAB-CNT-PNC		DL-FUT-2SG.A-pass.through-PNC		MAN
if	just	you may want it		you will pass through it		thus

n-ę-hs-yeR-a?		wadę?	ę-gųy-atho·y-ę-?
PRT-FUT-2SG.A-do-PNC		INTR	FUT-1SG > 2SG-tell-BEN-PNC
how you will do it		what	I will tell it to you

If you want to survive, you will do what I tell you.

A rhetorical use of the optative habitual:

(148) Nayé? ne? hyá hwę́·dų de?ųgwaihahę́·gęh[100] sų́·ga·? nayé? <u>a·yųdųhék</u> gaihwiyóh, óhni? <u>a·yųdųhék</u> ga?shatsdę́·hsæ·?, óhni? ne? <u>a·yųdųhék</u> sgé·nų?, óhni? ne? <u>a·yųdųhék</u> ųda·nųhgwa? ne? ųgwe?dagwé·gih, <u>a·yųdųhék</u> gųnų́·gwe gagwegih deyųdęhnų́·dæ·?... (CTL32.3-33.1).

naye?	ne?	hya	hwędų	de?-ųgwa-Rihw-ahę·g-ęh		sų ga?	naye?
ASRT	NOM	NEG	INTR	NEG-1PL.P-matter-hear-STV		INDEF	ASRT
it's	the	not	when	we have not heard the matter		someone	it's

aa-yų-adų-k-k-Ø		ga-Rihw-iyo-h'		ohni?
OPT-3FI.A-say-HAB-CNT-PNC		3N/Z.SG.A-matter-be.good-STV		ADD
for someone say it		Good Message		also

aa-yų-adų-k-k-Ø		ga-?shatsdęhsR-a?	ohni?	ne?
OPT-3FI.A-say-HAB-CNT-PNC		NPF-power-NSF	ADD	NOM
someone might say it		power	also	the

aa-yų-adų-k-k-Ø		sgęnų?	ohni?	ne?	aa-yų-adų-k-k-Ø
OPT-3FI.A-say-HAB-CNT-PNC		NOUN	ADD	NOM	OPT-3FI.A-say-HAB-CNT-PNC
someone might say it		peace	also	the	someone might say it

ųdad-nųhgw-a?		ne?	(y)-ųgwe-?d-a-gweg-ih
3FI > 3FI-be.relatives-STV		NOM	3N/Z.SG.A-person-NOM-JN-all-STV
they are relatives		the	all of the people

aa-yų-adų-k-k-Ø		gųn-ųgweh		ga-gweg-ih
OPT-3FI.A-say-HAB-CNT-PNC		3FZ.PL.A-person:SUFF		3N/Z.SG.A-all-STV
someone might say it		women		it is all

de-yų-adę-hnųdR-a?	...
DL-3FI.A-SRF-follow-STV	
they are sisters	

Never have we heard anyone say 'the Good Message', also that someone might say
'Power', also that someone might say 'Peace', also that someone might say 'all of the
people are related', that someone might say 'the women are all sisters'...

---

[100] Utterance-final prosody and the retention of word-final *h* utterance-medially is because the source of the excerpt is a dictated text (see sec. 1.3).

In (148), the culture hero has introduced the warring nations to new key concepts intended to pacify them, and the people respond with surprise and wonder at these original ideas. The optative habitual occurs and reoccurs to fine effect.

4.6.3.3 The Future Stative

The future stative takes patient pronominal prefixes unless it occurs with a verb that is lexically specified to take agent prefixes in the stative aspect. The stative aspect alternants combine with the continuative as shown in Table 4.44 above. The meaning of the future stative inflection differs depending on whether the state expressed by the verb stem is a given or a resultant state (section 4.2.1.2 above); in addition, with basically active verbs, the meaning differs depending on whether the verb stem is consequential or not (section 4.4.2).

With basically stative verbs the future stative adds the meaning of a future state or condition:

(149) The future stative with basically stative verbs:
    a. ęwagathų·dek
       ę-wag-athųd-e?-k-Ø
       FUT-1SG.P-hear-STV-CNT-PNC
       I will be hearing it; I am going to be listening

    b. tho nęwa?sæ·dyék
       tho   n-ę-w-a?sæ·dye-?-k-Ø'
       MAN   PRT-FUT-3N/Z.SG.A-wide-STV-CNT-PNC
       how   wide it will be

With basically active consequential verbs (these are resultant states because they derive from an active verb inflected with the stative) a future perfect meaning is expressed:

(150) The future stative with basically active consequential verbs:
    a. ęhohdę́·dyųk
       ę-ho-ahdędyų-h-k-Ø
       FUT-3M.SG.P-move.on-STV-CNT-PNC
       he will have left

    b. ęyodegę́k
       ę-yo-adeg-ęh-k-Ø'
       FUT-3N/Z.SG.P-burn-STV-CNT-PNC
       it will have burnt

With basically active non-consequential verbs the meaning is future progressive:

(151) The future stative with basically active non-consequential verbs:
    a. ęho·dę·nó·dak
       ę-ho-ad-Ręn-od-a?-k-Ø
       FUT-3M.SG.P-song-raise.up-STV-CNT-PNC
       he will be singing

b. ęhodowædík
   ę-ho-adowæd-ih-k-Ø'
   FUT-3M.SG.P-hunt-STV-CNT-PNC
   he will be hunting

In narratives the future stative occurs most frequently with instructions and polite admonitions. Here a chief instructs two young men to watch out for fierce animals:

(152) Ẹ̱jyadatʔnigu̱hǽ·k óʔ. Seʔ khę̣ gana·gé·ʔ hwaʔtga·yóʔdage oʔdáhdę̣t (HW07).

ę-jy-adat-ʔniguhR-aR-aʔ-k-Ø	oʔ	seʔ khę̣ ga-nage·-ʔ
FUT-2DU-REF-mind-put.in-STV-CNT-PNC'	ADD	TAG 3FZ.SG-live-STV
you two will be watching out for yourselves	also	you know they live

h-waʔ-t-ga-Ryo-ʔd-a-ge-h'	o-iʔdahdęt-Ø
TRNS-FACT[101]-DL-3FZ.SG-animal-NOM-JN-amount.to-STV	3N/Z.SG.P-frightening-STV
plenty of animals	it is frightening

Also, you two should be watching out for yourselves. [Because] actually, you know, plenty of fierce animals of all kinds live [there].

In (153), a rabbit with magical powers instructs the hero what to do when he meets a monster:

(153) Ahgwí ęhsehda·gwá·hah! Seʔ khę̣ iʔ néʔ naʔ ẹ̱gẹ́k (HW07).

Ahgwi	ę-hse-hdagw-ah-ah	seʔ khę̣
NEG	FUT-2SG.A-be.afraid.of-INCH-IMP	TAG
don't	you will get scared	you know

iʔ	neʔ	naʔ	ę-ga-i-ʔ-k-Ø
PRON	NOM	ASRT	FUT-3N/Z.SG.A-be.all.of it-STV-CNT-PNC'
I	the	it's	it will be

"Don't get scared of it! Actually, you know, it will only be me."

4.6.3.4 The Optative Stative

The optative stative takes patient pronominal prefixes unless the inflection occurs with a verb that is lexically specified to take agent prefixes in the stative aspect. The stative aspect alternants combine with the continuative as shown in Table 4.44 above. As with the future stative, the meaning of the optative stative inflection differs depending on whether the state expressed by the verb stem is a given or a resultant state (section 4.2.1.2), and, in case they are basically active verbs, whether the verb stem is consequential or not (section 4.4.2). The differences are illustrated in the examples below.

With basically stative verbs the optative stative expresses a state that should continue:

---

[101] This basically stative stem has become lexicalized with a few forms that contain a factual prepronominal prefix prefix.

(154) <u>The optative stative with basically stative verbs:</u>
    a. a·hodiʔniguhæhní·k
      aa-hodi-ʔniguhR-a-hniR-ih-k-Ø
      OPT-3M.PL-P-mind-JN-be.sturdy-STV-CNT-PNC
      they should be resolute

    b. tshaʔ nų̇· a·hęʔdę́·dak
      tshaʔ   nų   aa-hę-iʔdęd-aʔ-k-Ø
      SUB   LOC   OPT-3M.SG.A-reside-STV-CNT-PNC
      the place where he might/could/would be living

With basically active consequential verbs an optative perfect meaning is expressed:

(155) <u>The optative stative with basically active, consequential verbs:</u>
    a. a·hawehsá·gik
      aa-haw-ehsag-ih-k-Ø
      OPT-3M.SG.P-search.for-STV-CNT-PNC
      he might/could/should have gone on looking for it

    b. a·yagoʔníkhųk
      aa-yago-ʔnikhų-ʔ-k-Ø
      OPT-3FI.P-sew-STV-CNT-PNC
      she might/could/should have gone on sewing

Basically active non-consequential verbs inflected with the optative perfect express an optative progressive state:

(156) <u>The optative stative with basically active, non-consequential verbs:</u>
    a. a·wagesdík
      aa-wag-e-sd-ih-k-Ø
      OPT-1SG.P-EP-use-STV-CNT-PNC
      I might/could/should be using it

    b. hya tha·yodóʔkdak
      hya th-aa-yo-ad-oʔkd-aʔ-k-Ø
      NEG CON-OPT-3N/Z.SG.P-SRF-finish-STV-CNT-PNC
      there may be no end to it

The optative stative is used in polite requests, surmises, and other irrealis contexts:

(157) a·sagayę́haʔ khę <u>da·dwík</u>
    aa-sa-gayę-h-aʔ   khę   d-aa-dw-i-h-k-Ø
    OPT-2SG.P-willing-INCH-PNC   QUE   DL-OPT-1IN.PL.A-be.all.of.it-STV-CNT-PNC
    would you agree   question [you and] we might stay together
    Would you agree to stay on with us?

An example from a narrative, (158), expresses a mother's surmise that she and her daughter would be safer in another location:

(158) Nayé? ne? agé·?ih nayé? gi?shę aga·gwé·nya? <u>a·ya·gnųnhék</u> ne? khehá·wah né?tho
      nų·we ha·ya·gyadegá?da? tsha? nų́· ne? hya sų́· ga·? da?deyųdawę·yétha? (CTL17.7-
      18.2).

naye?	ne?	ag-eR-?-ih	naye?	gi?shę	aa-ga-gweny-a?
ASRT	NOM	1SG.P-think-INCH-STV	ASRT	ALT	OPT-3N/Z.SG.A-possible-PNC
it's	the	I came to think	it's	instead	it may be possible

aa-yagn-ųnhe-?-k-Ø	ne?	khe-hawah	ne?tho	nųwe
OPT-1EX.DU.A-be.alive-STV-CNT-PNC	NOM	1SG > 3-mother/child	LOC	LOC
we two may survive	the	my daughter	there	place

h-aa-yagy-adega?d-a?	tsha?	nų·	ne?	hya	sų ga·?
TRNS-OPT-1EX.DU.A-light.a.fire-PNC	SUB	LOC	NOM	NEG	IND
we two would light a fire	that	place	the	not	someone

da?-de-yų-ad-awę·ye-t-ha?
NEG-DL-3FI.A-SRF-stir-CS-HAB
they don't roam about

*So I began to think, instead, it might be possible for me and my daughter to survive
somewhere by kindling a fire at a place where no one roams about.*

In (159), an excerpt from another narrative, a grandson complains to his grandmother
that she has been unfair to him:

(159) Hyah kshodahah de?oyane? tsha? nwa?cyeæ?, naye? hihya? ne? wa?tsdiha?da?, hya
      ni? de?sagayę?ih ne? <u>a·wa·gyędak</u> ne? a?ęna ohni? [ne? gahesga·?] (H646.1-3).[102]

hya	k-hsodahah	de?-o-yane·-?	tsha?	n-wa?-hs-yeR-a?
NEG	1SG.A-grandmother	NEG-3N/Z.SG.P-good-STV	SUB	PRT-FACT-2SG.A-do-PNC
not	my grandmother	it isn't good	that	you did it

naye?	hihya?	ne?	wa?-t-hs-diha?d-a?	hya	ne?	i?
ASRT	MOD	NOM	FACT-DL-2SG.A-differentiate.between-PNC	NEG	NOM	PRON
it's	indeed	the	you act unfairly	not	the	I

de?-sa-gayę-?-ih	ne?	aa-wag-yęd-a?-k-Ø	ne?	(w)-a?ęn-a?
NEG-2SG.P-be.willing-INCH-STV	NOM	OPT-1SG.P-have-STV-CNT-PNC	NOM	NPF-bow-NSF
you haven't consented	the	I could have it	the	bow

ohni?	ne?	ga-hesgaR-a?
ADD	NOM	NPF-arrow-NSF
also	the	arrow

*Grandmother, it isn't good what you did, indeed, you acted unfairly in not agreeing
to my having a bow and arrow.*

4.6.4 The Continuative Plural

The continuative plural is an Onondaga innovation that isn't shared by the other Five
Nations languages. It occurs in texts originating as far back as the late 1890s and is still

---

[102] Hewitt did not mark stress or vowel length in this excerpt.

used by contemporary speakers. The form of the continuative plural is -*s*. The suffix is attached to verbs that are inflected with the future stative (4.6.3.3 above) to express a situation that is distributed in future time.

(160) a. dęhęní?doks
    d-ę-h-ęni?do-?-k-Ø-s
    DL-FUT-3M.SG.A-fart-STV-CNT-PNC-PL
    he will keep on farting

   b. ęwagá·węks
    ę-wag-awę-h-k-Ø-s
    FUT-1SG.P-own-STV-CNT-PNC-PL
    I will be owning it

   c. ęyodogę́?iks
    ę-yo-dogę-?-ih-k-Ø-s
    FUT-3N/Z.SG.P-be.certain-INCH-STV-CNT-PNC-PL
    it will come to be certain

   d. ęwagadnawę́ks
    ę-wag-adnawę-h-k-Ø-s'
    FUT-1SG.P-keep.something.warm-STV-CNT-PNC-PL
    it will be keeping me warm (e.g., a new coat)

Constructions with the continuative plural freely incorporate nouns. The continuative plural projects the situation into the future, and implies that the referent of the incorporated noun is one of several:

(161) a. ęhahsęnówanęks
    ę-ha-hsęn-owanę-h-k-Ø-'s
    FUT-3M.SG.A-name-be.large-STV-CNT-PNC-PL
    he will be one of the Confederacy chiefs
            [literally: he will have one of the big names]

   b. ęwage?se·hdí·yoks
    ę-wag-e-?se·hd-iyo-h-k-s
    FUT-1.SG.P-EP-vehicle-be.good-STV-CNT-PL
    I will have [one of] the good cars

   c. ęganuhsáhseks
    ę-ga-nuhs-ahse-?-k-Ø-s
    FUT-3N/Z.SG.A-house-be.new-STV-CNT-PNC-PL
    it will be [one of] the new houses

In (162) the Founder of the Confederacy has described three major principles that will guide the Confederacy, and he is urging his followers to live by them:

(162) Onę ęwa·di·hwahdę́·dyaʔ neʔ gaihwiyóh óhniʔ neʔ gaʔshatsdę́hsæʔ óhniʔ neʔ sgę́·nųʔ
      nayéʔ díʔ ęgayaʔdagweniyók neʔ gagwé·gih neʔ dyųnhéhgwih nayéʔ <u>ęyoihó·wanęks</u>
      neʔ ųgwéhneh (CTL41.1-4).

onę	ę-w-ad-Rihw-ahdędy-aʔ		neʔ	ga-Rihw-iyo-h'	ohniʔ
TMP	FUT-3N/Z.SG.A-matter-move.on-PNC		NOM	3N/Z.SG.A-matter-be.good-STV	ADD
now	it will function		the	Good Message	also

neʔ	ga-ʔshatsdęhsR-aʔ	ohniʔ	neʔ	sgęnųʔ	nayeʔ	diʔ
NOM	NPF-power-NSF	ADD	NOM	NOUN	ASRT	LNK
the	power	also	the	peace	it's	moreover

ę-ga-yaʔd-a-gweniyo-h-k-Ø		neʔ	ga-gweg-ih	neʔ
FUT-3N/Z.SG.A-body-JN-principal-STV-CNT-PNC		NOM	3N/Z.SG.A-all-STV	NOM
it will be the main one		the	it is all	the

d-y-ųnhe-hgw-ih	nayeʔ	ę-yo-Rihw-owanę-h-k-Ø-s		neʔ
CIS-3N/Z.SG.A-live-INST-STV	ASRT	FUT-3N/Z.SG.P-matter-large-STV-CNT-PNC-PL		NOM
[they] live by it	it's	it will be one of the large matters		the

(y)-ųgweh = ne
NPF-person:SUFF = LOC
among the people

*Now they are functioning, the Good Message and also the Power and the Peace,
which are [our] main [values], [and] everyone among the people will live by them for
they will be the most important ones [among others].*

In (163) the Founder establishes the Iroquois Nations' geographical and deliberative
center. While each nation has its own central fireplace, that is, the place where it makes
decisions affecting the community, in this segment the Founder designates Onondaga as
the Central Fireplace of the Confederacy – with the use of the continuative plural it is
shown to be one among several nation fires – where the chiefs of the Confederacy are to
meet regularly to make decisions affecting their relations to the outside world:

(163) NéʔtHo ęyagoyųhá·dyeʔ tshaʔ nų́·we weʔdwanųhsyų́·nit tshaʔ nų́·we weʔdwajisdayę́ʔ
      néʔtHo nų́·we <u>nęgayaʔdagwení·yoks</u> neʔ gajisdowá·nęh ęyoyęʔgwaé·dak
      haʔdeyoęhyaʔésdih (CTL311.1-4).

neʔtho	ę-yago-yų-h-adye-ʔ		tshaʔ	nųwe	weʔ-dwa-nųhs-yųni-d-Ø
LOC	FUT-3FI.P-arrive-STV-PRG-PNC		SUB	LOC	FACT-1IN.PL.A-house-form-CS-PNC
there	they will keep on arriving		that	place	our Confederacy

tshaʔ	nųwe	weʔ-dwa-jisd-a-yę-ʔ'	neʔtho	nųwe
SUB	LOC	FACT-1IN.PL.A-fire-JN-lay-PNC	LOC	LOC
that	place	we laid the fire	there	place

n-ę-ga-yaʔd-a-gweniyo-h-k-s	neʔ	ga-jisd-owanę-h
PRT-FUT-3N/Z.SG.A-body-JN-principal-STV-CNT-PL	NOM	3N/Z.SG.A-fire-large-STV
it will be the principal one [of several]	the	large fire

ę-yo-yę?gwaR-od-a?-k-Ø   h-a?-de-yo-Ręhy-a-?esd-ih
FUT-3N/Z.SG.P-smoke-rise-STV-CNT-PNC   TRNS-FACT-DL-3N/Z.SG.P-sky-JN-collide-STV
smoke will keep rising up   it pierces the sky
They will keep going to the place where we established the Confederacy, the place of the Principal Fireplace, the place where smoke will keep rising, piercing the sky.

4.7 Prepronominal Prefixes

4.7.1. Introduction

Prepronominal prefixes occur at the very beginning of the verb, as shown in Table 4.45.

Table 4.45 Position of the prepronominal prefixes within the verb

		The	Verb				
Prepronominal Prefixes	Pronominal Prefixes	Reflexive	Noun Root	Verb Root	Root Suffixes	Aspect Suffixes	Expanded Aspects

Two kinds of prepronominal prefixes occur in this position, the modal and the non-modal prefixes. The modals express modal meanings, the non-modals express adverbial meanings. The two types occur singly and in combination. Whether or not the modal prepronominals must combine with non-modal prefixes depends on the aspect inflection of the verbs they modify. Thus with verbs inflected with the punctual aspect a modal must combine with the non-modal prefixes (section 4.2.1.3); with verbs inflected with the habitual or the stative aspects, non-modals occur without modals. The discussion in this section focuses on the non-modal prefixes, their interactions with each other and with modals. The basic forms of the non-modal prepronominal prefixes and how they combine with modals is shown in Table 4.46.

Table 4.46 Forms of prepronominal prefixes with and without modals

Prefix	Form	with Future	with Factual	with Optative
Partitive	ni-	nę-	nwa?-	naa-
Coincident	tci-	tshę-	tsha?-	tshaa-
Contrastive	thi-	thę-	tha?-	thaa-
Negative	de?-[103]			
Translocative	he-	hę-	hwa?-	haa-
Dualic	de-	dę-	wa?d-	daa-
Repetitive[104]	s-	ęs-	sa-	ų(·)sa-
Cislocative	t-/d-	ęd-	da-	ų(·)da-

---

[103] Lounsbury (1953) named this prefix the *negative auxiliary*.

[104] Lounsbury (1953) named this prefix the *iterative*, and following him, so did Chafe (1967, 1970) and Abbott (1981, 1984, and 2000). More recently (Chafe (2015), Michelson & Doxtator (2002), Michelson et al. (2016), Woodbury (2003), *repetitive* has been used for the prefix.

Table 4.48[105] lists each non-modal prepronominal prefix with and without a modal together with the conditions of alternation of the different alternants. In the table, the first column identifies the non-modal prepronominal prefix(es) by name, the second column shows the alternants without a modal, the third column combines the future prepronominal prefix with the several alternants, the fourth combines the prefix alternants with the factual prepronominal prefix, and the fifth with the optative prepronominal prefix. The rows list all of the permissible prefix combinations.

Non-modals can combine with one another as shown in Table 4.48. Table 4.47 shows how non-modals do so within their position class:

Table 4.47 Order of non-modal prepronominal prefixes

Prepronominal Prefixes			
Partitive Coincident Negative	Translocative	Dualic	Repetitive Cislocative
Contrastive			

Prefixes that occupy the same position are mutually exclusive; they cannot combine in any one construction. Nor can prepronominals that are semantically incompatible. When partitive meanings coincide with the coincident, contrastive, or negative, the partitive prefix drops away (sections 4.7.4 and 4.7.8). The coincident and the contrastive are both positionally and semantically incompatible. When repetitive and cislocative meanings combine in a given construction, the dualic replaces the repetitive to express repetitive meanings (section 4.7.7). The contrastive and the translocative do not co-occur. When these two meanings are expressed by the same verb, the locative particle *(ne?)tho* precedes a verb with a contrastive prefix and the translocative drops away (section 4.7.5). The translocative and the cislocative do not co-occur. They are semantically incompatible. The negative cannot co-occur with the modal prefixes that are required by the punctual aspect inflection. To negate a modalized verb, the contrastive (combined with the optative) replaces the negative prefix (section 4.7.5). The negative does not occur in imperative clauses. Negative imperatives require a different construction (sec. 4.2.1.4.3).

---

[105] The table is modeled after one devised by Lounsbury (1953:45-50) for Oneida.

Table 4.48 Prepronominal prefixes

PREFIX CATEGORIES	NON-MODAL	FUTURE	FACTUAL	OPTATIVE
Modals		ę-	waʔ- weʔ-$_2$ ų-$_1$ -aʔ-$_c$ -a-$_c$ ų-a-$_c$	a- a·- ae-$_2$ aų-$_1$ ųų-a-$_c$
Repetitive*	s- j-$_v$ ji-$_2$ t-$_s$	ęs- ęj-$_v$ ęji-$_2$ ęt-$_s$	sa- se-$_2$ sų-$_1$	ų(·)sa- ų(·)se-$_2$
Cislocative*	t- d-$_{w.v}$ di-$_2$	ęt- ęd-$_{w.v}$ ędi-$_2$	da- de-$_2$ dų-$_1$	ų(·)da-/aųda- ų(·)de-/aųde-$_2$
Dualic	de-	dę-	waʔt- waʔd-$_{w,y}$ waʔdi-$_2$	da(·)- dae-$_2$
Translocative*	he-	hę-	hwaʔ- hweʔ-$_2$ hų-$_1$	ha(·)- hae-$_2$
Dualic and repetitive	des- dej-$_y$ deji-$_2$ det-$_s$	dęs- dęj-$_y$ dęji-$_2$ dęt-$_s$	dųsa- dųse-$_2$	dų(·)sa-/daųsa- dų(·)se-$_2$
Dualic and cislocative	det- ded-$_{w.v}$ dedi-$_2$	dęt- dęd-$_{w.v}$ dędi-$_2$	dųda- dųde-$_2$	dų(·)da- dų(·)de-$_2$
Translocative and repetitive	hes- hej-$_v$ heji-$_2$ het-$_s$	hęs- hęj-$_v$ hęji-$_2$ hęt-$_s$	hųsa- hųse-$_2$	hų(·)sa-/haųsa- hų(·)se-$_2$
Translocative and dualic	haʔde-	haʔdę-	hwaʔt- hwaʔd-$_{w.v}$ hwaʔdi-$_2$	haʔda(·)- haʔdae-$_2$
Translocative, dualic, and repetitive*	haʔdes- haʔdej-$_y$ haʔdeji-$_2$ haʔdet-$_s$	haʔdęs- haʔdęj-$_y$ haʔdęji-$_2$ haʔdęt-$_s$	hwaʔdųsa- hwaʔdųse-$_2$	haʔdų(·)sa- haʔdų(·)se-$_2$
Partitive*	ni-	nę-	nwaʔ- nweʔ-$_2$ nų-$_1$	na(·)- nae-$_2$
Partitive and repetitive*	nis- nij-$_v$ niji-$_2$ nit-$_s$	nęs- nęj-$_v$ nęji-$_2$ nęt-$_s$	nųsa- nųse-$_2$	nų(·)sa- nų(·)se-$_2$
Partitive and cislocative*	nit- nid-$_{w.v}$ nidi-$_2$	nęt- nęd-$_{w.v}$ nędi-$_2$	nųda- nųde-$_2$	nų(·)da-/naųda- nų(·)de-$_2$
Partitive and dualic*	naʔde-	naʔdę-	nwaʔt- nwaʔd-$_{w.v}$ nwaʔdi-$_2$	naʔda(·)- naʔdae-$_2$
Partitive and translocative	nhe-	nhę-	nhwaʔ- nhweʔ-$_2$	nha(·)- nhae-$_2$
Partitive, dualic, and repetitive	naʔdes- naʔdej-$_y$ naʔdeji-$_2$ naʔdet-$_s$	naʔdęs- naʔdęj-$_y$ naʔdęji-$_2$ naʔdet-$_s$	naʔdųsa- naʔdųse-$_2$	naʔdų(·)sa- naʔdų(·)se-$_2$
Partitive, dualic, and cislocative	naʔdet- naʔded-$_{w,y}$ naʔdedi-$_2$	naʔdęt- naʔdęd-$_{w,y}$ naʔdędi-$_2$	naʔdųda- naʔdųde$_2$	naʔdų(·)da- naʔdų(·)de-$_2$
Partitive, translocative, and repetitive	nhes- nhej-$_y$ nheji-$_2$ nhet-$_s$	nhęs- nhęj-$_y$ nhęji-$_2$ nhęt-$_s$	nhųsa- nhųse-$_2$	nhų(·)sa-/nhaųsa- nhų(·)se-$_2$
Partitive, translocative, and dualic	nhaʔde-	nhaʔdę-	nhwaʔt- nhwaʔd-$_{w.y}$ nhwaʔdi-$_2$	nhaʔda(·)- nhaʔdae-$_2$

Table 4.48 (Continued)

PREFIX CATEGORIES	NON-MODAL	FUTURE	FACTUAL	OPTATIVE
Partitive, translocative dualic, and repetitive	nha?des- nha?dej-$_y$ nha?deji-$_2$ nha?det-$_s$	nha?dẹs- nha?dẹj-$_y$ nha?dẹji-$_2$ nha?det$_s$	nha?dųsa- nha?dųse-$_2$	nha?dų(·)sa- nha?dų(·)se-$_2$
Coincident	tc(i)-	tshẹ-	tsha?- tshe?-$_2$ tshų-$_1$	tsha(·)- tshae-$_2$
Coincident and other prepronominals	The coincident is attested with the dualic; repetitive; cislocative; dualic and repetitive, and the dualic and cislocative. Substitute tc- or tsh- for the n- of the partitive.			
Contrastive	thi-	thẹ-	tha?- the(?)-/the-$_2$ tha-$_6$ the-$_{2,6}$	tha(·)- thae-$_2$
Contrastive and other prepronominals	The contrastive is attested with the dualic; repetitive; cislocative; dualic + repetitive; dualic + cislocative. Substitute th- for the n- of the partitive.			
Negative	de?-	substitute the contrastive for forms with modal prefixes		
Negative and other prepronominals	The negative is attested with the dualic, the cislocative, the repetive, the dualic + repetitive, dualic + cislocative. Substitute da?- for all partitives beginning in na?-; substitute de?- for all other partitives except those beginning in nh-. The negative is also attested in non-modal forms: with the translocative as the?- and the translocative + repetitive as the?s-.			

Distribution of alternants:

Second person imperatives of categories marked (*) take prefixes from the factual column. Insufficient data for rows 14 and beyond.

Subscript $_y$ marks an alternant that occurs with a pronoun beginning in y.

Subscript $_2$ marks an alternant that occurs with second person dual or plural agent, any second person patient, or the first person dual or plural inclusive pronominal prefixes.

Subscript $_s$ marks an alternant that occurs with a pronoun beginning in s or hs other than the second person pronouns described in subscript $_2$.

Subscript $_1$ marks an alternant in which ų optionally replaces the sequence $wa? + wa$ or $a + wa$.

Subscript $_c$ marks alternants that occur when a prefix category combines with one or more other prefix categories.

Subscript $_w$ marks an alternant that occurs with a pronoun beginning in w.

Subscript $_6$ marks alternants as they are pronounced in the Six Nations dialect of Onondaga.

Non-modal prepronominal prefixes can be optional or obligatory. A prefix is optional if there is an otherwise identical verb stem without that prefix. The optional prefix modifies the meaning of the non-derived verb stem; the obligatory prepronominal is lexicalized as an integral part of a verb stem's meaning.[106] In (164) the repetitive prepronominal is optional:

(164) s̲hoda?gái·de?
    s̲-ho-ada?gaide-?
    REP-3M.SG.P-be.healthy-STV
    he has recovered, he is healthy again
        cf. without the repetitive: hoda?gái·de? *he feels good*

In (165) the repetitive prefix is obligatory; the stem is meaningless without it.

(165) s̲kheya·háhgwẹnik
    s̲-khey-a·hahgwẹni-k
    REP-1SG > 3-remind.someone-HAB
    I remind her/them

4.7.2 The Locative Prepronominal Prefixes: The Translocative and the Cislocative

The translocative and the cislocative, contrast semantically. They have in common that both express locational and directional meanings with and without points of reference; both extend these meanings in various ways that are discussed in the next sections.[107] The forms of the cislocative and translocative are given in Tables 4.46 and 4.47 above. With verbs whose meanings involve motion (section 4.5 and Table 4.31), the translocative adds the meaning *direction away from* the speaker or another third person, and the cislocative adds the meaning *direction toward the speaker* or another third person. In these combinations the locatives derive a directional motion verb from a motion verb that is non-directional:

(166) a. Motion verb with the translocative:
      hwa?é·yụ?
      h-wa?-e-yụ-?
      TRNS-FACT-3FI.A-enter-PNC
      she arrived there, she entered there

   b. Motion verb with the cislocative:
      dayé·yụ?
      d-a-ye-yụ-?
      CIS-FACT-3FI.A-arrive-PNC

---

[106] In the Onondaga Dictionary (Woodbury 2003) entries of verb stems with obligatory prepronominal prefixes are cited with a period (.) instead of a dash (-) preceding the stem. Forms with non-obligatory prepronominal prefixes are cited as sub-entries of the plain stem.

[107] Abbott (1981) describes the meaning and distribution of the locative prepronominal prefixes in Oneida. The situation in Onondaga overlaps with his description as far as the major functions are concerned, but differs in some details.

she arrived here cf. *waʔé·yų́ʔ* she arrived

This is true of inherent non-directional manner-of-motion verbs (167) as well as derived ones (168):

(167) a. <u>Manner-of-motion verb with translocative:</u>
hwaʔhadákheʔ
h-waʔ-ha-dakhe-ʔ
TRNS-FACT-3M.SG.A-run-PRP
he is running there

  b. <u>Manner-of-motion verb with cislocative:</u>
dahadákheʔ
d-a-ha-dakhe-ʔ
CIS-FACT-3M.SG.A-run-PRP
he is coming running; he is running this way
          cf. <u>Without a locative prefix</u>: hadákheʔ *he is running*

(168) a. <u>Derived manner-of-motion verb with translocative:</u>
hwaʔhodowædihá·dyeʔ
h-waʔ-ho-adowæd-ih-adye-ʔ
TRNS-FACT-3M.SG.P-hunt-STV-PRG-PRP
he is hunting right along as he goes there

  b. <u>Derived manner-of-motion verb with cislocative:</u>
dahodowædihá·dyeʔ
d-a-ho-adowad-ih-hadye-ʔ
CIS-FACT-3M.SG..P-hunt-STV-PRG-PRP
he is hunting right along as he comes from there
          cf. <u>Without a locative prefix</u>: hodowædihá·dyeʔ *he is hunting along*

Combined with verbs that do not involve motion, the translocative indicates that the action or process takes place in a location away from the speaker or another third person as in (169). The cislocative functions in one of two ways: (i) to indicate relative nearness of the action to the speaker or a third person (170a), or (ii), where relative distance is of no importance, the cislocative functions as an all-purpose locative (170b).

(169) a. tho nų́ heyowǽ·dih
       tho   nų   he-yo-aæt-ih
       LOC   LOC   TRNS-3N/Z.SG.P-lie.down-STV
       there   place   it is lying there
       it's lying over there at that place; the place over there, where it is lying
               cf. *ęgáæt I will lie down*

  b. gęhsáʔge heho·dyaʔdáʔdiʔ
     ga-ihs-aʔ = ge   he-ho-ad-yaʔd-aʔdi-ʔ
     NPF-wall-NSF-LOC   TRNS-3M.SG.P-SRF-body-lean-STV
     at the wall   he is leaning against it there
     he is leaning against the wall there
             cf. hodyaʔdaʔdíʔ *he is leaning against something.*

(170) a. thodegá?dih
      t-ho-adeg-a?d-ih
      CIS-3M.SG.P-burn-CS-STV
      he has kindled a fire here
           cf. honadegá?dih *they have kindled a fire.*

   b. dahadųwishę?
      d-a-h-adųwishę-?
      CIS-FACT-3M.SG.A-rest-PNC
      he rested there
           cf. wa?hadųwishę? *he rested*

In (171) the speaker deploys the locatives to convey situational details. The founder has appointed the chiefs of each of the Nations. He instructs them where to stand as follows:

(171) Naye? ís ohę·dų heswá·da? swashųhne hagwá thadí·da? ne? swędyohgwá?shų? (CTL305.3-4).

naye?	is	o-hęd-ųh	he-swa-d-a?	swa-shųh = ne
ASRT	PRON	3N/Z.SG.P-be.in.front-STV	TRNS-2PL-stand-STV	2PL-back = LOC
it's	you	it is in front	you are standing there	at your back

hagwa	t-hadi-d-a?	ne?	swę-idyohgw-a? = shų?
DIR	CIS-3M.PL.A-stand-STV	NOM	2PL-group-NSF = PL
direction	they are standing here	the	your groups

So as to you [chiefs] you stand there in front of your groups [of people], [and] they stand here at your backs.

Verbs that take locative prepronominals are often modified by locative or directional particles which further specify locational meanings, as in (172) and (173):

(172) Ónę wa?hatdóga? tshá? sí thoyó?de? né? dehyadęhnų́dæ? né? Oháhæ? (H212.10).[108]

onę	wa?-h-at-dog-a?	tsha?	si	t-ho-yo?de-?
TMP	FACT-3M.SG.A-SRF-certain-PNC	SUB	LOC	CIS-3M.SG.P-work-STV
then	he noticed	that	over there	he is working there

ne?	de-hy-adę-hnųdR-a?	ne?	Ohahæ?
NOM	DL-3M.DU.A-SRF-link-STV	NOM	NAME
the	they are brothers	the	Flint

Then he noticed that his brother, Flint, was at work over there.

(173) Tho nų́· nhęhsdakhé? nęgę́ nheyothahinų́h (HW07).

tho	nų	n-h-ę-hs-dakhe-?	nęgę	n-he-yo-at-hah-in-ųh
LOC	LOC	PRT-TRNS-FUT-2SG.A-run-PRP	DEM	PRT-TRNS-3N/Z.SG.P-SRF-path-lead-STV
there	place	you will be running there	this	where the path leads

You'll run to the place where this path leads.

---

[108] Stress as provided by Hewitt. He did not mark vowel length in this excerpt.

As mentioned, numerous verbs select locatives in terms of the direction of the action; these verbs must take a locative, but which is selected depends on the direction of the action. Most of the verbs involve motion or some form of transmission. For example:

(174) <u>Verbs that select locative prepronominals directionally</u>:

With Translocative	With Cislocative
a. hehahgwehnętha?	thahgwehnętha?
he-h-ahgwehnęt-ha?	t-h-ahgwehnęt-ha?
TRNS-3M.SG.A-descend-HAB	CIS-3M.SG.A-descend-HAB
he goes downstairs	*he comes downstairs*
b. hesá·dih	disá·dih
he-s-adi-h	di-s-adi-h
TRNS-2SG.IMP-throw-IMP	CIS-2SG.IMP-throw-IMP
Throw it [there]!	*Throw it [my way]!*
c. hekheyadwęnųdá·?sek	dyųga·dwęnųdá·?sek
he-khey-ad-węn-ųdaR-?se-k	d-yųg-ad-węn-ųdaR-?se-k
TRNS-1SG > 3-SRF-voice-put.in-BEN-HAB	TRNS-3F.SG > 1SG-SRF-voice-put.in-BEN-HAB
I telephone her	*she telephones me*
d. hwa?ųnųhsadahsé?	dayųnųhsadahsé?
h-wa?-ų-a-nųhs-a-dahse-?	d-a-yų-a-nųhs-a-dahse-?
TRNS-FACT-3FI.A-SRF-house-JN-circle.around-PNC	CIS-FACT-3FI.A-SRF-house-JN-circle.around-PNC
she went around a house	*she came around a house*

4.7.2.1 Special Uses of the Translocative

(i) <u>Intensification</u>: Speakers use the translocative to expresses intensification of certain properties or processes or to emphasize the presence of those properties:

(175) a. <u>heyots?áhdih</u>
    he-yo-ats?ahd-ih
    <u>TRNS</u>-3N/Z.SG.P-get.used.up-STV
    It is <u>completely</u> used up, it is <u>all gone</u>
        cf. <u>Without the translocative</u>: ots?áhdih *it is used up*

   b. Ná·ye? né? <u>heyodųgóhdih</u> węhsægá?wih (H190.2).[109]

naye?	ne?	he-yo-ad-ųgohd-ih	w-ęhsR-a-ga?w-ih
ASRT	NOM	TRNS-3N/Z.SG.P-SRF-go.beyond-STV	3N/Z.SG.A-odor-JN-be.appetizing-STV
it's	the	it passed beyond	it is an appetizing odor

    It is an exceedingly appetizing odor.
        cf. <u>Without the translocative</u>: odųgóhdih *it has passed by.*

---

[109] Stress and vowel length as provided by Hewitt.

c. <u>he</u>yagósthwih
    he-yago-asthw-ih
    TRNS-3FI.P-be.less-STV
    she is the youngest
        cf. <u>Without the translocative</u>: ósthwih *it is less*

(ii) <u>Multiplicity</u>: Combined with the dualic prepronominal prefix and number or amount verbs the translocative expresses a multitude of kinds or the full extent:

(176) a. ha?dewahsųdagéh
        ha?-de-w-ahsųd-a-ge-h'
        TRNS-DL-3N/Z.SG.A-night-JN-amount.to-STV
        every night
            cf. <u>Without the translocative</u>: dewahsųdagéh *two nights*

    b. ha?dé·yųh
        ha?-de-y-ų-h
        TRNS-DL-3N/Z.SG.A-be.an.amount-STV
        the whole amount, all of it
            cf. nę gwa? níyųh *a small amount*

(iii) <u>Extension</u>: With certain verbs of physical motion the translocative adds the meaning of reaching out to perform the motion:

(177) a. hegyé·naųs
        he-g-yena-ųs
        TRNS-1SG.A-grab-HAB
        I reach out and grab it
            cf. <u>Without the translocative</u>: gyé·naųs *I grab it.*

    b. hehodya?gaisdih
        he-ho-ad-ya?gaR-is-d-ih
        TRNS-3M.SG.A-SRF-waist-be.long-CS-STV
        he is reaching
            cf. <u>Without the translocative</u>: hodya?gáisdih *he is stretching*

    c. hegadiyętha?
        he-g-adiyęt-ha?
        TRNS-1SG.A-pull-HAB
        I reach out and pull it
            cf. <u>With the cislocative</u>: tgadiyętha? *I pull it toward me*

(iv) <u>Lexicalizations</u>: Some verbs are lexicalized with the translocative. The verb stem *.yesd-* + dualic means 'to mix, or mingle'; with the translocative replacing the dualic, the verb stem means 'add to':

(178) hegayésdih
    he-ga-yesd-ih
    TRNS-3N/Z.SG.A-add-STV
    someone has added it
           cf. <u>With the dualic</u>: degayésdih *someone has mixed [them] together.*

Two more, among numerous other examples that take the translocative obligatorily, are
.*adę̈nę̈sgwahd-* + translocative 'sneak up on something', and .*ųnęhd-* + translocative
'swallow' :

(179) a. thó· hwaʔgadę̈nę̈sgwáhdaʔ.
      tho·   h-waʔ-g-adę̈-nę̈sgw-ahd-aʔ
      LOC   TRNS-FACT-1SG.A-SRF-steal-CS-PNC
      I snuck up on it

    b. hwaʔhų·nę̈hdaʔ
      h-waʔ-h-ųnęhd-aʔ
      TRNS-FACT-3M.SG.A-swallow-PNC
      he swallowed

4.7.2.2 Special Uses of the Cislocative

(i) <u>Second person on first person imperatives</u>: The cislocative occurs with imperatives in
which a second person is to act on a first person (section 4.2.1.4.1).

(180) a. dasgatshohgwáę̈nyųh
      d-a-sg-at-hsohgw-aR-ųnyų-h
      CIS-FACT-2SG > 1SG-lip-apply-DST-IMP
      Kiss me!

    b. dasgę̈niháhdę̈h
      d-a-sg-ę̈nih-ahd-ę̈-h
      CIS-FACT-2SG > 1SG-borrow-CS-BEN-IMP
      Lend it to me! Let me borrow it!

(ii) <u>Responding</u>: The cislocative converts verbs of saying into *response*-verbs:

(181) a. daha·dá·dyaʔ
      d-a-h-adady-aʔ
      CIS-FACT-3M.SG.A-speak-PNC
      he answered
           cf. <u>Without the cislocative</u>: waʔha·dá·dyaʔ *he talked, he spoke*

    b. dahę̈hę́·ʔ
      d-a-hę̈-ihę̈·-ʔ'
      CIS-FACT-3M.SG.A-say-PNC
      he replied
           cf. <u>Without the cislocative</u>: waʔhę̈hę́·ʔ *he said*

(iii) <u>Degree</u>: With verbs that describe property concepts, the cislocative marks the superlative:

(182) a. tga?sés
    t-ga-?s-es-Ø
    CIS-3N/Z.SG.A-EMPTY.NOUN-be.long-STV
    it goes the furthest
        cf. iyų́s *it is long*

    b. dyeksa?gó·nah
    d-ye-ksa?gona-h
    CIS-3FI.A-be.pretty-STV
    she is the prettiest
        cf. eksa?gó·nah *she is pretty*

(iv) <u>Unpredictable meanings</u>: With a number of verbs the cislocative derives unpredictable meanings. Some examples are:

(183) a. dahęnųhdų́?
    d-a-h-ęnųhdų-?
    CIS-FACT-3M.SG.A-know-PNC
    he took charge
        cf. <u>Without the cislocative</u>: honų́hdų? *he knows*

    b. dawagá?ga·k
    d-a-wag-a?gaR-k
    CIS-FACT-1SG.P-get.dark-PNC
    I fainted
        cf. <u>Without the cislocative</u>: wa?ó?ga·k *it became night, at night*

    c. dyųdwęnagę?shǽ·ha?
    d-yų-adwęnagę?shR-aha?
    CIS-3FI.A-corroborate-HAB
    she acts as a witness
        cf. <u>Without the cislocative</u>: ęyų·dwęnagę́?shę·? *she will corroborate it*

    d. dagátga?k
    d-a-g-atga?k-Ø
    CIS-FACT-1SG.A-let.go.of-PNC
    I contributed
        cf. <u>Without the cislocative</u>: ęgátga?k *I will leave it, I will let go of it*

(v) <u>More lexicalizations</u>: Other examples of verb stems that take the cislocative obligatorily.

(184) a. dwagetgwęhsó·daʔ
    d-wage-tgwęhs-od-aʔ
    CIS-1SG.P-blood-stand-STV
    I am bleeding

  b. ętgayęʔgwáe·dę́ʔ
    ę-t-ga-yęʔgwaR-od-ęʔ
    FUT-CIS-3N/Z.SG.A-smoke-stand-PNC
    it will smoke

  c. thahdahgwíʔse·ʔ
    t-h-ahdahgw-iʔse·-ʔ
    CIS-3M.SG.A-shoe-drag-PRP
    he is shuffling

  d. dahaægwáhdaʔ
    d-a-ha-Rægw-ahd-aʔ
    CIS-FACT-3M.SG.A-choose-CS-PNC
    he grabbed it

4.7.3 The Partitive

The forms of the partitive prepronominal prefix are given in Table 4.46 and 4.47 above. The partitive is added to *manner*-expressions that involve, size, quantity, extent, and location, so that it frequently occurs with verbs that are modified by expressions containing locational, extent and manner particles or classifiers.[110] The subordinating particle *tshaʔ* is often followed by a verb with the partitive, and the interrogative particles *do* 'how' and *gaę* 'which [one]', 'where (i.e., which place)' typically occur with partitive verbs. The examples given below show that these elements often co-occur. Finally, there are numerous verbs which take the partitive obligatorily.

  (i) <u>With the extent classifier particle *nigę*</u>:

(185) Néʔtho hụ́ <u>nigę naʔdewadehgwáʔthaʔ</u> tsháʔ nigaę́hes néʔ ohnéhdaʔ (H760.8-9).[111]

neʔtho	hụ	nigę	naʔ-de-w-ad-hgwaʔd-haʔ	tshaʔ
LOC	MOD	EXT	PRT-DL-3N/Z.SG.A-SRF-hold.up-HAB	SUB
there	perhaps	extent	thus it rises up	that

ni-ga-Ręh-es-Ø		neʔ	o-hnehd-aʔ
PRT-3N/Z.SG.A-tree-long-STV		NOM	NPF-pine-NSF
how high the tree is		the	pine tree

It rises up perhaps as much as a tall pine tree.

---

[110] It is notable that a number of these particles, although not actually analyzable, begin with *n*.

[111] Stress as provided by Hewitt.

(186) Sí· <u>nigę́ nhwaʔhadakhéʔ</u> ... (HW07)

si·	nigę	n-h-waʔ-ha-dakhe-ʔ
LOC	EXT	PRT-TRNS-FACT-3M.SG.A-run-PRP
over there	extent	thus he is running

He is running that far...

(ii) <u>With directional and locative particles and expressions:</u>

(187) Thohgé ó·nę sahųhdę́·dyaʔ <u>neʔthó nhųsahęnéʔ</u> tshaʔ nų́·we tyonéhdih (CTL16.1-2).

thohge	onę	s-a-hų-ahdędy-aʔ		neʔtho
LOC	LOC	REP-FACT-3M.PL.A-depart-PNC		LOC
then	now	they went home		there

n-h-ųsa-hęn-e-ʔ		tshaʔ	nųwe	t-yon-e-hd-ih
PART-TRNS-REP:FACT-3.M.PL.A-walk-PNC		SUB	LOC	CIS-3FZ.NSG.P-walk-CS-STV
they all went back		that	place	where they came from

Then they (M) went home, returning to the place they (FZ) had come from.[112]

(188) <u>Tho nha·héʔ</u> ahá·yoʔ (HW07).

tho	n-h-aa-h-e-ʔ		aa-ha-Ryo-ʔ
LOC	PRT-TRNS-OPT-3M.SG.A-walk-PRP		OPT-3M.SG.A-kill-PNC
there	he would go there		he would kill it

He went there to kill it.

(189) Onę hyaʔ ų <u>tho sgę́ha gátgaʔ nú· nigę́ʔdę́·ʔ</u> neʔ ná·yeʔ (HW07).

onę	hyaʔ	ų·	tho	sgęha	gatgaʔ	nų·
TMP	MOD	MOD	LOC	LOC	INTR	LOC
now	indeed	probably	there	near	somewhere	place

ni-ga-iʔdę·-ʔ		neʔ	nayeʔ
PRT-3FZ.SG.A-reside-STV		NOM	ASRT
thus she lives		the	it's

Now it's probably, close by, the place where she lives, that's it.

(iii) <u>With the subordinator particle *tshaʔ*:</u>

(190) a. <u>tshaʔ nųwe naʔdeyųgyadæʔih</u> (H683.18).[113]

tshaʔ	nųwe	naʔ-de-yųgy-adæ·ʔ-ih
SUB	LOC	PART-DL-1DU.P-meet.by.chance-STV
that	place	thus we two have met

the place where you and I have met by chance.

---

[112] The choice of different pronominal prefixes for the two verbs is explained by the fact that the referents of the two verbs are overlapping, but not identical: A mother and a daughter (feminine-zoic dual pronominal) left the original village. Meanwhile the daughter had a male child, so that when they returned to the original place there were three of them, a mixed male-female group (hence a masculine plural pronominal).

[113] Hewitt did not mark stress and vowel length in this excerpt.

b. <u>tsha?</u> <u>ni</u>dyagodó·dih

    tsha?   ni-d-yago-adodi-h

    SUB   PRT-CIS-3FI.P-grow-STV

    that   thus one has grown

    at their age

c. <u>tsha?</u> <u>ni</u>yodoháeh

    tsha?   ni-yo-ad-ohae-h'

    SUB   PRT-3N/Z.SG.P-SRF-wash-STV

    that   thus it is washed

    how clean it is

d. <u>tsha?</u> <u>ni</u>yų·dų·nhyę́ha?

    tsha?   ni-yų-adųnhyę-ha?

    SUB   PRT-3FI.A-preserve.food-HAB

    that   thus they preserve food

    the food they preserve

e. <u>tsha?</u> <u>n</u>ęsatgęisdihadye? (H682.12)[114]

    tsha?   n-ę-s-atgęisd-ih-adye-?

    SUB   PRT-FUT-2SG.P-move.over-STV-PRG-PRP

    that   thus you will be moving closer

    you will be moving closer

(iv) <u>Manner expressions</u>: Speakers use the partitive to derive *manner*-verbs:

(191) né?tho <u>ni</u>gayanó·we?

    ne?tho   ni-ga-yanoRe-?

    MAN   PRT-3FZ.SG.A-run.fast-STV

    how   thus she runs fast

    how fast she runs.

               cf. <u>Without the partitive</u>: hadiyanó·we? *they are fast runners.*

(v) When a quality or manner verb with the partitive occurs preceded by the subordinator *tsha?* and the intensity particle *gwas* the phrase expresses a special intensity of the quality:

(192) Gwas o? ayę́·? <u>tsha?</u> <u>n</u>wa?hadi·hwahǽ·hda? (LG24).

    gwas   o?   ayeę?   tsha?   n-wa?-h-adihwahæhd-a?

    INTNS ADD   SIM   SUB   PRT-FACT-3M.SG.A-act.excited-a?

    very   also   seems like that   he was excited

    He seemed <u>*so*</u> *excited.*

(193) Gwas yágę? nę́gę yá de?jyohsų́hda·?, <u>tsha?</u> <u>ni</u>yo·dǽ·nye? (HW07).

    gwas   yagę?   nęgę   hya   de?-s-yo-hsųhd-aR-?   tsha?

    INTNS HRSY   DEM   NEG NEG-REP-3N/Z.SG.P-bark-be.in-STV   SUB

    really   they say   this   not   there's no more bark on it   that

---

[114] Stress as provided by Hewitt. He did not mark vowel length in this excerpt.

<u>ni-yo-adæ·nye-ʔ</u>
PRT-3N/Z.SG.P-get.worn-STV
how worn it is
Really, they say, there's no longer bark on it, <u>that's how worn it is</u>.
        cf. <u>Without the partitive</u>: odǽ·nyeʔ / odæ·nyéh[115] *it is worn off from rubbing*

(vi) With the interrogative particles *do·* or *gaę*:

(194) a. Do· niyoshé·dih
       do   ni-yo-ashed-ih
       INTR   PRT-3N/Z.SG.P-count-STV
       what   thus it is counted
       What size is it? What number is it?

     b. ...gaę gwaʔ nigá·æʔ... (CTL260.1)
       gaę   gwaʔ   ni-ga-R-aʔ
       INTR   APPROX PRT-3N/Z.SG.A-be.in-STV
       which just   it is in it
       ...whatever is in there, which ever one...

     c. Sęnų́hdụʔ khę gaę nų́ ní·yęʔsæ... (NC01)
       s-ęnųhdụ-ʔ   khę   gaę   nų   ni-yę-e-ʔs
       2SG.P-know-STV QUE   INTR   LOC   PRT-3FI.A-walk-HAB
       you know it   question which place thus she is around
       Do you know where she is?

(vii) <u>Counting verbs</u>: with numbers greater than two:

(195) Ahsę́h <u>niwędagé</u> nęyųnísheʔ ęyųgwahdędyų́k (CTL15.4-5).
       ahsę   ni-w-ęd-a-ge-h'[116]   n-ę-y-ųnishe-ʔ
       NUMBER PRT-3N/Z.SG.A-day-JN-amount.to-STV PRT-FUT-3N/Z.SG.A-take.a.long.time-STV
       three   so many days   how long it will take

       ę-yųgw-ahdędyų-(h)-k-Ø
       FUT-1PL.P-depart-STV-CNT-PNC
       we will have departed
       In three days time we will have departed.

(196) Hwíks nwaʔhųdyaʔdíhsʔaʔ (H141.3).[117]
       hwiks   n-waʔ-hų-ad-yaʔd-ihsʔ-aʔ
       NUMBER PRT-FACT-3M.PL.A-SRF-body-finish-PNC
       five   generations
       Five generations.

---

[115] The different pronunciations are due to speaker variation.

[116] Recall that words ending in /h/ typically lose it utterance-medially.

[117] Hewitt did not mark second syllable vowel length in this excerpt.

(197) Nayé? ne? jyá·dak niyowęyųhga·géh nęhsihnadéjik (CTL698.3).

    naye?   ne?   jyadak   ni-yo-węyųhgaR-ge-h'
    ASRT   NOM   NUMBER   PRT-3N/Z.SG.P-thumb-amount.to-STV
    it's   the   seven   how many inches

    n-ę-hs-ihn-a-dęs-ih-k-Ø
    PRT-FUT-2SG.A-skin-JN-thick-STV-CNT-PNC
    how thick your skin will be
    Your skin will be seven inches thick.

  (viii) <u>Lexicalizations</u>: Frequently occurring stems with obligatory partitives:

(198) tho <u>nųgya?dawęha?</u>

    tho   n-wa?-wag-ya?d-a-węh-a?
    MAN   PRT-FACT-1SG.P-body-JN-happen-PNC
    how   thus it happened to me
    That is what happened to me.

(199) onó?jya? <u>nwa?gaędó?dę?</u> (H173.3).[118]

    o-no?jy-a?   n-wa?-ga-Ręd-o?dę-?
    NPF-tooth-NSF   PRT-FACT-3N/Z.SG.A-tree-be.a.kind-STV
    tooth   the kind of tree it is
    'Tooth' is the species of the tree.

(200) né?tho gehé? <u>na·gyé·æ?</u>.

    ne?tho   g-eR-he?   n-aa-g-yeR-a?
    MAN   1SG.A-want-HAB   PRT-OPT-1SG.A-do-PNC
    how   I want   how I would do it
    That's how I want to do it.

4.7.4. The Coincident

The forms of the coincident prepronominal prefix are given in Tables 4.46 and 4.47. The coincident indicates simultaneity in time, and *identity, sameness* or *similarity* in space or manner.

  (i) <u>Simultaneity</u>: with temporal expressions.

(201) <u>Tcihe?</u> gwa? wa?thahgwa? ne? onęya? (H668.21).[119]

    <u>tci-h-e-?</u>   gwa?   wa?-t-ha-hgw-a?   ne?   o-nęy-a?
    COIN-3M.SG.A-walk-PRP   RSTR   FACT-DL-3M.SG.A-pick.up-PNC   NOM   NPF-stone-NSF
    as he's walking   just   he picks it up   the   stone
    He picks up a stone as he walks.

---

[118] Stress as marked by Hewitt.

[119] Hewitt did not mark stress or vowel length in this excerpt.

(202) Onę di? <u>tsha?hathahí·ne?</u> wa?há·gę? niwa?á ganyá·dae? (CTL326.8).

onę	di?	tsh-a?-h-at-hah-ine-?		wa?-ha-gę-?
TMP	LNK	COIN-FACT-3M.SG.A-SRF-path-have.a.course-PRP		FACT-3M.SG.A-see-PNC
now	moreover	as he is following the path		he saw it

ni-w-a?a-h[120]	ga-nyadaR-e-?
PRT-3N/Z.SG.A-be.small-STV	3N/Z.SG.A-lake-exist-STV
it is small	lake

He saw a small lake as he followed the path.

   (ii) <u>Calendric references</u>: The coincident indicates the most recent occurrence of a recurring calendric event:[121]

(203) a. tcigaęhyáhęh
      tci-ga-Ręhy-a-hę-h
      COIN-3N/Z.SG.A-sky-JN-be.in.the.middle-STV
      this noon (if said after 12 p.m.); *yesterday noon* (if said before 12 p.m.)
           cf. <u>Without the coincident</u>: gaęhyáhę hagwáh *south, noon*

   b. tciwędado·gęhdih
      tci-w-ęd-a-dogę-hd-ih
      COIN-3N/Z.SG.A-day-JN-be.certain-cs-STV
      last Sunday
           cf. <u>Without the coincident</u>: awędado·gęhdih *Sunday*

   (iii) <u>Similarity with non-temporal expressions</u>: Determining similarity often involves comparing actions, events, or situations. For this reason the coincident often pairs up with the dualic prepronominal prefix (section 4.7.7) as it does in examples (205) and (206).

(204) Na? <u>tcigé·he?</u>
      na?   tci-g-eR-he?
      ASRT   COIN-1SG.A-think-HAB
      it's   as I think
      That's what I'm thinking.

(205) Nayé? gé·da? ne? sahsę·na? nayé? ne? gagwé·gih[122] <u>tsha?dęhcyé·æ?</u> (CTL370.8-371.1).

naye?	ga-id-a?	ne?	sa-hsęn-a?	naye?	ne?
ASRT	3N/Z.SG.A-mean-STV	NOM	2SG.P-name-NSF	ASRT	NOM
it's	it means	the	your name	it's	the

---

[120] Words ending in /h/ typically lose it utterance-medially.

[121] I thank Jay Meacham of Onondaga Nation for this insight.

[122] Utterance-final prosody and the retention of word-final *h* utterance-medially is because the source of the excerpt is a dictated text (see sec. 1.3).

ga-gweg-ih   tshaʔ-d-ę-hs-yeR-aʔ
3N/Z.SG.A-be.all-STV   COIN-DL-FUT-2SG.A-do-PNC
it is all   you will do the same
Your name means that you will treat them all equally.

(206) Sgá·da ęyųgwadeksayędák gę́·daʔ neʔ gagwé·gi <u>tshaʔde·dwayaʔdagwe·ní·yoʔ</u>
(CTL458.8-499.2).

sgada	ę-yųgw-ade-ks-a-yęd-ah-k-Ø	ga-id-aʔ	neʔ
NUMBER	FUT-1PL.P-SRF-dish-JN-have-STV-CNT-PNC	3N/Z.SG.A-mean-STV	NOM
one	we will be having a dish	it means	the

ga-gweg-ih[123]   tshaʔ-de-dwa-yaʔd-a-gweniyo-ʔ
3N/Z.SG.A-be.all-STV   COIN-DL-1IN.PL.A-body-JN-be.most.important-STV
it is all   we will have the same importance
We will have a single dish, [which] means that we all have equal authority.

(207) tshaʔda·yawę́haʔ
    tshaʔ-d-aa-yaw-ęh-aʔ
    COIN-DL-OPT-3N/Z.SG.P-happen-PNC
    it may happen the same way; it may come out even
          cf. <u>Without the coincident and dualic</u>: tshaʔ nwaʔawę́haʔ *what*
          happened

  (iv) <u>Lexicalizations with the coincident:</u>

(208) a. tshaʔgé·hdaʔ
      tsh-aʔ-g-eR-hd-aʔ
      COIN-FACT-1SG.A-think,want-CS-PNC
      I intended to do it; I did it on purpose

     b. tshaʔgá·dah
      tsh-aʔ-ga-d-ah
      COIN-FACT-3N/Z.SG.A-be.the.same-STV
      it is the same

  (v) <u>Lexicalizations with the coincident and dualic:</u>

(209) a. Tshaʔdé·gnaʔ
      tshaʔ-de-gn-a-ʔ
      COIN-DL-3FZ.DU.A-be.a.size-STV
      They two are the same size

     b. tshaʔdehniyaʔtoʔtę́h
      tshaʔ-de-hni-yaʔd-oʔdę-h'
      COIN-DL-3M.DU.A-body-be.a.kind-STV
      they two look alike

---

[123] Words ending in /h/ typically lose it utterance-medially.

c. tsha?deyųhá·dye?
    tsha?-de-y-ų-h-adye-?
    COIN-DL-3N/Z.SG.A-be.an.amount-STV-PRG-PRP
    they are equal amounts

(vi) <u>Loss of the partitive in the presence of the coincident</u>: As noted above, the partitive and coincident cannot co-occur. When a verb with an obligatory partitive expresses a coincident meaning, the partitive drops away. For example, the verb stem *.ųnho?dę-* + partitive 'be a lifestyle, be a way of thinking' is lexicalized with the partitive, as is the verb stem *.ęh-* + partitive 'happen'. In the derived constructions (207) above and (210) the coincident preempts the partitive:

(210)   tsha?dehnųnho?dę́h
        tsha?-de-hn-ųnh-o?dę-h´
        COIN-DL-3M.DU.A-life-be.a.kind-STV
        they two think alike
                    cf. <u>Without the coincident</u>: nigųnho?dę́h *my lifestyle, my attitudes*

4.7.5 The Contrastive

The forms of the contrastive are shown in Tables 4.46 and 4.47. The contrastive expresses *difference* or *contrast*. In some contexts it is used to indicate situations that are *unusual* or *excessive*. Also, the contrastive takes over the function of the negative with verbs inflected with the punctual. The contrastive and the translocative do not co-occur. When these two meanings are expressed by a verb, the locative particle *(ne?)tho* precedes a verb with a contrastive, the particle taking over for the translocative.

  (i) <u>Marking contrast or difference</u>:

(211) Onę́ gáę gwa? hagwá <u>tha?tgųgohdahgwáhę·?</u> (CTL591.3-4).
        onę   gaę   gwa?   hagwa   <u>th-a?-d-g-ųgohd-ahgw-hę·-?</u>
        TMP   INTR   APPROX   DIR   CON-FACT-DL-1SG.A-pass.through-INST-DST-PNC
        then   which just   direction I passed it the wrong way
        Then I performed [the ceremony] in the wrong way.
                    cf. <u>Without the contrastive</u>: dehaųgóhdih *he has passed it*

(212) Da· dogá?t he? enųda?gegá? nęgę́ <u>thiho·nyakhé?i</u> na? gó? hya? go·wę́sgwa?, na? dí?
        hya? tsha? nwa?awę́ha? (LG17).
        da   doga?t   he?   e-nųd-a? = ge = ga·?'   nęgę
        LNK   HYP   REP   3FI.A-hill-NSF = LOC = CHAR   DEM
        so   if   in turn   Onondaga woman   this

        <u>thi</u>-ho-nyak-he?-ih   na?   go·?   hya?   go-awę-s-gwa?   na?
        CON-3M.SG.P-marry-INCH-STV   ASRT   CTR   MOD   3FI.P-have-HAB-HBPST   ASRT
        had he gotten married   it's   however   indeed   she used to have it   it's

di?   hya?   tsha?   n-wa?-aw-ęh-a?
LNK   MOD   SUB   PART-FACT-3N/Z.SG.P-happen-PNC
moreover   indeed   that   thus it happened
So if he had married an Onondaga woman instead, she would have owned this home.
> cf. <u>Without the contrastive</u>: honyakhé?ih *he has gotten married*

(ii) To express unusual intensity:

(213)   thiwagadyéhwada?
      thi-wag-adyehwad-a?
      CON-1SG.P-be.wakeful-PNC
      I was excessively wakeful
> cf. <u>Without the contrastive</u>: aga·dyéhwada? *I am wakeful.*

(214)   Shę́·hge gwá? <u>thihų́nhe?</u>.
      shęhge   gwa?   <u>thi-h-ųnhe-?</u>
      DGR   APPROX   CON-3M.SG.A-be.alive-STV
      hardly   just   he is barely alive
      He's just barely alive
> cf. <u>Without the contrastive</u>: hų́nhe? *he is alive.*

(iii) <u>Replacing the negative *de?-* in verbs inflected with the punctual aspect</u>:

(215)   ...hya tha·ye?nyagę́?nha? (NC01).
      hya   thaa-ye-yagę?-nha?
      NEG   CON-OPT-3FI.A-excape-PNC
      not   she mustn't escape
      ...she mustn't escape.
> cf. <u>Inflected with the stative (and repetitive)</u>: hya de?jyodiya·gę́?ih *they
> did not get out again* (H196:13-14)

(216) hya thųdahayéisda?.
      hya   th-ųd-aa-ha-yei-sd-a?
      NEG   CON-CIS-OPT-3M.SG.A-be.right-CS-PNC
      not   he didn't do it correctly
      He didn't do it correctly.
> cf. <u>Inflected with the habitual</u>: hya de?thayéistha? *he doesn't do it
> correctly.*

(iv) <u>Lexicalizations with the contrastive</u>:

(217) <u>Thęyų·dyéę?</u> na? tho hadá·dye?s.
      th-ę-yų-adyeę-?   na?   tho   ha-d-(a?)-adye-?s
      CON-FUT-3FI.A-surprise-PNC   ASRT   LOC   3M.SG.A-stand-STV-PRG-HAB
      she will be surprised   it's   there   he is standing along
      She will be surprised that he is suddenly standing there.

(218) thigá·de?
    thi-ga-de-?
    CON-3N/Z.SG.A-be.different-STV
    it is different

(219) hyá tha?deyeyá?dih
    hya   tha?-de-ye-ya?d-i-h
    NEG   CON-DL-3FI.A-body-be.the.total-STV
    not   she isn't alone
    She is pregnant

(v) <u>Combining contrastive and translocative meanings</u>: The translocative and the contrastive are positionally incompatible. With expressions that combine contrastive and translocative meanings, the translocative is dropped and a locative particle takes over the function of the missing translocative:

(220) hya tho tha·hé?
    hya   tho   th-aa-h-e-?
    NEG   LOC   CON-OPT-3M.SG.A-walk-PRP
    not   there   he won't be going
    He won't be going there.
            cf. <u>Without the locative particle</u>: hya tha·hé? *He won't be walking*

4.7.6 The Repetitive and the Repeater Clitic

The forms of the repetitive prepronominal prefix are given in Tables 4.46. and 4.47. The repetitive indicates one of two meanings: (i) repetition, either exact replays (i.e., he stood up again) or replays with alterations (she cooked another meal; they rekindled the fire) often expressed in translation with *again* or *another*, or (ii) a return to the default or original state, often expressed in translation with *back*. The repeater clitic may be used together with the repetitive as a method of disambiguation between the *back* and *again* meanings. The repetitive occurs (iii) in number expressions to mark the number *one*. It functions (iv) as a marker of proper names; and (v) it is lexicalized with various verbs.

(i) <u>Replays</u>:

(221) <u>s</u>ayųdegá?da?
    <u>s</u>-a-yų-adeg-a?d-a?
    <u>REP</u>-FACT-3FI.A-burn-CS-PNC
    she rekindled the fire

(222) Hya he? sdę? <u>de?shahá·wi?</u> (CTL44.3-4).
    hya   he?   sdę?   de?-<u>s</u>-ha-hawi-?
    NEG   REP   ASRT   NEG-<u>REP</u>-3M.SG.A-carry-STV
    not   again   something   he didn't carry it
    Again he wasn't carrying anything.

(223) Óyaʔ dųdahátgaʔk[124] (H189.5).
    (Ø)-oya-ʔ   d-ųda-h-atgaʔk-Ø
    3N/Z.SG.A-other-STV   DL-CIS:FACT-3M.SG.A-donate-PNC
    it is different   he donated it
    He contributed another one.

  (ii) <u>Return to the default state</u>:

(224) dęshatga·hadé·niʔ
    d-ę-s-h-at-ga·hadeni-ʔ
    DL-FUT-REP-3M.SG.A-SRF-turn.something.around-PNC
    he will turn back

(225) Hųsahadí·yųʔ tshaʔ ganadá·yęʔ (CTL16.2).
    h-ųsa-hadi-yų-ʔ   tshaʔ   ga-nad-a-yę-ʔ
    TRNS-REP:FACT-3M.PL.A-arrive-PNC   SUB   3N/Z.SG.A-village-JN-lie-STV
    they arrived back there   that   village
    They arrived back at the village.

<u>With the repeater clitic</u>:

The repeater clitic – a recent Onondaga innovation[125] – is attached by speakers to fully inflected repetitive verbs in order to disambiguate the two meanings 'back' and 'again' when both are possible interpretations. The form of the repeater clitic is = ʔé.

(226) a. dųsaháæhdatʔéh
        d-ųsa-h-aæhdat-Ø = ʔé
        DL-REP:FACT-3M.SG.A-run-PNC = REPEATER
        he ran again

                cf. <u>Without the repeater clitic</u>: dųsaháæhdat *he ran back* (or *again*)

     b. dųdahatgáthwaʔéh[126]
        d-ųda-h-atgathw-a(ʔ) = ʔé
        DL-CIS:FACT-3M.SG.A-look-PNC = REPEATER
        he looked again
                cf. <u>Without the repeater clitic</u>: dųdahatgáthwaʔ *he looked back* (or
                again)

---

[124] In this example the dualic is taking over the function of the repetitive because the cislocative and repetitive cannot co-occur (see sec. 4.7.1).

[125] It occurs in contemporary speech, but not in the older texts. Onondaga is the only Northern Iroquoian language with the repeater clitic.

[126] Here the dualic is substituting for the repetitive because the cislocative and the repetitive are positionally incompatible (sections 4.7.1 and 4.7.7).

(iii) <u>In number expressions in the meaning *'one'*:</u>[127]

(227) a. sgahwajíyædah
       s-ga-hwajiR-a-d-ah
       REP-3N/Z.SG.A-family-JN-be.one-STV
       one family

      b. swęhníʔdadah
       s-w-ęhniʔd-a-d-ah
       REP-3N/Z.SG.A-month-JN-be.one-STV
       one month

      c. jyeyáʔdadah
       s-ye-yaʔd-a-d-ah
       REP-3FI.A-body-JN-be.one-STV
       one woman

(iv) <u>Marking a form as a proper name:</u>

(228) a. sgahnehdá·dih
       s-ga-hnehd-adi-h
       REP-3N/Z.SG.A-pine-be.the.other.side-STV
       Albany, New York, Schenectady, NY [literally: on the other side of the pines]

      b. shayaʔdés
       s-ha-yaʔd-es-Ø
       REP-3M.SG.A-body-be.long-STV
       Black Snake [literally: he of the long body]

      c. jyonųdowanęhé·nų́ʔ
       s-yo-nųd-owanę-(h)=he·nų́ʔ
       REP-3N/Z.SG.P-hill-be.large-STV=POP
       Seneca People [literally: people of the large hill]

(v) <u>Other Lexicalizations:</u>

(229) a. ęsgahdę́·dyaʔ
       ę-s-g-ahdędy-aʔ
       FUT-REP-1SG.A-depart-PNC
       I will go home

      b. ętsheihwiyósdę́ʔ
       ę-s-she-Rihw-iyo-sd-ę-ʔ
       FUT-REP-2SG>3-matter-be.good-CS-BEN-PNC
       you will apologize to her

---

[127] It is perhaps notable in this context that *sgá·dah* the number one, begins with *s*.

c. ęshagé·jyę?t
   ę-s-hage-jyę?t-Ø
   FUT-REP-3M.SG > 1.SG-heal.someone-PNC
   he will heal me

d. swak?nigų·hę?ih
   s-wak-?nigų·hę?-ih
   REP-1SG.P-forget-STV
   I have forgotten

4.7.7 The Dualic

The forms of the dualic prepronominal prefix are given in Tables 4.46 and 4.47. More frequently than not, verbs are lexicalized with the dualic. The basic meaning of the dualic is *doubling*. The dualic occurs (i) in counting words when the number is *two*; (ii) in reciprocal constructions; (iii) in verbs implicating two participants or two entities; (iv) in verbs involving doubling or layering; (v) in verbs involving a change of state, a change of position, a change of location or direction, changes in the times of day, and changes in weather conditions; and (vi) in verbs involving comparisons or competitions of various sorts. With some of these verbs the dualic is lexicalized, and with others there is also a form of the verb without the dualic. In addition, (vii), the dualic functions as a replacement for the repetitive when the latter combines with the cislocative.

(i) <u>Counting two entities</u>: When counting objects, a dual pronominal prefix is required.

(230) a. degniya?dagéh
     de-gni-ya?d-a-ge-h'
     DL-3FZ.DU.A-body-JN-amount.to-STV
     two women

   b. degniya?dagé dagós
     de-gni-ya?d-a-ge-h'   dagos
     DL-3FZ.DU.A-body-JN-amount.to-STV   NOUN
     two cats

   c. deyohsi?dagéh
     de-yo-ahsi?d-a-ge-h'
     DL-3N/Z.SG.P-foot-JN-amount.to-STV
     two feet [measure]

   d. degętshe?dagéh
     de-ga-itshę?d-a-ge-h'
     DL-3N/Z.SG.A-bottle-JN-amount.to-STV
     two bottles

   e. dewędagéh
     de-w-ęd-a-ge-h'
     DL-3N/Z.SG.A-day-JN-amount.to-STV
     two days

(ii) <u>The dualic marks a reflexive construction as reciprocal:</u>

The only difference between (231) a and b is the presence of the dualic in the reciprocal construction (section 4.8.4.2).

(231) a. <u>Reciprocal Construction:</u> waʔtgyadátgę?
     waʔ-t̲-gy-adat-gę-ʔ
     FACT-DL-3FZ.DU.A-REF-see-PNC
     they two saw each other, they met up

    b. <u>Reflexive Construction:</u> waʔgyadátgę?
     waʔ-gy-adat-gę-ʔ
     FACT-3FZ.DU.A-REF-see-PNC
     they two saw themselves [mirrored]

(iii) <u>With action verbs implicating two participants, objects, or body parts:</u>

(232) a. deyagodų̱tgó·da?
     de-yago-adų̱tgod-a?
     DL-3FI.P-kneel-STV
     she is kneeling

    b. dehowæt?ę́h
     de-ho-aæt?-ęh'
     DL-3M.SG.P-put.on.shoes-STV
     he is putting on shoes

    c. deyų̱shę́thwas
     de-yų̱-ashę̱thw-as
     DL-3FI.A-cry-HAB
     she is crying

    d. degyadęhnų́·dæ·?
     de-gy-adę-hnų̱dR-a?
     DL-3FZ.DU.A-SRF-follow.behind.something-STV
     they two are sisters

    e. waʔthyadadyená?
     waʔ-t-hy-adad-yena-?'
     FACT-DL-3M.DU.A-REF-grab-PNC
     they wrestled

    f. deya·gyadæ·?negę́h
     de-yagy-ad-Ræ?negę-h'
     DL-1EX.DU.A-SRF-put.together-STV
     we two are sitting next to each other

g. dehodítha·ʔ
   de-hodi-thaR-aʔ
   DL-3M.NSG.P-talk.to.somebody-STV
   they are having a conversation

(iv) <u>With verbs involving layering or doubling</u>:

(233) a. dehathnaʔnétʔas (JB)
     de-h-at-hnaʔnetʔ-as
     DL-3M.SG.A-SRF-double.something-HAB
     he puts on two layers of clothes

   b. deyagóthę·ʔ
     de-yago-at-hę·-ʔ
     DL-3FI.P-SRF-fill.something-STV
     she is full; she is pregnant

   c. dewathwají·yaʔks (JB)
     de-w-at-hwajiR-yaʔk-s
     DL-3N/Z.SG.A-SRF-family-break.off-HAB
     it is hatching

   d. degaędó·daʔ
     de-ga-Ręd-od-aʔ
     DL-3N/Z.SG.A-wood-set.up-STV
     the wood has been stacked

(v) <u>With 'change' verbs</u>: change of state, changes of position, changes of location or direction, bi-directional motion, changes in the times of day, and changes in weather conditions:

(234) a. deyagodųkhwáʔih
     de-yago-dųkhwaʔ-ih
     DL-3FI.P-sweat-STV
     she is sweating

   b. dehaʔnisgwęhdá·haʔ
     de-ha-ʔnisgwęhdaR-haʔ
     DL-3M.SG.A-turn.something.upside.down-HAB
     he turns it upside down

   c. waʔtgų·dí·dęʔ
     waʔ-t-gųdi-dę-ʔ
     FACT-DL-3FZ.PL.A-fly-PNC
     they flew (away)

    d. dehoyaʔdę́·dųs
       de-ho-yaʔd-ędų-s
       DL-3M.SG.P-body-sway-HAB
       he sways, he is staggering

    e. dehatsgáʔthaʔ
       de-h-atsgaʔd-haʔ
       DL-3M.SG.A-chew-HAB
       he's chewing

    e. deyóʔga·s
       de-yo-aʔgaR-as
       DL-3N/Z.SG.P-become.dark-HAB
       it is getting dark

    f. dęwathowǽ·dyeʔ
       de-w-athoR-Ø-adye-ʔ
       DL-3N/Z.SG.A-be.cold.weather-STV-PRG-PRP
       it is getting cold

 (vi) <u>With verbs involving comparisons or competition:</u>

(235) a. dęhayaʔdowehdahę́·ʔ
       d-ę-ha-yaʔdowehd-ahę·-ʔ'
       DL-FUT-3M.SG.A-consider-DST-PNC
       he will think it over, he will meditate on it

    b. waʔtgadeʔnyędę́sdaʔ
       waʔ-d-g-adeʔnędę-sd-ih
       FACT-DL-1SG.A-measure-CS-STV
       I compared it, I copied it

    c. dehonatgę·nyų́h (JB)
       de-hon-at-gęny-ųh'
       DL-3M.NSG.P-SRF-outdo-STV
       they are competing

    d. dehonęnidyohgwagę·nyų́h (JB)
       de-hon-ęn-idyohgw-gęny-ųh
       DL-3M.NSG.P-SRF-group-outdo-STV
       they are voting

 (vii) <u>As a replacement for the repetitive</u>: When repetitive and cislocative meanings combine in a given construction, the dualic replaces the repetitive to express repetitive meanings; this is so, because the repetitive and the cislocative are positionally incompatible (Table 4.48):

(236) a. Oˑ ya naʔ stę́ʔ, dętgųdodyágaʔ náʔ, neʔ agnáʔgaˑʔ (NC02).

oˑ	hya	naʔ	stę́ʔ	d-ę-t-gų-adodyag-aʔ	naʔ
EXC	NEG	ASRT	INDF	DL-FUT-CIS-3FZ.PL.A-grow-PNC	ASRT
oh	not	it's	something	they will grow again	it's

neʔ	ag-naʔgaR-aʔ
NOM	1SG.P-antlers-NSF
the	my antlers

Oh that's nothing, my antlers will grow again.

    b. dųdakhé·yųʔ

d-ųda-khey-ų-ʔ
DL-CIS:FACT-1SG > 3-give-PNC

I handed it back to her

4.7.8 The Negative

The forms of the negative prepronominal prefix are listed in Tables 4.46 and 4.47. The basic negative construction (i) consists of a particle *(h)ya* 'not' preceding a verb with the negative prefix *deʔ-*. The particle and the negative prefix, together, negate the meaning of the clause. As noted above, the negative prefix cannot combine with the partitive, the contrastive, or the coincident, and it cannot combine with modal prefixes. When a past negative meaning is to be expressed, the *(h)ya...deʔ-* frame occurs with a verb inflected with the stative aspect. To express a generic or habitual disinclination to do something (ii) the *(h)ya...deʔ-* frame occurs with a verb inflected with the habitual. When a factual, future, or optative meaning is to be expressed (iii), the contrastive plus optative take the place of the negative with a verb inflected with the punctual aspect. In Onondaga the negative prefix can combine (iv) with the repetitive, the cislocative, and (unlike the other Northern Iroquoian languages) with the dualic and the translocative. Constructions with the negative (or contrastive) prefix occur in indicative (i-iv) and (rarely) interrogative (v) clauses. (The negative imperative requires a different construction and is discussed in section 4.2.1.4.3). In addition, (vi), the negative prepronominal occurs with the verb root -*i*- in a copula-like construction, to negate a nominal.

    (i) <u>The basic construction</u>: The negative particle *(h)ya* together with the negative prefix *deʔ-* expresses clause-negation. The particle either immediately precedes the verb it modifies as in (237), or it occurs at the beginning of a clause separated from the verb by other modifying elements that are, typically, in the scope of the negative, as in (238). The negative prefix occurs only with verbs inflected with the habitual or the stative aspects.

(237) <u>Hya deʔwagęnųhdų́ʔ</u> do hų nigahwisdagé deyagohwisdáųh (LG17).

hya	deʔ-wag-ęnųhdų-ʔ	do	hų	ni-ga-hwisd-a-ge-h'
NEG	NEG-1SG.P-know-STV	INT	MOD	PART-3N/Z.SG.A-money-JN-amount.to-STV
not	I don't know	how	probably	the amount of money it is

de-yago-hwisd-a-ųh
DL-3FI.P-money-take.hold.of-STV
she got money

I don't know how much money she got.

(238) Waʔgaihwísheʔ neʔtho ní·yot <u>hya</u> hwędų́ sdęʔ <u>deʔhá·dųk</u> (CTL44.6).

waʔ-ga-Rihw-ishe-ʔ	neʔtho	niyot	hya	hwędų	sdęʔ
FACT-3N/Z.SG.A-matter-long.time-PNC	MAN	MAN	NEG	INTR	ASRT
it was a long time	thus	how it is	not	when	something

de?-h-adų-k
NEG-3M.SG.A-say-HAB
he doesn't say it
For a long time that's how it is: he never says anything.

   (ii) <u>Negative habitual</u>: The uses range from expressing general disinclinations, to describing negative character traits:

(239) a. hya deʔkhé·thaʔ
          hya deʔ-k-he·t-haʔ
          NEG NEG-1SG.A-smoke-HAB
          I don't smoke

       b. hya deʔha·gwé·nyųs
          hya deʔ-ha-gweny-ųs
          NEG NEG-3M.SG.A-be.able.to.do-HAB
          he can't do it; he is incompetent

       c. <u>Hya gwas deʔhoyoʔdę́hs</u> neʔ hųwáhawah, gaʔt khę́·, hya
          deʔdęhayoʔdę́hse·węʔnhaʔ (LG08).

hya	gwas	deʔ-ho-yoʔd-ęh-s	neʔ	hųwa-hawah	gaʔt khę
NEG	INTS	NEG-3M.SG.P-work-INCH-HAB	NOM	3 > 3M.SG-parent/child	HYP QUE
not	very	he doesn't work	the	her son	maybe

hya	deʔ-d-ę-ha-yoʔd-ęhsR-owęʔ-nhaʔ
NEG	NEG-DL-FUT-3M.SG.A-work-NOM-find-PNC
not	he can't find work

Her son doesn't (like) to work, or he can't find a job.

   (iii) <u>Negative constructions inflected with the punctual</u>. Irrealis (future or optative) meanings are expressed by prefixing the combined contrastive plus optative in place of the negative prefix, as in (240) and (241), respectively.

(240) Hya tha·gi·hwahníhdaʔ.

hya	th-aa-g-Rihw-a-hniR-hd-aʔ
NEG	CON-OPT-1SG.A-matter-JN-sturdy-CS-PNC
not	I won't agree

I won't agree to it

(241) <u>Hya</u> ų̃h <u>thahgwenya?</u> swa?jik dę?gi o?ksde? (H634.1).[128]

hya	ų̃h	thaa-k-gweny-a?	swá?jik	dę?gi	o-?ksdę?-ih
NEG	MOD	OPT-1SG.A-be.able.to.do-PNC	DGR	DGR	3N/Z.SG.P-heavy-STV
not	probably	I can't [do it]	too much	too	it is heavy

I probably can't [do it], it is much too heavy.

    (iv) <u>Other prepronominal prefixes combinations</u>: The negative prepronominal is positionally incompatible with the partitive, the coincident and the contrastive, but it *can* combine with the dualic (242), cislocative (243), translocative (244) and repetitive (245):

(242) <u>Negative and dualic</u>: Hya <u>da?deyago·dá?ih</u> (H156.13).

hya	da?-de-yago-da?-ih
NEG	NEG-DL-3FI.P-stop-STV
not	she did not stop

She did not stop.

(243) <u>Negative and cislocative</u>: Hya sų̃·ga? <u>de?thoyų̃h</u> (CTL178.5).

hya	sų̃ ga·?	de?-t-ho-yų̃-h'
NEG	IND	NEG-CIS-3M.SG.P-arrive-STV
not	somebody	he didn't arrive

No one arrived

(244) <u>Negative and translocative</u>: Hya hwędų̃ <u>the?kheyadwęnų̃da·?séh</u>

hya	hwędų̃	the?-khey-ad-węn-ų̃daR-?se-h'
NEG	INTR	NEG:TRNS-1SG > 3-SRF-voice-put.in-BEN-STV
not	when	I didn't telephone her

I have never telephoned her.

(245) <u>Negative and repetitive</u>: Sahadatgę?é hya <u>de?shona?gáe·da?</u> (NC02).

s-a-h-adat-gę-(?) = ?é	hya	de?-s-ho-na?gaR-od-a?
REP-FACT-3M.SG.A-REF-see-PNC = REP	NEG	NEG-REP-3M.SG.P-antler-stick.up-STV
he saw himself again	not	he didn't have antlers anymore

He saw himself again [i.e., his reflection in the water], he didn't have antlers anymore.

    (v) <u>The negative in interrogative clauses</u>: Constructions taking the negative prefix occur in polar questions (sec. 7.10.1). In polar questions, a question particle *khę* occurs, with a few exceptions, as the second constituent of the clause. In (246) *khę* occurs immediately after the negative particle.

(246) <u>Hya khę sdę? de?sé·he?,</u> dyę gwa?, tho ó? na? ayų̃·nų̃hwét ne? Clyde, tsha? nų̃ dyų̃gnidá?kstha?... (NC01)

hya	khę	sdę?	de?-s-eR-he?	dyę gwa?
NEG	QUE	INDF	NEG-2SG.A-think-want-HAB	HYP RSTR
not	question	something	you don't think	if

---

[128] Hewitt did not mark stress and vowel length in this excerpt.

tho	oʔ	naʔ	aa-yų-ęnųhwet-Ø		neʔ	Clyde	tshaʔ	nų
LOC	ADD	ASRT	OPT-3FI.A-spend.the.night-PNC		NOM	NAME	SUB	LO
there	also	it's	one can spend the night		the	Clyde	that	place

d-yųgn-idaʔk-st-haʔ
CIS-1DU.P-sleep-use-HAB
we use it to sleep there = bedroom
Do you mind if Clyde would spend the night in our bedroom? [Literally: you don't think anything of it, do you, if Clyde would spend the night in our bedroom?]

(vi) <u>Negating a nominal</u>: To negate a nominal the negative particle *hya* and the verb form *déʔgęh* are used. The verb form consists of the stative verb *-i-* 'be the total of, be all of it, be the only' prefixed with the negative prepronominal *deʔ-* as in (247a) and (248). Just like any other negativized verb, the verb form is preceded by *hya*, the negative particle, and note that the negated nominal must occur within the *hya ... deʔ-* frame. Example (247b) changes the polarity of (247a):

(247) a. <u>Hya</u> naʔ dagós <u>déʔgęh</u>.

hya	naʔ	dagos	deʔ-gę-i-h
NEG	ASRT	NOUN	NEG-3N/Z.SG.A-be.the.total.of-STV
not	it's	cat	it isn't

It isn't a cat

    b. naʔ nę́·gę dagós.

naʔ	nęgę	dagos
ASRT	DEM	NOUN
it's	this	cat

This [is] a cat.

(248) <u>Hya</u> naʔ ų́gwe <u>déʔgę́ʔ</u> sgęhnáksę sawá·dųʔ (H635.17-18).

hya	naʔ	(y)-ųgweh	deʔ-ga-i-ʔ		sgęhnáksę
NEG	ASRT	NPF-person:SUFF	NEG-3N/Z.SG.A-be.the.total.of-STV		NOUN
not	it's	person	it isn't		fox

s-a-w-adų-ʔ
REP-FACT-3N/Z.SG.A-become-PNC
it became again
It is not a human, it has become a fox again

4.8 The Verb Stem

4.8.1 Stems and Stem Derivation

Table 4.49 (repeat of Table 4.1) shows the position of the verb stem within the verb as a whole and how its components line up from left to right. The verb root, the only obligatory element of the stem, can form a stem by itself or it can combine with any one or more of the morphemes in the three other positions internal to the stem. Complex stems are, typically, hierarchically organized, deriving verb stems from verb stems by means of layered derivations. Combining a verb root with a noun root affects the lexical content of the stem; combinations with the reflexives and several of the root suffixes affect the number of the stem's semantic arguments. Other root suffixes have diverse functions that are detailed in the following sections. But as a whole the components of the verb stem function to create the verbal lexicon of the Onondaga language. The verb stem as a whole is subject to the verb's inflectional morphology.

Table 4.49 The verb stem position within the fully expanded verb

Inflect./Deriv.	Inflectional	Derivational	Lexical		Derivational	Inflectional	
Prepronominal and Modal Prefixes	Pronominal Prefixes	Reflexives	Noun Root or Stem	Verb Root	Root Suffixes	Basic Aspect Suffixes	Expanded Aspect Suffixes
			Verb Stem				

Some of the stems that are the result of combining the verb root with derivational suffixes have become lexicalized, others have not. Recall that the concept of lexicalization is used here to describe any combination of morphemes that is either semantically or morphologically non-compositional, such that its combined form or meaning cannot be predicted from the parts of which it is composed.

4.8.2 The Verb Root

The verb root position is filled by an obligatory verbal element, consisting either of a simple verb root or a lexicalized verbal element that gives signs of being more complex but which is no longer analyzable into its component morphemes.

(249) <u>Verb stems consisting of a simple verb root:</u>
    a. agí·daʔks
        ag-<u>idaʔk</u>-s
        1SG.P-sleep-HAB
        I am sleepy

    b. ęhá·yek
        ę-ha-<u>yek</u>-Ø
        FUT-3M.SG.A-wake.up-PNC
        he will wake up

(250) <u>Verb stems consisting of a lexicalized expression:</u>
    a. waʔkhne·gíhæʔ
        waʔ-k-<u>hnegihR</u>[129]-aʔ
        FACT-1.SG.A-drink-PNC
        I drank (it)

---

[129] The stem probably contains the noun root -*hneg*- 'liquid'.

b. eksaʔgó·nah
   e-ksaʔgona[130]-h
   3FI.A-be.pretty-STV
   she is pretty

4.8.2.1 Verb Root Alternations

Apart from their phonological variants, most verb roots occur in the same form in different morphological contexts. But a number of roots have alternating forms, depending on the basic aspect inflection with which they occur. Some of these are suppletive, that is, their forms are phonologically unrelated, others share some phonology. An example of a set of suppletive verb root alternants is *-adǫ-/-ę-/-ihę·-* 'say' where *-adǫ-* is selected by the habitual aspect, *-ę-* by the stative aspect, and *-ihę·* by the punctual aspect:

(251) a. iga·dǫk
         i-g-adǫ-k
         EP-1SG.A-say-HAB
         I say, I'm saying

      b. naʔ agę́h
         naʔ ag-ę-h'
         ASRT 1SG.P-say-STV
         that's what I've said

      c. waʔgihę́·ʔ
         waʔ-g-ihę·-ʔ'
         FACT-1SG.A-say-PNC
         I said (it)

An example of a set of phonologically related verb root alternants is *-atgaʔk-/-atgaʔ-/-atgaʔw-* 'let go of' which, are selected by the habitual, the stative, and the punctual aspects, respectively. A set of alternants that is partly suppletive and partly phonologically related is *-adęhǫgaR-/-ade·hw-/-ade·hg-* 'invite, act as host'.

Table 4.50 lists verb stems whose alternants vary with the three basic aspect inflectional categories:

Table 4.50 Verb root alternations conditioned by the basic aspects

Habitual	Stative	Punctual	Gloss
-a-	-awi-	-(y)ǫ-	*give to*
-adaʔae·R-	-adaʔae·R-	-adaʔaehg-	*wear a veil*
-adaʔgwahę·-	-adaʔgwahę·-	-adaʔgwahę·g-	*put on a belt*
.adats?- +dualic	.adatsha?- +dualic	.adats?- +dualic	*argue, quarrel*
-ade·t-	-ade·hw-	-ade·hg-	*assemble, gather together*
-adęhǫgaR-	-ade·hw-	-ade·hg-	*invite, act as host*

---

[130] The stem probably contains the noun root *-ksaʔ-* 'child'.

Table 4.50 (Continued)

Habitual	Stative	Punctual	Gloss
-ade?hoR-/-at-N-oR-[131]	-ade?hoR-/-at-N-oR-	-ade?ho·hg-/-at-N-o·hg-	*cover up, get covered*
.adę?ts?- +dualic	.adę?tsha?- +dualic	.adę?ts?- +dualic	*earn*
-adody-	-adody-	-adodyag-	*grow, grow up*
-adų-	-ę-	-ihę·-	*say*
-adųgwet-	-adųgwe-	-adųgwe-	*feel healthy, recover*
-ahdųwek-	-ahdųwe-	-ahdųwek-	*dive*
.adyę·- +contrastive	.adyę·- +contrastive	.adyR-/.adyehR-[132] +contrastive	*become quiet*
-ahdędyų-/ -at-N-ahdędyų-[133]	-ahdędyų-/ -at-N-ahdędyų-	-ahdędy-/ -at-N-ahdędy-	*leave, depart*
-ahsa·-/-ahsaų-[134]	-ahsaw-	-ahsaw-	*begin, start*
-akdų-	-akdų-	-akd-	*visit, drop in*
-asdest-	-asdest-	-asdesg-	*evaporate*
-atga?k-	-atga?-	-atga?w-	*let go of, leave*
-athahit?-	-athahida?-	-athahit?-	*take to the road.*
-athoR-	-athoR-	-athowæsg-	*feel cold, be cold*
-atho·y-	-athowi-	-atho·y-	*tell*
-Ret-	-Rehw-	-Rehg-	*gather, collect*
-ęnihdyę-	-ęnihdyę-	-ęnihdyag-	*put around one's neck*
-ę?daR-	-ę?da·w-	-ę?daR-	*burn something*
.ę?nhe- +dualic	.ę?nhe- +dualic	.ę?nhegw- +dualic	*play ball, play baseball.*
.gęnyų- +dualic	.gęnyų- +dualic	.gęny- +dualic	*beat, outdo*
-hga·k-/-ga·k-[135]	-hgae?-/-gae?-	-hgaehR-/-gaehR-	*make a noise, make a sound*
-hnegiR-	-hnegihR-	-hnegihR-	*drink*
-hse·-	-hsR-	-hse·-[136]	*chase, follow*
-hsi-	--	-hsihw-	*get hungry*
-iheyų-	-iheyų-	-ihey-	*die*
-ida?k-	-ida?w-	-ida?-	*sleep, be sleepy*
-N-ine-[137]	-N-i-	-N-in-	*lead somewhere*
-nų?-	-nųhn-	-nų?-	*stand guard*
-ody-	-ody-	-odyag-	*raise a child*

The verb roots listed in Table 4.51 alternate according to basic and expanded aspects (section 4.6) and selected root suffixes, e.g., *-i?dę-/-i?dęd-* 'live, reside', where the first alternant occurs with the basic aspects, and the second with expanded aspects.

---

[131] The second alternants of this set occur with incorporation. Capital N indicates that the stem requires an incorporated noun.

[132] Alternation is due to speaker variation.

[133] The second alternants of this set occur obligatorily with incorporation.

[134] Alternation is due to speaker variation.

[135] The second alternants of this set occur optionally with incorporation.

[136] This alternant is also selected by the purposive aspect.

[137] Capital N indicates that the stem must incorporate a noun.

Table 4.51 Verb root alternations conditioned by the expanded aspects

Basic Aspects	Expanded Aspects	*Gloss*
-ahdyawæ-	-ahdyawæ·d-	*be forbidden*
-ahgwishę-	-ahgwishęd-	*try hard*
-gehę·-	-gehęd-	*lay something down, set something down*
-hashę-	-hashęd-	*counsel, have a council*
-i?dę·-	-i?dę·d-	*live, reside, be in place*
-yę-	-yęd-	*put down, lay down, have*

(252) a. Tho nę gí?dę?.

    tho   nę   g-i?dę-?
    LOC   PRES 1SG.A-live-STV
    there here I reside
    I live here.

  b. ...tsha? nų· ęgi?dę́·dak.

    tsha?   nų   ę-g-i?dęd-a(h)-k-Ø
    SUB   LOC   FUT-1SG.A-live-STV-CNT-PNC
    that   place I will be residing
    where I will be living, where I will be staying.

Numerous other verb roots with alternating forms depending on whether or not they combine with noun roots divide into two formally distinct groups. One group has alternants such that the non-incorporating alternant has an initial increment that is lacking in the incorporating alternant. The other group is either suppletive in relation to incorporation or there are numerous differences between two phonologically related alternants. An example of the first kind is *.ahdoha·k-* / *.oha·k-* + dualic 'squeeze, squash, pin down' in which the non-incorporating alternant contains the initial sequence *ahd* lacking in the incorporating alternant:

(253) a. wa?tgahdohá·k

    wa?-t-g-<u>ahdoha·k</u>-Ø
    FACT-DL-1SG.A-squeeze-PNC
    I squeezed it

  b. wa?tsge?nyohá·k

    wa?-t-sge-?ny-<u>oha·k</u>-Ø
    FACT-DL-2SG > 1SG-hand-squeeze-PNC
    you squeezed my hand

Following Lounsbury (1953:75), Iroquoianists usually analyze these verbs as *requiring* incorporation, and treat the initial increments as *empty* morphs that represent a missing noun root. They are listed in this section because the extra increments are unable to occur as independent nominals and therefore cannot be regarded as true incorporated nouns by our definition (section 4.8.3). Table 4.52 lists incorporation-dependent alternations with initial increments. Similarities can be recognized in the alphabetized table:

Table 4.52 Verb root alternations conditioned by noun incorporation (1)

Non-incorporating Alternant	Incorporating Alternant	Gloss
-Rægew-	-gew-	*wipe*
.Ræʔnegar- + dualic -	.ʔnegar- + dualic	*burst something*
.Ræʔnegę- + dualic	.negę- + dualic	*lay side by side, put together*
-Ræʔnędak-	-nędag-	*stick to*
-adagwęhd-	-gwęhd-	*be wide*
.adagwęhdę- + dualic	.gwęhdę- + dualic	*flatten, get flattened*
.ahdoha·k- + dualic	.oha·k- + dualic	*squeeze, squash, pin down*
-ahgasd-	-gasd-	*be tough*
-aʔdaih-	-daih-	*be hot*
-aʔsęhd-	-ęhd-	*push down, drop something*
-aʔshędaʔ-	-ędaʔ-	*finish, conclude, complete*
-dagwa·s-	-gwa·s-	*bruise something*
-dagwaihcy-	-gwaihcy-	*straighten, align, enlighten*
.dagwaihd- + dualic	.gwaihd- + dualic	*open fully*
-ek-	-k-	*eat*
-ęnih-	-nih-	*borrow*
-ęno·yęʔ-	-no·yęʔ-	*be a lie*
-gowanę-	-owanę-	*be large, be great*
-ha·dat-	-dat-	*lift up, raise up*
-hęʔdų-	-ęʔdų-	*dangle, hang from*
.hnaʔnetʔ-/.hnaʔned- + dualic[138]	.netʔ-/.ned- + dualic	*double something*
-hnyot-	-ot-	*stand upright, protrude, have*
.hsaʔkdų- + dualic	.aʔkdų- + dualic	*bend something*
-hųʔji-	-ji-	*be black, be dark in color*
.hwadahse- + dualic	.dahse- + dualic.	*make something go around, twist around*
.hwahnh- + dualic	.hnh- + dualic	*form a circle*
-hwaʔe-/-hwaʔegw-[139]	-ʔe-/-ʔegw-	*bat , strike, hit*
-naʔnawę-	-nawę-	*melt, be damp, be wet*
-naʔno-	-no-	*be cold to the touch*
-ųnishe-	-ishe-	*take a long time, be a long time*
.yahyaʔk- + dualic	.iyaʔk- + dualic	*cross over*
.yaʔshr- + dualic	.aʔshr- + dualic	*layer something, double over, put on top of*
-ʔhor-/-ʔho·hg-[140]	-or-/-o·hg-	*cover something*
-ʔnhyenęʔ-/-ʔhyenęʔ-[141]	-yenęʔ-	*fall over*
-ʔsgoʔ-	-oʔ-	*drown, fall into the water*

---

[138] The first alternants in this set are selected by the habitual and the punctual aspects, the second by the stative.

[139] The first alternants in this set are selected by the habitual and the stative aspects, the second by the punctual.

[140] The first alternants in this set are selected by the habitual and the stative aspects, the second by the punctual.

[141] The first non-incorporating alternant is used by Six Nations speakers, the second by Onondaga Nation speakers.

The second group of incorporation-dependent verb root alternations are characterized by a variety of phonological relationships, for example, an added initial segment in the incorporating alternant as in *-jyęhd-/-ojyęhd-* 'dip a liquid', or *-idę·t-/-nidę·t-* 'be poor, be pitiful', or suppletive alternants as in *.ahsęnų-/.hę-* +coincident and dualic 'be in the middle, be between', etc. Table 4.53 lists incorporation-dependent alternations with these characteristics:

Table 4.53 Verb root alternations conditioned by noun incorporation (2)

Non-incorporating Alternant	Incorporating Alternant	*Gloss*
-R-	-aR-	*put in, incorporate*
-R-	-aR-	*apply, put on*
.Ræhwęd- +dualic	.?gwęd- +dualic	*be an opening, be a space*
.ady- +cislocative or translocative	.ųdy- +cislocative or translocative	*throw*
-ady(e)-(deriv)	-ųdy(e)-	*abandon, throw*
.ahsęnų- +coincident and dualic	.hę- +coincident and dualic	*be in the middle, be between.*
-ehsak-	-ihsak-	*look for, search, be lonely for*
.haų-/.hw-[142] +cislocative or translocative	.ęhaų-/.ęhw- +cislocative or translocative	*bring, take*
-hw-	-ęhw-	*hold, have possession of*
-hawi-	-ęhawi-	*carry in one's hands or arms, have along, accompany*
-ha?t-	-tha?d-	*dry something out, dry something off*
-Rhę-	-thę-	*be dry, be desiccated.*
-hs?-/-hsa?-	-ihs?-/-ihsa?	*finish, eat up, use up*
-hwe?nųny-	-gwe?nųny-	*wrap, bundle, combine*
-(i)dye-	-ųdye-.	*propel in water or air, fly*
-idę·t-	-nidę·t-	*be poor, be pitiful, be a pity*
-jyęhd-	-ojyęhd-	*dip a liquid*
-ųs-	-es-/-is-[143]	*be long*
-ya?k-	-iya?k-	*break or cut something off*
-yų-	-inyų-	*arrive, enter*
-?se·-/-?sR-[144]	-i?se·-/-i?sR-	*drag, ride in a vehicle*

Several of the verb root alternations listed in the two tables are conditioned by both incorporation and aspect selection. An example is the verb root *-?hoR- / -?ho·hg- / -oR- / -o·hg-* 'cover something': the alternants *-oR- / -o·hg-* occur with optionally incorporated nouns, *-?hoR- / -oR-* occur with the habitual and stative aspects, and *-?ho·hg- / -o·hg-* occur with the punctual aspect.

---

[142] The first alternants in this set are selected by the habitual and the stative aspects, the second by the punctual.

[143] The incorporating alternants are lexically selected by the incorporated noun root.

[144] The first alternants in this set are selected by the purposive, the habitual, and the punctual aspects, the second alternants are selected by the stative aspect.

(254) a. waʔeʔhó·hgaʔ
    waʔ-e-ʔho·hg-aʔ
    FACT-3FI.A-cover-PNC
    she covered it

    b. waʔkhehnaʔtshó·hgaʔ
      waʔ-khe-hnaʔtsh-ohg-aʔ
      FACT-1SG>3-buttock-cover-PNC
      I put pants on her.

    c. geʔhó·s
      ge-ʔhoR-s
      1SG.A-cover-HAB
      I cover [things]

    d. khenųhe·s
      khe-nųhR-oR-s
      1SG>3-scalp-cover-HAB
      I am putting on her hat. Literally: I am covering her scalp

4.8.3 The Incorporated Noun

4.8.3.1 The Noun Position

Table 4.54 The noun position

Inflect./Deriv.	Inflectional	Derivational	Lexical		Derivational	Inflectional	
Prepronominal and Modal Prefixes	Pronominal Prefixes	Reflexives	Noun Root or Stem	Verb Root	Root Suffixes	Basic Aspect Suffixes	Expanded Aspect Suffixes
		Verb Stem					

The noun position is immediately to the left of the verb root. The position is filled by a *noun stem* consisting of (i) a noun root, or (ii) a verb root plus nominalizer morpheme. The nominalizer alternants are: *-hsR- / -tshR- / -ʔtshR- / -ʔshR-, -ʔt-*. The distribution of the alternants is lexicalized and in addition there is some speaker variation. When a noun stem ending in a consonant is combined with a verb stem beginning in a consonant, the stem-joiner *a* occurs between the two morphemes.

(255) <u>Verb root combined with a noun root in the three basic aspects:</u>
    a. gnę́haks
      g-nęh-a-k-s
      1SG.A-corn-JN-eat-HAB
      I eat corn

    b. agnęhá·gih
      ag-nęh-a-g-ih
      1SG.P-corn-JN-eat-STV
      I am eating corn

   c. wa?gnẹhák
      wa?-g-nẹh-a-k-Ø´
      FACT-1SG.A-corn-JN-eat-PNC
      I ate corn

(256) <u>Verb root combined with a derived noun stem:</u>
   a. gadẹna?tshæhní·nựk
      g-adẹna?t-shR-a-hninự-k
      1SG.A-<u>take.provisions</u>-NOM-JN-buy-HAB
      I'm buying groceries

   b. wa?agathowæhsí·nyự?s
      wa?-ag-<u>athowæ</u>-hsR-inyự-?s-Ø
      FACT-1SG.P-<u>feel.cold</u>-NOM-enter-BEN-PNC
      I caught a cold

In addition to incorporation of the type shown in (255) and (256), there are examples –
they are far less frequent – in which much more complex sequences that themselves
contain a noun-verb combination occur in either the noun position with and without a
nominalizer morpheme as in (257) or in the verb position as in (258).

(257) <u>Verb root combined with a complex noun stem:</u>
      ẹgnẹhohgự·nya?
      ẹ-g-<u>nẹh</u>-o-hgw-ựny-a?
      FUT-1SG.A-<u>corn-put.in.liquid</u>-INST-make-PNC
      I will make corn soup
              cf. onẹhóhgwa? *corn soup*

In (257) the verb stem *-nẹhohgựny-* consists of one noun root, two verb roots, and an
instrumental suffix. But this is a layered derivation: the inner layer consists of a verb
stem *-nẹhohgw-* which combines the verb stem *-o-hgw-* 'use something to put into liquid'
with the noun root *-nẹh-* 'corn', giving the complex noun stem *-nẹhohgw-*, 'corn soup', and
the second layer consists of combining the first layer with the verb root *-ựny-* 'make
something'.

(258) <u>Complex verb stem combined with a noun root</u>
      niyo?gæ·hnodés (LG12)
      ni-yo-<u>a?gR</u>-hnod-es-Ø
      PRT-3N/Z.SG.P-<u>snow</u>-depth.of.a.substance-be.long-STV
      how deep the snow is
              cf. ohnó·des *(it is) deep water*

The verb stem in (258) consists of two noun roots and one verb root; the sequence of the
layering is as follows: (i) the noun root *-hnod-* 'depth of a substance' is combined with the
verb root *-es-* 'be long', forming a complex verb stem, which subsequently (ii) combines
with the noun root *-a?gR-* 'snow'. Examples like *ẹgnẹhohgự·nya?* and *niyo?gæ·hnodés*
clearly illustrate the often hierarchical organization of derived verb stems in this language.

When speakers combine a verb root with a loan word, they mark the nominal element as a loan by attaching a nominalizer:

(259) <u>Verb root combined with a loan word and a nominalizer:</u>
    a. sadiʔtshǽ·yęʔ   khę
       sa-<u>di</u>-ʔtshR-a-yę-ʔ   QUE
       2SG.P-tea-NOM-JN-have-STV   QUESTION
       Do you have tea?

    b. waʔhatshoda·ʔtshę́·nyaʔ (JB)
       waʔ-h-at-<u>shoda</u>-ʔtshR-ųny-aʔ
       FACT-3M.SG.A-SRF-soldier-NOM-make-PNC
       he enlisted [literally: he made himself a soldier]

4.8.3.2 The Process of Noun Incorporation

The process of combining nouns with verbs is referred to as *noun incorporation* (see Sapir 1911 for an early work, and Woodbury (1975), Mithun (1984), and Michelson (2011), as sources dealing extensively with how the process plays out in the Iroquoian languages).[145] Noun incorporation is a derivational process that derives a new, more complex verb stem from a source verb. Sapir's dictum that to count as noun incorporation a noun that occurs as a part of the verb stem must also be able to occur as an independent entity expression outside of a verb, is widely accepted in this and other contemporary studies. The two examples below show a verb with an incorporated noun (260a), and the same verb with the same noun as an independent entity (260b).

(260) a. waʔgnęhayę́thwaʔ
       waʔ-g-<u>nęh</u>-a-yęthw-aʔ
       FACT-1.SG.A-<u>corn</u>-JN-plant-PNC
       I planted corn; I corn-planted

---

[145] Sapir (1911) compares noun incorporation in numerous Native American languages arguing (against Kroeber 1909) that noun incorporation is a syntactic process; Woodbury (1975) – a Ph.D. dissertation – is a study of the grammatical and semantic functions of the different types of noun incorporation in Onondaga. Mithun (1984), comparing the process in several North American languages – posits four largely functional stages of noun incorporation's development. She argues that in the first stage, the incorporated noun loses its nominal status and functions solely to qualify the incorporating verb's meaning to express institutionalized activities. In the second stage noun incorporation impacts the clause's case-role structure. In the third stage noun incorporation impacts information structure in that speakers signal new or more salient information with independent nouns, using incorporation to background old or less salient information. The fourth stage – exemplified by the Iroquoian languages – is classificatory incorporation, in which an independent noun, which co-occurs in addition to the incorporated noun, functions at the discourse level in much the same way as the independent noun does at stage three. She argues that the four stages form an implicational hierarchy, such that a language that displays any one of the advanced stages, will also display each earlier stage. Michelson (2011) describes the current status of noun incorporation in Oneida. She investigates ways of assessing the semantic-syntactic consequence of independently occurring and incorporated nouns and concludes that where permitted, noun incorporation is the norm and independently occurring nouns "are used for contrast or when they are particularly salient (p.8)."

b. wa?gyęthwá? ne? onę́ha?
   wa?-g-yęthw-a?   ne?   o-nę̨h-a?
   FACT-1.SG.A-plant-PNC   NOM   NPF-corn-NSF
   I planted corn

Comparison of the two examples reveals several properties of noun incorporation: (i) As pointed out, it is the noun *root* or *stem* without inflectional affixes that is incorporated; (ii) A verb with an incorporated noun retains its morphological integrity as a verb in that incorporation affects neither the aspectual status of the stem nor, with just one exception (section 4.4.3.4), does it affect the selection of pronominal prefix categories, which in both cases is determined by the verb. And note that the dyadic verb *-yęthw-* takes the same intransitive agent prefix in both examples – intransitive because, non-animates are not referenced by the pronominal prefix when the other argument is animate. There is no real semantic difference between the two examples; the incorporated noun (260a) perhaps narrows the meaning of the verb much as that happens in English gerund clauses like *deer-hunting is my favorite activity*, that is to say, deer-hunting is a kind of hunting that is confined to a special class of animal, whereas the external noun simply further specifies the meaning of the pronominal prefix and some speakers say that when an external noun occurs the speaker has a specific entity in mind. So that there is a subtle difference in discourse properties between the (a) and (b) examples: (a) might be uttered by a speaker who is focusing on describing an activity; (b) might be uttered by a speaker who is focusing on or identifying the object that is affected by the activity or of marking it as especially salient.

4.8.3.3 Eligible Noun-Verb Combinations

Semantic roles of nouns that are eligible for incorporation are *patient, theme, factitive theme, location, path, and instrument*, although the most frequent incorporations are of *patient* and *theme* arguments. The only ineligible roles appear to be those of agent, beneficiary, source and goal:

Incorporation into active verbs:

(261) Patient Incorporation: wa?eksoháe?
   wa?-e-ks-ohae-?'
   FACT-3FI.A-dish-wash-PNC
   she washed dishes; she dish-washed

(262) Theme Incorporation: wa?hanehsohní·nų?
   wa?-ha-nehso-hninų-?
   FACT-3M.SG.A-cabbage-buy-PNC
   he bought cabbage; he cabbage-bought

(263) Factitive Theme Incorporation: wa?khæ·hgų́nya?
   wa?-g-hæ·hgw-ųny-a?
   FACT-1.SG.A-bread-make-PNC
   I made bread; I bread-made

(264) <u>Path Incorporation</u>: waʔtha·hí·yaʔk
    waʔ-t-ha-hR-iyaʔk-Ø
    FACT-DL-3M.SG.A-forest-go.across-PNC
    he crossed the forest; he forest-crossed

(265) <u>Instrument Incorporation</u>: waʔthashegwa·ʔésdaʔ
    waʔ-t-ha-shegwaR-ʔe-sd-aʔ
    FACT-DL-3M.SG.A-spear-strike-CS-PNC
    he poked it with a spear, he speared it

(266) <u>Location Incorporation</u>: honathahidákheʔ
    hon-at-hah-idakhe-ʔ
    3M.NSG.P-SRF-path-run-PRP
    they are running on a path

Incorporation occurs with active, stative, as well as motion verbs. In the corpus, 19% of active verbs, 23% of stative verbs, and 10% of motion verbs are attested in constructions with incorporated nouns. It is likely that the actual incidence is much higher. Active monadic verbs are ineligible for incorporation because of the ban on agent incorporation. Other constraints are mainly lexical.

<u>Incorporation into stative verbs</u>:

(267) a. gaæhgwahséʔ
      ga-Ræhgw-ahse-ʔʼ
      3N/Z.SG.A-sun,moon-be.new-STV
      (it is a) new moon

    b. dyotshęʔdagé·dat
      d-yo-itshęʔd-a-gedat-Ø
      CIS-3N/Z.SG.P-fly-JN-be.annoying-STV
      (it is a) pesky fly

Certain stative verbs require incorporation, for example, counting expressions (sec. 4.8.3.7 below) and certain stative verbs with positional, property, and situational meanings.

<u>Obligatory incorporation into selected statives with positional, property, or situational meanings</u>:

(268) a. waʔę·ná·deʔ
      w-aʔęn-ade-ʔ
      3N/Z.SG.A-pole-be.in.a.suspended.position-STV
      (it is a) suspended pole

    b. ohæ·hgwagáʔdeʔ
      o-hæ·hgw-a-gaʔd-eʔ
      3N/Z.SG.P-bread-JN-be.plentiful-STV
      it's lots of bread

    c. nigaęnoʔdę́h
      ni-ga-Ręn-oʔdę-h'
      PRT-3N/Z.SG.A-song-be.a.kind-STV
      the kind of song it is

Motion verbs that incorporate:

(269) a. owihsoʔgǽ·dyeʔ
      o-wihs-oʔgR-adye-ʔ
      3N/Z.SG.P-ice-float-PRG-PRP
      there is ice floating along in the water

    b. ejyųʔdahni·nų́he·ʔ
      e-ijyųʔd-a-hninų-hR-eʔ
      3FI.A-fish-JN-buy-DSLC-PRP
      she's here to buy fish

Noun incorporation is, for the most part, independent of other derivational processes in the sense that both simple and derived verb stems are able to incorporate.[146]

Incorporation into derived verb stems:

(270) a. <u>Verb stem derived with the semireflexive:</u> odę·ga·yáʔgih
      o-<u>ad</u>-RęgaR-yaʔk-ih
      3N/Z.SG.P-SRF-branch-break.off-STV
      the branch has broken off
          cf. Without the noun: deyo·dyáʔgih *it is broken, it has broken off*

    b. <u>Verb stem derived with the causative:</u> waʔhaʔnųdahní·hdaʔ
      waʔ-ha-ʔnųd-a-hniR-<u>hd</u>-aʔ
      FACT-3M.SG.A-leg-JN-be.sturdy-CS-PNC
      he braced his leg
          cf. Without the noun: waʔhahní·hdaʔ *he tightened it, he tamped it down*

    c. <u>Verb stem derived with the benefactive:</u> waʔkhekhwahní·nųʔs
      waʔ-khe-khw-a-hninų-<u>ʔs</u>-Ø
      FACT-1SG > 3-food-JN-buy-BEN-PNC
      I bought food for them
          cf. Without the noun: waʔkhehní·nųʔs *I bought it for them*

    d. <u>Verb stem derived with the distributive:</u> gaʔwahæ·niyų́·dųʔ (H162.10)
      ga-ʔwahR-a-niyųd-<u>u</u>-ʔ
      3N/Z.SG.A-meat-JN-hang-DST-STV
      pieces of meat are hanging [from it]
          cf. Without the noun: ganiyų́·dųʔ *it is hanging [from it], hanging objects*

---

[146] Exceptions are derivational affixes whose presence together with an incorporated noun lexicalize the derived stem, often the instrumental suffix, and, not infrequently, the semireflexive.

4.8.3.4 Classificatory Incorporation

A special kind of noun incorporation has been referred to as *classificatory incorporation* (Chafe 1970, Woodbury 1975, Mithun 1984).[147] It forms a clause that consists of a verb that includes an incorporated noun in addition to an external nominal that refers, without redundancy, to the same entity as the incorporated noun. The difference between the incorporated and the external occurrence is that the external nominal refers more specifically than does the incorporated one. The verb and the external nominal can occur in either order as shown in examples (271) and (272), although the verb far more frequently occurs to the left of the external nominal.

(271) Naʔ yágęʔ nęgę hę́·gweh <u>honasgwayę́ʔ</u> <u>ji·há</u> hyá yagęʔ gwás deʔhanasgwanų́hweʔs (HW05).

naʔ	yagęʔ	nęgę	hR-ųgweh	ho-<u>nasgw</u>-a-yę-ʔ	ji·hah	hya
ASRT	HRSY	DEM	3M.SG.A-person:SUFF	3M.SG.P-pet-JN-have-STV	NOUN	NEG
it's	they say	this	man	he has a pet	dog	not

yagęʔ	gwas	deʔ-ha-nasgw-a-nųhweʔ-s
HRSY	INTNS	NEG-3M.SG.A-pet-JN-like-HAB
they say	very	he doesn't like pet

They say this man <u>had a pet dog</u>, [and] they say he doesn't much like the pet.

(272) Dyęhaʔ gwaʔ <u>otgwę́hsaʔ</u> ętgahne·gó·dęʔ ęsné·æʔ ųgwa·dæ·ʔshwahetgę́hdęʔ (CTL51.5).

dyęhaʔ	gwaʔ	o-<u>tgwęhs</u>-aʔ	ę-t-ga-<u>hneg</u>-od-ęʔ	ę-sn-eR-aʔ
HYP	RSTR	NPF-blood-NSF	FUT-CIS-3N/Z.SG.A-liquid-protrude-PNC	FUT-2DU-think-PNC
if	blood	liquid will flow	you two will think

waʔ-wag-adæ·ʔshw-ahetgę-hd-ę-ʔ
FACT-1SG.P-luck-be.bad-CS-BEN-PNC
it has caused me bad luck

If <u>blood flows</u> [from the notched tree] you two will conclude that I have had bad luck.

The external, more specific, nominal of classificatory incorporations can involve any word or phrase that functions as a referring expression. In (273) the independent nominal *agathųwihsáʔi* 'I finished [making] a boat' is morphologically a verb that functions semantically in the same way as morphological nominals. Note that the classificatory noun and the independent nominal as a whole refer to the same entity:[148]

(273) ... tho hędwéʔ tshaʔ nų́· tgahųwá·yęʔ <u>agathųwihsáʔih</u> (CTL53.5-7).

tho	h-ę-dw-e-ʔ	tshaʔ	nų	t-ga-<u>hųw</u>-a-yę-ʔ
LOC	TRNS-FUT-1EX.PL.A-walk-PNC	SUB	LOC	CIS-3N/Z.SG.A-boat-JN-lay.down-STV
there	we will go there	that	place	the boat was placed there

---

[147] This is Mithun's stage 4 noun incorporation (see sec. 4.8.3.2, fn145).

[148] Constructions like this function much like relative clauses do.

<u>ag-at-hųw-ihsaʔ-ih</u>
1SG.P-SRF-boat-finish-STV
the boat I have finished [making]
We will go to the place where <u>the boat I finished making was placed</u>.

4.8.3.5 Productivity and Lexicalization

That noun incorporation is often a productive process is perhaps most clearly demonstrated by the fact that speakers to this day incorporate loan words (259a and b above). The process is used freely to create words as needed (Mithun's stage 1, see section 4.8.3.2, fn.145), some just for the present moment, and some for posterity, the latter eventually gaining currency among speakers and becoming lexicalized in one way or another, as activities or names of objects as in (274) and (275):

(274) <u>Activities</u>:
    a. godnęnohgwadaiháʔdih
       go-ad-nęnohgw-a-daihaʔd-ih
       3FI.P-SRF-potato-JN-heat-STV
       she is heating [herself] potatoes

    b. heyų·dwęnų́·da·s
       he-yų-ad-węn-ųdaR-s
       TRNS-3FI.A-SRF-word-put.in-HAB
       she is telephoning

(275) <u>Names</u> of <u>Objects</u>:
    a. (e)jisdodákhwaʔ
       e-jisd-od-akhw-aʔ
       3FI.A-light-set.up-INST-STV
       lamp

    b. gahnhóhwaʔes
       ga-hnho-hwaʔe-s
       3N/Z.SG.A-door-strike-HAB
       door-knocker

But the process of noun incorporation is only partly productive: both verbs and nouns vary greatly in the extent to which they combine with one another. The ability to do so is a lexical property of a given verb or noun. A fair number of verbs are never attested with a noun, others cannot occur without one. Some verbs can only occur with one or two noun roots, others with a large variety. Interestingly, it seems that nearly all morphological nouns can be incorporated to some extent. But like verbs, some nouns can be incorporated into any number of verbs, others are attested in just a very few. Some nouns only rarely occur independently, e.g. nouns describing large immovable referents and natural features; others only rarely combine with a verb, e.g., nouns describing persons and animals. These characteristics of individual nouns and verbs are evidenced in the productivity of the process in naturally occurring discourse. For example, it is almost inconceivable that a speaker talking about 'making something' would not incorporate the 'something' into the verb stem *-ǫny-* 'make', whether or not the particular combination had ever occurred before, and it would surely be considered poor form by competent speakers not to do so. For example, a person would inevitably say:

(276) waʔkhæ·hgṹ·nyaʔ
      waʔ-k-hæ·hgw-ǫny-aʔ
      FACT-1.SG.A-bread-make-PNC
      I made bread
                    But not: *waʔǫnyáʔ neʔ ohǽ·hgwaʔ

But the verb can and does occur *without* an incorporated noun when the formal characteristics of the nominal rules out incorporation. For example, the founder of the Iroquoian Confederacy says to the chiefs at a meeting of the nations:

(277) Sgahwajíyæda ǫgyǫ·níh (CTL461.5).
    s-ga-hwajiR-ada-h   ǫgy-ǫni-h'
    REP-3N/Z.SG.A-family-be.one-STV   1PL.P-make-STV
    (it is) one family   we made it
    We all have created a single family, we are one family

Although morphologically a verb, *sgahwajíyæda* 'one family' functions as a referring expression in (277). But it is not one that can be incorporated in the form given in the example, so that in this particular case *-ǫny-* shows up without an incorporated noun. On the other hand, enumeration verbs like *.N-ada-* + repetitive 'be one' *cannot* occur without an incorporated noun that describes the counted object, so in (277) it is Onondaga grammar that obliges *-ǫny-* 'make' to occur free of incorporation, but the enumeration verb is lexically specified to require a noun.

Apart from the incorporation characteristics of individual nouns and individual verbs, there are numerous noun-verb combinations that have become lexicalized over time, as has been pointed out earlier on. Lexicalized verb-noun combinations can be identified in one of four partly overlapping ways: (i) the analytic version is unacceptable to speakers as in (276); (ii) the meaning is non-compositional: the component meanings do not predict the combined meaning as in (278b); (iii) the lexical meaning of the analytic version differs from that of the incorporation version (278a and b); or (iv) the combined roots may have fused to such an extent that they are no longer identifiable, as is the case with many of the personal names. Typically, more than one of these are present. Examples of noun-verb stems whose *meanings* have become lexicalized but in which the component morphemes are easy to identify are:

(278) a. waʔshagohsóhgwak
        waʔ-shago-hsohgw-a-k-Ø
        FACT-3M.SG > 3-lip-JN-eat-PNC
        he kissed her
                cf. ehsohgwáʔgeh *her lip(s)*
                  waʔhék *he ate it*
                But not *waʔshagok neʔ ehsohgwáʔgeh

b. wa?hadi·ho·náhda?
wa?-hadi-Rihw-o·nahd-a?
FACT-3M.PL.A-matter-enlarge-PNC
they announced it
      cf. wa?hago·náhda? *he enlarged it*
        óihwa? *the reason*
     But not *wa?hago·nahda? ne? oihwa?

Both of these examples contain verb roots and noun roots that occur alone in other contexts, but they are unacceptable or make no sense when they occur together in analytic expressions as in (278).

The degree to which lexicalization is a factor in the process of noun incorporation is relevant to an issue that has been raised by Mithun (1984): It is the use of noun incorporation by speakers at the level of discourse (her stage 3) to mark new and old information. She found, in Mohawk, that when introduced as new information, a nominal will occur outside a verb as a separate constituent. After that, once its information-value is no longer salient, the information is backgrounded by incorporating the noun. This function, if it exists at all in Onondaga, is not reliably exploitable by speakers given the degree to which the process of noun incorporation is lexicalized, both in terms of the variability of individual nouns' and verbs' abilities to incorporate, and in terms of the existence of lexicalized noun-verb combinations. When Onondaga speakers have a choice with regard to incorporation, it seems speakers incorporate when the salient issue is the situation and they use the noun syntactically when the entity is to be foregrounded. Speakers' intuitions are that when incorporation is possible, that it is more natural to incorporate than not, and that not incorporating under those circumstances feels like "saying it in a round about way" (the late Harry Webster p.c.).

4.8.3.6 Incorporation and Possession

Two verb classes, positional verbs and a subclass of stative-only verbs with property meanings, express possession predicatively with incorporation *when they occur in the stative aspect with animate pronominal prefixes*. In constructions with these verbs the incorporated entity is possessed, and the pronominal prefix identifies the possessor. The specifics of pronominal selection of both these groups of verbs are discussed in section 4.4.3.4 above. The first group of verbs – the positional verbs – classifies the incorporated nominal in terms of characteristics of size, shape and position. Two of these verbs, -N-ade- and -ada-, are stative only and three -hnyod-/-od-, -ųd-, and -yę-, are active verbs. The positional verbs are:

-N-ade-   be unattached: of large unmovable or shapeless objects
-ada-   be contained: of contained objects
-hnyod-/-od-   be rooted, stick up: of standing or growing objects
-ųd-   be dangling: of objects with a secondary attachment to an intervening object
-yę-   lay down, place: of extended entities and all otherwise unclassified entities

In (279) constructions with a positional verb, in this case -yę-, show how possession is signaled only when the verb is inflected with the stative aspect, and only when it occurs with an animate pronominal prefix:

<u>Possession with incorporating positional verbs</u>:
(279) a. In the stative aspect with animate prefix:
      hoʔse·hdá·yę?
      ho-ʔse·hd-a-yę-ʔ
      3M.SG.P-car-JN-lay.down-STV
      he <u>has</u> a car

    b. In the punctual aspect with animate prefix:
      ęhasdęʔshæ·yę́?
      ę-ha-sdęʔshR-yę-ʔ'
      FUT-3M.SG.A-corn.braid-lay.down-PNC
      he will <u>lay down</u> the braid of corn

    c. In the stative aspect with non-animate prefix:
      tsha? gana?jyá·yę?
      tsha?   ga-na?jy-a-yę-?
      SUB   3N/Z.SG.A-bucket-JN-lay.down-STV
      where the bucket <u>is sitting</u> (someone has set it down there)

<u>Possession with incorporating stative-only verbs with property meanings</u>:
(280) a. With animate patient prefix
      honasgwiyóh
      <u>ho</u>-nasgw-iyo-h'   jí·ha
      3M.SG.P-domestic.animal-be.good-STV   dog
      he <u>has</u> a nice dog; his dog is nice

    b. With animate agent prefix
      hanasgwiyóh
      <u>ha</u>-nasgw-iyo-h'   jí·ha
      3M.SG.A-domestic.animal-be.good-STV   dog
      he <u>is</u> a nice dog

    c. With non-animate prefix
      waʔsgwehsiyóh
      <u>w</u>-asʔsgwehs-iyo-h'
      3N/Z.SG.A-ax-be.good-STV
      it <u>is</u> a nice ax

The following is a partial list of incorporating verbs for which 'possession' meanings with animate pronominals are attested:

Verb	Gloss	Verb	Gloss
-ahse-	*be new*	-N-ga?d-	*be plentiful*
.a?a- +partitive	*be small*	-is-	*be long*
-dęs-	*be thick*	.N-o?dę- +partitive	*be a kind*

4.8.3.7 Incorporation into Enumeration Verbs

All of the Five Nations languages have a set of three stative-only verb stems that enumerate entities. In Onondaga these stems are *.N-d-* +repetitive 'be one', *.N-ge-* +dualic 'be two', and *.N-ge-* +partitive 'be three or more', where *N* in the citations indicates that incorporating a noun is obligatory and the period (.) preceding the citation indicates that the cited prepronominal prefix is lexicalized for the given meaning. The incorporated noun marks the entity that is counted. When the counted entities are animate, the enumeration verbs must incorporate the noun *-ya?d-* 'body' (see below) which behaves as a classifier noun for an optionally co-occurring independent nominal that further specifies the counted entity. The enumeration word or phrase as a whole functions as a nominal in the clause, that is, the counting verb cannot predicate (Koenig & Michelson 2009, 2010a, 2012). In (281) there are two enumeration expressions. The incorporated nouns *-hwisd-* 'money = dollar' and *-ęd-* 'day' express the counted entities:

(281) Odiyo?dé? o·hę?sę́·k odyá?k, <u>áhya?k</u> gadé? <u>jyadák nigahwisdagé</u> ęyų̄tgwenyá? ne?
<u>jyę́dada</u> odyá?k dé·gę·? (LG11).

odi-yo?de-?		o·hę?sę·k	odya?k	<u>ahya?k</u>	gade?	<u>jyadak</u>
3FZ.NSG.P-work-STV		TMP	QNT	NUM	CNJ	NUM
they work		daily	some	six	or	seven

<u>ni-ga-hwisd-a-ge-h'</u>	ę-yų-at-gweny-a?	ne?
PRT-3N/Z.SG.A-money-JN-amount.to-STV	FUT-3FI.A-SRF-be.able-PNC	NOM
so many dollars	they will earn	the

<u>s-y-ęd-a-d-'ah</u>[149]	odya?k	de·gę·?
REP-3N/Z.SG.A-day-JN-be.one-STV	QNT	NUMBER
one day	some	eight

[The women] work every day and some earn <u>six or seven dollars</u> a day and some get eight.

An expression with *.N-ge-* +partitive 'be a number greater than two' must be accompanied by a number word or a quantifier. This is not so with the other two enumeration stems, which signal the amount unambiguously, as shown in (282) with *.N-ge-* +dualic 'be two' and in (283) with *.N-d-* +repetitive 'be one'.

(282) Thohgé ó·nę Hayęhwátha? wa?shagodę·nyéhda? <u>dehniya?dagé</u> wa?hųwęhnų́ksha?
(CTL122.7-8).

thohge	onę	Hayęhwatha?	wa?-shago-adęnyehd-a?
TMP	TMP	NAME	FACT-3M.SG > 3-send-PNC
then	now	Hiawatha	he sent them

<u>de-hni-ya?d-a-ge-h'</u>	wa?-hųwę-ihnųk-hs-a?
DL-3M.DU.A-body-JN-amount.to-STV	FACT-3 > 3M.SG-fetch-DSLC-PRP
two [men]	they went to fetch him

Then Hiawatha sent two men, [who] went to fetch him.

---

[149] Words ending in /h/ typically lose it utterance-medially.

Enumeration verbs can, as noted, participate in classificatory incorporation as in (283):

(283) Ónę éʔ sayų·gwáhdų?, sgayáʔdadah niyaguʔú gítgit (NC01).

onę	eʔ	s-a-yųgw-ahdų-ʔ	s-ga-yaʔd-a-d-'ah
TMP	REP	REP-FACT-1PL.P-lose-PNC	REP-3FZ.SG.A-body-JN-be.one-STV
now	again	we lost it again	one animate being

ni-yag-ųʔų-h'	gitgit
PRT-3FI.A-be.small-STV	NOUN
it's a small one	chicken

Now we've lost one more baby chick.

4.8.3.8 The Classifier Nouns *-yaʔd-*, *-Rihw-*, and *-ʔnigųhR-*

Three noun roots with special characteristics as incorporated nouns are *-yaʔd-* 'body', *-Rihw-* 'thing, matter', and *-ʔnigųhR-* 'mind, thought'. They are nouns with broad meanings relating to animacy, abstractness, and mental activity, respectively. These three nouns are incorporated with greater frequency than any others, and they combine with a greater variety of verbs than any others. The Onondaga Dictionary (Woodbury 2003) cites 203 verb stems with *-yaʔd-*, 192 stems with *-Rihw-*, and 54 stems with *-ʔnigųhR-*. Verb-noun combinations with these nouns are nearly always lexicalized, mainly because their meanings tend to be non-compositional. Consequently, verb stems containing them typically do not have analytic counterparts.

The "animacy" noun *-yaʔd-*: The first of the nouns, *-yaʔd-* 'body', occurs with verbs that describe situations involving the whole person and verbs involving physical contact with an animate patient participant.

With verbs whose meanings involve the whole person:
(284) ...déʔseʔ neʔ hųdęnóthaʔ waʔhųdę·nodéʔ tshaʔ hayaʔdá·hgwaʔ seʔ neʔ Tom, neʔ
      hųdę·nóthaʔ, neʔ ųnísʔih (LG05).

dęʔseʔ	neʔ	hų-ad-Ręn-ot-haʔ	waʔ-hų-ad-Ręn-od-ęʔ	tshaʔ
CNJ	NOM	3M.PL.A-SRF-song-raise-HAB	FACT-3M.PL.A-SRF-song-raise-PNC	SUB
and	the	band	they played songs	as

ha-yaʔd-aR-h-gwaʔ	seʔ	neʔ	Tom	neʔ	hų-ad-Ręn-ot-haʔ
3M.SG.A-body-be.in-HAB-PST	MOD	NOM	NAME	NOM	3M.PL.A- SRF-song-raise-HAB
he used to be in it	actually	the	Tom	the	band

neʔ	ųnisʔi
NOM	TMP
the	long time ago

...and the band played, [because] Tom actually had joined the band a long time ago.

The noun root -yaʔd- occurs obligatorily with dyadic verbs involving physical contact with an animate patient participant:

<u>With verbs involving physical contact between animate participants:</u>
(285) Oné néʔtho hadidakhenų́·dyeʔ hadíhse·ʔ neʔ ga·yoʔá <u>waʔtshagodiyaʔdahí·hdaʔ</u> neʔ
    Hayęhwáthaʔ shagóhawah waʔagonų́hyaʔk (CTL137.8-138.1).

oné	neʔtho	hadi-dakhe-nų-adye-ʔ	hadi-hse·-ʔ	neʔ	ga-Ryo = ʔá
TMP	LOC	3M.PL.A-run-STV-PRG-PRP	3M.PL.A-chase-PRP	NOM	NPF-animal = DIM
now	there	they are running along	they are chasing it	the	bird

<u>waʔ-t-shagodi-yaʔd-a-hi·hd-aʔ</u>		neʔ	Hayęhwathaʔ	shago-hawah
FACT-DL-3M.NSG > 3-body-JN-smash-PNC		NOM	NAME	3M.SG > 3-parent/child
they smashed into her		the	Hiawatha	his daughter

waʔ-ago-nųhyaʔk-Ø
FACT-3FI.P-hurt-PNC
she got hurt

As they are running along, chasing the bird, they smash into Hiawatha's daughter,
hurting her.

The contrast between animate and non-animate patient participants is shown clearly in
(286a and b):

(286) a. waʔkheyaʔdoháeʔ
      waʔ-khe-<u>yaʔd</u>-ohae-ʔ'
      FACT-1SG > 3-<u>body</u>-wash-PNC
      I washed her/them; I bathed her/them
                 But not: *waʔkheyohaeʔ

     b. waʔgoháeʔ
      waʔ-g-ohae-ʔ'
      FACT-1SG.A- wash-PNC
      I washed it

Physical contact verbs can usually replace *-yaʔd-* with other body-part nouns (with
transitive prefixes and possessive interpretations) as in (287a), and they can often
incorporate non-animate nouns (with intransitive prefixes) as in (287b):

(287) a. waʔshagogų́hsoháeʔ
      waʔ-shago-gų̨hs-ohae-ʔ'
      FACT-3M.SG > 3-face-wash-PNC
      he washed her face

     b. waʔhaʔse·hdoháeʔ
      waʔ-ha-ʔse·hd-ohae-ʔ'
      FACT-3M.SG.A-vehicle-wash-PNC
      he washed a car; he car-washed

While the great majority of physical contact verbs must always incorporate *-yaʔd-* with
animate patients, a small subset of these verbs has two senses with animate patients
depending on whether *-yaʔd-* is present or not; the first describes primary or direct physical
contact, e.g. 'carry someone' as in (288a), the second describes secondary, indirect, or

partial contact, e.g. 'take someone along, escort someone' as in (288b). The incorporated noun *-yaʔd-* occurs only in the first of these:

(288) a. <u>Primary contact</u>: shagodiyaʔdęhá·wiʔ
      shagodi-yaʔd-ęhawi-ʔ
      3M.NSG > 3-body-carry-STV
      they are carrying her

   b. <u>Secondary contact</u>: shagodihá·wiʔ
      shagodi-hawi-ʔ
      3M.NSG > 3FI-carry-STV
      they are taking her along, they are escorting her

Other verbs with separate primary and secondary contact meanings are:

Primary contact meaning with *-yaʔd-*	Secondary contact meaning without *-yaʔd-*
waʔga·dyaʔdíhsʔaʔ *I got old*	waʔgadéhsʔaʔ *I got ready*
shagoyaʔdíʔse·ʔ *he's (physically) dragging her*	shagóʔse·ʔ *he's pulling her [e.g., in a wagon]*
gadyaʔdíʔse·ʔ *I'm dragging myself*	gadéʔse·ʔ *I'm crawling*
waʔheyaʔdagá·hadu̜k *I rolled him*	waʔhegá·hadu̜k *I rotated him [e.g., in a wheel]*
waʔthu̜wayaʔdga·hadé·niʔ *they rolled him around [on the ground]*	waʔthu̜waga·hadé·niʔ *they turned him [e.g., in a revolving chair]*
waʔshagoyaʔdá·gwʔ *they chose her*	waʔshagó·gwaʔ *they nominated her*
heyaʔdanú̜hna? *I'm his body guard*	henú̜hna? *I'm watching over him*
waʔtheyaʔtgwáihcyaʔ *I'm straightening [his body]*	waʔthedagwáihcyaʔ *I gave him counsel*
waʔtyu̜·gyaʔdashá·nyeʔ *she rubbed me all over*	waʔtyu̜gashá·nyeʔ *she rubbed me in one place*
waʔga·dyaʔdoháeʔ *I bathed*	waʔgadoháeʔ *I washed [e.g. my hands]*
waʔheyaʔdahséhdaʔ *I hid him*	waʔheyahséhdaʔ *I robbed him*
ęheyaʔdaniyú̜·dęʔ *I'll hitch him up*	ęheniyú̜·dęʔ *I'll follow him*

<u>The "abstraction" noun *-Rihw-*</u>: Incorporating *-Rihw-* 'matter, thing', has the general effect of expressing an action or state that is abstract of in some way *intangible*, so that, for example, the meaning of *-u̜dy-* alone is 'abandon or throw away an object' but the meaning of *-Rihu̜dy-* is 'to leave word' (the sequence *wu̜ > u̜* by regular rule). Unlike *-Rhu̜dy-*, most lexicalizations with *-Rihw-* are non-compositional to a far greater extent. Incorporation of *-Rihw-* is very extensive, and is, for the most part lexicalized. In (289) *-Rihw-* is incorporated into the verb stem *-hni·hd-* 'tighten, tamp down', resulting in the combined stem's meaning 'confirm, affirm [something]':

(289) Naʔ néʔ tshaʔ <u>waʔhaihwahnihdáʔ</u> tshaʔ hoʔtshatsdęhse·wanę́h dę́ʔseʔ hadahu̜hsadáts
     neʔ gaihsę·hdáʔ do· niyót tshaʔ ęhó·yu̜ʔs (HW07).

naʔ	neʔ	tshaʔ	waʔ-ha-<u>Rihw</u>-a-hniR-hd-aʔ	tshaʔ
ASRT	NOM	SUB	FACT-3M.SG.A-matter-JN-be.strong-CS-PNC	SUB
it's	the	that	he confirmed it	that

ho-ʔtshatsdęhsR-owanę-h	dę́ʔseʔ	h-ad-ahu̜hsad-at-s	neʔ
3M.SG.P-power-large-STV	CNJ	3M.SG.A-SRF-be.listening-CS-HAB	NOM
the Creator	and	he gets to listen	the

ga-Rihsę·hd-aʔ	do	niyot	tshaʔ	ę-ho-yų-ʔs-Ø
NPF-dream-NSF	INTR	MAN	SUB	FUT-3M.SG > 3M.SG-enter-BEN-PNC
dream	how	how it is	that	he will visit him

That's how He affirmed that He was the Creator, and that he gets to listen to dreams, which is how He will communicate with him.

The effect of incorporating *-Rihw-* is shown also by the following pair:

(290) a. hoihwihsáʔih
   ho-Rihw-ihsaʔ-ih
   3M.SG.P-matter-finish-STV
   he has promised (it), he has decreed (it)

  b. hohsáʔih
   ho-hsaʔ-ih
   3M.SG.P-complete-STV
   he's completed (it); he ate up; he's used it up

The <u>"mental activity/mental state" noun *-ʔnigųhR-*:</u> Verbs incorporating *-ʔnigųhR-* 'mind, thought', express a variety of mental activities and mental states:

(291) Hátsgwih, gadogę́ khę <u>nisaʔnigųheʔdę́h</u> (HW07).

hatsgwih	ga-dogę-h		khę	ni-sa-<u>ʔnigųhR</u>-oʔdę-h'
EXCL	3N/Z.SG.A-be.the.same-STV		QUE	PRT-2SG.P-mind-be.a.kind-STV
OK	it is the same		question	what your mind-set is

Ok, are you [still] of the same mind?

(292) Onę ęyagothų́·dek neʔ gędyohgwagwé·gih, ó·nę <u>ęhsʔnigųhæyędáhdaʔ</u> nwa·hóʔdęʔ sí·daʔ (CTL36.6-7).

onę	ę-yago-athų́de-(ʔ)-k-Ø		neʔ	ga-idyohgw-a-gweg-ih	onę
TMP	FUT-3FI.P-listen-STV-CNT-PNC		NOM	3N/Z.SG.A-crowd-JN-all-STV	TMP
now	they will be listening		the	the whole crowd	now

ę-hs-ʔnigųhR-yęd-ahd-aʔ		nwa·hoʔdęʔ	s-id-aʔ
FUT-2SG.A-thought-place-CS-PNC		INTR	2SG.A-mean-STV
you will explain		what	you mean (it)

Now the whole crowd will be listening when you explain what you mean.

The following pair further highlights the effect of incorporating *-ʔnigųhR-:*

(293) a. waʔháhdų?
   waʔ-h-ahdų-ʔ
   FACT-3M.SG.A-disappear-PNC
   he disappeared, he went out of sight

  b. waʔhoʔnigųhǽ·hdų?
   waʔ-ho-ʔnigųhR-ahdų-ʔ
   FACT-3M.SG.P-mind-disappear-PNC
   he fainted

4.8.4 The Reflexives

The reflexives, when they occur, are the left-most elements of the stem.

Table 4.55 The reflexive position

Inflect./Deriv.	Inflectional	Derivational	Lexical		Derivational	Inflectional	
Prepronominal and Modal Prefixes	Pronominal Prefixes	Reflexives	Noun Root or Stem	Verb Root	Root Suffixes	Basic Aspect Suffixes	Expanded Aspect Suffixes
			Verb Stem				

There are two reflexive morphemes. Some Iroquoianists, following Lounsbury (1953), refer to them as the *semireflexive* (SRF) and the *(full) reflexive* (REF), others (Mithun, Chafe) refer to the first of these as the *middle voice* morpheme. In each case, the precise effect of the reflexives depends upon the source verb to which it attaches. Of the two types of reflexive, only the semireflexive affects the argument structure of the source verb.

4.8.4.1 The Semireflexive (SRF)

The distribution of the semireflexive's alternants is in part predictable on phonological grounds and in part lexicalized. The forms of the semireflexive alternants are *-a- / -ad- / -ade- / -adę- / -ah- / -an- / -aR- / -as- / -at- / -ę- /-ęn-*. The occurrence of *-at-* and *-ad-* vastly outnumbers that of all other forms. The alternant *-a-* occurs with selected stems beginning in *h* or *?*. The alternants *-ade-* and *-adę-* occur before stems that begin with certain consonant clusters [150] such that attaching them directly to -at- or -ad- would produce an impermissible sequence of consonants. The choice between *-ade-* and *-adę-* is lexically determined. The alternant *-at-* occurs before stems beginning with *d, g, j, tc,* clusters consisting of *h* and any of the resonants *w, n, y, R,* the cluster *hs,* [151] and some stems beginning with the clusters *s?* and *?n*. The alternant *-ad-* occurs before vowels (except *i*)[152] and with any of the resonants *w, n, y, R*. The alternant *-an-* occurs before selected *i-* and *y*-stems; *-ęn-* occurs before selected *i*-stems. The alternant *-ah-* occurs before selected stems beginning in *j*. The alternant *-aR-* occurs before selected *a*-stems; *-ę-* occurs before some stems beginning with *n, ?n,* and *hn*.[153]

The outcomes of derivations with the semireflexive are diverse, depending on the transitivity and meaning of the source verb, but its most predictable action is to

---

[150]The consonant clusters are (i) two obstruents; (ii) an obstruent and a laryngeal (except certain stems beginning with *s?*, (iii) an obstruent (other than surface *j* deriving from internally complex *ts*) and a resonant; (iv) two resonants; (v) a resonant and a laryngeal; (vi) a laryngeal and and obstruent (with the exception of certain stems beginning with *ht* and *hts*); (vii) a laryngeal and two resonants; (viii) a laryngeal followed by a resonant and a laryngeal; or (ix) two laryngeals.

[151]The cluster *hs* becomes *sh* when it follows *-at-*.

[152]An exception to this exception is the stem *-i-* 'to be all of it, to be the only one'.

[153]An additional form *-as-* is obsolete. It occurred in the turn of the century speech of John Arthur Gibson with stems beginning with *j,* but is replaced by contemporary speakers with -at-.

detransitivise the source verb; and often, though not invariably, affect a verb's meaning by identifying the agent of the action with the entity that is acted upon. Occasionally the semireflexive changes a verb's category from stative to active. And finally, it has a variety of unpredictable semantic effects. All of these are detailed in subsections (i) through (vi), below.

(i) <u>Triadic verbs with two animate and one non-animate argument</u>:

In (294a and b) a transitive pronominal prefix references the two animate arguments (agent and goal); the semireflexive detransitivises the stem; an intransitive agent pronominal prefix references only the agent argument of the verb.

(294) a. waʔtshagonų́hę·ʔ   >   waʔthų̨dę́nų̨hę́·ʔ
       waʔ-t-shago-nų̨hę·-ʔ   waʔ-t-hų̨-<u>adę</u>-nų̨hę·-ʔ
       FACT-DL-3M.SG.>3-greet,thank-PNC   FACT-DL-3M.PL.A-<u>SRF</u>-greet,thank-PNC
       he greeted/thanked her   *they gave greetings/thanks*

     b. ęshagá·ų̨ʔ   >   ęhá·dų̨ʔ
       ę-shaga-ų̨-ʔ   ę-h-<u>ad</u>-ų̨-ʔ
       FUT-3M.SG>3-give-PNC   FUT-3M.SG.A-<u>SRF</u>-give-PNC
       he will give it to her/them   *he will give (it)*

There are only a few non-derived triadic verb stems[154] in Onondaga, but two others that follow this pattern are:

-ahę·dų̨- *ask someone [about something]*	>	-adahę́·dų̨ʔ- *ask about something*
-nyehd- *send something with someone*	>	-adęnyehd- *send something or someone*

The stems derived with the semireflexive as well as the source stems can incorporate, though not always with predictable meanings.

(295) a. ...hehéʔ a·hadęnásgų̨ʔ (HW05).
       h-eR-heʔ   aa-h-<u>adę</u>-nasgw-ų̨-ʔ
       3M.SG.A-want-HAB   OPT-3M.SG.A-SRF-pet-give-PNC
       He wants to give away his pet

     b. waʔshagohwísdų̨ʔ
       waʔ-shago-<u>hwisd</u>-ų̨-ʔ
       FACT-3M.SG>3-money-give-PNC
       he gave her/them money

     c. ęyų̨·di·hwadahędų́ʔ
       ę-yų̨-<u>ad</u>-Rihw-adahędų̨-ʔ'
       FUT-3FI.A-SRF-matter-ask.for-PNC
       she will question the matter

---

[154] The majority of triadic verbs are derived with the benefactive suffix (4.8.5.1).

d. hakhwahę́·dųk
   ha-<u>khw-ahędų</u>-k
   3M.SG.a-food-ask.for-HAB
   he is asking for food

(ii) <u>Dyadic verb stems with one animate and one non-animate argument</u>:

The semireflexive derivation can mark an action as one that is self-agentive as in (a) – an outcome that is sometimes described as *middle voice* – or as one that is reflexive as in (b). Because the semantic patient of the source verb is non-animate, there is no pronominal shift.

(296) a. tho waʔeyę́ʔ   >   waʔų·dyę́ʔ
       tho   waʔ-e-yę-ʔ'   waʔ-ų-<u>ad</u>-yę-ʔ'
       LOC   3FI.A-set.down-PNC   FACT-3FI.A-<u>SRF</u>-set.down-PNC
       she set it down there   *she sat down*

     b. waʔgéhsʔaʔ   >   waʔgadéhsʔaʔ
       waʔ-ge-hsʔ-aʔ   waʔ-g-<u>ade</u>-hsʔ-aʔ
       FACT-1.SG.A-complete.something-PNC   FACT-1.SG.A-<u>SRF</u>-complete.something-PNC
       I finished it, I ate it up   *I got ready*

Other verb stems that follow patterns in (ii) are:

-ahseht- *hide something*	>	-adahseht- *hide*
-Rægw- *choose, pick something*	>	-adæ·gw- *make a claim*
-dagwaihcy- *straighten something*	>	-atdagwaihcy- *straighten out, straighten up*
.deny- +dualic *change something*	>	.atdeny- +dualic *change, change places*
-Ret- / -Rehw- / -Rehg- *gather something*	>	-ade·t-/-ade·hw-/-ade·hg- *assemble*
-ohae- *wash sthg., bathe someone*	>	-adohae- *wash*

(iii) Many verb stems derived with the semireflexive can incorporate nouns. The noun is incorporated between the semireflexive morpheme and the verb root. With an incorporated noun, the semireflexive derivation marks an action as one in which the actor acts on his or her possession or benefits himself through his possession.

(297) a. waʔgathe·hnayę́ʔ
     waʔ-g-<u>at</u>-he·hn-a-yę-ʔ'
     FACT-1SG.A-<u>SRF</u>-bundle,luggage-JN-set.down-PNC
     I set down my luggage

     b. waʔgathe·hníhsʔaʔ
     waʔ-g-<u>at</u>-he·hn-ihsʔ-aʔ[155]
     FACT-1.SG.A-<u>SRF</u>-bundle,luggage-complete.something-PNC
     I got my luggage ready

---

[155] *-ihsʔ-* is the incorporating alternant of this verb stem.

240 The Verb

    c. hathwisdayę́haʔ
       h-at̲-hwisd-a-yę-haʔ
       3M.SG.A-SRF-money-JN-set.down-HAB
       he saved money

(iv) <u>Deriving an anticausative construction</u>: an anticausative construction results when a verb stem describing a causative process occurs with the semireflexive and non-animate pronominals. Such stems select agent or patient prefixes in accordance with the patterns of their active counterparts – agent forms with habitual and punctual inflections and patient forms with the stative – even though it is the semantic patient of the action that is identified by the pronominal in this type of construction.[156]

(298) a. há·yaʔks   >   wá·dyaʔks
       ha-yaʔk-s   w-ad̲-yaʔk-s
       3M.SG.A-break.off-HAB   3N/Z.SG.A-SRF-break.off-HAB
       he breaks it   *it breaks*

     b. hoyáʔgih   >   odyáʔkih
       ho-yaʔk-ih   o-ad̲-yaʔg-ih
       3M.SG.P- break.off-STV   3N/Z.SG.P- SRF-break.off-STV
       he has broken it   *it is broken; it has broken off*

     c. ę́·gyaʔk   >   ęwá·dyaʔk
       ę-g-yaʔk-Ø   ę-w-ad̲-yaʔk-Ø
       FUT-1SG.A-break.off-PNC   FUT-3N/Z.SG.A-SRF-break.off-PNC
       I will break it off   *it will break off*

Other verb stems that follow this pattern are:

-awęhæ·t- *move something up and over*	>	-adawęhæ·t- *overflow*
-awęhdų- / -awęhd- *tear something off*	>	-adawęhdų- / -adawęhd- *chip, rip*
.yaʔk- + dualic *break something in two*	>	.adyaʔk- + dualic *break in two, break off*
.owę- + dualic *split something*	>	.adowę- + dualic *split, crack*
.Ræʔnegaʀ- + dualic *burst something*	>	.adæ·ʔnegaʀ- + dualic *burst, explode*

The derived stem *-adawęhdų- / -adawęhd-* 'chip, rip' is interesting in that it can denote causative as well as anticausative meanings depending on whether a non-animate agent or non-animate patient pronominal is selected in the stative aspect:[157] with the non-animate patient pronominal the meaning is anticausative, with the non-animate agent prefix it is the nearest thing that Onondaga has to expressing a passive meaning (section 4.4.3.2). The construction with non-animate agent pronominal implies the existence of a causer without identifying him or her. The contrast exists only in the stative inflection and only with non-animate pronominals.

---

[156] The shift from animate to non-animate pronominal prefix in this type of derivation was first remarked on by Koenig & Michelson (2012).

[157] Recall that the feminine-zoic singular prefixes (*ga-* and *o-* or their alternants) are default prefixes for non-animate (neuter) participants, and that they are identified as 3N/Z.SG.A and 3N/Z.SG.P in the morpheme identification line of the examples.

(299) a. <u>In the habitual with anticausative meaning</u>: wada·wéhdųs
    w-<u>ad</u>-awęhdų-s
    3N/Z.SG.A-SRF-chip,rip-HAB
    it chips, it rips

    b. <u>In the punctual with anticausative meaning</u>: waʔwadawéhdaʔ
       waʔ-w-<u>ad</u>-awęhd-aʔ
       FACT-3N/Z.SG.A-SRF-chip,rip-PNC
       it chipped, it ripped

    c. <u>In the stative with non-animate *patient* prefix and anticausative meaning</u>:
       oda·wéhdųh
       <u>o</u>-ad-awęhdų-h
       <u>3N/Z.SG.P</u>-SRF-tear.something.off-STV
       it has chipped, it has split off

    d. <u>In the stative with non-animate *agent* prefix and *causative* meaning</u>:
       wada·wéhdųh
       <u>w</u>-ad-awęhdų-h
       <u>3N/Z.SG.A</u>-SRF-tear.something.off-STV
       it was chipped, it was split off [by someone]

Like other derived forms, anticausative verb stems can incorporate nouns. Examples are:

(300) a. odųhwęjiyáʔgih
       o-<u>ad</u>-ųhwęjy-iyaʔg-ih[158]
       3N/Z.SG.P-<u>SRF</u>-earth-break.off-STV
       the earth has caved in; it has earth-caved

    b. waʔdwadeéʔgwaʔné·ga·ʔ
       waʔ-d-w-<u>ade</u>-Reʔgw-a-ʔnegaR-ʔ
       FACT-DL-3N/Z.SG.A-<u>SRF</u>-bubble,balloon-JN-burst-PNC
       the bubble or balloon burst

    c. deho·dnųʔwáewęh
       de-ho-<u>ad</u>-nųʔwaR-owę-h
       DL-3M.SG.P-<u>SRF</u>-head-split-STV
       his head split, he has a cut in his head

(v) <u>Change of category</u>:

Adding the semireflexive may derive an active verb that can occur in all three basic aspects from a stative-only verb without changing the number of roles that are expressed:

---

[158] *-iyaʔg-* is one of the incorporating alternants of this verb stem.

(301) a. waʔųtgahǽ·ęʔ
        waʔ-ų-<u>at</u>-gahæ-ęʔ
        FACT-3FI.A-<u>SRF</u>-look-PNC
        she watched, she paid attention
                cf. dehagáhæ·ʔ *he is looking, he is gazing*

    b. waʔųdehnhų́·dęʔ
        waʔ-ų-<u>ade</u>-hnhųd-ęʔ
        FACT-3FI.A-<u>SRF</u>-have.in.mouth-PNC
        she put it in her mouth
                cf. gohnhų́·daʔ *she has it in her mouth*

(vi) <u>Additional, unpredictable, effects of the semireflexive:</u>

  (1) Adding the semireflexive changes the direction of the action:

(302) a. waʔhadęhní·nųʔ
        waʔ-h-<u>adę</u>-hninų-ʔ
        FACT-3M.SG.A-<u>SRF</u>-buy-PNC
        he sold it
                cf. Without the semireflexive: waʔhahní·nųʔ *he bought it*

    b. hotgá·yaʔks
        ho-<u>at</u>-ga·yaʔk-s
        3M.SG.P-SRF-pay-HAB
        he gets paid
                cf. Without the semireflexive: hagá·yaʔks *he pays*

    c. waʔhathe·wáhdaʔ
        waʔ-h-at-he·wahd-aʔ
        FACT-3M.SG.A-SRF-punish.somebody-PNC
        he got punished
                cf. Without the semireflexive: waʔshagohe·wáhdaʔ *he punished her*

  (2) Changed meanings with added semireflexive:

(303) a. waʔhadekhų́·nyaʔ
        waʔ-h-<u>ade</u>-khw-ųny-aʔ
        FACT-3M.SG.A-SRF-food-make-PNC
        he ate [a meal]
                cf. Without the semireflexive: waʔhakhų́·nyaʔ *he cooked [a meal]*

    b. waʔgadé·yoʔ
        waʔ-g-<u>ade</u>-Ryo-ʔ
        FACT-1.SG.A-SRF-kill-PNC
        I fought
                cf. Without the semireflexive: waʔgé·yoʔ *I killed (it)*

c. waʔhadęnoyę́hdaʔ
   waʔ-h-ad-ęnoyęhd-aʔ
   FACT-3M.SG.A-SRF-lie-PNC
   he denied it
               cf. Without the semireflexive: waʔhęnoyę́hdaʔ *he lied*

d. waʔhatgwé·nyaʔ
   waʔ-h-at-gweny-aʔ
   FACT-3M.SG.A-SRF-be.able.to.do-PNC
   he won, he earned [something]
               cf. Without the semireflexive: waʔhagwé·nyaʔ *he could do it*

4.8.4.2 The Full Reflexive (REF)

The full reflexive morpheme's alternants are *-adad- / -adade- / -adadę- / -adat- / -adęn-*. The distribution of these alternants is only partially predictable on phonological grounds and is similar to that described for semireflexive alternants in the previous section. The alternant *-adad-* occurs with stems that begin in a vowel or a resonant consonant; *-adat-* occurs with stems that begin in a consonant; *-adade-* and *-adadę-* occur with selected stems that begin in consonant clusters, the choice between them is lexically selected; *-adat-* occurs with stems that begin in obstruents or laryngeals; *-adęn-* occurs with selected stems that begin in *i*. The full reflexive has two functions, it derives *reflexive* and *reciprocal* verb stems from dyadic source verbs. The first of these creates a stem whose agent and undergoer roles are enacted by the same participant; the second creates a stem whose agent and undergoer roles are enacted by the participants upon one another.

The Reflexive:

The reflexive derives a stem whose agent and undergoer roles are enacted by the same participant. The derived stem can occur with a singular, dual, or plural pronominal prefix which indexes two semantic roles performed by the same participant(s). Unlike the source verb, it cannot occur with a transitive prefix.

(304) a. ...waʔhadátgęʔ tshaʔ ohné·goʔ (NC02).
         waʔ-h-adat-gę-ʔ   tshaʔ   o-hneg-o-ʔ
         FACT-3M.SG.A-REF-see-PNC   SUB   3N/Z.SG.P-liquid-be.immersed-STV
         he saw himself   that   it is immersed in water
         ...*he saw his reflection in the water.*
                   cf. waʔshagó·gęʔ *he saw her/them*

b. waʔhyadadé·yoʔ
   waʔ-hy-adade-Ryo-ʔ
   FACT-3M.DU.A-REF-kill-PNC
   they killed themselves
               cf. ę(s)hesní·yoʔ *you two will kill him*

c. waʔhųdadekhų́·nyę?
   waʔ-<u>hų-adade</u>-khw-ųny-ę-ʔ
   FACT-3M.PL.A-REF-meal-make-BEN-PNC
   they cooked for themselves
          cf. ęs<u>g</u>ekhų́·nyę? *you will cook a meal for me*

<u>The Reciprocal:</u>

The reciprocal derives a stem whose agent and undergoer roles are enacted by a number of participants upon one another. The stem is identical to the reflexive, except that it requires a dualic prepronominal prefix. The reciprocal occurs only with non-singular intransitive pronominal prefixes. Reciprocals tend to lexicalize with specialized meanings as in (305).

(305) a. waʔthya·dá·dų?
      waʔ-t-hy-adad-ų-ʔ
      FACT-DL-3M.DU.A-REF-give-PNC
      they two traded/bartered with each other

   b. waʔtgyadátgę?
      waʔ-t-gy-adat-gę-ʔ
      FACT-DL-3FZ.DU.A-REF-see-PNC
      they two saw each other, they met up

4.8.5 The Root Suffixes

The position of the root suffixes is shown in Table 4.56:

Table 4.56 Position of the root suffixes

Inflect./Deriv.	Inflectional	Derivational	Lexical		Derivational	Inflectional	
Prepronominal and Modal Prefixes	Pronominal Prefixes	Reflexives	Noun Root or Stem	Verb Root	Root Suffixes	Basic Aspect Suffixes	Expanded Aspect Suffixes
			Verb Stem				

Table 4.57 is an alphabetical list of the root suffixes with each suffix's basic meaning, its alternants, and the aspect class it takes if it occurs as the last element of the verb stem.

Table 4.57 The root suffixes

Name	Suffixes and Alternants[159]	Aspect Class
Ambulative: *do something as one walks*	-(a)h- -(a)hn-	H2
Benefactive/Dative (Applicative): *do for, do to*	-(a)hse-/-(a)s-[160] -(a)ni-/-ę- -(a)ni-/-s- -(a)ʔse-/-(a)ʔs- -ęni-/-as- -ęni-/-ę- -(ę)ni-/-has-	A3
Causative:[161] *cause, make, use*	-(a)ht-/-(a)hd-[162] -(a)st-/-(a)sd- -(a)t-/-(a)d- -(a)ʔt-/-(a)ʔd- -(a)t- -hw-	E1 E1 E3 E1 A E2
Dislocative: *go somewhere or intend to do something*	-(a)h- -(a)hR- -(a)hn- -(a)hs- -hsR- -(a)ʔn-	H2
Distributive: *do distributively, severally*	-(a)dų- -(a)hę·- -(a)hų- -nyų- -shę·- -shų- -ų- -(a)yų-	B4

---

[159] A suffix occurs with the parenthesized segment *a* in this column when combining the root suffix with an adjacent morpheme would result in a cluster of two or more consonants.

[160] All benefactive alternants are suppletive conditioned by aspect as indicated here by a slash (/). The alternants to the left of the slash occur with the habitual and stative aspects, those to the right occur with the punctual.

[161] The alternants ending in voiceless consonants occur before consonants, those ending in voiced consonants occur before vowels.

[162] The alternants with the joiner vowel occur with stems ending in a consonant; the alternants -ht-/-hd- occur with stems ending in a sonorant (including vowels); the alternants -t-/-d- occur with stems ending in an oral obstruent; in addition, the sequence hth is realized as th.

Table 4.57 (Continued)

Name	Suffixes and Alternants	Aspect Class
Inchoative: *become*	-(a)ʔ-	E4
	-(a)h-/-(a)ʔ-	E3
	-(a)ʔkheʔ-/-(a)ʔheʔ-[163]	E3
	-ęh-/-ęʔ-[164]	E3
	-heʔ-[165]	E3
Instrumental (Applicative): *do with, use for*	-(a)hgw-	E1
Intensifier: *very, really*	-(a)ji-	
	-jihw-	G2
	-(a)hjihw-	
	-(a)sjihw-	
	-(a)ʔjihw-	
Nominalizer	-ęhsR-	
	-hsR-	
	-shR-	NA
	-tshR-	
	-ʔshR-	
	-ʔtshR-	
Reversative: *undo or reverse action of the verb*	-(a)hcy-	A2
Reversative-multiplier: *undo; do a lot*	-(a)hgw-	G2
	-gw-/-ųgw-	

Root suffixes are a powerful instrument of lexical expansion. Many verb roots can co-occur with numerous root suffixes to produce different meanings. The verb root .*hsihaR-* + *dualic* 'plug up [a hole]' can serve as one of many possible examples:

(306) a. <u>Without root suffix</u>: waʔthahsiháę́ʔ
    waʔ-t-ha-hsihaR-ęʔ
    FACT-DL-3M.SG.A-plug.up-PNC
    he plugged it up

   b. <u>With reversative</u>: waʔthahsihá·gwaʔ
    waʔ-t-ha-hsihaR-gw-aʔ
    FACT-DL-3M.SG.A-plug.up-<u>REV</u>-PNC
    he opened it up

   c. <u>With causative</u>: waʔthahsihá·hdaʔ
    waʔ-t-ha-hsihaR-hd-aʔ
    FACT-DL-3M.SG.A-plug.up-<u>CS</u>-PNC
    he caused it to get plugged up

---

[163] The two alternants represent variation among individual speakers. Both take the -Ø punctual aspect which occurs with stems ending in -ʔ.

[164] The -ęh-/-ęʔ- and -(a)h-/-(a)ʔ- alternants of the inchoative are suppletive in relation to aspect. The alternants ending in *h* occur with the habitual and the punctual aspects, the alternants ending in ʔ occur with stative apect.

[165] The alternant -heʔ- takes the -Ø punctual aspect.

d. <u>With inchoative</u>: dẹgahsihá·ʔnhaʔ
d-ẹ-ga-hsihaR-ʔ-nhaʔ
DL-FUT-3N/Z.SG.A-plug.up-<u>INCH</u>-PNC
it will get stuck

e. <u>With benefactive</u>: deyagohsihá·ʔsek
de-yago-hsihaR-ʔse-k
DL-3FI.P-plug.up-<u>BEN</u>-HAB
she is choking [literally: it is plugging it up on her]

f. <u>With causative and distributive</u>: waʔthahsiha·hdahệ·ʔ
waʔ-t-ha-hsihaR-hd-ahẹ·-ʔ
FACT-DL-3M.SG.A-plug.up-<u>CS</u>-DST-PNC
he caused several of them to get plugged up [e.g. several gaps]

Each root suffix can occur as a single element between the verb root and the aspect suffix. In addition, all but the intensifier suffix are able to combine with other root suffixes. The linear sequence in which they combine depends on the order of the derivations. Table 4.58 shows the root suffixes that will combine with the root suffix listed in the first column. However, they cannot all combine at any one time. At a maximum three root suffixes are attested as part of a single verb stem. Details of the combinations and their sequencing are presented separately for each suffix in sections 4.8.5.1 to 4.8.5.8.

Table 4.58 Attested root suffix combinations

	Ben	Instr	Caus	Inch	Rev	Distr	Disloc	Amb
Benefactive		x	x	x	x	x		
Instrumental	x		x			x		x
Causative	x	x	x	x	x	x	x	
Inchoative	x		x			x	x	x
Reversative/Multiplier	x		x			x	x	
Distributive	x	x	x	x	x	x	x	x
Dislocative			x	x	x	x		
Ambulative		x		x		x		

The discussion in the following sections will proceed in terms of the role the suffixes play in the derivational morphology of the Onondaga verb. Sections 4.8.5.1 to 4.8.5.3 will deal with the suffixes that affect the participant structure of the verb, that is, the two applicative suffixes (the benefactive and the instrumental), and the causative; sections 4.8.5.4 to 4.8.5.7 will deal with the inchoative, the reversatives, the distributive, and the intensifier suffixes, which affect the meaning of the source verb in a variety of ways. The ambulative and dislocative suffixes are discussed in section 4.8.5.8. Their aspectual and modal characteristics have been discussed in section 4.5.3.1 above, in section 4.8.5.8 their other derivational and combinatorial properties will be described.

4.8.5.1 The Benefactive/Dative (Applicative)

All benefactive alternants come in pairs: they are suppletive in relation to aspect as indicated here by a slash (/). The forms of the benefactive alternants are *-(a)hse- / -(a)s-; -(a)ni- / -ę-; -(a)ni- / -s-; -(a)ʔse- / -(a)ʔs-; -ęni- / -as-; -ęni- / -ę-; -(ę)ni- / -has-*. The alternants to the left of the slash occur with the habitual and stative aspects, those to the right occur with the punctual. The parenthesized *a* is a joiner vowel that intervenes when combining the root suffix with an adjacent morpheme would result in a cluster of two or more consonants. The choice among alternant-sets is lexicalized to each verb stem and speakers learn them together with the stem. The benefactive combines with active, stative, and motion verbs, although combinations with active verbs predominate in the corpus (90%). The benefactive derivation derives polyadic stems which mark a peripheral participant who may be positively or negatively affected, as a core participant of a verb. Onondaga differs from many other languages across the world in that applicative derivations are obligatory in the sense that there is no contrasting expression with the applicative argument in peripheral function.[166] Dixon (2010-2012:3:299f) refers to the obligatory type as "quasi-applicative".

The benefactive suffix is added to monadic (307a) or to dyadic (307b) verb stems to derive dyadic or triadic stems, respectively:

(307) a. Tshaʔ niyogęhnhanóh naʔ nęgę́hah, hya gwas de?odiyanę·?sé ne?
　　　　Clifford hoyęthwáhų? (LG02).

tshaʔ	ni-yo-gęhnh-a-no-h		naʔ	nęgę = há	hya	gwas
SUB	PRT-3N/Z.SG.P-sumer-JN-cold-STV		ASRT	DEM = DIM	NEG	INTNS
that	it's a cold summer		it's	this particular	not	very

de?-odi-yanę·-?se-h'	ne?	Clifford	ho-yęthw-ahų-?
NEG-3FZ.NSG.P-good-BEN-STV	NOM	NAME	3M.SG.P-plant-DST-STV
it wasn't good for them	the	Clifford	he has planted [things]

　　　　This summer was cool [and] it wasn't good for Clifford's garden
　　　　[= plantings].

　　b. Wa?shagotho·yę́? ę· nhaųsahę·né? (LG06).

wa?-shago-atho·y-ę-?	ę·	n-h-aųsa-hęn-e-?'
FACT-3M.SG > 3-tell-BEN-PNC	DIR-C	PRT-TRNS-OPT:REP-3M.PL.A-walk-PNC
he told them	other direction	they should go back there

　　　　He told them to move away

As was pointed out above, the derivation changes a peripheral participant, here beneficiary/recipient, into a core participant. The animate participant(s) are referenced by the pronominal prefix.[167] Since benefactor and beneficiary are typically animate, both are identified by pronominals from the transitive series as in (307b) and (308).

---

[166] This is true also of the instrumental applicative (section 4.8.5.2).

[167] Recall that in the presence of animate participants non-animate participants are not expressed in the pronominal prefix and that dyadic stems with one non-animate participant and monadic stems both take intransitive pronominal prefixes.

<u>The benefactive derives a dyadic from a monadic stem</u>. In the derived form, the
pronominal prefix identifies the benefactor and beneficiary participants:

(308) ų̇no·yę́tha?   >   shagono·yę́hdanik
      ų-(ę)no·yęt-ha?   shago-(ę)no·yęhd-<u>ani</u>-k
      3FI.A-lie-HAB   3M.SG > 3-lie-<u>BEN</u>-HAB
      <u>she</u> is lying   <u>he's</u> lying to <u>her/them</u>

<u>The benefactive derives a triadic from a dyadic stem</u>. The pronominal prefix identifies
the benefactor and beneficiary participants in the derived form. The (non-animate) affected
participant is not expressed in the verb:

(309) ęhadiyæ·gwa?   >   wa?shagowǽ·gwa?s
      ę-<u>hadi</u>-Ręgw-a?   wa?-<u>shago</u>-Ręgw-a?s-Ø
      FUT-3M.PL.A-choose-PNC   FACT-3M.SG > 3-choose-BEN-PNC
      <u>they</u> will choose (<u>it</u>)   <u>he</u> chose (it) for <u>her/them</u>

When the expected transitive prefix is replaced by a pronominal prefix from the
intransitive series, it is usually the case that the benefactor is non-animate as in (310), or
that a benefactive stem has been detransitivised by a semireflexive as in (311):

<u>A beneficiary stem with a non-animate benefactor participant</u>. The pronominal prefix
identifies the beneficiary participant; the benefactor is not expressed:

(310) Nę yágę? sthwihá nęgę wa?hode?shæ·yędá?s ne? gahahsę·dyethá?... (HW07)
      onę   yagę?   sthwiha   nęgę   wa?-<u>ho</u>-ade?shR-a-yęd-<u>a?s</u>-Ø   ne?
      TMP   HRSY   QNT   DEM   FACT-<u>3M.SG</u>.P-luck-JN-have-<u>BEN</u>-PNC NOM
      then   they say   little bit this   he was lucky [= luck was to him]   the

      gahahsędyetha?
      NOUN
      lion
      Then, they say, the lion had a bit of luck...

Other benefactive stems with non-animate benefactors that take patient prefixes are:

-Ręhgwęni-/-Ręhgwę-	*itch* (= it makes someone itch)
.hsiha·?se-/.hsiha·?s- + dualic	*choke* (= it chokes someone)
-i?dahni·?s-	*get constipated* (= it hardens someone's feces)
-nųhwakdęni-/-nųhwakdani-/-nųhwakdę-	*get ill, sick* (= it sickens someone)

<u>A detransitivised benefactive stem without a beneficiary participant is derived with the</u>
<u>semireflexive from a beneficiary stem with a beneficiary participant</u>: The pronominal
prefix identifies the benefactor participant:

(311) wa?shagoniháhdę?   >   wa?hadęniháhdę?
      wa?-<u>shago</u>-nihahd-ę-?   wa?-<u>h</u>-adę-nihahd-ę-?
      FACT-3M.SG > 3-lend-BEN-PNC   FACT-3M.SG.A-SRF-lend-BEN-PNC
      <u>he</u> lent it to her/them   <u>he</u> lent it out

Which of the participants is removed by the process of detransitivising the stem depends on the order of derivations. The set in (312) shows that unlike (311) the verb root *-yę-* 'put something down' was detransitivised first, yielding *-adyę-* 'sit down' (312b), losing the patient participant, and then re-transitivised with the benefactive suffix *-adyę+ni-* 'for something/someone to settle on [=sit down on] something' (312c), which does have a beneficiary participant but lacks a patient.

<u>A detransitivised benefactive stem without a patient participant</u>. The pronominal prefix identifies the beneficiary:

(312) a. waʔgyę́ʔ
      waʔ-g-yę-ʔ'
      FACT-1.SG.A-place-PNC
      I put it down

    b. waʔgadyę́ʔ
      waʔ-g-ad-yę-ʔ'
      FACT-1SG.A-SRF-place-PNC
      I sat down

    c. aga·dyę·níh
      ag-ad-yę-ni-h'
      3FZ.SG>1SG-SRF-place-BEN-STV
      it settled on me [e.g., a stray dog adopting a new master]

Pronominal prefixes cannot identify more than two participants, so the third participant of the derived ditransitive – the patient – remains unexpressed in the pronominal. This is always the case when that participant is non-animate. But it is also the case when there are three animate participants. In that (unusual) event, the patient participant is expressed in an external nominal expression:

<u>A benefactive construction with three animate participants</u>. The pronominal prefix identifies agent and beneficiary participants. The animate patient participant occurs as an independent nominal:

(313) Onę ęgwanaʔdų́s neʔ <u>dędji·swayená?</u> (CTL692.2-3).
    onę   ę-gwa-naʔdų-s-Ø   neʔ   d-ę-s-swa-yena-ʔ'
    TMP   FUT-1PL>2PL-show-BEN-PNC   NOM   DL-FUT-REP-2PL-accept-PNC
    now   we (pl) will show you (pl)   the   you (pl) will work together
    Now we will show you your colleague

In (313) one group (moiety) of Iroquoian Chiefs has just appointed a new chief (to replace a chief who has died). They present the new chief to the second group (moiety), saying 'we will show you your colleague'. The phrase *neʔ dędji·swayená?* 'your colleague' though morphologically a verb, functions as a nominal in the clause. The peculiar use of a plural pronominal to represent a single participant in the derived nominal is a comitative construction, common in the Iroquoian languages. The clause says, literally, 'we will show you [the one who you and he will work together]' where the segment in square brackets is a derived nominal referring to the animate patient of the clause, i.e., the new chief.

The benefactive suffix also occurs in reflexive expressions in which the actor is both benefactor and beneficiary as in (314), or the benefactor and beneficiary act reciprocally as in (315):

(314) <u>A reflexive stem with the benefactive.</u> Benefactor and beneficiary roles are enacted by the same participant, who is identified by an intransitive pronominal prefix:
 waʔhadathǫ́·nyęʔ
 waʔ-<u>h</u>-adat-hah-ǫny-ę-ʔ
 FACT-3M.SG.A-REF-trail-make-BEN-PNC
 <u>he</u> made <u>himself</u> a trail

(315) <u>A reciprocal stem with the benefactive.</u> Benefactor and beneficiary act on each other and are identified by an intransitive non-singular pronominal prefix:
 dehyadadniyǫ́·dęnik
 de-<u>hy</u>-adad-niyǫd-ęni-k
 DL-3M.DU.A-REF-hang.up-BEN-HAB
 <u>they</u> exchange gifts [literally: <u>they</u> hang up things for <u>each other</u>]

Root suffix combinations with all but the ambulative and dislocative suffixes have been attested for the benefactive. Combinations and their sequencing are shown in Table 4.59:

Table 4.59 Attested root suffix combinations with the benefactive

		causative	benefactive		
		instrumental	benefactive		
	instrumental	causative	benefactive		
root		distributive	benefactive		aspect
		inchoative	benefactive		
			benefactive	inchoative	
		reversative	benefactive		
	reversative	causative	benefactive		

Examples of each of these complex stems, a number of them with non-compositional meanings, are:

(316) a. <u>Causative and benefactive:</u> hǫwatgathwahdęníh
 hǫw-atgathw-ahd-ęni-h'
 3 > 3M.SG-look.at-CS-BEN-STV
 they have displayed it to him
 b. <u>Instrumental and benefactive:</u> dęsheyadǫhwaęhę́hgwęʔ
 d-ę-shey-adǫhwaęhę-hgw-ę-ʔ
 DL-FUT-2SG > 3-get.scared-INST-BEN-PNC
 you will scare her [with it]

 c. <u>Instrumental, causative, and benefactive:</u> dęsheyadǫhwaęhęhgwáʔdęʔ
 d-ę-shey-adǫhwaęhę-hgw-aʔd-ę-ʔ
 DL-FUT-2SG > 3-get.scared-INST-CS-BEN-PNC
 you will cause her to get scared [with it]

d. <u>Distributive and benefactive</u>: waʔhųwatho·yahę́·ʔs
   waʔ-hųw-atho·y-ahę·-ʔs-Ø
   FACT-3 > 3M.SG-tell-DST-BEN-PNC
   they told him many things

e. <u>Inchoative and benefactive</u>: dayesawęnítgęʔs
   d-a-yesa-węn-itgę-ʔ-s-Ø
   CIS-FACT-3FI > 2SG-word-emerge-INCH-BEN-PNC
   they spoke out to you

f. <u>Benefative and inchoative</u>: ęyagonowęʔséʔkheʔ
   ę-yago-nowę-ʔse-ʔkheʔ-Ø
   FUT-3FI.P-fail.to.do-BEN-INCH-PNC
   she will get lazy

g. <u>Reversative and benefactive</u>: ęsga·dyaʔdų·dá·gwaʔs
   ę-sg-ad-yaʔd-ųdaR-gw-aʔs-Ø
   FUT-2SG > 1SG-SRF-body-put.into.a.container-REV-BEN-PNC
   you will leave me [literally: you will disconnect from me]

h. <u>Reversative, causative, and benefactive</u>: ęsathaha·gwáhdę?
   ę-s-at-hah-aR-gw-ahd-ę-ʔ
   FUT-2SG.P-SRF-path-put.in-REV-CS-BEN-PNC
   it will lead you astray

4.8.5.2 The Instrumental (Applicative)

The form of the instrumental suffix is *-(a)hgw-*. The parenthesized *a* is a joiner vowel that intervenes when combining the root suffix with an adjacent morpheme would result in a cluster of two or more consonants. The instrumental is added to a semantically dyadic or monadic verb, deriving a polyadic verb, that treats the semantic instrument as a patient participant. As is the case with the benefactive derivation, the instrumental derivation is obligatory in the sense that there is no contrasting expression in which the applicative argument occurs in peripheral function. Since instruments are always non-animate and are typically used by animate actors, and neuter is not expressed in the pronominal prefix unless it is the only argument, the pronominal prefix of the derived verb cannot identify an instrument argument; it can only express an animate or non-animate user of the instrument argument.

Example (317) is from a story in which a tree with many blossoms has lit up the newly created world of humans. The non-animate patient prefix *-yo-* references the semantic agent (the tree) in the derived instrumental verb. The instrument itself is identified by an independent expression.

(317) …néʔtho dógęs gǽ·heʔ tshaʔ ganųhsákdaʔ neʔ Onóʔjyaʔ nwaʔgaędóʔdęʔ, nayeʔ neʔ
      tshaʔ deyawęhahá·gih nayeʔ <u>deyohatheʔdáhgwih</u> tshaʔ néʔtho dyųhwęjyá·deʔ
      (H158.2-4).

neʔtho	dogęs	gæ·heʔ	tshaʔ	ga-nųhs-akd-aʔ	neʔ
LOC	MOD	NOUN	SUB	3N/Z.SG.A-house-be.near-STV	NOM
there	it's true	standing tree	at	near a house	the

o-noʔjy-aʔ	n-waʔ-ga-Rẹd-oʔdẹ-ʔ		naye?	ne?	tsha?
NPF-tooth-NSF	PRT-FACT-3N/Z.SG.A-tree-kind.of-PNC		ASRT	NOM	SUB
Tooth	the kind of tree it is		it's	the	that

de-yaw-ẹhahag-ih	naye?	de-yo-hathe-ʔd-ahgw-ih		tsha?	neʔtho
DL-3N/Z.SG.P-be.blooming-STV	ASRT	DL-3N/Z.SG.P-be.light-CS-INST-STV		SUB	LOC
it is blooming	it's	it has used it to make light		at	there

d-y-ųhwẹjy-ade-ʔ
CIS-3N/Z.SG.A-earth-exist-STV
where the earth is

…*there near a house stood a tree, the Tooth variety; it was in bloom [and] that's what it used to light up the earth.*

cf. <u>Without the instrumental</u>: deyohathéʔdih *it is making light*

In (318) the pronominal prefix *-dwa-* references an animate user, the presence of an instrument argument is marked in the verb with the instrumental suffix; the instrument is identified by an independent nominal.

(318) Nayéʔ <u>ẹdwanaʔdúhgwaʔ</u> neʔ <u>gaya·nẹ·hsæ·ʔgó·nah</u> (CTL239.2).

naye?	ẹ-dwa-naʔdų-hgw-a?	ne?	ga-yan-ẹhsR-a? = gona
ASRT	FUT-1IN.PL.A-identify.something-INST-PNC	NOM	NPF-good-NOM-NSF = AUG
it's	we will identify it with it	the	Great Law

This is what we will use to name it: the 'Great Law'.

Example (319) is a kinship expression that is used by a woman to refer to her sister's daughter in order to differentiate her from her own daughter. The user and patient arguments are both animate and expressed by the transitive prefix *-khe-*, the instrument is the kinship term *khehawáh* 'my daughter', and it occurs as a separate nominal.

(319) <u>khehawá</u> dekhenųhẹ·<u>khwa?</u>

khe-hawa	de-khe-nųhẹ·-hgw-ha?[168]
1SG > 3-mother/daughter	DL-1SG > 3-greet.with.a.kin.term-INST-HAB
my daughter	I use the kin term to greet her

niece [literally: I use the kin term 'my daughter' to greet her with]

In (320) The instrumental suffix combines with a manner-of-motion verb. A mother and her daughter have decided to leave the populated places, where they suffered from marauders, to go to live in the forest. The animate user argument (the people) is identified with an agent prefix, the instrumental suffix marks the presence of an instrument, which occurs independently as the place classifier expression *tshaʔ nų́·we.*

---

[168] Recall that the sequence *hgw-haʔ* is pronounced *khwaʔ.*

(320) Naye? ne? akdá? nhwa?gné? ne? tsha? nǘ·we hadi·ná·ge·?, í·nų ne? ga·hagǘ·wa
ne?tho wa?gyęnadayę? ne?tho wa?gyadegá?da? tsha? nǘ·we hya de?ęhdákhwa? ne?
ǘ·gweh (CTL2.5-8).

naye?	ne?	akda?	n-h-wa?-gn-e-?		ne?	tsha?	nųwe
ASRT	NOM	LOC	PRT-TRNS-FACT-3FZ.DU.A-walk-PNC		NOM	SUB	LOC
it's	the	nearby	they two went there		the	that	place

hadi-nage·-?	inų	ne?	ga-Rh-agųwa	ne?tho
3M.PL.A-live-STV	LOC	NOM	NPF-forest-LOC	LOC
they live	far	the	in the forest	there

wa?-gy-ę-nad-a-yę-?'		ne?tho	wa?-gy-ade-ga?d-a?
FACT-3FZ.DU.A-SRF-camp-JN-place-PNC		LOC	FACT-3FZ.DU.A-SRF-kindle.a.fire-PNC
they two set up camp		there	they two kindled a fire

tsha?	nųwe	hya	de?-ę-ehd-ahgw-ha?		ne?	hR-ųgweh
SUB	LOC	NEG	NEG-3FI.A-go.somewhere-INST-HAB		NOM	3M.SG.A-person:SUFF
at	place	not	they don't use it to go [there]		the	people

*They two left the place nearby where they lived, going far into the forest, where
they set up camp [and] kindled a fire at a place that people don't use to travel.*

In (321) the instrumental occurs with a triadic verb. It is a common way to announce the
subject of a story by the narrator. The animate user argument (the narrator) is expressed
with an agent prefix, the presence of an instrument (the topic of the story) is marked on the
verb by the root suffix, and is identified in a separate nominal (locusts).

(321) Na? ǘhgę? ęgethá·hgwa?, ne? o?gwę·yó?da? (LG01).

na?	ųhgę?	ę-ge-thaR-hgw-a?		ne?	o?gwę·yó?da?
ASRT	TMP	FUT-1SG.A-talk.about-INST-PNC		NOM	NOUN
it's	at this time	I'll use it to tell		the	locust(s)

So now I am going to talk about locusts. [Literally: I'll use locusts for telling]

A second, and very productive use of the instrumental suffix is to create names of
objects, especially for items that have been newly introduced to the culture. Usually, but
not inevitably – e.g. (322h) – these lexicalized expressions are inflected with the habitual
aspect and prefixed with a feminine-indefinite agent pronominal prefix identifying the user
argument. Although they are morphologically verbs, they function as nominals in clauses.

(322) Use of the instrumental to create names of objects:
    a. edęhdá·khwa?
       e-dęhdaR-hgw-ha?
       3FI.A-spread.out-INST-HAB
       carpet [literally: one uses it to spread out]

    b. ųde?nyędęsdákhwa?
       ų-ade?nyędęsd-ahgw-ha?
       3FI.A-compare-INST-HAB
       ruler [literally: one compares with it]

c. ųdnųhsodákhwaʔ
   ų-ad-nųhs-od-ahgw-haʔ
   3FI.A-SRF-house-set.up-INST-HAB
   umbrella [literally: one uses it to set up one's house]

d. ųwęʔdákhwaʔ
   ų-aęʔd-ahgw-haʔ
   3FI.A-blow-INST-HAB
   horn [literally: one blows with it]

e. ohsóhgwaʔ
   o-ahso-hgw-aʔ
   NPF-color.something-INST-NSF
   paint, color [literally: it is used to color with]

f. ehyadų́khwaʔ
   e-hyadų-hgw-haʔ
   3FI.A-write-INST-HAB
   pencil, pen [one writes with it]

g. ewihsayędákhwaʔ
   e-wihs-a-yęd-ahgw-aʔ
   3FI.A-ice-JN-place-INST-HAB
   refrigerator [one uses it to place ice]

h. ehwishéhgwih
   e-hwishe-<u>hgw</u>-ih
   3FI.A-be.powerful-<u>INST</u>-STV
   her strength, her respiration [literally: she uses it for strength/breathing]

Nominals created with the instrumental suffix can be possessed, just like morphological nouns, in that they can be prefixed with a possessive pronominal prefix (323a), and they can be incorporated into another verb by adding a nominalizer (323b):

(323) a. hodyędákhwaʔ
         ho-adyęd-ahgw-haʔ
         3M.SG.P-sit.down-INST-HAB
         his chair

     b. waʔha·dyędakhwaʔtshé·dęʔ
        waʔ-h-adyęd-ahgw-haʔ-ʔtshR-od-ęʔ
        FACT-3M.SG.A-sit.down-INST-HAB-NOM-set.up-PNC
        he set up the chair(s)

A fair number of instrumental stems can function grammatically as both verbs (324a), and nominals (324b).

(324) a. wadega?dáhgwih
    w-ade-ga?d-ahgw-ih
    3N/Z.SG.A-SRF-light.a.fire-INST-STV
    it was used to light a fire

   b. ų̱dega?dákhwa?
    ų̱-ade-ga?d-ahgw-ha?
    3FI.A-SRF-light.a.fire-INST-HAB
    kindling; matches

The following root suffix combinations that include the instrumental have been attested; combinations and their sequencing are shown in Table 4.60:

Table 4.60 Attested root suffix combinations with the instrumental

		causative	instrumental			
			instrumental	causative	benefactive	a
r			instrumental	benefactive		s
o		distributive	instrumental			p
o			instrumental	distributive		e
t	distributive	causative	instrumental			c
		causative	instrumental	distributive		t
			instrumental	ambulative		

Examples of each of these complex stems, a number of them with non-compositional meanings, are:

(325) a. <u>Causative and instrumental</u>: deyohathe?dáhgwih (H158.4).
    de-yo-hathe-?d-ahgw-ih
    DL-3N/Z.SG.P-give.off.light-CS-INST-STV
    it makes light with it

   b. <u>Instrumental, causative, and benefactive</u>: See (316)
   c. <u>Instrumental and benefactive</u>: See (316)

   d. <u>Distributive and instrumental</u>: wa?tgwa?nęyahnhahų̱hgwa?
    wa?-t-gwa-?nęy-a-hnha-hų-hgw-a?
    FACT-DL-1EX.PL > 2PL-bone-JN-encircle-DST-INST-PNC
    we (excl.) used it to tie up your bones

   e. <u>Instrumental and distributive</u>: honadi·hų̱dahgwáhę·?
    hon-ad-Rihw-ų̱d-ahgw-hę·?
    3M.NSG.P-SRF-matter-have.attached-INST-DISTR-STV
    their responsibilities

f. <u>Distributive, causative,[169] and instrumental</u>: ęwadeʔnyędęshę·dáhgwik
ę-w-ade-ʔnyędę-shę·-d-ahgw-ih-k-Ø
FUT-3N/Z.SG.A-SRF-measure-DST-CS-INST-STV-CNT-PNC
it will be used as a symbol [literally: it will be used to measure with]

g. <u>Causative, instrumental, and distributive</u>: deyeyahyaʔkdahgwáhę·k
de-ye-yahyaʔk-d-hgw-ahę·-k
DL-3FI.A-cross.over-CS-INST-DST-HAB
they use [a path] to cross over [a river].

h. <u>Instrumental and ambulative</u>: oʔnahgųdahgwáhneʔ
o-ʔnahg-ųd-ahgw-ahn-eʔ
3N/Z.SG.P-drum-be.attached-INST-AMB-PRP
bee; wasp [it stings as it goes]
        cf. *oʔnahgųthaʔ* 'it stings' [= bee]

4.8.5.3 The Causative

The forms of the causative followed by their aspect class in the order of frequency with which they occur as components of derived verb stems are: *-(a)ht-/-(a)hd-* (E1), *-(a)st-/-(a)sd-* (E1), *-(a)t-/-(a)d-* (E3), *-(a)ʔt-/-(a)ʔd-* (E1), *-(a)t-* (A) *and -hw-* (E2). The parenthesized *a* is a joiner vowel that intervenes when combining the root suffix with an adjacent morpheme would result in a cluster of two or more consonants. The alternants are cited as pairs. The members ending in voiced consonants occur before vowels, those with voiceless consonants occur before consonants by regular rule. The causative is added to active, stative, and motion verbs. Except for the *-(a)t-* alternant of the causative, which has somewhat different characteristics from the other suffixes, the causative derives an active verb that can be inflected with all three aspects. The alternant *-(a)t-* mentioned above, derives attributive stative verbs from active or stative verbs (see below).

Dixon (2012:240) lists four canonical features of causative constructions (characterized here in terms adapted to the approach used to analyze Onondaga): a. the derivation applies to monadic verbs and derives dyadic verbs; b. the non-derived single argument is encoded as patient in the derived form; c. the new causer argument is encoded as agent; d. there is some explicit formal marking of the causative construction. The Onondaga causative derivation exceeds or extends these criteria in a number of ways.

    i. The derivation applies to monadic and polyadic verbs.
    ii. The derivation applies to active, stative, and motion verbs.
    iii. The derivation may involve a change in verb class affiliation (Table 4.61 below).
    iv. The derivation does not always change the participant structure of the verb, so that monadic verbs may remain monadic, and polyadic verbs may remain polyadic. When the participant structure remains the same, there are either semantic effects in the derived stems, involving intensity and the application of

---

[169] In Woodbury et al. (1992) the *-t-/-d-* causative was identified as an instrumental.

extra force; or the derived form replaces the participant of the source verb with a causer participant.

v. Although frequently, the pronominal prefix will reference a causer argument, a number of the suffixes, may show up in examples with instrumental meanings especially *-(a)ht-/-(a)hd-*, *-(a)st-/-(a)sd-* and *-(a)ʔt-/-(a)ʔd-*.[170]

vi. Although the choice of causative suffix is established for each verb stem and learned with it by speakers, some verbs occur with several different causative alternants in different meanings.

vii. Causatives sometimes occur in deverbal expressions describing various every-day objects.

viii. There are numerous derived stems with idiosyncratic meanings.

Table 4.61 lists the derivational characteristics of the causative in terms of the verb class affiliation of source and derived stems, and the argument structure changes brought about by the derivation.[171]

Table 4.61 Causative characteristics (N = 126)

Verb Class Change source stem > derived stem	Argument Structure Change source stem > derived stem
active > active (58%)	monadic > dyadic (39%) dyadic > triadic (21%) monadic > monadic (11%) dyadic > dyadic (28%) triadic > triadic (1%)
stative > active (35%)	monadic > dyadic (70%) dyadic > triadic (2%) monadic > monadic (19%) dyadic > dyadic (9%)
motion > active (7%)	monadic > monadic (89%) dyadic > dyadic (11%)

The table shows that the causative derives active verbs, i.e., verbs that inflect for the three basic aspects, regardless of the source verb's category; that the derivation applies to polyadic as well as monadic stems; and that it frequently fails to change the participant structure of the stem. Note that with motion verbs as source verbs the argument structure never changes. Each of the possibilities listed in the table are exemplified next.

(i) <u>Active source verbs</u>

<u>Deriving a causative dyadic stem from an active monadic stem</u>. The new causer argument is encoded as agent or patient depending on aspect (326a,b), the causee, if non-animate is unmarked (326a,c), or if animate, the causer and causee are marked by a transitive prefix (326b):

---

[170] Abbott (2000) classifies all of the cognate Oneida alternants as instrumentals; Lounsbury (1953) and Abbott (2006) treat them as two sets of suffixes – causative and instrumental – with identical forms.

[171] *-(at)-* causative data, are dealt with separately (see below and Table 4.62).

(326) a. wa?tgʊdóꞏgwa? (H669.10) > wa?thadogwáhda?
    wa?-t-gʊ-adogw-a?   wa?-t-<u>h</u>-adogw-<u>ahd</u>-a?
    FACT-DL-3FZ.PL.A-scatter,disperse-PNC   FACT-DL-<u>3M.SG.A</u>-scatter-CS-PNC
    they dispersed [going to different   *he scattered it* [literally: he caused it
    locations]   to scatter]

          In the stative aspect with patient prefix:
          dehodogwáhdih *he has scattered it*
          de-<u>ho</u>-adogw-<u>ahd</u>-ih
          DL-<u>3M.SG.P</u>-scatter-CS-STV
          he has scattered it

  b. ęgeꞏjyáꞏgę? > wa?hagejyagę́sda?
    ę-ge-jyagę-?   wa?-<u>hage</u>-jyagę-<u>sd</u>-a?
    FUT-1SG.A-try.hard-PNC   FACT-<u>3.SG > 1SG</u>-try.hard-CS-PNC
    I will try hard   *he encouraged me*

  c. deyosdáꞏthek[172] > dehasdaꞏthé?tha?
    de-yo-sdaꞏthe-k   de-ha-sdaꞏthe-?t-ha?
    DL-3N/Z.SG.P-shine,gleam-HAB   DL-3M.SG.A-shine,gleam-CS-HAB
    it shines, it gleams   *he polishes it*

<u>Deriving a causative triadic stem from and active dyadic stem</u>: The new causer argument
is referenced as agent or patient depending on aspect; the causee and third argument, when
non-animate, are unmarked.

(327) wa?hahsę́ꞏnya? > na? wa?hahsęꞏnyá?da?
    wa?-ha-hsęny-a?   na? wa?-ha-hsęꞏny-a?d-a?
    FACT-3M.SG.A-make-PNC   ASRT FACT-3M.SG.A-make-CS-PNC
    he made it   *that's what he made it with* [= he caused it to make it]

<u>Deriving a causative monadic stem from an active monadic stem</u>: No change in
participant structure, but meaning change in terms of intensity of the action.
(328) wa?hadidáꞏhgwa? > dahadidaꞏhgwá?da?
    wa?-ha-adidaR-hgw-a?   d-a-ha-adiaR-hgw-a?d-a?
    FACT-3M.SG.A-get.in-REV-PNC   CIS-FACT-3M.SG.A-get.in-REV-CS-PNC
    he got out   he jumped out

<u>Deriving a causative dyadic stem from an active dyadic stem</u>: No change to the
participant structure, but semantic change in terms of intensity of the action.
(329) thodiyę́thwih > thodiyęthwáhdih
    t-ho-adyęthw-ih   t-ho-adiyęthw-<u>ahd</u>-ih
    CIS-3M.SG.P-tug.at-STV   CIS-3M.SG.P-tug.at-CS-STV
    he is tugging at it   *he is jerking it*

<u>Deriving a triadic causative verb from a triadic stem</u>: No change to the participant
structure, but semantic change in terms of the degree to which the action is performed.

---

[172] The source verb *.staꞏthe-* + dualic takes patient prefixes in all aspects.

260 The Verb

(330) waʔthahę̇·ʔ   >   waʔthahę̇·hdaʔ
       waʔ-t-ha-hę̇·-ʔ'   waʔ-t-ha-hę̇·-hd-aʔ
       FACT-DL-3M.SG.A-put.sthg.in.sthg-PNC   FACT-DL-3M.SG.A-put.sthg.in.sthg-CS-PNC
       he filled it   *he filled it all the way to the top*

(ii) <u>Stative Source Verbs</u>

<u>Deriving a causative dyadic stem from an agent-only (331a) or patient-only (331b) stative
monadic stem</u>: a new causer argument is added in the derived form.

(331) a. wahétgęʔ   >   waʔkhetgę́hdaʔ
         w-ahetgę-ʔ   waʔ-k-hetgę-hd-aʔ
         3N/Z.SG.A-be.bad-STV   FACT-1SG.A-be.bad-CS-PNC
         it is bad   *I spoiled it*

      b. onaʔnóh   >   waʔgnaʔnósdaʔ
         o-naʔno-h   waʔ-g-naʔno-sd-aʔ
         3N/Z.SG.P-be.cold.to.the.touch-STV   FACT-1SG.A-be.cold.to.the.touch-CS-PNC
         it is cold to the touch   *I cooled it*

<u>Deriving a causative triadic stem from a patient only stative dyadic stem</u>: a new causer
argument is added in the derived form.

(332) agehnhų́·daʔ   >   ųgehnhų́thwih
       age-hnhųd-aʔ   ųge-hnhųt-hw-ih
       1SG.P-have.sthg.in.one's.mouth-STV   3FI/Z>1SG-have.sthg.in.one's.mouth-CS-STV
       I have it in my mouth   *she has put it in my mouth*

<u>Deriving a causative monadic stem from an agent only stative monadic stem</u>: the
argument of the source verb is replaced by a causer argument.

(333) tgayé·iʔ   >   daha·yéit
       t-ga-ye·i-ʔ   d-a-ha-ye·i-t-Ø
       CIS-3N/Z.SG.A-be.right,correct-STV   CIS-FACT-3M.SG.A-be.right,correct-CS-PNC
       it is right   *he acted correctly*

<u>Deriving a causative dyadic stem from an agent only stative dyadic stem</u>: the derived
verb replaces the original agent argument with a causer argument.
(334) gyę·déih   >   waʔgyędé·hdaʔ
       g-yędeR-ih   waʔ-g-yędeR-hd-aʔ
       1SG.A-know.something-STV   FACT-1SG.A-know.something-CS-PNC
       I know (it)   *I displayed [my] knowledge*

(iii) <u>Motion Verbs as Source Verbs</u>

<u>Deriving a causative monadic stem from a monadic motion verb</u>: with non-compositional
semantic change:

(335) haya?dagu̧dá·dye?   >   hwa?haya?dagu̧da·dyéhda?
    ha-ya?dagu̧dadye-?   h-wa?-ha-ya?dagu̧dadye-hd-a?
    3M.SG.A-continue.moving-PRP   TRNS-FACT-3M.SG.A-continue.moving-CS-PNC
    he keeps right on moving   *he went there permanently*

<u>Deriving a causative dyadic stem from a dyadic motion verb</u>: with semantic change in terms of the force that is wielded.

(336) wa?hahá·wi?   >   wa?hahawíhda?
    wa?-ha-hawi-?   wa?-ha-hawi-hd-a?
    FACT-3M.SG.A-carry.in.one's.hands-PRP   FACT-3M.SG.A- carry.in.one's.hands-cs-PNC
    he is carrying it along   *he grabbed it*

Instrumental Meanings

As has been pointed out above, examples that are glossed with instrumental meanings are quite common. The source verbs are always dyadic. For the most part these appear to come about because the causative translation is infelicitous in English. In (337) the causative stem *-nu̧hya?kd-* 'cause somebody to hurt' was glossed as an instrumental in the text:

(337)…ẹyagonu̧hyá?kda? ne? ú̧·gweh ne? ená·ge·?… (CTL317.8-318.1).
    ẹ-yago-nu̧hya?k-<u>d</u>-a?   ne?   (y)-u̧gweh   ne?   e-nage·-?
    FUT-3FI.P-hurt-CS-PNC   NOM   NPF-person:SUFF   NOM   3FI.A-reside-STV
    it will cause them to hurt   the   people   the   they live [here]
    …it will be used to hurt the people living [here]… [referring to the ill-will of possible enemies].
        cf. Without the causative: wa?shagonú̧hya?k *he hurt her*

In (338) there are two causative verbs, one of them glossed as an instrumental: *-hẹ·-* + <u>*sd*</u>- 'tie with = [cause something to tie something]', and the second glossed as a causative: *-hniR* + <u>*hd*</u>- 'make sturdy'. Here the causee argument, *sgẹnu̧dú̧? ojinu̧hya?dá?* 'deer sinew', occurs as a separate nominal expression.

(338) Thohge ó·nẹ sgẹnu̧dú̧? ojinu̧hya?dá? nayé? <u>wa?hahé·sda?</u> <u>wa?hahní·hda?</u> hwiks
    nwa?hahé·ga? tsha? nigahesga·ís (CTL302.7-8).
    thohge onẹ   sgẹnu̧du̧?   o-jinu̧hya?d-a?   naye?   wa?-ha-hẹ·-<u>sd</u>-a?
    TMP   TMP   NOUN   NPF-sinew-NSF   ASRT   FACT-3M.SG.A-tie-CS-PNC
    thereafter   deer   sinew   it's   he caused it to tie it

    wa?-ha-hni·-<u>hd</u>-a?   hwiks   n-wa?-ha-hẹ·g-a?   tsha?
    FACT-3M.SG.A-sturdy-CS-PNC   NUM   PRT-FACT-3M.SG.A-tie-PNC   SUB
    he made it sturdy   five   thus he tied it   that

    ni-ga-hesgaR-is-Ø'
    PRT-3N/Z.SG.A-arrow-be.long-STV
    how long the arrows are
    Then he used deer sinew to tie the long arrows five times to make it sturdy.
        cf. Without the causative: khẹ́·s *I tie [things]*

The *-(a)t-* Causative

In Onondaga, the semantic role of *stimulus* is treated as a kind of *causer*. There is a small group of affect verbs like *get exhausted, slip, suffer [pain], feel surprise, grieve, worry, fear, satisfy, amuse, know, pity, see, etc.*, that serve as source verbs for the *-(a)t-* causative. Attached to these, the causative derives a stative verb and replaces the argument(s) of the affect verb with an argument that expresses the role of *stimulus*.

Table 4.62 Characteristics of the *-(a)t-* causative (N = 16)

Verb Class Change source stem > derived stem	Argument Structure Change source stem > derived stem
va > vs (75%)	monadic > monadic (45%) dyadic > monadic (55%)
vs > vs (25%)	monadic > monadic (75%) dyadic > monadic (25%)

The table shows that the derivation applies to both active and stative affect verbs, and that the derivation invariably results in a monadic verb stem. Each of the possibilities listed in the table are exemplified next.

Deriving stative stems with attributive meanings: The causative suffix *-(a)t-* derives stative stems with attributive meanings from active (339a) or stative (339b) stems:

(339) a. wa?há·gę?   >   ó·gęt
    wa?-ha-gę-?   o-gę-t̲-Ø
    FACT-3M.SG.A-3-see-PNC   3N/Z.SG.P-see-CS-STV
    he saw (it)   *it is visible*

   b. agade·yę?dó·da?   >   ode·yę?dó·dat
     ag-ade·yę?dod-a?   o-ade·yę?dod-a̲t̲-Ø
     1SG.P-be.worried-STV   3N/Z.SG.P-be.worried-CS-STV
     I am worried   *it is worrisome, dangerous*

   c. ak?nigųhiyóh   >   o?nigųhí·yot (H660.12)
     ak-?nigųhR-iyo-h'   o-?nigųhR-iyo-t-Ø
     1SG.P-mind-good-STV   3N/Z.SG.P-mind-good-CS-STV
     I am satisfied / content   *it is pleasing*

The *-(a)t-* causative functions attributively:

(340) The derived verb modifies a nominal phrase:
    ...oyę́·det ne? gohá·wah goksa?dayę·dá?she·? (CTL3.4).
    o-yędeR-t̲-Ø   ne?   go-hawah   go-ksa?d-a-yęd-a?-hsR-e?
    3N/Z.SG.P-know-CS-STV   NOM 3FZ.SG>3-mother/child 3FI.P-child-JN-have-INCH-DSLC-PRP
    it is noticeable   the   her daughter   she is going to have a child
    ...it is noticeable [that] her daughter is expecting a child.
          cf. Without the causative: gyędé·ih *I know, I have an inkling*

(341) <u>The derived verb is modified by a degree particle:</u>
Gųdáʔ goʔ naʔ geʔsé·ʔs nęgę́ ųhgę́ʔ ya go·ʔ deʔskheyaʔdanę́hgwik, <u>jíh gaęhyá·gęt</u>
(LG10).

gųdaʔ	go·ʔ	naʔ	ge-ʔse·-ʔs	nęgę	ųhgęʔ
MOD	CTR	ASRT	1SG.A-drive-HAB	DEM	TMP
by necessity	however	it's	I drive around	this	at this time

hya	deʔ-s-khe-yaʔd-a-nęhgwi-k	jik	ga-Ręhyagę-t̲-Ø
NEG	NEG-REP-1SG>3-body-JN-haul-HAB	DGR	3N/Z.SG.A-be.in.pain-CS-STV
not	I'm not a taxi driver anymore	too much	it's painful

I do drive at this time, but I'm not a taxi driver anymore, it's too much of a struggle.
cf. <u>Without the causative:</u> gowęhyagę́h *she is suffering, she is in pain*

It was pointed out that some verb stems are lexicalized with more than one alternant of
the causative suffix. For example, *-yędeR-* 'know' occurs with the *-(a)st-/-(a)sd-* alternant,
with the *-(a)ht-/-(a)hd-* alternant and with the *-(a)t-* alternant. The derived stems in (a-b)
are active verbs, the stem in (c) is stative. Each derived stem has a different meaning:

(342) a. gyędé·sthaʔ
    g-yędeR-st-haʔ
    1SG.A-know, have.an.inkling-CS-HAB
    I am making it known

    b. hniyędé·thaʔ
    hni-yędeR-ht-haʔ
    3M.DU.A-know-CS-HAB
    they two show know-how, expertise

    c. oyę́·det
    o-yędeR-t-Ø
    3N/Z.SG.P-know-CS-STV
    it is noticeable

<u>Deverbal causatives:</u>

(343) a. deyųdadnųhæhgwáʔthaʔ
    de-yų-adad-nųhæhgw-aʔt-ha?
    DL-3FI.A-REF-scalp.someone-CS-HAB
    tomahawk

    b. heyų·dwęnųdá·sthaʔ
    he-yų-ad-węn-ųdaR-st-haʔ
    TRNS-3FI.A-SRF-voice-put.in-CS-HAB
    telephone

    c. gaʔse·hdaʔ
    ga-ʔseR-hd-aʔ
    NPF-drag-CS-NSF
    car, vehicle

d. tsha? nų hehųwadi?nųhdá·tha?

   tsha?   nų   he-hųwadi-?nųhdaR-t-ha?
   SUB   LOC   TRNS-3 > 3M.NSG-bury-CS-HAB
   that   place they cause them to get buried there
  graveyard

The following root suffix combinations that include the causative have been attested; combinations and their sequencing are shown in Table 4.63:

Table 4.63 Attested root suffix combinations with the causative

		causative	causative		
		causative	benefactive		
	instrumental	causative	benefactive		
		causative	instrumental		
		causative	instrumental	distributive	
root	distributive	causative	instrumental		aspect
		causative	dislocative		
		causative	distributive	dislocative	
		causative	distributive		
	reversative	causative			
	reversative	causative	benefactive		
		causative	inchoative		

Examples of each of these complex stems – a number of them with non-compositional meanings – are:

(344) a. <u>Causative and causative</u>: ętgadiyęthwáhda?

     ę-t-g-adiyęt-hw-ahd-a?
     FUT-CIS-1SG.A-pull-CS-CS-PNC
     I will yank it

  b. <u>Causative and benefactive</u>: See (316)
  c. <u>Instrumental, causative, and benefactive</u>: See (316)
  d. <u>Causative and instrumental</u>: See (325)
  e. <u>Causative, instrumental, and distributive</u>: See (325)
  f. <u>Distributive, causative, and instrumental</u>: See (325)

  g. <u>Causative and dislocative</u>: deshagodæ·hdáhne?

     de-shago-adR-ahd-ahn-e?
     DL-3M.SG > 3-meet-CS-DSLC-PRP
     he is going to meet her; he is here to meet her

  h. <u>Causative, distributive, and dislocative</u>: hawęhæ·sdahę́·hne?

     h-awęhR-asd-ahę́·-hn-e?
     3M.SG.A-move.something.upward-CS-DST-DSLC-PRP
     he is going to move [things] up [there]; he is here to move [things] up [there]

   i. <u>Causative and distributive</u>: wa?thahsiha·hdahę·?
    wa?-t-ha-hsihaR-hd-ahę·-?
    FACT-DL-3M.SG.A-be.tight-CS-DST-PNC
    I plugged up [the gaps]

   j. <u>Reversative and causative</u>: ętgahæ·gwáhda?
    ę-t-ga-R-hR-agw-ht-a?
    FUT-CIS-3N/Z.SG.A-wind-put.up.on-REV-CS-PNC
    [the] wind will take it off of it

   k. <u>Reversative, causative, and benefactive</u>: See (316)

   l. <u>Causative and inchoative</u>: wa?gę?dųhgwésthe?
    wa?-ga-i?dųhgw-es-t-he?-Ø
    FACT-3N/Z.SG.A-flame-long-CS-INCH-PNC
    it caused the flame to become long[er]

4.8.5.4 The Inchoative

The inchoative morpheme alternants are *-(a)?-; -(a)h-/-(a)?-; -ęh-/-ę?-; -he?-, -(a)(?)khe?-.*[173] The pairs of alternants separated by slashes, are grammatically conditioned by aspect category.[174] The parenthesized *a* is a joiner vowel that intervenes when combining the root suffix with an adjacent morpheme would result in a cluster of two or more consonants. The choice of inchoative suffix is lexicalized for each verb stem and learned with it by speakers. For the suppletive forms, the alternant ending in *h* occurs with the habitual and punctual aspects, and the one ending in *?* occurs with the stative aspect. Inchoative forms take the aspect classes E3 and E4 when the suffix occurs as the last element of a verb stem.

   The inchoative derives an active verb that can be inflected with the three basic aspects from active or stative stems. The derived verb changes the viewpoint of the source verb to a focus on the onset of an event. The derivation does not effect a change in participant structure, thus a monadic verb will be derived from a monadic source verb, and a dyadic verb from a dyadic source. The derivation is semantically compositional in most, but not all, cases.

<u>Deriving active inchoative verbs from active source verbs:</u>
Active source verbs are often verbs describing involuntary actions, positional verbs, and weather verbs. For example, the stem *-hsi-/-hsihw-* '[be] hungry' is, in Onondaga, an active, involuntary action verb that takes patient prefixes in all aspects. With the inchoative, the pronominal selection remains unchanged, but the meaning changes to 'get hungry':

---

[173] The parenthesized glottal stop *(?)* indicates speaker variation.

[174] Chafe (1967) ranks the cognate alternants in Seneca into three groups. in terms of their relative closeness to the verb root when they combine with other root suffixes. Chafe (1996) refers to the Seneca cognates of the suppletive alternants as the *archaic inchoatives* because of their limited distribution in Seneca. In Onondaga there is little difference in the frequency with which the alternants occur.

(345)   waʔhohsíhweʔ   >   waʔhohsíʔkheʔ
        waʔ-ho-hsihw-eʔ   waʔ-ho-hsi-ʔkheʔ-Ø[175]
        FACT-3M.SG.P-be.hungry-PNC   FACT-3M.SG.P-be.hungry-INCH-PNC
        he is hungry   *he got hungry*

An example with a positional verb is the secondary attachment verb *-ųd-/-ųt-* 'attach, put forth, project outward'. With the inchoative, the meaning changes to 'get attached':

(346)   áų·daʔ   >   audáʔih
        a-ųd-aʔ   a-ųd-aʔ-ih
        3N/Z.SG.P-attach-STV   3N/Z.SG.P-attach-INCH-STV
        it is attached   *it has become attached*

An example with a weather verb is *-nųnyayę-* 'freeze'. With the inchoative, the meaning changes to 'become frozen':

(347)   onųnyá·yęʔ   >   onų·nyayę́ʔih
        o-nųnyayę-ʔ   o-nųnyayę-ʔ-ih
        3N/Z.SG.P-freeze-STV   3N/Z.SG.P-freeze-INCH-STV
        it is frozen   *it has become frozen*

<u>Deriving an active inchoative verb from a stative source verb:</u>
Much more frequently (74% of source verbs), the inchoative occurs with a stative source verb. The verb *-yędeR-* 'know' is a mental state verb that takes agent prefixes. With the inchoative, pronominal selection changes to the predominant active verb pattern of agent prefixes in the habitual and punctual aspects, and patient prefixes in the stative, and the meaning changes from 'know (something)' to 'understand' [literally, come to know (something)]:

(348)   gyę́·di·h   >   waʔgyędé·ʔnhaʔ
        g-yędeR-ih   waʔ-g-yędeR-ʔ-nhaʔ
        1SG.A-know-STV   FACT-<u>1SG.A</u>-know-INCH-PNC
        I know, I have an inkling   *I understood*
                 cf. In the stative aspect: hyá deʔ<u>agyę</u>·dé·ʔih *I didn't understand it*

The verb *-ksdęʔ-* 'be old [of animates]' is a stative verb with attributive meaning that takes patient prefixes. The inchoative derives a stem that takes patient prefixes in all three of the basic aspects; the meaning changes to 'get old':

(349)   goksdęʔáh   >   waʔagoksdęʔáʔkheʔ
        go-ksdęʔ-áh   waʔ-ago-ksdęʔ-aʔkheʔ-Ø
        3FI.P-be.old-STV   FACT-3FI.P-be.old-INCH-PNC
        she is old, old lady   *she got old*

---

[175] *-hsi-* is the alternant of the stem that occurs with derivational suffixes.

The verb *-ya?dashaye-* 'be slow-moving' is a stative physical activity verb that takes patient prefixes. The inchoative derives a stem that takes patient prefixes in all three of the basic aspects; the meaning changes to 'get delayed':

(350) agoya?dasha·yẹh   >   wa?agoya?dasha·yẹha?
       ago-ya?d-a-shayẹ-h   wa?-ago-ya?d-a-shayẹ-h-a?
       3FI.P-body-JN-be.slow.moving-STV   FACT-3FI.P-body-JN-be.slow.moving-INCH-PNC
       she is slow-moving   *she got delayed*

The inchoative is extremely productive in discourse where it functions to activate states and situations and add the meaning of incipience as noted above. An example with an inchoative derivation from an active positional source verb is:

(351) Gwas ganyó? <u>odinakdodẹhá?</u> tshe? gwa? degų́tkhwa? (LG14).
       gwas   ganyo?   odi-nakd-od-ẹh-a?   tshe? gwa?
       INTNS   TMP   3FZ.NSG.P-space-protrude-<u>INCH</u>-STV   TMP
       very   as soon as they got a chance   already

       de-gų-atgw-ha?
       DL-3FZ.PL.A-dance-HAB
       they dance
       Every chance they got, immediately they danced.

An example with an inchoative derivation from a mental state source verb is:

(352) Gadogẹ ųgwayo?déhgwa?, thogẹ ne? hayẹthwás ohyá? Hitchings hayá·ji?. Thohge
       nų <u>dedyųgwadadyẹdé·?ih</u> (LG07).
       ga-dogẹ-h   ųgwa-yo?de-h-gwa?   thogẹ   ne?   ha-yẹthw-as
       3N/Z.SG.A-certain-STV   1PL.P-work-HAB-PST   DEM   NOM   3M.SG.A-plant-HAB
       it is the same   we used to work   that   the   he plants

       o-ahy-a?   Hitchings   ha-yas-ih   thohge   nų
       NPF-apple-NSF   NAME   3M.SG.A-be.named-STV   TMP   LOC
       apple   Hitchings   he is called   then   place

       de-d-yųgw-adad-yẹdeR-?-ih
       DL-CIS-1PL.P-REF-know-<u>INCH</u>-STV
       <u>we got to know each other</u>
       We used to work together for Hitchings, [as] he is called, he grows apples, [and]
       that's where we got to know each other.

Table 4.64 shows attested root combinations with the inchoative:

Table 4.64 Attested root suffix combinations with the inchoative

		inchoative	dislocative			
		inchoative	distributive			
root		inchoative	distributive	distributive	ambulative	aspect
	causative	inchoative				
	benefactive	inchoative				
		inchoative	benefactive			

Examples of each of these complex stems – a number of them with non-compositional meanings – are:

(353) a. Inchoative and dislocative: hoyoʔdę́hse·ʔ
      ho-yoʔd-<u>ęh-she·</u>-ʔ
      3M.SG.P-work-INCH-DSLC-PRP
      he is going to work

    b. Inchoative and distributive: waʔtgaihwayędáʔshę·ʔ
      waʔ-t-ga-Rihw-a-yęd-<u>aʔ-shę·</u>-ʔ
      FACT-DL-3N/Z.SG.A-matter-JN-lay.down-INCH-DST-PNC
      the various decisions that were made

    c. Inchoative, distributive, distributive, and ambulative: desagahsęʔdųnyų́hne?
      de-sa-gahsR-ę-<u>ʔ-dų-nyų-hn</u>-e?
      DL-2SG.P-tear(s)-move.down-INCH-DST-DST-AMB-PRP
      you are crying as you come

    d. Causative and inchoative: See (344)
    e. Benefactive and inchoative: See (316)
    f. Inchoative and benefactive: See (316)

4.8.5.5 The Reversatives[176]

Two reversatives affect the meaning of the verb stem in slightly different ways. The first, *-(a)hcy-*, reverses the action of the verb stem, e.g., *-adyaʔdawiʔd-* 'get dressed' > *-adyaʔdawiʔdahcy-* / *-adyaʔdawihcy-* 'get undressed'; the second, the reversative-multiplier *-(a)hgw-*, *-ųgw-/-gw-* [177] either reverses the stem's meaning, e.g., *-adeʔsgųd-* 'put in the oven' > *-adeʔsgųdagw-* 'take out of the oven', or multiplies its action in unpredictable ways, e.g., *-yena- catch, grab, accept* > *-yenaųgw-* 'have seizures', or does both, e.g., *-adehnhodų-* 'for a door to close' > *-adehnhodųgw-* 'for a place to be open to the public'. The parenthesized *a* is a joiner vowel that intervenes when combining the root suffix with an adjacent morpheme would result in a cluster of two or more consonants. The choice of reversative alternant is lexicalized for each verb stem and learned with it by speakers.

<u>Reversative Meanings</u>

The meaning of *-adidaR-* is 'get into something, board something'; with the reversative the meaning is 'get out of something':

---

[176] Cognates in the other Iroquoian languages are called 'infective (undoer)' (Lounsbury 1953); 'oppositive' Chafe (1967), and 'undoer' (Chafe 1996, Abbott 2000, 2006), 'reversative' (Michelson & Doxtator 2002).

[177] *-ųgw-* follows a consonant, *-gw-* follows a vowel.

(354) ... neʔ ogwę·yoʔdá·ʔ nę hęnehéʔ <u>ęshųdidá·hgwaʔ</u> neʔ nę deʔsgųdákhwaʔgé waʔgá·ęʔ (LG07).

neʔ	ogwę·yoʔdá·ʔ	nę	hęn-eR-heʔ	ę-s-hų-adidaR-<u>hgw</u>-aʔ
NOM	NOUN	TMP	3M.PL.A-want-HAB	FUT-REP-3M.PL.A-get.in-<u>REV</u>-PNC
the	locusts	then	they want	they jump back out

neʔ nę	deʔsgųdakhwaʔ = ge	waʔ-ga-R-ęʔ
NOM TMP	frying.pan = LOC	FACT-3N/Z.SG.A-be.in-PNC
when	at the frying pan	it is in it

... the locusts want to jump back out of the frying pan when they're in it.

The meaning of *-ahsęny-* is 'get dressed'; with the reversative the meaning is 'get undressed':

(355) Agwegíh <u>waʔų̨ʔshę·nyahcyáʔ</u> tho niyót thogę́ é·daʔ, yáh sdęʔ deʔsgęhnáhæ·ʔ (LG09).

agwegih	waʔ-ų̨-ahsę·ny-<u>ahsy</u>-aʔ	tho niyot	thogę
QNT	FACT-3FI.A-get.dressed-<u>REV</u>-PNC	MAN	DEM
all	she got undressed	how it is	that

e-d-aʔ	hya	sdęʔ	deʔ-s-ga-ihn-a-hR-aʔ
3FI.A-stand-STV	NEG	IND	NEG-REP-3N/Z.SG.A-skin-JN-be.on-STV
she is standing	not	something	it isn't on the skin

She got completely undressed and there she stood with nothing on.

<u>With Multiplier effect on the action:</u>

The verb *.ahdędy-* + repetitive means 'go home' [literally, go back]. In this example, the reversative marks the fact that a whole group of persons are returning each to their own home:

(356) Thohgé ó·nę gędyóhgwaʔ tshaʔ <u>sahų̨hdę·dyų́·gwaʔ</u> (CTL171.6).

thohge onę	gę-idyohgw-aʔ	tshaʔ	s-a-hų-ahdędyų-<u>gw</u>-aʔ
TMP TMP	NPF-crowd-NSF	SUB	REP-FACT-3M.PL.A-leave-<u>REV</u>-PNC
thereafter	the crowd [of people]	that	they went home [multiply]

Then the crowd left to go home.

The following root suffix combinations that include the reversative have been attested; combinations and their sequencing are shown in Table 4.65:

Table 4.65 Attested root suffix combinations with the reversative

		reversative	reversative/multiplier		
		reversative	causative		
		reversative	causative	benefactive	
root		reversative	benefactive		aspect
	distributive	reversative			
		reversative	distributive		
		reversative	dislocative		

Examples of each of these complex stems – a number of them with non-compositional meanings – are:

(357) a. <u>Reversative and reversative/multiplier</u>: ęhakhahcyǫ́·gwaʔ
    ę-ha-kh-ahcy-ǫgw-aʔ
    FUT-3M.SG.A-partition-MLT-PNC
    he will distribute it; he will divide it up

    b. Reversative and causative: See (344)
    c. Reversative, causative and benefactive: See (316)
    d. Reversative and benefactive: See (316)

    e. <u>Distributive and reversative</u>: ędyęnǫhdǫ·nyǫ́·gwaʔ
    ę-dy-ęnǫhdǫ-nyǫ-gw-aʔ
    FUT-1IN.DU.A-know-DST-MLT-PNC
    we two (incl.) will think it over

    f. <u>Reversative and distributive</u>: waʔeniyǫdagwahǫ́ʔ
    waʔ-e-niyǫd-agw-ahǫ-ʔ
    FACT-3FI.A-hitch.up-REV-DST-PNC
    she took off [several] [e.g. laundry off of a clothes line]

    g. <u>Reversative and dislocative</u>: ęhaniyǫdagwáhaʔ (H204.6)
    ę-ha-niyǫd-agw-ah-aʔ
    FUT-3M.SG.A-hitch.up-REV-DSLC-PNC
    he will go to unhitch it

4.8.5.6 The Distributive

The distributive alternants are *-(a)dǫ-; -(a)hę·-/-(a)hǫ-; -(ǫ)nyǫ-; -shę·-/-shǫ-; -ǫ-/-(a)yǫ-.*[178] The parenthesized *a* is a joiner vowel that intervenes when combining the root suffix with an adjacent morpheme would result in a cluster of two or more consonants. The choice of distributive is lexicalized for each verb stem and learned with it by speakers. The alternants *-nyǫ-* and *-ǫnyǫ-* are phonologically conditioned; *-nyǫ-* occurs after a vowel, and *-ǫnyǫ-* after a consonant (including underlying R). Semantically, the suffix *distributes* the action denoted by a stem in terms of temporal or spatial dimensions or over the participants of a given verb. The suffix co-occurs with other root suffixes either to its left or to its right. The distributive's scope extends over the portion of the stem that is to its left.

The distributive occurs with active, motion, and stative verbs. Adding the distributive typically does not change the category of the verb, although there are a few exceptions. An example is the stative verb *-ęnǫhdǫ-* 'think' that becomes, with the distributive, the active verb *-ęnǫhdǫnyǫ-* 'think about, ponder' which can be inflected with the three basic aspects. But change of category is not a defining feature of the suffix.

---

[178] Note that each of the alternants includes the vowel *ǫ* (*ę·* derives from underlying *Rǫ* by regular rule). Note also the, undoubtedly, related verb stem *.ǫ-* + partitive 'be an amount'.

There are a few verb stems that can take either of two different alternants of the distributive with changed meaning. An example is the stative verb *-dogę-* 'be certain, be a certain one, be the same': With the distributive *-(a)hę·-* the meaning becomes 'be certain ones'; with the distributive *-(a)hų-* the meaning is lexicalized as 'be square'.

Depending on the meaning of the original stem, the addition of the distributive introduces numerous subtle distinctions that the following in-context examples help to reveal.

A. <u>Distributed action in time</u>

<u>Repetitive actions:</u>
(358) <u>Waʔthahwaʔesdahę̇·ʔ</u> ehų̇ʔgwa·ʔgé tshaʔ nigę́ waʔaihé·yaʔ (LG09).

waʔ-t-ha-hwaʔe-sd-<u>ahę̇·</u>-aʔ	e-hų̇ʔgwaR-aʔ = ge	tshaʔ nigę
FACT-DL-3M.SG.A-strike-CS-DST-PNC	3FI.A-throat-NSF = LOC	SUB EXT
<u>he pierced it repeatedly</u>	(on) her throat	until

waʔ-a-ihey-aʔ
FACT-3FI.A-die-PNC
she died
He kept piercing her throat [with the knife] until she died.

(359) Dę́ʔseʔ neʔ nę ęshadiyų́ʔdaʔ, <u>dęhadiyaʔkhų́ʔ</u> neʔ ęwadésdaʔ, ęjyekhųnyáʔdaʔ (LG11).

dęʔseʔ	neʔ nę	ę-s-hadi-yų-ʔd-aʔ	d-ę-hadi-yaʔk-<u>hų</u>-ʔ
CNJ	NOM TMP	FUT-REP-3M.PL.A-arrive-CS-PNC	DL-FUT-3M.PL.A-cut-DST-PNC
and	when	they will bring it back	<u>they will cut it [into pieces]</u>

neʔ	ę-w-ade-sd-aʔ	ę-s-ye-khw-ųny-aʔd-aʔ
NOM	FUT-3N/Z.SG.A-SRF-use-PNC	FUT-REP-3FI.A-meal-make-CS-PNC
the	it gets used	they will cook with it

And when they bring [the log] back, they <u>chop it into pieces,</u> so it can be used to cook with.

<u>Sequential actions</u> (repetitive sets of actions in sequence):

(360) Nęgę́ diʔ hyaʔ dyotgų́t haʔdéyųh <u>hahsę·nyáhę·k</u> thogę́ neʔ ohnáʔgę hagwá tshaʔ nų́ waʔgadęhnyodáʔ nęgę́ neʔ mací·n (LG13).

nęgę	diʔ	hyaʔ	dyotgut	haʔ-de-y-ų-h'
DEM	LNK	MOD	TMP	TRNS-DL-3N/Z.SG.A-be.an.amount-STV
this	moreover	indeed	always	all kinds [of things]

ha-hsę·ny-<u>ahę̇·</u>-k	thogę	neʔ	o-hnaʔgę-h	hagwa	tshaʔ	nų
3M.SG.A-make-DST-HAB	DEM	NOM	3N/Z.SG.P-behind-STV	DIR	SUB	LOC
he's making [things]	that	the	it is behind	direction	that	place

waʔ-g-adę-hnyod-aʔ	nęgę	neʔ	machine
FACT-1SG.A-SRF-set.up-PNC	DEM	NOM	NOUN
I set it up for myself	this	the	machine

He was <u>always making things,</u> using the back of my machine.

<u>Continuing states:</u>
In this story a boy wakes up to realize that his cat, who is suspected of killing the family's chickens, and who the boy is supposed to be watching, has disappeared from his room. He jumps up and...

(361) <u>Osnowé·nyu̧ʔ</u>, waʔhahsę́·nyaʔ (NC01).
      o-snowe-<u>nyu̧</u>-ʔ   waʔ-h-ahsę·ny-aʔ
      3N/Z.SG.P-fast-DST-STV   FACT-3M.SG.A-get.dressed-PNC
      quickly   he got dressed
      He got dressed <u>quickly</u>

The meaning in (361) is, perhaps, that the boy keeps up his speed with each piece of clothing that he gets into.

B. <u>Activities and events that take place in stages:</u>

<u>Recurring calendric events:</u>
A chief in the sky-world (before humans peopled the earth) finds that his young wife's 'life has changed' [= she is pregnant], an unheard of condition that is without explanation in that place:

(362) Néʔtho níyot tshaʔ <u>wę̇dadényu̧ʔ</u> <u>wahsu̧dadényu̧ʔ</u> óhniʔ dehoyaʔdowéhdih (H167.5-6).
     neʔtho   niyot   tshaʔ   w-ęd-ade-<u>nyu̧</u>-ʔ   w-ahsu̧d-ade-<u>nyu̧</u>-ʔ
     MAN   MAN   SUB   3N/Z.SG.A-day-exist-DST-STV   3N/Z.SG.A-night-exist-DST-STV
     thus   how it is that   <u>daily</u>   <u>nightly</u>

     óhniʔ   de-ho-yaʔdowehd-ih
     ADD   DL-3M.SG.P-consider-STV
     also   he is pondering
     That is why <u>daily</u> and also <u>nightly</u>, he is pondering [it].

<u>Recounting events in stages:</u>
A hero returns home and tells the villagers all that had happened to him:

(363) Hu̧sahayú̧ʔ nęgę́ neʔ <u>waʔhatho·yahę́·ʔ</u> tshaʔ nwaʔawę́haʔ:
     h-u̧sa-ha-yu̧-ʔ   nęgę   neʔ   waʔ-h-atho·y-<u>ahę·</u>-ʔ
     TRNS-REP:FACT-3M.SG.A-arrive-PNC   DEM   NOM   FACT-3M.SG.A-tell-DST-PNC
     when he got back   this   the   <u>he told them [in stages]</u>

     tshaʔ   n-waʔ-aw-ęh-aʔ
     SUB   PRT-FACT-3N/Z.SG.P-happen-PNC
     that   what happened
     When he got back home, this one told them what had happened:

     tshaʔ óʔ waʔha·yóʔ yu̧gwé neʔ Tsgęihdiʔgó·na;
     tshaʔ   oʔ   waʔ-ha-Ryo-ʔ   neʔ   Tskęihdiʔgó·na
     SUB   ADD   FACT-3M.SG.A-kill-PNC   NOM   NAME
     that   also   he killed it   the   Big Lizard
     how he killed Big Lizard;

tsha? ó? tsha? niyót tsha? sahųwa?nyagéhda?, ne? aho·yohná? gwa?yę?á
wa?ho·ya?dagehnhá? tsha? gáyę? ne? gwás tgá·e?... (HW07)

tsha?	o?	tsha?	niyot	s-a-hųwa-?nyagęhd-a?		ne?
SUB	ADD	SUB	MOD	REP-FACT-3 > 3M.SG-help.escape-PNC		NOM
that	also	that	how it is	someone helped him escape		the

aa-ho-Ryo-h-na?		gwa?yę?á	wa?-ho-ya?dagehnh-a?	tsha? gayę?
OPT-3FZ.SG > 3M.SG-kill-STV-STVPST		NOUN	FACT-3M.SG > 3M.SG-help-PNC	REL
she could have killed him		rabbit	he helped him	the one

ne?	tgae?
NOM	DGR
the	the smallest

*also, how he was helped by rabbit, the very smallest one, to escape from the one
who could have killed him; ...*

The narration of the hero's experiences continues on in many stages, each described in
one or more clauses.

<u>Conditioned Periodic Activity</u>:

The speaker describes eating locusts, a local, somewhat unsightly delicacy:

(364) Ogá?wi go·? ná?, gwa? hya? <u>dehsatgahgwékhųk</u> ne? do gá·? hwędúh gwa? ęhsek
(LG07).

o-ga?w-ih		go·?	na?	gwa?	hya?
3N/Z.SG.P-taste.good-STV		CTR	ASRT	RSTR	MOD
it tastes good		however	it's	just	indeed

de-hs-at-gahgwek-hų-k	ne?	do	ga·?	hwędų	gwa?
DL-2SG.A-SRF-close.eyes-dst-HAB	NOM	INTR	IND	INTR	RSTR
<u>you close your eyes repeatedly</u>	the	how	something	whenever	just

ę-hs-e-k-Ø
FUT-2SG.A-eat-PNC
you will eat it

They taste good, as long as <u>you close your eyes whenever you eat one</u>.

C. <u>Distributed action in space</u>

<u>Distributed Activity in several locations</u>: A chief describes how to get to where two
travelers want to go, the localities they will pass, and how long it will take them:

(365) Dá· nę wa?shagotho·yę? gáę nų· nhęhné?, do· ó? nigęh, niyų hęhyęnųhwét, <u>tho ó?</u>
<u>dęhyadųgohdahę·?</u> tsha? nų·, hadinagé·? ne? yá de?tgaihwayéi?s, hųdę·yós , oyá?
hęnųgwehų́·weh (HW07).

da	nę	wa?-shago-atho·y-ę-?	gaę	nų
LNK	TMP	FACT-3M.SG > 3-tell-BEN-PNC	INT	LOC
so	now	he told them	where	place

n-h-ę-hn-e-ʔ'		do	oʔ	nigę	niyų
PRT-TRNS-FUT-3M.DU.A-walk-PNC		INT	ADD	EXT	AMT
so they two will go		how	also	extent	how much

h-ę-hy-ęnųhwet-Ø		tho	oʔ	d-ę-hy-adųgohd-ahę̄-ʔ
TRNS-FUT-3M.DU.A-overnight-PNC		LOC	ADD	DL-FUT-3M.DU.A-pass.through-DST-PNC
they will stay overnight there		there	also	they two will pass through several

tshaʔ	nų	deʔ-t-ga-Rihw-a-yei-ʔs		hų-adeˑyo-s
SUB	LOC	NEG-CIS-3N/Z.SG.A-matter-JN-be.right-PL		3M.PL.A-kill-HAB
that	place(es)	it is unreliable		they are killers

(y)-oyaʔ	hęn-ųgweh = ųwe
3N/Z.SG.A-different-STV	3M.PL.A-person:SUFF = AUTH
it is different	Indians

So he told them the way to go; also how often they'll stay overnight, also, the places they will pass through where the evil killers of other Indians live.

Distributed activity in different directions:

(366) Nę góˑʔ hyáʔ nęgę́, waʔhadikhwęˑdaʔháʔ tshaʔ hagwá neʔ waʔhadinųˑnyęˑdaʔháʔ, onę́ nęgę́, <u>waʔhųnųhwethų́ʔ</u>, dųsaˑhųwéˑnyaʔ (HW07).

nę	goˑʔ	hya?	nęgę	waʔ-hadi-khw-ęda?-nha?		tsha?	hagwa
TMP	CTR	MOD	DEM	FACT-3M.PL.A-meal-finish-PNC		SUB	DIR
now	however	indeed	this	they finished eating		that	directions

ne?	wa?-hadi-nųny-ęda?-nha?		onę	nęgę	wa?-hų-ęnųhwet-<u>hų-?</u>
NOM	FACT-3M.PL.A-dance-end-PNC		TMP	DEM	FACT-3M.PL.A-stay.overnight-DST-PNC
the	they finished dancing		now	this	<u>they overnighted in various places</u>

d-ųsa-hų-aeny-aʔ
DL-REP:FACT-3M.PL.A-disperse-PNC
they dispersed

However, when they are done eating and dancing, these [people] disperse, <u>going to stay overnight in various places</u>.

Repetitive action in space:

(367) Naʔ diʔ hyáʔ nęgę́, tho yúgęʔ nigayanowéʔ nigę́ neʔ ayę́ˑæʔ gahwęhdáʔ gadakhéʔ ųhwęˑjyáʔge, gaędagehę́ʔ gwáʔ <u>dewadųʔtgwaʔdáhęˑk</u> (HW07).

na?	di?	hya?	nęgé	tho	yagę?	ni-ga-yanoR-e?
ASRT	LNK	MOD	DEM	MAN	HRSY	PRT-3FZ.SG.A-run.fast-STV
it's	moreover	indeed	this	thus	they say	how fast she runs

nigę	ne?	ayęæ?	ga-hwęhd-a?		ga-dakhe-?	Ø-ųhwęjy-a? = ge
CLSF	NOM	SIM	NPF-snowsnake-NSF		3N/Z.SG.A-run-PRP	NPF-earth-NSF = LOC
extent	the	like	snowsnake		it's running	on the earth

ga-Ręd-a-gehę·-ʔ'   gwaʔ   de-w-adųʔtgwaʔd-<u>hę</u>·-k
3N/Z.SG.A-log-JN-set.down-STV   RSTR   DL-3N/Z.SG.A-skip.over-DST-HAB
logs are heaped   just   <u>it bounces over it.</u>
Indeed, this one, runs so fast, it's like a snowsnake running on the ground, that's
<u>bouncing</u> right over heaped logs.

D. <u>Multiple participants</u>

<u>Distributed reciprocal action:</u>

(368) Da· gųhwaʔá neʔ gųgwehųwé thųgyoʔdęháʔ dęʔseʔ go·ʔ hyaʔ naʔ
    <u>deyagwadadyęde·ʔshę́·ʔ</u> neʔ gųʔshę́·nih (LG14).

da	g-ųhw-aʔ = á		neʔ	g-ųgweh = ųwe
LNK	1SG.A-self-NSF = DIM		NOM	1SG.A-person:SUFF = AUTH
so	I alone		the	I'm an Indian

th-aʔ-wag-yoʔd-ęh-aʔ		dęʔseʔ	go·ʔ	hyaʔ	naʔ
CON-FACT-1SG.P-work-INCH-PNC		CNJ	CTR	MOD	ASRT
I got to work there		and	but	indeed	that

de-yagw-adad-yędeR-ʔ-shę·-ʔ'		neʔ	gų-aʔshę·nih
DL-1EX.PL.A-REF-know-INCH-DST-STV		NOM	3FZ.PL.A-white.person
<u>we got to know one another</u>		the	white women

So I was the only Indian that got to work there, but of course <u>the white women and I</u>
    <u>got to know each other.</u>

<u>Action by multiple agents on multiple patients:</u>

(369) Onę thohgé dwagęní·hęʔ, nęgę́ neʔ tho hųgyoʔdęháʔ nęgę́ tshaʔ nų́ neʔ haʔdeyų́
    <u>agwahsę·nyáhę·k</u>, neʔ..neʔ wadésdaʔ neʔ gahsųwæʔshųʔá naʔ oʔ nęgę́ gųdidyéʔs si
    naʔ (LG14).

onę	thohgę	d-wag-ęni·hę-ʔ	nęgę	neʔ	tho
TMP	TMP	CIS-1SG.P-quit-STV	DEM	NOM	LOC
now	then	I quit here	this	the	there

h-waʔ-wag-yoʔd-ęh-aʔ	nęgę	tshaʔ	nų	neʔ
TRNS-FACT-1.SG.P-work-INCH-PNC	DEM	SUB	LOC	NOM
I worked there	this	that	place	the

haʔ-de-y-ų-h'		agwa-hsę·ny-<u>ahę</u>·-k		neʔ	w-ade-sd-aʔ
TRNS-DL-3N/Z.SG.A-amount-STV		1EX.PL.A-make-<u>DST</u>-HAB		NOM	3N/Z.SG.A-SRF-use-STV
everything		<u>we make several</u>		the	it uses it

ga-hsųR-aʔ = shųʔá	naʔ	oʔ	nęgę	gųdi-dye-ʔs	si	naʔ
NPF-gun-NSF = PL	ASRT	ADD	DEM	3FZ.PL.A-fly-HAB	LOC	ASRT
guns	it's	also	this	airplane	far	it's

I quit this [job] and worked at a place where <u>we made all kinds of things</u> that are
used for guns and airplanes.

<u>Distributed experiences</u>:

(370) Onę nęgę, <u>waʔhụdętga·dụ́ʔ</u>, gwas igę́h... (HW07)

onę	nęgę	waʔ-hụ-ad-ętgad-ụ-ʔ'		gwas	i-ga-i-h
TMP	DEM	FACT-3M.PL.A-SRF-have.fun-<u>DST</u>-PNC		INTS	EP-3N/Z.SG.A-be.all.of-STV
now	thi	<u>they each of them had fun</u>		very	it is all of it

Now all these [people] enjoy themselves very much...

E. <u>Lexicalized stems</u>

A fair number of verb stems with a distributive are lexicalized as stems that can function as either stative verbs *or* nominals. With some exceptions, these are stems which already function ambiguously as both nominals and statives, and the distributive merely signals the distribution of the multiple referents in space. Most have an incorporated noun and are based on positional verbs. Examples are:

(371) a. gahne·gó·nyụʔ

   ga-hneg-o-nyụ-ʔ
   3N/Z.SG.A-water-be.in.water-DST-STV
   (be) puddles [all over]
          cf. gahné·goʔ '(be a) puddle'

   b. hodigwęhę́·nyụʔ

   hodi-gwęhR-ụnyụ-ʔ
   3M.NSG.P-settlement-DST-STV
   their various settlements
          cf. hodigwę́hæ·ʔ *they are a settled group* (H612.1)

   c. odaʔaædé·nyụʔ

   o-ad-aʔaR-ade-nyụ-ʔ
   3N/Z.SG.P-SRF-veil-exist-DST-STV
   cobwebs [all over]
          cf. odaʔáæde? *(it is a) cobweb*

A more contemporary example is (372). It has no incorporated noun, and though it describes a non-animate referent, it has an animate pronominal prefix, due to the fact the referent has moving parts:

(372) odiyoʔdé·nyụʔ (LG13)

   odi-yoʔde-<u>nyụ</u>-ʔ
   3FZ.NSG.P-be.work-DST-STV
   machinery

F. <u>Stems with incorporated nouns</u>:

Glosses in English not withstanding, the distributive does *not* pluralize the incorporated noun; its scope, rather, is over the incorporating stem as a whole.

(373) Odyá?k o? <u>hodi?se·hdayędú?</u>, ne? automobile dewatgęnyús tgę?í· ho?se·hdiyóh, na?
tsha? ihswá? hutgwé·nyus, gonugwe ó? dehodiye·náuh (LG11).

odya?k	o?	hodi-?se·hd-a-yęd-u-?'			ne?	automobile
QNT	ADD	3M.NSG.P-vehicle-JN-have-DST-STV			NOM	NOUN
some	also	<u>they have vehicles</u>			the	automobile

de-w-atgęny-us		tgę?i	ho-?se·hd-iyo-h'		na?	tsha?	ihswa?
DL-3N/Z.SG.A-compete-HAB		COMP	3M.SG.P-vehicle-good-STV		ASRT	SUB	QNT
it competes		more	he has a nice car		it's	that	a lot

hu-atgweny-us	gun-ugweh		o?	de-hodi-yena-uh
3M.PL.A-win-HAB	3FZ.PL.A-person:SUFF		ADD	DL-3M.NSG.P-catch-STV
they are winners	women		also	they all took part

*Some of them had cars, they competed whose is the nicer car; there were lots of
winners, women too, they all took part.*

The following root suffix combinations that include the distributive have been attested;
combinations and their sequencing are shown in Table 4.65:

Table 4.66 Attested root suffix combinations with the distributive

			distributive			
			distributive	distributive		
			distributive	dislocative		
		causative	distributive	dislocative		
		causative	distributive			
			distributive	causative[179]	instrumental	
root			distributive	ambulative		aspect
		inchoative	distributive			
		inchoative	distributive	distributive	ambulative	
			distributive	instrumental		
		instrumental	distributive			
	causative[180]	instrumental	distributive			
			distributive	reversative		
		reversative	distributive			
			distributive	benefactive		

Examples of each of these complex stems – some with non-compositional meanings – are:

(374) a. <u>Distributive and distributive:</u> dęyudadidę·hę·nyú?
d-ę-yudad-idęR-hę·-nyu-?
DL-FUT-3FI > 3FI-help.out-DST-DST-PNC
they will console them

b. <u>Distributive and dislocative:</u> dehaęhiya?khúhne? (H205.11)
de-ha-Ręh-iya?k-hu-hn-e?
DL-3M.SG.A-treetop-cross.over-DISTR-DSLC-PRP
he is going to cross over the treetops

---

[179] listed as DIST-INST-INST in Woodbury et al. (1992)
[180] listed as INST-INST-DIST in Woodbury et al. (1992)

    c. <u>Causative, distributive, and dislocative</u>: See (344)
    d. <u>Causative and distributive</u>: See (344)
    e. <u>Distributive, causative, and instrumental</u>: See (325)

    f. <u>Distributive and ambulative</u>: ųnųhdųnyų́hne?
       ų-ęnųhd-ųnyų-hn-e?
       3FI.A-think-DST-AMB-PRP
       she is thinking about it as she goes

    g. <u>Inchoative and distributive</u>: See (353)
    h. <u>Inchoative, distributive, distributive, and ambulative</u>: See (353)
    j. <u>Distributive and instrumental</u>: See (325)
    k. <u>Instrumental and distributive</u>: See (325)
    l. <u>Causative, instrumental, and distributive</u>: See (325)
    m. <u>Distributive and reversative</u>: See (357)
    n. <u>Reversative and distributive</u>: See (357)
    o. <u>Distributive and benefactive</u>: See (316)

4.8.5.7 The Intensifier

The form of the intensifier suffix is *-jihw-; -(a)ji-; -(a)hjihw-; -(a)?jihw-; -(a)sjihw-* with some speaker variation with regard to the choice of suffix with a given stem. All take the G2 aspect alternants *[-as, -ęh-, a?]*. The suffix occurs with active and stative verbs. There is no attestation of the intensifier combining with other root suffixes. Semantically, it marks either (i) an intensification of the activity, event, or attribute described by the verb, or (ii) a situation that takes place suddenly or quickly. The suffix is attested with only nine stems, all of which are listed below:

Derived Verb	Source Verb
.adya?kjihw- +contrastive *break off suddenly, end suddenly.*	-adya?k- v.a. *break off*
-N-Risjihw- *be overly done/ripe*	-Ri- v.a. *get done, get cooked, ripen*
-atdoga?jihw- *notice at once.*	-atdog- v.a. *notice, sense, become aware*
-athųdesjihw- *hold a full hearing.*	-athųd(e)- v.s. *have hearing, hear, listen*
.dęsdaji- +dualic and cislocative *stand up quickly, leap up*	.dęsd- +dualic and cislocative v.a. *jump up, stand up*
-ęheyasjihw- *be long dead*	-ihey- /-ęhey- v.a. *die*
.hnawadetsjihw- +cislocative *be an extra strong current*	-det- v.s. *be vigorous, be strong, be lively*
-hnyodasjihw- / -hnyodahjihw- *be really steep*	-hnyod- v.a. *stand upright, protrude*
-Ręhyagę?jihw- *suffer intensely*	-Ręhyagę- v.a. *suffer pain*

Although the intensifier suffix is used by contemporary speakers, it is apparently no longer productive in the sense that new stems are formed with it. Instead, intensification is typically signaled with one of several particles. Examples with each of the attested verbs are:

(375) a. ohyaisjíhwęh
    o-ahy-a-Ri-sjihw-ęh
    3N/Z.SG.P-berry-JN-be.ripe-INTNS-STV
    the berries are overly ripe

  b. thęwa·dyaʔkjíhwaʔ
    th-ę-w-ad-yaʔk-jihw-aʔ
    CON-FUT-3N/Z.SG.A-SRF-break.off-INTNS-PNC
    it will break off, or end, suddenly

  c. hattdogaʔjíhwas
    h-atdog-aʔjihw-aʔ
    3M.SG.A-notice-INTNS-HAB
    he notices it at once

  d. ęsathųdesjíhwęk (Hms856:17)
    ę-s-athųde-sjihw-ę(h)-k-Ø
    FUT-2SG.P-hear/listen-INTNS-STV-CNT-PNC
    you will be holding a full hearing

  e. dųdayedęsdá·jiʔ (H205.9)
    d-ųda-ye-dęsd-aji-ʔ
    DL-CIS:FACT-3FI.A-stand.up-INTNS-PNC
    she leapt up

  f. hawęheyasjíhwęh (H633.10)
    haw-ęhey-asjihw-ęh
    3M.SG.P-die-INTNS-STV
    he is long dead

  g. dyohnawadetsjíhwęh
    d-yo-hnaw-a-det-sjihw-ęh
    CIS-3N/Z.SG.P-current-JN-be.vigorous-INTNS-STV
    there's a really strong current

  h. gahnyodasjíhwęh *or* gahnyodahjíhwęh
    ga-hnyod-asjihw-ęh
    3N/Z.SG.A-stand.upright-INTNS-STV
    it is really steep

  i. ęyeęhyagęʔjíhwaʔ (H669.7)
    ę-ye-Ręhyagę-ʔjihw-aʔ
    FUT-3FI.A-suffer-INTNS-PNC
    one will suffer intensely

4.8.5.8 The Dislocative and the Ambulative

The forms of the *dislocative* are *-(a)h-, -(a)hR, -(a)hn-, -(a)hs-, -hsR-, -(a)ʔn-*. The *ambulative* morpheme has two alternants, *-(a)h- and -(a)hn-*, that are formally identical to two of the dislocative alternants. The parenthesized *a* is a joiner vowel that intervenes when combining the root suffix with an adjacent morpheme results in a cluster of two or more consonants. The dislocative morpheme adds the meaning that performing the action described by the verb involves going somewhere else. The ambulative adds the meaning that the actor is performing the action described by the verb as he is walking. In Onondaga it is impossible to tell on formal grounds when the *-(a)h-* and the *-(a)hn-* suffixes function as dislocative and when as ambulative, although with verbs whose meanings lack intentionality or goal-orientation, the dislocative interpretation rarely makes sense. Nevertheless, the two suffixes are treated as distinct here, because there is overlap in the form and function of only two of the dislocative alternants, because their combinatorial characteristics with other root suffixes differ, and, finally, because there is at least one verb, *-atgathw-* 'look at' that takes both the dislocative and the ambulative with different meanings; together with the dislocative *-(a)hn-* it means 'go [somewhere] to look at [something]', together with the ambulative *-(a)h-* it means 'look at [something] as one goes'. There are 107 dislocative verbs in the corpus, and 40 ambulative verbs.

Both suffixes derive manner-of-motion verbs from active verbs, which means that they can be inflected with a fourth aspect – the purposive – in addition to the three basic aspects. The purposive aspect together with the dislocative expresses a participant's having gone somewhere with the intention to perform an activity. The two suffixes' aspectual and modal characteristics are discussed in section 4.5.3.1. The derivations apply to monadic and dyadic stems, but only the dislocative has been attested with transitive prefixes. Neither suffix changes a verb's participant structure.

(376) <u>The dislocative with a monadic verb stem:</u> degadawę·yéhse·ʔ
      de-g-adawę·ye-hsR-eʔ
      DL-1SG.A-roam.about-DSLC-PRP
      I am here [intending to] take a walk
            cf. dehadawę́·yek *he roams about*

(377) <u>The dislocative with a dyadic verb stem:</u>
      hehsákheʔ
        h(a)-ehsak-h-eʔ
        3M.SG.A-look.for-DSLC-PRP
        he is here [intending] to look for it
            cf. héhsaks *he looks for it*

(378) <u>The ambulative with a monadic verb stem:</u> dęhohęehdáhneʔ
      d-ę-ho-hęehd-ahn-eʔ
      DL-FUT-3M.SG.P-shout-AMB-PRP
      he will shout as he goes
            cf. dęhohę́ehdaʔ *he will shout*[181]

---

[181] -hęehd-is a verb stem that takes patient pronominal prefixes in all aspects.

(379) <u>The ambulative with a dyadic verb stem</u>: dahsatgathwáhe?
        d-a-hs-atgathw-ah-e?
        CIS-FACT-2SG.A-look.at-AMB-PRP
        you are looking at it as you go
                cf. gatgáthwas *I am looking at it*

The following root suffix combinations that include the dislocative have been attested; combinations and their sequencing are shown in Table 4.67:

Table 4.67 Attested root suffix combinations with the dislocative

root		inchoative	dislocative	aspect
		distributive	dislocative	
		instrumental	dislocative	
		causative	dislocative	
	causative	distributive	dislocative	
		reversative	dislocative	

(380) a. <u>Inchoative and dislocative</u>: goksa?dayẹ·dá?she·?
        go-ksa?d-a-yẹd-a?-hsR-e?
        3FI.P-child-JN-have-INCH-DSLC-PRP
        she is going to have a child

    b. <u>Distributive and dislocative</u>: See (374)
    c. <u>Causative and dislocative</u>: See (344)
    d. <u>Causative, distributive, and dislocative</u>: See (344)
    e. <u>Reversative and dislocative</u>: See (357)

The following root suffix combinations that include the ambulative have been attested; combinations and their sequencing are shown in Table 4.68:

Table 4.68 Attested root suffix combinations with the ambulative

			instrumental	ambulative	
root			distributive	ambulative	aspect
	inchoative	distributive	distributive	ambulative	

(381) a. <u>Instrumental and ambulative</u> (Repeated from (325): o?nahgụdahgwáhne?
        o-?nahg-ụd-ahgw-ahn-e?
        3N/Z.SG.P-drum-be.attached-INST-AMB-PRP
        bee; wasp [literally, it stings as it goes]
                cf. *o?nahgụtha?* 'it stings' [= bee]

    b. <u>Distributive and ambulative</u>: See (374)
    c. <u>Inchoative, distributive, distributive, and ambulative</u>: See (353)

5 The Noun and Nominal Expressions

5.1 Introduction

The three Iroquoian lexical categories – noun, verb, and particle – are established on the basis of their morphological characteristics. Roots are lexically marked as either noun roots or verb roots; each follows different inflectional patterns. However, numerous words that are morphologically verbs or particles, and words that have morphological characteristics of both nouns and verbs (e.g., kinship terms), are lexicalized as referring expressions and are nearly always marked in context with the nominal particle *ne?*. Verbal nouns of this kind refer, typically, to household objects, buildings or parts of buildings, plants, animals, foods, the weather, directions – in short, objects or processes encountered in everyday life. The morphologically distinct groups of nominals mentioned above are described together in the present chapter because of similarities in their distribution. The inflectional characteristics of nominals differ depending on whether they denote animate or non-animate referents, whether they refer to humans or non-humans, to kin or non-kin, and how and whether they can be possessed. These differences are taken up as the discussion proceeds from morphological nouns in section 5.2, to verbal nouns in section 5.3, to relationship terms in section 5.4, to particle nouns in section 5.5, to independent personal pronouns in section 5.6.[1] The chapter ends with a discussion of complex nominal expressions in section 5.7.

5.2 The Morphological Noun

The structure of the minimal morphological noun is shown in Table 5.1:

Table 5.1 The structure of the morphological noun

The Morphological Noun		
Noun prefix	Noun Root	Noun Suffix
	Verb Root + Nominalizer	
	Noun Stem	

5.2.1 The Noun Prefix (NPF)

5.2.1.1 Animacy

---

[1] In this chapter independent pronouns are merely documented. A more thoroughgoing discussion can be found in chapter 6 on Pro-Forms.

The primary way to mark the difference between nouns denoting animate and non-animate referents is by the choice of the noun prefix. Animate nouns take prefixes that code for person, number, and feminine or masculine gender; non-animate nouns take non-animate prefixes:

(1) a. haksaʔáh
    ha-ksaʔ = áh
    3M.SG.A-child = DIM
    boy

   b. ganáʔjyaʔ
    ga-naʔjy-aʔ
    NPF-pail-NSF
    pail

The prefix of noun roots denoting non-animate referents is lexically assigned: either *ga-* (or its morphophonologically selected alternants *gę-, Ø-*)[2] or *o-* (or its alternants *a-, aw-*). The prefixes, are formally identical to the non-animate agent and patient verbal pronominal prefixes. Both types code for person, number and gender, but they differ functionally from each other in that verbal prefixes code for semantic case whereas noun prefixes are merely a formal requirement of a well-formed noun.

(2) a. *ga-noun*: gahų́·waʔ
    ga-hųw-aʔ
    NPF-canoe,boat-NSF
    canoe

   b. *o-noun*: óhyaʔ
    o-ahy-aʔ
    NPF-fruit-NSF
    fruit

A few noun stems occur with both of the prefixes and changed meanings, as in (3):

(3) a. ohųwéʔdaʔ
    o-hųweʔd-aʔ
    NPF-horn-NSF
    horn

   b. gahųwéʔdaʔ
    ga-hųweʔd-aʔ
    NPF-horn-NSF
    chimney, conduit, pipe

---

[2] *Ø-* is the word initial alternant of *w-* (before *a-, e-, and ę-*stems) or word initial *y-* (before *o-* or *ų-*stems). Word-initial *w-* is dropped by the majority of morphological and verbal nouns; word initial *y* is dropped everywhere.

Of 253 morphological nouns in the corpus, 101 are attested as *ga*-nouns, 146 are attested as *o*-nouns, and 6 are attested as taking both *ga*- and *o*- prefixes with different meanings.[3]

Nouns denoting animal names occur lexicalized with masculine or feminine-zoic prefixes.

(4) a. hanyáhdęh
    ha-nyahdęh
    NPF-snapping turtle
    snapping turtle

  b. ga·yoʔáh
    ga-Ryo = ʔáh
    NPF-game.animal = DIM
    bird

  c. ojiʔnų́·waʔ
    o-jiʔnųw-aʔ
    NPF-bug,worm-NSF
    maggot, worm, insect

5.2.1.2 Marking the Noun for Possession[4]

To inflect a morphological noun for possession, the *ga*- or *o*-prefix is replaced by a prefix that codes for the possessor's person, number, and gender. The possessed entity (the referent of the construction) is not marked pronominally (recall, however, that a non-animate never is pronominally marked unless it is the only argument). Possessive prefixes are formally identical to the pronominal prefixes of the agent or patient series of pronominal prefixes for verb stems. But, like noun prefixes, they differ in that they do not mark semantic case relationships as do the verbal prefixes. Rather, the choice of prefix from one of the two intransitive series depends on how the entity denoted by the noun is possessed: alienably or inalienably.

---

[3] The count does not include the 11 animal names that are probably morphological nouns because their suffixes tend to be difficult to segment; nor does it include terms that denote body parts exclusively; it does include roots that denote both an object and a body part. Body parts are discussed in section 5.2.1.2.2.

[4] Possession is expressed in a variety of ways in Onondaga. These are described in section 7.11. The present section deals with the details of marking possession morphologically on the noun.

5.2.1.2.1 Alienably Possessed Nouns

Alienably possessed nouns – these denote objects that can be taken or given away, or that are impermanent in some way – select prefixes from the patient series of pronominal prefixes. Both *ga*- and *o*-nouns take identical prefixes to mark possession as shown in (5):

(5) a. hohų́·waʔ
    ho-hųw-aʔ
    3M.SG.P-canoe,boat-NSF
    his canoe
            cf. <u>*gahų́·waʔ*</u> 'boat, canoe'

  b. hóhyaʔ
    ho-ahy-aʔ
    3M.SG.P-fruit-NSF
    his fruit
            cf. <u>*óhyaʔ*</u> 'fruit'

Alienable possession may involve animate beings. If these are animals, possession is marked as with non-animate objects (6a), if possession expresses a temporary relationship between humans, then it is marked with a transitive prefix as in (6b) where *the possessor is in the patient position*:[5]

(6) a. ...sahayenáʔ hotshenę́h... (LG23)
    s-a-ha-yena-ʔ'   <u>ho</u>-tshenę-h
    REP-FACT-3M.SG.A-take-PNC   3M.SG.P-pet-NSF
    he took back his pet

  b. ųkhiyadejyę́ʔtshæ·ʔ (LG20)
    ųkhiy-ade-jyęʔt-shR-aʔ
    3 > 1NSG-SRF-heal-NOM-NSF
    our doctor

While kin are for the most part treated as inalienable possessions, at least one term, -ųgweʔd- which denotes a group of kin is treated as alienable, by marking the possessor with a simple patient prefix:

(7)   haųgwéʔdaʔ (H152.3; LG05)
    ha-ųgwe-ʔd-aʔ
    3M.SG.P-person-NOM-NSF
    his people; his lineage

In conversation, or while telling a story, English nouns are sometimes borrowed. Borrowings, whether they denote animate or non-animate possessions, are prefixed with a

---

[5] In contrast to many kinship terms where the selection among transitive prefixes is made by comparing the ages of the two participants to the relationship (see section 5.4).

patient prefix like an alienably possessed morphological noun, except that a semireflexive is inserted between the prefix and the borrowed noun.

(8) Possession with borrowed words:

    a. agatmachí·n (LG13)
       ag-at-machi·n
       1SG.P-SRF-machine
       my machine

    b. ųgwatbós (LG12)
       ųgw-at-bos
       1PL.P-SRF-boss
       our boss

5.2.1.2.2 Inalienably Possessed Nouns

Two groups of nominals are inalienably possessed in Onondaga, (i) nouns denoting body parts and (ii) certain kinship terms. Kinship terms are discussed in a separate section (sec. 5.4) because of their many unique characteristics; this section looks at how body part terms are marked for possession.

The majority of body part nouns select prefixes that are identical to the agent series of pronominal prefixes to mark the possessor. In addition, possessed body part terms nearly always require the locative clitic = ge / = ne[6] as in (9):

(9) a. hgihiʔnáʔge
      k-gihiʔn-aʔ = ge
      1SG.A-knee-NSF = LOC
      (on) my knee

    b. khųʔgwáʔge
      k-hųʔgw-aʔ = ge
      1SG.A-throat-NSF = LOC
      (on) my throat

    c. geshų́hne
      ge-shųh = ne
      1SG.A-back = LOC
      (on) my back

    d. kʔnahsíʔge
      k-ʔnahs-iʔ = ge
      1SG.A-tongue-NSF = LOC
      (on) my tongue

---

[6] The choice of locative clitic alternants is phonologically conditioned: = *ne* after *h*; = *ge* elsewhere.

Of 69 body part terms in the corpus, 52 take possessive prefixes from the agent series; 9 take possessive prefixes from the patient series; 8 take possessive prefixes from both the agent and the patient series. Body exudations like 'tears', 'saliva', 'feces', 'urine', etc. are treated like alienably possessed nouns.

The nine exceptional body part terms that take possessive prefixes from the patient series are for the most part ones that are not under voluntary control of the possessor (Woodbury 1975:34):

Root	Gloss	Root	Gloss
-e·yahs- / -e·yah-	*heart*	-nųhR-	*scalp*
-gahe·hd-	*eyelashes*	-nų?khwe?R-	*hair*
-hdegaR-	*rib*	-thwęhs-	*liver*
-jinųhya?d-	*vein, cord*	-yųR-	*intestine*
-ji?sæwęhd-	*brain*		

Six of these, *-ji?sæwęhd, -hdegaR-, -jinųhya?d-, -nų?khe?R-, -thwęhs-,* and *-nųhR-* do not take the locative clitic when possessed. An example is:

(10) agehdé·ga·?
      age-hdegaR-a?
      1SG.P-rib-NSF
      my rib

The eight body part terms that take possessive pronouns from both the agent and the patient series are:

Root	Gloss	Root	Gloss
-ihcyųhd-	*abdomen, lower*	-yeę?d- / -yę·?d-	*body, corpse*
-nosgR-	*beard*	-?ehd-	*claw, finger- or toenail*
-no?jy-	*tooth*	-?nigųhR-	*mind, thought*
-sdyę?d-	*bone*	-?nųd-	*leg*

Usually substituting a patient prefix for an agent prefix changes the status of the body part from inalienable to alienable, and the version with the patient prefix lacks the locative clitic, e.g.:

Inalienable	Alienable
k?ehdá?geh *my finger- or toenail*	ak?é·hda? *my claw* [e.g. of lobster]
gno?jyá?geh *my tooth*	agnó?jya? *my [false] tooth*
k?nų·dá?geh *my leg*	ak?nų·da? *my [wooden] leg*
gnosgæ·?geh *my whiskers*	onósgæ·? *[fake] beard*
gesdyę?dá?geh *my bone*	agesdyę?da? *my [e.g., chicken] bone*

Many body part terms can occur with a non-animate prefix, but then the body part is understood to be disconnected from a possessor. Of the 73 documented body part terms, 16 are not attested with non-animate prefixes; they take only possessives. They are:

Root	gloss	Root	Gloss
-aʔsR- / -ʔsR-	wrist	-jiʔsæwęhd-	brain
-gęʔgw-	eyebrow	-nųhehd-	nipple
-gęʔjy-	forehead	-nyęd-	leg below knee
-hsehd-	nape of neck	-shųh- / -shųhw-	back
-hsohgw- / -hsohg-	lip	-yahgw-[7]	abdomen, pelvis
-hswaʔ-	spine	-yųhd-	gum
-ihcyųhd-	abdomen (lower)	-ʔahs-	breast, chest
-ihnų- / -ihn-	skin	-ʔnyųhs- / -ʔnyų-	nose

With body part terms, non-animate prefixes do not mark possession, and do not take a locative clitic. When these nouns occur with the non-animate prefix, they do so with regular noun morphology as in (11):

(11) oʔnǫ́·daʔ
     o-ʔnǫd-aʔ
     NPF-leg-NSF
    leg

        cf. geʔnųdáʔgeh *my leg*

When body part nouns do occur with non-animate prefixes, they are always the *o*-prefixes, except for a small number that can take both *ga-* and *o*-prefixes with changes in their denotation, e.g.:

o-noun	*ga*-noun	possessed
ojíhgwaʔ *fist*	gajíhgwaʔ *hammer*	gjihgwáʔgeh *my fist*
ogų́hsaʔ *face*	gagų́hsaʔ *mask*	hgųhsíʔgeh *my face*
oyáʔdaʔ *body*	gayáʔdaʔ *doll*	gyaʔdíʔgeh *my body*

5.2.2 The Noun Stem

The noun stem can be a simple noun root as in examples (1)-(11) above,[8] or a derived noun stem that consists of a verb root followed by a nominalizer suffix, as in (12) or, less frequently, a verb root plus derivational suffix that functions as a nominalizer, as in (13), or, on exceedingly rare occasions, a noun plus incorporating verb plus nominalizer, as in (14).[9] The alternants of the nominalizer suffix are -(ę)hsR-/-shR-/-tshR-/-ʔ(t)shR- (Table 4.57). The distribution of alternants is lexicalized. When a noun stem ending in a consonant cluster combines with a nominalizer suffix, a joiner vowel is inserted, as in (12c):

---

[7] No longer in use.

[8] In the Onondaga Dictionary (Woodbury 2003) bases consisting of a simple noun root are designated *n*.

[9] In the Onondaga Dictionary (Woodbury 2003) derived noun bases are designated *v>n*.

(12) <u>Verb root plus nominalizer</u>:
    a. gahyadų́hsæ·ʔ
      ga-hyadų-hsR-aʔ
      NPF-write-NOM-NSF
      book
          cf. <u>khyá·dų</u>k *I write*

    b. hadihnháʔtshæʔ
      hadi-hnhaʔ-<u>tshR</u>-aʔ
      3M.PL.A-hire.someone-NOM-NSF
      hired men
          cf. hag<u>ęhnhá</u>ʔih *he has hired me*

    c. sayaʔdowehdáshæ·ʔ
      sa-yaʔdowehd-<u>ashR</u>-aʔ
      2SG.P-think.about-NOM-NSF
      your judgment
          cf. waʔthniya<u>ʔdowéhda</u>ʔ *they two thought it over*

    d. ęʔnhéʔtshæʔ
      Ø-ęʔnhe-<u>ʔtshR</u>-aʔ
      NPF-play.ball-NOM-NSF
      ball
          cf. deg<u>ę́ʔnhe</u>s *I play ball*

(13) <u>Verb plus derivational suffix</u>:
    a. gaʔsé·hdaʔ
      ga-ʔseR-<u>hd</u>-aʔ
      NPF-drag-CS-NSF
      vehicle, car
        cf. gé<u>ʔse·</u>ʔ *I am dragging it*

    b. ohsóhgwaʔ
      o-ahso-<u>hgw</u>-aʔ
      NPF-paint.something-INST-NSF
      paint
        cf. hahsós *he paints*

(14) <u>Noun plus incorporating verb plus nominalizer</u>:
    a. ganadagayų́shæʔ
      ga-nad-a-gayų-shR-aʔ
      NPF-town-JN-be.old-NOM-NSF
      old [abandoned] town
        cf. ogá·yų̨h *it is old*

b. onhæhdágwaʔtshæʔ
o-nhR-a-hdagw-ʔtshR-aʔ
NPF-disease-be.afraid-NOM-NSF
smallpox [literally, dreaded disease]
    cf. hahdá·gwas *he fears it, he is afraid*

5.2.2.1 Incorporating a Noun Stem into a Verb

One of the characteristics that distinguishes a noun root from a verb root is the fact that a noun root can be incorporated into a verb.[10] Derived noun stems are incorporated into a verb stem just like plain noun roots, as shown in (15).

(15) a. <u>Incorporated noun root</u>: othųwahdę·dyų́h
       o-at-<u>hųw</u>-ahdędyų-h'
       3N/Z.SG.P-SRF-canoe-depart-STV
       the canoe has departed

   b. <u>Incorporated derived noun</u>: hęwagęʔnheʔtshę́·diʔ
      h-ę-wag-ęʔnhe-ʔtshR-ųdi-ʔ
      TRNS-FUT-1SG.P-ball-NOM-throw-PNC
      I will throw a ball

5.2.2.2 Counting Morphological Nouns

To count entities, the counted noun must be incorporated in one of three enumeration verbs: .*d-* + repetitive 'be one'; .*ge-* + dualic 'be two'; or .*ge-* + partitive 'be three or more'. A non-animate noun retains its lexicalized prefix in such a construction.[11] In expressions that count one or two objects a number particle is omitted. In those constructions the number is expressed by the prepronominal prefix. In numbers above that, a number particle is required:

(16) <u>Counting a *ga*-noun</u>:
    a. sganų́hsadah
       s-ga-nųhs-a-d-'ah
       REP-3N/Z.SG.A-house-JN-be.one-STV
       one house

    b. deganųhsagéh
       de-ga-nųhs-a-ge-h'
       DL-3N/Z.SG.A-house-JN-amount.to-STV
       two houses

---

[10] For a discussion of the characteristics of nouns that are subject to incorporation, see section 4.8.3.3.

[11] See section 4.4.3.4 which discusses incorporating constructions in which the lexically assigned prefix category of the incorporated noun governs pronominal selection.

    c. ahsę́ niganųhsagéh
      ahsę ni-ga-nųhs-a-ge-h'
      NUM PRT-3N/Z.SG.A-house-JN-amount.to-STV
      three houses

(17) <u>Counting an *o*-noun</u>:
    a. jyohnyų́hsadah
      s-yo-hnyųhs-a-d-'ah
      REP-3N/Z.SG.P-squash-JN-be.one-STV
      one squash

    b. deyohnyų́hsagéh
      de-yo-hnyųhs-a-ge-h'
      DL-3N/Z.SG.P-squash-JN-amount.to-STV
      two squashes

    c. ahyá?k niyohnyų́hsagéh
      ahya?k ni-yo-hnyųhs-a-ge-h'
      NUM PRT-3N/Z.SG.P-squash-JN-amount.to-STV
      six squashes

A different pattern of enumeration occurs when counting animate nouns: A classificatory noun is incorporated into the enumeration verb as in (15) whose agent pronominal prefix codes for person number and gender. Frequently the count expression is accompanied by an external noun that further specifies the counted entity as in (19). In counting humans the classificatory noun *-ya?d-* 'body' is incorporated into the counting verb when counting one or two persons; when counting three or more persons *.adi-* + partitive 'be a total of [entities]' is the counting verb without classificatory incorporation:

(18) <u>Counting human nouns with incorporated classifiers</u>:
    a. shayá?dadah
      s-ha-ya?d-a-d-'ah
      REP-3M.SGA-body-JN-be.one-STV
      one [man]

    b. dehniya?dagéh
      de-hni-ya?d-a-ge-h'
      DL-3M.DU.A-body-JN-amount.to-STV
      two [men; a man and a woman][12]

    c. ahsę́ nigų́nadi
      ahsę ni-gųn-ad-i-h
      NUM PRT-3FZ.PL.A-SRF-be.a.total.of-STV
      three [women]

---

[12] Recall that dual and plural masculine prefixes are used for mixed male and female groups.

(19) <u>Counting human nouns with classifier and specifying external noun:</u>

    a. jyeyáʔdada eksaʔáh

        s-ye-yaʔd-a-d-'ah   e-ksaʔ = á

        REP-3FI.A-body-JN-be.one-STV   3FI.A-child = DIM

        one girl

    b. dehniyaʔdagé hnihędaʔgehé·nų?

        de-hni-yaʔd-a-ge-h'   hni-hęd-aʔ = ge = henų?

        DL-3M.DU.A-body-JN-amount.to-STV   3M.DU.A-field-NSF = LOC = POP

        two farmers

    c. ahsę nigųnadí gųnų́·gweh

        ahsę   ni-gųn-ad-i-h   gųn-ųgweh

        NUM   PART-3FZ.PL.A-SRF-be.a.total.of-STV   3FZ.PL.A-person:SUFF

        three women

    d. gayéi nihęnadí shagonóʔshųʔáh[13]

        gayei   ni-hęn-ad-i-h   shago-noʔ = shųʔá

        NUM   PRT-3M.PL.A-SRF-be.a.total.of-STV   3M.SG > 3-step.parent/step.child = PL

        his four step-children; he has four step-children

The pattern for non-human animate nouns – i.e., nouns denoting animals – depends on whether or not a general term is available and incorporable. The procedure follows the pattern for human nouns closely: either a general term denoting the animal is incorporated into the number verb, or if, for structural reasons, that noun is not incorporable, then the general term used for human referents, i.e., -yaʔd- is used and followed by a more specific verbal or particle noun. One way in which nouns that denote humans differ from nouns denoting non-humans, is that .adi- + partitive is used to count three or more human referents as in (19c and d), whereas .ge- + partitive is used to count three or more non-human, animate referents.

(20) <u>Counting non-human animate nouns that can be incorporated:</u>

    ahsę niyojyųʔdagéh

    ahsę   ni-yo-jyųʔd-a-ge-h'

    NUM   PRT-3N/Z.SG.P-fish-JN-amount.to-STV

    three fish

(21) <u>Counting non-human animate nouns that cannot be incorporated:</u>

    ahsę nigųdiyaʔdagé dagós

    ahsę   ni-gųdi-yaʔd-a-ge-h'   dagos

    NUM   PRT-3FZ.PL.A-body-JN-amount.to-STV   cat

    three cats

---

[13] Words with clitics, especially multi-syllabic clitics, frequently are pronounced with two stresses.

5.2.3 The Noun Suffix

The Noun suffix is attached directly to the stem. Its form is *-aʔ / -iʔ*. The alternant *-iʔ* occurs with selected body part terms and the morphological noun *-ihs-* 'wall, ceiling', *-aʔ* occurs elsewhere (see examples (1) through (13)). The noun suffix contributes no meaning to the word except to mark it as a noun.

5.3 Verbal Nouns

Verbal nouns are, morphologically, verbs that have become lexicalized as nominals and that function semantically and in the discourse structure as referring expressions.[14] Typically, a verbal noun describes an important characteristic of the referent. Included in this class of nouns are proper names, some place names, various abstract concepts, a few body part words, a few relationship terms, a few words denoting human beings, numerous animal names, numerous words describing objects added to the cultural repertoire since contact. Verbal nouns comprise a larger class of nominals than do morphological nouns.[15] Examples of verbal nouns used in utterances are given in (22):

(22) a. ... déʔseʔ neʔ <u>hųdęnóthaʔ</u> oʔ waʔhųdę·nodęʔ... (LG05)
      dęʔseʔ   neʔ   hų-ad-Ręn-ot-haʔ   oʔ   waʔ-hų-ad-Ręn-od-ęʔ
      CNJ   NOM   3M.PL.A-SRF-song-raise-HAB   ADD   FACT-3M.PL.A-SRF-song-raise-PNC
      and   the   band   also   they played songs
      ... and the band also played songs...

    b. Dahayáʔkdaʔ neʔ <u>gahahsę·dyéthaʔ</u> (HW07).
      d-a-ha-yaʔk-d-aʔ   neʔ   ga-hahsR-ųdye-t-haʔ
      CIS-FACT-3M.SG.A-break.off-CS-PNC   NOM   3N/Z.SG.A-flame-throw-CS-HAB
      he ripped it off   the   lion
      The lion had ripped it off.

5.3.1 Characteristics of Verbal Nouns

A. <u>Verbal nouns are lexicalized as fully inflected forms</u>: With very few exceptions, verbal nouns are lexicalized as fully inflected forms with a given set of prefixes and suffixes – usually the habitual or stative. Thus if any part of the word is changed, it no longer functions as a nominal. For example in (22a) above, a change from habitual to punctual aspect marks the different functions of two words both built on the otherwise identical stem *-ad-Ręn-ot-*; in (23) a change of pronominal prefix marks the difference: the *a*-example functions as a nominal, the *b*-example does not.

---

[14] In the Onondaga Dictionary (Woodbury 2003) verbal nouns are designated *V > N*.

[15] 475 verbal nouns are listed in the Onondaga Dictionary (Woodbury 2003); additional examples have been collected since its publication. Verbal nouns are an open class that is still being added to by contemporary speakers (cf. Koenig & Michelson (2016) for Oneida).

(23) a. gayé·naųs
    ga-yena-ųs
    3N/Z.SG.A-catch,grab-HAB
    trap [literally: it catches it]

  b. hayé·naųs
    ha-yena-ųs
    3M.SG.A-catch,grab-HAB
    he catches it, he grabs it

Because verbal nouns are lexicalized as whole words, the usual inflectional repertoire of nouns is not available to them. Thus a verbal noun cannot, in unaltered form, be incorporated into a verb stem and with very few exceptions, the possessive pronominal prefix cannot replace the lexicalized pronominal prefix.[16] Example (24) shows how one speaker deals creatively with the fact that most verbal nouns cannot accept possessive prefixes by substituting the English word *machine* in a possessive construction for the Onondaga term *odiyo?dé·nyų?* 'machine' that occurs earlier on in the utterance:

(24) Dyę gwa? nę, tsha? hya? niyohgáe?i nęgę <u>odiyo?dé·nyų?</u>, dahodí? sdę? gwa? wa?ha·gyęhda?, dyę hwa?gatgathwá?, tha?nyadé? ne? hya? na? wa?tgdęsda?, ne? <u>agatmací·n</u> tho nhwa?gé?, daho?nyoha·gwá? na? né?, niha?nyowanę hya? finger (LG13).

dyę gwa? nę	tsha?	hya?	ni-yo-hgae?-ih		nęgę	odi-yo?de-nyų-?
COND RST TMP	SUB	MOD	PRT-3N/Z.SG.P-noisy-STV		DEM	3FZ.NSG.P-work-DST-STV
after a while	that	indeed	how noisy it was		this	machine

d-a-ho-adi-?		sdę?	gwa?	wa?-hag-yęhd-a?		dyę
CIS-FACT-3M.SG.P-throw-PNC		INDF	RST	FACT-3M.SG > 1SG-hit-PNC		TMP
he threw it		something	just	he hit me with it		until

h-wa?-g-atgathw-a?		t-ha-?ny-ade-?		ne?	hya?	na?
TRNS-FACT-1.SG.A-look.at-PNC		CIS-3M.SG.A-finger-exist-STV		NOM	MOD	ASRT
I looked there		there's his finger		the	indeed	it's

wa?-t-g-dęsd-a?		ne?	ag-at-macin		tho
FACT-DL-1SG.A-stop.something-PNC		NOM	1SG.P-SRF-machine		LOC
I stopped it		the	my machine		there

n-h-wa?-g-e-?		d-a-ho-?ny-ohaR-gw-a?		na?
PRT-TRNS-FACT-1SG.A-walk-PNC		CIS-FACT-3M.SG.P-finger-put.on.the.tip-REV-PNC		ASRT
I went there		it took off the tip of his finger		it's

ne?	ni-ha-?ny-owanę-h		hya?	finger
NOM	PRT-3M.SG.A-finger-big-STV		MOD	NOUN
the	he has a big finger		indeed	finger

This machine was so noisy [that I couldn't hear, so] he threw something at me and hit me with it until I looked up, [and] there's his finger; indeed, I stopped my machine [and] went there: it took off the tip of his finger, his big finger.

---

[16] Exceptions cited in Woodbury (2003) are verbal nouns with the meaning *apron, pin, and chair.*

B. <u>Verbal nouns are lexicalized together with clitics</u>: Even though clitics typically are loosely attached to fully inflected nouns and verbs, they appear to be lexicalized together with some verbal nouns. Notice that (25a and b) have identical structures except for the clitic =*shųʔá*, and yet they have different meanings:

(25) a. ohnyųhsagáhdeʔ
      o-hnyųhs-a-gahde-ʔ
      3N/Z.SG.P-squash,melon,pumpkin-JN-raw-STV
      watermelon

   b. ohnyųhsagahdeʔshųʔáh
      o-hnyųhs-a-gahde-ʔ = shųʔá
      3N/Z.SG.P-squash,melon,pumpkin-JN-raw-STV = PL
      vegetables, squashes, melons, pumpkins

Other examples of verbal nouns with clitics are:

(26) a. ųgwehųwéhneh
      (y)-ųgweh = ųwe = hne
      NPF-person:SUFF = AUTH = LOC
      (on the) reservation

   b. gajyęʔgekháʔ (6N)[17]
      ga-jyę-ʔ = ge = khaʔ
      NPF-bowl-NSF = LOC = CHAR
      Bowl Game

C. <u>Verbal nouns end in the habitual or the stative aspect</u>: There are isolated examples of verbal nouns ending in a noun suffix. They never end in the punctual.

(27) <u>Verbal nouns ending in the habitual aspect</u>:
   a. deyoyęhsæ·sdá·thek
      de-yo-yęhsR-a-sta·the-k
      DL-3N/Z.SG.P-blanket-JN-gleam-HAB
      silk

   b. dewatjisdó·gwaʔs
      de-w-at-jisd-ogw-aʔs
      DL-3N/Z.SG.A-SRF-ember-scatter-HAB
      sparks, scattered lights

(28) <u>Verbal nouns ending in the stative aspect</u>:
   a. oʔdųyó·daʔ
      o-iʔdųyod-aʔ
      3N/Z.SG.P-pile.up-STV
      heap, pile

---

[17] The Onondaga Nation term for the same game lacks the clitics; it is simply *gajyęʔ*.

b. odęháe·da?
o-adęhaR-od-a?
3N/Z.SG.P-sunlight,moonlight-be.upright-STV
sunshine, moonshine

(29) Verbal nouns ending in a noun suffix:
a. Sganya·dái·yo?
s-ga-nyadaR-iyo-?
REP-3N/Z.SG.A-lake-beautiful-NSF
Handsome Lake [name of the Seneca Prophet]
Note: the stative of -iyo- is -h

b. gajihgwa?é? (6N)
ga-jihgw-a-?e-?'
3N/Z.SG.A-fist,knot-JN-bat,hit-NSF
Lacrosse
Note: the stative of -?e- is -h

c. gajyęhayę·dáhsæ·?
ga-jyęh-a-yęd-ahsR-a?
3N/Z.SG.A-fire-JN-extend-NOM-NSF
the Council Way

D. Verbal nouns often contain incorporated nouns: Examples are

(30) a. degahwisdohá·gih
de-ga-hwisd-oha·g-ih
DL-3N/Z.SG.A-metal-squeeze-STV
newspaper, press

b. dewahų́hdes
de-w-ahųhd-es-Ø
DL-3N/Z.SG.A-ear-long-STV
donkey, mule

c. degagáhi·s
de-ga-gahR-is-Ø
DL-3N/Z.SG.A-eye-be.long-STV
telescope

E. Verbal nouns are often derived with root suffixes: This is especially so for names of tools or objects around the house. Note also that many of these begin in the feminine-indefinite agent pronominal prefix and end in the habitual aspect:

(31) a. eksoháetha?
e-ks-ohae-t-ha?
3FI.A-dish-wash-CS-HAB
dishpan [literally: one washes dishes with it]

b. esthu̜·dæ·yędákhwaʔ
 e-sthu̜dR-yęd-ahgw-haʔ
 3FI.A-hay-place-INST-HAB
 barn [literally: one uses it to put hay]

c. ejihgwęhdákhwaʔ
 e-jihgw-ęhd-ahgw-haʔ
 3FI.A-fist,knob-push.down-INST-HAB
 hammer [literally: one pushes down with it]

d. deyoihwado·gę́hdih
 de-yo-Rihw-a-dogę-hd-ih
 DL-3N/Z.SG.P-matter-JN-be.certain-CS-STV
 the Bible [Literally: it has caused it to be true]

e. odiyoʔdé·nyu̜ʔ
 odi-yoʔde-nyu̜-ʔ
 3FZ.PL[18]-work-DST-STV
 machinery

F. <u>Verbal nouns can occur as a compound nominal expressions:</u>

(32) a. ...né? <u>gawęheyú̜ ganę́hgwik</u> naʔ hwaʔagóhwaʔ (LG09)
 ne?   gaw-ęheyu̜-h'[19] ga-nęhgwi-k   naʔ   h-waʔ-ago-hw-aʔ
 NOM   3FI.P-die-STV 3N/Z.SG.A-haul.away-HAB ASRT   TRNS-FACT-3FI.P-take-PNC
 the   dead-wagon   it's   it took her
 ... a hearse came and took [this woman].

b. gayaʔdá·haʔ gahu̜hsé·daʔ
 ga-yaʔd-aR-haʔ   ga-hu̜hsR-od-aʔ
 3N/Z.SG.A-body-put.in-HAB   3N/Z.SG.A-box-stand-STV
 television [literally: a picture is in a box]

c. sdęʔ deʔgásthaʔ
 sdęʔ   deʔ-ga-st-haʔ
 INDF   NEG-3N/Z.SG.A-use-HAB
 junk [literally: something [that] isn't used]

d. ú̜·gwe gó·yos (CTL447.5)
 (y)-u̜gweh   go-Ryo-s
 NPF-person:SUFF   3FI.P-kill-HAB
 weapon, disease [literally: it kills people]

---

[18] Sometimes objects with moving parts, although non-animate, are lexicalized with zoic pronominal prefixes.
[19] Recall that word-final *h* drops in utterance-medial forms.

G. <u>Initial syllable drop</u>: Not infrequently speakers drop the first syllable of a verbal noun. Sometimes the first syllable is recoverable by speakers as in the *a*-example, sometimes not as in the *b*-example:

(33) a. deʔsgųdákhwaʔ [from adeʔsgųdákhwaʔ]
      Ø-[a]deʔsgųd-ahgw-haʔ
      3N/Z.SG.A-fry,bake,roast-INST-HAB
      frying pan

    b. naga·yáʔgih
      [ʔ]-nagaR-yaʔg-ih
      [ʔ]-pole-break.something.off-STV
      beaver

H. <u>The repetitive prefix marks some verbal nouns as proper names</u>:

(34) a. Shonųhses
      s-ho-nųhs-es-Ø
      REP-3M.SG.P-house-long-STV
      an Onondaga chief's title

    b. Sgahnehdá·dih
      s-ga-hnehd-adi-h
      REP-3N/Z.SG.A-pine.tree-other.side-STV
      Albany, NY; Schenectady, NY

I. <u>Variation among speakers</u>: When it comes to the uses of verbal nouns, speakers, within the two communities as well as between them, differ fairly frequently. The variation consists of both differences in the forms of the words and differences in the denotations of words:

(35) <u>Differences in form</u>:
    a. ojiʔtgwaiyóh (ON)   ojiʔtgwá·jik (6N)
      o-jiʔtgwaR-iyo-h'   o-jiʔtgwaR-jik-Ø
      3N/Z.SG.P-yellow-good-STV   3N/Z.SG.P-yellow-dark-STV
      orange [color]   *orange [color]*

    b. dehųtjihgwaʔéh (ON)   gajihgwaʔéʔ (6N)
      de-hų-at-jihgw-a-ʔe-h'   ga-jihgw-a-ʔe-ʔ
      DL-3M.PL.A-SRF-fist,knot-JN-bat, hit-STV   NPF-fist,knot-JN-bat, hit-NSF
      Lacrosse   *Lacrosse*

(36) <u>Difference in denotation</u>:
    a. degahæ·hgwáʔshæ·ʔ
      de-ga-hæ·hgw-aʔshR-aʔ
      DL-3N/Z.SG.A-bread-layer.something-STV
      layer cake (ON); *pie* (6N)

  b. ųthǽ·stha?
   ų-at-hR-st-ha?
   3FI.A-SRF-put.on.top.of-CS-HAB
   blanket (ON); *collar over a native dress* (6N)

5.4 Kinship and Other Relationship Terms[20]

Kinship terms are composed of a pronominal prefix and a stem that, typically, specifies one member of a reciprocal kin relationship, i.e., the referent. In addition, kinship terms can have attached certain clitics: (i) the diminutive clitic – as a sign of affection, (ii) the pluralizer clitic – for plural referents, or (iii) the decessive clitic – when the term refers to a deceased relative. The structure of kinship terms is:

pronominal prefix   -kin relation [referent]   = (clitic)

The choice of pronominal prefix depends on whether the kinship term is one that marks (i) age differences e.g., parent-child, older sibling-younger sibling, etc. or (ii) a relation in which relative age is ignored. If age differences are marked, then the pronominal prefix is chosen from the transitive series, such that, the agent portion of the prefix expresses the older of the two kintypes and the patient portion the younger. Thus, the prefix as a whole identifies the possessor and the referent in terms of person, number and gender, but whether the referent is expressed as agent or patient depends on whether (s)he is the older or the younger of the two. For example, in (37a) the referent is the older, in (37b) the referent is younger. [Note that the convention used in identifying the relationship morpheme is that the *referent* of the term is italicized and placed to the left of the possessor. A period separates the reciprocals of the relationship]: [21]

---

[20] Iroquoian kinship terms have been discussed extensively by Morgan (1871), Lounsbury (1964) and Koenig & Michelson (2010b). In addition, Mithun (2010a) has discussed irregularieties and gaps in the patterning of Mohawk kin terms. Morgan compiled extensive lists of attested kinship terms of a great many languages of the world, among them the Five Nations Iroquoian languages; Lounsbury analyzed the semantic structures underlying the set of Seneca kinship terms employing componential analysis; Koenig & Michelson present a detailed analysis of Oneida kinship expressions, pointing out their dual nature as both verbal and nominal entities. Apart from a few differences in detail, the semantic and morphosyntactic structures of the Onondaga set of terms coincides with that of the other Five Nations Iroquoian languages. The description of Onondaga terms presented here benefits greatly from the many important insights to be found in Lounsbury (ibid.), a seminar in the Oneida language conducted by Lounsbury during the academic year 1971-2 at Yale University (documented in my lecture notes), and in the detailed analysis provided by Koenig & Michelson (ibid.). The Onondaga data are from lists of contemporary usages provided by Jay Meacham, my own fieldwork, and, for attestations of early usages, from Morgan's tables.

[21] Contemporary speakers frequently use *gnóha?* 'my mother' and *g?níha?* 'my father' with first person *agent* intransitive prefixes when referring to their own parents, but switch to transitive prefixes when referring to someone else's parents.

(37) <u>Age differences marked</u>:
    a. <u>akshodaháh</u>[22]
      ak-hsod = ahá
      3FZ.SG > 1SG-*grandparent*.grandchild = DIM
      [she is] my (dear) grandmother

    b. <u>kheyá·de·ʔ</u>
      khey-ade·ʔ
      1SG > 3-*grandchild*.grandparent
      [she is] my grandchild

On the other hand, if the term expresses a relation in which age differences are unmarked, a dual or plural prefix from the agent or patient series is selected:

(38) <u>Age differences not marked</u>:
    a. <u>ugyáæʔseʔ</u>
      ugy-aæʔseʔ
      1DU.P-*cousin*.cousin
      my cousin [literally: we two [are] cousins]

    b. <u>ugwáæʔseʔ</u>
      ugw-aæʔseʔ
      1PL.P-*cousin*.cousin
      our/my cousin(s) [literally: we all [are] cousins]

Table 5.2 lists relationship stems describing 'blood' (consanguineal) relationships, relationships by adoption and marriage, and other, non-kinship relationships:

---

[22] The prefix *-ak-* 3FZ.SG > 1SG in this example is formally identical to the intransive prefix *-ak-* 3FZ.SG.P. It is one of a series of patient prefixes with first, second, and third person patients all of which are formally identical to transitives that include feminine-zoic agents. Until Karin Michelson brought this to the attention of a group of Iroquoianists during a conference, this portion of the kinship system had been assumed to have intransitive prefixes and therefore was thought to introduce an irregularity into the paradigm (See also Koenig & Michelson 2010b:178).

Table 5.2 Onondaga relationship terms

Consanguineal ("Blood") Relatives			
	Stem	Relationship	Focal Denotata[23]
Older Relatives	-hsodah / -hsodahah	*grandparent*.grandchild	grandmother, grandfather
	-noha?	*mother*.child	mother, aunt[24]
	-?nih / -?nihah	*father*.child	father
	-no?sęh / -no?sęhah	*uncle*.nephew/niece	mother's brother, father's brother[25]
	-htci?ah / -tci?ah	*older sibling*.younger sibling	older sister, older brother
Younger Relatives	-ade·?	*grandchild*.grandparent	granddaughter, grandson
	-hawah	*child*.parent	daughter, son[26]
	-ęhwadę?	*niece/nephew*.aunt/uncle	brother's child, sister's child[27]
	-?gę? /-?gę?ah	*youngersibling*.older sibling	younger sister, younger brother
No relative age	.adęhnųdę? + dualic	*(be) siblings*	sister, brother
	.aæ?se?	*cousin*	mother's sister's or mother's brother's child; father's sister's or father's brother's child[28]
	-nųhgwa?	*relative*	all consanguineal relatives
Relatives by Marriage and Adoption			
Older *and* Younger Relatives	-no?	*step-child; step-parent*	stepmother; stepfather; stepdaughter, stepson
	-hsa?wah	*parent-in-law; child-in-law*	a woman's: mother-, father-, daughter-, or son-in-law
	-nehnhųs	*parent-in-law; child-in-law*	a man's: mother-, father-, daughter-, or son-in-law

---

[23] Listed in this column are the immediate family members denoted by the terms. They also apply to more distant members in other generations by regular rule, for example, the grandmother term also applies to the mother's mother's sister, etc.

[24] Traditionally, the term was used to refer to one's mother and mother's sister. Contemporary speakers have extended its meaning to refer to the father's sister as well. When referring to the aunt, speakers use the full expression *gnohá? dekhenų́hę·khwa?* literally: my mother, I use it to greet her with.

[25] Traditionally, the term was used to refer to one's mother's brother (Morgan, ibid). Contemporary speakers use it for one's father's brother as well.

[26] Traditionally, the term also included a woman's sister's child, and a man's brother's child (Morgan, ibid.).

[27] Traditionally, the term was used to refer to a woman's brother's child, or a man's sisters child (Morgan, ibid.).

[28] Traditionally, the term was used to refer to a mother's brother's child, or a father's sister's child (Morgan, ibid.).

Table 5.2 (Continued)

	Stem	Relationship	Focal Denotata
No relative age distinction	-a·yẹh / -ya·yẹh	*sibling-in-law*	sister-in-law; brother-in-law
	-adẹnowẹʔ	*co-parents-in-law*	daughter's husband's parents; son's wife's parents
Non-kin Relationships			
No relative age distinction	-atciʔ -ẹnụhsanegẹh	*friend* *neighbor*	*friend* *neighbor*

Table 5.3 shows the distribution of transitive pronominal prefixes over age-differentiating consanguineal kinship terms with first person, second person, and third person possessors:

Table 5.3 Pronominal prefix selection with age-differentiating kin terms

Referent		1st person possessor	2nd person possessor	3rd person ♂ possessor	3rd person ♀ possessor
O L D E R ♀	grand-mother	akshodaháh 3FZ.SG > 1SG	sahsodaháh 3FZ.SG > 2SG	hohsodáh 3FZ.SG > 3M.SG	gohsodáh 3FZ.SG > 3FI
	mother	agnóhaʔ 3FZ.SG > 1SG	sanóhaʔ 3FZ.SG > 2SG	honóhaʔ 3FZ.SG > 3M.SG	gonóhaʔ 3FZ.SG > 3FI
	aunt	agnoháʔ dekhenụ́hẹ·khwaʔ 3FZ.SG > 1SG	sanoháʔ deshenụ́hẹ·khwaʔ 3FZ.SG > 2SG	honoháʔ deshagonụ́hẹ·khwaʔ 3FZ.SG > 3M.SG	gonoháʔ deyụdadnụ́hẹ·khwaʔ 3FZ.SG > 3FI
	sister +	aktciʔáh 3FZ.SG > 1P	sahtciʔáh 3FZ.SG > 2SG	shagohtciʔáh 3M.SG > 3FI	ụdadehtciʔáh 3FI > 3FI
Y O U N G E R ♀	younger sister	kheʔgẹʔáh 1SG > 3FI	sheʔgẹʔáh 2SG > 3FI	shagoʔgẹʔáh 3M.SG > 3FI	ụdadeʔgẹʔáh 3FI > 3FI
	daughter	khehawah 1SG > 3FI	shehawah 2SG > 3FI	shagohawah 3M.SG > 3FI	ụdathawah 3FI > 3FI
	niece	kheyẹhwá·dẹʔ 1SG > 3FI	sheyẹhwá·dẹʔ 2SG > 3FI	shagohwádẹʔ 3M.SG > 3FI	ụdadẹhwádẹʔ 3FI > 3FI
	grand-daughter	kheyá·de·ʔ 1SG > 3FI	sheyá·de·ʔ 2SG > 3FI	shagó·de·ʔ 3M.SG > 3FI	gó·de·ʔ 3FZ.SG > 3FI
O L D E R ♂	grand-father	hakhso·daháh 3M.SG > 1SG	hyahsó·dah 3M.SG > 2SG	hohsó·dah 3M.SG > 3M.SG	hụwahsó·dah[29] 3 > 3M.SG
	father	hakʔniháh 3M.SG > 1SG	hyaʔniháh 3M.SG > 2SG	hoʔníh 3M.SG > 3M.SG	hụwáʔnih 3 > 3M.SG
	uncle	hagnoʔsẹ́hah 3M.SG > 1SG	hyanoʔsẹ́hah 3M.SG > 2SG	honoʔsẹ́hah 3M.SG > 3M.SG	hụwanoʔsẹ́hah 3 > 3M.SG
	older brother	haktciʔáh 3M.SG > 1SG	hyatciʔáh 3M.SG > 2SG	hohtsciʔáh 3M.SG > 3M.SG	hụwahtsciʔáh 3 > 3M.SG
OLDER MEMBER OF THE RELATIONSHIP IS AGENT					MIXED

---

[29] In the other Five Nations Iroquoian languages *hụwa-* (prefix #33) 'he > him' in the darkly shaded areas of the table occurs with *ho-* 'he, he > him'. Recall that the 6N dialect replaces *ho-* in the meaning 'he > him' with *hụwa-*. However, the ON dialect does not, except for these four relationship terms.

Table 5.3 (Continued)

Referent		1st person possessor	2nd person possessor	3rd person ♂ possessor	3rd person ♀ possessor
Y O U N G E R ♂	brother –	he?gę?áh 1SG>3	hese?gę?áh 2SG>3	ho?gę?áh 3M.SG>3M.SG	hųwa?gę?áh 3>3M.SG
	son	hehá·wah 1SG>3	heshá·wah 2SG>3	hohá·wah 3M.SG>3M.SG	hųwáhawah 3>3M.SG
	nephew	heyęhwá·dę? 1SG>3	hesęhwá·dę? 2SG>3	hawęhwá·dę? 3M.SG>3M.SG	hųwęhwá·dę? 3>3M.SG
	grandson	heyá·de·? 1SG>3	hesá·de·? 2SG>3	hó·de·? 3M.SG>3M.SG	hųwá·de·? 3>3M.SG
OLDER MEMBER OF THE RELATIONSHIP IS AGENT					MIXED

In Table 5.3, note that the portion of the table with darker shading specifies the only areas in the paradigm where the pronominal prefix has the younger of the two relatives in the agent position. Another noteworthy feature of the paradigm is the selection of prefixes for female relatives. As a rule, for prefixes with female interactants, the feminine-zoic occurs in the agent position, and the feminine-indefinite in the patient position. But in the last column, some of the female-female relationships – highlighted with lighter shading – select the feminine-indefinite in the agent position, whereas the rest of the female-female relationships – no highlight – select the feminine-zoic in the agent position. Pronoun selection is lexicalized for each term, and the two are learned together by speakers as a single unit.[30]

As noted above, when relative age is not specified by a kin term, then a dual or plural prefix is selected from the agent or patient series, depending on which of these is lexicalized with the stem. This is illustrated in Table 5.4:

Table 5.4 Pronominal prefix selection with non-age-differntiating kin terms

Referent	1st person	2nd person	3rd person ♂	3rd person ♀
sibling	deyagyadęhnų́·dæ·? 1IN.DU.A	dejyadęhnų́·dæ·? 2DU	dehyadęhnų́·dæ·? 3M.DU.A	degyadęhnųdæ·? 3FZ.DU.A
cousin	ugyáæ?se? 1DU.P	jyáæ?se? 2DU	honáæ?se? 3M.NSG	onáæ?se? 3FZ.NSG

A small number of kinship stems can be inflected to denote both members of a reciprocal relationship at once. This is done by inserting the full reflexive morpheme (section 4.8.4.2) between the pronominal prefix and the stem, and replacing the transitive pronominal prefix with a non-transitive, non-singular prefix. The joint reference shows clearly in (39):

(39) Na? ų́hgę? né?, thoné honadathawá hninagé·? nęgę́ ugwehųwę́hneh (LG08).

na?	ų́hgę?	ne?	thonę	hon-adat-hawa	hni-nage·-?
ASRT	TMP	NOM	LOC	3M.NSG.P-REP-*child.parent*	3M.DU.A-reside-STV
it's	next	the	here	mother and son	they two live

---

[30] Mithun (2010a) points out similar areas of irregularity in the Mohawk paradigm and relates them to earlier stages in the development of the pronominal paradigm originating in a simple specific vs.non-specific third person system. See also Chafe's (1977b) description of the evolution of third person pronominal prefixes from simple to complex.

nẹgẹ   (y)-ugweh = ųwe = hne
DEM   NPF-person:SUFF-AUTH = LOC
this   reservation
So there's a mother and son living here on the reservation.

With a transitive prefix and without the reflexive, the term denotes just one member of the relationship:

(40)   hehá·wah
        he-hawah
        1SG > 3M-*child*.parent
        my son

Attested terms that can be inflected to denote both members of the relationship are shown in Table 5.5:

Table 5.5 Terms that refer to both members of the relationship

Referent	1st person	2st person	3rd person ♂	3rd person ♀
child.parent	dwadáthawah 1EX.PL.A	jyadáthawah 2DU	honadáthawah 3M.NSG.P	onadathawaháh 3FZ.NSG.P
younger siblings[31]	dwadade?gẹ́? 1EX.PL.A	jyadade?gẹ́? 2DU	hụdade?gẹ́? 3M.PL.A	not attested
relatives	ųgyadadnų́hgwa? 1DU.P	jyadadnų́hgwa? 2DU	honadadnų́hgwa? 3M.NSG.P	onadadnų́hgwa? 3FZ.NSG.P

5.4.1 Verbal and Nominal Characteristics of Kinship Terms

As was noted in the introduction to this chapter, kinship terms have some verbal attributes, some nominal attributes, and some features that are peculiar to the kinship vocabulary. The present section describes these special characteristics.

Verbal Characteristics: There are four ways in which kinship terms are like verbs: (i) some terms include transitive prefixes; (ii) some terms include a reflexive morpheme; (iii) one term, *-adẹhnụdæ·?* 'sibling', is attested with expanded aspects; (iv) incorporated terms require the nominalizer. Terms with features (i) and (ii) have been discussed in the previous section. As to (iii) expanded aspect, one kinship stem, *.adẹhnụdR-* + dualic 'sibling' – it occurs in (41) and (42) – is attested exclusively with verbal morphology.

To mark a deceased relative, *.adẹhnụdR-* + dualic 'sibling' occurs with the habitual past, it *cannot* occur with the decessive clitic:

(41) Thohgé go·? na? ne? <u>dyagyadẹhnụdǽ·hgwa?</u>, da·nyátgẹhǽ·? na? hodi·yóh gwas hya?
     hwa?gahs?áhda? ne? tsha? nihadihwají·yæ? (LG20).
     thohge   go·?   na?   ne?   de-yagy-adẹhnụdR-ah-gwa?   danyat = gẹhæ?
     TMP   CTR   ASRT   NOM   DL-1EX.DU.A-be.siblings-HAB-PST   Daniel = DEC
     then   however it's   the   my former sibling   the late Daniel

---

[31] With the addition of the reflexive, this term is lexicalized to refer to the relationship between members of the same moiety.

na?	hodi-Ryo-h'	gwas	hya?	h-wa?-ga-hs?-ahd-a?
ASRT	3M.NSG.P-kill-STV	INTNS	MOD	TRNS-FACT-3N/Z.SG.A-finish.all-CS-PNC
it's	it has killed them	very	indeed	it destroyed

ne?	tsha?	ni-hadi-hwajiR-a-a?
NOM	SUB	PRT-3M.PL.A-family-be a size-NSF
the	that	their whole family

But at that time my late brother Daniel's entire family was killed, [the influenza] destroyed them.

The same stem (with the distributive and without the dualic prefix) is also extended to refer to colleagues in the Confederacy Council:

(42) Oné ga·yę·nędá?i deswana?gaę̇·da? nayé? <u>swadęhnų́·dę·?</u>... (CTL382.6-7)

oné	ga-Wyę·n-ęda?-ih[32]	de-swa-na?gaR-ųd-a?	naye?	sw-adęhnųdR-ų-?'
TMP	3N/Z.SG.A-task-finish-STV	DL-2PL-antler-have.on-STV	ASRT	2PL-sibling-DST-STV
now	the task is finished	you have antlers on	it's	you are colleagues

Now it is done, you have on antlers, you [now] are colleagues...

The stem in (42) is also attested with the progressive morpheme and inflected for all aspects in the meaning *act as colleagues*, e.g. *wa?hųdęhnųdę́·dye?* [wa?-hų-adęhnųdR-ų-(a)dye-?] 'they acted as colleagues' (W425.2). When used to refer to a relative or to a colleague, it seems best to analyze this term as a verbal noun (section 5.3 above). But the fact that the version with the progressive can be inflected for all three aspects demonstrates that it is a full-fledged verb.[33]

(iv) <u>Incorporation</u>: Incorporation is uncommon, but it is documented with a few relationship terms. The fact that they must include the nominalizer shows them to be verbs.[34] An example is:

(43) a. thatcihsi·yóh
    t-h-atci-<u>hsR</u>-iyo-h'
    CIS-3M.SG.A-be.friends-NOM-good-STV
    he is the best of friends

   b. hode·?tciyóh
    ho-ade·?-<u>tshR</u>-iyo-h'
    3M.SG.P-*grandchild*.grandparent-NOM-be.good-STV
    he has a nice grandchild

<u>Nominal Characteristics</u>: A number of kinship term characteristics are nominal in character or are simply peculiar to kinship expressions: (i) in discourse, kinship expressions are referring expressions; (ii) kinship expressions can take the nominal particle *ne?*; (iii) they are negated like nouns, not verbs; (iv) transitive prefixes are selected on the

---

[32] Recall that words ending in /h/ typically lose it utterance-medially.

[33] Recall that verbal nouns are attested mainly in the habitual or the stative aspects.

[34] Note also that the incorporating verb in (43a) inflects for the superlative just like other verbs with adjectival meanings (see section 4.7.2.2).

basis of age differences of referents, a characteristic that is specific to kinship expressions; (iv) they are pluralized like nominals.

(i) <u>Discourse Function</u>: In discourse, kinship expressions function as nominals, as shown in (44) where *hakʔnihá́ʔgęhǽʔ* 'my late father' is an external nominal that is in apposition to the pronominal prefix *-ha-* of *waʔhęhę́·ʔ* 'he said':

(44) Nę hyaʔ naʔ néʔ <u>hakʔnihá́ʔgęhǽ·ʔ</u> waʔhęhę́·ʔ ęganųhsagęisdík diʔ hyaʔ nę·gę́ tho séʔ
     hędjidwadę́·ʔ ganadagų́·wah (LG16).

nę	hyaʔ	naʔ	neʔ	hak-ʔnihaʔ = gęhæʔ		waʔ-ha-ihę-·ʔ'
TMP	MOD	ASRT	NOM	3M.SG > 1SG-*father*.child = DEC		FACT-3M.SG.A-say-PNC
now	indeed	it's	the	my late father		he said

ę-ga-nųhs-a-gęisd-i-k-Ø		diʔ	hyaʔ	nęgę	tho	seʔ
FUT-3N/Z.SG.A-house-JN-move-STV-CONT-PNC		LINK	MOD	DEM	LOC	MOD
the house will be moved		so	indeed	this	there	actually

h-ę-s-dw-ad-R-ęʔ	ga-nad-agųwa
TRNS-FUT-REP-1IN.PL-SRF-put.in-PNC	3N/Z.SG.A-town-LOC
we will put it back in there	in the town

Then my late father said, "The house will be moved back into the town."

(ii) <u>Negation</u>: Nouns and nominal expressions cannot take the negative prepronominal prefix *deʔ-*, as verbs do (section 4.7.8); kinship expressions, just like all other nominals, are negated with the special predicator *déʔgę?* 'it isn't'.[35]

(45) a. Ya naʔ hakʔnihá <u>déʔgęh</u> (EO/JM)

hya	naʔ	hak-ʔnih-ah	deʔ-ga-i-h
NEG	ASRT	3M > 1SG-father-DIM	NEG-3N/Z.SG.A-be-STV

    he's not my father

   b. Ya naʔ Mary gnohá? <u>déʔgęh</u> (EO/JM)

hya	naʔ	Mary	g-noha?	deʔ-ga-i-h
NEG	ASRT	NAME	1SG.A-mother	NEG-3N/Z.SG.A-be-STV

    Mary is not my mother

(iii) <u>Semantic dimensions encoded by pronominal prefixes attached to kinship terms</u>: As noted, terms that refer to one of the members of a bipolar relationship involving different generations – e.g., grandparent, grandchild – or that mark other age-distinctions, e.g., older sibling, younger sibling, are morphologically marked with transitive pronominal prefixes. The transitive prefixes code for person, gender, and number as do verbal prefixes, but crucially, the juxtaposition of persons encoded by transitives codes for generational and age differences in kinship terms rather than for semantic case as it does in verbs. Specifically, what is the agent position in verbs is replaced by the older of the two relatives, and similarly the patient position is replaced by the younger of the two relatives:

---

[35] The only exception to this statement is *-adęhnųdR-* 'be siblings' which negates like a verb and also has additional verbal characteristics not shared with other kin terms (see above).

(46) a. hakshodaháh
    hak-hsod-ahah
    3M.SG > 1SG-grandparent-DIM
    my grandfather

  b. haktciʔáh
    hak-tciʔah
    3M.SG > 1SG-older.sibling
    my older brother

  (iv) Kinship terms are pluralized like nominals, with the plural clitic =*shųʔá*.[36]

(47) …kheya·de·ʔshųʔá dehniyaʔdagé ásde neʔ naʔ heʔ íthneʔs (EO01).

khey-ade·ʔ = shųʔá	de-hni-yaʔd-a-ge-h'		asde	neʔ naʔ	heʔ
1SG > 3-grandchild = PL	DL-3M.DU.A-body-JN-amount.to-STV		LOC	FOCUS	REP
my grandchildren	two of them		outdoors	it's this	again

    i-t-hn-e-ʔs
    EP-CIS-3M.DU.A-walk-HAB
    they are around
    … my two grandchildren are outdoors again.

5.5 Particle Nouns

Particles, by definition, are forms that lack internal structure; unlike morphological nouns, they cannot be incorporated, and although they take the occasional clitic, their ability to take other affixes is non-existent or extremely limited. In the Iroquoian languages, particles have many different functions: syntactic, adverbial, discourse, pragmatic, etc. One group of particles – they are designated *N* in the Onondaga Dictionary (Woodbury 2003) – always function as nominals in that they denote entities. Just like every other nominal, they are nearly always preceded by the nominal particle *neʔ*. Often they are plant or animal names and some are borrowings from other languages, i.e., *dagós* 'cat', which may be a borrowing from the Dutch. Some animal names derive from the sounds speakers make to attract an animal, e.g. *gítgit* 'chicken', or they are forms that look like they might have been formed from Onondaga roots but have become structurally and/or semantically opaque, e.g. dadekháhgwaʔ 'strawberry'. These words are classified as nouns solely on the basis of their meaning and their distribution, for example:

(48) a. Tcihéʔs neʔ <u>jí·ha</u> seʔ khę dahųwasháędę? (HW05).

tci-h-e-ʔs	neʔ	<u>jí·hah</u>	seʔ	khę	d-a-hųw-ashaed-ę?
COIN-3M.SG.A-walk-HAB	NOM	NOUN	TAG		CIS-FACT-3 > 3M.SG-tie.up-PNC
he's around	the	dog	you know?		somebody tied him up

    While the dog was there, you know, someone tied him up.

---

[36] Verb forms are 'pluralized' with the distributive morpheme.

b. Sẹnų́hdų́ʔ khẹ tshaʔ ni·yų́h, waʔų·gwanasgwahdų́ʔ neʔ gítgit, nigųnaʔsʔáh.
(NC01)

s-ẹnųhdų-ʔ	khẹ	tshaʔ	niyų	waʔ-ųgwa-nasgw-ahdų-ʔ
2SG.P-know-STV	QUE	SUB	AMT	FACT-1PL.P-pet-disappear-PNC
you know	question	that	amount	we lost our pets

neʔ	gitgit	ni-gųn-aʔsʔa-h'
NOM	NOUN	PRT-3FZ.PL.A-small-STV
the	chicken	they are small

Do you know how many little chickens we have lost ?"

5.6 Independent Personal Pronouns

Pronouns are substitutes for lexical nouns whose referents are identifiable either by contextual information or because they have been identified by a previous use of the noun. In the Iroquoian languages, independent personal pronouns are typically used for special emphasis, or to foreground a participant. They are, morphologically, particles (first and second person pronouns) or an independent noun form consisting of a third person patient pronominal prefix and a noun stem *-ųhwaʔ* (third person pronouns). Third person pronouns distinguish between singular and plural number, first and second person pronouns do not as can be seen in Table 5.6. (For a detailed discussion of independent pronouns and their distributional characteristics see section 6.2).

Table 5.6 Independent personal pronouns

Person-Gender-Number	Pronoun	Gloss
1st person	iʔ/niʔ[37]	*I; we*
2nd person	is/nis	*you; you two or more*
3rd person masculine singular	háųhwaʔ	*he*
3rd person feminine-zoic singular	áųhwaʔ	*she*
3rd person feminine-indefinite singular	gáųhwaʔ	*she, one*
3d person masculine non-singular	honų́hwaʔ	*they two or more[38]*
3d person feminine-zoic non-singular	onų́hwaʔ	*they two or more women*

Examples of the use of independent pronouns are:

(49) a. ...gehéʔ hẹsgatho·yáʔ tshaʔ nya·wẹ́ʔih neʔ nẹ́, iʔ waʔhgẹiʔdák (LG07).

g-eR-heʔ	h-ẹ-s-g-atho·y-aʔ	tshaʔ	ni-yaw-ẹ-ʔ-ih
1SG.A-want-HAB	TRNS-FUT-REP-1SG.A-tell-PNC	SUB	PRT-3N/Z.SG.P-happen-INCH-STV
I want	I will tell again	that	thus it has happened

neʔ nẹ	iʔ	waʔ-k-gẹiʔd-ak
NOM TMP	PRON	FACT-1SG.A-fry-PNC
when	I/we	I fried it

...I want to tell again what happened when I fried [the locusts].

---

[37] First and second person pronouns occur with and without initial *n.* The *n* may be a partitive or the forms with the *n* may be a contraction of *neʔ iʔ* and *neʔ is.*

[38] Recall that dual or plural masculine pronouns are used for males or mixied groups of males and females.

b. Nę né? na? tsha? nwa?hadéhęha? ne? <u>háuhwa?</u>, wa?hayagę?nhá? ná? (LG09).

nę	ne?	na?	tsha?	n-wa?-ha-adehęh-'a?		ne?
TMP	NOM	ASRT	SUB	PRT-FACT-3M.SG.A-get.embarrassed-PNC		NOM
then	the	it's	that	how embarrassed he got		the

ha-uhw-a?	wa?-ha-yagę?-nha?	na?
3M.SG.P-self-NSF	FACT-3M.SG.A-emerge-PNC	ASRT
he, himself	he went out	it's

As for him, he got so embarrassed, he went out and left [the room].

5.7 Complex Nominal Expressions

A variety of constructions can function as independent noun phrases with a single referent.[39] Like morphological nouns, verbal nouns, and selected particles, these nominal expressions refer to entities. They are organized here into five (somewhat overlapping) groups. Except for free relatives these expressions can occur either before or after the verb just like any other independent noun,[40] and just like nouns, they can be preceded by the nominal particle *ne?*, a demonstrative particle (*négę* or *thógę*), or both, and, again as with nouns, the nominal particle typically does not occur utterance-initially.

A. <u>Noun-noun compounds</u>: Note that the nominal particle *ne?* can occur before both parts of the compound as in (50) or before the compound's head as in (51). The two nouns are adjoined. The phrase as a whole refers to one of the nouns contained within it: [[NP*i* NP*j*]]NP*j*

(50) Na? yá·gę? hadisthá? <u>ne? onę?dá? owę́·ga?</u>... (HW07)

na?	yagę?	hadi-st-ha?	ne?	o-nę?d-a?	o-RęgaR-a?
ASRT	HRSAY	3M.PL.A-use-HAB	NOM	NPF-hemlock-NSF	NPF-branch-NSF
it's	they say	they use it	the	hemlock	branch

They say they use a hemlock branch...

(51) Wa?há·gę? <u>osdę́hæ? ne? gahú·wa?</u> (CTL67.5).

wa?-ha-gę-?	o-sdęhR-a?	ne?	ga-huw-a?
FACT-3M.SG.A-see-PNC	NPF-stone-NSF	NOM	NPF-boat-NSF
he saw it	stone	the	boat

He saw a stone boat.

In (52) the compound consists of an incorporated noun and an independent noun. Here neither is marked by the nominal particle.

(52) ... [[wa?hó·gę? ne? hę́·gweh] [onę́ha? gahę·dákta?]]... (CTL182.5)

wa?-ho-gę-?	ne?	hR-ugweh	o-nęh-a?
FACT-3M.SG > 3M.SG-see-PNC	NOM	3M.SG.A-person:SUFF	NPF-corn-NSF
he saw him	the	man	corn

---

[39] See Koenig & Michelson 2009 for an analysis of the internal structure of nominal expressions in Oneida

[40] Free relatives are attested only to the right of the verb.

ga-hẹd-akd-aʔ
3N/Z.SG.A-field-near-STV
near the field
...he saw the man near the corn field...

B. <u>Nominal expressions with two or more nominals in apposition:</u>

(i) Nominal demonstratives: The demonstrative functions as an independent nominal so that the particle and the nominal are in apposition. The referent of the phrase as a whole is identical to the referent of both of the nouns it contains: [[NP$_i$ NP$_j$]]$_{NPi}$

<u>A demonstrative particle and noun</u>: without the nominal particle in (53a); with the nominal particle before each, the demonstrative and the proper noun (53b):

(53) a. Naʔ yágẹʔ <u>nẹgẹ hẹgwé</u> honasgwayẹʔ ji·háh... (HW05).

na?	yage?	nẹgẹ	hR-ụgweh	ho-nasgw-a-yẹ-?	jihah
ASRT	HRSAY	DEM	3M.SG.A-person:POSS	3M.SG.P-pet-JN-have-STV	NOUN
it's	they say	this	man	he has a pet	dog

They say this man had a dog...

    b. Ga·nyóʔ hesni·yụ́h, ís ẹhsathụga·yáʔk, ẹhsjisdẹ́hdaʔ, tshaʔ nụ́· gẹʔdẹ́·ʔ <u>neʔ nẹgẹ neʔ Otsgẹihdiʔgó·na</u> (HW07).

ganyó?	he-sni-yụ-h'		is	ẹ-hs-at-hụga·ya?k-Ø		
INDF	TRNS-2DU-arrive-STV		PRON	FUT-2SG.A-SRF-draft.someone-PNC		
whenever	you two have arrived there		you	you will volunteer		

ẹ-hs-jisd-ẹhd-a?	tsha? nụ́	ga-i?dẹ-?	ne?	nẹgẹ	ne?
FUT-2SG.A-fire-drop-PNC	SUB LOC	3.FZ.SG.A-dwell-STV	NOM	DEM	NOM
you will drop fire	place where	she dwells	the	this	the

Otsgẹihdi?gona
NAME
Great Lizard

As soon as you two get there, you're the one, you will volunteer to drop the fire into the place where she lives, this one, the Great Lizard

<u>A demonstrative particle and a noun-noun compound:</u>

(54) ...háụ? di? dásha[41] <u>thogẹ́ ohwahdáʔ oʔẹ́·naʔ</u>... (HW03)

hau?	di?	d-a-s-hawa-h	thogẹ	o-hwahd-a?	o-a?ẹn-a?
INST	LNK	CIS-FACT-2IMP-bring-IMP	DEM	NPF-maple-NSF	NPF-stick-NSF
alright	moreover	bring it!	that	maple	stick

...all right, so bring me that maple stick...

<u>A demonstrative particle and an internally headed relative clause</u> (see sec. 7.5.1): the IHRC can be preceded by the nominal particle as in (55):

---

[41] An elliptical form of dáshawah *bring it!* The base is .haụ- / .ẹhaụ- / .haw- / .hw / .ẹhw- / -ya?dẹhaw- + cislocative or translocative v.a. *bring, take.*

(55) ... waʔgahnodų́ʔ nigę̨ hya diʔ gwas deʔodų́ neʔ, tho naʔ dahų̨dawę·yéʔ <u>nę̨gę̨ neʔ</u>
    <u>hodiʔse·nų́·dyeʔs</u> (LG03).

waʔ-ga-hnod-ų-ʔ'		nigę̨	hya	diʔ	gwas
FACT-3N/Z.SG.A-be.deep-DST-PNC		EXT	NEG	LINK	INTS
it flooded		extent	not	moreover	very

deʔ-o-adų-h'	neʔ	tho	naʔ	d-a-hų-ad-awę·ye-ʔ	nę̨gę̨
NEG-3N/Z.SG.P-become-STV	NOM	LOC	ASRT	CIS-FACT-3M.PL.A-SRF-stir-PNC	DEM
it isn't possible	the	there	it's	they wander about	this

neʔ	hodi-ʔse·-nų-(a)dye-ʔs
NOM	3M.NSG.P-drag-STV-PRG-HAB
the	they drive

...it was so flooded that it wasn't possible for them to get around, these ones who drive.

<u>An internally headed relative clause and a noun:</u>

(56) Nę̨·gę̨ ų́hgę̨ʔ hodinasgwahdų́·nik, <u>neʔ nigų̨naʔsʔá gítgit</u> (NC01).

nę̨gę̨	ų́hgę̨ʔ	hodi-nasgw-ahdų-ni-k	neʔ	ni-gų̨n-aʔsʔa-h
DEM	TMP	3M.PL.P-pet-lose-BEN-HAB	NOM	PART-3FZ.PL.A-be.small.ones-STV
right now		they lose their pets	the	little ones

gitgit
NOUN
chicken

Right now, they are loosing their baby chicks.

C. <u>Expressions with possessed nominals</u>

(i) A possessed noun and a second noun. One noun is more specific than the other.

(57) <u>Agetshenę́ʔshų̨ʔ, jíhah gá·eʔ dų̨désneh</u> (H153.14).

age-tshenę-ʔ = shų̨ʔ	jihah	gaeʔ	dl-de-sn-e-h
1SG.P-pet-NSF = PL	NOUN	DGR	DL-CIS-2DU-walk-IMP
my pets	dog	less	come here!

Hurry up [and] come here, my dogs!

(ii) A kinship expression and a proper noun:

(58) Ų̨hgę̨ʔ <u>neʔ khehawá dekhenų̨hę·khwáʔ Dorothy</u>, tciyeksaʔá gwaʔ tho neʔ, enų̨hwéʔs
    gę̨s neʔ, sų̨ gáʔ oyáʔ a·yų̨dadyaʔdagéhnhaʔ (LG08).

ų̨hgę̨ʔ	neʔ	khe-hawah	de-khe-nų̨hę·-hgw-haʔ	Dorothy
TMP	NOM	1SG > 3-parent.child	DL-1SG > 3-greet-INST-HAB	NAME
next	the	my niece[42]		Dorothy

---

[42] Literally, 'my daughter [that's what] I greet her with it'.

tci-ye-ksaʔ = á			gwaʔ	tho	neʔ	e-nųhweʔ-s	gęs	neʔ	sų gaʔ
COIN-3FI.A-child = DIM			RST	MAN	NOM	3FI.A-like-HAB	CST	NOM	INDF INDF
when she was a little girl			just	thus	the	she likes	usually	the	someone

(y)-oya-ʔ	aa-yųdad-yaʔdagehnh-aʔ
3N/Z.SG.A-different-STV	OP-3FI > 3FI-help-PNC
different one	she would help them

Next, my niece, Dorothy, when she was a little girl, she liked to help others.

(iii) A kinship expressions and an internally headed relative clause:

(59) Naʔ díʔ hyaʔ <u>deyagyadęhnųdǽ·hgwaʔ</u>, neʔ <u>thagówanę</u>, tho nhwaʔhéʔ... (LG20)

naʔ	diʔ	hyaʔ	de-yagy-adęhnųdR-ah-gwaʔ	neʔ	t-ha-gowanę-'h
ASRT	LNK	MOD	DL-1EX.DU.A-be.siblings-STV-HBPST	NOM	CIS-3M.SG.A-big-STV
it's	moreover	indeed	we two had been siblings	the	he is older

tho	n-h-waʔ-h-e-ʔ
LOC	PRT-TRNS-FACT-3M.SG.A-walk-PNC
there	he went there

Indeed, my [deceased] sibling, the oldest one, went there...

D. <u>Expressions in which one nominal further specifies another</u>

(i) A noun and a conjoined NP. The noun has a more general meaning than the two nouns composing the conjoined NP. The nominal particle precedes the entire expression.

(60) Dęʔseʔ <u>neʔ gatshenę jihá· dagós oʔ</u> tshaʔ niyót odigáʔhwaʔ ... (LG01)

dęʔseʔ	neʔ	ga-tshenę-h	jí·hah	dagós	oʔ	tshaʔ	ni-yo-hd-Ø
CNJ	NOM	NPF-pet-NSF	NOUN	NOUN	ADD	SUB	PRT-3N/Z.SG.P-how.it.is-STV
and	the	pet(s)	dog(s)	cat(s)	also	that	how it is

odi-gaʔhw-aʔ
3FZ.NSG-like.the.taste-STV
they like the taste

And the pets, dogs and cats, they like the taste [of locusts] ...

(ii) An expression consisting of a noun compound specifying the meaning of a noun incorporated into a verb:

(61) ...nęhshų́·yok neʔ onę́·yaʔ gahų́·waʔ... (CTL55.7-8)

n-ę-hs-hųw-o-k[43]	neʔ	o-nęy-aʔ	ga-hųw-aʔ
PRT-FUT-2SG.A-boat-float-PNC	NOM	NPF-stone-NSF	NPF-boat-NSF
you will launch a boat	the	stone	boat

...you will launch a stone boat...

E. <u>Free relatives</u> marked with the relative marker *tshaʔ gayę́ʔ* 'the one (animate) who/that' in (62), or *tshaʔ nwadę́ʔ* 'the one (animate or non-animate that) in (63):[44]

---

[43] *w > y /_o* by regular rule.

(62) Oyáʔ néʔ waʔeyenáʔ <u>tshaʔ gáyę̣́ shago·nṵhgwaʔ</u> (LG17).

   (y)-oya-ʔ   neʔ   waʔ-e-yena-ʔ´   tshaʔ gayę̣́
   3N/Z.SG.A-different-STV   NOM   FACT-3FI.A-accept-PNC   REL
   it is different   the   she got it   the one who

   shago-nṵhgw-aʔ
   3M.SG > 3-have.relatives-STV
   his relative(s)
   The other one got it [the inheritance], *the one who is his relative.*

(63) Onę hę̣· waʔgṵye·nawáʔs waʔgṵ́·yṵʔ, <u>tshaʔ nwádę̣ sehsagihá·dyeʔ</u> (HW06).

   onę   hę̣·   waʔ-gṵ-yenawaʔs-Ø   waʔ-gṵy-ṵ-ʔ   tshaʔ nwadę̣
   TMP   AFF   FACT-1SG > 2SG-help.someone-PNC   FACT-1SG > 2SG-give-PNC   REL
   then   yes   I helped you   I gave it to you   that which

   s-ehsag-ih-adye-ʔ
   2SG.P-look.for-STV-PRG-STV
   you're searching along
   Now indeed, I'm helping you, I'm giving you what you're searching for as you go.

---

[44] Some speakers use different relative markers for animate and non-animate referents, others use *tshaʔ gayę̣́* for both animate and non-animate referents.

6 Pro-Forms

6.1 Introduction

Pro-forms are words or affixes that substitute for nouns, or nominal expressions. Their meanings are recoverable from the linguistic context or from the speech situation. Onondaga pro-forms can be classified in terms of their formal characteristics or their functions. Formally, pro-forms are either independent words or bound morphemes. They comprise personal pronouns, various indefinite expressions, interrogatives, and demonstratives. Independent pro-forms are morphologically diverse: they occur as particles or as nouns. Personal pronouns occur in two forms that can occur together in a single clause: as pronominal prefixes – a complex system of obligatory bound morphemes on verbs and nouns (secs. 4.3 and 5.2.1) – and as independent words. The second group – independently occurring pro-forms – are discussed in this chapter. They are personal pronouns (*I, you, he, she*, etc.), interrogative particles (*who, what, when, where*, etc.), indefinite particles (*something, somebody, somewhere, sometime*, etc.), and demonstrative particles (*this, that*). Possession is marked obligatorily by pronominal prefixes on nouns; there is no independent pro-form performing this function.[1] Section 6.2 deals with independent personal pronouns, section 6.3 with interrogative pronouns, section 6.4 with indefinite expressions, and section 6.5 with demonstratives.

Table 6.1 summarizes the distribution of pro-forms on the basis of their formal characteristics. It shows, among other things, that personal and indefinite pro-forms occur as both pronominal prefixes and independent words, that possessives occur only as prefixes, and that demonstratives and interrogatives occur only as independent words or phrases.

Table 6.1 Distribution of Onondaga pro-forms

Function	Affix-Type	Independent word
personal	verbal/nominal prefix	particle, noun, or verb
indefinite	verbal/nominal prefix	particle or particle cluster
possessive	nominal prefix	–
demonstrative	–	particle
interrogative	–	particle or particle cluster

---

[1] Onondaga differs in this from Mohawk and Oneida. The equivalent of a possesive pronoun is expressed by the morphologically stative verb stem *-awę–* 'own something'.

6.2 Personal Pronouns

Unlike pronominal prefixes, independent personal pronouns are optional; they serve to signal various types of prominence relations in Onondaga. In that function they occur, with a few exceptions, in apposition to obligatory verbal pronominal prefixes. First and second person pronouns – the deictic pronouns – foreground the speaker and addressee in discourse. Third person pronouns can substitute for or co-occur with a person's name or a phrase characterizing an individual. First and second person pronouns are, formally, particles. Neither distinguishes singular from plural. Third person pronouns are morphological nouns. They consist of a patient pronominal prefix that distinguishes person, number, and gender, combined with a noun base *-ųhwaʔ* that is glossed 'self' in this work. Third person independent pronouns are limited to animate referents. The quantity forms *.jyaę-* + dualic 'be both' and *-gweg-* 'be all' occur as verbs with animate, agent, non-singular pronominal prefixes and as particles when the distinctions of person, number, and gender are irrelevant. The inventory of independent pronouns that is attested in the corpus is:

Table 6.2 Inventory of independent pronouns

Person-Gender-Number	Pronoun	Gloss
1st person	iʔ/niʔ[2]	*I; we*
2nd person	is/nis	*you; you two or more*
3rd person masculine singular	háųhwaʔ	*he, him*
3rd person feminine-zoic singular	áųhwaʔ	*she, her*
3rd person feminine-indefinite singular	gáųhwaʔ	*she, her, one*
3d person masculine non-singular	honúhwaʔ	*they two or more,[3] them*
3d person feminine-zoic non-singular	onúhwaʔ	*they two or more women*
Quantified pronominals[4]	dedni·jyá·ęh	*we both (inclusive)*
	desni·jyá·ęh	*you both*
	dehni·jyá·ęh	*they both (M)*
	degni·jyá·ęh	*they both (FZ)*
	agwagwé·gih	*we all (exclusive)*
	dwagwé·gih	*we all (inclusive)*
	swagwé·gih	*you all*
	gųdigwé·gih	*they all (FZ)*
	hadigwé·gih	*they all (M)*

Examples with first, second, and third person pronouns used for emphasis are:

---

[2] Recall that first and second person pronouns occur with and without initial *n*. It is not clear whether the *n* is a partitive or whether the form with the *n* is a contraction of *neʔ iʔ* and *neʔ is*.

[3] Recall that dual or plural masculine pronouns are used for males or mixied groups of males and females.

[4] Quantified pronominals differ formally from the set of independent personal pronouns in that they are derived from verb stems.

(1) a. Do· í?, kjiná ne? ni?á hyá ni? sdę? de?kdá·gwas (HW07).

do·	i?	k-jina-Ø	ni? = á	hya	ni?
INTR	PRON	1SG.A-brave-STV	PRON = DIM	NEG	PRON
how	I	I am brave	I only	not	I

sdę?	de?-k-dagw-as
INDF	NEG-1SG.A-fear.something-HAB
anything	I don't fear things

How about me? I'm brave, I'm the only one who isn't afraid of anything.

  b. Wadę? nis cyá·jih.

wadę?	nis	hs-yas-ih
INTR	PRON	2SG.A-be.named-STV
what	you	you are called

As to you, what is your name?
    cf. wadę? cyá·jih 'What is your name?'

  c. Háuhwa? gwas tho?se·hdiyóh.

ha-uhwa?	gwas	t-ho-?se·hd-iyo-h'
3M.SG.P-self	INTNS	CIS-3M.SG.P-car-be.nice-STV
he himself	very	his car is the nicest[5]

It's he [that has] the very nicest car.

Note that in (1a-c) the independent pronoun is coreferential with the pronominal prefix of the following verb. The pronominal prefix is the obligatory element that identifies the argument(s) in each of the clauses in terms of person, gender, and number; the independent pronouns are optional. But although utterances with independent pronouns characteristically include verbs with coreferential pronominal prefixes, this is not always so, as is shown in example (2):

(2) I? hí·hya? ne? jyadahę·dųk sų́· ne? hoyá·neh (CTL208.3-4).

i?	hí·hya?	ne?	sy-ad-ahędų-k	sų	ne?	ho-yane-h
PRON	MOD	NOM	2DU-SRF-ask.someone-HAB	INTR	NOM	3M.SG.P-be.chief-STV
I	indeed	the	you two ask about	who	the	he is chief

Indeed, I am the one about whom you ask, "who is the chief?"

Independent pronouns can also occur with a second and even a third coreferential independent nominal. Example (3), a verbless clause contains three nominals referring to the same referent:

(3) Is khę shugwe ne? sathędanų́?as tsha? ganęhayę́thwih (CTL191.2).

is	khę	hs-ugweh	ne?	s-at-hęd-a-nų?-as
PRON	QUE	2SG.A-person:SUFF	NOM	2SG.A-SRF-field-JN-guard-HAB
you	QUESTION	you, a person	the	you guard the field

---

[5] Recall that with a group of verbs with adjectival meanings, including -iyo-, the entity referenced by the incorporated noun is understood as possessed under certain circumstances (sec. 4.4.3.4).

tsha? ga-nęh-a-yęthw-ih
SUB 3N/Z.SG.A-corn-JN-plant-STV
where corn field

[Are] you the person, guarding the cornfield? [Literally: Are you, person, the one guarding the field, where the corn is planted?]

Quantified pronominals are stative verbs, morphologically:

(4) Quantified Pronominals:
 a. desni·jyáę jyahdę́·dyah!
  de-sni-jyaę-h   sy-ahdędy-ah
  DL-2DU-be.both-STV 2.DU-move.on-IMP
  Both of you, go!

 b. dwagwé·gih dwanųhsanų́hwe?s.
  dwa-gweg-ih   dwa-nųhs-a-nųhwe?-s
  1EX.PL.A-be.all-STV 1EX.PL.A-house-JN-like-HAB
  we all (excl.) like the house

6.2.1 Personal Pronouns and Clitic Combinations

Personal pronouns can combine with the diminutive, the plural, and the locative clitics with added meanings:

Table 6.3 Pronoun and clitic combinations

Pronoun	Clitic	Combined Gloss
i?, is, haųhwa?, etc.	diminutive = ?á/ = á/ = há	*only; alone*
	plural = shų?	*even, also*
	locative = ge	*at, there*

The diminutive clitic is added to personal pronouns to add the meaning 'only, alone' as in examples (1a) above and (5):

(5) a. haųhwa?á hoyó?de?
  ha-ųhwa? = á ho-yo?de-?
  3M.SG.P-self = DIM 3M.SG.P-work-STV
  he only   he is working
  <u>*Only he* is working</u>

 b. Onę ęshadęnó·dę? haųhwa?á, ęhęhę́·?, ... (CTL627.2).
  onę ę-s-h-ad-Ręn-od-ę?   ha-ųhwa? = á ę-ha-ihę·-?'
  TMP FUT-REP-3M.SG.A-SRF-song-raise.up-PNC 3M.SG.P-self = DIM FUT-3M.SG.A-say-PNC
  then he will sing again   he alone   he will say
  Then he will sing again, <u>he alone</u>, [and] he will say,...

Combining the diminutive clitic with the cislocative, expresses unique or superlative qualities as in (6a and b):

(6) a. Naʔ <u>thauhwaʔá</u> neʔ jí·ha hatcihsǽ·yęk (HW05).

naʔ t-ha-uhwaʔ=á | neʔ | jiha | h-atci-hsR-a-yę-k
ASRT CIS-3M.SG.P-self=DIM | NOM | NOUN | 3M.SG.A-friend-NOM-JN-know.how-HAB
it's he's the most and only | the | dog | he knows how to be friends

The dog is the only one who knows how to be friends.

b. Nayéʔ <u>thonuhwaʔá</u> thodiʔshasdęhse·wá·nęh neʔ thonę uhwę·jyáʔgeh (CTL285.2).

naye? t-hon-uhwaʔ=á | t-hodi-ʔshasdęhsR-owanę-h | neʔ | thonę
ASRT CIS-3M.NSG.P-self=DIM | CIS-3M.NSG.P-power-big-STV | NOM | LOC
it's only they | they are most powerful | the | here

Ø-uhwęjy-aʔ=ge
NPF-earth-NSF-LOC
on earth

They, [are] the most powerful [persons] here on earth.

The plural clitic *-shuʔ* in combination with the personal pronoun adds the meaning 'even, also':

(7) Hauhwaʔshúʔ hoyóʔdeʔ

ha-uhwaʔ=shúʔ | ho-yoʔde-ʔ
3M.SG.P-self=PL | 3M.SG.P-work-STV
he [and others] | he is working

<u>*Even he*</u> *is working.*

The external locative clitic is added to mark the referent as a location. In (8a) the referent is the semantic source; in (8b) the referent is the semantic goal:

(8) a. …nayeʔ tho ęhęnagǽ·t <u>gauhwáʔge</u> neʔ Gahę·déhsuk neʔ hę·gwe neʔ haksaʔáh
(CTL3.3-4).

naye? tho ę-h-ę-nagR-at-Ø | ga-uhwaʔ=ge
ASRT LOC FUT-3M.SG.A-SRF-live-CS-PNC | 3FZ.SG.A-self=LOC
that's it there he will get born | at herself

neʔ Gahę·déhsuk | neʔ | hR-ugweh | neʔ | ha-ksaʔ=á
NOM NAME | NOM | 3M.SG.A-person:SUFF | NOM | 3M.SG.A-child=DIM
the Gahę·déhsuk | the | male | the | boy

He, the male child, will be born there of Gahę·déhsuk herself.

b. Waʔgyenáʔ tshaʔ níyu nigawęnagéh waʔsha·dá·dyaʔ neʔ <u>iʔge</u> hagwá (CTL94.5-6).

waʔ-g-yena-ʔ' | tshaʔ | niyu | ni-ga-węn-a-ge-h'
FACT-1SG.A-accept-PNC | SUB | AMT | PART-3N/Z.SG.A-word-JN-amount.to-STV
I accept it | that | how many | the number of words

waʔ-hs-adady-aʔ | neʔ | iʔ=ge | hagwa
FACT-2SG.A-talk-PNC | NOM | PRON=LOC | DIR
you talked | the | at me | direction

I accept the several words you are saying to me. [Literally: I accept the number of words you talk in my direction.]

6.3 Interrogative Pronouns

Interrogative pronouns are, formally, particles and particle clusters. They are used in content questions which elicit information about persons, things, and events (sec. 7.10.3). The interrogative pronouns are also used in embedded questions. Embedded questions are discussed in sections 6.3.1 and 7.4.2. Interrogatives also occur as elements of many indefinite pro-forms. Indefinite expressions with interrogatives are discussed in section 6.4.

An appropriate response to a question formed with an interrogative pronoun is an utterance in which the question word is replaced by the noun or noun phrase that identifies the questioned entity. An example in English is, 'Who did it?' to which an appropriate response is 'John did it', or merely 'John'. In Onondaga, interrogative pronouns distinguish animate (who) from non-animate (what) referents. In addition, interrogatives or interrogative phrases are used in questions regarding the reasons for actions (why), times and locations of actions or events (when, where), in alternative- or choice-questions (which), and questions concerning scalable concepts (how far, how many, etc.) Table 6.4 lists the basic interrogative particles, some of which occur only with two or more, modifying, particle.

Table 6.4 Inventory of interrogative particles

Interrogative Particles	Gloss
sǫ	*who, whose*
nwadę́? / wadę́? / nwa·hó?dę?[6]	*what*
(h)ot (arch.)	*what*
hwę́·dųh	*when*
gaę (+ verb with locative prepronominal)	*where*
do (+classifier word or particle)	*how, how about*

Interrogative phrases with *do, gaę, and (n)wadę́?* are composed of an interrogative particle followed by a classifier verb or particle. They are listed in Table 6.5:

Table 6.5 Interrogative expressions

Interrogative phrase	Gloss
sǫ (nwadę?)	*who*
do nigę́	*how [extent]*
do nigę́ niyų́	*how often [extent, amount]*
do niyų́	*how many, how much*
do ga?t	*what if*
gae nų́	*where [place]*
gaę nę (> ganę́)	*where [nearby]*
gaę tho gwa?	*where [just there]*
gaę nigahá·wi?	*when [literally: where time]*
gaę nigá·æ?	*which [literally: where it's in it]*
(h)ot nwa·hó?dę? (arch.)	*what; why*
(n)wadę́? ní·yot	*why [literally: what how it is]*
(n)wadę́? óihwa?	*why [literally: what reason]*
(n)wadę́? ó·ya?	*what else [literally: what other]*

---

[6] The three variants of the non-animate interrogative *nwadę́? / wadę́? / nwa·hó?dę?* all derive, ultimately, from the verb form *nwa?oihó?de?* [nwa?-o-Rihw-o?dę-?] '[the] kind of thing [it is]'.

The interrogative pronoun precedes every other word in the clause that contains it. The animate interrogative *sų* 'who' frequently occurs in combination with *nwadę́ʔ* 'what' the form contemporary speakers use for the non-animate interrogative.[7] Together the two interrogatives are glossed 'who'. The animate interrogative pronoun and the pronominal prefix of the predicating verb are coreferential. The choice of pronominal prefix depends on the circumstances. If the gender of the participant is unknown or presumed to be feminine, as in (9), a feminine-indefinite pronominal is prefixed to the verb that specifies the questioned entity or event. If the participant is presumed to be a man, then the masculine occurs, as in (10). Where the verbs require interactive prefixes, similar choices occur, as in (11) and (12):

(9) <u>Sų nwadę́ʔ</u> í·yę̌ʔs.

sų	nwadę́ʔ	i-yę-e-ʔs
INTR	INTR	EMPTY-3FI.A-come.go-HAB
who	what	someone is around

Who is here?

(10) <u>Sų nwadę́ʔ</u> í·hę̌ʔs.

sų	nwadę́ʔ	i-ha-e-ʔs
INTR	INTR	EMPTY-3M.SG.A-come.go-HAB
who	what	he is around

Who is here?

(11) <u>Sų́·</u>[8] <u>nwa·hóʔdę́ʔ</u> dah<u>ya</u>dęnyéhda? (CTL75.2).

sų	nwa·hoʔdę?	d-a-hy-adęnyehd-a?
INTR	INTR	CIS-FACT-3M.SG > 2SG-send-PNC
who	what	he sent you this way

Who sent you here?

(12) <u>Sų́·</u> <u>nwa·hóʔdę́ʔ</u> waʔ<u>es</u>athó·yę? (CTL71.6).

sų	nwa·hoʔdę?	waʔ-es-atho·y-ę-ʔ
INTR	INTR	FACT-3FI > 2SG-tell-BEN-PNC
who	what	someone told you

Who told you about it?

The same interrogative phrase, *sų́· nwadę́ʔ*, is used in questions asking the identity of a possessor. The possessive prefix of the possessed noun is then coreferential with the interrogative pronoun.

---

[7] In texts dating from sometime early in the 20th century or before, the question form for non-animate objects or events is attested as *hot nwa·(oi)hóʔdęh*, literally, 'what kind of matter'. In contemporary speech *hot* is no longer used, and the original qualifier, which is most frequently reduced to *nwadę́ʔ*, has become the non-animate interrogative word.

[8] Accent and length are given as they were marked in the original text.

(13) <u>Sų hų·</u> <u>nwadę́ʔ</u> goʔsé·hdaʔ.

sų	hų	nwadę́ʔ	<u>go-ʔse·hd-aʔ</u>
INTR	MOD	INTR	3FI.P-car-NSF
who	perhaps	what	<u>somebody's</u> car

Whose car [is it], I wonder?

The non-animate interrogative *(n)wadę́ʔ* 'what' is used in examples (14) - (16):

(14) <u>Wadę́ʔ</u> niyó·dyęh.

(n)wadę	ni-yo-adyeR-ęh
INTR	PART-3N/Z.SG.P-go.on-STV
what	how it's going on

What is going on?

In (14) the interrogative pronoun is coreferential with the verb's non-animate pronominal prefix. However, in examples (15) - (17) the morphological representation of a non-animate argument is lacking altogether. Recall that this is because non-animate semantic arguments are not referenced morphologically in verbs that also have animate arguments, and because, in any event, there is no provision in verbs for marking three arguments morphologically.

(15) <u>Nwa·hóʔdę́ʔ</u> ahgwé·nyaʔ na·gųyadyé·æʔs (CTL278.7).

nwa·hoʔdęʔ	ak-gweny-aʔ[9]	n-aa-gųy-ad-yeR-aʔs-Ø
INTR	1SG.P-be.able-STV	PART-OPT-1SG > 2SG-SRF-do-BEN-PNC
what	I can	thus I may do it for you

What can I do for you?

(16) <u>Nwa·hóʔdę́ʔ</u> naʔ snaʔjyęhá·wiʔ (CTL85.3-4).

nwa·hoʔdęʔ	naʔ	s-naʔjy-ęhawi-ʔ
INTR	ASSRT	2SG.A-pail-carry-STV
what	that's it	you are carrying a pail

What is that pail you are carrying?

An example with the archaic interrogative phrase *hót nwa·hóʔdęʔ* is:

(17) <u>Hot</u> <u>nwa·hóʔdę́ʔ</u> sayóʔdeʔ (H676.17-18).

hot	nwa·hoʔdęʔ	sa-yoʔde-ʔ
INTR	INTR	2SG.P-work-STV
what	kind of thing	you are working

What are you working at?

In *why*-questions the non-animate interrogative occurs together with the manner classifier *ní·yot* 'how it is' and the questioned event occurs in a clause marked by the subordinating particle *tshaʔ*:

---

[9] Recall that the sequence k > h/_k (sec. 2.2.2.2)

(18) <u>Nwadę́?</u> <u>ní·yot</u> tsha? thonę́ íhse?s.

nwadę?	ni-yo-hd-Ø		tsha?	thonę	i-hs-e-?s
INTR	PART-3N/Z.SG.P-how.it.is-STV		SUB	LOC	EMPTY-2SG.A-come.go-HAB
what	thus it is		that	here	you are around

Why are you here?

(19) <u>Nwadę́?</u> <u>ní·yot</u> tsha? wa?esathó·yę?.

nwadę?	ni-yo-hd-Ø		tsha?	wa?-es-atho·y-ę-?
INTR	PART-3N/Z.SG.P-how.it.is-STV		SUB	FACT-3 > 2SG-tell-BEN-PNC
what	thus it is		that	she told you

Why did she tell you?

Questions about the timing of an event use the interrogative *hwę́·dų* 'when':

(20) <u>Hwędų́</u> disayų́h.

hwędų	di-sa-yų-h'
INTR	CIS-2SG.P-enter-STV
when	you entered here

When did you get here?

(21) <u>Hwędų́</u> dęhsadųhwęjyónik ne? ohwísda?.

hwędų	d-ę-s-adųhwęjyoni-k	ne?	o-hwisd-a?
INTR	DL-FUT-2SG.A-want-PNC	NOM	NPF-money-NSF
when	you will want it	the	money

When do you want the money?

In location questions, the particle *gaę* 'where' may occur alone as in (22a), co-occur with the location particle *nų* 'place' as in (22b), or co-occur with a motion verb with the translocative or cislocative as in (22c).   Presence or absence questions (22a), may lack the particle *nų(we)* and the prepronominal prefix.

(22) a. <u>Gaę</u> di? ne? wa?hųwadihųgá·ya?k (CTL349.3).

gaę	di?	ne?	wa?-hųwadi-hųga·ya?k-Ø
INTR	LINK	NOM	FACT-3 > 3M.NSG-appoint-PNC
where	moreover	the	someone appointed them

Where are the appointed ones (are they present or absent)?

b. <u>Gaę</u> nų́ ne? wa?hųwadihųgá·ya?k.

gaę	nų	ne?	wa?-hųwadi-hųga·ya?k-Ø
INTR	LOC	NOM	FACT-3 > 3M.NSG-appoint-PNC
where	place	the	someone appointed them

Where are the appointed ones [located]?

c. <u>Gaę</u> na? <u>nhe</u>honenųh ne? sahwajiyæ? (H615.9).

gaę	na?	n-he-hon-e-nųh	ne?	sa-hwajiR-a?
INTR	ASRT	PRT-TRNS-3M.NSG.P-walk-STV	NOM	2SG.P-family-NSF
where	it's	they have gone there	the	your family

Where have your family gone?

Alternative-questions differ from all others in that they ask to identify one or more of a group of known referents, whether or not they are mentioned in the same clause. In Onondaga such questions begin in *gaę nigá·æʔ* literally, 'which of what is contained in it'.

(23) <u>Gaę nigá·æʔ</u> sé·heʔ.

gaę	ni-ga-R-aʔ	s-eR-heʔ
INTR	PART-3N/Z.SG.A-be.in-STV	2SG.P-want-HAB
which	it is in it	you want it

Which one do you want?

(24) <u>Gaę</u> diʔ <u>nigá·æʔ</u> hago·wá·nęh.

gaę	diʔ	ni-ga-R-aʔ	ha-gowanę-h
INTR	LINK	PART-3N/Z.SG.A-be.in-STV	3M.SG.A-big-STV
which	moreover	it is in it	he is big

Which [boy] is bigger?

The interrogative particle *do* 'how' occurs in questions about various scalable concepts, like measurements (25), quantity (26), time (27), etc.:

(25) <u>Do</u> <u>nitgá·deʔ</u>.

do	ni-t-ga-de-ʔ
INTR	PART-CIS-3N/Z.SG.A-be.at.a.level-STV
how	it is that high

How high is it?

(26) <u>Do·</u> <u>niyų́</u> sawi·yǽ·yęʔ.

do	niyų	sa-wiR-a-yę-ʔ
INTR	AMT	2SG.P-baby-JN-have-STV
how	amount	you have a baby

How many babies do you have?

(27) <u>Do·</u> hų <u>nigaihwís</u> neʔtho nidyawę́ʔih (H788.18).

do	hų	ni-ga-Rihw-is-Ø	neʔtho
INTR	MOD	PART-3N/Z.SG.A-matter-long-STV	MAN
how	perhaps	long time	thus

ni-d-yaw-ę-ʔ-ih
PART-CIS-3N/Z.SG.P-happen-INCH-STV
thus it came to happen
How long since it happened?

Do· is paired with *gaʔt* 'if' for hypothetical questions:

(28) ...<u>do·</u> <u>gaʔt</u> neʔ ų́hgęʔ ęyųkhí·yoʔ... (CTL129.3-4)

do	gaʔt	neʔ	ų́hgęʔ	ę-yųkhi-Ryo-ʔ
INTR	COND	NOM	TEMP	FUT-3 > 1NSG-kill-PNC
what	if	the	presently	they will kill us

...what if, soon, they'll kill us...?

6.3.1 Interrogatives in Embedded Questions

Interrogative Pronouns introduce the subordinate clause of embedded questions:

<u>Embedded questions with the animate interrogative:</u>
(29) Oihwiyó? igę́ tsha? sęnų́hdų? [sų́ nwa·hó?dę? sniksa?dayędá?she·?] (CTL5.8-6.1).

o-Rihw-iyo-?		i-ga-i-Ø		tsha?	s-ęnųhdų-?
3N/Z.SG.P-matter-good-STV		EP-3N/Z.SG.A-be-STV		SUB	2SG.P-know-STV
surely		it is		that	you know

sų	nwa·ho?dę?	sni-ksa?d-a-yęd-a-?-she·-?
INTR	INTR	2DU-child-JN-have-INCH-DSLC-PRP
who	what	you two are going to have a child

Surely you know who you are having a child with? [Literally, it is certain that you know who you two are having a child?]

(30) Onę́ ųk?nigųhæyę·dá?nha? [sų́· nís] (CTL70.2-3).

onę	wa?-wag-?nigųhR-a-yęd-a?-nha?	sų	ne?	is
TEMP	FACT-1SG.P-mind-JN-place-INCH-PNC	INTR	NOM	PRON
now	I came to understand	who	the	you

Now I realize who you [are].

<u>Embedded questions with the non-animate interrogative:</u>

(31) Hya de?agęnųhdų́? [nwadę́? ę́·he?].

hya	de?-wag-ęnųhdų-?	nwadę?	ę-eR-he?
NEG	NEG-1SG.P-know-STV	INTR	3FI.A-want-HAB
not	I don't know	what	she wants (it)

I don't know what she wants.

(32) Thohge ne? goksdę?á hya de?agoihwagweniyósdi [nwa·hó?dę? wa?ahę́·? ne? ųdáthawah] (CTL4.3-4).

thohge	ne?	go-ksdę?a	hya	de?-ago-Rihw-a-gweniyo-sd-ih
TEMP	NOM	3FI-old.person	NEG	NEG-3FI.P-matter-JN-main.one-CS-STV
then	the	old lady	not	she didn't believe it

nwa·hó?dę?	wa?-a-ihę·-?'	ne?	ųdat-hawah
INTR	FACT-3FI.A-say-PNC	NOM	3FI > 3FI-child&parent
what	she said	the	her daughter

Then the old lady didn't believe what her daughter said.

<u>Embedded question with the locative interrogative:</u>

(33) Hya de?agęnųhdų́? [gaę nų́ niwé?s ne? dagús] (NC01).

hya	de?-wag-ęnųhdų-?	gaę	nų	ni-w-e-?s
NEG	NEG-1SG.P-know-STV	INTR	LOC	PART-3FZ.SG.A-walk-HAB
not	I don't know	where	place	she's around

    ne?   dagus
    NOM   NOUN
    the   cat
I don't know where the cat is.

Embedded question with temporal interrogatives:
(34) ... hya de?wagatdó·gęh [<u>hwę́·dų thoyų́h</u>...] (CTL178.3-5)
    hya   de?-wag-atdogę-h   hwędų   t-ho-yų-h'
    NEG   NEG-1SG.P-notice-STV   INTR   CIS-3M.SG.P-arrive-STV
    not   I didn't notice   when   he arrived
    ...I didn't notice when he arrived here... [Literally, I didn't notice, 'When has he
        arrived'?]

Embedded question with the interrogative of choice:
(35) ...ęhathó·ya? [<u>gaę nigá·æ?</u> ęhaihwahní·hda?] (CTL260.3).
    ę-ha-atho·y-a?   gaę   ni-ga-R-a?
    FUT-3M.SG.A-tell-PNC   INTR   PART-3N/Z.SG.A-be.in-STV
    he will tell   which   it is in it

    ę-ha-Rihw-a-hniR-hd-a?
    FUT-3M.SG.A-matter-JN-strong-CS-PNC
    he will strenthen the matter
    He will announce which [opinion] he will ratify.

Embedded question with a scalable interrogative:
(36) Sęnų́hdų? khę́h [<u>do nigę́</u> dayų·gní?se·k]
    s-ęnųhdų-?   khę   do   nigę   d-a-yųgn-i?se·-?
    2SG.P-know-STV   QUE   INTR   EXT   CIS-FACT-1DU.P-drag-PNC
    you know   question how   extent we drove here
    Do you know how far we drove?

6.4 Indefinite Pro-forms

Indefinite pro-forms occur as particle clusters. They mark referents, events, or states, as
unknown, uncertain, or in some way not identifiable. Indefinite expressions often include
interrogative particles, but these lose their identities as question words in that context. The
only interrogative that does not occur as a part of indefinite expressions is the non-animate
interrogative *nwadę́?* 'what'. The non-animate indefinite is *sdę?* or the cluster *sdę? gwa?*
'something, anything'. Table 6.6 lists indefinite pro-forms and their glosses:

Table 6.6 Indefinite pro-forms

	Particle cluster	Particle Identifications	Gloss
Animate	sǫ gwaʔ	interrogative + restrictive	*somebody (indefinite)*
	sǫ ga·ʔ	interrogative + non-specific	*somebody (non-specific)*
	hya sǫ ga·ʔ	negative + interrogative + non-specific	*nobody*
Non-animate	sdęʔ sdęʔ gwaʔ	indefinite indefinite + restrictive	*something, anything whatever*
	hya sdęʔ	negative + indefinite	*nothing*
	gaę gwaʔ	interrogative + restrictive	*whichever, wherever, however + complement*
	hwędų́ gwaʔ	interrogative + restrictive	*sometime, whenever*
	hya hwę́·dų	negative + interrogative	*never*
	gá(ʔ)tgaʔ[10]	non-specified location	*anywhere*
	hya gá(ʔ)tgaʔ	negative + unspecified location	*nowhere*
	gaʔ gwaʔ nigę	non-specific + restrictive + extent classifier	*indefinite extent of time or space*
	gaʔ gwaʔ nų	non-specific + restrictive + location classifier	*some place; in the vicinity*
	do gwaʔ nwaʔųnísheʔ	interrogative + restrictive + time classifier	*some length of time*
	do ga·ʔ	interrogative + non-specific	*several [time periods]*

As the table shows, indefinites distinguish between animate and non-animate referents. The interrogative particle *sǫ·* 'who' followed by the particles *gwaʔ* or *ga·ʔ* refers to indefinite or non-specific animate entities, respectively, as can be seen by comparing (37) with (38).

(37) Sǫ gwáʔ dayǫ·dwęnǫ́·da·k.

    sǫ gwaʔ   d-a-yǫ-ad-węn-ųdaR-k'

    INDF   CIS-FACT-3FI.A-SRF-voice-put.in.a.container-PNC

    someone   one telephoned

Someone telephoned.

(38) Sǫ gá·ʔ khę éʔdę·ʔ.

    sǫ ga·ʔ   khę   e-iʔdę-ʔ

    INDF   QUE   3FI.A-be.in.place-STV

    somebody,anybody   question   someone is in place

Is anybody / somebody home?

The difference between the sequences *sǫ gwáʔ* and *sǫ gá·ʔ* is the difference between an indeterminate person (one of several possible persons) and a non-specific person (a person who may or may not exist); in (37) someone called, but his or her identity is uncertain; in (38), there may be no one at home. When restrictive *gwaʔ* or non-specific *ga·ʔ* combine

---

[10] The two pronunciations were given by different speakers. The older texts record the particle both ways.

with an interrogative, it has the effect of changing an interrogative phrase to an indefinite one.[11]

The indefinite non-animate particle *sdę?* occurs with or without the restrictive particle *gwa?*.

(39) <u>Sdę́? gwa?</u> hé·he?

sdę? gwa?	h-eR-he?
INDF	3M.SG.A-want-HAB
something	he wants it

Whatever he wants.

(40) Gwas go·? ųwé hya thagadųwishę́? tsha? nigę́ <u>sdę́?</u> ęhenų́·da?, ... (LG24)

gwas	go·?	ųwe	hya	th-aa-g-adųwishę-?´	tsha?	nigę	sdę?
INTS	CTR	AUTH	NEG	CON-OPT-1.SG.A-rest-PNC	SUB	EXT	INDF
very	however	really	not	I can't rest		that	until	something

ę-he-nųd-a?
FUT-1SG > 3M.SG-feed-PNC
I will feed him

And this [cat], I can't rest until I give him something to eat ...

The particle cluster *gaę gwa?* occurs as an element of temporal (41a), locative (41b), and 'choice' clauses (41c), among others. The cluster may be glossed 'whichever, wherever, anywhere, however, whenever' in context.

(41) a. Thohge onę ne?tho e?dę·? <u>gaę gwa?</u> nwa?gaihwishe? (H629.5).

thohge	onę	ne?tho	e-i?dę-?	gaę gwa?
TEMP	TEMP	LOC	3FI.A-reside-STV	INTR
then	now	there	she resided	whichever

n-wa?-ga-Rihw-ishe-?
PART-FACT-3N/Z.SG.A-matter-length.of.time-PNC
how long it was

Then she stayed there for a certain length of time.

b. Nayé? gę́·da? ne? <u>gaę gwa?</u> nędwé? (CTL308.8).

naye?	ga-id-a?	ne?	gaę gwa?	n-ę-d-w-e-?
ASSRT	3N/Z.SG.A-mean-STV	NOM	INTR	PART-FUT-CIS-3N/Z.SG.A-come-PURP
that's it	it means	the	wherever	it will come

That means it could come from anywhere.

c. Hodi?shasdęhsǽ·yę? ne? <u>gaę gwa? nigá·ǽ?</u> ne? degní ęhadiyǽ·gwa? sgá·da ęhadi·hwahní·hda? (CTL444.1-3).

hodi-?shasdę-hsR-a-yę-?		ne?	gaę gwa?	ni-ga-R-a?
3M.NSG.P-strong-NOM-JN-have-STV		NOM	INTR	PART-3N/Z.SG.A-be.in-STV
they have power		the	whichever	it is in it

---

[11] In that context it is interesting that Hewitt sometimes glosses the restrictive as 'seemingly' (e.g., H680.7)

neʔ	degni	ę-hadi-Rægw-aʔ		sgada	ę-hadi-Rihw-a-hniR-hd-aʔ
NOM	NUM	FUT-3M.PL.A-choose-PNC		NUM	FUT-3M.PL.A-matter-JN-strong-CS-PNC
the	two	they will choose		one	they will confirm a matter

They have the power to pick one of the two decisions [on the table], [and] they will confirm just one of them. [Literally: ...to pick whichever of the two is in it...]

In (42) the cluster *hwędų gwaʔ* 'whenever' introduces an indefinite conditional time clause:

(42) Nayeʔ diʔ tshaʔ nęyawę́haʔ neʔ hwędų gwaʔ ę[ji]sga·háʔnhaʔ[12] ęhsihę́·ʔ gęs,
  "Dehadųhwęjyę́·dųs" (H621.16-17).

naye?	di?	tsha?	n-ę-yaw-ęh-a?		ne?	hwędų gwaʔ
ASSRT	LINK	SUB	PART-FUT-3N/Z.SG.P-happen-PNC		NOM	INTR
that's it	moreover	that	thus it will happen		the	whenever

ę-ji-sg-a·haʔ-nhaʔ		ę-hs-ihę·-ʔ'	gęs
FUT-REP-3SG > 1SG-remember-PNC		FUT-2SG.A-say-PNC	CST
you will remember me		you will say	usually

de-h-ad-ųhwęjy-ędų-s
DL-3M.SG.A-SRF-earth-shake-HAB
He Shakes The Earth[13]

Moreover, this is what will happen: Whenever you remember me, you will [call me] "He Shakes The Earth".

An example with the extent particle sequence *gaʔ gwaʔ nigę́* 'just about so [much, far, etc.]' is:

(43) ... nę gaʔ gwaʔ nigę́ nhęgadyéʔ tshaʔ gęs nigaʔsés (LG21).

onę	gaʔ gwaʔ nigę	n-h-ę-ga-dye-?		tsha?	gęs
TMP	INDF	PRT-TRNS-FUT-3N/Z.SG.A-fly-PNC		SUB	CST
then	about so [far]	it will fly there		that	usually

ni-ga-ʔses-Ø'
PRT-3N/Z.SG.A-go.far-STV
it goes a long way

...then it will fly just about so [far], going usually a long way.

Examples with the locational indefinites *ga(ʔ)tgaʔ* 'somewhere, anywhere' and *gaʔ gwaʔ nų* 'some place [nearby]' are:

(44) a. ...hya <u>gáʔtgaʔ</u> deʔshųwagę́h (CTL119.2).

hya	gaʔtgaʔ	deʔ-s-hųwa-gę-h'
NEG	INDF	NEG-REP-3 > 3M.SG-see-STV
not	anywhere	they didn't see him

...they didn't see him anywhere.

---

[12] In Hewitt's text the form is transcribed as ęsga·háʔnhaʔ, but the base requires a repetitive prefix, so the correct form would be ęjisga·háʔnhaʔ.

[13] A proper name.

b. Gaʔt khę̂, oyá̧ʔ, <u>gaʔ gwaʔ nų́·</u> thadina·gé·ʔ... (HW07).

gaʔt	khę	(y)-oya-ʔ		ga? gwa? nų	t-hadi-nage·-ʔ
HYP	QUE	3N/Z.SG.A-different-STV		INDF	CIS-3M.PL.A-live-STV
if	question	it is different		someplace [near]	they live

Perhaps others live in the vicinity...

In (45) the particle sequence *do· gwaʔ* 'several, a few, some' introduces an indefinite amount clause:

(45) <u>Do· gwaʔ niwę̂dage</u> onę heʔ sayeyagę́ʔnhaʔ waʔeyę̂dagwahaʔ? (H636.22).

do	gwaʔ	ni-w-ęd-a-ge-h'		onę	heʔ
INTR	RST	PART-3N/Z.SG.A-day-JN-amount.to-STV		TEMP	REP
how	just	that many days		now	again

s-a-ye-yagę-ʔ-nhaʔ	waʔ-e-yęd-agw-ahaʔ
REP-FACT-3FI.A-come.out-INCH-PNC	FACT-3FI.A-wood-pick.up-PNC
she came out again	she picked up wood

After a few days, she went out again to fetch wood.

6.4.1 Negative Indefinite Expressions

To negate an indefinite clause the word that otherwise functions as an interrogative expression is inserted between the negative particles *hya* 'not' or *áhgwih* 'don't' and the negated verb.[14] The restrictive particle *gwaʔ* is not attested with negated indefinite expressions; instead, the nonspecific particle *ga·ʔ* replaces *gwaʔ* with animate indefinite referents (46), and *sdęʔ* occurs without a restrictive with non-animate indefinites (47) and (48). (48) is an example with the negative imperative *áhgwih*.

(46) ... <u>hya sų ga·ʔ</u> deʔagonųhdų́ʔ gaę nų́ nihéʔs... (LG09)

hya	sų ga·ʔ	deʔ-ago-ęnųhdų-ʔ	gaę nų	ni-h-e-ʔs
NEG	INDF	NEG-3FI.P-know-STV	INTR LOC	PRT-3M.SG.A-walk-HAB
not	anybody	they don't know	where	thus he is around

...nobody knows where he is...

(47) <u>Hya sdę̂ʔ</u> deʔwagę́h (EO01)

hya	sdęʔ	deʔ-wag-ę-h'
NEG	INDF	NEG-1SG.P-say-STV
not	anything	I haven't said

I haven't said anything.

(48) Naʔ néʔ <u>áhgwi díʔ sdę̂ʔ</u> ahodiʔnya·æ̂ʔnháʔ neʔ ode·yoʔdatgíʔ ga·yoʔdaná·ge·ʔ (HW07)

naʔ	neʔ	ahgwi	diʔ	sdęʔ	aa-hodi-ʔnyaR-aʔ-nhaʔ
ASSRT	NOM	NEG	LNK	INDF	OPT-3FZ.SG > 3M.NSG-handle-INCH-PNC
that's it	the	don't	moreover	anything	it may molest them

---

[14] See sections 4.2.1.4.3 and 4.7.8 on negating verbs.

ne?   o-ade-Ryo?d-a-tgi-?   ga-Ryo?d-a-nage·-?
NOM   3FZ.SG.P-SRF-animal-JN-wild-STV   3FZ.SG.A-animal-JN-be.plentiful-STV
the   wild beast   it is plentiful

This is so that some of the plentiful wild beasts shouldn't molest them.

6.5 Demonstratives

Demonstratives are, formally, particles. In discourse, they are attested as nominal expressions with deictic or anaphoric functions, or as elements of complex noun phrases consisting of a demonstrative in apposition to a lexical nominal. When demonstratives occur as simple nouns their distribution is no different from lexical nouns. They occur with or without the nominal particle, before or after the main verb. As a part of complex noun phrases, the demonstrative typically precedes the lexical nominal.

In Onondaga, demonstratives distinguish two degrees of proximity:

Table 6.7: Demonstrative particles

	Demonstratives	Gloss
Proximal or Neutral	né·ge	this [near], this [unspecified distance]
Distal	thó·ge	that [not near]

The proximal/neutral demonstrative is much more frequent in discourse than is the distal. In addition to signaling proximity, speakers manipulate the semantic dimension of proximity to accomplish numerous discourse and narrative tasks, e.g., to track narrative participants, to distinguish primary from secondary actors, to indicate insider or outsider status, etc.

Like independent pronouns, the demonstratives can take a clitic. But unlike pronouns, the demonstratives are attested with only the diminutive, i.e., *negeháh* 'this little/only/specific one'; *thogeháh* 'that little/only/specific one'.

Speakers' deictic use of simple demonstratives to point to some aspect of the speech situation is described in section 6.5.1. Demonstratives occur anaphorically as a substitute for a previously identified referent during the course of a speech event. This use is described in section 6.5.2. Complex noun phrases with demonstratives were illustrated in section 5.7 above. Additional examples of complex noun phrases with demonstratives are provided in section 6.5.3.. Section 6.5.4 describes miscellaneous additional uses of demonstratives. The strategic use of demonstratives in discourse is pointed out as the discussion proceeds.

6.5.1 Deictic Uses of Demonstratives

Speakers can use a demonstrative to point to a person, object, or other aspect of the speech situation. In this use, only the participants in the speech event can identify the exact referent of the demonstrative, and typically the proximal or distal demonstratives are chosen on the basis of their distance from some focal center such as the speaker himself or the addressee. A pointing gesture often accompanies the deictic use of demonstratives. Very frequently the assertion particle *na?* 'it's' precedes the demonstrative when it is used in this way.

332 Pro-Forms

(49) a. Wadę́? na? né·gę?
     INTR   ASSRT   DEM
     what   that's it   this
     What's this [here]?

   b. Wadę́? na?   thó·gę?
     INTR   ASSRT   DEM
     what   that's it   that
     What's that [there]?

(50) Na? nę́gę gehé? ękhní·nų?.
     na?   nę̨gę   g-eR-he?   ę-k-hní·nų-?
     ASSRT   DEM   1SG.A-want-HAB   FUT-1SG.A-buy-PNC
     that's it   this   I want   I will buy (it)
     It's this one [close by] I want to buy.

(51) Na? thó·gę ųgyátcih.
     na?   thogę   ųgy-atci-h
     ASSRT   DEM   1DU.P-be.friends-STV
     that's it   that   we're friends / my friend
     That one [there] is the one [who's] my friend.

(52) Dahę̨hę́·? ne? né?tho nihoyéęh: "Nę́gę." (H186.3-4)
     d-a-ha-ihę̨·-?'   ne?   ne?tho   ni-ho-yeR-ęh   nę̨gę
     CIS-FACT-3M.SG.A-say-PNC   NOM   MAN   PART-3M.SG.P-do-STV   DEM
     he said   the   thus   thus he has done   this
     He answered, He did it: this one.

6.5.2 Anaphoric Uses of Demonstratives

Anaphoric demonstratives help to track narrative participants. An anaphoric demonstrative recalls a referent that was active earlier on in the discourse. In the first utterance of example (53), the speaker describes artifacts he has fashioned; in the second, he refers to them anaphorically with the demonstrative:

(53) Onę́ wa?gadéhs?a? niganahsagwa?s?á ne? agwę́na? na? ęthonętcík ne? hę́·gweh. Naye?
     dí? hęsníhwa? nę́·gęh (CTL146.7-147.1).
     onę   wa?-g-adehs?-a?   ni-ga-nahs-agwa = ?s = ?á   ne?
     TEMP   FACT-1SG.A-finish-PNC   PART-3N/Z.SG.A-strand-small = PL = DIM   NOM
     now   I finished   small strands   the

     ag-węn-a?   na?   ę-t-ho-nętsh-i-k   ne?   hR-ųgweh.
     1SG.P-word-NSF   ASSRT   FUT-CIS-3M.SG.P-lead-STV-MOD   NOM   3M.SG.A-person:SUFF
     my word(s)   that's it   it will be leading him [this way]   the   man

naye?	di?	h-ẹ-sni-hw-a?		nẹgẹ.
ASSRT	LINK	TRNS-FUT-2DU-take.along-PNC		DEM
that's it	moreover	you two will take it along		this

Now I finished [making the] small strands, [representing] my words, which will lead the man here. Moreover, these are what you two will take along.

In (54) *nẹgé* refers anaphorically to participants that were identified in the previous utterance which describes their getting together for a celebration.

(54) Oné nẹgé, wa?hụdẹtga·dụ? (HW07).

onẹ	nẹgẹ	wa?-hụ-adẹtgadụ-?'
TEMP	DEM	FACT-3M.PL.A-have.fun-PNC
now	this	they had fun

Now these [people][15] were enjoying themselves

In (55) *nẹgẹ* refers anaphorically to a participant who was described in the previous utterance as receiving a pension for his service in World War I. Then the speaker thought of another bit of information about him and added the following utterance:

(55) Dẹ?se? hanụda?gegá? nẹ́·gẹ (LG17).

dẹ?se?	ha-nụd-a? = ge = ga?	nẹgẹ
CNJ	3M.SG.A-hill-NSF = LOC = CHAR	DEM
and	he [is] Onondaga	this

And he this [man] is Onondaga.

Examples (53) and (54) show that the demonstrative particle can occur before or after the main verb, just like an ordinary noun. (55) is a verbless clause.

6.5.3 Demonstratives as Elements of Complex Nominal Expressions

As part of a complex nominal expression, demonstratives function as specifiers. In example (56), a chief identifies a particular tree he wants people to uproot:

(56) Ẹswaẹdodá·gwa? nẹgẹ gǽhe?, onó?jya? gayá·jih (H171.10-11).

ẹ-swa-Rẹd-od-agw-a?	nẹgẹ	g-Rǽhe-?	o-no?jy-a?
FUT-2PL-tree-stand-REV-PNC	DEM	NPF-growing.tree-NSF	NPF-tooth-NSF
you all will pull up a tree	this	growing tree	tooth

ga-yas-ih
3N/Z.SG.A-be.named-STV
it is called

You will all pull up this live tree, called Tooth.

One way of tracking participants in discourse is to use the distal demonstrative to reintroduce an actor from an earlier scene. In (60) *thó·gẹh dehniya?dagé ne? hnụ́·gwe*

---

[15] Recall that the masculine plural prefix, here *-hụ-*, can refer to groups of men or to mixed groups of men and women.

'those two men' are recalled from an earlier scene of a council session in which it was decided what the chiefs' duties in the Iroquoian Confederacy were to be:

(57) <u>Thó·gę dehniya?dagé ne? hnų́·gwe</u> nayé? ęyetciyų? ne? ga?shasdę́hsæ·? ęthyęnųhdųhék ne? hodiskę?ægéhdah tsha? niyųgyųhwęjyagéh… (CTL272.1-3)

thogę	de-hni-ya?d-a-ge-h'		ne?	hn-ųgweh[16]	naye?
DEM	DL-3M.DU.A-body-JN-amount.to-STV		NOM	3M.DU.A-person:SUFF	ASRT
that	two persons		the	they two men	it's

ę-yetciy-ų-?	ne?	ga-?shasdę-hsR-a?	ę-t-hy-ęnųhdų-he-k
FUT-2NSG > 3-give-PNC	NOM	NPF-strong-NOM-NSF	FUT-CIS-3M.DU.A-know-HAB-MOD
you will give them	the	power	they will exercise control

ne?	hodi-skę?Rægehdah	tsha?	ni-yųgy-ųhwęjy-a-ge-h'
NOM	3M.NSG.P-warrior:SUFF	SUB	PART-1PL.P-nation-JN-amount.to-STV
the	warriors	that	the number of our nations

You will give those two men the power to control the warriors of our several nations…

In narrative, the proximal and distal demonstratives can be used to distinguish in-group participants from newcomers or outsiders. In example (58) the chief, an insider, has been informed of the odd behavior of *thogę́ hę·gweh* 'that man,' a stranger. He thinks this over, and responds:

(58) Thohge ó·nę ne? hahsęnowá·nęh[17] wa?hęhę́·?, "agęnų́hdų? onę nwahó?dę? deyodųhwę·jyóhwih <u>thogę́ hę́·gwe</u> nayé? hoiho·náhdih…" (CTL147.3-4).

thohge	onę	ne?	ha-hsęn-owanę-h	wa?-ha-ihę·-?'
TEMP	TEMP	NOM	3M.SG.A-name-be.large-STV	FACT-3M.SG.A-say-PNC
then	now	the	chief	he said

ag-ęnųhdų-?	onę	nwaho?dę?	de-yo-adųhwęjyo-hwih	thogę
1SG.P-know-STV	TEMP	INTR	DL-3N/Z.SG.P-need-STV	DEM
I know	now	what	it is needed	that

hR-ųgweh	naye?	ho-Rihw-o·náhd-ih…
3M.SG.A-person:SUFF	ASSRT	3M.SG.P-matter-enlarge-STV
man	that's it	he is announcing it

Thereupon the chief said, "I know now what is needed, what it is that man is announcing…"

In example (59) the tension between insider and outsider is encoded in the juxtaposition between the first person inclusive plural pronominal prefix with the distal demonstrative. The pronominal prefixes reference both speaker and addressee in the expression *ędwa·gwé·nyæ? ędwa·di·hwagwe?nų́·nya?* 'we (speaker and addressees, the in-group) will be able to agree' setting off the 'others', *thó·gę dehnų́·gwe* 'those two men'. The deft use of

---

[16] Words ending in /h/ typically lose it utterance-medially.

[17] Utterance-final prosody and the presence of word-final *h* utterance-medially is because the source of the excerpt is a dictated text (see sec. 1.3).

options provided by the pronominal system and the distal demonstrative together highlight the difficulty of the negotiation between 'us' and 'them' described in the text.

(59) Oné wa?ų·gwadæ·?shwiyó?khe? dyęhá? gwa? ędwa·gwé·nya? ędwa·di·hwagwe?nų́·nya? thó·gę dehnų́·gweh (CTL284.8-285.9).

onę	wa?-ųgw-adæ?shwiyo-?khe?-Ø	dyęha?	gwa?	ę-dwa-gweny-a?
TEMP	FACT-1PL.P-good.luck-INCH-PNC	COND	RST	FUT-1IN.PL.A-be.able-PNC
now	we are getting lucky	if	just	we (I and you all) will be able

ę-dw-adi·hwagwe?nųny-a?	thogę	de-hn-ųgweh
FUT-1IN.PL.A-agree-PNC	DEM	DL-3M.DU.A-person:SUFF
we (I and you all) will agree	that	two men

Now we are fortunate if we all (incl.) [and] those two men will be able to agree.

6.5.4 Other uses of Demonstratives

A. <u>Adding the diminutive</u>: Exclusivity can be marked morphologically by adding the diminutive clitic to the demonstrative. Example (60) is about a family that for reason of safety moved to an isolated location deep in the forest:

(60) Ne?tho nų́·we nęgęhá_hodigwę́hæ? tsha? nihadi·hwají·yæ? (H612.1).

ne?tho	nųwe	nęgę = há	hodi-gwęhR-a?	tsha?
LOC	LOC	DEM = DIM	3M.NSG.P-group-NSF	SUB
there	place	this only	their group	that

ni-hadi-hwajiR-a-?
PART-3M.PL.A-family-be.a.size-NSF
their family

[It was] a place where <u>only this group</u> located their [whole] family.

In (61) the founders of the Iroquois Confederacy are discussing how they might persuade two reluctant Seneca Chiefs to join them in the Confederacy by assigning them special powers. Adding the diminutive indicates that they are singling them out from among a larger group. Note also the social distance being projected by the use of the distal demonstrative:

(61) Sgada gę́· gwa? tsha? niyo·dyéæ?di aedwade?nyę́·dę? ne? aedwęhę́·? <u>thogę́ha</u> dehnų́·gweh, is hí·hya? ne? snisgę?ægehdagó·na sníhwa? etciyadwęnodáhgwi ne? gędyohgwá?geh (CTL266.5-6).

sgada	gę gwa?	tsha?	ni-yo-ad-yeR-a?d-ih	ae-dw-ade?nyędę-?
NUM	RSTR	SUB	PART-3N/Z.SG.P-SRF-do-CS-STV	OPT-1IN.PL.A-measure-PNC
one	only	that	the direction it goes	we [and you] should try it

ne?	ae-dwa-ihę·-?'	thogę = há	de-hn-ųgweh	is	hihya?
NOM	OPT-1IN.PL.A-say-PNC	DEM = DIM	DL-3M.DU.A-person:SUFF	PRON	MOD
the	we [and you] should say	that only	two men	you	indeed

ne?   sni-sgę?ægehda = gona   sni-hw-a?   etciy-ad-węn-od-a-hgw-ih
NOM   2DU-warrior = AUG   2DU-hold-STV 3 > 2NSG-SRF-word-stand-INST-STV
the   you [two] great warriors you hold it   they trust you

ne?   ga-idyohgw-a?-ge
NOM   NPF-crowd-NSF-LOC
the   at the crowd

The only way to proceed is for us to try [to single out] those *two men, saying "You two great warriors, indeed you hold the trust of the people."*

B. <u>Extending the meaning of proximity</u>: The proximal demonstrative is used to mark closeness in time as well as closeness in space when it modifies temporal expressions:

(62) a. nęgę ų́hgę?

    nęgę   ųhgę?
    DEM   TEMP
    this   soon
    right now; this time

   b. nęgę wędá·de?

    nęgę   w-ęd-ade-?
    DEM   3N/Z.SG.A-day-exist-STV
    this   day
    today

   c. nęgę ęyó?ga·k

    nęgę   ę-yo-?gaR-k
    DEM   FUT-3N/Z.SG.P-night-MOD
    this   night; it will be night
    tonight

   d. nęgę tcihę?géhjik

    nęge   tci-hę?gehjik
    DEM   COIN-morning
    this   when it is morning
    this morning

C. <u>Demonstratives as components of utterance-initial particle groupings</u>: Demonstratives are frequently attested as components of utterance-initial particle clusters. These clusters can function as links to the preceding utterance as in (63) and (64). When they contain demonstratives, the clusters are often initiated by the assertion particle:

(63) <u>Na? nęgę gęs tsha? niyót</u> tsha? ne? tciyagwaksa?shų?á ųgwa·di·hwayęní gęs gayo?dę́hsæ·?, ne? agwaksa?shų?áh (HW02).

    na?   nęgę   gęs   tsha?   niyot   tsha?   ne?   tci-yagwa-ksa?-shų?a
    ASRT   DEM   CST   SUB   MAN   SUB   NOM   COIN-1EX.PL.A-child-PL
    it's   this   usually   that   how it is   that   the   when we children

ųgw-ad-Rihw-yę-ni-h'		gęs	ga-yoʔdę-hsR-aʔ	neʔ	agwa-ksaʔ-shųʔa
1PL.P-SRF-matter-have-BEN-STV		CST	NPF-work-NOM-NSF	NOM	1EX.PL-child-PL
our responsibility		usually	work	the	we children

So normally, how it was when we were children, we had responsibilities, work, we children.

(64) <u>Naʔ diʔ hyáʔ nęgę́</u> neʔ thonę hana·gé·ʔ nęgę́ neʔ, degyadęhnųdǽ·ʔ henáʔ hajihęsdají Wesleyan minister (LG07).

naʔ	diʔ	hyaʔ	nęgę	neʔ	thonę	ha-nage-ʔ		nęgę	neʔ
ASRT	LINK	MOD	DEM	NOM	LOC	3M.SG.A-reside-STV		DEM	NOM
it's	so	indeed	this	the	here	he is residing		this	the

de-gy-adęnųdR-aʔ		henaʔ	ha-jihęsdajih		Wesleyan	minister
DL-3FZ.DU.A-be.siglings-STV		NOUN	3M.SG.A-be.a.minister		NAME	NOUN
her sister		spouse	he is a minister		Wesleyan	minister

And so this one residing here, her brother-in-law, he is a Wesleyan minister.

D. <u>A possible presentational use of the proximal demonstrative</u>: In this example *nęgę* is neither anaphoric, nor does it point to an aspect of the situation. Rather, 'the ones driving' are being introduced as new participants, so that *nęgę* appears to be performing a presentational function.

(65) ...hya diʔ gwas deʔodų́ neʔ, tho naʔ da·hųdawę·yéʔ <u>nęgę́ neʔ hodiʔse·nų́·dyeʔs</u> (LG03).

hya	diʔ	gwas	deʔ-o-adų-h'		neʔ	tho	naʔ
NEG	LINK	INTS	NEG-3N/Z.SG.P-be.possible-STV		NOM	LOC	ASRT
not	moreover	very	it isn't possible		the	there	it's

d-aa-hų-ad-awę·ye-ʔ		nęgę	neʔ	hodi-ʔse·-nų-(a)dye-ʔs
CIS-OPT-3M.PL.A-SRF-stir-PNC		DEM	NOM	3M.NSG.P-drag-STV-PRG-HAB
they wander about		this	the	they drive around

...it wasn't possible for them to get around, these ones driving.

7 Syntactic Constructions

7.1 Introduction

The relatively simple organization of the Iroquoian languages at the syntactic level is a reflection of the Iroquoian verb's abundant and complex morphological patterning. Much of what is accomplished by the rules of syntax in other languages takes place at the morphological level in Onondaga.[1] If syntax is taken to consists of the rules that combine words and phrases into clauses and sentences, the Iroquoian family of languages is a special case in that verbs, with their elaborate morphology collapse the distinction between word and clause. Whereas in languages like English the arguments of verbs are realized by separate words, in Onondaga arguments are referenced morphologically by obligatory pronominal prefixes within the verb and separate words simply add additional information. Thus the Onondaga verb is able to express propositional meanings, just like a clause can.

Iroquoianists generally analyze discourse in terms of intonationally defined units involving accent placement, pitch contours, pauses, and various phonological markers rather than sentences (secs. 2.7.2 and 2.7.6). The languages differ intonationally, but in all of them utterance-medial and utterance-final patterns are not difficult to identify (see Chafe 2015:167 for Seneca, Michelson et al. 2016:371 for Oneida, Mithun 2010b:24f for Mohawk); the intonationally recognized unit – here referred to as an *utterance* – can consist of a single intonation unit with utterance-final intonation or several intonation units, each ending in utterance-medial intonation (demarcated with a comma) and with a final unit ending with utterance-final intonation (demarcated with a period).

This chapter describes some of the basic regularities of forming clauses, and combining clauses into utterances. While the verb is the central member of every clause, a clause without one or, more frequently, more than one particle is a rarity. Particles occur with greater frequency than any of the other two morphologically defined word classes – verbs and nouns (see chapter 3). For this reason, the discussion of syntactic structures begins, in section 7.2, with an introduction to the functions of the most frequently occurring particles

---

[1] See Koenig & Michelson (2015a), who argue that Iroquoian syntax is not selectional. They describe the syntax of closely related Oneida as "DIRECT, i.e. not mediated by the selection by the heads of dependants realizing their semantic arguments." Their claim is, furthermore, that in Iroquoian the grammatical roles of semantic arguments are "not syntactic, but inflectional in nature." Chafe (2015b), developing a discourse oriented account of these languages' polysynthetic characteristics, describes Seneca syntax in terms of "the ways in which elements inside a word, or sometimes an entire word, are *amplified* by elements outside a word" (Ibid., p.112). But see Baker (1996) on Mohawk syntax.

in the grammar of Onondaga. Section 7.3 discusses clause structure. Sections 7.4 and 7.5 look at utterances that include argument clauses and relative clauses, respectively. Section 7.6 deals with clauses that include location and time expressions. Section 7.7 reviews looser kinds of dependencies that can relate clauses. Sections 7.8 - 7.11 deal with negation, modality, question formation, and possession, respectively, and section 7.12 discusses quantification, counting, degree, and comparison.

7.2 Particles and Their Functions

Particles comprise the class of uninflected words. As languages go, the Onondaga lexicon contains an unusually large number of individual particles. A clause without a particle is rare indeed! Particles serve as both content and function words. In terms of the traditional notion of word class, particles are diverse, showing up as all of the following: nouns, verbs, adverbs, adjectives, pro-forms of all types, conjunctions, subordinators, numbers, and interjections. In addition to their functions as single words, particles often form lexicalized clusters whose elements may or may not modify one another.

This section takes a look at the most frequently occurring particles and their functions as constituents of phrases, clauses, and multi-clausal utterances. That subclass – approximately 185 + particles – can be loosely divided into four categories: (i) pro-forms, (ii) adverbials, (iii) particles with grammatical functions, and (iv) particles with discourse-pragmatic functions.

For a detailed discussion of the group of particles functioning as *pro-forms* see chapter six. These particles function to identify and keep track of participants. They consist of personal pronouns (sec. 6.2 above), interrogative particles (sec. 6.3 above), indefinite particle clusters (sec. 6.4 and table 6.2 above), and demonstrative particles (sec. 6.5 above).

Adverbials function much of the time to describe details of temporal and locational settings (sec. 7.6). Examples of temporal particles are *ahsé·de* 'yesterday', *ahsų́he* 'at night', *hya áhsų* 'not yet', and the temporal deictic particles *ó·nę* 'now', *thóhge* 'later', etc. Examples of locational particles are *ásde* 'outdoors', *nęgę́ nų́* 'this place' or directionals like *hehdáʔge* 'below' or *heʔtgę* 'above' and deictic particles like *néʔtho* 'there', *thó·nę* 'here, this way'.

The *grammatical* particles function mainly at the level of the clause. The assertion particle *naʔ* or *ná·yeʔ* which has variants in each of the Northern Iroquoian languages, is the second most frequently occurring particle in the corpus on which this grammar is based.[2] The particle is often glossed 'that's it, it is it' by speakers[3] and in the morpheme gloss line in this volume it is glossed as 'it's'.[4] There is no equivalent of *naʔ* in the English language. The particle typically occurs at least once, and often more than once in most multi-clausal utterances. Frequently, it is the first word of an utterance, alone or as a part of a group of particles that establish the topic, modality and setting of the utterance. When

---

[2] The most frequent is the nominal particle *neʔ* (see below).

[3] Hewitt glossed it 'that (it is)'.

[4] As late as 1912 the assertion particle *ná·yeʔ* is attested as distributionally distinct from *naʔ* with different but related meanings. *Ná·yeʔ* occurred clause-initially, *naʔ* preceding a nominal. In the League text (Woodbury et. al, 1992) *ná·yeʔ* is identified as DEC (declarative) and *naʔ* as CONTR (contrastive). At some time after 1912, with only very few exceptions (usually when the longer form occurs in clause-final position), the two have merged, both occurring as *naʔ*. However, the related, but now only distributionally identifiable functions, have been retained. In this work *naʔ*, is uniformly marked ASRT.

it occurs inside a clause, sometimes followed by an accented version of the nominal particle *ne?*, it contrastively recalls a referent or a topic introduced earlier on. *Na?* sometimes occurs in otherwise verbless clauses, serving as a kind of predicative element. Lounsbury (1953:100), discussing the function of the Oneida variant *né·* of Onondaga's *na?*, describes it's functions this way:

> ...similar to that of a generalized third person independent or demonstrative pronoun...[which] is nearly always a predicative element in a sentence...Such a predication is then usually followed in turn by a descriptive phrase standing in apposition to *né·* and describing it...

Chafe (2015:125) describes the function of the Seneca variant *ne:?* when followed by Seneca's variant of the nominal particle as follows:

> ...[the assertion particle] implies the vague neutral referent that is captured by 'it' in the translation 'it is'. That referent triggers the need for the further information that is supplied by a following amplification.

The excerpt in (1) illustrates both the occurrence of *na?* within an introductory particle cluster as well as its contrastive function utterance-internally:

(1) <u>Na?</u> gwá? hya? ʉ́·, tsha? <u>na?</u> dehonadʉhwęjyoník ne? hʉ?shę·ní e? <u>na?</u> ahʉ·dyenawasdá? nęgę́ ne? ʉhwę́·jya? (LG04).

na?	gwa?	hya?	ʉ		tsha?	na?	de-hon-adʉhwęjyoni-k		ne?
ASRT	RSTR	MOD	MOD		SUB	ASRT	DL-3M.NSG.P-need,want-HAB		NOM
it's	just	indeed	probably		that	it's	they want it		the

hʉ-a?shę·nih		e?		na?	a-hʉ-ad-yenaw-asd-a?
3M.PL.A-white.man		REP		ASRT	OPT-3M.PL.A-SRF-hold.on-CS-PNC
white men		repeatedly		it's	they can hold onto it

nęgę	ne?	(y)-ʉhwęjy-a?
DEM	NOM	NPF-earth,land-NSF
this	the	land

It's a fact, probably, that what the white men want is that they keep holding on to this land.

The nominal particle *ne?*, which is glossed 'the' by speakers, is another particle that has variants in all of the Northern Iroquoian languages, although its frequency varies in the different languages. In Onondaga, as represented in our corpus, it is the most frequently occurring of all the particles. As its name implies, it functions to mark a following word or phrase as a referring expression. The utterance in (2) consists of a set of particles, the main verb *dahatgahægétsgwa?* 'he looks up', pronounced with phrase-final intonation, the nominal particle *ne?* and a nominal expression which further specifies the entity that is identified by the main verb's pronominal. When the main verb precedes the referring expression as in this example, speakers often pause between the nominal particle and the nominal, despite the fact that the two are elements of a single intonational contour.

342 Syntactic Constructions

(2) Gwás nẹh dahatgahægétsgwaʔ, neʔ osgẹnụdụ́ʔ (NC02).

gwas onẹ	d-a-h-at-gahR-a-getsgw-aʔ		neʔ	osgẹnụdụ́ʔ
INTS TMP	CIS-FACT-3M.SG.A-eye-JN-raise.up-PNC		NOM	NOUN
just then	he looks up		the	deer

Just then the deer looks up.

The nominal particle always precedes the modified expression and the two are always
contiguous. When an utterance begins in a referring expression, *neʔ* is typically omitted.
(There is only one example in the corpus where *neʔ* begins an utterance.) It is important to
note, that the particle's identification as 'the' in the examples is misleading to the extent that
neʔ has few of the characteristics of the English determiner *the*. Thus, *neʔ* does not
distinguish definite from indefinite referents, nor does it mark generic meanings.
Distributionally, *the* and *neʔ* differ in that *neʔ* in contrast to *the,* occurs with proper nouns,
pronouns, demonstratives, and possessed nominals including kinship terms.

In (1) above, the particle marks two nouns, *hụʔshẹ́·ni* 'white men' and *ụhwẹ́jyaʔ* 'earth,
land'. In (3) the verb *hohsé·ʔ* preceded by *neʔ* is interpreted as an internally headed relative
clause, i.e., 'the one she's chasing' (sec. 7.4.1). It is not uncommon for the demonstrative
particle and the nominal particle to occur together before a nominal as they do in the
phrase *nẹgẹ́ neʔ shayaʔdadáh* 'this one man' in (3):

(3) Gwas yágẹʔ nẹ gẹ́s waʔdwákdaʔ, nẹgẹ́ hehonahdụ́h <u>neʔ hohsé·ʔ</u> nẹgẹ́ neʔ
    shayáʔdadah, nẹ hothụ·déʔ dayohsụwæ·gáehæʔ (HW07).

gwas	yagẹʔ	nẹ	gẹs	waʔ-t-w-akd-aʔ		nẹgẹ
INTNS	HRSY	TMP	CST	FACT-DL-3FZ.SG.A-get.close-PNC		DEM
very	they say	now	repeatedly	she got close		this

he-hon-ahdụ-h'		neʔ	ho-hse·-ʔ		nẹgẹ	neʔ
TRNS-3M.NSG.P-disappear-STV		NOM	3FZ.SG > 3M.SG-chase-PRP		DEM	NOM
they have disappeared		the	she is chasing him		this	the

s-ha-yaʔd-a-d-'ah		nẹ	ho-athụd-eʔ	de-yo-hsụR-a-gaehR-aʔ
REP-3M.SG.A-body-JN-be.one-STV		TMP	3M.SG.P-hear-STV	DL-3N/Z.SG.P-gun-JN-noise-STV
one man		now	he hears it	a gun makes a noise

*They say she kept getting closer, [and] when these [persons] had disappeared, [she
and] <u>the one she's chasing</u>, <u>this man</u> hears a gun shot.*

The nominal particle with a proper name (a), and a kinship term (b):

(4) a. Thohge <u>neʔ Gahẹ·déhsụk</u> waʔahẹ́·ʔ ... (CTL4.1)

thohge	neʔ	Gahẹ·déhsụk	waʔ-a-ihẹ·-ʔ'
TMP	NOM	NAME	FACT-3FI.A-say-PNC
then	the	Gahẹ·déhsụk	she said

Then Gahẹ·déhsụk said ...

b. Tho waʔagyadųgohdáʔ sgáda <u>neʔ khehawá dekhenųhę́·khwaʔ.</u>[5] (LG03)

Tho	waʔ-agy-ad-ųgohd-aʔ	sgada	neʔ	khe-hawah
LOC	FACT-1EX.DU.A-SRF-pass-PNC	NUMBER	NOM	1SG > 3-child
there	we two passed by	one	the	[my daughter

de-khe-nųhę́·-hgw-haʔ
DL-1SG > 3-greet-INST-HAB
I greet her with a kin term
= my niece]
LG: Once, my niece and I went through there.

Discussing the Seneca variant of the nominal particle which he glosses 'namely', Chafe (2012b; 2015:123) focuses on a discourse property of the particle, which consists of amplifying the meaning of a word or phrase preceding it. This may occur at two levels: either to amplify the meaning of the pronominal prefix attached to a clause's main verb, or to amplify information about a topic discussed in a prior utterance.[6]

Among frequently occurring particles with grammatical functions are two negative particles, *hya* 'not' and *ahgwih* 'don't'. The negative particle *hya* together with the prepronominal prefix *deʔ-* or the contrastive prepronominal *th-* negates a morphological verb. A negative imperative is expressed with the negative imperative particle *ahgwih* followed by an imperative verb or a punctual verb inflected with the future or optative (see section 7.8 where these are discussed and exemplified in detail).

Other examples of frequent particles with grammatical functions are a group of connective particles which link utterances, clauses, and intra-clausal constituents. Examples are the conjunctions *dę́ʔseʔ* 'and', *gadéʔ* 'or', *gíʔshę* 'alternatively' *góʔ* 'however', the additive *óhniʔ/oʔ* 'also', the cluster *do gaʔt* which is both an indefinite as well as a conditional particle.

Of a group of subordinating particles or particle clusters – *tshaʔ* 'that, where', *naʔ gwaʔ* 'because', *ganyoʔ* 'as soon as' – the most frequent is the *tshaʔ*-subordinator. This particle may mark clausal arguments (sec.7.4), certain relative clauses (sec. 7.5), and it combines with the classifier particles (see below) to mark amount, direction, extent, location and manner expressions. The particle cluster *naʔ gwaʔ* marks *because*-clauses (sec. 7.7.2), and *ganyóʔ* marks certain temporal dependencies.

A group of *classifier* particles mark expressions dealing with amount, direction, extent, manner, location, and size. They are *n(i)yų́h* 'amount', *hagwá* 'direction', *nigę́* 'extent [of time, space, or amount]',[7] *nų́·we* or *nų́* 'place' and *n(í·)yot* 'how it is [manner]'. Apart from pairing up with these adverbial expressions, they are also similar in the way they combine with certain other particles: when preceded by the subordinator *tshaʔ* they mark free relative clauses with the above values (sec. 7.5.2); when preceded by the locative/manner particle *(neʔ)tho* they often mark relative-correlative clauses (sec. 7.5.3); when preceded by interrogative particles, they mark questions (sec. 7.10) or indirect questions (sec. 7.4.2).

---

[5] *khehawá dekhenųhę́·khwaʔ* the phrase means 'my niece' [literally: I use the kinterm 'daughter' to greet her with] This locution distinguishes the niece from the daughter, who would be referred to by *khehawáh.*

[6] Chafe notes that in Seneca, the particle is included as the final element of the intonational contour of the phrase that immediately precedes it. In Onondaga the particle initiates an intonational contour as noted above.

[7] The particle marks terminal points, cf., German *bis, zu, bis dann, bis jetzt, bis dort.*

The excerpts in (5) provide examples of the classifiers as they combine with the subordinator *tsha?*:

(5) Classifier particles combined with the *tsha?* subordinator:
  a. ...nųda·gy[e]ǽ·? dogę ne? <u>tsha? nyų́ wagnakdodęhá?</u>... (LG23)

n-ųda-g-yeR-a?		dogę	ne?	tsha?	niyų	wag-nakd-od-ęh-a?
PRT-CIS:FACT-1.SG.A-do-PNC		MOD	NOM	SUB	AMT	1SG.P-space-stand-INCH-STV
I handled it		surely	the	that	much	I got a chance

  ...I handled it every chance I got...

  b. Né?tho ęshátga?k <u>tsha? hagwá hęní?tę·?</u> (CTL441.8).

ne?tho	ę-s-h-atga?k-Ø		tsha?	hagwá	hęn-i?dę·-?
LOC	FUT-REP-3M.SG.A-let go-PNC		SUB	DIR	3M.PL.A-be.situated-STV
there	he will let go of it		that	direction	they are situated

  He will let go of it towards where they are seated.

  c. ...nhwa?séh, gae? <u>tsha? nigę́ ęthe?</u> nę́·gę! (HW07)

n-h-wa?-s-e-h		gae?	tsha?	nigę	ę-t-h-e-?		nęgę
PRT-TRNS-FACT-2SG.IMP-walk-IMP		DGR	SUB	EXT	FUT-CIS-3M.SG.A-walk-PNC		DEM
go!		less	that	extent	he'll come here		this

  ...get going, before this one gets here!

  d. ...tho he·yagwé?s gwá? tcithaya?dahǽ?neh, <u>tsha? nų́ dehosnyé?ih</u> undertaker... (LG05)

tho	he-yagw-e-?s		gwa?	tci-t-ha-ya?d-a-hR-a? = neh
LOC	TRNS-1EX.PL.A-walk-HAB		RST	COIN-CIS-3M.SG.A-body-JN-put.up.on-STV = LOC
there	we are there		just	funeral parlor

tsha?	nų	de-ho-snye-?-ih		undertaker
SUB	LOC	DL-3M.SG > 3M.SG-take.care.of-INCH-STV		NOUN
that	place	he has taken care of him		

  ...we were at the funeral parlor where he was laid out, ...[Literally: we were at the funeral parlor, the place where the undertaker had taken care of him...]

  e. Wa?heyatho·yę́? nęgę́ <u>tsha? niyót hona·dnadayę́?</u>, ... (LG06)

wa?-hey-atho·y-ę-?		nęgę	tsha?	niyot
FACT-1SG > 3M.SG-tell-BEN-PNC		DEM	SUB	MAN
I told him		this	that	how it is

hon-ad-nad-a-yę-?
3M.NSG.P-SRF-village-JN-place-STV
they have set up camp

  I told him about how these [people] have set up camp ...

<u>Particles with discourse-pragmatic functions</u>. Many of the most frequent particles in this category are modal, marking speakers' attitudes toward the reliability of their information (sec. 7.9). One or another of these occurs in most utterances, frequently right up front. Examples are the hearsay particle *yágę?* 'they say', particles that express likelihood, for example *ayé·ę?* or *ayę́·?* 'it seems like' or certainty, e.g., *dó·gęs* 'for sure, truly', or the

cluster *naʔ séʔ* 'in fact'. Other modal particles express necessity, such as *gų́·daʔ* 'it must be', possibility, such as *gęhjihwę́h* 'apparently' or the cluster *hyaʔ ų* 'indeed, probably'.

Other discourse particles are the linking particles *diʔ* 'moreover, so' and *da* 'so (then)'. They occur in clusters that introduce utterances and express coherence between what went before in the story and what is to follow. Examples of such utterance-initial clusters are *Naʔ díʔ hyaʔ...* 'So, moreover, indeed it's...' *Onę diʔ hyaʔ yágę?...* 'So then indeed they say...', or *Ayę́·ʔ go·ʔ, hya hų·...* 'However, it doesn't seem like...', *Da nęgę ų́hgę?...* 'So then now...' These particles are discussed in detail in section 7.7.1.

Other discourse particles are the deictic particles that point to pragmatic factors of the situation. The most frequent of these are *ó·nę* 'now' and *thohge* '*then, later*'. In addition to signaling situation time, these also organize discourse sequencing. Locative deictics are *(neʔ)tho* the distance neutral deictic glossed 'there' and the proximal deictic *tho(nę)* 'here'. *Nę* 'this one, this here' is also used as a presentational particle. The distance neutral deictic *(neʔ)tho* is homonymous with the manner particle *(neʔ)tho* 'thus' which is also used to express approval: 'there you are, that's it, that's OK'.

7.3 The Clause

A clause is understood in this work to consist, minimally, of a verb form. But simple clauses occur with a variety of additional constituents. Ignoring linear order for the moment, the elements (words) constituting a simple clause can be: a single verb form (sec. 7.3.1); a verb form and one or more particles (sec. 7.3.2); a verb form, one or more noun forms or nominal expressions, and one or more particles (sec. 7.3.3). Clauses consisting of only a verb form and a noun form but lacking one or more particles do not occur in the corpus of texts, although such a clause can easily be elicited.

7.3.1 Verb-Only Clauses

Although the great majority of Onondaga clauses and utterances in connected discourse contain numerous words, verb-only utterances do occur, and they show, as noted above, that the verb on its own is able to express a complete proposition. Verb-only clauses are recognizable as complete utterances because they unfailingly are pronounced with utterance-final intonation patterns (section 2.7.6), are typically followed by a longer than average pause, and if followed by another utterance, that utterance will typically begin with a pitch reset. Verb-only clauses usually express mood-like distinctions. For the most part, they are used in discourse as exclamations, emphatic comments, commands, etc. The excerpt in (6a), from a story, is an exclamation that was preceded by a description of a scary-looking killer animal; the narrator in (6b) calls attention to the magical power of an animal that entered the forest as a rabbit and reappeared as a lion; in (6c), a child has overstayed his welcome with his grandfather and he is told to leave:

(6) a. Exclamation: Oʔdáhdęt! (HW07)
    o-iʔdahdęt-Ø
    3N/Z.SG.P-be.terrifying-STV
    It is terrifying!

   b. Narrator's interpolation to listeners: Dehotdé·nyų̈h (HW07).
      de-ho-at-deny-ų̈h
      DL-3M.SG.P-SRF-deny-STV
      He has transformed [himself]!

   c. Command: Hwaʔséh! (HW03)
      h-waʔ-s-e-h
      TRNS-FACT-2SG.IMP-walk-IMP
      Go away!

7.3.2 Clauses Consisting of a Verb and One or More Particles

Clauses consisting of a verb and one or more particles, are more frequent than verb-only clauses in connected discourse. As was pointed out above, Onondaga's many particles occur at all levels of the language. Some of this diversity is illustrated below:

A. <u>Clauses with temporal, locative, and manner particles</u>

Adverbial particles often precede the modified verb form. A verb preceded by a temporal or locative particle, or both, can occur as a complete utterance to locate events or activities in space and time. Locative particles often co-occur with locative prepronominal prefixes (sec. 4.7.2) on verb forms that express directional and locational meanings as they do in (8a) and (9a and b):

(7) Verb and temporal particle(s):
   a. Nę waʔhyahdę́·dyaʔ (HW07).
      onę   waʔ-hy-ahdędy-aʔ
      TMP   FACT-3M.DU.A-move.on-PNC
      then   they two departed
      Then the two [men] departed.

   b. Thohgé ó·nę waʔthadidáʔnhaʔ (CTL26.3-4).
      thohge onę   waʔ-t-hadi-d-aʔ-nhaʔ
      TMP   TMP   FACT-DL-3M.PL.A-stand-INCH-PNC
      thereupon   they all stood up
      Thereupon they all stood up.

(8) Verb with locative particle(s):
   a. Tho nhę·dnéʔ (HW07).
      tho   n-<u>h</u>-ę-dn-e-ʔ'
      LOC   PRT-<u>TRNS</u>-FUT-1IN.DU.A-walk-PNC
      there   we two will go there
      We'll go there.

   b. Tho nų́hge ená·ge·ʔ (LG17).
      tho   nųh = ge   e-nage·-ʔ
      LOC   LOC = LOC   3FI.A-live-STV
      there   at a place   she resides
      Where she lives [literally, the place she lives at].

(9) Verb and temporal and locative particles:
a. <u>Thohge</u> nų dedyųgwadatyędé·ʔih (LG07).

thohge	nų	de-d-yųgw-adad-yędeR-ʔ-ih
TMP	LOC	DL-CIS-1PL.P-REF-know-INCH-STV
then	place	we got to know each other <u>there</u>

Later, we got to know each other there.

b. ...naʔ ų̄hgę́ʔ tho dyená·ge·ʔ (LG16).

naʔ	ų̄hgęʔ	tho	d-ye-nage·-ʔ
ASRT	TMP	LOC	CIS-3FI.A-live-STV
it's	at this time	there	she resides <u>there</u>

...she lives there at this time.

Manner particles may co-occur with a verb form that includes the partitive prefix:

(10) Verb and <u>manner particle</u>:
a. ...<u>tho</u> nęgyé·æʔ (HW07).

tho	n-ę-g-yeR-aʔ
MAN	PRT-FUT-1SG.A-do-PNC
thus	<u>how</u> I'll do it

...that's how I'll do it.

b. <u>Tho</u> néʔ <u>ni</u>hadatjí·nah (LG12).

tho	neʔ	ni-ha-adatjina-h
MAN	NOM	PRT-3M.SG.A-be.plucky-STV
thus	the	<u>how</u> plucky he is

That's how plucky he is / He's the plucky one.

B. <u>Clauses with mixed particle groupings</u>

Particle groupings are a frequent part of connected discourse, though less so in elicited examples. Perhaps this is an indication of the degree to which discourse cohesion is signaled by particles. Thus it is very common to find that an utterance occurs with an introductory grouping of particles that orients the listener in terms of discourse and setting details.

In (11) a discourse particle, *da·*, links the expression to a previous topic (in this example that topic is how modern kids harm their teeth eating too much candy); the modal particle *dogęs* indicates the speaker's level of confidence regarding the statement she is making, the nominal particle *neʔ* marks the following temporal expression as a nominal:

(11) Linking, modal, nominal, and adverbial particles: Da· dogę́s neʔ ų̄nísʔi,
hadinoʔji·yóʔsgwaʔ (LG20).

da·	dogęs	neʔ	ų̄nisʔih	hadi-noʔjy-iyo-ʔs-gwaʔ
LNK	MOD	NOM	TMP	3M.PL.A-tooth-be.good-STVPL-HBPST
so	truly	the	past time	they used to have good teeth

So for sure in the past, they used to have really good teeth.

In (12) the intensifier particle *gwas* modifies the manner clause *tsha?
nwa?hadi·hwahǽ·hda?*, showing that the modifier and the modified constituent need not
occur contiguously; the additive *o?* is cohesive, it links the utterance to what went before in
the text; *ayę́·?* is a modal expression; the subordinator particle *tsha?* together with the
partitive prefix *n-* describe the manner of the participant's behavior.

(12) Intensifier, additive, modal, and subordinative: Gwas o? ayę́·?, tsha?
     nwa?hadi·hwahǽ·hda? (LG24).

gwas	o?	ayeę?	tsha?	n-wa?-h-adihwahæhd-a?
INTNS	ADD	MOD	SUB	PRT-FACT-3M.SG.A-act.excited-a?
very	also	seem like	that	how excitedly he acts

Also, it seems that he's really excited.

The negative particle *hya* and the negative prefix *de?-* are obligatory parts of certain
negative expressions (section 7.8). The particle can occur either immediately before the
negated verb, or the two can be separated by additional particles as in (13). Here the
intervening particles are the contrast marking connective *go·?* and an interrogative particle
hwędųh:

(13) Negative, modal, and indefinite: Hya gó·? hwędų́h de?wagadyę·níh (LG10).

hya	go·?	hwędųh	de?-wag-adyeę-ni-h'
NEG	CTR	INTR	NEG-1SG.P-have.an.accident-BEN-STV
not	however	when(ever)	I haven't had an accident

However, I've never had an accident.

In (14) the demonstrative particle *nęgę* refers anaphorically to a previously described
family whose members weren't fond of working hard for a living. In that context the
demonstrative, apart from functioning as a proform that is appositional to the verb's
pronominal prefix *-hodi-*, also serves to provide discourse coherence. The contrary
connective *go·?* marks situations or outcomes that are contrary to either the protagonists' or
the narrator's expectation.

(14) Demonstrative and contrast particle: Nęgę́ go·? wa?hodihsí?he? (LG08).

nęgę	go·?	wa?-hodi-hsi-?he?-Ø
DEM	CTR	FACT-3M.NSG.P-hungry-INCH-PNC
these	however	they got hungry

However, these [guys] got hungry.

7.3.3 Clauses with Verbs and External Nouns, Demonstratives, or Pronouns

There are four important points to make about clauses consisting of a verb with one or
more external nominals (referring expressions that occur outside the verb): (i) External
nominals are optional in Onondaga (section 7.3.1 above). When they occur, they further
specify the verbs' semantic arguments (Koenig & Michelson 2015a:8). (ii) The linear order
of verbs and external nominals is discourse, rather than syntactically, determined (Mithun
1987). (iii) External nominals can be expressed via a morphological noun, as in (19), (21)
and (22) below, or a variety of simple and complex nominal expressions such as an
internally headed relative clause as in (16) and (20), a free relative as in (17b), a proper

name as in (17a) and (19) a demonstrative particle as in (18c), or a personal pronoun as in (18d).[8] Any one of these is likely to be preceded by the nominal particle *ne?*. (iv) The pronominal prefixes that attach to external nominals do not have to agree in number, person, or gender with the pronominal prefixes of the verb. This *dis*-agreement can take several forms as shown in (24) to (26).

The Linear order of verbs and external nominals is not syntactically determined: The examples below illustrate all possible linear orders of verbs and their external nominals. As noted above, the linear order of verbs and external nominals is determined by discourse considerations. A number of discourse patterns are especially frequent. Typically, external nominals preceded by various particle clusters introduce new participants to the discourse, or recall ones that were introduced previously. When a nominal occurs early on in a clause, perhaps preceded by the assertion particle *na(ye)?* and ahead of the verb, it indicates a shift in the topic of discourse, or a contrast of some other kind. The examples below illustrate combinations of verbs and their external nominals:

<u>External agent or patient nominals:</u>

(15) Verb and following external agent nominal:
    a. Na? gę́s ne? shųgwa·jyapshæwíh, <u>k?nihagęhǽ?</u>... (HW02)

na?	gęs	ne?	shųgwa-jyap-hsR-awi-h'	k-?niha = gęhæ?
ASRT	CST	NOM	3M.SG > 1PL-job-NOM-give-STV	1SG.A-father = DEC
it's	usually	the	he gave us a job	my late father

    Usually, my late father gave us a job...

    b. Sahahdędyá? ne? <u>Shohé·yis</u> (HW06).

s-a-h-ahdędy-a?		ne?	Shohé·yis
REP-FACT-3M.SG.A-move.on-PNC		NOM	NAME
he returned home		the	Shohé·yis

    Shoheyis returned home.

(16) Verb and preceding external agent nominal:
    a. ...dę́?se? ne? <u>hųdęnótha?</u> o? wa?hųdę·nodę́?... (LG05)

dę́?se?	ne?	hų-ad-Ręn-ot-ha?	o?	wa?-hų-ad-Ręn-od-ę?
CNJ	NOM	3M.PL.A-SRF-song-raise-HAB	ADD	FACT-3M.PL.A- SRF-song-raise-PNC
and	the	band	also	they played

    ...and the band played, too.

    b. Nę ne? <u>gų?shę·níh</u> dęgų́tgwa?na? (LG14).

onę	ne?	gų-a?shę·nih	dę-gų-atgw-a?n-a?
TMP	NOM	3FZ.PL.A-white.person	DL-FUT-3FZ.PL.A-dance-DSLC-PRP
then	the	white women	they will go to dance

    And the white girls will go to dance.

---

[8] Relative clauses are discussed in section 7.5.

350 Syntactic Constructions

(17) Verb and following external patient nominal:
    a. Ahsedéh seʔ waʔshagwaʔnųhdá·k <u>Tom Green</u> (LG05).

ahsedeh	seʔ	waʔ-shagwa-ʔnųhdaR-k	Tom Green
TMP	MOD	FACT-1EX.PL > 3M.SG-bury-PNC	NAME
yesterday	actually	we buried him	Tom Green

Yesterday, we actually buried Tom Green.

    b. Nę́, waʔhododahcyę́ʔ <u>nęgę́ neʔ tshaʔ gayę́ʔ ohnaʔgę́ hétha</u>ʔ (HW07).

onę	waʔ-ho-ad-odahcy-ę-ʔ		nęgę	neʔ	tshaʔ gayę́ʔ
TMP	FACT-3M.SG > 3M.SG-SRF-appear-BEN-PNC		DEM	NOM	REL
now	he appeared to him		this	the	who

o-hnaʔgę-h	h-e-t-haʔ
3N/Z.SG.P-be.behind-STV	3M.SG.A-walk-CS-HAB
behind	he goes

Then he appeared to him, [to] this one who walked behind.

Verb and preceding external patient nominal. The external nominals in (18a and b) are internally headed relative clauses; in (18c) the external nominal is an anaphoric demonstrative; the external nominal in (18d) is a personal pronoun:

(18) a. Nayéʔ dehonadawę·yéh deyohada·yę́·dų́ʔ <u>ena·gé·nyų</u>ʔ dehadinųhǽkhwaʔ (CTL1.4-6).

nayeʔ	de-hon-ad-awę·ye-h'	de-yo-had-a-yęd-ų-ʔ	e-nage·-nyų-ʔ
ASRT	DL-3M.NSG.P-SRF-stir-STV	DL-3N/Z.SG.P-bush-JN-lie-DST-STV	3FI.A-live-DST-STV
it's	they are roaming	across the bush	inhabitants

de-hadi-nųhR-a-hgw-haʔ
DL-3M.PL.A-scalp-JN-lift-HAB
they scalp

They are roaming about across the bush, scalping inhabitants.

    b. <u>Gędyohgówanę</u> oné, hųwanaʔwę́thwih (HW07).

ga-idyohgw-owanę-'h	onę	hųwan-aʔwę́thw-ih
3N/Z.SG.A-crowd-be.large-STV	TMP	3 > 3M.PL-slaughter-STV
it is a large crowd	now	they have slaughtered them

They have slaughtered lots of people by now.

    c. Naʔ <u>thogę́</u> dęyų·wę·yéʔ (LG01).

naʔ	thogę	d-ę-yų-awę·ye-ʔ'
ASRT	DEM	DL-FUT-3FI.A-stir-PNC
it's	that	they stir it.

They stir that [i.e., the locusts and the pork fat in the pan].

    d. ... <u>haųhwá</u>ʔ séʔ onę́ nę́·gę ęshohsé·k (HW07).

ha-ųhwaʔ	seʔ	onę	nęgę	ę-s-ho-hse·-k'
3M.SG.P-self	MOD	TMP	DEM	FUT-REP-3FZ.SG > 3M.SG-chase-PNC
he himself	actually	then	this	she will chase him next

... it's him, actually, this one will chase next.

Less frequently several external nominals occur in the same clause. The linear order of the elements in such clauses is also determined by discourse factors.

(19) Verb and preceding external agent nominal and following external patient nominal:
Thohgé ó·nę ne? <u>Deganawí·da?</u> wa?haga·háthwa? <u>gahú·wa?</u> (CTL55.1-2).

thohge onę	ne?	<u>Deganawi·da?</u>	wa?-ha-ga·hathw-a?	<u>ga-hųw-a?</u>
TMP	NOM	<u>NAME</u>	FACT-3M.SG.A-turn.over-PNC	<u>NPF-boat-NSF</u>
thereupon	the	<u>Deganawida?</u>	he turned it over	<u>boat</u>

Then Deganawí·da? turned over the boat.

<u>External applicative nominals</u>: If the applicative nominal is animate, as in (20), it is expressed via the verb's patient pronominal prefix in addition to the external nominal (Sections 4.8.5.1 and 4.8.5.2).[9]

(20) Verb and following external beneficiary nominal:
... hya gwas de?odiyanę·?sé ne? <u>Clifford hoyęthwáhų?</u> (LG02).

hya	gwas	de?-odi-yanę·-?se-h'	ne?	Clifford	ho-yęthw-ahų-?
NEG	INTS	NEG-3FZ.NSG.P-good-BEN-STV	NOM	NAME	3M.SG.P-plant-DST-STV
not	very	it wasn't good for them	the	Clifford	he has planted them

... it hasn't been good for Clifford's plantings.

Example (21) contains two external nominals:

(21) Verb and preceding external patient and following beneficiary nominal:
...ne? thogę ne? <u>ohwísda?</u> wa?ųkhiga·yá?ks <u>djeya?dadáshų?</u> (LG19).

ne?	thogę	ne?	o-hwisd-a?	wa?-ųkhi-ga·ya?k-s-Ø
NOM	DEM	NOM	NPF-money-NSF	FACT-3 > 1NSG-pay.out-BEN-PNC
the	that	the	money	they paid us

s-ye-ya?d-ada-Ø = shų?
REP-3FI.A-body-have.in-STV = PL
each person

... that money they paid us, each of us.[10]

(22) Verb and preceding external instrument:[11]
...nęgę ne? hęgwéh wa?sha·gó·yo?, ne? hé·na?, a?shá·? wa?hásda? (LG09).

nęgę	ne?	hR-ųgweh	wa?-shago-Ryo-?	ne?	he·na?	(Ø)-a?shaR-?
DEM	NOM	3M.SG.A-man:SUFF	FACT-3M.SG > 3-kill-PNC	NOM	NOUN	NPF-knife-NSF
this	the	man	he killed her	the	spouse	knife

wa?-ha-sd-a?
FACT-3M.SG.A-use-PNC
he used

...this man killed his wife using a knife.

---

[9] This excerpt followed a discussion of how dry the summer had been. The animate pronominal prefix was chosen to reference the plants perhaps because it was their growth that was at issue.

[10] The reference is to monthly payments by the state to Onondaga Nation members.

[11] Recall that unlike most beneficiaries, instruments are non-animate, thus they are semantic, but not morphological arguments of the verb (see sec. 4.8.5.2).

(23) Verb and following external instrument:
      Naʔ ų́hgęʔ <u>ęgethá·hgwaʔ</u>, neʔ <u>oʔgwę·yóʔdaʔ</u> (LG01).

naʔ	ųhgęʔ	ę-ge-thaR-<u>hgw</u>-aʔ	neʔ	oʔgwę·yóʔdaʔ
ASRT	TMP	FUT-1SG.A-talk.about-<u>INST</u>-PNC	NOM	NOUN
it's	at this time	I'll use it to tell	the	locust(s)

      Next I am going to talk about locusts. [Literally: I'll use locusts to tell about]

<u>Mismatches: Agreement between verbal prefixes and external nominals is not required in Onondaga</u>: In (24) the referent of the nominal *honóhaʔ* 'his mother', literally, she is his mother, is expressed pronominally with the transitive prefix *ho-* 'she (feminine-zoic agent) > him (masculine patient)', whereas the verb identifies the identical referent with the feminine-indefinite prefix -(y)e- 'she' (feminine-indefinite agent):

(24) ... ónę híhyaʔ neʔ honóhaʔ néʔtho waʔé·yų̧ʔ... (H144.3)

onę	hihyaʔ	neʔ	ho-noha?	neʔtho	waʔ-e-yų-?
TEMP	MOD	NOM	3FZ.SG > 3M.SG-mother	LOC	FACT-<u>3FI.A</u>-arrive-PNC
then	indeed	the	his mother	there	she arrived

      ...then, indeed, his mother arrived there...

Similarly (25), where the pronominal prefix marking the internally headed relative clause meaning *lion* (literally: the one who throws flames) is prefixed with the third person feminine-zoic prefix *ga-* and the verb's pronominal prefix that refers to the same entity is the third person masculine agent *-ha-*:[12]

(25) Dahayáʔkdaʔ, neʔ gahahsę·dyéthaʔ (HW07).

d-a-ha-yaʔkd-aʔ	neʔ	ga-hahsR-ųdy-eht-haʔ
DL-FACT-<u>3M.SG.A</u>-rip.off-PNC	NOM	<u>3FZ.SG.A</u>-flame-throw-cs-HAB
he ripped it off	the	lion

      He ripped it off, the lion [did].

In excerpt (26) the verb, though semantically dyadic, is, in the meaning 'have', morphologically intransitive and lexicalized with a stative pronominal prefix to express the experiencer nominal (sec. 4.3). Thus the animate referent of the external noun is not referenced by the pronominal prefix of the main verb:

(26) Da· ųgwayę́ʔ neʔ hathwisdanų́hnaʔ (LG19).

da	ųgwa-yę-ʔ	neʔ	ha-at-hwisd-a-nųhn-aʔ
LINK	1PL.P-have-STV	NOM	3M.SG.A-SRF-money-JN-guard-STV
so	we have	the	treasurer

      And we have a treasurer.

---

[12] Internally headed relative clauses are discussed in section 7.5.1 below.

7.3.3.1 Clauses with Possessed External Nominals[13]

The nominal particle *ne?*, a demonstrative particle, or both, nearly always precede external possessed nominals, but neither particle is obligatory. The external noun in (27) is composed of a possessive prefix and a morphological noun:

(27) ...hya s<u>ǫ</u>·gaʔ neʔ <u>ǫ</u>·gwe thayésdaʔ <u>neʔ akhǫ·waʔ</u>... (CTL46.6)

hya	sǫ· gaʔ	neʔ	(y)-ǫgweh	th-a·-ye-sd-aʔ	neʔ	ak-hǫw-aʔ
NEG	INDF	NOM	NPF-person:SUFF	CON-OPT-3FI.A-use-PNC	NOM	1SG.P-boat-NSF
not	somebody	the	person	one shouldn't use it	the	my boat

...no one should use my boat...

The external noun in (28) is derived with the nominalizer from a verb stem:

(28) Thohge ó·nę ędwatgáthwaʔ <u>neʔ hoyoʔdéhsæ·ʔ</u> (CTL25.4).

thohge onę	ę-dw-atgathw-aʔ	neʔ	ho-yoʔdę-hsR-aʔ
TMP	FUT-1IN.PL.A-look.at-PNC	NOM	3M.SG.P-work-NOM-NSF
thereafter	we will look at it	the	his work

Thereafter we will look at his work.

The external noun in (29) is a body part noun, requiring an agent-series possessive prefix and a locative clitic:

(29) Waʔthahwaʔesdahę́·ʔ, <u>ehǫʔgwa·ʔgé</u> tshaʔ nigę́ waʔaihé·yaʔ (LG09).

waʔ-t-ha-hwaʔe-sd-ahę·-aʔ'	e-hǫʔgwaR-aʔ = ge	tshaʔ nigę
FACT-DL-3M.SG.A-strike-CS-DST-PNC	3FI.A-throat-NSF = LOC	SUB EXT
he struck it several times	her throat	until

waʔ-a-ihey-aʔ
FACT-3FI.A-die-PNC
she died

He kept striking her throat until she died.

The external noun in (30) contains a borrowing, which requires that the possessed form includes the semireflexive morpheme:

(30) ...naʔ díʔ hyaʔ <u>neʔ ǫgwatbós</u> waʔhęhę́·ʔ... (LG12)

naʔ	diʔ	hyaʔ	neʔ	<u>ǫgwa-at-bos</u>	waʔ-ha-ihę·-ʔ'
ASRT	LINK	MOD	NOM	<u>1PL.P-SRF-boss</u>	FACT-3M.SG.A-say-PNC
it's	so	indeed	the	<u>our boss</u>	he said

...so our boss said...

The kinship term in (31) marks the elder person as acting on the younger:[14]

---

[13] See section 5.2.1.2 on the possessed noun construction, and section 7.11 on the different ways of expressing possession in Onondaga.

[14] See section 5.4 for the special treatment accorded kinship terms in the Iroquoian languages.

(31) Nę hya? na? <u>né? hak?nihá?gęhǽ·?</u>[15] wa?hęhę́·? ęganųhsagęisdík... (LG16)

nę	hya?	na?	ne?	hak-?niha?=gęhæ?	wa?-ha-ihę·-?'
TMP	MOD	ASRT	NOM	3M.SG>1SG-father=DEC	FACT-3M.SG.A-say-PNC
now	indeed	it's	the	my late father	he said

ę-ga-nųhs-a-gęisd-i-k-Ø
FUT-3N/Z.SG.A-house-JN-move-STV-CONT-PNC
the house will be moved
Then it's my late father, who said, "the house will be moved..."

The external nominal phrase in (32) consists of a complex kinship term – *my mother's sister's daughter* – including one involving a same-generation relationship – *sister* – requiring a non-singular pronominal prefix that includes both the possessor and the possessed as referents:

(32) ...nęgę́ <u>ne? gnohá?gęhǽ·?</u>[16] degyadęhnų·dǽ·? na? dí? hya? ne? <u>ųdáthawah</u> na? tho niyót
     gowæ·?é nęgęhá? (LG20).

nęgę	ne?	g-noha?=gęhæ?	de-gy-adęhnųdR-a?	na?	di?	hya?
DEM	NOM	1SG.A-mother=DEC	DL-3FZ.DU.A-be.siblings-STV	ASRT	LNK	MOD
this	the	my late mother	they are sisters	it's	moreover	indeed

ne?	ųdat-hawah	tho	niyot	go-Ræ?=?é	nęgę=há
NOM	3FI>3FI-parent.*child*	MAN	MAN	3FI.P-get.a.disease=REP	DEM=DIM
the	her daughter	thus	how it is	she got the disease again	this, specifically

...this [one], my late mother's sister,[17] *indeed it's her daughter, she's the next one who caught the disease.*

7.3.3.2 Clauses with Compound External Nominal

In (33) the external nominal expression consists of a demonstrative that is in apposition to the compound nominal phrase; in (34) the nominal expression's head noun *-hųw- / -hųy-* 'boat, canoe' occurs twice, once referring generally as a classifier noun incorporated into the verb, and once as a part of the more specific compound *onę́·ya? gahų́·wa?* 'stone canoe'.

(33) ...háų? di? dásha,[18] <u>thogę́ ohwáhda? o?ę́·na?</u>... (HW03)

hau?	di?	d-a-s-hawa-h	thogę	o-hwahd-a?	o-a?ęn-a?
INST	LNK	CIS-FACT-2IMP-bring-IMP	DEM	NPF-maple-NSF	NPF-stick-NSF
alright	moreover	bring it!	that	maple	stick

...all right, so bring me that maple stick...

---

[15] Words with clitics, especially two-syllable clitics, often receive two stresses.

[16] Recall that contemporary speakers may use intransitive agent prefixes with first person possessor parent terms.

[17] Literally: my late mother, they two are sisters.

[18] *dásha* is an elliptical form of dáshawah *bring it!* The base is .haų- / .ęhaų- / .haw- / .hw / .ęhw- / -ya?dęhaw- + cislocative or translocative v.a. *bring, take.*

(34) ...nęhshų́·yok <u>neʔ onę́·yaʔ gahų́·waʔ</u>... (CTL55.7-8)

n-ę-hs-hųw-o-k[19]		neʔ	o-nęy-aʔ	ga-hųw-aʔ
PRT-FUT-2SG.A-boat-float-PNC		NOM	NPF-stone-NSF	NPF-boat-NSF
you will launch a boat		the	stone	boat

...you will launch a stone boat...

The external nominal in (35) is derived from a positional verb inflected for verbal possession (sec. 7.11.2):

(35) <u>Ųgyųhwęjyayę́ʔ</u> thónę néʔ ęhadiyastháʔ ganęhæ·gwegí gó·wę (LG19).

ųgy-ųhwęjy-a-yę-ʔ	thonę	neʔ	ę-hadi-yas-t-haʔ
1PL.P-land-JN-have-STV	LOC	NOM	FUT-3M.PL.A-be.named-INST-HAB
our property[20]	here	the	they call it

ga-nęhR-a-gweg-ih	go-awę-h
3N/Z.SG.A-group-JN-all-STV	3FI.P-own-STV
the whole group	they own it

Our property here, that's what they call it, it belongs to the whole group.

7.4 Clausal Arguments

A different kind of complex nominal from those described in section 7.3.3.2 is one that is a complete clause in its own right, but instead of occurring as a separate clause, it is linked as an external nominal to another clause. Such a clausal argument describes a situation or a proposition. A second type of clausal argument, occurs in utterances that include indirect questions. The characteristics of clausal arguments and a sub-type of these, indirect questions, are discussed in section 7.4.1 and 7.4.2, respectively.

7.4.1 Clauses with Clausal Arguments

When an utterance includes a clausal argument, it may be simply juxtaposed to the main verb, or the relationship may be marked with the subordinator *tshaʔ*, or a variety of adverbial particles or particle clusters; alternatively, the predicate of the argument clause may be morphologically marked with the optative. The choice among these alternatives depends on requirements *internal to the argument clause*. Main verbs whose meaning involves uncertain or hypothetical outcomes (e.g., *hope, want,* etc.) are apt to occur with clausal arguments that include optative modal prepronominal prefixes, and factive main verbs – verbs whose meaning presupposes the truth of the argument clause (e.g., *regret, remember* etc.) – are apt to occur with the subordinator *tshaʔ*.[21]

---

[19] Recall that *w* > *y* /_*o* by regular rule.

[20] Literally, *the land we have lying to us.*

[21] Koenig & Michelson (in press) and Michelson et al. (2016) were the first to note similar co-occurrences in Oneida, where semantic constraints on clausal arguments are associated with the forms of the argument clauses, such that argument clauses beginning with the subordinator (in Oneida the cognate form to *tshaʔ* is *tsiʔ*) co-occur with factual situations, argument clauses whose verbs begin in the optative co-occur with irrealis situations, and argument clauses with neither of these expresses a speaker's lack of commitment to factuality.

In examples (36) the main and argument clauses are juxtaposed (argument clauses are underlined in the examples). Frequently, two juxtaposed clauses are pronounced within a single intonational contour. In example (36a), the main clause *nę hothų·déʔ* 'then he heard it' consists of a temporal particle and a semantically dyadic perception verb, and the argument clause, a verb form, describes the situation that is perceived, *dayohsųwæ·gáehæʔ* 'a gun sounded out'. The two clauses were pronounced within a single intonational contour. In (36b) the argument clause of the aspectual verb *-ahsaw-* 'begin' describes the situation of the old lady getting angry:

(36) a. ... nę hothų·déʔ dayohsųwæ·gáehæʔ (HW07).

onę	ho-athude-ʔ	d-a-yo-hsųR-a-gaehR-aʔ
TMP	3M.SG.P-hear-STV	CIS-FACT-3N/Z.SG.P-gun-JN-make.a.noise-PNC
then	he hears it	a gun sounded out

... then he's hearing a gun sound out.

    b. Thohge ó·nę neʔ goksdęʔá waʔųhsawę́ʔ waʔagonaʔkhwę́haʔ... (CTL4.4)

thohge ó·nę	neʔ	go-ksdęʔa	waʔ-ų-ahsaw-ęʔ	waʔ-ago-naʔkhwęh-aʔ
TMP TMP	NOM	3FI.P-old.person	FACT-3FI.A-begin-PNC	FACT-3FI.P-get.angry-PNC
thereafter	the	old lady	she began it	it got her angry

Thereafter the old lady began to get angry...

An argument clause marked for the optative mode, *a·hadęnásgų* 'he should give away his pet', is juxtaposed to a main clause with the desiderative verb -eR- *'want, think'* in (37a). Similarly, an argument clause morphologically marked for the optative mode, *a·ye·yaʔdagéhnhaʔ* 'she can/may help', is juxtaposed to a main clause with *-nųhwe-* 'like' in example (37b), presumably because the situation of helping is conditioned on numerous uncertain real-world factors. In both examples the argument clause expresses an irrealis situation:

(37) a. Do gá·ʔ nwaʔwá·dyetʔaʔ gęs hehéʔ a·hadęnásgųʔ (HW05).

do ga·ʔ	n-waʔ-w-adyetʔ-aʔ	gęs	h-eR-heʔ
INDF	PRT-FACT-3N/Z.SG.A-number.of.times-PNC	CST	3M.SG.A-want-HAB
some	number of times	usually	he wants

aa-h-ad-nasg-ų-ʔ
OPT-3M.SG.A-pet-give-PNC
he should give his pet

He frequently wants to give [away] his pet.

    b. Nę héʔ naʔ néʔ, tho góʔ niyót tshaʔędageha·dyéʔ enųhwéʔs a·ye·yaʔdagehnháʔ gaʔ gwaʔ nų́· (LG08).

nę	heʔ	naʔ	neʔ	tho	goʔ	niyot
TMP	REP	ASRT	NOM	MAN	CTR	MAN
then	again	it's	the	thus	however	how it is

tsh-aʔ-(w)-ęd-a-ge-h'-adye-ʔ	e-nųhwe-ʔs
COIN-FACT-3N/Z.SG.A-day-JN-amount.to-STV-PRG-PNC	3FI.A-like-HAB
as days went along	she likes it

aa-ye-yaʔdagehnh-aʔ   gaʔ gwaʔ nų·
OPT-3FI.A-help-PNC   IND RSTR LOC
she can help   some place
But the way it was as time went on, she liked helping at various places.

Depending on the situation described by the argument clause, certain main verbs can co-occur with argument clauses that begin with different 'complementizers', or simply juxtaposed to the main clause. The verb *-atdog-* is such a verb. In (38a) the argument is a temporal clause marked with the temporal particle *onę* 'now, then', in (38b) the juxtaposed argument clause is unmarked; in (38c) the argument clause occurs with the *tshaʔ* subordinating particle.

(38) a. ...hya deʔhonatdó·gęh <u>onę waʔtshagodiyaʔdahí·hdaʔ neʔ kheháwah</u> (CTL169.3-4).

    hya   deʔ-hon-atdog-ęh   onę   waʔ-t-shagodi-yaʔd-a-hi·-hd-aʔ
    NEG   NEG-3M.NSG.P-notice-STV   TMP   FACT-DL-3.M.NSG > 3FI-body-JN-smash-PNC
    not   they didn't notice   when   they smashed into her

    neʔ   khe-hawah
    NOM   1SG > 3-child
    the   my child
    ...they didn't notice when they smashed into my daughter.

  b. ...ęhųtdógaʔ <u>hya thaʔde·jyodę·nų·dak aųsahadaʔgaitát</u> (CTL487.1-2).

    ę-hų-atdog-aʔ   hya   thaʔ-de-s-yo-ad-Ręn-ųdaR-k
    FUT-3M.PL.A-notice-PNC   NEG   CON-DL-REP-3N/Z.SG.P-SRF-song-put.in-HAB
    they will notice it   not   it isn't hopeful anymore

    aųsa-ha-adaʔgaid-at-Ø
    OPT:REP-3M.SG.A-recover-CS-PNC
    he can recover
    ...they will notice [that] there is no hope for his recovery.

  c. Waʔhatdogáʔ nęgę <u>tshaʔ daga·ǽ·deʔ</u> (HW07).

    waʔ-h-atdog-aʔ   nęgę   tshaʔ   d-a-ga-Ræde-ʔ
    FACT-3M.SG.A-notice-PNC   DEM   SUB   CIS-FACT-3FZ.SG.A-climb-PRP
    he noticed   this   that   she is climbing up
    He notices that she's climbing up [inside the tree].

<u>Linear Order</u>: Main and argument clauses are linearly ordered: the argument clause occurs to the right of the main verb as seen in all the examples above. But the sequence can be interrupted by other constituents or by supplement expressions, expressions that are not otherwise integrated into the clause. In (39), a supplement expression – *nę gwaʔ oyé·det* 'it's just barely noticeable' – is interpolated commentary by the story-teller. That is then followed by the underlined argument clause:

(39) Nę́ gwáʔ nigę́ nhehonenų́h nę waʔhyatdogáʔ, nę gwáʔ oyędét <u>nęgę́ tshaʔ nų́·</u>
<u>dewadawę·yéʔthaʔ neʔ nęgę́ nwaʔgayáʔdoʔdę́ʔ</u>[22] (HW07).

nę	gwaʔ	nigę	nhe-hon-e-nųh		onę	waʔ-hy-atdog-aʔ
PRES	RSTR	EXT	PRT-TRNS-3M.NSG.P-walk-STV		TMP	FACT-3M.DU.A-notice-PNC
here	just	how far	thus they have gone		now	they two noticed

nę gwaʔ	o-yędeR-t-Ø		nęgę	tshaʔ	nų·	de-w-ad-awę·ye-ʔt-haʔ
QNT	3N/Z.SG.P-know-CS-STV		DEM	SUB	LOC	DL-3FZ.SG.A-SRF-stir-CS-HAB
little bit	it is noticeable		this	that	place	she frequents [the place]

neʔ	nęgę	n-waʔ-ga-yaʔd-oʔdę-ʔ
NOM	DEM	PRT-FACT-3FZ.SG.A-body-kind.of-STV
the	this	thus kind of being

*They've gone just a little way, when they notice – it's just barely noticeable – that this
is the place she frequents, this, like animal.*

Argument clauses can be nested, one within the other (marked in the example by square
brackets), as in (40):

(40) … [ₛwaʔhonehæ·gwáʔ hyaʔ ų nęgę́ [ₐᵣ₉tshaʔ [ₛwaʔhgwe·nyáʔ [ₐᵣ₉waʔga·dyę́ʔ]]]]
(LG23).

waʔ-ho-nehæ·gw-aʔ	hyaʔ	ų	nęgę	tshaʔ	waʔ-k-gweny-aʔ
FACT-3M.SG.P-surprise-PNC	MOD	MOD	DEM	SUB	FACT-1SG.A-can.do-PNC
it surprised him	indeed	probably	this	that	I was able to do it

waʔ-g-adyę-ʔ´
FACT-1SG.A-sit.down-PNC
I sat down

…indeed it surprised this [horse] that I was able to sit down.

7.4.2 Embedded (Indirect) Questions[23]

The linear order of embedded, or indirect questions is the same as that of argument
clauses, discussed in section 7.4.1 above, that is, the embedded question clause follows the
clause containing the main verb. And again, like clauses with clausal arguments, when
there are embedded questions, the verbs of the two clauses need not be adjacent. A feature
of embedded question clauses in Onondaga is that the form of the question clause is not
altered from the form of a question that is not embedded (sec. 7.10). Thus, if the embedded
clause consists of a content (or open) question, it begins with a question word or phrase
and is followed by a verb form that describes the questioned situation or entity; if the
embedded clause consists of a polar (or closed) question, then the question particle *khę*
follows as the second element of the clause just as it does when the question clause is not
embedded.

---

[22] *nwaʔgayáʔdoʔdę́ʔ* is pronounced with a whispered final syllable. Note that predicted penultimate
utterance-final stress is moved to the antepenultimate syllable.

[23] Embedded questions are also discussed in section 6.3.1.

<u>Embedded content questions</u>: Embedded content questions are shown in examples (41) - (45). They begin with interrogative particles or two-particle expressions. The latter often consist of an interrogative particle followed by a classifier particle that specifies the type of information that is sought as in (43) - (45):

(41) Waʔhatho·yáʔ <u>wadę́ʔ</u> nwaʔha·dyé·æʔ (LG09).

waʔ-ha-atho·y-aʔ	wadęʔ	n-waʔ-ha-ad-yeR-aʔ
FACT-3M.SG.A-tell-PNC	INTR	PRT-FACT-3M.SG.A-SRF-do-PNC
he told	what	thus he did it

He told us what he had done.

(42) …waʔtgaihwayędaʔnháʔ <u>sų́·</u> nęhajisdę́hdaʔ (HW07).

waʔ-t-ga-Rihw-a-yęd-aʔ-nhaʔ	sų	n-ę-ha-jisd-ęhd-aʔ
FACT-DL-3N/Z.SG.A-matter-JN-place-INCH-PNC	INTR	PRT-FUT-3M.SG.A-fire-drop-PNC
it was agreed	who	how he will drop the fire

… they agreed on who will toss the fire [into the tree].

(43) …dęgaihwayę·dáʔnhaʔ, <u>do· nyų́</u> ęhá·gwaʔ, neʔ ęhatgwé·nyaʔ (HW04).

d-ę-ga-Rihw-a-yęd-aʔ-nhaʔ	do	nyų	ę-ha-gw-aʔ
DL-FUT-3N/Z.SG.A-matter-JN-place-INCH-PNC	INT	AMT	FUT-3M.SG.A-accomplish-PNC
it will be decided	how	amount	he accomplishes it

neʔ	ę-h-at-gweny-aʔ
NOM	FUT-3M.SG.A-SRF-be.able-PNC
the	he will win

It will be decided how much the winner must accumulate.

(44) Hya deʔswagá·haʔs, <u>do nigę́</u> nhwaʔwéʔ seʔ góʔ hyaʔ ęhagwá dewęʔnyaʔé neʔ degrís (LG12).

hya	deʔ-s-wag-a·haʔ-s	do·	nigę	n-h-waʔ-w-e-ʔ
NEG	NEG-REP-1SG.P-remember-HAB	INTR	EXT	PRT-TRNS-FACT-3N/Z.SG.A-walk-PNC
not	I don't remember	how	extent	there it went

seʔ	go·ʔ	hyaʔ	ęhagwa	dewęʔnyaʔe	neʔ	degrees
MOD	CTR	MOD	DIR	NUMBER	NOM	NOUN
actually	however	indeed	other side = beyond	one hundred	the	degrees

I don't remember just how far [the temperature] went, but likely it was over 100 degrees.

(45) … nhehawé·nų, hya sų gá·ʔ deʔagonųhdų́ʔ <u>gaę nų́</u> nihéʔs, nęgę́ ų́hgęʔ (LG09).

n-he-haw-e-nų	hya	sų ga·ʔ	deʔ-ago-ęnųhdų-ʔ	gaę nų
PRT-TRNS-3M.SG.P-walk-STV	NEG	INTR IND	NEG-3FI.P-know-STV	INTR LOC-C
he has gone away	not	somebody	they don't know	where

ni-h-e-ʔs	nęgę ųhgęʔ
PRT-3M.SG.A-walk-HAB	DEM TMP
he is around	at present

… he's gone away, and nobody knows where he is now.

An embedded questions can occur as a constituent of an argument clause. In (46) *ahatho·yá?* 'for him to tell' *wadę? oí·hwa? nęgę tsha? nwa?ha·yǽ·?* 'why he did it' is an argument clause containing a reason clause of *tcihahsá? hya tha·hųwanakdothás* 'at first they didn't give him a chance' (the clause structure is marked by square brackets):

(46) …tcihahsá? hya tha·hųwanakdothás [ahatho·yá?, [wadę́? oí·hwa? nęgę́ tsha? nwa?ha·yéæ?]] (LG09).

tci-hahsa?	hya	th-aa-hųwa-nakd-ot-has-Ø	aa-ha-atho-y-a?
COIN-TMP	NEG	CONT-OPT-3 > 3M.SG-space-set.up-BEN-PNC	OPT-3M.SG.A-tell-PNC
at first	not	they didn't give him a chance	for him to tell

wadę?	o-Rihw-a?	nęgę	n-wa?-ha-yeR-a?
INTR	NPF-matter-NSF	DEM	PRT-FACT-3M.SG.A-do-PNC
what	the reason	this	thus he did it

…at first they didn't give him a chance to tell why [lit., the reason] *he had done it.*

Just as words and phrases can occur between a main verb and its clausal argument, so can they occur between the main verb and an embedded question. In (47) *sgadahá* 'even once' occurs between the main verb and the embedded question:

(47) Hya go·? ni?á de?ųgahędų́? sgadahá nwádę? nwa?awę́ha?da?… (LG13)

hya	go?	ne?	i? = á	de?-ųg-ahę-dų-?	sgada = há
NEG	CTR	NOM	PRON = DIM	NEG-3 > 1SG-ask.someone-STV	NUMBER = DIM
not	however	the	I/we = only	they didn't ask me	even one [time]

nwadę?	n-wa?-aw-ęh-a-?d-a?
INTR	PRT-FACT-3N/Z.SG.P-happen-CS-PNC
what	it caused it to happened

But they didn't ask me, even once, what caused it to happen…

And the interrogative particle need not occur immediately next to the main verb of the embedded question clause: In (48) the modal particle *hų* separates the interrogative particle *do* from the counting expression that describes the questioned expression:

(48) Hya de?wagęnųhdų́? do hų nigahwisdagé deyagohwisdáųh (LG17).

hya	de?-wag-ęnųhdų-?	do	hų	ni-ga-hwisd-a-ge-h'
NEG	NEG-1SG.P-know-STV	INT	MOD	PART-3N/Z.SG.A-money-JN-amount.to-STV
not	I don't know	how	perhaps	the amount of money it is

de-yago-hwisd-a-ųh
CIS-FACT-3FI.P-money-JN-take.hold.of-STV
she got money

I don't know how much money she got.

<u>Embedded polar questions</u>: In (49) the question particle *khę* is the second constituent of the embedded question:

(49) Hya deʔwagęnųhdų́ʔ otgųhsotshǽ·ʔ khę hų́ neʔ wadá neʔ hagahíʔge (LG24).

hya	deʔ-wag-ęnųhdų-ʔ	o-atgųhsotshR-aʔ	khę	hų	neʔ
NEG	NEG-1SG.P-know-STV	NPF-glass-NSF	QUE	MOD	NOM
not	I don't know	glass	question	maybe	the

w-ada-h	neʔ	ha-gahR-iʔ = ge
3N/Z.SG.A-inside-STV	NOM	3M.SG.A-eye-NSF-LOC
it is inside	the	his eye

I don't know, whether he has a glass eye [literally: is there glass maybe inside his eye?].

Embedded alternative questions: Examples (50) and (51) contain alternative questions (section 7.10.2); the former describes two hypothetical situations: 'has she stolen the chicken or has she bought it?', and the latter questions the truth or falsehood of a single situation, 'is it a good gun or not?':

(50) Hya deʔwagęnųhdų́ʔ nęgę onęsgwę́· khę hų́ neʔ gitgít gayaʔdęhawí gaʔt khę ohni·nų́h (LG06).

hya	deʔ-wag-ęnųhdų-ʔ	nęgę	o-nęsgw-ęh	khę	hų	neʔ	gitgit
NEG	NEG-1SG.P-know-STV	DEM	3FZ.SG.P-steal-STV	QUE	MOD	NOM	NOUN
not	I don't know	this	she has stolen it	question	maybe	the	chicken

ga-yaʔd-ęhawi-h		gaʔd	khę	o-hninų-h´
3FZ.SG.A-body-carry.in.one's.hands-STV		HYP	QUE	3FZ.SG.P-buy-STV
she is holding it in her hands		or if	question	she has bought it

I don't know, has she stolen it, this chicken she is holding in her hand, or has she bought it?

(51) …hya deʔhonęnúhdų́ʔ, dogę́s khę hų́·, gahsųwiyó gaʔd khę hiyáh (LG17).

hya	deʔ-hon-ęnųhdų-ʔ	dogęs	khę	hų	ga-hsųR-iyo-h'
NEG	NEG-3M.NSG.P-know-STV	MOD	QUE	MOD	3N/Z.SG.A-gun-be.good-STV
not	they don't know	it's true	is it?	maybe	good gun

gaʔt khę	hiyah
INDF QUE	NEG
or is it?	not

…they don't know whether it is a good gun or not.

7.5 Relative Clauses

In languages like English, relative clauses function as nominal modifiers. In the Iroquoian languages, relative clauses are headless. They do not function as modifiers. Rather, they supplement information about a semantic argument of a main verb just like any other external nominal expression does. In Onondaga, relative clauses are either (i) internally headed – these are clauses composed of verbal expressions that function as nominals; or (ii) free relatives – these are clauses that either supplement information about a semantic argument of the main verb or provide situational information regarding time, space, or manner; or (iii) relative-correlative constructions. There is no restriction on the order of occurrence between main verb and relative clause, although preposed relative clauses are much less frequent than are ones that follow the main verb.

7.5.1 Internally Headed Relative Clauses

An internally headed relative clause is one in which the entire clause denotes an entity. Typically, such a constituent can function as a verb in one context and as a nominal in another. For example, the verb form *ęhatgwé·nyaʔ* can mean 'he will win' in one context, and 'the one who will be the winner' in another (as in example 52). When a verb form like this functions as a relative clause, it is often preceded by the nominal particle *neʔ*, or less frequently, by either one of the demonstratives. Note also that the relative clause in a number of these examples contains an incorporated noun.

(52) …dęgaihwayę·dáʔnhaʔ, do· nyų̀ ęhá·gwaʔ, <u>neʔ ęhatgwé·nyaʔ</u> (HW04).

d-ę-ga-Rihw-a-yęd-aʔ-nhaʔ	do	nyų
DL-FUT-3N/Z.SG.A-matter-JN-place-INCH-PNC	INT	AMT
it will be decided	how	amount

ę-ha-gw-aʔ	neʔ	ę-h-at-gweny-aʔ
FUT-3M.SG.A-accomplish-PNC	NOM	FUT-3M.SG.A-SRF-be.able-PNC
he accomplishes it	the	he will win / the winner

It will be decided how much the winner must accumulate.

(53) Ogayų́ neʔ <u>waʔonųhsadé·gaʔ</u>.

o-gayų-h	neʔ	waʔ-o-nųhs-adeg-aʔ
3N/Z.SG.P-old-STV	NOM	FACT-3N/Z.SG.P-house-burn-PNC
it's old	the	[the] house burned

The house that burned down was old.

Example (54) contains two internally headed relative clauses in apposition: both *hadáʔ* 'the one who is standing' and *haʔwasdę́hwaʔ* 'the one holding sticks' refer to the same participant. The contrastive particle cluster *nęgę neʔ naʔ* 'this [other] one' disambiguates the two third person masculine participants marked by the verb's pronominal prefix, as indicated by the subscripts in the translation:

(54) Nę gó·ʔ hyaʔ nęgę́ naʔ waʔhoʔnigųhæhnih·dáʔ <u>nęgę́ neʔ ná̧ʔ hadáʔ haʔwasdę́hwaʔ</u>. (HW07)

onę	go·ʔ	hyaʔ	nęgę	naʔ	waʔ-ho-ʔnigųhR-a-hniR-hd-aʔ
TMP	CTR	MOD	DEM	ASRT	FACT-3M.SG > 3M.SG-mind- JN-sturdy-JN-CS-PNC
then	however	indeed	this	it's	he$_i$ gave him$_j$ confidence

nęgę neʔ naʔ	ha-d-aʔ	ha-ʔwasd-ęhw-aʔ
CONTRASTIVE	3M.SG.A-stand-STV	3M.SG.A-stick-hold-STV
this [other] one$_j$	he's$_j$ standing / the one standing	he's$_j$ holding sticks / the one holding sticks

But actually this is [how] he$_i$ gives him$_j$ confidence, this standing one$_j$, the one$_j$ holding the sticks.

(55) Hya go·ʔ naʔ deʔu̲gwanasgwáye̲ʔ, <u>neʔ e̲yu̲khinasgwané̲sgwaʔ</u> (LG06).

hya	go·ʔ	naʔ	deʔ-u̲gwa-nasgw-a-ye̲-ʔ	neʔ	e̲-yu̲khi-nasgw-ne̲sgw-aʔ
NEG	CTR	ASRT	NEG-1PL.P-pet-JN-have-STV	NOM	FUT-3 > 1NSG-pet-steal-PNC
not	however	it's	we don't have pets	the	she/they will steal a pet from us

But actually we don't have pets, ones she might steal.

Clauses specifying numbers of objects as in (56) also function as internally headed relative clauses that are adjoined to the main verb (Koenig & Michelson 2009, 2010c):

(56) E̲hayáʔk oʔ ne̲gé̲, <u>hwíks nigahu̲dagéh</u> (HW07).

e̲-ha-yaʔk-Ø	oʔ	ne̲ge̲	hwiks	ni-ga-hu̲d-a-ge-h'
FUT-3M.SG.A-cut-PNC	ADD	DEM	NUM	PRT-3N/Z.SG.A-whip-JN-amount.to-STV
he will cut	also	this	five	that number of whips

Also, he should cut five whips [Literally, he should cut, whips that number five].

7.5.2 Free Relative Clauses

Free relative clauses may be preceded by (i) *tshaʔ gáye̲ʔ* 'the one who' marking animate referents, (ii) by *tshaʔ* followed by one of the classifier particles, e.g., *tshaʔ nu̲* 'the place' where, *tshaʔ nigé̲* 'the extent of *time/place that*', etc., or (iii) by *tshaʔ* followed by one of a small number of verbs that take the partitive prepronominal prefix obligatorily, e.g., *.e̲h-/.e̲ʔ-/.yaʔdawe̲h-/.we̲h-* + partitive 'happen', *.athawi-/.at-N-e̲hawi-* + partitive 'time passing', etc., referring to referents that do not fit into the classes marked by classifiers. In the examples below the relative clauses are underlined.

(i) Free relatives with *tshaʔ gáye̲ʔ* 'the one that':

(57) Oyáʔ né̲ʔ waʔeyenáʔ <u>tshaʔ gáye̲ʔ shago·nú̲hgwaʔ</u> (LG17).

(y)-oyaʔ-aʔ		ne̲ʔ	waʔ-e-yena-ʔ´	tshaʔ gaye̲ʔ
3N/Z.SG.A-different-STV	NOM	NOM	FACT-3FI.A-accept-PNC	REL
it is different		the	she got it	the one who

shago-nu̲hgw-aʔ
3M.SG > 3-have.relatives-STV
his relative(s)

A different one got [the house], the one who was his relative.

In example (58) the *tshaʔ gayé̲ʔ* clause occurs before the main clause verb:

(58) Naʔ hyaʔ neʔ <u>tshaʔ gáye̲ʔ shu̲gwanasgwawí</u> hoge̲he̲níhgwaʔ, ... (LG24)

naʔ	hyaʔ	neʔ	tshaʔ gaye̲ʔ	shu̲gwa-nasgw-awi-h'
ASRT	MOD	NOM	REL	3M.SG > 1PL-pet-give-STV
it's	indeed	the	the one who	he has given us a pet

ho-ge̲he̲ni-k-gwaʔ
3M.SG > 3M.SG-abuse-HAB-HBPST
he used to abuse him

The one who gave us the pet, used to abuse him [the pet]...

(ii) Free relatives with *tsha?* and a classifier particle:

tsha? and the locative classifier:

(59) Na? nẹgẹ́ nẹ̆· e?dẹ̆·? na? tsha? thosgẹha, ne? <u>tsha? nṵ· dyagoyó?de?</u> (LG07).

na?	nẹgẹ	nẹ	e-i?dẹ̆·?	na? tsha?	thosgẹha	ne?
ASRT	DEM	LOC	3FI.A-reside-STV	ASRT SUB	LOC	NOM
it's	this	here	she is residing	because	close by	the

tsha?	nṵ	d-yago-yo?de-?
SUB	LOC	CIS-3FI.A-work-STV
that	place	she works here

She lives here with us because the place where she works is close by.

tsha? and the extent classifier:

(60) ...ẹhsa·dnṵhdṵ́?da? <u>tsha? nigẹ́ ẹya·gwadéhs?a?</u> (CTL96.7).

ẹ-hs-adnṵhdṵ?d-a?	tsha?	nigẹ	ẹ-yagw-ad-ehs?-a?
FUT-2SG.A-wait-PNC	SUB	EXT	FUT-1EX.PL.A-SRF-finish-PNC
you will wait	that	extent	we will get ready

...you will wait until [the time that] *we are ready*

tsha? and the amount classifier:

(61) Na? di? hya? nẹgẹ́ Dorothy, hya sṵ gá? de?agonṵhdṵ́? <u>tsha? niyṵ́ gó? dyẹ</u>
    <u>wa?ehninṵnyṵ́? iyéks</u>[24] (LG08).

na?	di?	hya?	nẹgẹ	Dorothy	hya	sṵ ga?	de?-ago-ẹnṵhdṵ-?	tsha?
ASRT	LINK	MOS	DEM	NAME	NEG	INT IND	NEG-3FI.P-know-STV	SUB
it's	so	indeed	this	Dorothy	not	someone	they didn't know	that

niyṵ	go·?	dyẹ	wa?-e-hninṵ-nyṵ·?	i-ye-k-s
AMT	CTR	HYP	FACT-3FI.A-buy-DST-PNC	EP-3FI.A-eat-HAB
amount	however	perhaps	she bought several times	food / they eat it

So as to Dorothy, no one knew the number of times she bought food.

tsha? and the manner classifier:

(62) Onẹ dí? dẹga·dá?nha? <u>tsha? niyót</u> odi·hwahdẹ·dyṵ́ ne?tho ṵhwẹ·jyá·de? hehdá?ge?
    nwa?gaẹhyádi?... (CTL30.2-4)

onẹ	di?	de-ga-d-a?-nha?	tsha?	niyot
TMP	LNK	DL-3N/Z.SG.A-stand-INCH-PNC	SUB	MAN
now	moreover	it will stop	that	how it is

o-ad-Rihw-ahdẹdyṵ-h'	ne?tho	Ø-ṵhwẹjy-ade-?	hehda?ge
3N/Z.SG.P-SRF-matter-move.on-STV	LOC	3N/Z.SG.A-earth-exist-STV	DIR
it is functioning	here	[on] earth	below

---

[24] Note that the verb form *iyéks* 'food [= what they eat] / they eat it' is an internally headed relative clause.

n-wa?-ga-Rųhy-adi-?
PRT-FACT-3N/Z.SG.A-sky-be.a.side.of-STV
side of the sky
Now it will stop how things are functioning here on earth, beneath the sky.

(iii) Free relatives with *tsha?* and a verb that requires the partitive prepronominal prefix:

(63) Na? gęs ne? nę· ųgwę·nų́hdų?, <u>tsha? niga·hawí? dę́the?, ęshá·yų?</u> (HW02).

na?	gęs	ne? nę	ųgw-ęnųhdų-?	tsha?	ni-ga-hawi-?
ASRT	CST	NOM TMP	1PL.P-know-STV	SUB	PRT-3N/Z.SG.A-carry-STV
it's	usually	when	we know	that	it's time for it

d-ę-t-h-e-?	ę-s-ha-yų-?
DL-FUT-CIS-3M.SG.A-walk-PNC	FUT-REP-3M.SG.A-arrive-PNC
he will come back	he will return home

Usually, that's when we know it's time for him to get back home [literally: the time that he will come back, returning home].

(64) Wa?hęhę́·? yágę?, ęgųyatho·yę́? <u>tsha? nęhcyé·æ?</u> (HW07).

wa?-ha-ihę-?'	yagę?	ę-gųy-atho·y-ę-?	tsha?
FACT-3M.SG.A-say-PNC	HRSY	FUT-1SG > 2SG-tell-BEN-PNC	SUB
he said	they say	I will tell you	what

n-ę-hs-yeR-a?
PRT-FUT-2SG.A-do-PNC
thus you will do it

He says, "I will tell you what to do."

(65) …na? gęs honathowíh <u>tsha? niya·wę́?ih, ne? thóhge</u> (LG20).

na?	gęs	hon-athowi-h'	tsha?	ni-yaw-ę?-ih	ne? thogę
ASRT	CST	3M.NSG.P-tell-STV	SUB	PART-3N/Z.SG.P-happen-STV	NOM TMP
it's	usually	they are telling	what	thus it happened	at that time

…usually they were talking about what happened in those times [lit: the way that it happened]

(66) Dahadadyá? wa?hęhę́·? hya go·? hya? na? hé? í? de?wa·gí·hwa?, <u>tsha? nigya?do?dę́h.</u> (EO01)

d-a-ha-adady-a?	wa?-ha-ihę·?'	hya	go·?	hya?	na?
CIS-FACT-3M.SG.A-answer-PNC	FACT-3M.SG.A-say-PNC	NEG	CTR	MOD	ASRT
he answered	he said	not	however	indeed	it's

ne?	í?	de?-wag-Rihw-a?	tsha?	ni-g-ya?d-o?dę-h'
NOM	PRON	NEG-1SG.P-matter-NSF	SUB	PRT-1SG.A-body-kind-STV
the	I/we	it isn't my fault	that	the kind of body I have

He answered, [and] said, "But it isn't my fault what I look like [literally, the kind of body I have]."

7.5.3 Relative-Correlative Constructions

Michelson et al. (2016) and Koenig & Michelson (2014) describe a relative-correlative construction that is frequent in Oneida, but less so in Onondaga. Relative-correlative constructions consist of two clauses that share an element – in Onondaga that element appears to be confined to location expressions (sec. 7.6.1); one clause describes a situation in a given location and begins in *tho nų* 'that's where', and the other is a free relative beginning in *tshaʔ nų* 'the place where' or *tshaʔ* and a verb with locative prepronominal prefixes. The two clauses can occur in either order.

(67) …naʔ dę·dyéʔ nęgé tshaʔ nų ganųhsayéʔ neʔ hodiksdęʔá <u>tshaʔ nų</u>
<u>hodinųhsayę·dáhgwaʔ, tho nų ęshadiyaʔdá·ʔnhaʔ</u> (LG18).

naʔ	d-ę-d-yę-e-ʔ		nęgę	tshaʔ nų	ga-nųhs-a-yę-ʔ		neʔ
ASRT	DL-FUT-CIS-3FI.A-walk-PNC		DEM	SUB LOC	3N/Z.SG.A-house-JN-lie-STV		NOM
it's	someone will come back		this	place where	house		the

hodi-ksdęʔa-h		tshaʔ nų	hodi-nųhs-a-yęd-ahgwaʔ		tho	nų
3M.NSG.P-be.old-STV		SUB LOC	3M.NSG.P-house-JN-have-HBPST		LOC	LOC
old folks		place where	they used to have their home		there	place

ę-s-hadi-yaʔda·ʔ-nhaʔ
FUT-REP-3M.PL.A-join.in-PNC
they will come back together

…they'll return to the place where there's a house, the old folks, the place where they used to have their home, that's the place where they'll get together again.

(68) Naʔ diʔ hyaʔ niʔá neʔ, <u>tho nhwaʔgéʔ tshaʔ thanagé·ʔ</u> nęgé neʔ, ęhm, justice-of-peace hyaʔ ų· hayá·jih (LG06).

naʔ	diʔ	hyaʔ	neʔ	iʔ = á	neʔ	tho	n-h-waʔ-g-e-ʔ
ASRT	LINK	MOD	NOM	PRN-DIM	NOM	LOC	PRT-TRNS-FACT-1SG.A-walk-PRP
it's	so	indeed	the	I, alone	the	there	I went there

tshaʔ	t-ha-nage·-ʔ		nęgę	neʔ	ęhm	hyaʔ	ų·
SUB	CIS-3M.SG.A-dwell-STV		DEM	NOM	FILLER	MOD	MOD
that	where he lives		this	the	ah	indeed	probably

justice of the peace	ha-yas-ih
NOMINAL	3M.SG.A-be.named-STV
justice of the peace	he is called

As for me, I went to the place where the Justice of the Peace resided.

(69) Nęgé, <u>tho nų goyoʔdéʔ tshaʔ nų neʔ dry cleaning plant</u> (LG07).

nęgę	tho	nų	go-yoʔde-ʔ	tshaʔ	nų	neʔ	dry-cleaning plant
DEM	LOC	LOC	3FI.A-work-STV	SUB	LOC	NOM	NOUN
this	there	place	she is working	that	place	the	dry-cleaning plant

The place where she's working is the place where there's the dry-cleaning plant.

7.6 Clauses with Location and Time Expressions

7.6.1 Location Expressions

In chapter 4, section 4.7.2 the functions and distribution of the translocative and cislocative prepronominal prefixes are discussed. They mark location, directionality, or relative proximity to a reference point, depending on the class of verb with which they occur. These prefixes function to modify the meanings of the verb stems to which they are attached. The discussion in the present section concerns expressions that specify locational properties of the clause as a whole.

In Onondaga, location is expressed as a kind of participant by the following types of noun forms or nominals: (i) expressions with deictic location particles; (ii) a noun form; (iii) a nominal expression that includes a positional verb; (iv) a free relative that includes a locative particle (see also the discussion in section 7.5.2 above); (v) expressions with particles that reference specific locations; (vi) a location expression that functions as an argument clause. All of these may be preceded by the nominal particle *neʔ*, either one of the demonstrative particles, or the nominal particle and a demonstrative particle, just like regular externally occurring nouns or nominals (sec.7.3.3).

(i) <u>Expressions with deictic locative particles</u> (*neʔtho / tho*, the distance-neutral locative 'here / there'; *thonę / nę* 'here'; *sígę / sí·* 'over there, yonder'): The example in (70b) shows that the location deictics can occur with classes of verbs other than motion verbs. The locative particle may occur before or after the verb it modifies, although it is much more frequent before the verb. The particle-plus-verb sequence may also be interrupted by other constituents as shown in (70d):

(70) a. ...waʔhęhę·ʔ sų́· nwahoʔdę? <u>dashejyadęnyéhdaʔ</u> <u>neʔtho</u>... (CTL205.8)

waʔ-ha-ihę·-ʔ'	sų·	nwahoʔdę?	d-a-shejy-adęnyehd-aʔ	neʔtho
FACT-3M.SG.A-say-PNC	INTR	INTR	CIS-FACT-3M.SG > 2DU-send-PNC	LOC
he said	who	what	he sent you two	here/there

...who sent you here...?

  b. Naʔ óʔ dogá·ʔ nihodi·yó <u>thonę́h</u> (LG20).

naʔ	oʔ	doga·ʔ	ni-hodi-Ryo-h'	thonę
ASRT	ADD	QNT	PRT-3M.NSG.P-kill-STV	LOC
it's	also	a few	it has killed them	here

It (the epidemic) killed several [persons] here.

  c. ...onę si <u>hwaʔhayę́ʔ</u> honųnawę́ʔdaʔ (CTL204.3-4).

onę	si	h-waʔ-ha-yę-ʔ'	ho-nųnawę́ʔd-aʔ
TMP	LOC	TRNS-FACT-3M.SG.A-place-PNC	3M.SG.P-pipe-NSF
then	over there	he placed it	his pipe

Then he placed his pipe aside.

d. Seʔá gwaʔ go·ʔ, <u>tho</u> naʔ <u>dųdayųgniʔsé·ʔgeh</u> (LG03).

seʔ=á	gwaʔ	go·ʔ	tho	naʔ	d-ųda-yųgni-ʔse·-ʔ-geh
MOD=DIM RSTR	CTR		LOC	ASRT	DL-CIS:FACT-1DU.P-drag-PNC=LOC
in fact		however	there	it's	we drove through there

Actually though, we did drive through there.

(ii) <u>Noun forms</u>: Location expressions composed of morphological nouns are suffixed with either the internal locative suffix or the external locative clitic as in (71a and b). Place names and borrowed location terms as in (72) occur without these. Location nouns can occur before or after the main verb:

(71) Noun forms with (a) internal locative suffix and (b) external locative clitic:
a. Naʔ óʔ <u>neʔ onųdaguwá</u> thoyęthwíh… (LG02)

naʔ	oʔ	neʔ	o-nųd-agųwa	t-ho-yęthw-ih
ASRT	ADD	NOM	NPF-hill-LOC	CIS-3M.SG.P-plant-STV
it's	also	the	below the hill	he has planted it there

He's also planted it there below the hill…

b. Ųnisʔíh diʔ naʔ nęgę <u>neʔ ganedáʔge</u>, hona·dnadayędáhgwaʔ (LG06).

ųnisʔih	diʔ	naʔ	nęgę	neʔ	ga-ned-aʔ=ge
TMP	LINK	ASRT	DEM	NOM	NPF-rise-NSF=LOC
past time	moreover	it's	this	the	on the rise

hon-ad-nad-a-yęd-ahgwaʔ
3M.NSG.P-SRF-village-JN-place-HABPST
they used to make camp

Some time ago, they made camp on the hill [above us].

(72) Place names (a) and borrowed location terms from English (b-c):
a. Thohge ó·nę dwagahdędyú <u>neʔ ganyéʔge</u>[25] (CTL170.6).

thohge	onę	d-wag-ahdędyų-h'	neʔ	ganyéʔge
TMP	TMP	CIS-1SG.P-depart-STV	NOM	NAME
thereafter		I departed from there	the	Mohawk Territory

Then I departed from Mohawk Territory.

b. …naʔ diʔ hyaʔ <u>saikhyús</u> ųgéʔse·k, ųgadeʔnyędęʔ gó·ʔ hyaʔ do· nihgahiyóh (LG10).

naʔ	diʔ	hyaʔ	saikhyus	waʔ-wag-eʔse·-ʔ	waʔ-wag-adeʔnyędę-ʔ
ASRT	LINK	MOD	NAME	FACT-1SG.P-drive-PNC	FACT-1SG.P-try-PNC
it's	so	indeed	Syracuse	I drove	I was tested

go·ʔ	hyaʔ	do	ni-k-gahR-iyo-h'
CTR	MOD	INTR	PRT-1SG.A-eye(s)-be.good-STV
however	indeed	how	how good my eyes are

…so I drove to Syracuse [and] had my eyes tested [literally: so I drove to Syracuse, I was tested how good my eyes are].

---

[25] *ganyéʔge* is no longer analyzable. It is thought to mean 'flint place'. The final syllable is probably the locative clitic =*ge*.

c. Ihswáʔ honų̄hwakdę́ <u>neʔ hospital</u> (LG05).

ihswaʔ	ho-nų̄hwakd-ę-h'	neʔ	hospital
QNT	3M.SG.P-hurt-BEN-STV	NOM	NOUN
a lot	he was ill	the	hospital

He was very ill in the hospital.

(iii) <u>Location expressions that include a positional verb</u>: These may be preceded by the *tshaʔ* subordinator particle or a locative particle and they may be inflected with the cislocative to indicate a location. Typically, the main verb is a motion verb of some sort. As the examples show, the location expression may precede or follow the main verb:

(73) a. Ę̄hsgwe·nyá́ʔ hę̄hcyų́ʔ <u>tshaʔ tgana̧ʔahgá·deʔ</u> (HW07).

ę-hs-gweny-aʔ	h-ę-hs-yų-ʔ	tshaʔ	t-ga-naʔahgaR-ade-ʔ
FUT-2SG.A-can.do-PNC	TRNS-FUT-2SG.A-arrive-PNC	SUB	CIS-3N/Z.SG.A-shore-exist-STV
you'll be able to do it	you'll get there	that	at the shore

You'll be able to get to the shore

b. ...si· <u>nwaʔgą̄ehyadéʔ</u> thawehdíh... (HW07)

si·	n-waʔ-ga-Rę̄hy-ade-ʔ	t-haw-e-hd-íh
LOC	PRT-FACT-3N/Z.SG.A-sky-exist-PNC	CIS-3M.SG.P-walk-CS-STV
far away	where the sky is	he has come from there

...he has come from the far side of the sky...

c. Nę̄ waʔeyǽthę́ʔ <u>tshaʔ wadekhwahǽ·tcedaʔ</u> (LG09).

nę	waʔ-e-Rǽthę-ʔ	tshaʔ	w-ade-khw-a-hR-atshR-od-'aʔ
TMP	FACT-3FI.A-climb.up-PNC	SUB	3N/Z.SG.A-SRF-food-JN-put.on-NOM-stand.up-NSF[26]
then	she climbed up	that	table

She climbed up on the table

d. ... waʔhayų́ʔ <u>tshaʔ gana̧ʔahga·déʔ</u>... (HW07)

waʔ-ha-yų-ʔ	tshaʔ	ga-naʔahgaR-ade-ʔ
FACT-3M.SG.A-arrive-PNC	SUB	3N/Z.SG.A-shore-exist-STV
he arrived	that	at the shore

...he arrived at the shore...

(iv) <u>Location expressions formed from relative clauses</u> (secs. 7.5.1-7.5.3):

(a) With internally headed relative clauses: In (74) the internally headed relative clause is composed of the nominal particle and the location verb *-ada-* 'be inside':

(74) Hya deʔwagę̄nų̄hdų́ʔ otgų̄hsotshǽ·ʔ khę̄ hų́ <u>neʔ wadá</u> neʔ hagahíʔgeh (LG24).

hya	deʔ-wag-ę̄nų̄hdų-ʔ	o-atgų̄hsotshR-aʔ	khę̄	hų	neʔ
NEG	NEG-1SG.P-know-STV	NPF-glass-NSF	QUE	MOD	NOM
not	I don't know	glass	question	maybe	the

---

[26] Because the prefix is verbal and there is no nominalizer after the verb root, the suffix might also be analyzed as a stative aspect suffix.

    w-ada-h   ne?   ha-gahR-i?=ge
    3N/Z.SG.A-inside-STV   NOM   3M.SG.A-eye-NSF-LOC
    it is inside   the   his eye

I don't know if he has a glass eye? [Literally: I don't know, is the inside at his eye, glass?].

  (b) With free relatives: Note that in (75) the translocative prefixed to the main verb *hęjyáu̧·dę?* 'it will reattach there' and the cislocative prefixed to *dwa·gyá?kdih* 'I have ripped it off from there' allow us to interpret the expression as a whole as both a source and a goal argument. But the two prefixes have no syntactic function, they are a part of the lexical meanings of the verb forms.

(75) Ęhsa·de·yó? ahgwí hęjyáu̧·dę?, <u>ne? tsha? nu̧· dwa·gyá?kdih</u> (HW07).

    ę-hs-ade-Ryo-?   ahgwih   h-ę-s-ya-u̧d-ę?   ne?   tsha?
    FUT-2SG.A-SRF-kill-PNC   NEG   TRNS-FUT-REP-3N/Z.SG.P-attach-PNC   NOM   SUB
    you will fight   not   it will reattach to there   the   that

    nu̧·   d-wag-ya?k-d-ih
    LOC   CIS-1SG.P-break.off-CS-STV
    place   I have ripped it off from there

You will have to fight for it not to reattach to the place from which I ripped it off.

  (c) With relative-correlative constructions: Relative-correlative constructions contain two locative expressions.

(76) a. Tho nhęhsé? <u>tsha? tgęhyu̧hwadá·dye?</u> (HW07).

    tho   n-h-ę-hs-e-?   tsha?   t-ga-ihyu̧hw-d-adye-?
    LOC   PRT-TRNS-FUT-2SG.A-walk-PNC   SUB   CIS-3N/Z.SG.A-river-stand-PRG-PRP
    there   you will go there   where   at the flowing river

"You should go to the river."

  b. ...tho hwa?hęné? <u>tsha? disanu̧hsá·yę?</u> (EO01).

    tho   h-wa?-hęn-e-?   tsha?   di-sa-nu̧hs-a-yę-?
    LOC   TRNS-FACT-3M.PL.A-go-PRP   SUB   CIS-2SG.P-house-JN-lie-STV
    there   they are going there   where   at your house

They're going to your house.

  (v) <u>Expressions with particles that specify locations</u>: These include directions (left, right, outside, inside), locations in relation to other objects (above, beneath, nearby), and particles that reference specific locations (outdoors, indoors). All of these may oprtionally be marked with the nominal particle *ne?* just like external nouns.

(77) a. Onę dí? dęga·dá?nha? tsha? niyót odi·hwahdę·dyú̧ ne?tho u̧hwę·jyá·de? <u>hehdá?ge</u>
       <u>nwa?gaęhyádih</u>... (CTL30.2-4)

        onę   di?   de-ga-d-a?-nha?   tsha?   niyot
        TMP   LNK   DL-3N/Z.SG.A-stand-INCH-PNC   SUB   MAN
        now   moreover it will stop   that   how it is

o-ad-Rihw -h'   ne?tho Ø-ųhwęjy-ade-? hehda?ge
3N/Z.SG.P-SRF-matter-move.ON-STV LOC 3N/Z.SG.A-earth-exist-STV DIR
it is functioning   there [on] earth   beneath

n-wa?-ga-Rųhy-adi-?
PRT-FACT-3N/Z.SG.A-sky-side.of-STV
side of the sky
Now it will stop how things are functioning on earth, beneath the sky.

b. ...onę he? dųdahatgáthwa? <u>ne? hé?tgę</u> tsha? hegayę?gwaitgé?tha?... (CTL81.7-8)

onę he? d-ųda-h-atgathw-a?   ne? he?tgę tsha?
TMP REP DL-CIS:FACT-3M.SG.A-look.at-PNC NOM DIR   SUB
then again he looked at it   the above at

he-ga-yę?gwaR-itgę-?-t-ha?
TRNS-3N/Z.SG.A-smoke-emerge-INCH-INST-HAB
smoke hole
...then he looked again [from] above [through] the smoke hole...

c. ...thogę nęh ęhahe?dęsda? <u>ne? ásde hagwá</u>, osgų·da·nędagí nęha·?ó? <u>tsha? ne?</u>
<u>ha?gų́·wah</u>, ęhahsę·nyá? thogę ne? whistle... (LG24)

thogę nę ę-ha-hę?dę-sd-a?   ne? asde hagwa
DEM   TMP FUT-3M.SG.A-soft-CS-PNC NOM LOC   DIR
that   then he will soften it   the outside direction

o-sgųdaR-nędag-ih   n-ę-ha-R?o-?   tsha? ne? ha?gųwa
3N/Z.SG.P-bark-stick.to-STV PRT-FUT-3M.SG.A-notch-PNC SUB NOM DIR
bark sticks on   thus he will notch it   that the below

ę-ha-hsę·ny-a?   thogę ne? whistle
FUT-3M.SG.A-make-PNC DEM NOM LEX
he will make it   that   the whistle
...then he'll soak [off] the outside bark, notch the bottom, [and] make that [into] a
whistle...

d. Na? nęgę nę́· e?dę́·? na? tsha? <u>thosgę́hah</u>, ne? tsha? nų́· dyagoyó?de?. (LG07)

na?   nęgę nę e-i?dę·-?   na? tsha? thosgęha ne?
ASRT DEM PRES 3FI.A-reside-STV ASRT SUB LOC   NOM
it's   this here she is residing because close by the

tsha? nų   d-yago-yo?de-?
SUB   LOC CIS-3FI.A-work-STV
that   place she works here
She lives here because the place where she works is close by.

e. Da <u>akdá?</u> di? hya? nhesonenų́h (LG06).

da   akda? di?   hya? n-he-s-on-e-nųh'
LINK LOC   LINK MOD PRT-TRNS-REP-3FZ.NSG.P-walk-STV
so   nearby moreover indeed they have gone back there
So they went [somewhere] nearby [literally: so nearby is where they went].

f. Na? gwá? tsha? tho gó·? niyót <u>ne? akdá?</u> nihẹni?dẹ́·dụ?, hya?
honadadya?dagéhnhẹh (LG18).

na?	gwa?	tsha?	tho	go·?	niyot	ne?	akda?
ASRT	RSTR	SUB	MAN	CTR	MAN	NOM	LOC
it's	just	that	thus	however	how it is	the	nearby

ni-hẹn-i?dȩ̣·-dụ-?		hya?	hon-adad-ya?dagehnh-ẹh
PRT-3M.PL.A-reside-DST-STV		MOD	3M.NSG.P-REF-help-STV
thus they are residing severally		indeed	they are helping themselves

But actually, the way it is, they live nearby [in houses] that they take care of.

g. Nẹ tho gó·? wa?dya·gnithá·ẹ?, <u>ásdeh</u> (EO01).

nẹ tho	go·?	wa?-d-yagni-thaR-ẹ?	asdeh
PRES LOC	CTR	FACT-DL-1EX.DU.A-converse-PNC	LOC
right here	however	we two talked	outdoors

However, we two talked right here, outside.

(vi) <u>Location expressions that function as argument clauses:</u>

The cislocative prefix of *nidyawenụ́h* 'she's come from there' in (a) is a part of the verb
stem's lexical meaning. In (b) the location particle *tho* 'there' marks the location expression
ne? tho naụdahé? 'he would go there' whose meaning is further specified by the free
relative *tsha? nụ́ níkda?* 'the place where I was standing' (the relationships are marked with
square brackets):

(78) a. ...ẹhatdogá? <u>nẹ nụ· nidyawenụ́h</u> (HW07).

ẹ-h-atdog-a?		nẹ	nụ·	ni-d-yaw-e-nụh
FUT-3M.SG.A-notice-PNC		PRES	LOC	PRT-CIS-3FZ.SG.P-walk-STV
he will notice		here	place	she's come from there

...he'll realize she's left this place [literally, he'll realize it's this here place she's
come from].

b. [Hya de?hogwenyụ́] [[ne? tho naụdahé?] [tsha? nụ́ níkda?]]]... (LG13)

hya	de?-ho-gweny-ụh		ne?	tho	n-aụda-h-e-?
NEG	NEG-3M.SG.P-be.possible-STV		NOM	LOC	PRT-OPT:CIS-3M.SG.A-walk-PNC
not	he wasn't able [to do it]		the	there	he would come

tsha?	nụ	ni-k-d-a?
SUB	LOC	PRT-1SG.A-stand-STV
that	place	I'm standing

He wasn't able to come to where I was standing...

Apart from locative elements described in this section, there are numerous verb bases in
Onondaga that describe relative location. They are shown in Table 7.1, but are not further
discussed in this section. Inflected forms of all of them can be found in the Onondaga
Dictionary (Woodbury 2003).

Table 7.1 Relative location verbs

Verb	Type	Gloss
-R-/-aR-	v.a.	*put/be in*
-R-/-aR-	v.a.	*put/be on, apply*
-ada-	v.s.	*be inside*
.ade·- + partitive and dualic	v.s.	*be a distance between*
.adi- + partitive or repetitive	v.s.	*be on a side of something*
.adyeæʔt- / .adyeæʔd- + partitive	v.a.	*face a direction*
-akd-/-yaʔdakd-	v.s.	*be nearby, be beside*
.ahsęnų-/.hę– + coincident and dualic	v.s.	*be in the middle, between*
-akdųdye-/-yaʔdakdųdye-	v.m	*be alongside, in the vicinity*
.de- + cislocative	v.s.	*be a certain level*
.de- + coincident, dualic, and cislocative	v.s.	*be on the same level*
-Ręnyų-	v.s.	*be in various locations*
.ga·di- + repetitive	v.s.	*be on one side*
-hR-	v.a.	*put/be on top of something*
-hęd-/-hęt-	v.m.	*walk ahead, be in front of*
-hnaʔgę-	v.s.	*later, be behind*
-hnųdR-	v.a.	*follow behind something*
-yęne·hgw- hagwáh	v.s.	*be the right side*
.yęnoʔga·di- hagwáh	v.s.	*be the left side*
-yęsd-	v.s.	*be the right side*

7.6.2 Time Expressions

The discussion is divided into three parts:[27] (i) deictic expressions of time which relate events to the time of utterance (e.g., I saw her yesterday/last winter/last month); (ii) the expression of events in terms of non-deictic temporal divisions and cyclical events (e.g., he skates in the winter); (iii) expressions relating an event to situation-time (e.g., it rained while I slept).

(i) Deictic Expressions of Time:

Numerous particles and verb forms name recurring time periods that relate a situation to the time of utterance:[28]

(79) a. <u>Ahsedéh</u> seʔ waʔshagwaʔnųhdá·k, Tom Green (LG05).

ahsedeh	seʔ	waʔ-shagwa-ʔnųhdaR-k	Tom Green
TMP	MOD	FACT-1EX.PL > 3M.SG-bury-PNC	NAME
yesterday	actually	we buried him	Tom Green

Yesterday we actually buried Tom Green.

---

[27] Morphologically marked temporal dimensions relating to aspect and mode are discussed in section 4.2 above.

[28] Interestingly, in narratives, the deictic temporal particles *onę* 'now' and *thohge* 'then' are – with few exceptions – employed to mark discourse level information, rather than extra-linguistic context.

b. Onę gó·ʔ hyáʔ nęgę waʔhnihę́·ʔ, "Ęyo·hę́ʔnháʔ gó·ʔ hyaʔ tho nhę·dnéʔ" (HW07).

onę	go·ʔ	hyaʔ	nęgę	waʔ-hn-ihę̨·-ʔ'	ę-yo-Rhęʔ-nhaʔ
TMP	CTR	MOD	DEM	FACT-3M.DU.A-say-PNC	FUT-3N/Z.SG.P-become.day-PNC
now	however	indeed	this	they two said	tomorrow

go·ʔ	hyaʔ	tho	n-h-ę-dn-e-ʔ'
CTR	MOD	LOC	PRT-TRNS-FUT-1IN.DU.A-walk-PNC
however	indeed	there	thus you and I will go there

But then, indeed, these two say, "Tomorrow, we'll go there."

Some deictic expression of this kind may be modified with prepronominal prefixes and/or with demonstratives to distinguish repetitions of past or future time periods in relation to the speech event. For example:

Preceding period of past events: add cislocative and coincident:	ahsé·deh *yesterday*	tcidwahsé·deh *day before yesterday*
Following period of future events: add translocative and repetitive:	ęyo·hę́ʔnhaʔ *tomorrow*	hęjyo·hę́ʔnhaʔ *day after tomorrow'*

In (80a) the speaker uses the coincident and cislocative prefixes and the proximal demonstrative *nęgę* to reference the winter that immediately preceded the time of the speech event. In (80b) the translocative is used to mark a future event:

(80) a. Nęgę́ tcidyohsǽ·ʔ, gwas tshaʔ niwa·gá·haʔs, ayéę́ʔ tshaʔ niyotho·wéhgwaʔ, dę́ʔseʔ si niyų́ waʔoʔgę·díʔ... (LG03)

nęgę	tci-d-y-ohsR-aʔ	gwas	tshaʔ	ni-wag-a·haʔ-s
DEM	COIN-CIS-NPF-winter/year-NSF	INT	SUB	PRT-1SG.P-remember-HAB
this	last winter/year	very	that	I remember

ayeęʔ	tshaʔ	ni-yo-athowe-h-gwaʔ	dę́ʔseʔ	si	niyų
SIM	SUB	PRT-3N/Z.SG.P-be.cold-HAB-HBPST	CNJ	LOC	AMT
like	that	how cold it used to be	and	far	a lot

waʔ-o-aʔgę·di-ʔ
FACT-3N/Z.SG.P-snow-PNC
it snowed

I remember, this last winter, how cold it was and how much it snowed...

b. ...néʔtho hęya·gní·yų́ʔ neʔ hagyaʔdanų́hnaʔ neʔ ó·yaʔ hęjyo·hę́ʔnhaʔ (CTL280.7-8).

neʔtho	h-ę-yagni-yų-ʔ	neʔ	hag-yaʔd-a-nųhn-aʔ	neʔ
LOC	TRNS-FUT-1EX.DU-arrive-PNC	NOM	3M.SG > 1SG-body-JN-guard-STV	NOM
there	we two will arrive there	the	my deputy	the

(y)-oyaʔ	h-ę-s-yo-Rhęʔ-nhaʔ
3N/Z.SG.A-other-STV	TRNS-FUT-REP-3N/Z.SG.P-become.day-PNC
it is another	day after tomorrow

...my deputy and I will arrive there day after tomorrow.

To specify the present period or cycle of a repetitive event, the proximal demonstrative *nęgę* 'this one' or *nęgę́hah* 'this particular one' is used together with the name of the event as in (81). The demonstrative can occur before (a) or after (b) the event expression:

(81) a. Nayéʔ diʔ <u>nęgę́ wędá·deʔ</u> onę sagní·yųʔ (CTL23.4-5).

nayeʔ	diʔ		nęgę	w-ęd-ade-ʔ		onę	s-a-gni-yų-ʔ
ASRT	LNK		DEM	3N/Z.SG.A-day-exist-STV		TMP	REP-FACT-3FZ.DU.A-arrive-PNC
it's	moreover		this	day		now	they returned home

So today, the two [women] returned home.

b. <u>Tshaʔ niyogęhnhanóh naʔ nęgę́hah</u>, hya gwas deʔodiyanę·ʔsé neʔ Clifford hoyęthwáhųʔ (LG02).

tshaʔ	ni-yo-gęhnh-a-no-h		naʔ	nęgęhah		yah	gwas
SUB	PRT-3N/Z.SG.P-sumer-JN-cold-STV		ASRT	DEM		NEG	INTS
that	it's a cold summer		it's	this particular one		not	very

deʔ-odi-yanę·-ʔse-h'		neʔ	Clifford	ho-yęthw-a-hų-ʔ
NEG-3FZ.NSG.P-good-BEN-STV		NOM	NAME	3M.SG.P-plant-JN-DST-STV
it wasn't good for them		the	Clifford	he has planted [things]

This summer it's been cold [and] it hasn't been good for Clifford's garden.

A number expression and one of several ways to mark past time are used to specify a particular number of years in the past. Two approaches are shown in (82):

(82) a. Onę hyáʔ ų <u>deyohsæ·gé tshaʔ nwaʔųnísheʔ</u>, nęgę́ tho nidyawę́ʔi, nęgę́ neʔ hęgwéh waʔsha·gó·yoʔ, neʔ hé·naʔ, aʔshá·ʔ waʔhásdaʔ (LG09).

onę	hyaʔ	ų	de-y-ohsR-a-ge-h´		tshaʔ	nwaʔųnisheʔ
TMP	MOD	MOD	DL-3N/Z.SG.A-winter-JN-amount.to-STV		SUB	TMP
Now	indeed	probably	it is two years		that	how long ago

nęgę	tho	ni-d-yaw-ęʔ-ih		nęgę	neʔ	hR-ųgweh
DEM	MAN	PRT-CIS-3N/Z.SG.P-happen-STV		DEM	NOM	3M.SG.A-man:SUFF
this	thus	thus it happened here		this	the	man

waʔ-shago-Ryo-ʔ		neʔ	he·naʔ	(w)-aʔshaR-ʔ[29]	waʔ-ha-sd-aʔ
FACT-3M.SG > 3-kill-PNC		NOM	NOUN	NPF-knife-NSF	FACT-3M.SG.A-use-PNC
he killed her		the	spouse	knife	he used

It must be about two years ago [that] this man killed his wife with a knife.

b. Nę hyáʔ ų́·, gaʔt <u>sí nę gwáʔ hwíks niyohsæ·gé</u> onę tshųgeʔsé·ʔ kheyaʔdanęhgwih… (LG10)

nę	hyaʔ	ų·	gaʔt	si	nę	gwaʔ	hwiks
TMP	MOD	MOD	HYP	LOC	TMP	RSTR	NUM
now	indeed	perhaps	maybe	far	now	just	five

---

[29] Recall that nouns normally drop initial *w-* pronominal.

    ni-y-ohsR-a-ge-h'   onę   tshaʔ-wage[30]-ʔse·-ʔ

    PRT-3N/Z.SG.A-year-JN-amount.to-STV   TMP   COIN-OPT-1SG.P-ride-PRP

    so many years   now   while I was riding

    khe-yaʔd-a-nęhgwi-k

    1SG > 3-body-JN-haul-HAB

    I'm a taxi-driver

    It must be about five years ago when I drove a taxi...

<u>General reference to the past and the present</u>: Variants of the temporal expression *ųnísʔih / nwaʔųnísheʔ* refer to past time in general; the particle cluster *nęgę ų́hgę(ʔ)* refers to the present. Frequently one of these occurs as a part of an introductory particle sequence that provides the setting for the utterance that follows:

(83) a. Naʔ óʔ <u>neʔ ųnisʔí</u> tshaʔ nigųdineʔnoʔdęʔsgwáʔ neʔ odiksdęʔshųʔáh, hya tho deʔóʔ
    tshaʔ ųhgęʔ niyót <u>nęgę́ ų́hgęʔ</u> (LG21).

    naʔ   oʔ   neʔ   ųnisʔih   tshaʔ   ni-gųdi-neʔn-oʔdę-ʔs-gwaʔ   neʔ

    ASRT ADD NOM TMP   SUB   PART-3FZ.PL.A-clothes-kind-HAB-HBPST   NOM

    it's   also   the   past time   that   the kind of clothes they used to have   the

    odi-ksdęʔ + shųʔáh   hya tho deʔ-oʔ   tshaʔ ųhgęʔ niyot   nęgę ųhgęʔ

    3FZ.NSG.P-old.person-PL   NEG MAN NEG-ADD   SUB TMP MAN   DEM TMP

    old ladies   not the same   how it is now   at present

    Also, in the past they used to dress like old ladies, but it's different at present.

  b. Da· dogę́s <u>neʔ ųnísʔi</u>, hadinoʔji·yóʔsgwaʔ (LG21).

    da·   dogęs   neʔ   ųnisʔih   hadi-noʔjy-iyo-ʔs-gwaʔ

    LNK   MOD   NOM   TMP   3M.PL.A-tooth-be.good-STV.PL-HBPST

    so   truly   the   past time   they used to have good teeth

    In the past, really, they used to have good teeth.

  c. Da· <u>nęgę́ ų́hgęʔ</u> nigahawíʔ gotgaʔdéʔ niyagotnoʔjyų́·daųh (LG20).

    da   nęgę ųhgęʔ   ni-ga-hawi-ʔ   go-atgaʔt-eʔ

    LNK   DEM TMP   PART-3N/Z.SG.A-carry-PRP   3FI.P-be.many-STV

    so   at present   the time it is   lots of them

    ni-yago-at-noʔjy-ųdaR-ųh

    PRT-3FI.P-SRF-tooth-put.in.a.container-STV

    they have false teeth

    At this time there are a lot of people who wear false teeth.

  (ii) The Expression of Events in Terms of Non-deictic Temporal Divisions and Cyclical Events:

To express periodic events non-deictically, the event is named without a demonstrative:

---

[30] The combination tshaʔ + wag > tshųg by regular phonological rule.

(84) a. Dę?se? ne? nę <u>hwíks wadų?thá?</u> wa?ųhdędyá? gęs khwesásneh nhwa?ę?... (LG07)

dę?se?	ne?	nę	hwiks	w-adų?d-ha?	wa?-ų-ahdędy-a?	gęs
CNJ	NOM	TMP	NUM	3N/Z.SG.A-be.a.sequence-HAB	FACT-3FI.A-leave-PNC	CST
and		when		Friday	she left	usually

Khwesasneh	n-h-wa?-ę-(e)-?'
NAME	PRT-TRNS-FACT-3FI.A-go-PNC
Akwesasne	she went there

And on Fridays [literally, when it's Friday] *she usually left to go to Akwesasne...*

b. <u>Gohsæ·?gé</u>, tho ó? na? ní·yot, gadé? sų gá·? dahodųhwę́·jyos, ne? oyędá? hahsá? oné ęhųnidyohgųnyá? nęgę́ha ga·hagų́wa nhęhęné? ęhadiyę́·diya?k (LG11).

g-ohsR-a? = ge		tho	o?	na?	niyot	gadé?	sų	ga?
NPF-winter-NSF = LOC		MAN	ADD	ASRT	MAN	CNJ	INTR	IND
in the winter		how	also	it's	how it is	maybe	somebody	

d-aa-ho-adųhwęjyo-s-Ø	ne?	o-yęd-a?	hahsa? onę
DL-OPT-3M.SG.P-want-BEN-PNC	NOM	NPF-wood-NSF	TMP TMP
he may want it	the	wood	right away

ę-hų-ęn-idyohgw-ųny-a?	nęgę = há	ga-Rh-agųwa
FUT-3M.PL.A-SRF-group-make-PNC	DEM = DIM	NPF-forest-LOC
they'll form group	this specific one	in the forest

n-h-ę-hęn-e-?	ę-hadi-yęd-iya?k-Ø
PRT-TRNS-FUT-3M.PL.A-walk-PNC	FUT-3M.PL.A-wood-cut-PNC
there they will go	they will cut wood

And in the winter, there may be someone who wants wood; right away, [the men] get together [and] go into the forest to cut wood.

<u>Extent</u>: To express the extent of a time period that has a specified terminal point, the extent classifier *nigę́* is used.

(85) a. <u>Do gá·? niwędagéh nigę́</u> tho ihé?s, nę dųdahahdę́·dya? (HW05).

do	ga?	ni-w-ęd-ge-h'	nigę	tho	i-h-e-?s
INTR	IND	PRT-3N/Z.SG.A-day-amount.to-STV	EXT	LOC	EP-3M.SG.A-walk-HAB
A few		so many days	extent	there	he is around

nę	d-ųda-h-ahdędy-a?
TMP	DL-CIS:FACT-3M.SG.A-depart-PNC
then	he went back home

He stayed around there for several days, then he returned home.

b. <u>...ęhsa·dnųhdų́?da? tsha? nigę́</u> ęya·gwadéhs?a? (CTL96.7).

ę-hs-adnųhdų?d-a?	tsha?	nigę	ę-yagw-ad-ehs?-a?
FUT-2SG.A-wait-PNC	SUB	EXT	FUT-1EX.PL.A-SRF-finish-PNC
you will wait	that	extent	we will get ready

...you will wait until we are ready

   c. ...nhwáʔseh, <u>gaeʔ tshaʔ nigę ęthéʔ</u> nę́·gę! (HW07)

n-h-waʔ-s-e-h		gaeʔ	tshaʔ	nigę	ę-t-h-e-ʔ		nęgę
PRT-TRNS-FACT-2SG.IMP-walk-IMP		DGR	SUB	EXT	FUT-CIS-3M.SG.A-walk-PNC		DEM
go there!		less	that	extent	he'll come here		this

...get going, before this one gets here!

A time period without specific terminal points is expressed using indefinite temporal expressions like *dyę gwaʔ onę* 'eventually' or *dyę gwaʔ ųhgęʔ* 'soon', omitting the extent particle:

(86) a. Gwas yágę́ʔ tho niyo·dyeęhadyéʔ <u>dyę́ gwaʔ ónę</u> thohá gagwegí otciʔgé·ʔ tshaʔ gaęhyá·deʔ (HW07).

gwas	yagę́ʔ	tho	ni-yo-adyeR-ęh-adye-ʔ		dyę gwaʔ onę	thohah
INTS	HRSY	LOC	PRT-3N/Z.SG.P-do-STV-PRG-PRP		INDF RSTR TMP	DGR
very	they say	there	it keeps doing it		after a while	almost

ga-gweg-ih		o-atciʔge·-ʔ		tshaʔ	ga-Ręhy-ade-ʔ
3N/Z.SG.A-be.all-STV		3N/Z.SG.P-be.cloudy-STV		SUB	3N/Z.SG.A-sky-be.located-STV
it is all		it is cloudy		that	in the sky

[The clouds] really keep multiplying there [and] after a while it's just about all clouds   in the sky.

   b. ...dehonadawę·yé neʔ hya deʔakhiyędé·ih <u>dyęhaʔ gwaʔ ų́hgęʔ</u> nayéʔ ęhadihetgę́hdaʔ... (CTL191.7-8)

de-hon-ad-awę·ye-h'	neʔ	hya	deʔ-akhi-yędeR-ih		dyęhaʔ gwaʔ ųhgęʔ
DL-3M.NSG.P-SRF-stir-STV	NOM	NEG	NEG-1NSG > 3-know-STV		INDF RSTR TMP
they roam about	the	not	we don't know them		soon

nayeʔ	ę-hadi-hetgę-hd-aʔ
ASRT	FUT-3M.PL.A-bad-CS-PNC
it's	they will spoil it

...strangers are roaming about [and] soon they will spoil it...

<u>Frequency</u>: To express the frequency of a cyclical event non-deictically, the period is named as a part of a counting expression. This may be done by adding (a) a number term, (b) a descriptive verbal expression, or (c) a particle referring to a cyclical event:

(87) a. <u>Jyadáh gahé·ʔ niyohsæ·gé naʔdegųdéʔ</u> naʔ de·gáęʔ hadí·yųk (LG01).

jyadak gahe·ʔ		ni-y-ohsR-a-ge-h'
NUM NUM		PRT-3N/Z.SG.A-year-JN-amount.to-STV
seventeen		so many years

naʔ-de-gų-ade·-ʔ			naʔ	degaęʔ	hadi-yų-k
PART-DL-3FZ.PL.A-distance.between-STV			ASRT	TMP	3M.PL.A-arrive-HAB
the distance between them			it's	how often	they arrive

They [the locusts] arrive every seventeen years.

b. Né?tho ní·yot <u>ha?dewẹdagé</u> ohni? ne? <u>ha?dewahsụdagé</u> gona?khwẹ?i ne?
   goksdẹ?áh… (CTL4.6-7)

ne?tho	niyot	ha?-de-w-ẹd-a-ge-h'		ohni?	ne?
MAN	MAN	TRNS-DL-3N/Z.SG.A-day-JN-amount.to-STV		ADD	NOM
thus	how it is	every day		also	the

ha?-de-w-ahsụd-a-ge-h'	go-na?khwẹ?-ih	ne?	go-ksdẹ?ah
TRNS-DL-3N/Z.SG.A-night-JN-amount.to-STV	3FI.P-get.angry-STV	NOM	3FI.P-old.person
every night	she got angry	the	old woman

So every day and every night, the old woman got angry…

c. Odiyo?dé? <u>o·hẹ?sẹ́·k</u> odyá?k, áhya?k gadé? jyadák nigahwisdagé ẹyụtgwenyá? ne?
   jyẹ́dada odyá?k dé·gẹ·? (LG11).

odi-yo?de-?	o·hẹ?sẹ·k	odya?k	ahya?k	gade?	jyadak
3FZ.NSG.P-work-STV	TMP	QNT	NUM	CNJ	NUM
they work	daily	some	six	or	seven

ni-ga-hwisd-a-ge-h'	ẹ-yụ-at-gweny-a?	ne?
PRT-3N/Z.SG.A-money-JN-amount.to-STV	FUT-3FI.A-SRF-be.able-PNC	NOM
how many dollars	they earned	the

s-y-ẹd-a-d-'ah	odya?k	de·gẹ·?
REP-3N/Z.SG.A-day-JN-be.one-STV	QNT	NUMBER
one day	some	eight

The women do daily work, some earn six or seven dollars a day [literally: one day]
and some get eight.

(iii) Relating an Event to Situation-Time

Two events may happen at the same time, the onset time of one event depends on the
occurrence of another event, or situations are sequenced in relation to one another. These
alternatives all consist of two clauses that are temporally related.

<u>Temporal coincidence</u>: To mark the fact that two situations coincide temporally, the verb
form that frames the time period is prefixed with the coincident prepronominal prefix (see
also section 4.7.4); thus, in (88a) what happens to the dog occurs while he is at a certain
place; in (88b) the two men are worrying while they are lying down resting:

(88) a. <u>Tcithé?s ne? jí·ha</u> se? khẹ dahụwasháẹdẹ? (HW05).

tci-t-h-e-?s	ne?	ji·hah	se? khẹ	d-a-hụw-ashaed-ẹ?
COIN-CIS-3M.SG.A-walk-HAB	NOM	NOUN	TAG	CIS-FACT-3 > 3M.SG-tie.up-PNC
while he is around there	the	dog	you know	someone tied him up

While the dog was there, you know, someone had him tied up.

b. Na? yágẹ? nẹgẹ <u>tsha?dehnidagǽ·?</u> nẹ hyẹnụhdú·nyụk, wadẹ? di? nẹhni·yé·æ?.
   (HW07)

na?	yagẹ?	nẹgẹ	tsha?-de-hn-idagR-a?	onẹ
ASRT	HRSY	DEM	COIN-DL-3M.DU.A-be.lying.down-STV	TMP
it's	they say	this	while they two are lying down	now

    hy-ęnųhdų-nyų-k   wadę?   di?   n-ę-hni-yeR-a?
    3M.DU.A-know-DST-HAB   INTR   LNK   PRT-FUT-3M.DU.A-do-PNC
    they are thinking about it   what   moreover   thus they two will do it
    They say that while these two are lying down, they keep pondering, how they will do it.

The coincident prepronominal prefix *tci-* typically occurs with a verb, but it can also be attached to stage-of-life terms as in (89):

(89) Ųhgę? ne? khehawá dekhenųhę·khwá? Dorothy, <u>tciyeksa?á</u> gwa? tho ne?, enųhwé?s gęs ne?, sų gá·? oyá? a·yųdadya?dagéhnha? (LG08).

    ųhgę?   ne?   khe-hawah   de-khe-nųhę·-hgw-ha?   Dorothy
    TMP   NOM   1SG>3-parent.*child*   DL-1SG>3-greet-INST-HAB   NAME
    next   the   my niece[31]   Dorothy

    tci-ye-ksa?=á   gwa?   tho   ne?   e-nųhwe?-s   gęs   ne?
    COIN-3FI.A-child=DIM   RST   MAN   NOM   3FI.A-like-HAB CST   NOM
    while she was a little girl   just   thus   the   she likes   usually   the

    sų ga·?   (y)-oya?   aa-yųdad-ya?dagehnh-a?
    IND IND   3N/Z.SG.A-different-STV   OP-3FI>3FI-help-PNC
    someone   it is different   she would help them
    Next [it's about] my niece Dorothy; when she was a little girl, she liked helping out others.

Temporal coincidence can also be marked with the particle sequence *ne? nę* 'when, at the time that...' preceding a situation expression. The *ne? (o)nę* clause can precede (90a) or follow (90b) the main clause:

(90) a. Na? <u>né? nę dųdayágne?</u>, na? né? gwas wé deyohahiyá?ki o?, gah<u>négo?</u>[32] (LG03).

    na?   ne? nę   d-ųda-yagn-e-?   na?   ne?   gwas   we
    ASRT   NOM TMP   DL-CIS:FACT-1EX.DU.A-walk-PNC   ASRT   NOM   INTS   QNT
    it's   when   we two came back   it's   the   very   a lot

    de-yo-ahah-iya?k-ih   o?   ga-hneg-o-?
    DL-3N/Z.SG.P-road-cross.over-STV   ADD   3N/Z.SG.A-water-immerse.in.fluid-STV
    it crossed the road   also   it was immersed in water
    When we came back, [water] had also completely crossed over the road, [which] was submerged.

    b. Onę tho, na? wa?hadihęt ne? hųdę·nótha?, <u>ne? nę wa?shagwa?nųhdá·ha?</u> (LG05).

    onę   tho   na?   wa?-hadi-hęt-Ø'   ne?   hų-ad-Ręn-ot-ha?
    TMP   LOC   ASRT   FACT-3M.PL.A-walk.ahead-PNC   NOM   3M.PL.A-SRF-song-raise-HAB
    then   there   it's   they walked ahead   the   band

---

[31] Literally, 'my daughter [that's what] I greet her with it'.

[32] The underline identifies whispered pronunciation.

```
ne? onę       wa?-shagwa-?nųhdaR-h-a?
NOM TMP       FACT-1EX.PL > 3M.SG-bury-DSLC-PRP
when          we went to bury him
```
The band walked ahead when we went to bury him.

c. Tho né? na? wa?aihé·ya?, <u>ne? nę</u> shagoyenawá?khų? (LG20).

```
tho    ne?    na?    wa?-a-ihey-a?        ne?  nę    shago-yenawa?k-hų-?
LOC    NOM    ASRT   FACT-3FI.A-die-PNC   NOM  TMP   3M.SG > 3-hold.onto-DST-STV
there  the    it's   she died             when       he was holding her
```
She died while he was holding her.

<u>Temporal dependency</u>: The indefinite temporal subordinator *ganyó?* 'whenever, as soon as' introduces the dependent clause. The main- and dependent clauses can occur in either order. In (91a) the dependent clause precedes the main clause; in (91b) the dependent clause follows it:

(91) a. <u>Ganyó?</u> ędwahgwehnę́hda?, ęhohsé·k thogę ne? shaya?dadáh, tsha? gáyę? hadatjí·nah (HW07).

```
ganyo?     ę-d-w-ahgwehnęhd-a?              ę-ho-hse·-k                    thogę   ne?
INDF       FUT-CIS-3FZ.SG.A-descend-PNC     FUT-3FZ.SG. > 3M.SG-chase-PNC  DEM     NOM
as soon as she will come down               she will chase him             that    the
```

```
s-ha-ya?d-a-d-ah'            tsha? gayę?      h-adat-jina-h
REP-3M.SG.A-body-JN-be.one-STV   REL          3M.SG.A-REF-be.male-STV
one man                      the one who      he is a show-off
```
"As soon as she descends [from the tree], she will chase the other guy, the one who is   a show-off."

b. Sé? khę yágę? ędyohsųwægaehǽ? <u>ganyó?</u> hęhohǽ·?nha?. (HW07)

```
se? khę    yage?       ę-d-yo-hsųR-a-gaehR-a?                 ganyo?
TAG        HRSY        FUT-CIS-3N/Z.SG.P-gun-JN-make.noise-PNC INDF
you know   they say    there'll be a gun-sound towards here    as soon as
```

```
h-ę-ho-hR-a?-nha?
TRNS-FUT-3FZ.SG. > 3M.SG-be.on-INCH-PNC
she will catch up with him
```
"You know, a gun will sound out as soon as she catches up with him."

<u>Temporal Sequence</u>: Expressing sequences of events often involves particle clusters that include the extent classifier *nigę́* 'extent of time, space, or amount':

(92) a. ...wa?hęhę́·?, "Gáe? tsha? nigę́ ętgaæhgwitgę́?nha?, ęjyahdę́·dya?" (HW07).

```
wa?-ha-ihę·-?"              gae?    tsha?   nigę    ę-t-ga-Ræhgw-itgę?-nha?
FACT-3M.SG.A-say-PNC        DGR     SUB     EXT     FUT-CIS-3N/Z.SG.A-sun-become.visible-PNC
he said                    less    that    extent  sun will rise
```

```
ę-jy-ahdędy-a?
FUT-2DU-move.on-PNC
you two will leave
```
...he said: "Before the sun rises, you two should leave."

b. Dá·ne dętkhwę?ga·sthwáhda?, <u>tsha? nigé</u> tho nęyo?ksdék tsha? nitshe·yésdih (HW03).

dane	d-ę-t-k-hwę?gaR-asthw-hd-a?		tsha?	nigę	tho
LNK	DL-FUT-CIS-1SG.A-splint-diminish-CS-PNC		SUB	EXT	MAN
SO	I'll whittle the splint		that	extent	thus

n-ę-yo-?ksd-e-k-Ø	tsha?	ni-t-hs-yęsd-ih
PRT-FUT-3N/Z.SG.P-heavy-STV-CNT-PNC	SUB	PRT-CIS-2SG.A-be.appropriate-STV
how heavy it will be	that	it is appropriate for you

So then I'll whittle the stick, until its weight is appropriate for you.

7.7 Other Relationships between Clauses

This section deals with loser relationships between clauses. They involve neither subordinate clauses, argument clauses nor adjunct expressions. Strings of such clauses frequently make up intonationally recognizable entities referred to here as utterances (see sec. 2.7.4 for a description of the intonational properties of utterances; see also sec. 7.1, the introduction to this chapter).

7.7.1 Connectives

The term *connective* is used to describe particles that link neighboring clauses and that combine their primary function of clause linkage with a variety of textual and discourse functions. The particles together with a major function and frequent glosses are listed in Table 7.4.

Table 7.4 Connective particles

Function	Particle	Frequent glosses
coordinative	dę́?se?	*and*
alternative	gadé? gí?shę ga?t khę	*or, alternatively, maybe* *alternatively, or else, or maybe* *or maybe*
additive	óhni?, ó? di?	*also* *moreover*
contrary	gó?	*however, but, actually*
conditional	(do)ga?t dyę́(ha?) gwa?	*if* *maybe, perhaps, if*
sequence	dá(ne)	*so, so then*
paired particles	há·dye? … na? go·?... gányo?… da ó·nę	*even though...never-the-less...* *as soon as …so then...*

(i) Linking clauses with the coordinative carticle *dę́?se?* 'and':

The coordinating conjunction *dę́?se?* links elements of the same syntactic status; two clauses as in (93a) or two utterances as in (93b). The particle occurs between the two linked entities. In (93a) the second clause elaborates the information provided by the first clause. In (93b) *dę́?se?*, which occurs at the beginning of the utterance, forms a link to a prior statement regarding the absence of the children's father. That the particle can also link two external nominals, is shown in (93c).

(93) a. [Gwas yágę? dųsayohnegawatgá?] d**ę́?se?**, [dayo·yahęhá? ayę́æ? nę sahahdųwék ne?, Gashaisdo·wá·nęh] (HW07).

gwas	yagę?	d-ųsa-yo-hneg-watg-a?	dę?se?
INTS	HRSY	DL-REP:FACT-3N/Z.SG.P-liquid-churn-PNC	CNJ
really	they say	water churned up again	and

d-a-yo-Ryahęh-a?		ayę́æ?	nę	s-a-h-ahdųwek-Ø
CIS-FACT-3N/Z.SG.P-come.to.a.boil-PNC		SIM	LOC	REP-FACT-3M.SG.A-dive-PNC
it boiled up		seems like	here	he dove back in

ne?	ga-shaisd-owanę-h
NOM	3N/Z.SG.A-snake-be.large-STV
the	Great Sake

The water really churned up and it seems like it boiled up as the Great Snake dove back in.

b. D**ę́?se?** ne? shagohawashų́?a, hajihęsdají? na?, honųhsgų́wa tho honi?dę́?,… (LG09)

dę?se?	ne?	shago-hawah + shų?á	hajihęsdaji?	na?	ho-nųhs-agųwa
CNJ	NOM	3M.SG > 3-parent.*child* = PL	NOUN	ASRT	3M.SG.P-house-LOC
and	the	his children	minister	it's	in his house

tho	hon-i?dę·-?
LOC	3M.NSG.P-reside-STV
there	they are living

And his children are living in the minister's house…

c. … akhninų́h [ne? gohsá·dęs], d**ę́?se?** [ne? saddle] (LG23).

wak-hninų-h'	ne?	gohsá·dęs	dę?se?	ne?	saddle
1SG.P-buy-STV	NOM	LEX	CNJ	NOM	LEX
I've bought it	the	horse	and	the	saddle

I had bought the horse and the saddle.

   (ii) Linking clauses with the alternative particles *gadé?* 'or, maybe', *gí?shę* 'or else', or the particle cluster *ga?t khę* 'maybe':

Like the coordinative particle *dę́?se?*, the alternative particle *gadé?* links elements of the same syntactic status and occurs between the linked elements as in (94a-c). In (94a) these are clauses, in (94b) they are nominals, and in (94c) they are number expressions.

(94) a. …nę hehé? [_CL_dęhahgwe?dá·?] **gadé?** [_CL_hgųhsi?gé ne? nęthayeǽ·?] … (LG24)

nę	h-eR-he?	d-ę-hak-gwe?daR-?	gade?
TMP	3M.SG.A-want-HAB	DL-FUT-3M.SG > 1SG-scratch-PNC	ALT
when	he wants	he will scratch me	or.maybe

    k-gųhs-iʔ = ge   neʔ   n-ę-t-ha-yeR-aʔ
    1SG.A-face-NSF = LOC   NOM   PRT-FUT-CIS-3M.SG.A-do-PNC
    on my face   the   he will touch it
    ...when he wants something, he will scratch me, or he may touch my face...

b. Khawíʔ gęs oʔ [_{NOM}sdęʔ ęhéʔ] <u>gadéʔ</u> [_{NOM}owęnawęʔdaę·nyųʔshųʔá tshaʔ gęs
   niho·gáʔhwaʔ] (LG28).

    k-hawi-ʔ   gęs   oʔ   sdęʔ   ę-(e)R-heʔ   gade?
    1SG.A-bring.along-PRP   CST   ADD   INDF   3FI.A-want-HAB   ALT
    I'm bringing it along   usually also   something one wants it   or

    o-Ręnawęʔd-ųnyų-ʔ + shųʔá   tshaʔ   gęs   ni-ho-gaʔhw-aʔ
    3N/Z.SG.P-be.sweet-DST-STV = PL   SUB   CST   PRT-3M.SG.P-like.to.eat-STV
    sweet things   that   usually he likes to eat it
    Usually I also bring something that is wanted, or sweet things that he likes to
    eat.

c. Odiyoʔdéʔ o·hęʔsę́·k odyáʔk, [áhyaʔk] <u>gadéʔ</u> [jyadák] nigahwisdagé ęyųtgwenyáʔ
   neʔ jyędada odyáʔk dé·gę·ʔ (LG11).

    odi-yoʔde-ʔ   o·hęʔsę·k   odyaʔk   ahyaʔk   gadeʔ   jyadak
    3FZ.NSG.P-work-STV   TMP   QNT   NUM   CNJ   NUM
    they work   daily   some   six   or   seven

    ni-ga-hwisd-a-ge-h'   ę-yų-at-gweny-aʔ   neʔ
    PRT-3N/Z.SG.A-money-JN-amount.to-STV   FUT-3FI.A-SRF-be.able-PNC NOM
    how many dollars   they earned/won   the

    s-y-ęd-a-d-'ah   odyaʔk   de·gę·ʔ
    REP-3N/Z.SG.A-day-JN-be.one-STV   QNT   NUMBER
    one day   some   eight
    The women work every day and some get six or seven dollars a day and some get
    eight.

Unlike *gadéʔ*, the alternative particle *giʔshę́* is not coordinative in the sense that it must
link grammatically identical elements. It often occurs after the second element as in (95a).
Example (95b) is from a myth in which the chief of the sky world has a bad dream that
must be guessed in order to release him from its prophecy. In the utterance preceding the
excerpt he complains to the addressee that his family hasn't come to help with the
guessing. The alternative particle links the utterance semantically to the preceding
statement.

(95) a. Hya díʔ deʔtga·nyóʔ gwaʔ hwędų́ a·tcihę́·ʔ [_{CL}nę ęga·dwędéhdaʔ, neʔ jí·hah],
        [_{CL}ęgadęnasgų́ʔ] <u>giʔshę́h</u> (HW05).

        hya   diʔ   deʔ-t-ganyoʔ   gwaʔ   hwędųh   aa-hs-ihę·-ʔ'   onę
        NEG   LNK   NEG-CIS-IND   RSTR   INTR   OPT-2SG.A-say-PNC TMP
        not   moreover   not whenever   just   when   you should say   now

ę-g-adwędehd-aʔ   neʔ   ji·hah   ę-g-adę-nasgw-ų-ʔ   giʔshęh
PRT-1SG.A-let.go.of-PNC   NOM   NOUN   FUT-1SG.A-SRF-pet-give-PNC   ALT
I'll let it go   the   dog   I will pet-give   or else

And you shouldn't, just anytime [it pleases you], say, "I'll let go of the dog", or
"I'll give away my pet."

b. Dyęhaʔ gwaʔ giʔshę is swagwenyų aeswaihwaʔsægwaʔ tshaʔ nigayéhaʔ neʔ
   agʔniguhæʔ (H617:20-21).[33]

   dyęhaʔ   gwaʔ   giʔshę   is   swa-gweny-ų   ae-swa-Rihwaʔsæ·gw-aʔ
   INDF   RSTR   ALT   PRON   2PL-be.able-STV   OPT-2PL-answer-PNC
   maybe   just   alternatively   you   you are able to   you could answer

   tshaʔ   ni-ga-yeR-haʔ   neʔ   ag-ʔniguhR-aʔ
   SUB   PRT-3N/Z.SG.A-do-HAB   NOM   1SG.P-mind-NSF
   that   how it does it   the   my mind

   Alternatively, you might be able to answer what [it is] that is agitating my
   mind.

The particle cluster *gaʔt khę* combines the particle *gaʔt* that marks both indefinite and
hypothetical expressions with the question particle *khę* that, in other contexts, marks polar
questions. This combination adds a modal component, marking the alternatives as
somewhat of a guess on the part of the speaker:

(96) Hya gwas deʔhoyoʔdęhs neʔ hųwáhawah, <u>gaʔt khę·</u>, hya deʔdęhayoʔdęhse·węʔnhaʔ
     (LG08).

   hya   gwas   deʔ-ho-yoʔdęh-s   neʔ   hųwa-hawah   gaʔt khę   hya
   NEG   INTS   NEG-3M.SG.P-work-HAB   NOM   3>3M.SG-parent.*child*   INDF QUE   NEG
   not   very   he doesn't work   the   her son   maybe   not

   deʔ-d-ę-ha-yoʔd-ęhsR-owęʔ-nhaʔ
   NEG-DL-FUT-3M.SG.A-work-NOM-find-PNC
   he can't find work

   Her son doesn't much [like to] work or maybe he can't find a job?

   (iii) The Additive Linking Particle *óhniʔ/óʔ* 'also':

The additive particle *óhniʔ/óʔ* frequently follows the constituent that is "added," especially
when it connects two situations. The particle also connects clauses, or smaller constituents
into an "additive chain" as in (100). In (97) the particle connects two clauses:

(97) a. Gwas yágęʔ négę gwaʔ thigaʔnahsaniyų́·daʔ, oʔdaegų́ʔá <u>oʔ</u>... (HW07)
     gwas   yagęʔ   nęgę   gwaʔ   thi-ga-ʔnahs-a-niyųd-aʔ
     INTS   HRSY   DEM   RSTR   CON-3N/Z.SG.A-tongue-JN-hang-STV
     very   they say   this   just   tongue is hanging way out

---

[33] Hewitt did not mark stress and vowel length in this excerpt except as shown.

    o-ʔdaR-ogų-ʔ = á   oʔ
    3N/Z.SG.P-mud-be.only-STV = DIM   ADD
    muddy all over   also
    Really, he is just panting, also he's muddy all over...

b. Honatciʔáh yá·gęʔ, hehniwęnóha·ʔ, hyadatjína <u>óʔ</u> (HW07).
    hon-atci-ʔ = á   yagęʔ   he-hni-węn-ohaR-aʔ
    3M.NSG.P-friend-NSF = DIM   HRSY   TRNS-3M.DU.A-voice-raise-STV
    they are friends   they say   they two are boisterous

    hy-adat-jina-h   oʔ
    3M.DU.A-REF-be.male-STV   ADD
    they two are show showing off also
    They say two pals are boisterous, they're showing off, too.

The utterance in (98a) is the third in a series of utterances that list the living arrangements of the protagonist; the excerpt in (98b) follows a description of the weather's negative effects on the summer gardening efforts that were described in the preceding utterance:

(98) a. <u>Honasgwayęʔ</u> óʔ gatshé·nęʔ, gųniʔdę́·ʔ gaʔęhægų́wah (HW01).
    ho-nasgw-a-yę-ʔ   oʔ   ga-tshenę-ʔ   gųn-iʔdę-ʔ
    3M.SG.P-animal-JN-have-STV   ADD   NPF-pet-NSF 3FZ.PL.A-reside-STV
    he has animals   also   pet(s)   they live

    ga-ʔęhR-agųwa
    NPF-fence-LOC
    in the yard
    Also, he has [domesticated] animals living in the yard.

b. Naʔ <u>óʔ</u> neʔ, dogęs néʔ naʔ si nigáę osdáę·dyeʔs (LG02).
    naʔ   oʔ   dogęs   neʔ   naʔ   si nigaę   o-sdaR-ųdye-ʔs
    ASRT ADD MOD   NOM ASRT LOC EXT   3N/Z.SG.P-rain-throw.away-HAB
    it's   also truly the   it's   long interval it rains
    Also, it's been a long time between rain showers.

In (99), the additive *oʔ* connects *hniyędéthaʔ* 'they demonstrate' to the preceding situation, and note that *oʔ* intervenes between the main verb of the second clause and its argument clause:

(99) Hó·· ʔé··, tshaʔ nihyadatjináh; [<u>hniyędetháʔ oʔ</u> [tshaʔ nęthni·yé·æʔ, neʔ nę
    dęhų·dæ·ʔnháʔ]]... (HW07)
    ho· ʔeh tshaʔ   ni-hy-adat-jina-h   hni-yędet-haʔ   oʔ
    EXCL   SUB   PRT-3M.DU.A-REF-be.male-STV   3M.DU.A-show.knowledge-HAB   ADD
    oh my! that   thus they two are showing off they two demonstrate   also

n-ẹ-t-hni-yeR-aʔ   neʔ onẹ   d-ẹ-hụ-adæ·ʔ-nhaʔ
PRT-FUT-CIS-3M.DU.A-do-PNC   NOM TMP   DL-FUT-3M.PL.A-meet.by.chance-PNC
thus they two will do it   when   they all will meet up

Oh my! How they're showing off; they demonstrate too what they'll do when they all meet up...

An example of a chain of *additive* clauses is (100):

(100) Dá· nẹ waʔshagotho·yẹ́ʔ gáẹ nụ́· nhẹhnéʔ, do· ó̰ʔ nigẹ́h, niyụ́ hẹhyẹnụhwét, tho ó̰ʔ dẹhyadụgohdahẹ́·ʔ tshaʔ nụ́·, hadinagé·ʔ neʔ yá deʔtgaihwayéiʔs, hụdẹ·yós, oyáʔ hẹnụgwehụ́·weh (HW07).

daneh	onẹ	waʔ-shago-atho·y-ẹ-ʔ		gaẹ	nụ·
LNK	TMP	FACT-3M.SG > 3-tell-BEN-PNC		INTR	LOC
so	now	he told them		where	place

n-h-ẹ-hn-e-ʔ		do	oʔ	nigẹ	niyụ
PRT-TRNS-FUT-3M.DU.A-walk-PNC		INTR	ADD	EXT	AMT
they two will go there		how	also	extent	how much

h-ẹ-hy-ẹnụhwet-Ø		tho	oʔ	d-ẹ-hy-adụgohd-ahẹ·-ʔ
TRNS-FUT-3M.DU.A-overnight-PNC		LOC	ADD	DL-FUT-3M.DU.A-pass.through-dst-PNC
they two will spend the night there		there	also	they will pass through several

tshaʔ	nụ·	hadi-nage·-ʔ	neʔ	ya	deʔ-t-ga-Rihw-a-yei-ʔs
SUB	LOC	3M.PL.A-dwell-STV	NOM	NEG	NEG-CIS-3N/Z.SG.A-matter-JN-right-STVPL
that	place	they live	the	not	it is unreliable

hụ-adẹ·yo-s	(y)-oyaʔ	hẹn-ụgweh = ụwe
3M.PL.A-kill-HAB	3N/Z.SG.A-different-STV	3M.PL.A-person:SUFF = AUTH
they kill	it is different	human being

So then he told them the way to go; also, how often they'll stay over night; also, the places they will pass through where the evil killers of other human beings live.

In (101) the additive particle connects two or more nominal constituents:

(101) a. Dẹ́ʔseʔ neʔ, gatshenẹ jihá· dagós oʔ tshaʔ niyót odigáʔhwaʔ... (LG01)

dẹʔseʔ	neʔ	ga-tshenẹ-h	jíhah	dagós	oʔ	tshaʔ
CNJ	NOM	NPF-pet-NSF	NOUN	NOUN	ADD	SUB
and	the	pet(s)	dog(s)	cat(s)	also	that

ni-yo-ht-Ø		odi-gaʔhw-aʔ
PRT-3N/Z.SG.P-how.it.is-STV		3FZ.NSG.P-like.the.taste-STV
how it is		they like the taste

And the pets, the dogs, also the cats, like the taste of [locusts]...

    b. Nẹ ẹga·dnẹhohgụ́nyaʔ, naʔ neʔ niʔá· gwaʔ gyẹ́·dei, neʔ naʔ agụnhéhgwi, onẹhóhgwaʔ, gage·hótcyụh, ojísgwaʔ óhniʔ (PJ02).

Nẹ	ẹ-g-ad-nẹh-o-hgw-ụny-aʔ		naʔ	neʔ	niʔ = á	gwaʔ
PRS	FUT-1SG.A-SRF-corn-put.in.water-INST-make-PNC		ASRT	NOM	PRN = DIM	RSTR
here	I will make corn soup		it's	the	I/we	just

g-yędeR-i		ne?	na?	ag-ųnhe-hgw-i		o-nęh-o-hgw-a?
1SG.A-know-STV		NOM	ASRT	1SG.P-live-INST-STV		NPF-corn-put.in.water-INST-NSF
I know it		the	it's	I live by it		corn soup

ga-ge·hotcyųh	o-jisgw-a?	ohni?
NPF-corn.bread	NPF-mush-NSF	ADD
cornbread	mush	also

I'll make corn soup, it's what I know and I live by it, corn soup, cornbread, and also mush.

(iv) Linkages with the Contrary Particle *gó·?* 'however, but':

The particle typically introduces an utterance that contrasts or disagrees with a prior statement. In addition to contrast, the particle may also express unexpectedness, or surprise on the part of the speaker as in (102a). Combined with the assertion particle *na?* special attention is directed to the contrast, as in (102b) which is preceded by a discussion of the difficulty of getting wood out of the forest in the winter. When *go·?* modifies a negative expression, it follows the particle *hya* as in (102c):

(102) a. Ogá?wi <u>go·?</u> ná?, gwa? hyá? dehsatgahgwekhúk ne? do gá·? hwędúh gwa? ęhsek (LG07)

o-ga?w-ih		go·?	na?	gwa?	hya?
3N/Z.SG.P-taste.good-STV		CTR	ASRT	RSTR	MID
it tastes good		however	it's	just	indeed

de-hs-at-gahgwek-hų-k		ne?	do ga·?	hwędų	gwa?
DL-2SG.A-SRF-close.eyes-dst-HAB		NOM	INT IND	TMP	RSTR
you close your eyes		the	several	whenever	just

ę-hse-k-Ø
FUT-2SG.A-eat-PNC
you will eat it

They [locusts] *are delicious, but actually, when you eat them you want to shut your eyes.*

b. <u>Na? gó?</u> ná? gęs ne? í?, dehniksá?ah nę hniniyųthá? oyędá? ne? akhi·gá·ya?ksek, honathwisdųní sthwíhah (LG03).

na?	go·?	na?	gęs	ne?	i?	de-hni-ksa?ah	nę
ASRT	CTR	ASRT	CST	NOM	PRN	DL-3M.DU.A-child	PRES
it's	however	it's	usually	the	I/we	two boys	here

hni-niyųt-ha?		o-yęd-a?		ne?	(aa-y)akhi-gaya?k-s-ek-Ø
3M.DU.A-hitch.up-HAB		NPF-firewood-NSF		NOM	OPT-1EX.NSG > 3-pay-HAB-CONT-PNC
they hitch it up		firewood		the	that we should pay them

hon-at-hwisd-ųni-h'   sthwiha
3M.NSG.P-SRF-money-make-STV QNT
they are earning money   a little bit
But as for us, we have two little boys that bring wood because they want to make a little bit of money.

c. Hya go·ʔ naʔ deʔųgwanasgwáyę̨ʔ, neʔ ę̨yų̨khinasgwanę̨́sgwaʔ (LG06).

hya	go·ʔ	naʔ	deʔ-ųgwa-nasgw-a-yę̨-ʔ	neʔ	ę̨-yų̨khi-nasgw-nę̨sgw-aʔ
NEG	CTR	ASRT	NEG-1PL.P-pet-JN-have-STV	NOM	FUT-3 > 1NSG-pet-steal-PNC
not	however	it's	we don't have pets	the	she/they will steal our pet

But we didn't have any pets for her to steal [literally, but we don't have pets, pets she will steal].

  (v) Conditional Clauses: *if (protasis)…then (apodosis)*:

These utterances begin with the conditional particle *gaʔt / dogaʔt* 'if' or the indefinite expression *dyę̨(haʔ) gwaʔ* 'maybe, perhaps, if'. The clause that states the consequence is not marked with a special particle. The utterance expresses hypothetical situations and their consequences. In our corpus the clause stating the condition always precedes the clause describing the consequence.

(103) a. [Gaʔt odų̨hwę̨·jyagwaihsyų̨́] [inų̨́ nhę̨́·weʔ neʔ gahwę̨́hdaʔ]… (HW04)

gaʔt	o-ad-ų̨hwę̨·jy-gwaihcy-ų̨h	inų̨́	n-h-ę̨-w-e-ʔ	neʔ
HYP	3N/Z.SG.P-SRF-earth-go.straight-STV	LOC	PRT-TRNS-FUT-3N/Z.SG.A-go-PNC	NOM
if	the land is level	far	thus it will go there	the

ga-hwę̨hd-aʔ
NPF-snowsnake-NSF
snowsnake
If the land is level, the snowsnake will go far…

b. [Dogáʔt sdę̨ʔ agihę̨́·ʔ] [dahadadyáʔ óʔ] (LG24).

do gaʔt	sdę̨ʔ	aa-g-ihę̨·-ʔ'	d-a-h-adady-aʔ	oʔ
INT HYP	INDF	OPT-1SG.A-say-PNC	CIS-FACT-3M.SG.A-answer-PNC	ADD
if	something	I would say it	he answered	also

If I should say something, he'd also answer back.

c. …[dyę̨ gwáʔ ahsehék dę̨hsadų̨góhdaʔ], [tho nę̨hcyé·æʔ, [wádę̨ʔ ę̨gų̨yathó·yę̨ʔ]] (HW07).

dyę̨ gwaʔ	aa-hs-eR-heʔ-k-Ø	d-ę̨-hs-ad-ų̨gohd-aʔ	tho
INDF	OPT-2SG.A-want-HAB-CNT-PNC	DL-FUT-2SG.A-SRF-pass.through-PNC	MAN
if, maybe	you may want it	you will survive	thus

n-ę̨-hs-yeR-aʔ	wadę̨ʔ	ę̨-gų̨y-atho·y-ę̨-ʔ
PRT-FUT-2SG.A-do-PNC	INTR	FUT-1SG > 2SG-tell-BEN-PNC
you will do it	what	I will tell you

"If you want to survive, you will do what I tell you."

(vi) Links with *da·* / *dá·ne* '(and) so':

Da·/dá·nẹ expresses event-continuation and sequencing. In (104a) the particle expresses a continuation of events: A man takes his wife to a dance where there is drinking, <u>so</u> his wife starts to drink. In (104b) a man lists the sequence of steps it takes to whittle a snowsnake. The excerpt is followed by a number of utterances all beginning with *dá·ne*. Different characteristics of sequences are expressed by combining *dá·ne* with other particles. In (104c) *dá·ne* occurs followed by the repetitive *he?* 'next, again', with a focus on the repetitive nature of sequencing. In (104d) it occurs in a conditional clause where it combines with the temporal particle with a focus on the temporal element of sequencing.

(104) a. <u>Da·</u> na? nẹgẹ́ ne? he·ná? wa?ehnegihǽ? o? ná? (LG09).

da·	na?	nẹgẹ	ne?	hena?	wa?-e-hnegihR-a?	o?	na?
LNK	ASRT	DEM	NOM	NOUN	FACT-3FI.A-drink-PNC	ADD	ASRT
so	it's	this	the	spouse	she drank		also	it's

So his wife also got to drinking.

    b. <u>Dá·ne</u> dẹtkhwẹ?ga·sthwáhda?, tsha? nigẹ́ tho nẹyo?ksdék tsha? nitshe·yẹ́sdih (HW03).

dane	d-ẹ-t-k-hwẹ?gaR-sthw-hd-a?		tsha?	nigẹ	tho
LNK	DL-FUT-CIS-1SG.A-splint-be.less-CS-PNC		SUB	EXT	MAN
so	I'll whittle at the splint		that	extent	thus

n-ẹ-yo-?ksd-e-k-Ø		tsha?	ni-t-hs-yẹsd-ih
PRT-FUT-3N/Z.SG.P-heavy-STV-CNT-PNC		SUB	PRT-CIS-2SG.A-be.appropriate-STV
how heavy it will be		that	it is appropriate for you

So then I'll whittle away (the) stick, until it's weight is appropriate for you.

    c. <u>Da·né hé?</u> ẹsge·há?da?... (HW03)

dane	he?	ẹ-s-ge-ha?d-a?
LNK	REP	FUT-REP-1SG.A-dry-PNC
so	next	I will dry it out

So next I will dry it out...

(vii) Clauses connected with paired particles:

Connection between clauses is sometimes expressed by paired particles, in which each of the pairs introduces a separate clause. Examples are *há·dye?* ... *na? go·?* 'even though'...'never-the-less'...' in (105a) and *ganyó?...da ó·nẹ...* 'as soon as...then' in (105b):

(105) a. Dẹ́?se? ne? <u>há·dye</u>, ne? hegagwegí thotgwenyụ́, ne? oyá·? né? na? nwa?haụhwẹjyó?dẹ?, <u>na? gó·?</u> gowẹ́ ne? agụ́·gwe, tsha? onụda?gegá? se? ná? (LG18).

dẹ?se?	ne?	hadye	ne?	he-ga-gweg-ih
CONJ	NOM	DIS	NOM	TRNS-3N/Z.SG.A-be.all-STV
and	the	never mind	the	everything

t-ho-at-gweny-ųh'		ne?	(y)-oya?		ne?	na?
CIS-3M.SG.P-SRF-be.able.to.do-STV		NOM	3N/Z.SG.A-be.different-STV		NOM	ASRT
he has earned it		the	different one		the	it's

n-wa?-ha-ųhwęjy-o?dę-?		na?	go·?	go-awę-h	ne?
PRT-FACT-3M.SG.P-nation-kind.of-PNC		ASRT	CTR	3FI.P-own-STV	NOM
his [Iroquois] nation		it's	however	she owns it	the

ag-ųgweh	tsha?	o-nųd-a? = ge = ga?		se?	na?
3FI.A-person:SUFF	SUB	NPF-hill-NSF = LOC = CHAR		MOD	ASRT
woman	that	Onondaga		actually	it's

And even though he has earned everything, he's from a different nation, so the Onondaga woman actually owns it.

d. <u>Ganyó?</u> dęyosda·thę́ha?, da· ó·nę ęgna?nawęhse·há·ę?, onų?wá?geh (HW03).

ganyo?	d-ę-yo-sda·th-ęh-a?	da·	onę
TMP	DL-FUT-3N/Z.SG.P-shine-INCH-PNC	LNK	TMP
as soon as	it will shine	so	now

ę-g-na?nawę-hsR-ohaR-ę?	o-nų?waR-a? = ge
FUT-1SG.A-melt-NOM-put.on.top-PNC	NPF-head-NSF-LOC
I will put lead on the top	on it's head

As soon as it's shiny, I'll put lead on its tip [literally, *I'll put lead on the top of its head*].

7.7.2 Reason and Because-Clauses

The expressions *na? dyoíhwa?* and *na? gánya? / na? ganyáha?*, 'it's the reason',[34] and *na? gwa?* 'because', relate two clauses such that one – the *reason*-clause – provides an explanation, a reason, or a cause, of the situation provided by the other – the *situation*-clause.

<u>Clauses with *na? dyoíhwa?*</u>. The *reason*-clause can precede the *situation*-clause as in (106a) or follow it (as in106b):

(106) a. [Na? dyoíhwa? ųgwa·haé? dęthé?] [tsha? ųgwaihwayé·idih, ne?
ųgwayo?dę́hsæ·?] (HW02).

na?	d-yo-Rihw-a?	ųgwa-Rhae-?	d-ę-t-h-e-?	tsha?
ASRT	CIS-NPF-matter-NSF	1PL.P-expect-STV	DL-FUT-CIS-3M.SG.A-walk-PNC	SUB
it's	the reason	we expect	he will come back	that

ųgwa-Rihw-a-yei-d-ih	ne?	ųgwa-yo?dęhsR-a?
1PL.P-matter-JN-complete-CS-STV	NOM	1PL.P-work-NSF
we have completed it	the	our work

The reason we're expecting him to come back is that we've finished our task.

---

[34] *ganya? / ganyáha?* probably derives from *gaihų·nyáha?*, i.e., *ga-Rihw-ųny-aha?* literally, 'it makes a matter'. This is the form used in similar contexts in the text transcribed by Hewitt from speakers at the end of the 19th century.

b. ...[dyųgwa·dé?gwęh[35] tsha? tganadá·yę?] [naye? dyoíhwa? swá?jik ade·yohsæ·?
odi·hwahdędyų́h]. (CTL69.5-6)

d-yųgw-ade?gw-ęh	tsha?	t-ga-nad-a-yę-?		naye?	d-yo-Rihw-a?
CIS-1PL.P-flee-STV	SUB	CIS-3N/Z.SG.A-village-JN-lie-STV		ASRT	CIS-NPF-matter-NSF
we have fled	that	village		it's	the reason

swa?jik	Ø-ade-Ryo-hsR-a?	o-ad-Rihw-ahdędyų-h'
INT	NPF-SRF-fight-NOM-NSF	3N/Z.SG.P-SRF-matter-move.on-STV
too much	warfare	it's going on

We fled the village because there was too much fighting going on.

Clauses with *na? ganyá(ha)?*. Like *na? dyoíhwa?*, the expression *na? ganyá(ha)?* 'the reason' occurs with the *reason*-clause:

(107) [Na? ganyá? gęs hya de?hanųhwé?s thogę ne? ashagohnha?nhá? ne?, nęgę ne?,
ganadá?ge nithoné·nų hų?shę·níh] [jik hya de?tha·di·hwayéi?s hya
de?honadi·hwagwaihcyų́h] (LG15).

na?	ganya?	gęs	hya	de?-ha-nųhwe?-s		thogę	ne?
ASRT	RSN	CST	NEG	NEG-3M.SG.A-like-HAB		DEM	NOM
it's	the reason	usually	not	he doesn't like it		that	the

aa-shago-hnha?-nha?	ne?	nęgę	ne?	ga-nad-a? = ge
OPT-3M.SG.A > 3-hire-PNC	NOM	DEM	NOM	NPF-town/city-NSF = LOC
he would hire them	the	this	the	at the city

ni-t-hon-e-nų	hų-a?shę·nih	jik	hya
PRT-CIS-3M.NSG.P-walk-STV	3M.PL.A-white.person	DGR	NEG
they come from there	white people	too much	not

de?-t-hadi-Rihw-a-yei-?s	hya	de?-hon-ad-Rihw-a-gwaihcy-ųh
NEG-CIS-3M.PL.A-matter-JN-correct-PL	NEG	NEG-3M.NSG.P-SRF-matter-JN-straight-STV
they aren't righteous	not	they aren't truthful

The reason he doesn't like to hire those white people from the city, is that they aren't trustworthy.

Reason clauses with *na? ganyá(ha)?* also occur as independent utterances as in (108):

(108) [Na? dę?se?, tsha? niyeksá?gona nęgę ne? hé·na?]. [Na? hyá? ų ganyá? tsha?
niyagodna·gé·hgwa? (LG09).

na?	dę?se?	tsha?	ni-ye-ksa?gona-h		nęgę	ne?	hena?	na?	hya?
ASRT	CNJ	SUB	PRT-3FI.A-nice.looking-STV		DEM	NOM	NOUN	ASRT	MOD
it's	and	that	she is good looking		this	the	spouse	it's	indeed

ų	ganya?	tsha?	ni-yago-ad-nage·-h-gwa?
MOD	RSN	SUB	PRT-3FI.P-SRF-be.plentiful-HAB-HBPST
probably	the reason	that	they used to be plentiful

And his wife was good looking. It's probably the reason she had plenty [of friends].

---

[35] Utterance-final prosody and the presence of word-final *h* utterance-medially is because the source of the excerpt is a dictated text (see sec. 1.3).

<u>Clauses with *naʔ gwaʔ* 'because'</u>: The expression *naʔ gwaʔ* occurs with the *reason*-clause
The two clauses can occur in either order as shown in (109):

(109) a. [Hya go·ʔ éʔ niʔá hwędų́ tshaʔ deʔwagatdó·gę,] [<u>naʔ gwáʔ</u> tshaʔ jik ihswáʔ
dewakdųkhwá·sʔih] (LG12).

hya	go·ʔ	eʔ	neʔ	iʔ	hwędų	tshaʔ	deʔ-wag-atdog-ęh
NEG	CTR	REP	NOM	PRON	INTR	SUB	NEG-1SG.P-notice-STV
not	however	again	the	I/we	when	that	I didn't notice

naʔ gwaʔ	tshaʔ	jik	ihswaʔ	de-wak-dųkhwaR-sʔih
ASRT RST	SUB	SCAL	QNT	DL-1SG.P-sweat-FCL
because	that	too	a lot	I'm sweating

However, I never noticed [the heat] because I was sweating a lot.

b. ...[<u>naʔ gwáʔ</u> tshaʔ hya deʔwahgayęʔíh neʔ awagegkdų́ʔ] [nę waʔwǽ·ʔ
dewa·gnųhyá·niʔks] (LG06).

naʔ gwaʔ	tshaʔ	hya	deʔ-wak-gaR-yę-ʔ-ih		neʔ
ASRT RSTR	SUB	NEG	NEG-1SG.P-price-have-INCH-STV		NOM
because	that	not	I won't pay		the

aa-wage-kdų-ʔ'		nę	waʔ-w-eR-aʔ	de-wag-nųhyaniʔk-s
OPT-3FZ.SG > 1SG-examine-PNC		TMP	FACT-3FZ.SG.A-think-PNC	DL-1SG.P-be.stingy-HAB
for her to tell my fortune		now	she thought	I am stingy

... it's because I won't pay for her to tell my fortune, [that] she thinks I'm stingy.

Given its intonation pattern with a pause and pitch reset following the first occurrence of
the assertion particle *naʔ*, example (110) may also be a *because*-clause:

(110) Naʔ go·ʔ neʔ oné sahayų́ʔ [waʔha·dyę́·ʔgwaʔ naʔ, [tho náʔ shatgodáʔ ganųhsákdaʔ,
neʔ jí·hah]] (HW05).

naʔ	go·ʔ	neʔ oné	s-a-ha-yų-ʔ		waʔ-h-adyęʔgw-aʔ
ASRT	CTR	NOM TMP	REP-FACT-3M.SG.A-arrive-PNC		FACT-3M.SG.A-surprise-PNC
it's	however	when	he got home		he was surprised

naʔ	tho	naʔ	s-ha-tgod-aʔ	ga-nųhs-akd-aʔ		neʔ	ji·hah
ASRT	LOC	ASRT	REP-3M.SG.A-sit-STV	3N/Z.SG.A-house-near-STV		NOM	noun
it's	there	it's	he's sitting again	near the house		the	dog

*When he got home, however, he was surprised [because], there the dog was sitting
again near the house. [Literally, when he got home, however, he was surprised it's
[pause and pitch reset], there he's sitting again...]*

7.8 Negation

The morphology of negative constructions is discussed in sections 4.2.1.4.3 and 4.7.8. Here
we recall that information as needed, but are concerned mainly with how negation is
expressed within the clause.

7.8.1 Verbal Negation

A morphological verb is negated by combining the negative particle *hya* with a verb that is prefixed with a negative or a contrastive prepronominal prefix. Recall that the contrastive does the work of the negative in the presence of modal prepronominals, because the negative and the modals cannot co-occur in the same morphological slot.

A negative imperative is expressed with the negative imperative particle *ahgwih* followed by an imperative verb or a punctual verb inflected with the future or optative. In addition, the imperative suffix can replace the punctual suffix in the latter construction. Infrequently, the particle cluster *ya gęk* 'it shouldn't be' is used in place of *ahgwi*.[36] The name *negative imperative* is somewhat misleading, since these constructions are used as much to mark precepts, decrees, injunctions, or instructions as they are to mark commands.

While the two elements of negation are ordered – the negative particle must precede the verb – the two need not occur adjacently. Very frequently they are separated by one or more particles:

(111) a. …dogá·ʔ niyohsæ·gé neʔ <u>hyá hwędų sų́·gaʔ neʔ hę́·gwe deʔshagonadahę·ʔséh</u> (CTL3.1-2).

doga·ʔ	ni-y-ohsR-a-ge-h'		ne?	hya	hwędų	sų ga?
QNT	PRT-3N/Z.SG.A-year-JN-amount.to-STV		NOM	NEG	INTR	INDF
several	thus many years		the	not	when	somebody

ne?	hR-ųgweh	de?-shago-nadahR-ę?se-h'
NOM	3M.SG.A-person:SUFF	NEG-3M.SG > 3-visit-BEN-STV
the	man	he didn't visit them

…for several years never did any man visit them.

b. Nę go·ʔ hyaʔ agwegí waʔhadidogęsdahę́·ʔ, neʔ nęgę́ gahnyodųnyų́ʔ deyotdé·nyųʔ, neʔ <u>ahgwí sų ga·ʔ ędyagoyé·nah</u> (LG13).

onę	go·?	hya?	agwegi	wa?-hadi-dogęst-ahę·-?'
TMP	CTR	MOD	QNT	FACT-3M.PL.A-straight-CS-DST-PNC
then	however	indeed	all	they fixed several

ne?	nęgę	ga-hnyod-ų-nyų-?'	de-yo-at-deny-ų-?
NOM	DEM	3N/Z.SG.A-protrude-DST-DST-STV	DL-3N/Z.SG.P-SRF-change-DST-STV
the	this	guards	they got changed

ne?	ahgwih	sų	ga·?	ę-d-yago-yena-h
NOM	IMPNEG	INTR	IND	FUT-CIS-3FI.P-catch-IMP
the	don't	somebody		it should catch someone

But then they fixed [the machines], changing the guards, so no one should get caught in them.

7.8.2 Negative Questions

Negative questions are rare in the corpus, but when they do occur, they are used as polite requests. The construction consists of the negative particle *hya,* followed by the question

---

[36] The particle cluster *ya gęk* is probably derived from *hya agęk* which is composed of the negative particle, the optative aa-, the non-animate agent pronominal -ga- the verb root -i- 'be, be all, be the total of', and the continuative suffix -k.

particle *khę* and a verb with either an optative or a negative prepronominal prefix as in (112a and b), respectively. Again, the two elements of the negative construction need not occur adjacently, as shown in (112b):

(112) a. <u>Hya khę thahsathųdát</u> ayųgninyakheʔ (H634.21-22).[37]

hya	khę	th-aa-hs-athųd-at-Ø	aa-yųgni-nyak-heʔ-Ø
NEG	QUE	CON-OPT-2SG.A-hear-CS-PNC	OPT-1DU.P-marry-INCH-PNC
not	question	you shouldn't agree	we two should get married

Wouldn't you agree we two should get married?

   b. <u>Ya khę sdęʔ deʔséheʔ</u>, dyę gwaʔ, tho óʔ naʔ ayų·nųhwét neʔ Clyde, tshaʔ nų dyųgnidáʔkstha?... (NC01)

hya	khę	sdęʔ	deʔ-s-eR-heʔ	dyę gwaʔ	tho	oʔ	naʔ
NEG	QUE	INDF	NEG-2SG.A-want,think-HAB	INDF	LOC	ADD	ASRT
not	question	some	you don't want it	if, maybe	there	also	it's

aa-yų-ęnųhwet-Ø	neʔ	Clyde	tshaʔ	nų	d-yųgn-idaʔk-st-ha?
OPT-3FI.A-spend.the.night-PNC	NOM	NAME	SUB	LOC	CIS-1DU.P-sleep-INST-HAB
one may spend the night	the	Clyde	that	place	our bedroom

Do you mind [literally: don't you want] *if Clyde spends the night in our bedroom...?*

7.8.3 Negative Expressions with Dependent Clauses

The polarity of dependent clauses is independent of the main clause's polarity. Thus, a main verb of either polarity, can occur with an argument clause of either polarity, as shown in (113) to (116).

   (i) Positive main verb, positive argument clause:

(113) ...[[waʔhgwe·nyáʔ] [waʔga·dyęʔ]] (LG23).

waʔ-k-gweny-aʔ	waʔ-g-adyę-ʔ´
FACT-1SG.A-can.do-PNC	FACT-1SG.A-sit.down-PNC
I was able to do it	I sat down

I was able to sit down.

   (ii) Positive main verb, negative argument clause:

(114) ...[[ęhųtdógaʔ] [hya thaʔde·jyodę·nų́·dak aųsadaʔgaidát]] (CTL487.1-2).

ę-hų-atdog-aʔ	hya	thaʔ-de-s-yo-ad-Ręn-ųdaR-k
FUT-3M.PL.A-notice-PNC	NEG	CON-DL-REP-3N/Z.SG.P-SRF-song-put.in-HAB
they will notice it	not	it isn't hopeful anymore

aųsa-ha-adaʔgaid-at-Ø
OPT:REP-3M.SG.A-recover-CS-PNC
for him to recover

...they will notice that there is no hope for his recovery.

---

[37] Hewitt did not mark stress or vowel length in this excerpt.

(iii) Negative main verb, positive argument clause:

(115) ... hya seʔ thahgwé·nyaʔ, a·gadadyaʔdagehnháʔ... (PJ01)

hya	seʔ	th-a-k-gweny-aʔ	aa-g-adad-yaʔdagehnh-aʔ
NEG	MOD	CON-OPT-1SG.A-be.able-PNC	OPT-1SG.A-REF-help-PNC
not	actually	I'm not able to	I help myself

...I'm not able to help myself...

(iv) Negative main verb, negative argument clause:

(116) ...[[hya deʔoyá·ne·ʔ] [neʔ ų́gwe hya daʔdeyų̄dadnowę̄́khwaʔ]] (CTL14.2-3).

hya	deʔ-o-yane·-ʔ	neʔ	(y)-ų̄gweh	hya
NEG	NEG-3N/Z.SG.P-good-STV	NOM	NPF-person:SUFF	NEG
not	it isn't good	the	person(s)	not

daʔ-de-yų̄dad-nowęhgw-haʔ
NEG-DL-3FI > 3FI-act.kindly-HAB
they aren't kind to one another.

...it isn't good that the people aren't kind to one another.

Like argument clauses, the polarity of the main clause and a relative clause (a) or the main clause and an embedded question (b) are independent of each other. If a verb's argument is expressed with a verb form that functions as an internally headed relative clause, the predicate expression and the argument expression are marked separately with the negative prepronominal prefix as shown in (117):[38]

(117) a. ...ahsų̄ [[deʔjyų̄gweʔdadah] [deʔagogwathwih neʔ thonę]] (H617.19).[39]

ahsų̄	deʔ-s-y-ų̄gwe-ʔt-ada-h	deʔ-ago-gwathw-ih
TMP	NEG-REP-3FZ.SG.A-person-NOM-be.one-STV	NEG-3FI.P-drop.in-STV
still = not yet	not one woman	she hasn't visited

neʔ	thonę
NOM	LOC
the	here

Still not a single woman has come here to visit [literally: she hasn't visited here yet, not a person who is singly a woman].

b. [[Hya deʔwagę̄nųhdų́ʔ] [do hų̄ nigahwisdagé deyagohwisdáų̄h]] (LG17).

hya	deʔ-wag-ę̄nųhdų-ʔ	do	hų̄	ni-ga-hwisd-a-ge-h'
NEG	NEG-1SG.P-know-STV	INT	MOD	PART-3N/Z.SG.A-money-JN-amount.to-STV
not	I don't know	how	probably	the amount of money it is

---

[38] The temporal particle *ahsų̄* can replace the negative particle as the first element in negative expressions.

[39] Hewitt did not mark stress and vowel length in this excerpt.

de-yago-hwisd-a-ųh
DL-3FI.P-money-take.hold.of-STV
she got money
I don't know how much money she got.

7.8.4 Negating a Nominal

To negate a nominal the negative particle *hya* and the verb form *déʔgęh* are used. While the two negation elements are ordered, the verb form *déʔgęh* can occur on either side of the negated nominal, as shown in (118).

(118) a. <u>Hya</u> naʔ ųgwe <u>deʔgęh</u> sgęhnáksę sawadų́ʔ (H635.17-18).[40]

hya	naʔ	(y)-ųgweh	deʔ-ga-i-h	sgęhnaksę
NEG	ASRT	NPF-person:SUFF	NEG-3N/Z.SG.A-be.all-STV	NOUN
not	it's	person(s)	it isn't	fox

s-a-w-adų-ʔ
REP-FACT-3N/Z.SG.A-become-PNC
it became again
It is not a human, it has become a fox again.

b. <u>Hya</u> naʔ néʔ Bob hagnoʔsę́hah <u>déʔgę</u>, ųgyaæʔséʔ naʔ neʔ Bob (JM/EO).

hya	naʔ	neʔ	Bob	hag-noʔsęhah	deʔ-ga-i-h
NEG	ASRT	NOM	NAME	3M.SG > 1SG-uncle	NEG-3N/Z.SG.A-be.all-STV
not	it's	the	Bob	my uncle	it isn't

ųgy-aæʔseʔ	neʔ	Bob
1DU.P-cousin	NOM	NAME
we two cousins	the	Bob

Bob isn't my uncle, he's my cousin.

c. …<u>hya</u> naʔ <u>deʔgę́</u> neʔ gwas ų́·we hodųwędá·dyeʔ, desgya·dyéę gó·ʔ (HW06).

hya	naʔ	deʔ-ga-i-h	neʔ	gwas ųwe	ho-adųwęd-adye-ʔ
NEG	ASRT	NEG-3N/Z.SG.A-be.all-STV	NOM	INTS AUTH	3M.SG.P-chant-PRG-STV
not	it's	it isn't	the	authentic	his chanting

de-s-gy-adyeR-ęh	go·ʔ
DL-REP-3FZ.DU.A-similar-STV	CTR
they two are similar	however

… this isn't normal chanting, but the two are similar.

d. Gehéʔ <u>hyá</u> íʔ <u>deʔgę́</u> neʔ tshaʔ oyáʔ níyot tshaʔ sų́nheʔ (H168.13).

g-eR-heʔ	hya	iʔ	deʔ-ga-i-h	neʔ	tshaʔ
1SG.A-think-HAB	NEG	PRON	NEG-3N/Z.SG.A-be.all-STV	NOM	SUB
I think	not	I	it isn't	the	that

---

[40] Hewitt did not mark stress and vowel length in this excerpt.

(y)-oya?	ni-yo-ht-Ø	tsha? s-ųnhe-?
3N/Z.SG.A-different-STV	PRT-3N/Z.SG.P-how.it.is-STV	SUB 2SG.A-be.alive-STV
it is different	how it is	your life

I think it is not I who [caused] your life to change.

7.8.5 Other Forms of Negation

With very few exceptions (see below), Onondaga's particles express positive polarity. Two methods of achieving negative polarity are (a) creating a particle cluster consisting of *hya* and a particle (119a), and with a combination of *hya* and the negative prepronominal *de?-* affixed to the particle (119b). The choice between the two is lexicalized.

(119) a. "Hótgi? ų́hdeh," hahsá? saho·ha?nhá? Clyde <u>hya gátga?, hya ó?</u> ná? ne? hohsó·dah (NC01).

ho-tgi-?	ų̨hdeh	hahsa?	s-a-ho-a·ha?-nha?
3M.SG.P-filthy-STV	INTS	TMP	REP-FACT-3M.SG.P-remember-PNC
he's filthy	extremely	right away	he remembered

Clyde	hya	gatga?	hya	o?	na?	ne?	ho-hsodah
NAME	NEG	INDF	NEG	ADD	ASRT	NOM	3M.SG.P-grandfather
Clyde	not	somewhere	not	also	it's	the	his grandfather

"Oh darn it," right away he remembers, [but] Clyde [is] nowhere [around], nor is his grandfather.

b. Da· [a]yę́? di? na? <u>hya hų́·</u> gwás <u>de?dogę́s</u> ne? ná? dyóihwa?... (LG04)

da	ayę·?	di?	na?	hya	hų	gwas	de?-dogęs
LINK	SIM	LINK	ASRT	NEG	MOD	INTS	NEG-true
so	it seems	moreover	it's	not	probably	really	not true

ne?	na?	d-yo-Rihw-a?
DEM	ASRT	CIS-NPF-matter-NSF
the	it's	reason

So it seems it probably wasn't true, [that that was] the reason...

Two particles – *wa?jik?á /gwajik?á* 'nearly, almost' and *ahsų* 'still not, not yet' – can replace *hya* in a negative expression:

(120) a. wa?jik?á í? de?wage·yóh (H668.15).

wa?jik?á	i?	de?-wage-Ryo-h'
DGR	PRON	NEG-1SG.P-kill.someone-STV
almost	I, we	it hasn't killed me

It nearly killed me

b. ...wa?hęhę́·?, hehohyadų́h nęn, dewęhni?dagé tsha? nwa?ųníshe?, <u>ahsų da?dethadihyadųk</u> (LG19).

wa?-ha-ihę·-?´	he-ho-hyadų-h	onę
FACT-3M.SG.A-say-PNC	TRNS-3M.SG.P-write-STV	TMP
he said	he has written there	now

de-w-ęhni?d-a-ge-h´	tsha?	nwa?ųnishe?	ahsų
DL-3N/Z.SG.A-month-JN-amount.to-STV	SUB	TMP	TMP
it's two months	that	long time	not yet

da?-de-t-hadi-hyadų-k
NEG-DL-CIS-3M.PL.A-write-HAB
they don't write here
...he said, he wrote him as long as two months ago [and] still they haven't written here.

7.9 Modality

Modality is a semantic category that deals with the expression of (i) a speaker's commitment to the factuality of the situation expressed by a clause or (ii) the speaker's commitment to the necessity of a situation's accomplishment. An English example of a modalized expression of the first kind is *she may be late* [as against the non-modalized statement *she is late*] Here the inclusion of the modal auxiliary *may* shows that the speaker is somewhat doubtful about the factuality of the situation. An example, of the second kind is *you must wash the dishes.* Here the modal auxiliary *must* marks the fact that the speaker is imposing a strong obligation on someone to bring about the event. Important dimensions of modality are the concepts of *necessity, possibility,* and certain *inherent characteristics* of a participant, such as the *ability* or *inclination* of a participant to accomplish the task expressed by the situation. The first example – *she may be late* – expresses *possibility*; the second example – *you must wash the dishes* – expresses *necessity*; a third set of examples – *she can wash the dishes* vs. *she could wash the dishes* – expresses *ability* and, in at least one reading, *inclination*, respectively.

Linguists frequently divide modality into three categories that, to some extent, overlap the distinctions discussed in the previous paragraph. They are (i) epistemic modality, (ii) deontic modality, and (iii) dynamic modality. <u>Epistemic modality</u> is concerned with the expression of necessity and possibility in terms of a speaker's commitment to the truth of the proposition, that is, does the speaker have a strong (necessity) or a weakened (degrees of possibility) commitment to its factuality. For example: *He must have arrived by now* (strong commitment) vs. *He may have arrived by now* (weak commitment). <u>Deontic modality</u> can emanate from different sources; either the speaker himself, or rules, regulations, social conventions, etc. can serve as deontic sources. The modality is concerned with the expression of necessity and possibility in terms of the strength of the obligation (various degrees of necessity and possibility) the deontic sources impose. For example: You *must* get to school on time (strong obligation) vs. You *may* read, if you want (weak obligation). <u>Dynamic modality</u> differs from epistemic and deontic modality in that it involves characteristics, i.e., abilities or dispositions of persons who are referred to in the clause. It can also involve the concepts of necessity and possibility, for example, in terms of their strength. Thus *He needs some sleep* (necessity) vs. *He hopes for some sleep* (possibility) expresses a weaker one. In turn, *he can get you there in a hurry* expresses, a participants ability to do something.

Onondaga lacks modal auxiliaries like English *may, should, must, can etc.*; it expresses modality either lexically, mainly with morphological verbs, or with modal particles. Finally, as was discussed in chapter 4, section 4.2 above, the modal prepronominal prefixes –the factual, future, and optative prefixes of verbs – and the different uses of the imperative, are the grammaticalized resources Onondaga speakers use to express modality.[41]

Sections 7.9.1 - 7.9.3 deal with how modality is expressed using Onondaga's verbal and particle resources. Each section looks at these in terms of the semantic categories of necessity and possibility.[42]

7.9.1 Epistemic Necessity and Possibility

The Onondaga language expresses epistemic necessity and possibility as a graded series, ranging from a speaker's certainty that what he is saying is factual to various degrees of reservation on that score. The modality is expressed both lexically by several verb forms and by particles. For example, the morphological verb *-ęnųhdų–* 'know' frequently is used to express certainty:

(121) a. ...<u>agęnųhdų́·ʔ</u> waʔgihę́·ʔ neʔ wadę́ʔ niyót neʔ ohędų́ʔ neʔ ęyo·hę́·ʔnha? (LG06).

ag-ęnųhdų-ʔ	waʔ-g-ihę·-ʔ´		neʔ	wadęʔ	niyot	neʔ
1SG.P-know-STV	FACT-1SG.A-say-PNC		NOM	INT	MAN	NOM
I know	I said		the	what	how it is	the

o-hęd-ų		neʔ	ę-yo-Rhę·ʔ-nha?
3N/Z.SG.P-be.ahead-STV		NOM	FUT-3N/Z.SG.P-become.day-PNC
it is ahead		the	tomorrow

...I said, I know what's ahead, in the future.

b. Naʔ gęs neʔ nę· <u>ųgwę·nų́hdų?,</u> tshaʔ niga·hawíʔ dę́theʔ, ęshá·yų? (HW02).

naʔ	gęs	neʔ nę	ųgw-ęnųhdų-ʔ	tshaʔ	ni-ga-hawi-ʔ
ASRT	CST	NOM TMP	1PL.P-know-STV	SUB	PRT-3N/Z.SG.A-carry-STV
it's	usually	when	we know	that	it's time

d-ę-t-h-e-ʔ		ę-s-ha-yų-ʔ
DL-FUT-CIS-3M.SG.A-walk-PNC		FUT-REP-3M.SG.A-arrive-PNC
he will come back		he will return home

Usually, that's when we know it's time for him [father] to get back home.

The stative verb form *oyę́·det* 'be noticeable, show' consists of the non-animate pronominal prefix *o-*, the verb root *-yędeR-* 'know' and a causative suffix. Despite its English glosses, in context it signals epistemic necessity. For example:

(122) a. <u>Oyędé·t</u> tshaʔ niwahétgęh, neʔ naʔ éstha? (LG09).

o-yędeR-t-Ø		tshaʔ	ni-w-ahetgę-h		neʔ	naʔ	e-st-ha?
3N/Z.SG.P-know-CS-STV		SUB	PRT-3N/Z.SG.A-be.bad-STV		NOM	ASRT	3FI.A-use-HAB
it shows		that	how bad it is		the	it's	one uses it

It <u>goes to show</u> how bad it is to use it [i.e., whiskey].

---

[41] See especially the discussion in section 4.2.1.3 on the punctual aspect and marking mood.

[42] The expression of modality in the Iroquoian languages and its development over time are discussed in Mithun (2016). Expressions of modality in Seneca are discussed in Chafe (2015), in Oneida in Michelson, et al. (2016).

b. Naʔ <u>gayȩdéthaʔ</u>, tshaʔ agwaksaʔdiyóʔsgwaʔ, tshaʔ nwaʔonísheʔ hohdȩdyų́h (HW02).

naʔ	ga-yȩdeR-t-haʔ	tshaʔ	agwa-ksaʔd-iyo-ʔs-gwaʔ	tshaʔ
ASRT	3N/Z.SG.A-know-CS-HAB	SUB	1EX.PL.A-child-be.good-STVPL-HBPST	SUB
it's	it shows	that	we've been good children	that

n-waʔ-y-ųnishe-ʔ	ho-ahdȩdyų-h'
PRT-FACT-3N/Z.SG.A-length.of.time-PNC	3M.SG.P-depart-STV
length of time	he's been gone

It's what shows that we've been good children while he was gone.

The morphological verb *-eR-* 'think, want', especially when it is inflected with a first person pronominal prefix, is used to signal reduced certainty, as in (123):

(123) a. <u>Gehéʔ</u> naʔ hyaʔ ų· tshaʔ gųgwehų́·we (LG12).

g-eR-heʔ	naʔ	hyaʔ	ų·	tshaʔ	g-ųgweh-ųweh
1SG.A-think-HAB	ASRT	MOD	MOD	SUB	1SG.A-person:SUFF-AUTH
I think	that's it	indeed	probably	that	I am an Indian

I suppose it was because I was Indian.

b. Ȩ· hya gó·ʔ ų <u>gehéʔ</u> deʔshoyoʔdę́ʔih... (LG13)

ę·	hya	go·ʔ	ų	g-eR-heʔ
FILLER	NEG	CTR	MOD	1.SG.A-think-HAB
ah	not	however	probably	I think

deʔ-s-ho-yoʔdę-ʔ-ih
NEG-REP-3M.SG.P-work-INCH-STV
he didn't get to work again

I don't believe he worked again... [literally, I think he didn't work again].

The particle variously pronounced *ayę́·æʔ/ayeęʔ/ayę́·ʔ/ayǽ·ʔ* 'it seems, it's like' which probably derives from the verb form a-y-eR-aʔ [OPT-3FI.A-think-PNC] 'one might think' has a similar effect:

(124) <u>Ayę́·ʔ</u> go·ʔ, hya hų· gwas, tháyodiyanę́·sdę́ʔ (LG02).

ayę́·ʔ	go·ʔ	hya	hų	gwas	th-aa-yodi-yanę·-sd-ę-ʔ
SIM	CTR	NEG	MOD	INTS	CON-OPT-3FZ.NSG.P-good-CS-BEN-PNC
seems like	however	not	probably	very	it will cause it to be good for them

Seems like [the plants] aren't going to do well at all.

Many modal particles express epistemic modality; *dogȩ(s)* 'for sure, truly' and *(naʔ) séʔ* 'actually, in fact' are used to signal necessity:

(125) a. Naʔ óʔ neʔ, <u>dogȩs</u> néʔ naʔ si nigáȩ ostáȩ·dyeʔs (LG02).

naʔ	oʔ	dogȩs	neʔ	naʔ	si nigaȩh	o-staR-ųdye-ʔs
ASRT	ADD	MOD	NOM	ASRT	LOC EXT	3N/Z.SG.P-rain-throw.away-HAB
it's	also	truly	the	it's	long extent	it rains

Additionally, for sure, it's been a long time between showers.

b. Ahsedéh se? wa?shagwa?nųhdá·k Tom Green (LG05).

ahsedeh	se?	wa?-shagwa-?nųhdaR-k	Tom Green
TMP	MOD	FACT-1EX.PL > 3M.SG-bury-PNC	NAME
yesterday	actually	we buried him	Tom Green

Yesterday we actually buried Tom Green.

Strong possibility is expressed by the particle *gęhjihwę́h*, 'it must be, apparently, I think that...'

(126) a. Dųdawado?kdę́? gęs, na? dí? hya? ųhgę? nęgę́ ų, tsha? nwa?awę́ha?, gęhjihwę́h jih stroke (LG05).

d-ųda-w-ado?kd-ę?	gęs	na?	di?	hya?	ųhgę?	nęgę	ų
DL-CIS:FACT-3N/Z.SG.A-end-PNC	CST	ASRT	LINK	MOD	TMP	DEM	MOD
it reversed	usually	it's	so	indeed	this time		maybe

tsha?	n-wa?-aw-ęh-a?	gęhjihwęh	ga-yas-i	stroke
SUB	PRT-FACT-3N/Z.SG.P-happen-PNC	MOD	3N/Z.SG.A-be.named-STV	NOUN
that	thus it happened	surely	it is called	stroke

He gets better [usually], but this time what happened __must have__ been a stroke.

b. Na? deshagosnye?íh gęhjihwę́ ó? odya?kshų?á tho nihadiyé·ha? (LG20).

na?	de-shago-snye-?-ih	gęhjihwęh	o?
ASRT	DL-3M.SG > 3-take.care.of-INCH-STV	MOD	ADD
it's	he took care of them	surely	also

odya?k = shų?á	tho	ni-hadi-yeR-ha?
QNT = PL	MAN	PART-3M.PL.A-do-HAB
various	thus	the way they do it

He took care of his family and __surely__ various [others] did the same thing.

The particle cluster *hyá? ų* 'indeed, probably' expresses a relatively strong commitment to factuality:

(127) a. Onę hyá? ų deyohsæ·gé tsha? nwa?ųníshe?, nęgę́ tho nidyawę́?i, nęgę́ ne? hęgwéh wa?sha·gó·yo?, ne? hé·na?, a?shá·? wa?hásda? (LG09) .

onę	hya?	ų	de-y-ohsR-a-ge-h´	tsha?	nwa?ųnishe?
TMP	MOD	MOD	DL-3N/Z.SG.A-winter-JN-amount.to-STV	SUB	TMP
now	indeed	probably	it is two years	that	how long ago

nęgę	tho	ni-d-yaw-ę?-ih	nęgę	ne?	hR-ųgweh
DEM	MAN	PRT-CIS-3N/Z.SG.P-happen-STV	DEM	NOM	3M.SG.A-man:SUFF
this	thus	thus it happened here	this	the	man

wa?-shago-Ryo-?	ne?	he·na?	(Ø)-a?shaR-?	wa?-ha-sd-a?
FACT-3M.SG > 3-kill-PNC	NOM	NOUN	NPF-knife-NSF	FACT-3M.SG.A-use-PNC
he killed her	the	spouse	knife	he used

__It must be__ about 2 years ago it happened, this man killed his wife with a knife.

b. Naʔ diʔ hyaʔ niʔá neʔ, tho nhwaʔgéʔ tshaʔ thanagé·ʔ nęgę́ neʔ, ęhm, justice-of-peace <u>hyaʔ ų·</u> hayá·jih (LG06).

naʔ	diʔ	hyaʔ	neʔ	iʔ = á	neʔ	tho	n-h-waʔ-g-e-ʔ
ASRT	LINK	MOD	NOM	PRN-DIM	NOM	LOC	PRT-TRNS-FACT-1SG.A-walk-PNC
it's	so	indeed	the	I, alone	the	there	I went there

tsha?	t-ha-nage·-ʔ		nęgę	neʔ	ęhm	hyaʔ	ų·
SUB	CIS-3M.SG.A-dwell-STV		DEM	NOM	FILLER	MOD	MOD
that	where he lives		this	the	ah	indeed	probably

justice of the peace	ha-yas-ih
NOMINAL	3M.SG.A-be.named-STV
justice of the peace	he is called

And I myself went to the man who <u>I guess</u> he is called Justice of the Peace.

7.9.2 Deontic Necessity and Possibility

Deontic modality, as was pointed out above, can emanate from different sources, either the speaker himself, or rules and regulations, social conventions, etc. It is concerned with the expression of necessity and possibility in terms of the strength of the obligation the deontic source imposes. In Onondaga these range from lexicalized verb forms like *tgagų́·daʔ* 'it must be', to morphological verbs like *-atho·yę–* 'tell someone to do something' and *-adų-* 'be possible', where the strength of the obligation also sometimes is mitigated by the prepronominal prefix that is chosen by the speaker when specifying the obligation.

<u>Obligation</u>

The lexicalized verb form/particle *tgagų́·daʔ / gų́·daʔ* 'it must be' expresses a very strong obligation. In (128a) the quoted speaker is the deontic source; in (128b) the deontic source is someone other than the speaker, someone who is conveying local hiring rules:

(128) a. Tgagų́·daʔ, yágę? waʔhęhę́·ʔ, tshaʔ, tho nęhcyeǽʔ nwadę́ʔ gųyathó·yęnik (HW07).

t-ga-gųd-aʔ		yagę?	waʔ-ha-ihę·-ʔ		tshaʔ	tho
CIS-3N/Z.SG.A-be.essential-STV		HRSY	FACT-3M.SG.A-say-PNC		SUB	MAN
it is essential		they say	he said		that	thus

n-ę-hs-yeR-aʔ	nwadę?	gųy-atho·y-ęni-k
PRT-FUT-2SG.A-do-PNC	INTR	1SG > 2SG-tell-BEN-HAB
you'll do it a certain way	what	I tell you

"It is essential," they say, he said, "that you do what I tell you."

b. … waʔhųwatho·yę́ʔ <u>gųdáʔ</u> oʔ naʔ neʔ hų?shę·níh ęshagohnhaʔnháʔ nęgę, neʔ hadinadáʔgehé·nųʔ (LG15).

waʔ-hųwa-atho·y-ę-ʔ		gųda?	o?	naʔ	neʔ	hų-aʔshę·nih
FACT-3 > 3M.SG-tell-BEN-PNC		MOD	ADD	ASRT	NOM	3M.PL.A-white.person
they told him		it must be	also	it's	the	white guys

ẹ-shago-hnhaʔ-nhaʔ   nẹgẹ   neʔ   hadi-nad-aʔ = ge = he·nụʔ
FUT-3M.SG > 3-hire-PNC   DEM   NOM   3M.PL.A-town-NSF-LOC-POP
he will hire them   this   the   city people
...they told him he <u>must</u> hire white guys from the city.

<u>Orders</u> (129) and <u>requests</u> (130) impose obligations of various strengths. Together with a following optative verb form, the stem *-atho·yẹ–* 'tell someone' comes across as an order:

(129) <u>Waʔshagotho·yẹ́ʔ</u> ẹ· nhaụsahẹ·néʔ (LG06).
       waʔ-shago-atho·y-ẹ-ʔ   ẹ·   n-h-aụsa-hẹn-e-ʔ'
       FACT-3M.SG > 3-tell-BEN-PNC   DIR-C   PRT-TRNS-OPT:REP-3M.PL.A-walk-PNC
       he told them   away   they should go back there
       He told them to move away.

<u>Permission and requests for permission</u> are often expressed with the morphological verb *-adụ-* 'be possible'. In (130a) a minister is cited as having given permission to the speaker to buy his horse; in (130b) *-adụ-* is used together with the question particle to ask for permission:

(130) a. ... nẹgẹ́ naʔ hajihẹsdajíʔ waʔhẹhẹ́·ʔ <u>ẹwadụ́ʔ</u> ẹkhninụ́ʔ ... (LG23)
         nẹgẹ   naʔ   ha-jihẹdaji-h   waʔ-ha-ihẹ·-ʔ'
         DEM   ASRT   3M.SG.A-be.a.minister-STV   FACT-3M.SG.A-say-PNC
         this   it's   he is a minister   he said

         ẹ-w-adụ-ʔ   ẹ-k-hninụ-ʔ
         FUT-3N/Z.SG.A-be.possible-PNC   FUT-1SG.A-buy-PNC
         it will be   I will buy it
         ... this minister said [that] I <u>can</u> buy it [i.e., his horse] ...

      b. <u>Ẹwá·dụʔ</u> khẹ asdé nhẹgéʔ.
         ẹ-w-adụ-ʔ   khẹ   asde   n-h-ẹ-g-e-ʔ
         FUT-3N/Z.SG.A-be.possible-PNC   QUE   LOC   PRT-TRNS-FUT-1SG.A-walk-PNC
         it will be possible   question outside thus I will go
         <u>Can</u> I go outside?

<u>Giving advice</u> imposes a weak form of obligation. The lexicalized form *á·gẹk* an inflected form of the morphological verb *-i-* 'be, exist, make up the total, be all of it, be the only' is used in (131) to advise a person on how to avoid a confrontation with a dangerous animal:

(131) Da· nis <u>á·gẹk</u>, ẹtshahgwehnẹ́hdaʔ, ẹhsa·déʔgwaʔ (HW07).
       da   nis   aa-ga-i-k-Ø   ẹ-t-hs-ahgwehnẹhd-a?
       LNK   PRON   OPT-3N/Z.SG.A-be-CNT-PNC   FUT-CIS-2SG.A-descend-PNC
       so   you   it should be   you will come down

       ẹ-hs-adeʔgw-a?
       FUT-2SG.A-escape-PNC
       you will escape
       So, as to you, you <u>should</u> come down [and] escape.

The morphological verb *.adǫhwẹjyo-* + dualic 'be necessary' is used to express obligations that find their deontic source in social conventions:

(132) Onę diʔ híhyaʔ, aedwaʔnigǫhǽdák tshaʔ <u>deyodǫhwẹ·jyóhwih</u>, ae·dwadǫhehsę́·ʔ...
     (HW06)

onę	diʔ	hihyaʔ	ae-dwa-ʔnigǫhR-d-Ø-k-Ø	tshaʔ
TMP	LNK	MOD	OPT-1IN.PL.A-mind-stand-STV-CNT-PNC	SUB
now	moreover	indeed	we should be keeping in mind	that

de-yo-adǫhwẹjyo-hwi	ae-dw-adǫhehsę·-ʔ'
DL-3N/Z.SG.P-necessary-STV	OPT-1IN.PL.A-pray-PNC
it is necessary	we should pray

Now indeed, we should keep in mind that it is necessary for us to pray ...

7.9.3 Dynamic Necessity and Possibility

The verb form *tgagǫ́·daʔ* 'it must be' and the particle *gǫ́daʔ*, as we have seen in section 7.9.2, can express deontic necessity. It is also used to express dynamic necessity, and sometimes an expression will be ambiguous between the two meanings, depending on whether it expresses internal (dynamic) needs or externally sourced (deontic) obligation. The examples in (133) express internal needs and drives:

(133) a. Ę̀· onę díʔ hyáʔ nęgę́ yágęʔ waʔhęhę́·ʔ, tgagǫdáʔ niʔ ęsgadéʔgwaʔ (HW07).

ę·	onę	diʔ	hyaʔ	nęgę	yagęʔ	waʔ-ha-ihę·-ʔ'
FILLER	TMP	LNK	MOD	DEM	HRSY	FACT-3M.SG.A-say-PNC
ah	now	moreover	indeed	this	they say	he said

t-ga-gǫd-aʔ	ne? iʔ	ę-s-g-adeʔgw-aʔ
CIS-3N/Z.SG.A-be.necessary-STV	NOM PRON	FUT-REP-1SG.A-run.away-PNC
it must be	I/we	I will run back [home]

So then he says "I've <u>got</u> to get out of here."

b. Gǫdáʔ go·ʔ naʔ geʔsé·ʔs nęgę́ ǫhgę́ʔ ya go·ʔ deʔskheyaʔdanę́hgwik... (LG10)

gǫdaʔ	go·ʔ	naʔ	ge-ʔse·-ʔs	nęgę	ǫhgęʔ
MOD	CTR	ASRT	1SG.A-drive-HAB	DEM	TMP
by necessity	however	it's	I drive around	this	at this time

ya	deʔ-s-khe-yaʔd-a-nęhgwi-k
NEG	NEG-REP-1SG > 3-body-JN-haul-HAB
not	I'm not a taxi driver anymore

I must drive [for myself], but at this time I'm not a taxi driver any longer.

The morphological verb *-adǫ-* 'be possible' is another morphological verb that is used to express both deontic and dynamic modality. In (134a and b) it expresses <u>ability</u> and <u>inability</u>, respectively:

(134) a. Dogáʔt gowiyǽ·yęʔ, neʔ goyoʔdéʔ ęyųdadehnháʔnhaʔ, go·ʔ neʔ eksaʔáh neʔtho
nidyagododí neʔ <u>ęwá·dųʔ,</u> dęyesnyeʔnháʔ neʔ niyagaʔá (LG11).

dogaʔt	go-wiR-a-yę-ʔ		neʔ	go-yoʔde-ʔ	ę-yųdade-hnhaʔ-nhaʔ
ALT	3FI.P-child-JN-have-STV		NOM	3FI.P-work-STV	FUT-3FI > 3FI-hire-PNC
if	she has a child		the	she is working	she will hire her

go·ʔ	neʔ	e-ksaʔah	neʔtho	ni-d-yago-adodi-h	neʔ
CTR	NOM	3FI.A-child	MAN	PRT-CIS-3FI.P-grow.up-STV	NOM
however	the	girl	thus	she has grown up	the

ę-w-adų-ʔ	d-ę-ye-snye-ʔ-nhaʔ	neʔ
FUT-3N/Z.SG.A-become.possible-PNC	DL-FUT-3FI.A-look.after-INCH-PNC	NOM
it will be possible	she will take care of [things]	the

ni-yag-aʔa-h
PRT-3FI.A-be.small-STV
they are little

*If a woman who works has a child, she will hire a girl who has grown up [and]
who is able to take care of the little ones.*

b. <u>Hya oʔ thawá·dųʔ,</u> hyaʔ ahadiyagęʔnháʔ neʔ naʔ hodiyǽ·ʔi, neʔ ayehninųhǽ·ʔ sdęʔ
íyeks (LG20).

hya	oʔ	th-aa-w-adų-ʔ	hyaʔ	aa-hadi-yagę-ʔ-nhaʔ	neʔ
NEG	ADD	CON-OPT-3N/Z.SG.A-possible-PNC	MOD	OPT-3M.PL.A-emerge-PNC	NOM
not	also	it isn't possible	indeed	for them to come out	the

naʔ	hodi-yeR-aʔ-ih	neʔ	aa-ye-hninų-hR-aʔ	sdęʔ
ASRT	3M.NSG.P-do-INCH-STV	NOM	OPT-3FI.A-buy-DSLC-PNC	INDF
it's	they get to do it	the	for them to go to buy	some

i-ye-k-s
EP-3FI.A-eat-HAB
they eat it = food

The people who had smallpox couldn't go out to buy food.

Another morphological verb that is used to express ability is *-gweny-* 'be able, can do'.
It's negative *expresses in*ability:

(135) a. Ahgwíh ęhsgęhæʔs , naʔ dyóihwaʔ tshaʔ <u>ęhgwe·nyáʔ</u> tshaʔ tho, waʔhęhę́·ʔ,
ęgųyaʔdagéhnhaʔ (HW07).

ahgwih	ę-hs-gęhæʔs-Ø	naʔ	d-yo-Rihwa-ʔ	tshaʔ
NEG	FUT-2SG.A-despise-PNC	ASRT	CIS-3N/Z.SG.P-be.a.reason-STV	SUB
don't	you will despise it	it's	the reason	that

ę-k-gweny-aʔ	tshaʔ	tho	waʔ-ha-ihę·-ʔ'
FUT-1SG.A-be.able.to-PNC	SUB	MAN	FACT-3M.SG.A-say-PNC
I'll be able to	that	thus	he said

ę-gu-ya?dagehnh-a?
FUT-1SG > 2SG-help-PNC
I'll help you
"Don't despise [my advice]," he said, "because that's how <u>I'll be able</u> to help you."

b. Hya thauhsahgwé·nya?, ne? ihswá? wa?ge?se·shú? (LG10).

hya	th-ausa-k-gweny-a?		ne?	ihswa?	wa?-ge-?se·-shu-?'
NEG	CON-OPT:REP-1SG.A-be.able.to-PNC		NOM	QNT	FACT-1SG.A-drive-DST-PNC
not	I can't anymore		the	a lot	I drive around

I <u>can't</u> drive so much anymore.

Inflected with the non-animate agent pronominal, *-gweny-* is used to express potentialities that derive from rules or conditions outside the agent, such as social conventions or objective reality. This is illustrated by the question-answer pair in (136):

(136) Addition problem:
<u>Question</u>: do· niyú ęga·gwe·nyá? gayé·i dęhse? áhya?k? (EO/JM)

do	niyu	ę-ga-gweny-a?		gayei	dęhse?	ahya?k
INTR	AMT	FUT-3N/Z.SG.A-can.do-PNC		NUM	CNF	NUM
how	much	it can do it		four	and	six

How much will four and six add up to?

<u>Answer</u>: ęga·gwe·nyá? ne? washęh (EO/JM).

ę-ga-gweny-a?		ne?	washęh
FUT-3N/Z.SG.A-can.do-PNC		NOM	NUM
it can do it		the	ten

It will add up to ten.

A verb stem based on *.aduhwęjyo-* + dualic 'be necessary', the same root that is used to express deontic modality, is also used dynamically if it is derived with the benefactive, and inflected with animate pronominal prefixes. The derivation changes its meaning so we have *.aduhwęjyoni-/-aduhwęjyos-* + dualic *'need something'*:

(137) Na? gwá? hya? ú·, tsha? na? <u>dehonaduhwę·jyoník</u> ne? hu?shę·ní e? na?
      ahu·dyenawasdá? nęgę́ ne? uhwę́·jya? (LG04).

na?	gwa?	hya?	u	tsha?	na?	de-hon-aduhwęjyo-ni-k	ne?
ASRT	RSTR	MOD	MOD	SUB	ASRT	DL-3M.NSG.P-need,want-BEN-HAB	NOM
it's	just	indeed	probably	that	it's	they want/need it	the

hu-a?shę·nih	e?	na?	a-hu-ad-yenaw-asd-a?
3M.PL.A-white.man	REP	ASRT	OPT-3M.PL.A-SRF-hold.on-CS-PNC
white men	repeatedly	it's	they can hold onto it

nęgę	ne?	Ø-uhwęjy-a?
DEM	NOM	NPF-earth,land-NSF
this	the	land

It's a fact, I believe, that what the white men want is for them to keep holding on to this land.

7.10 Questions

In Onondaga, as in many languages of the world, questions occur in three varieties, depending on whether or not the number of appropriate answers is limited, and whether or not the questioner controls the wording of the answer. The three types are (i) *polar* (or *yes-no*) questions, (ii) *alternative* (or choice) questions, and (iii) *content* questions. The first two – polar questions and alternative questions – provide the questioner with the choice of words that describe the questioned entity or situation, constraining the answer to *yes* or *no*, or to the choice between the questioner's proposed alternatives; the respondent to a content question, on the other hand, is free to fashion an answer in his own words, and so can choose among an unlimited number of semantically appropriate answers. An example in English of a polar question is *Do you want to have lunch?* Examples of alternative questions that are constrained to various degrees are *Do you want a sandwich or a salad for lunch?* or *Which of these menu items do you want for lunch?* Alternative questions can also ask for the truth value of a proposition. For example, *Are you hungry or not?* An example of a content question is *What would you like for lunch?*

Sections 7.10.1 - 7.10.3, below, discuss the forms and uses of questions in Onondaga. The inevitable overlap with other sections of this grammar that focus on particular aspects of question formation will be held to a minimum here by careful cross-referencing. Thus, embedded questions were discussed above in the section on clausal arguments (7.4.2) which cites embedded examples of the three question-types but focuses on their function in the grammar of Onondaga. The distribution of interrogative pronouns is dealt with in detail above in chapter 6 (section 6.3), which also discusses their distribution in embedded questions.

7.10.1 Polar (Yes-No) Questions

The question particle *khę* marks polar questions. Usually, the particle occurs as the second word of a question clause, however, the linking particle *diʔ*, the restrictive particle *gwaʔ*, and the nominal particle *neʔ* may intervene, and will move it to third position as in (138d-f) respectively; if *khę* is a constituent of a particle clusters it is always the second element of the cluster even when the cluster is preceded by another word.

The excerpts in (138) show that *khę* can follow particles as well as words with lexical roots; (138c) contains two polar questions, one in which *khę* follows a particle, and one in which it follows a verb:

(138) a. Onę <u>khę</u> goyų́h neʔ agų́·gwe (H229.6).

onę	khę	go-yų-h'	neʔ	ag-ųgweh
TMP	QUE	3FI.P-arrive-STV	NOM	3FI.A-person:SUFF
now	question	she has arrived	the	woman

Has the woman arrived?

b. Is <u>khę</u> neʔ sų́·gwe sathędanų́ʔas tshaʔ ganęhayę́thwih (CTL191.2).

is	khę	neʔ	s-ųgweh	s-at-hęd-a-nųʔ-as
PRN	QUE	NOM	2SG.A-person:SUFF	2SG.A-SRF-field-JN-guard-HAB
you	question	the	you, a person	you guard a field

tsha?   ga-nęh-a-yęthw-ih
SUB   3N/Z.SG.A-corn-JN-plant-STV
that   corn has been planted
Are you the person guarding the field where corn has been planted?

c. ...wa?hęhę́·?, [thó·nę <u>khę́</u> sí?dę·?] [sędá?wi <u>khę́</u>] (CTL172.3-4).

wa?-ha-ihę·-?'   thonę   khę   s-i?dę·-?
FACT-3M.SG.A-say-PNC   LOC   QUE   2SG.A-be.situated-STV
he said   here   question you live

sa-ida?-wih   khę
2SG.P-asleep-STV   QUE
you are asleep   question
...he said, Are you home? Are you asleep?

d. Nayé? dí? <u>khę́</u> ne? a·yoyanǽ·dye? ne? sa?nigų́hæ·?... (CTL596.1-2)

naye?   di?   khę́   ne?   aa-yo-yanR-adye-?   ne?
ASRT   LNK   QUE   NOM   OPT-3N/Z.SG.P-good-PRG-PRP NOM
it's   moreover   question   the   it goes on well   the

sa-?nigųhR-a?
2SG.P-mind-NSF
your mind
Moreover, is your mind at ease?

e. Stę? gwa? <u>khę</u> ę́·he?.

sdę? gwa?   khę   ę-eR-he?
INDF   QUE   3FI.A-think,want-HAB
something   question   she wants it
Does she want something?

f. Nayé? ne? <u>khę́</u> ne? íswęh (CTL633.1).

naye?   ne?   khę   ne?   i-sw-ę-h
ASRT   NOM   QUE   NOM   EP-2PL-say-STV
it's   the   question   the   you all have said it
Is this what you all have said?

Polar questions with indefinite interrogatives:

(139) a. Sų́ ga·? <u>khę́</u> tho í·dyę?s.

sų ga·?   khę   tho   i-d-yę-e-?s
INTR   QUE   LOC   EP-CIS-3FI.A-walk-HAB
somebody   question   there   is she around?
Is somebody there?

b. Sdę? gwa? <u>khę</u> ę́·he?.

sdę?   gwa?   khę   ę-eR-he?
INTR   RSTR   QUE   3FI.A-want-HAB
something   just   question   she wants it
Does she want something?

Polar questions can combine with other clauses to form larger utterances as in (140):

(i) Polar question combined with a free relative clause:

(140) [[Sẹnų́hdų́ʔ <u>khẹ́</u>] [tshaʔ ni·yų́h, waʔų·gwanasgwahdų́ʔ neʔ gítgit, nigųnaʔsʔáh]]
     (NC01).

s-ẹnųhdų-ʔ	khẹ	tshaʔ	niyų	waʔ-ųgwa-nasgw-ahdų-ʔ	neʔ
2SG.P-know-STV	QUE	SUB	AMT	FACT-1PL.P-pet-disappear-PNC	NOM
you know	question	that	amount	our pets disappeared	the

gitgit	ni-gųn-aʔsʔa-h
NOUN	PRT-3FZ.PL.A-be.small-STV
chicken	they are little

Do you know how many of our baby chicks have disappeared?

(ii) Polar question combined with an embedded content question: This expression can be treated as either a polar question or a content question by answering 'yes' (I know his name) or by providing the name (see section 7.4.2):

(141) [[Sẹnų́hdų́ʔ khẹ́] [nwadẹ́ʔ hayá·jih]].

s-ẹnųhdų-ʔ	khẹ	nwadẹ́ʔ	ha-yas-ih
2SG.P-know-STV	QUE	INTR	3M.SG.A-be.named-STV
you know	question	what	he's called

Do you know what his name is?

Other uses of polar questions:

(i) Requests: Polar questions may be used to make a request. Often these include the verb root-*adų-* 'become, come to be possible'. The request itself then is prefixed with either the future or the optative prepronominal prefix. The example in (142a) is a direct request, that in (142b) is a reported request:

(142) a. Ẹwá·dų́ʔ <u>khẹ</u> asdé nhẹgéʔ.

ẹ-w-adų-ʔ	khẹ	asde	n-h-ẹ-g-e-ʔ
FUT-3N/Z.SG.A-be.possible-PNC	QUE	LOC	PRT-TRNS-FUT-1SG.A-walk-PNC
will it be possible	question	outside	I will go there

Can I go outside?

    b. Naʔ óʔ neʔ awet Methodist hodijihẹsdáh hodahẹdų́ oʔ naʔ neʔ <u>ẹwádų́ʔ khẹ á·hek</u>.
      (LG07).

naʔ	oʔ	neʔ	awet	Methodist	hodi-jihẹsdah	ho-ad-ahẹdų-h
ASRT	ADD	NOM	MOD	NAME	3M.NSG.P-minister	3M.SG.P-SRF-ask-STV
it's	also	the	it seems	Methodist	minister	he is asking

oʔ	naʔ	neʔ	ẹ-w-adų-ʔ	khẹ	aa-h-ek-Ø
ADD	ASRT	NOM	FUT-3N/Z.SG.A-be.possible-PNC	QUE	OPT-3M.SG.A-eat-PNC
also	it's	the	will it be possible	question	he can eat

Also, this Methodist minister, he asked, will it be possible for him to eat it?

(ii) Tag Questions: The particle cluster *seʔ khę̂* 'you know?' occurs as a tag question. These are not really questions, rather, they function as a social communication between speaker and audience or speaker and respondent, and they can mark the speaker's reduced commitment to the truth of a proposition (see the discussion of epistemic modality, above). Tag questions are included here because they illustrate yet another use of *khę*:

(143) a. Tcithéʔs neʔ jí·ha, <u>seʔ khę̂</u> dahųwasháędę? (HW05).

tcit-h-e-ʔs		neʔ	ji·hah	seʔ khę
COIN-3M.SG.A-walk-HAB		NOM	NOUN	MOD QUE
while he is around		the	dog	you know

d-a-hųw-ashaed-ę?	
CIS-FACT-3 > 3M.SG-put.a.halter.on-PNC	
someone tied him up	

While the dog was around, you know, someone had him tied up.

   b. <u>Seʔ khę̂</u> néʔ íʔ, yágę̂ waʔhę̧hę̧·ʔ, neʔ Gashaisdówanęh, ę̧sgahdųwék niʔá, ganųwagųwá nhę̧sgéʔ (HW07).

seʔ khę	neʔ	iʔ	yagę̂	waʔ-ha-ihę̧·-ʔ'	neʔ
MOD QUE	NOM	PRON	HRSY	FACT-3M.SG.A-say-PNC	NOM
you know?	the	I/we	they say	he said	the

ga-shaisd-owanę-'h	ę̧-s-g-ahdųwek-Ø	neʔ iʔ = á
3N/Z.SG.A-snake-be.large-STV	FUT-REP-1SG.A-dive-PNC	NOM PRON = DIM
Great Snake	I'll dive back down	I only

ga-nųw-agųwa	n-h-ę̧-s-g-e-ʔ'
NPF-water.surface-LOC	PRT-TRNS-FUT-REP-1SG.A-walk-PNC
under water	there I'll go back

"As for me, you know" the Great Snake says, "I will dive back down alone, I'll go back under the surface of the water."

(iii) Negative Questions: Negative questions can be used as polar questions as in (144), or as requests as in (145). The question particle occurs between the negative particle and the verb that expresses the content of the question. The negated verb is inflected with the contrastive and the optative as in (144)[43] and (145b and c), or with the negative prepronominal prefix as in (145a).

(144) a. <u>Hya khę̂</u> tha·hsgwé·nyaʔ.

hya	khę	th-aa-hs-gweny-aʔ
NEG	QUE	CON-OPT-2SG.A-can.do-PNC
not	question	you can't do it

Can't you do it?

---

[43] The examples in (144) were relayed to me by Jay Meacham who elicited them from his late aunt Eva Okun.

b. <u>Hya khę́</u> deʔawét tha·swadęhní·nu?.

hya	khę	deʔ=awet	th-aa-sw-adęhninų-ʔ
NEG	QUE	NEG=MOD	CON-OPT-2PL-sell-PNC
not	question	it isn't possible	you can't sell it

You can't sell it?

<u>Requests</u> can be formulated as negative questions:

(145) a. <u>Hya khę́</u> sdę́? <u>deʔshé·he?</u>, dyę́ gwa?, tho ó? na? ayų·nųhwét ne? Clyde, tsha? nų́
dyų̨gnidá?kstha? ...   (NC01)

hya	khę	sdę?	deʔ-hs-eR-he?	dyę gwa?	tho	o?	na?
NEG	QUE	INDF	NEG-2SG.A-want-HAB	INDF	MAN	ADD	ASRT
not	question	something	you don't want it	maybe	thus	also	it's

aa-yų-ęnųhwet-Ø	tsha?	nų	d-yų̨gn-ida?k-st-ha?
OPT-3FI.A-stay.overnight-PNC	SUB	LOC	CIS-1DU.P-sleep-CS-HAB
she might stay overnight	that	place	where we sleep

*Can Clyde (the cat) maybe spend the night in our bedroom... ? [Literally, you
don't want Clyde to spend the night in our bedroom...?]*

b. <u>Hya khę</u> thahsathų̨dat ayų̨gninyakhe? (H634.21).[44]

hya	khę	th-aa-hs-athų̨d-at-Ø	aa-yų̨gni-nyak-he?-Ø
NEG	QUE	CON-OPT-2SG.A-listen-CS-PNC	OPT-1DU.P-marry-INCH-PNC
not	question	you may agree to it	we two may get married

*Would you agree we get married? [Literally, you wouldn't agree we two should get
married?]*

c. <u>Hya khę</u> thahsathų̨dat ne? asgnų̨da? (H651.11-12).[45]

hya	khę	th-aa-hs-athų̨d-at-Ø	ne?	aa-sg-nų̨d-a?
NEG	QUE	CON-OPT-2SG.A-listen-CS-PNC	NOM	OPT-2SG>1SG-share.food-PNC
not	question	you wouldn't agree	the	you may share food with me

*Would you agree to share food with me? [Literally, you wouldn't agree to our
sharing food?]*

7.10.2 Alternative (Choice) Questions

The particle cluster *ga?t khę* combines the indefinite or hypothetical particle *ga?t* 'if,
maybe' with the question particle. The cluster is often used to mark hypothetical
statements. However, when two *ga?t khę* clauses are strung together as in (146) they
appear to function as a kind of alternative (choice) question.

(146) [Na? gó·? hya? nęgę́ ne? hęgwéh hya sų ga·? deʔagonų̨hdų́? gaę nų́ nihé?s], [<u>ga?t khę</u>
<u>hawęheyų́h</u>], [<u>ga?t khę hę́·nhe?</u>] (LG09).

na?	go·?	hya?	nęgę	ne?	hR-ų̨gweh	hya	sų ga?
ASRT	CTR	MOD	DEM	NOM	3M.SG.A-person:SUFF	NEG	INTR IND
it's	however	indeed	this	the	man	not	somebody

---

[44] Hewitt did not mark stress or vowel length in this excerpt.

[45] Hewitt did not mark stress or vowel length in this excerpt.

de?-ago-ęnyhdy-?   gaę ny   ni-h-e-?s   ga?t khę   haw-ęheyy-h'
NEG-3FI.P-know-STV   INTR LOC   PRT-3M.SG.A-walk-HAB HYP QUE   3M.SG.P-die-STV
they don't know   where   thus he is around   maybe   he has died

ga?t khę   hR-ynhe-?
HYP QUE   3M.SG.A-be.alive-STV
maybe   he is alive
This man, nobody knows where he is. Has he maybe died? Is he maybe alive?

The excerpts in (147) are hypothetical statements:

(147) a. Hya gwas de?hoyo?dęhs ne? hywáhawah, <u>ga?t khę·,</u> hya
        de?dęhayo?dęhse·wę?nha? (LG08).
        hya   gwas   de?-ho-yo?dęh-s   ne?   hywa-hawah   ga?t khę   hya
        NEG   INTS   NEG-3M.SG.P-work-HAB   NOM   3 > 3M.SG-parent.*child*   HYP QUE   NEG
        not   very   he doesn't work   the   her son   maybe   not

        de?-d-ę-ha-yo?d-ęhsR-owę?-nha?
        NEG-DL-FUT-3M.SG.A-work-NOM-find-PNC
        he can't find work
        Her son doesn't [like to] work [or] maybe he can't find a job.

    b. Ga?t khę oyú? ga? gwa? ny· thadina·gé·? hyde·yós da·hy·dǽ·?nha? (HW07).
        ga?t khę   (y)-oya?   ga?   gwa?   ny·   t-hadi-nage·-?
        HYP QUE   NPF-other-NFS   INDEF   RSTR   LOC   CIS-3M.PL.A-live-STV
        if   different   about   just   place   they live there

        hy-ade-Ryo-s   d-aa-hy-adæ·?-nha?
        3M.PL.A-SRF-kill.someone-HAB   DL-OPT-3M.PL.A-meet-PNC
        fighters   they all may meet up
        If others live in the vicinity, they may meet up with fighters.

Alternative questions can also be phrased as content questions, using a particle cluster consisting of the interrogative particle *gaę* followed by the classifier *nigá·æ?*. Together, they are glossed 'which [one].' Examples (repeated from chapter 6), are:

(148) a. Gaę nigá·æ? sé·he?.
        gaę   ni-ga-R-a?   s-eR-he?
        INTR   PART-3N/Z.SG.A-be.in-STV   2SG.P-want-HAB
        which   it is in it   you want it
        Which one do you want?

    b. Gaę di? nigá·æ? hago·wá·nęh.
        gaę   di?   ni-ga-R-a?   ha-gowanę-h
        INTR   LINK   PART-3N/Z.SG.A-be.in-STV   3M.SG.A-big-STV
        which   moreover it is in it   he is big
        Which [boy] is bigger?

7.10.3 Content Questions

Content questions elicit information about persons, things, and events. In contrast to polar and alternative questions, content questions have a potentially unlimited number of appropriate answers and can be worded by the respondent. A content questions is marked by the fact that an interrogative pronoun or expression occurs as the initial constituent of the clause. In this, Onondaga is much like English. An appropriate response to a question formed with an interrogative pronoun, is a sentence in which the question word is replaced by the nominal that identifies the questioned entity. In Onondaga, interrogative pronouns distinguish animate (who) from non-animate (what) referents. In addition, interrogative particles or interrogative expressions are used in questions regarding the reasons for actions (why), times and locations of actions or events (when, where), alternative- or choice-questions (which), and questions concerning scalable concepts (how far, how many, etc.). As a matter of convenience for the reader, tables 6.4 and 6.5 above are reproduced here as Tables 7.2 and 7.3. Table 7.2 lists the basic interrogative particles, some of which occur also with other, modifying, particles. These interrogative expressions are listed in Table 7.3.

Table 7.2 Inventory of interrogative particles

Interrogative Particles	Gloss
sų	*who, whose*
nwadę́ʔ / wadę́ʔ / nwa·hóʔdę́ʔ[46]	*what*
(h)ot (arch.)	*what*
hwę́·dųh	*when*
gaę + verb with locative prepronominal	*where*
do + classifier	*how, how about*

Table 7.3 Interrogative expressions

Interrogative phrase	Gloss
sų (nwadę́ʔ)	*who*
do nigę́	*how [extent]*
do nigę́ niyų́	*how often [extent, amount]*
do niyų́	*how many, how much*
do gaʔt	*what if*
gae nų́	*where [place]*
gaę nę (> ganę́)	*where [nearby]*
gaę tho gwaʔ	*where [just there]*
gaę nyóʔ (>ganyóʔ)	*when, as soon as, whenever*
gaę nigahá·wiʔ	*when [literally: where time]*
gaę nigá·æʔ	*which [literally: where it's in it]*
(h)ot nwa·hóʔdęʔ (arch.)	*what; why*
(n)wadę́ʔ ní·yot	*why [literally: what how it is]*
(n)wadę́ʔ óihwaʔ	*why [literally: what reason]*
(n)wadę́ʔ ó·yaʔ	*what else [literally: what other]*

---

[46] The three variants of the non-animate interrogative *nwadę́ʔ / wadę́ʔ / nwa·hóʔdę́ʔ* all derive, ultimately, from the verb form *nwaʔoihóʔdeʔ* [nwaʔ-o-Rihw-oʔdę-ʔ] '[the] kind of thing [it is]'

A set of examples of content questions with each of the interrogative pronouns including embedded content question are listed in section 6.3, embedded content questions are also cited in 7.4.2 above. Examples of sets of content questions asking for information about different entities and situations and their answers are shown in (149)-(154). All except one of the examples (150) were culled from textual sources.

(149) Q: Dó hų nigaihwís néʔtho nidiyawę́ʔih
    do   hų   ni-ga-Rihw-is-Ø   neʔtho   ni-di-yaw-ę́ʔ-ih
    INTR   MOD   PRT-3N/Z.SG.A-matter-long-STV   MAN   PRT-CIS-3N/Z.SG.P-happen-STV
    how   perhaps thus long   how   thus it has happened
    How long since it happened?

    A: Onę́ áhsę nwaʔųdiyaʔdíhsaʔ (H788.18-20).[47]
    onę   ahsę   n-waʔ-ų-ad-yaʔt-ihs-aʔ
    TMP   NUMBER   PRT-FACT-FI.A-SRF-body-finish-PNC
    now   three   thus their bodies were finished
    By now it is three generations. (literally: three times they have finished their bodies)

(150) Q: Do óʔ nigę́ niyohgáeʔih.
    do   oʔ   nigę   ni-yo-hgaeʔ-ih
    INTR   ADD   EXT   PRT-3N/Z.SG.P-make.noise-STV
    how   also   extent thus it makes noise
    How loud is it?

    A: tho góʔ niyohgaeʔíh deyodahųhsawę́·yat (elicited).
    tho   go·ʔ   ni-yo-hgaeʔ-ih   de-yo-ad-ahųhs-awę·y-at-Ø
    MAN   CTR   PRT-3N/Z.SG.P-make.noise-STV   DL-3N/Z.SG.P-SRF-hearing-stir-CS-STV
    thus   however thus it makes noise   it deafens
    It's so loud it deafens [one] [literally: it's so loud it obstructs hearing].

(151) Q: Sų́ nwa·hóʔdęʔ neʔ nę sniksaʔdayędaʔshe·ʔ.
    sų   nwa·hoʔdęʔ   neʔ   sni-ksaʔd-yęd-aʔshe·-ʔ
    INTR   INTR   NOM   2DL-child-have-DSLC-PRP
    who   what   the   you two are going to have a child
    Who is the father of the child you two are going to have?

    A: Gnóhaʔ hya deʔwagęnų́hdųʔ wadę́ʔ nwaʔawę́haʔ (CTL3.8-4.3).
    g-nohaʔ   hya   deʔ-wag-ęnųhdų-ʔ   wadęʔ   n-waʔ-aw-ęh-aʔ
    1SG.A-mother NEG   NEG-1SG.P-know-STV   INTR   PRT-FACT-3N/Z.SG.P-happen-PNC
    my mother   not   I don't know   what   thus it happened
    Mother, I don't know what happened.

The content question in (152) is answered in A$_1$ with a polar question followed by a reason, which in A$_2$ receives a response from the original questioner. The sequence shows how speakers can circumvent the restrictions of polar questions by negating a question and offering an alternative:

---

[47] Hewitt did not mark vowel length in this excerpt.

(152) Q: Sų· di? ęháæ?thę?, ęhajisdęhda?

sų	di?	ę-ha-Ra?thę-?	ę-ha-jisd-ęhd-a?
INTR	LNK	FUT-3M.SG.A-climb-PNC	FUT-3M.SG.A-fire-drop-PNC
who	moreover	he will climb up	he will drop the fire

Who, then, will climb up [and] toss the fire?

A₁: Do· í?, kjiná ni?á hyá ni? sdę? de?khdá·gwas (HW07).

do	i?	k-jina-h	hya	ne? i?	sdę?
INTR	PRON	1SG.A-be.male-STV	NEG	NOM PRON	INTR
how	I/we	I'm brave	not	I/we	something

de?-k-hdagw-as
NEG-1SG.A-afraid-HAB
I'm not afraid of it

How about me? I'm the only brave one, I'm not afraid of anything.

A₂: Hiyá i? gó·? hyá? ęgæ?thę? ękjisdęhda? (HW07).

hiyah	i?	go·?	hya?	ę-g-Ræ?thę-?	ę-k-jisd-ęhd-a?
NEG	PRON	MOD	MOD	FUT-1SG.A-climb-PNC	FUT-1SG.A-fire-drop-PNC
not	I	actually	indeed	I will climb	I will toss the fire

No, actually, I will climb up [and] I will toss the fire.

(153) Q: Gaę nų́we dáshawa?.

gaę	nųwe	d-a-hs-haw-a?
INTR	LOC	CIS-FACT-2SG.A-carry-PNC
where	place	you are carrying it this way

Where did you get this?

A: K?niháh hagawíh (H189.3).

k-?nihah	hag-awi-h'
1SG.A-father	3M.SG > 1SG-give-STV
my father	he gave it to me

My father gave it to me.

Finally, an example of a question with an evasive answer – one of the possible choices provided by content questions – is shown in (154):

(154) Q: Gaę na? nhehonenųh ne? sahwajiæ?

gaę	na?	n-he-hon-e-nųh		ne?	sa-hwajiR-a?
INTR	ASRT	PRT-TRNS-3M.NSG.P-walk-STV		NOM	2SG.P-family-NSF
where	it's	they have gone there		the	your family

Where have your family gone?

A: Hya de?hęni?dę? ne? gagwé·gih (H615.9-10).[48]

hya	de?-hęn-i?dę-?		ne?	ga-gweg-ih
NEG	NEG-3M.PL.A-be.in.place-STV		NOM	3N/Z.SG.A-be.all-STV
not	they aren't here		the	it is all

None of them are here

---

[48] Hewitt did not mark stress and vowel length in this excerpt.

<u>Hypothetical questions</u>:

Content questions can be used to pose hypothetical questions. This is done by beginning the question with the particle sequence *do ga?t* 'what if':

(155) a. Do· ga?t ne? ų́hgę? ęhų·dé·yo? (CTL129.3).

do ga?t	ne?	ųhgę?	ę-hų-ade·yo-?
INTR HYP	NOM	TMP	FUT-3M.PL.A-fight-PNC
what if	the	presently	they will fight

What if, eventually they fight?

b. Do· ga?t ųhgę? na? ne? hę́gwe wa?há·yų? (CTL96.6).

do ga?t	ųhgę?	na?	ne?	hR-ųgweh	wa?-ha-yų-?
INTR HYP	TMP	ASRT	NOM	3M.SG.A-person:SUFF	FACT-3M.SG.A-arrive-PNC
what if	presently	it's	the	man	he arrived

What if eventually the man got [here]?

7.11 Possession

Possession, a relation between a possessor and a possessed entity, is expressed using either morphological nouns (sec. 5.2.1.2), or two subclasses of verbs – positional verbs, and small set of verbs with adjectival meanings (sec. 4.8.3.6). How possession is marked on these constituents depends on whether the possession is alienable or not (morphological nouns and positional verbs), whether the possession is animate or not (verbs with adjectival meanings). Nominal possession is discussed in section 7.11.1; verbal possession is discussed in section 7.11.2.

7.11.1 Nominal Possession

Possession of an entity is expressed by attaching a possessive pronominal prefix to a nominal stem. Possessive prefixes are formally identical to the agent or patient series of verbal pronominal prefixes, but their meanings and distributions differ. The possessive prefix codes for the possessor's person, number, and gender – like a verbal pronominal prefix – but unlike a verbal pronominal prefix, it codes for possession rather than a case relationship. The possessed entity – the referent of the construction – is expressed lexically, but remains unmarked pronominally.

Grammatically, the possessed nominal occurs as an external nominal in apposition to the main verb:

(156) … sahayená? ne? <u>hotshenę́h</u>… (LG23)

s-a-ha-yena-?'	ne?	ho-tshenę-h
REP-FACT-3M.SG.A-take-PNC	NOM	3M.SG.P-pet-NSF
he took it back	the	his pet

…he took back his pet…

The possessed nominal may also occur as a kind of location participant (7.6.1 above):

(157) ...naʔ <u>honųhsgų́wa</u> tho honiʔdę́·ʔ... (LG09)

naʔ	ho-nųhs-<u>agųwa</u>	tho	hon-iʔdę·-ʔ
ASRT	3M.SG.P-house-LOC	LOC	3M.NSG.P-reside-STV
it's	in his house	there	they are living

...they are living in his house...

The possessed nominal may also be a borrowed term; however, in that case a semireflexive is inserted between the possessive pronominal and the borrowed term:

(158) ...waʔtgdę́sdaʔ neʔ, <u>agatmacíne</u>... (LG13)

waʔ-t-g-dęsd-aʔ		neʔ	ag-at-macine
FACT-DL-1SG.A-stop.something-PNC		NOM	1SG.P-SRF-machine
I stopped it		the	my machine

...I stopped my machine...

<u>Alienably possessed entities:</u> With a few exceptions (they are specified in detail in chapter 5 section 5.2.1.2.2), alienably possessed entities are entities that are not body parts or blood relatives (kin terms are discussed in chapter 5 section 5.4). They denote objects that can be taken or given away, or that are impermanent in some way. Animate (non-human) as well as non-animate entities may be alienably possessed. To mark possession of an alienably possessed morphological noun a possessive prefix identical to the patient series of prefixes is selected. This is so whether the particular stem takes a *ga-* or an *o-* nominal prefix in its basic form:

(159) a. agnáhdaʔ

    ag-nahd-aʔ

    1SG.P-comb-NSF

    my comb

        cf. *ganáhdaʔ* 'comb'

  b. ageʔnhų́hsaʔ

    age-ʔnhųhs-aʔ

    1SG.P-egg-NSF

    my egg

        cf. *oʔnhų́hsaʔ* 'egg'

  c. hotshé·nęh

    ho-tshenę-h

    3M.SG.P-pet-NSF

    his pet

Example (160a) shows that both non-derived – *akhų́·waʔ* 'my boat'– and derived noun stems – *agyoʔdę́hsæ·ʔ* 'my work'– may be marked for possession, and (160b) is an example of a possessed verbal noun; note that the entire stem (including the aspect suffix) is marked for possession by the pronominal prefix (section 5.3).[49]

---

[49] Possessed verbal nouns are one of the reasons that Iroquoianist destinguish between verbal stems and verbal bases. See Koenig & Michelson (2016 ms.), on lexical categories, where they discuss the significance of adding the possessive prefix to the stem rather than the base.

(160) a. Nayé? ne? ó·nę ęge·yęnędá?nha? ne? <u>agyo?dę́hsæ·?</u> thohgé ó·nę ne? <u>akhų́·wa?</u> hya
sų́·ga? ne? ų́·gwe[50] thayésda? ne? akhų́·wa?... (CTL46.4-7)

nayé?	ne? ó·nę	ę-ge-Wyęn-ęda?-nha?	ne?	ag-yo?dę-hsR-a?
ASRT	TMP	FUT-1SG.A-task-finish-PNC	NOM	1SG.P-be.working-NOM-NSF
it's	when	I will finish it	the	my work

thohge onę	ne?	ak-hųw-a?	hya sų ga?	ne?
TMP	NOM	1SG.P-boat-NSF	NEG INDF	NOM
then	the	my boat	nobody	the

Ø-ųgweh	th-aa-ye-sd-a?	ne?	ak-hųw-a?
3FZ.SG.P-person:SUFF	CON-OPT-3FI.A-use-PNC	NOM	1SG.P-boat-NSF
person	they shouldn't use it	the	my boat

When I've completed my work, then, as to my boat, nobody should use my boat...

b. gojisdodákhwa?
go-jisd-od-ahgw-ha?
3FI.P-ember-raise.upright-INST-HAB
her lamp [literally, [what] she uses to raise an ember]

Certain kin terms that denote groups of relatives, are treated morphologically like alienably possessed entities in that they select pronominals from the patient series. Examples are:

(161) a. ...dogę́s gotga?dé? ne? <u>haųgwé?da?</u> (LG05).

dogęs	go-atga?d-e?	ne?	ha-ųgwe-?d-a?
MOD	3FI.P-be.plentiful-STV	NOM	3M.SG.P-person-NOM-NSF
truly	they are plentiful	the	his people

...for sure, lots of them were his folks.

b. ...né?tho hęní?dę·? ne? <u>hodihwají·yæ?</u> (CTL66.1-2).

ne?tho	hęn-i?dę·-?	ne?	hodi-hwajiR-a?
LOC	3M.PL.A-dwell-STV	NOM	3M.NSG.P-family-NSF
there	they resided	the	their family

...that's where their family resided.

<u>Inalienably possessed entities</u>: With a few exceptions, body part terms are classified as inalienably possessed. Inalienably possessed entities are marked for possession with pronominal prefixes that are identical to the agent series of verbal pronominal prefixes as shown in (162). In addition, body part nouns typically occur with the locative clitic:

(162) a. Wa?thahwa?esdahę́·?, <u>ehų?gwa·?gé</u> tsha? nigę́ wa?aihé·ya? (LG09).

wa?-t-ha-hwa?e-sd-ahę-a?'	e-hų?gwaR-a?=ge	tsha? nigę
FACT-DL-3M.SG.A-strike-CS-DST-PNC	3FI.A-throat-NSF=LOC	SUB EXT
he pierced it several times	(on) her throat	until

---

[50] Words ending in /h/ typically lose it utterance-medially.

    wa?-a-ihey-a?
    FACT-3FI.A-die-PNC
    she died
    He kept slashing her throat until she died.

b. ...<u>khyagwiyæ?gé</u> wa?onṇhwakdę́ha? (LG23).
    k-hyagwiR-a? = ge   wa?-o-nṇhwakd-ęh-a?
    1SG.A-toe-NSF = LOC   FACT-3N/Z.SG.P-hurt-INCH-PNC
    (on) my toe   it began to hurt
    ...my toe began to hurt.

c. ...nę hehé? dęhahgwe?dá·? gadé? <u>hgṇhsi?gé</u>[51] ne? nęthayeæ̨·?... (LG24)
    nęh   h-eR-he?   d-ę-hak-gwe?daR-?   gade?
    TMP   3M.SG.A-want-HAB   DL-FUT-3M.SG > 1SG-scratch-PNC   ALT
    now   he wants   he will scratch me   maybe

    k-gṇhs-i? = ge   ne?   n-ę-t-ha-yeR-a?
    1SG.A-face-NSF = LOC   NOM   PRT-FUT-CIS-3M.SG.A-do-PNC
    on my face   the   he will touch it
    ...now he [the cat] *wants to scratch me or touch my face...*

The exceptional body part terms that take possessive prefixes from the patient series are for the most part ones that denote entities not under the voluntary control of the possessor, e.g., internal organs, hair, etc.; also body exudations, e.g., tears, saliva, etc., are treated like alienably possessed nouns. An example with *-e·yah-* 'heart', is:

(163) ...wa?tgahí·?nha? ne? hawe·yáhne... (CTL134.8)
    wa?-t-ga-hi·?-nha?   ne?   haw-e·yah = ne
    FACT-DL-3N/Z.SG.A-shatter-PNC   NOM   3M.SG.P-heart = LOC
    it broke it   the   (on) his heart
    ...it broke his heart...

There are two kinship terms – *-noha?* 'mother' and *-?nihah* 'father' that differ from all others, in that when inflected for a first person possessor they take the intransitive *agent* prefix *k-/g-* (pron. pref. #1) instead of a transitive prefix, thus marking them as inalienably possessed.

7.11.2 Verbal Possession

As was pointed out above, two sets of verbs, five positional verbs and a group of stative only verbs with adjectival meanings are used to indicate possession verbally (chapter 4 section 4.8.3.6). In addition, the verb root *-awę-* 'own something' is used to indicate possession lexically.

<u>Alienably possessed entities</u>: Inflected for the stative aspect, several positional verbs, but most often *-yę-,* are used to express possession of alienable entities. The possessor is

---

[51] Recall that *k > h before k or g* by regular rule.

referenced by the (patient) pronominal prefix, and, typically, the noun denoting the possessed entity is incorporated into the positional verb. Examples are:

(164) a. ...waʔhųwá·gęʔ neʔ hę·gwe dahá·yųʔ tshaʔ <u>odinųhsá·yęʔ</u>... (CTL6.7-8)

waʔ-hųwa-gę-ʔ	neʔ	hR-ųgweh[52]	d-a-ha-yų-ʔ
FACT-3 > 3M.SG-see-PNC	NOM	3M.SG.A-person:SUFF	CIS-FACT-3M.SG.A-arrive-PNC
she saw him	the	man	he arrived

tsha?   odi-nųhs-a-yę-ʔ
SUB   3FZ.NSG.P-house-JN-have.extended-STV
where   they have a house/their house
...*she saw the man arriving at their house...*

b. Gwas yágęʔ nęgę <u>onaʔgaedų́·nyųʔ</u>[53] (HW07).

gwas   yageʔ   nęgę   o-naʔgaR-ųd-ųnyų-ʔ
INTS   HRSY   DEM   3FZ.SG.P-horn-have.hanging-DST-STV
very   they say this   it has horns
They say this [creature] even has horns.

The positional verb may be inflected for the negative:

(165) Hya go·ʔ naʔ <u>deʔųgwanasgwayę́ʔ</u> neʔ ęyųkhinasgwanę́sgwaʔ (LG06).

hya   go·ʔ   naʔ   deʔ-ųgwa-nasgw-a-yę-ʔ   neʔ   ę-yųkhi-nasgw-nęsgw-aʔ
NEG   CTR   ASRT   NEG-1PL.P-pet-JN-have-STV   NOM   FUT-3 > 1NSG-pet-steal-PNC
not   however it's   we don't have pets   the   she/they will steal our pet
But we don't have any pets at this time, ones they'll steal.

The possessed entity may also be expressed by a general term that is incorporated into the positional verb followed by an external noun form with a more specific meaning (sec. 4.8.3.4):

(166) a. <u>Honasgwayę́ʔ</u> óʔ <u>gatshé·nęʔ</u>, gųniʔdę́·ʔ gaʔęhægų́·wah (HW01).

ho-nasgw-yę-ʔ   oʔ   ga-tshenę-ʔ   gųn-iʔdę·-ʔ
3M.SG.P-pet-have-STV   ADD   NPF-pet-NSF   3FZ.PL.A-dwell-STV
he has animal(s)   also   domesticated animal   they dwell

ga-ʔęhR-agųwah
NPF-fence-LOC
in the yard
Also, he has animals living in the yard.

b. Odyáʔk oʔ <u>hodiʔse·hdayę́dųʔ</u>, neʔ <u>automobile</u>... (LG11)

odyaʔk   oʔ   hodi-ʔse·hd-a-yęd-ų-ʔ   neʔ   automobile
QNT   ADD   3M.NSG.P-vehicle-JN-have-DST-STV   NOM   NOUN
some   also   they have vehicles   the   automobile
Also, some of them had cars...

---

[52] Words ending in /h/ typically lose it utterance-medially.

[53] *-naʔgaR-* 'horn, antler' is a body part term that is inflected like the alienable nouns.

<u>Inalienably possessed entities with positional verbs</u>: Verbal possession with inalienably possessed nouns (body parts) use the whole set of positional verbs, depending on the shape of the body part and how it is attached to the body. The excerpt in (167c) is especially interesting: it's about a man who got his finger cut off by a machine, hence the choice of *-ade-* 'exist in space, unattached' incorporating *-ʔny-* 'finger'. When attached to the hand the root takes *-ųd-* which denotes a secondary attachment.[54]

(167) a. Deyoyaʔdasdá·thek, gayaʔdasnóweʔ, <u>gayé·i nigaʔnųdó·daʔ</u> (HW07).

de-yo-yaʔd-a-sda·the-k	ga-yaʔd-a-snoR-eʔ	gayeih
DL-3FZ.SG.P-body-JN-gleam-HAB	3FZ.SG.A-body-JN-act.fast-STV	NUM
it gleams	she is swift	four

ni-ga-ʔnųd-od-aʔ
PRT-3FZ.SG.A-leg-have.sticking.out-STV
she has leg(s)
Her body gleams, she's swift, she has four legs.

b. ... nęgę́ ų́hgęʔ gwaʔ sgadá <u>dehagáhæda</u>... (LG24)

nęgę	ųhgęʔ	gwaʔ	sgada	de-ha-gahR-ada-'h
DEM	TMP	RSTR	NUM	DL-3M.SG.A-eye-have.contained-STV
at this time	only	one		he has eyes in him

...at this time, he has only one eye...

c. ...hwaʔgatgathwáʔ, <u>thaʔnyadéʔ</u>... (LG13)

h-waʔ-g-atgathw-aʔ	t-ha-ʔny-ade-ʔ
TRNS-FACT-1.SG.A-look.at-PNC	CIS-3M.SG.A-finger-exist.unattached-STV
I looked there	there's his finger

...I looked [and] over there is his [unattached] finger...

<u>Possessed entities and adjectival verbs</u>: The adjectival verbs that express possession with animate pronominal prefixes select, agent or patient pronominals depending on whether the incorporated entity stem is alienable or not, in the same way as positional verbs do (sec. 4.4.3.4 for the list of verbs and further details about prefix selection).

<u>Alienably possessed entities with adjectival verbs</u>: Patient prefixes identify the possessor; the stem describes the possessed entity:

(168) a. ...dyęháʔ gwaʔ neʔ ęgahnehdó·dęʔ thaihwayé·iʔ <u>hoyoʔdęhsí·yoh</u> ... hegagųdáhgwih hoihwayę·dáhgwih (CTL470.6-8).

dyęhaʔ	gwaʔ	neʔ	ę-ga-hnehd-od-ęʔ
HYP	RST	NOM	FUT-3N/Z.SG.A-pine-stand-PNC
if	just	the	pine tree chief

t-ha-Rihw-a-ye·i-ʔ	ho-yoʔdę-hsR-iyo-h'
CIS-3M.SG.A-matter-JN-be.right-STV	3M.SG.P-work-NOM-be.good-STV
he is righteous	his work is good

---

[54] A secondary attachment is one in which a body part, e.g., a hand, is attached to another attached body part, i.e. the arm.

<pre>
he-ga-gǫdahgw-ih   ho-Rihw-a-yęd-a-hgw-ih
TRNS-3N/Z.SG.A-continue-STV   3M.SG.P-matter-JN-have-INST-STV
it will continue   his duties
</pre>
...*if the one who was made Pine Tree [Chief] is righteous [and] his work is good...his duties will become permanent.*

b. Naʔ néʔ naʔ tho <u>niyųgwayanę·hseʔdę́h</u> (LG18).

<pre>
na?   ne?   na?   tho   ni-yųgwa-yanR-ęhsR-oʔdę-h´
ASRT NOM   ASRT MAN   PRT-1PL.P-be.good-NOM-be.a.kind-STV
it's the   it's how   how our law is
</pre>
That is our law [literally, our good kind of entity] .

c. Naʔ diʔ hyaʔ tshaʔ ų́ <u>nihowęhagaʔdéhgwaʔ</u>, ... (LG05)

<pre>
na?   di?   hya?   tsha? ų·
ASRT LINK   MOD   SUB   MOD
it's moreover indeed   that   probably
</pre>

<pre>
ni-ho-węh-a-gaʔde-h-gwa?
PRT-3M.SG.P-flower-JN-have.many-HAB-HBPST
he used to have lots of flowers
</pre>
And he used to have lots of flowers, ...

<u>Inalienably possessed entities</u>: with adjectival verbs

Agent prefixes identify the possessor, the stem describes the possessed entity:

(169) a. ...dahoʔnyohá·gwaʔ, naʔ néʔ <u>nihaʔnyowánę</u> ... (LG13)

<pre>
d-a-ho-?ny-ohaR-gw-a?   na?   ne?
CIS-FACT-3M.SG.P-finger-put.on.the.tip-REV-PNC   ASRT NOM
it took off the tip of his finger   it's the
</pre>

<pre>
ni-ha-?ny-owanę-h
PRT-3M.SG.A-finger-big-STV
his big finger
</pre>
...it took off the tip of his finger, his big finger...

b. ...dethagáhæ·ʔ, hoyaʔda·yęsdíh <u>haguhsiyóh</u> (CTL82.5).

<pre>
de-t-ha-gahR-a?   ho-ya?d-a-Węsd-ih   ha-gųhs-iyo-h'
DL-CIS-3M.SG.A-watch-STV   3M.SG.P-body-JN-handsome-STV   3M.SG.A-face-good-STV
he's gazing back at [him]   he's handsome   his face is good
</pre>
...he looks back at [him], he's handsome [and] has a nice face.

c. Nayéʔ neʔ jyá·dak niyowęyųhga·géh <u>nęhsihnadęjík</u> (CTL598.3).

<pre>
naye? ne?   jyadak   ni-yo-węyųhgaR-ge-h'
ASRT   NOM   NUM   PRT-3N/Z.SG.P-thumb-amount.to-STV
it's   the   seven   so many inches
</pre>

n-ę-hs-ihn-a-dęs-i-k-Ø
PRT-FUT-2SG.A-skin-JN-thick-STV-CNT-PNC
how thick your skin will be
Your skin will be seven inches thick.

The verb root *-awę-* 'own [something]' expresses possession lexically:

(170) Ųgyųhwęjyayę́? thónę né? ęhadiyasthá? ganęhæ·gwegí <u>gó·węh</u> (LG19).
     ųgy-ųhwęjy-a-yę-?   thonę   ne?   ę-hadi-yas-t-ha?
     1PL.P-land-JN-have-STV   LOC   NOM   FUT-3M.PL.A-be.named-INST-HAB
     our property[55]   here   the   they call it

     ga-nęhR-a-gweg-ih   go-awę-h
     3N/Z.SG.A-group-JN-all-STV   3FI.P-own-STV
     the whole group   they own it
     Our property here, that's what they call it, is owned by the whole group.

7.12 Quantification, Degrees, and Comparisons[56]

Onondaga quantity expressions are diverse; they may involve cardinal number words, numerous quantity particles, and special sets of verb and noun roots, some of which are lexicalized with particular prepronominal prefixes. Section 7.12.1 lists the number words and describes how they are combined into expressions that will form all possible numbers. Section 7.12.2 deals with ways of counting situation and entity expressions. Section 7.12.3 describes how possessed entities are counted. Section 7.12.4 discusses the uses of quantity particles. Section 7.12.5 looks at degree expressions. Section 7.12.6 deals with the formation of comparison expressions.

7.12.1 Cardinal Number Words and Expressions

Onondaga has a base 10 number system; it uses both multiplication and addition to form numbers beyond *twenty*. All number words involve the single numbers *1 - 10* in a variety of formulae. There appears to be no number word for the concept *zero*. When there is a need to express that concept, the expressions *ne? ya sdę?* (JM) – literally, it's not something – is used:
    The single numbers: *sgá·da* 'one', *dégni* 'two', *áhsę* 'three', *gayé·(i)* 'four', *hwíks* 'five', *áhya?k* 'six', *jyádak* 'seven', *dé·gę* 'eight', *wá?dę·* 'nine', *washę́* 'ten'.
    The teens: To form the numbers 11 to 19, the particle *gahé?* 'teens' is added to each cardinal number, e.g., *sgáda gahé?* 'eleven', *degní gahé?* 'twelve', *ahsę́ gahé?* 'thirteen', etc. [the formula: single number + *gahé?* 'teens'].
    Dewashę́ means 'twenty' – literally, two tens – where *washę́* 'ten' is inflected with the dualic prepronominal prefix. To form the numbers 21-29, a single-number particle is added to *dewashę́*, e.g., *dewashę́ sgá·dah* 'twenty-one', *dewashę́ dégni* 'twenty-two', etc. [the formula: 2 x 10 + single number].

---

[55] Literally, *the land we have lying to us.*

[56]See Koenig & Michelson (2010c) for a detailed examination of Iroquoian quantification; Michelson et al. (2016) Section 9, describes Oneida quantification expressions.

The *30* to *90* series counted in tens, differs from *dewashę́* 'twenty' only in that the numbers occur as expressions rather than single words. They are constructed by choosing one of the single numbers and following it by *niwashę́* literally, 'thus tens' where the *washę́* 'ten' is inflected with the partitive prepronominal prefix. Thus, *ahsę́ niwáshę* 'thirty [literally, three tens]' , *gayéi niwashę́h* 'forty [literally, four tens], *hwíks niwashę́* 'fifty', etc. [the formula: X x 10].

The series 31-39; 41-49, 51-59, etc., all the way to 99 are constructed by *following* the 30 to 90 numbers by singles. Thus *áhsę niwashę́ sgá·da* 'thirty-one', *gayéi niwashę́ dégni* 'forty-two, all the way to *waʔdę́· niwashę́ wáʔdę·* 'ninety nine'. [The formula: X x 10 + single number].

The hundreds: *sgadá dewęʔnyáʔeh* (ON) / *sgadá dewęʔnyá(ų)ʔ(w)eh* (6N) means 'one hundred [literally 'once the hand is struck']. To form the 'hundreds' series of numbers 200-900, *dewęʔnyáʔeh* follows the single cardinal numbers, e.g., *degní dewęʔnyáʔeh* 'two hundred', *áhsę dewęʔnyáʔeh* 'three hundred', etc., [the formula: X x 100]

The thousands: To form the 'thousands' series of numbers 1000, 2000 etc., involves the use of the counting verbs (for an analysis of these see section 7.12.2 below), e.g., *(sgadá) sgahųhsǽ·dah* [REP-3N/Z.SG.A-box-JN-be one-STV] 'one thousand [literally, 'one is the box'], *(degni) degahųhsagé* [DL-3N/Z.SG.A-box-JN-be two or more-STV] 'two thousand', *áhsę nigahų́hsageh* [PRT-3N/Z.SG.A-box-JN-be.three.or.more-STV] 'three thousand', *gayéi nigahų́hsageh* 'four thousand', etc.

The terms with the meanings 'hundred' and 'thousand' can also be modified by a preceding indefinite quantity particle, e.g., *dogá·ʔ niyohųhsæ·géh* 'several thousand' (LG17).

7.12.2 Counting Situations and Entities

Counting situations involves different strategies from counting entities. While entities must be counted using special counting and amount verbs, number words can combine directly with situation expressions.

7.12.2.1 Counting Situation Expressions

Cardinal number words modify situation expressions directly, as in (171). The number word precedes the situation expression it modifies, but the two need not be adjacent:

(171) a. <u>Jyádak</u>, yá·gę?, <u>nwaʔhowákdaʔ</u> ónę háhsaʔ waʔhaʔáhsæik (H162.14-163.1).[57]

jyadak	yagę?	n-waʔ-ho-wakd-aʔ	onę hahsaʔ
NUM	HRSY	PRT-FACT-3M.SG.P-shake-PNC	TMP TMP
seven	they say	he shook it	before

waʔ-ha-ʔahsR-a-Ri-k
FACT-3M.SG.A-basket-JN-get.done-PNC
he filled the basket
They say he shook it seven [times], before he filled the basket.

---

[57] Stress and vowel length as marked by Hewitt; he transcribed the last word of the example as *waʔhaʔáhseik*.

b. Néʔtho haʔdega·yéiʔ <u>degní waʔtgehsényaʔ</u> néʔ úgweh (H212.7-8).[58]

neʔtho	haʔ-de-ga-yei-ʔ		degni	waʔ-t-ge-hsę-ny-aʔ
MAN	TRNS-DL-3N/Z.SG.A-enough-STV		NUM	FACT-DL-1SG.A-create-PNC
thus	it is enough		two	I created it

neʔ	(y)-ugweh
NOM	NPF-person:SUFF
the	human

It's sufficient, that I've created the human being twice.

c. Thóhge ónę néʔ Odędųniʔá waʔthohę́éhdaʔ, ná·yeʔ <u>áhsęh nwaʔhadǽ·sdaʔ</u>, heyóheʔ ga·iʔsdowa·nęh (H728.21-22).[59]

thohge	onę	neʔ	Odędųniʔa	waʔ-t-ho-hęehd-aʔ	naye?	ahsę
TMP	TMP	NOM	NAME	FACT-DL-3M.SG.P-shout-PNC	ASRT	NUM
thereafter	the	Sapling	he shouted		it's	three

n-waʔ-h-adǽ·sd-aʔ	heyóheʔ	ga-Riʔsd-owan-ęh
PRT-FACT-3M.SG.A-repeat-PNC	DGR	3N/Z.SG.A-speech.sound-large-STV
he repeated it	exceedingly	loud voice

Then Odędųniʔa shouted, repeating it three [times], [in] an exceedingly loud voice.

7.12.2.2 Counting Entity Expressions with Counting Verbs

Counting verbs that occur with cardinal numbers and with certain quantifier particles are listed in Table 7.5, below. Which counting verb is selected depends on the number of entities being counted and on whether the counted entity is animate or not. The first four counting verbs are used to count non-animate entities, the fifth occurs with animate entities. Of the first group, the first two – they count one and two entities, respectively – never occur with independent cardinal number words; the number meanings – *one* and *two* – are expressed by their prepronominal prefixes and for that reason are a part of the meaning of the verb.

Table 7.5 The Counting verbs

Counting Verbs	Gloss
.COUNTED.NOUN.ROOT-d- + repetitive	*be one counted entity*
.COUNTED.NOUN.ROOT-ge- + dualic	*be two counted entities*
.COUNTED.NOUN.ROOT-ge- + partitive	*be three or more counted entities*
.COUNTED.NOUN.ROOT-ge- + translocative and dualic	*be every counted entity*
.ad-i- + partitive	*the number of [animate entities]*

Examples are given in (172) and (173). The third stem, which is used to count three or more entities and entities with indefinite amounts, always occurs with an external number word or quantifier particle as in (174) and (175). The first four counting verbs in the table take the (ga- or o-) lexicalized pronominal prefixes of the incorporated verb.[60] The fifth

---

[58] Stress and vowel length as marked by Hewitt.

[59] Stress and vowel length as marked by Hewitt.

[60] In this they differ from the cognate counting verbs in Oneida (see Michelson et al, secs. 9.1-9.3) which always take agent prefixes with incorporated non-animate entities.

counting verb – .ad-i- + partitive – takes agent prefixes. Grammatically, the counting verb and, if present, the number word or quantifier particle, form an internally headed relative clause that is adjoined to a main verb (7.5.1 above).

7.12.2.2.1 Counting Non-animate Entities

The first group of four verb bases must incorporate the noun root that denotes the counted entity; the fifth – .ad-i- + partitive – does not incorporate; with that base, the counted entity occurs as an external nominal.

Examples in (172) to (174) use the non-animate counting verbs for 'one', 'two', or 'three' or more entities:

(172) Thohge ó·nę neʔ Ganyęʔgegáʔ Hayęhwáthaʔ dahátgaʔk <u>sgahesgá·dah</u>… (CTL300.7)

thohge onę	neʔ	Ganyęʔgega?	Hayęhwatha?	d-a-h-atga?k-Ø
TMP TMP	NOM	NAME	NAME	CIS-FACT-3M.SG.A-let.go.of-PNC
thereafter the		Mohawk	Hiawatha	he contributed it

s-ga-hesgaR-a-d-ah
REP-3N/Z.SG.A-arrow-JN-be.one-STV
one arrow

Then the Mohawk [Chief], Hiawatha, contributed one arrow [literally, an arrow that is one…]

(173) Onę hyáʔ ų <u>deyohsæ·gé</u> tshaʔ nwaʔųnísheʔ, nęgę́ tho nidyawę́ʔi… (LG09)

onę	hyaʔ	ų	de-y-ohsR-a-ge-h´		tshaʔ	nwaʔųnishe?
TMP	MOD	MOD	DL-3N/Z.SG.A-winter-JN-amount.to-STV		SUB	TMP
Now	indeed	probably	it is two years		that	how long ago

nęgę	tho	ni-d-yaw-ęʔ-ih
DEM	MAN	PRT-CIS-3N/Z.SG.P-happen-STV
this	thus	thus it happened here

It must be about 2 years ago, when it happened …

(174) a. Ęhayáʔk oʔ nęgę́, <u>hwíks nigahųdagéh</u> (HW07).

ę-ha-ya?k-Ø		oʔ	nęgę	hwiks	ni-ga-hųd-a-ge-h'
FUT-3M.SG.A-cut-PNC		ADD	DEM	NUM	PRT-3N/Z.SG.A-whip-JN-amount.to-STV
he will cut		also	this	five	this number of whips

Also, he should cut five whips.

b. <u>Jyadáh[61] gahé·ʔ niyohsæ·gé</u> naʔdegųdé·ʔ naʔ de·gáęʔ hadí·yųk (LG01).

jyadak	gahe·ʔ	ni-y-ohsR-a-ge-h'
NUM	NUM	PRT-3N/Z.SG.A-year-JN-amount.to-STV
seventeen		so many years

---

[61] In this example, the speaker extends the rule which changes *kk* clusters to *hk* word internally, to accross a word boundary.

na?-de-gu-ade·-?   na?   degae?   hadi-yu-k
PART-DL-3FZ.PL.A-distance.between-STV   ASRT   TMP   3M.PL.A-arrive-HAB
the distance between them   it's   how often   they arrive
[The locusts] arrive every seventeen years.

Counting verbs may occur with quantifier particles instead of number words:

(175) <u>Dogá·? niwẹdagé</u> nigẹ́ tho ihé?s, nẹ́ dụdahahdẹ́·dya? (HW05).

doga·?   ni-w-ẹd-ge-h'   nigẹ   tho   i-h-e-?s
QNT   PRT-3N/Z.SG.A-day-amount.to-STV   EXT   LOC   EP-3M.SG.A-walk-HAB
A few   so many days   extent   there   he is around there

onẹ   d-ụda-h-ahdẹdy-a?
TMP   DL-CIS:FACT-3M.SG.A-wander-PNC
then   he went back home
He stayed around there for several days, then he returned home.

Some noun stems cannot be incorporated into counting verbs, for example, borrowings from other languages. In that case the number word immediately precedes the nominal and the counting verb is omitted. Morphological nouns inflected for possession, cannot be incorporated; in order to incorporate, they must occur with positional verbs when quantified; they are discussed below in section (7.12.3). An example with a borrowing is:

(176) Wa?hohninụ́? di? hyá?, ụhwẹ́·jya?, <u>degní é·git</u>, tsha? niyụ́h, nẹgẹ́ hẹ́·gweh (LG16).

wa?-ho-hninụ-?   di?   hya?   Ø-ụhwẹjy-a?   degni   egit
FACT-3M.SG > 3M.SG-buy-PNC   LINK   MOD   NPF-land-NSF   NUM   NOUN
he bought it from him   so   indeed   land   two   acre

tsha?   niyụ   nẹgẹ   hR-ụgweh
SUB   AMT   DEM   3M.SG.A-person:SUFF
that   so much   this   man
So he bought a piece of land – two acres – from this man.

When the counting verb root *-ge-* occurs with the translocative and dualic prepronominal prefixes, the meaning of the base is 'every' or 'every kind', with the quantified entity incorporated into the counting verb:

(177) Se? khẹ gana·gé·? <u>hwa?tga·yo?dagé</u> o?dáhdẹ·t (HW07).

se? khẹ   ga-nage·-?
MOD QUE   3N/Z.SG.A-be.plentiful-STV
you know?   it is plentiful

h-wa?-t[62]-ga-Ryo?d-a-ge-h'   o-i?dahdẹt-Ø
TRNS-FACT-DL-3N/Z.SG.A-animal-JN-amount.to-STV   3N/Z.SG.P-be.frightening-STV
every kind of animal   it is frightening
Actually, you know, every kind of fierce animal is plentiful [there].

---

[62] In older texts this stative verb took the prefix *hwa?t-* which includes the factual. The Onondaga Nation speaker who related the story apparently retained this as well. Contemporary speakers and Six Nations speakers use *ha?de-*.

7.12.2.2.2 Counting Animate Entities

Animate entities are counted using *.adi-* + partitive, a base that consists of the partitive prepronominal prefix, the semireflexive, and the verb root *-i-* 'be the total of'. If the counted entity is specified, it occurs as a separate nominal. *Animacy* includes animals and humans (including kin) as in (178a-c). The base also occurs with quantifiers, as in (178d):

(178) a. <u>Gayé·i nigųnadí gohsá·dęs</u>, nigųnų?s?ų́ ígę nwá·ho?dęh (HW01).

gayei	ni-gųn-ad-i-h		gohsá·dęs	ni-gųn-ų?s?ų-h
NUM	PRT-3FZ.PL.A-SRF-be.the.total-STV		NOUN	PRT-3FZ.PL.A-be.little-STV
four	how many there are		horse(s)	they are little

i-ga-i-h	nwa·ho?dęh
EMPTY-3N/Z.SG.A-be-STV	INTR
it is	what kind

There are four ponies [Literally: There are four horses, it's the little kind].

b. Degní dehowiyæyędáhgwa? ne? gwas háųhwa? degnų́·gwe onadade?gę?áh, nę hé? na? né? <u>gayéih nihęnadíh shagonó?shų?á</u> (LG05).

degni	de-ho-wiR-a-yęd-ah-gwa?		ne?	gwas	ha-ųhw-a?
NUMBER	DL-3M.SG.P-infant-JN-have-HAB-HBPST		NOM	INTS	3M.SG.P-self-NSF
two	he had two babies		the	really	he, himself

de-gn-ųgweh	on-adade?gę?ah		onę	he?
DL-3FZ.DU.A-person:SUFF	3FZ.NSG.P-be.a.younger.sibling		TMP	REP
two females	they are sisters		now	again

na?	ne?	gayeih	ni-hęn-ad-i-h
ASRT	NOM	NUMBER	PRT-3M.PL.A-SRF-be.the.total-STV
it's	the	four	thus many of them

shago-no? + shų?á
3M.SG > 3-stepparent.*stepchild*= PL
his stepchildren

He's had two children, two girls that are his own, and there are four stepchildren.

c. Onę́ hwa?wats?áhda? ne? áhsę nigųnadí ne? Hayęhwátha? shagohawashų?á (CTL138.3-4).

onę	h-wa?-w-at-s?a-hd-?		ne?	ahsę	ni-gųn-adi-h
TMP	TRNS-FACT-3N/Z.SG.A-SRF-be.used.up-CS-PNC		NOM	NUM	PRT-3FZ.PL.S-be.the.total-STV
then	it was the last one		the	three	thus many of them

ne?	Hayęhwátha?	shago-hawa + shų?á
NOM	NAME	3M.SG > 3-*child*.parent = PL
the	Hiawatha	his children

It was the last one of Hiawatha's three daughters.

d. Tho hé? nų ne? hęnųgwehųwé <u>dogá·?</u> <u>nihęnadíh</u> wa?hodiyo?déha? (LG04).

tho	he?	nų	ne?	hęn-ųgweh = ųwe		doga·?
LOC	REP	LOC	NOM	3M.PL.A-person:SUFF = AUTH		QNT
there	again	place	the	Indians		a few

ni-hęn-ad-i-h	wa?-hodi-yo?d-ęh-a?
PRT-3M.PL.A-SRF-be.the.total-STV	FACT-3M.NSG.P-work-INCH-PNC
the total of them	they worked

And some of the Indians went to the same place to work.

The counting stem *.adi-* + partitive, can occur with an external nominal expression that is, grammatically, an internally headed relative clause, as is *ganųhsgúwa hęní?dę?* 'the ones who resided in the lodge' in (179):

(179) Dá, ónę híhya? tshá? <u>nihęnadi</u> ne? <u>ganųhsgúwa hęní?dę?</u> hyá de?shonasdeísdih, né?tho gę́ gwa? dehadigáhæ? tsha? gododihádye? (H148.6-8).[63]

da	onę	hihya?	tsha?	ni-hęn-ad-i-h		ne?	ga-nųhs-agųwa
LNK	TMP	MOD	SUB	PRT-3M.PL.A-SRF-be.the.total-STV		NOM	3N/Z.SG.A-house-LOC
so	then	indeed	that	the total of them		the	in the house

hen-i?dę·-?	hya	de?-s-hon-asdeisd-ih	ne?tho	nęgę	gwa?
3M.PL.A-reside-STV	NEG	NEG-REP-3M.NSG.P-pay.attention-STV	MAN	DEM	RSTR
they reside	not	they no longer pay attention	thus	this	just

de-hadi-gahR-a?	tsha?	go-adodi-h-adye-?
DL-3M.PL.A-watch-STV	SUB	3FI.P-grow-STV-PRG-PRP
they are watching	that	she is growing along

So now indeed all the ones who were in the house no longer paid attention [to her], they just watched her grow.

Finally, *.adi-* + partitive can occur alone without a specifying nominal, as in (180). In that example the counted entity is identified pronominally within the main verb:

(180) Nayé? dí? ne? hadi·nyahdę́ áhsę nihęnadíh wa?hųwadiya?dá·gwa? (CTL336.1).

naye?	di?	ne?	hadi-nyahdęh	ahsę	ni-hęn-ad-i-h
ASRT	LNK	NOM	3M.PL.A-turtle	NUM	PRT-3M.PL.A-SRF-be.the.total-STV
it's	moreover	the	turtle clan	three	the number of [men]

wa?-hųwadi-ya?d-a-gw-a?
FACT-3 > 3M.NSG-body-JN-choose-PNC
they chose them

Moreover, they chose three (men) from the turtle (clan)

Two roots denoting humans, *-ksa?(ah)* 'child, children' and *-ųgweh* 'person', differ from noun or verb roots, in that they take nominal as well as verbal morphology. Both can occur with the dualic prepronominal prefix to form a counting expression as in (181):

---

[63] Stress and vowel length as marked by Hewitt; he did not mark vowel length in this excerpt.

(181) a. Naʔ góʔ náʔ gęs neʔ íʔ, <u>dehniksáʔah</u> nę hniyųtháʔ oyędáʔ... (LG03)

naʔ	go·ʔ	naʔ	gęs	neʔ	iʔ	de-hni-ksaʔah	nę
ASRT	CTR	ASRT	CST	NOM	PRN	DL-3M.DU.A-child	PRES
it's	however	it's	usually	the	I/we	two boys	here

hni-niyųt-haʔ	o-yęd-aʔ
3M.DU.A-hitch.up-HAB	NPF-firewood-NSF
they hitch it up	firewood

But as to us, two boys hitch up the firewood...

b. Thohge ó·nę neʔ <u>dehnų́·gwe</u> sahyahdę́·dyaʔ... (CTL206.5)

thohge	onę	neʔ	de-hn-ųgweh	s-a-hy-ahdędy-aʔ
TMP	TMP	NOM	DL-3M.DU.A-person:SUFF	REP-FACT-3M.DU.A-depart-PNC
thereafter	the	two persons	they two go home

Then the two men went back home...

7.12.2.3 Ordinal Number Expression

Ordinal numbers locate an entity or situation within a series. To form ordinal numbers in Onondaga, a cardinal number is followed by *wadų́ʔthaʔ* 'be one of a sequence', for example *sgadáh wadų́ʔthaʔ* '[it's] first, the first [time], *degní wadų́ʔthaʔ* '[it's] second, the second [time]', etc. There is, in addition, a base -adyęhd- + cislocative 'do first' which often replaces *sgadáh wadų́ʔthaʔ* with situation expressions, as in (182c).

(182) a. Neʔ ahsę́ wadųʔtháʔ wędá·deʔ hí·hyaʔ neʔ sayá·ne·h ís syaʔdagwe·ní·yoʔ neʔ
   gaihwiyóh (CTL93.1-2).

neʔ	ahsę	w-adų́ʔt-haʔ	w-ęd-ade-ʔ	hihyaʔ	neʔ
NOM	NUM	3N/Z.SG.A-one.of.a.sequence-HAB	3N/Z.SG.A-day-exist-STV	MOD	NOM
the	three	it's in a sequence	day	indeed	the

sa-yane·-h	is	s-yaʔd-a-gweniyo-ʔ	neʔ
2SG.P-peace.chief-STV	PRON	2SG.A-body-JN-important.one-STV	NOM
you, a peace chief	you	you, a leader	the

ga-Rihw-iyo-h'
3N/Z.SG.A-matter-good-STV
good message

[On] the third day, indeed, you, a peace chief, will be a leader of the Good Message.

b. ...degní wadų́ʔthaʔ áhsų héʔ sahęhę́·ʔ... (CTL199.8)

degni	w-adų́ʔt-haʔ	ahsų	heʔ	s-a-ha-ihę·-ʔ'
NUM	3N/Z.SG.A-be.in.a.sequence.HAB	REP	REP	REP-FACT-3M.SG.A-say-PNC
two	it's in a sequence	yet again	he repeated it

...he repeated it a second time...

c. Nayéʔ díʔ ędwa·dyę́ęhdaʔ tho hędwéʔ tshaʔ dyonųdáhæʔ.

naye?	di?	ę-dw-adyęhd-a?	tho	h-ę-dw-e-?
ASRT	LNK	FUT-1IN.PL.A-do.first-PNC	LOC	TRNS-FUT-1IN.PL.A-walk-PNC
it's	moreover	we all will do it first	there	we all will go there

```
tsha?    d-yo-nųd-a-hR-a?
SUB      CIS-3N/Z.SG.P-hill-JN-be.up.above-STV
that     up on the hill
```
First, we'll go to the top of the hill.

7.12.2.4 Counting Entity Expressions with Amount Verbs

Amount verbs are listed in Table 7.6. Each of the verbs can incorporate appropriate noun roots, but unlike the counting verbs listed in Table 7.5, they can also occur without incorporation.

Table 7.6 Amount verbs

Amount Verbs	Gloss
.ų- + partitive[64]	*be an amount, be a number of*
.ų- + translocative and dualic	*be everything, be all of it*
.ų- + coincident and dualic	*be the same amount*
-atga?d-	*be plentiful, be many, be a lot*

Expressions with the amount base *.ų-* + partitive 'be an amount' may or may not specify the precise number of entities, as in (183). As the examples show, the base may occur in relation to animate as well as non-animate referents, and it can incorporate appropriate noun roots. Also, note the quite unusual example in (183d) which omits the partitive prefix. All of the amount verbs based on the verb root *-ų-* take agent pronominal prefixes.

(183) a. Thohge ne? tciwade·yó tcidų·dyéęhda?, New Process Gear ni?á wa?ųgwayo?dęhá?
gwas nę <u>niya·gyų́h</u> ne? agyų́·gwe (LG13).
```
thohge    ne?    tci-w-ade-'                    tci-d-a-w-adyeęhd-a?
TMP       NOM    COIN-3N/Z.SG.A-SRF-kill-STV    COIN-CIS-FACT-N/Z.SG.A-first-PNC
then      the    as there was fighting          it was first


New Process Gear    ne?    i?=á            wa?-ųgwa-yo?dę-h-a?
NAME                NOM    INTS=DIM        FACT-1PL.P-work-INCH-PNC
New Process Gear    the    I/we specifically    we got to work


gwas    nę    ni-yagy-ų-h'                          ne?    agy-ųgweh
INTNS   LOC   PRT-1EX.PL.A-be.an.amount-STV         NOM    1EX.PL.A-person:SUFF
very    here  several of us                         the    we women
```
During the first world war <u>several of us</u> women got to work for New Process Gear.

b. Háų? gá·e? nųda·swéh <u>áhya?k</u> <u>nę́jyųk</u> né? dektcí·e? (H724.24-25).[65]
```
haų?     gae?        n-ųda-sw-e-h                 ahya?k
INSTG    DGR         PRT-CIS:FACT-2PL-walk-IMP    NUM
OK       less (space)    come this way             six
```

---

[64] Note that this is the verb base that has become lexicalized as the amount classifier *niyųh*.

[65] Stress and vowel length as marked by Hewitt.

    n-ę-sy-ų-Ø-k-Ø   neʔ   dekcí·eʔ
    PRT-FUT-2PL-be.an.amount-STV-CNT-PNC   NOM   NOUN
    the number of you   the   chickadee
Come hither, you six chickadees.

c. Waʔagwathúgayaʔk áhsę niwáshę <u>niya·gyųh</u> (H788.3).[66]

    waʔ-agw-at-hųga·yaʔk-Ø   ahsę niwashę   ni-yagy-ų-h
    FACT-1EX.PL.A-SRF-draft.sbdy-PNC   NUM   PRT-1EX.PL.A-be.an.amount-stv
    we volunteered   thirteen   the number we are
Thirteen was the number of us [who] volunteered.

d. nayeʔ néʔ hyá deʔų·gwę·núhdų́ʔ neʔ ohędų́ hagwá waʔwędade·nyų́·dyeʔ <u>wędų́</u> hų́
    dęji·dwadátgęʔ (CTL48.4-5).

    nayeʔ neʔ hya deʔ-ųgw-ęnųhdų-ʔ   neʔ o-hęd-ųh   hagwa
    ASRT   NOM NEG NEG-1PL.P-know-STV   NOM 3N/Z.SG.P-be.ahead-STV DIR
    it's   the not we don't know   the it's ahead   direction

    waʔ-w-ęd-ade-nyų-adye-ʔ   w-ęd-ų-h'   hų
    FACT-3N/Z.SG.A-day-exist-DST-PRG-PNC   3N/Z.SG.A-day-be.an.amount-STV   MOD
    days along   number of days   maybe

    d-ę-s-dw-adat-gę-ʔ
    DL-FUT-REP-1EX.PL.A-REF-see-PNC
    we will see each other again
*We don't know whether in [the number of] future days we will see each other
    again.*

The amount verb .ų- + partitive also occurs with the diminutive with the meaning 'few':

(184) Néʔtho díʔ níyot nę́gę odų́ni <u>niyų́hah</u> néʔ diyóhsawaʔ dę́ʔseʔ néʔ gų́díyoʔ <u>niyų́hah</u> óʔ
    náʔ néʔ tsháʔ diyóhsawaʔ... (H689.12-15)[67]

    neʔtho diʔ   niyot   nęgę o-ad-ųni-h'
    MAN   LNK   MAN   DEM   3N/Z.SG.P-SRF-make-STV
    thus   moreover how it is this it grows

    ni-y-ų = há   neʔ d-yo-ahsaw-aʔ   dęʔseʔ neʔ
    PRT-3N/Z.SG.A-be.an.amount = DIM   NOM CIS-3N/Z.SG.P-start-STV CNJ   NOM
    few   the it has started   and   the

    gų́di-Ryo-ʔ   ni-y-ų = há   oʔ   naʔ   neʔ
    3FZ.PL.A-animal-NSF   PRT-3N/Z.SG.A-be.an.amount = DIM   ADD ASRT NOM
    animals   few   also it's the

---

[66] Stress and vowel length as marked by Hewitt.

[67] Stress and vowel length as marked by Hewitt.

d-yo-ahsaw-aʔ
CIS-3N/Z.SG.P-start-STV
it has started
That's how it was with these growing [things], they were few in the beginning, and the animals, they too were few in the beginning...[Literally, the way it is, few growing things [in] the beginning and also few animals [in] the beginning].

The verb root -ų̈- in combination with the translocative and dualic prepronominal prefixes denotes 'many different' entities:

(185) Naʔ óʔ neʔ hwaʔųgwayoʔdęháʔ si tshaʔ nų hayęthwás, <u>haʔdeyų́</u> ohyaʔshų́ʔa...
   (LG15)

naʔ	oʔ	neʔ	h-waʔ-ųgwa-yoʔd-ęh-aʔ	si	tshaʔ	nų
ASRT	ADD	NOM	TRNS-FACT-1PL.P-work-INCH-PNC	LOC	SUB	LOC
it's	also	the	we worked there	there	that	place

ha-yęthw-as	haʔ-de-y-ų-h'	o-ahy-aʔ + shųʔá
3M.SG.A-plant-HAB	TRNS-DL-3N/Z.SG.A-be.an.amount-STV	NPF-berry,apple-NSF = PL
he farms/farmer	it's all of the different ones	fruits

We worked at a place where he grows all the different [kinds of] fruit...

The verb root -ų̈- in combination with coincident and dualic prepronominal prefixes denotes 'equal amounts' (sec 4.7.4):

(186) Nayéʔ neʔ shagwahsę́naʔ nayéʔ ęhakhahcyų́·gwaʔ <u>tshaʔdeyųhá·dyeʔ</u> ęyeyenáʔ neʔ
   ųgweʔdagwé·gih néʔtho ená·geʔ (CTL195.5-6).

nayeʔ	neʔ	shagwa-hsęn-aʔ	nayeʔ	ę-ha-khahcy-ųgw-aʔ
ASRT	NOM	1EX.NSG > 3MSG-name-NSF	ASRT	FUT-3M.SG.A-divide-MLT-PNC
it's	the	our chief	it's	he will distribute it

tshaʔ-de-y-ų-h'-adye-ʔ	ę-ye-yena-ʔ'	neʔ
COIN-DL-3N/Z.SG.A-be.an.amount-STV-CNT-STV	FUT-3FI.A-accept-PNC	NOM
they are equal amounts	they will accept it	the

Ø-ųgweʔt-a-gweg-ih	neʔtho	e-nage·-ʔ
3N/Z.SG.A-person-JN-all-STV	LOC	3FI.A-reside-STV
everyone	there	they reside

Our chief will distribute it [the harvest] and everyone who lives here will accept equal shares.

The amount base *-atgaʔd-* 'be many, be plentiful, have many' occurs with both animate and non-animate entities, and it is able to incorporate. It differs from the amount bases derived from the verb root -ų̈- in that it takes patient pronominal prefixes.

(187) a. Gwas nę niyagų́h naʔ neʔtho ihswáʔ naʔ góʔ dogę́s <u>gotgaʔdéʔ</u> neʔ haųgwéʔtaʔ
      (LG05).

gwas	nę	ni-yag-ų-h'	naʔ	neʔtho	ihswaʔ	naʔ	goʔ
INTS	LOC	PRT-3FI.A-be.an.amount-STV	ASRT	LOC	QNT	ASRT	MOD
very	here	thus they amount to	it's	there	a lot		but

dogȩs   go-at-ga?d-e?   ne?   ha-ųgwe?t-a?
MOD   3FI.P-SRF-be.plentiful-STV   NOM   3M.SG.P-kinsmen-NSF
for sure   they are plentiful   the   his folks
There was quite a number [of people] there, but a lot of them were his folks.

b. Nayé? hí·hya? ne? <u>odohsæ·gá?de</u> ųgyahdȩdyų ne? kheháwa ne?
Gahȩ·déhsųk (CTL17.4-5).

naye?   hihya?   ne?   o-ad-ohsR-a-ga?d-e?   ųgy-ahdȩdyų-h'
ASRT   MOD   NOM   3N/Z.SG.P-SRF-year-JN-plentiful-STV   1DU.P-depart-STV
it's   indeed   the   it's many years   we two have departed

ne?   Gahȩ·dehsųk
NOM   NAME
the   Gahȩ·dehsųk
Indeed, it's been many years since we left, my daughter Gahȩ·déhsųk and I.

7.12.3 Counting Possessed Entities

Positional verbs with incorporated nouns are used when counting possessed entities or
when referring to more than one possession:

Table 7.7 Positional verbs for counting possessed entities

Verb	Entities (classified by shape or manner of attachment)
-POSSESSED.NOUN.ROOT-ada-	have inside: contained entity
-POSSESSED.NOUN.ROOT-od-	have rooted, have sticking up: standing or growing object
-POSSESSED.NOUN.ROOT-ųd-	have dangling: objects with a secondary attachment to an intervening object
-POSSESSED.NOUN.ROOT-yȩ-	have lying in a neutral position: extended objects, all other entities

The possessed entity is typically identified by an incorporated noun as in (188a-d), but if
a particle or a morphological verb expresses the possessed entity as in (188e), it occurs
outside the positional verb. the The choice of pronominal prefix – from the agent or patient
series – depends on whether or not the entity is alienably possessed or not: alienable
possessions take patient prefixes, inalienable possessions take agent prefixes:

(188) a. ...dȩ?se? sgadá gȩ gwa? <u>ȩyų·gwadųnhehsǽ·dak</u> (CTL307.7).

dȩ?se?   sgada   [nȩ]gȩ   gwa?   ȩ-yųgw-ad-unhe-hsR-ada-Ø-k-Ø
CNJ   NUM   DEM   RSTR   FUT-1PL.P-SRF-life-NOM-be.inside-STV-CNT-PNC
and   one   this   just   we will have life inside us
...and we all will have just one life [among] us.

b. Deyoya?dasdá·thek, gaya?dasnówe?, <u>gayé·i niga?nųdó·da?</u> (HW07).

de-yo-ya?d-a-sda·the-k   ga-ya?d-a-snoR-e?   gayeih
DL-3FZ.SG.P-body-JN-gleam-HAB   3N/Z.SG.A-body-JN-act.fast-STV   NUM
she gleams   she is swift   four

ni-ga-ʔnųd-od-aʔ
PRT-3FZ.SG.A-leg-stick.out-STV
she has leg(s)
Her body gleams, she's swift, [and] she has four legs.

c. ...ųgwa·dę·dó·daʔ <u>gayé·i niyokdehę́·daʔ</u> (CTL353.2).

ųgw-ad-Rę́d-od-aʔ	gayei	ni-yo-kdehR-ųd-aʔ
1PL.P-SRF-tree-stick.up-STV	NUMBER	PRT-3N/Z.SG.P-root-extend-STV
we have a growing tree	four	it has roots extending from it

...we have a tree [that] has four roots [extending outward]

d. <u>Degní dehowiyæyędáhgwaʔ</u>, neʔ gwas háųhwaʔ degnų́·gwe onadadéʔgęʔáh... (LG05)

degni	de-ho-wiR-a-yęd-ah-gwaʔ[68]	neʔ	gwas	ha-ųhw-aʔ
NUMBER	DL-3M.SG.P-infant-JN-have-HAB-HBPST	NOM	INTS	3M.SG.P-self-NSF
two	he had two babies	the	really	he, himself

de-gn-ųgweh	on-adade-ʔgęʔah
DL-3FZ.DU.A-person:SUFF	3FZ.NSG-REF-be.a.younger.sibling
two females	they are sisters

He's had two children, they are his own, two sisters...

e. ... <u>gayéi é·git niyųhwę·jyáʔ hodí·yęʔ</u>... (HW01)

gayei	egit	ni-y-ųhwęjy-aʔ	hodi-yę-ʔ
NUM	NOUN	PRT-NPF-land-NSF	3M.NSG.P-have-STV
four	acres	of land	they have

...they had four acres of land...

Positional verbs may also be used with the distributive to mark several possessed entities:

(189) ...nę gó·ʔ naʔ, hododiʔsjíhwęh, honyagí oʔ <u>howiyæyę́dųʔ</u> oʔ (LG24).

nę	go·ʔ	naʔ	ho-adodi-ʔs-jihw-eh	ho-nyag-ih	oʔ
TMP	CTR	ASRT	3M.SG.P-grow.up-PL-INTS-STV	3M.SG.P-marry-STV	ADD
now	however	it's	he's fully grown up	he's married	also

ho-wiR-a-yęd-ų-ʔ	oʔ
3M.SG.P-infant-JN-have-DST-STV	ADD
he has babies	also

Now he's grown up, he's married, and he's also got several kids.

7.12.4 Expressions with Quantity Particles

Many of the quantity particles derive from verb stems. Table 7.8 lists the particles and, where derived, their probable verbal sources.

---

[68] The referent of the noun root *-wiR-* 'baby' is treated as an alienable possession in all of the Five Nations Iroquoian languages.

Table 7.8 Quantity particles with their verbal sources

Quantity Particles	Probable Sources	Gloss
agwé·gih[69]	-gweg- 'be all'	all
agwé·gi?s	agwegi = ?s	every, everyone
gagwé·gih		it is all
gu̧di·gwé·gih		it is all of them (zoic)
oihwagwé·gih	-Rihw-gweg- 'be all matters'	it is everything
dejyá(·)ȩh	.jyaȩ + dualic	both
dehnijyá·ȩh		both [men or mixed]
degnijyá·ȩh		both [women]
dó(·)ga(·)?		several
do·ga·?á	doga·? = DIM	few
íhswa?[70]	-ihsw- 'be lots'	a lot, many
nȩ gwa?[71]		little bit; less
ó·dya?k	-adya?k- 'break off'	some
odya?kshų́?a	-adya?k + shų?á	various, several
(o)sthwihá	-asthw- 'be less, be smaller'	a little bit, just barely

Agwé·gih 'all'

The particle or its inflected form occurs before or after the modified expression (190a and
b). The stem *-gweg-* also occurs fully inflected as a verb that can incorporate noun stems
(190b and c). In addition, it occurs with the plural clitic in the meaning 'everyone, each' as
in (190d).

(190) a. <u>Agwegí na? dahu̧wáhnhe?</u> (LG09).
     agwegih   na?   d-a-hu̧wa-hnhe-?
     QNT   ASRT   CIS-FACT-3 > 3M.SG-form.a.circle-PNC
     all   it's   they encircled him
     All [of them] supported him.

  b. Thohge onȩ wa?hodiya?da·yeik <u>gagwegih</u> (H632.13-4).[72]
     thohge onȩ   wa?-hodi-ya?dayei-k   ga-gweg-ih
     TMP   FACT-3M.NSG.P-assemble-PNC   3N/Z.SG.A-be.all-STV
     thereafter   they assembled   it is all
     Then they all assembled

  c. Ne?tho niwageihsȩhdo?dȩh; wa?gatgathwa? <u>oihwagwegh</u> tsha? nȩyawȩ́ha?
     (H630.5-6).[73]
     ne?tho   ní-wage-Rihsȩ·hd-o?dȩ-h'   wa?-g-atgathw-a?
     MAN   PRT-1SG.P-dream,sleep-kind-STV   FACT-1SG.A-look.at-PNC
     thus   thus is my dream   I looked at it

---

[69] The base has become lexicalized as a particle fairly recently. Hewitt cites the verb form *gagwé·gih*
[ga-gweg-ih] but glosses it 'all' rather than 'it is all'.

[70] Hewitt spells this word *iswa?*.

[71] nȩ gwa? functions as both a quantifier and degree particle.

[72] Vowel length as marked by Hewitt; he did not mark stress in this excerpt.

[73] Hewitt did not mark stress and vowel length in this excerpt; punctuation as marked by Hewitt.

o-Rihw-a-gweg-ih	tsha?	n-ę-yaw-ęh-a?
3N/Z.SG.P-matter-JN-be.all-STV	SUB	PRT-FUT-3N/Z.SG.P-happen-PNC
everything	that	thus it will happen

[In] my dream I saw everything that's going to happen.

d. Na? né? agwegí?s wa?hadiyená? sdę? gwa? nwadę? ... (LG18)

na?	ne?	agwegi = ?s	wa?-hadi-yena-?'	sdę? gwa? nwadę?
ASRT	NOM	QNT = PL	FACT-3M.PL.A-get-PNC	INDEF RSTR INTR
it's	the	everyone	they all got it	something

Everyone / each gets something...

Dejyá·ęh 'both'

The examples in (191) show that the form occurs as a particle (examples a-c) and as a stem with verb morphology (examples c and d where the stem is inflected with pronominal prefixes). In (191a) the particle precedes a locative expression *tsha? nų́·we* 'the place where', in (191b) it follows the verb form it modifies.[74] Note that while in (191c and d) the referents of the particle are specified by external nominals, the particle functions anaphorically as an entity expression in its own right in other examples. In (191c) the expression *degni·jyá·ęh* 'both women', is followed by a complex external nominal *ne? goksdę?áh ohni? ne? goháwah* 'the old lady and her daughter'. The same is true in example (191d), where the referent of *dehnijyáęh* 'both men' is further specified by the external nominal *ne? hnų́·gweh* 'the two men'.

(191) a. ...*dejyá·ęh tsha? nų́·we* dedyo·de·yę́?tha·t dękdę́sda? niyosnó·we? ęwá·dų?
(CTL72.8-73.2).

dejyaęh	tsha?	nųwe	de-d-yo-ade·yę?tha·t-Ø	d-ę-k-dęsd-a?
QNT	SUB	LOC	DL-CIS-3N/Z.SG.P-be.dangerous-STV	DL-FUT-1SG.A-stop-PNC
both	that	place	it is dangerous there	I will stop it

ni-yo-snoR-e?	ę-w-adų-?
PRT-3N/Z.SG.P-fast-STV	FUT-3N/Z.SG.A-become-PNC
it is fast	it will become

...both are places where it's dangerous [and] I will end [the danger] as fast as possible.

b. Tho gó·? na?dehná? ne? *dejyáęh* wa?a·gwék... (LG24)

[tho	go·?	na?-de-hn-a-?	ne?	dejyaęh]
MAN	CTR	PRT-DL-3M.DU.A-be.a.size-STV	NOM	QNT
thus	however	they two were a size	the	both

wa?-agw-ek-Ø
FACT-1EX.PL.A-eat-PNC
we ate it

But both [the fish] were large enough for us to eat...[literally, but thus was their two size [that] both we ate [them]].

---

[74] Evidence that *dejyaęh* modifies *na?dehna?* is the third person masculine dual pronominal prefix of the verb form.

c. [Onę [degni·jyá·ęh] [neʔ goksdęʔá ohniʔ neʔ goháwah]] [dejyá·ę
odiʔniguhæhétgęʔs] (CTL6.3-4).

onę	de-gni-jyaę-h		neʔ	go-ksdęʔah	ohniʔ	neʔ
TMP	DL-3FZ.DU.A-be.both-STV		NOM	3FI.P-old.person	ADD	NOM
then	both [women]		the	old lady	also	the

go-hawah	dejyaęh	odi-ʔniguhR-ahetgę-ʔs
3FZ.SG > 3FI-parent.*child*	QNT	3FZ.NSG.P-mind-bad-STVPL
her daughter	both	they are unhappy

Then both [women], the old woman and her daughter, both were unhappy.

d. Onę dehnijyáęh neʔ hnú·gwe néʔtho waʔthnidáʔnhaʔ hohę́·duh (CTL200.7-8).

onę	de-hni-jyaę-h		neʔ	hn-ugweh	neʔtho
TMP	DL-3M.DU.A-be.both-STV		NOM	3M.DU.A-person:SUFF	LOC
then	both [men]		the	two men	there

waʔ-t-hni-daʔ-nhaʔ	ho-hęd-uh
FACT-DL-3M.DU.A-stand.up-PNC	3M.SG.P-be.in.front.of-STV
they two stood up	in front of him

Then both men stood up in front of him

Dó·ga·ʔ 'several', *dogaʔá* 'a few'

The particles modify counting verbs, amount verbs and possessed counting constructions. Only rarely do they modify a simple (non-quantifying) verb form

With animate and non-animate counting verbs (also (175) above):

(192) a. Thohgé neʔ hahsęnowá·nęh waʔshagoyaʔda·gwáʔ dó·ga·ʔ nihęnadí neʔ
dęhudi·hogwáhdaʔ… (CTL180.1-2)

thohge	neʔ	ha-hsęn-owanę-h	waʔ-shago-yaʔd-a-gw-aʔ		do·ga·ʔ
TMP	NOM	3M.SG.A-name-big-STV	FACT-3M.SG > 3-body-JN-choose-PNC		QNT
then	the	chief	he chose them		few

ni-hęn-ad-i-h	neʔ	d-ę-hu-ad-Rihw-ogw-ahd-aʔ
PRT-3M.PL.A-SRF-be.the.total-STV	NOM	DL-FUT-3M.PL.A-SRF-matter-scatter-CS-PNC
the number of [men]	the	they will spread the news

Then the chief chose a few [men] who will spread the news...

b. …neʔtho gníʔdęʔ waʔgaihwísheʔ dogá·ʔ niyohshæ·gé neʔ hya hwędú sú· ga·ʔ neʔ
hę́·gwe deʔshagonadahę·ʔséh (CTL3.1-2).

neʔtho	gn-iʔdę·-ʔ	waʔ-ga-Rihw-ishe-ʔ		doga·ʔ
LOC	3FZ.DU.A-reside-STV	FACT-3N/Z.SG.A-matter-long-PNC		QNT
there	they two resided	it was a long time		several

<table>
<tr><td>ni-y-ohsR-a-ge-h'</td><td></td><td>hya</td><td>hwędų</td><td>sų ga·?</td><td>ne?</td></tr>
<tr><td>PRT-3N/Z.SG.A-year-JN-be.an.amount-stv</td><td></td><td>NEG</td><td>INTR</td><td>INDF</td><td>NOM</td></tr>
<tr><td>thus many years</td><td></td><td>not</td><td>when</td><td>somebody</td><td>the</td></tr>
</table>

<table>
<tr><td>hR-ųgweh</td><td>de?-shago-nadahR-ę?se-h'</td></tr>
<tr><td>3M.SG.A-person:SUFF</td><td>NEG-3M.SG > 3-visit-BEN-STV</td></tr>
<tr><td>man</td><td>he didn't visit them</td></tr>
</table>

...they lived there for a long time [and] for several years never did a man come to visit them.

With a possessive counting construction:

(193) Wa?gayų́? di? hya? ganų?wae·hahenų́? dę́?se? <u>dogá·?</u> niyo·wi·yǽ·yę?... (LG17)

<table>
<tr><td>wa?-ga-yų-?</td><td></td><td>di?</td><td>hya?</td><td>ganų?wae·hahenų?</td><td></td><td>dę?se?</td><td>doga·?</td></tr>
<tr><td>FACT-3FZ.SG.A-arrive-PNC</td><td></td><td>LINK</td><td>MOD</td><td>NAME</td><td></td><td>CONJ</td><td>QNT</td></tr>
<tr><td>she arrived</td><td></td><td>so</td><td>indeed</td><td>Oneida</td><td></td><td>and</td><td>several</td></tr>
</table>

<table>
<tr><td>ni-yo-wiR-a-yę-?</td></tr>
<tr><td>PART-3FZ.SG.P-child-JN-have-STV</td></tr>
<tr><td>so she had children</td></tr>
</table>

There was a woman who came from Oneida, and she had several children...

With simple (non-quantifying) verb forms:

(194) a. Na? ó? dogá·? nihodi·yó thonę́h (LG20).

<table>
<tr><td>na?</td><td>o?</td><td>doga·?</td><td>ni-hodi-Ryo-h'</td><td></td><td>thonę</td></tr>
<tr><td>ASRT</td><td>ADD</td><td>QNT</td><td>PRT-3M.NSG.P-kill-STV</td><td></td><td>LOC</td></tr>
<tr><td>it's</td><td>also</td><td>several</td><td>it has killed them</td><td></td><td>here</td></tr>
</table>

There are several [persons] here that have died from it [the disease].

b. Doga·?ah gęs nwa?thathwada[h]se? onę he? gęs hųsahayų? tsha? thodinųhsa·yę? (H646.16-18).[75]

<table>
<tr><td>doga·? = á</td><td>gęs</td><td>n-wa?-t-h-athwadahse-?</td><td></td><td>onę</td><td>he?</td><td>gęs</td></tr>
<tr><td>QNT = DIM</td><td>CST</td><td>PRT-FACT-DL-3M.SG.A-circle.around-PNC</td><td></td><td>TMP</td><td>REP</td><td>CST</td></tr>
<tr><td>few</td><td>usually</td><td>thus he circled around it</td><td></td><td>then</td><td>again</td><td>usually</td></tr>
</table>

<table>
<tr><td>h-ųsa-ha-yų-?</td><td></td><td>tsha?</td><td>t-hodi-nųhs-a-yę-?</td></tr>
<tr><td>TRNS-FACT:REP-3M.SG.A-arrive-PNC</td><td></td><td>SUB</td><td>CIS-3M.NSG.P-house-JN-have-STV</td></tr>
<tr><td>he arrived again</td><td></td><td>where</td><td>there they had there house</td></tr>
</table>

Customarily he circled around it a few times, then he arrived again at their house.

<u>*ihswa?*</u> *'a lot, many'*

The particle modifies non-quantifying verbs (195 a-d) and, less frequently in our corpus, amount verbs (196). The particle also occurs as an entity expression in its own right

---

[75] Vowel length as marked by Hewitt; he did not mark stress in this excerpt.

without further specification, as in (197). It quantifies over entities and also functions as a degree expression.

With non-quantifying verbs *ihswaʔ* can function as a degree term as in (195b and c):

(195) a. Thohge neʔ Deganawí·daʔ waʔhęhę́·ʔ "Is hí·hyaʔ neʔ sų́·gweh <u>ihswáʔ</u> sayoʔdę́ʔih neʔ tshaʔ ohá·deʔ ade·yóhsæ·ʔ" (CTL91.5-6).

thohge	neʔ	Deganawidaʔ	waʔ-ha-ihę·ʔ		is	hi·hyaʔ	neʔ
TMP	NOM	NAME	FACT-3M.SG.A-say-PNC		PRON	MOD	NOM
then	the	Deganawidaʔ	he said		you	indeed	the

s-ųgweh	ihswaʔ	sa-yoʔdę-ʔ-ih	neʔ	tshaʔ
2SG.A-person:SUFF	QNT	2SG.P-work-INCH-STV	NOM	SUB
you, a person	a lot	you have come to work	the	where

o-ahade-ʔ	Ø-ade·yo-hsR-aʔ
3N/Z.SG.P-be.a.path-STV	NPF-fight-NOM-NSF
it is a path	warfare

Then Deganawidaʔ said, "Indeed, you have worked a lot [in relation to] the war path."

b. <u>Ihswáʔ</u> honųhwakdę́ neʔ hospital (LG05).

ihswaʔ	ho-nųhwakd-ę-h'	neʔ	hospital
QNT	3M.SG.P-hurt-BEN-STV	NOM	NOUN
a lot	he was ill	the	hospital

He was very ill in the hospital.

c. Hya go·ʔ éʔ niʔá hwędų́ tshaʔ deʔwagatdógę̨ʔ, naʔ gwáʔ tshaʔ jik <u>ihswáʔ</u> dewakdųkhwá·s?ih (LG12).

hya	go·ʔ	eʔ	neʔ	iʔ	hwędų	tshaʔ	deʔ-wag-atdog-ęh
NEG	CTR	REP	NOM	PRON	INTR	SUB	NEG-1SG.P-notice-STV
not	however	again	the	I	when	that	I didn't notice

naʔ gwaʔ	tshaʔ	jik	ihswaʔ	de-wak-dųkhwaR-sʔih
ASRT RSTR	SUB	SCAL	QNT	DL-1SG.P-sweat-FCL
because	that	too	a lot	I'm sweating

However, I never noticed [the heat] because I was sweating a lot.

d. Hya thaųhsahgwé·nyaʔ, neʔ <u>ihswáʔ</u> waʔgeʔse·shų́ʔ (LG10).

hya	th-aųsa-k-gweny-aʔ		neʔ	ihswaʔ	waʔ-ge-ʔse·-shų-ʔ'
NEG	CON-OPT:REP-1SG.A-be.able.to-PNC		NOM	QNT	FACT-1SG.A-drive-DST-PNC
not	I can't anymore		the	a lot	I drive around

I can't drive so much anymore.

442 Syntactic Constructions

With amount verbs:

(196) Gwas nę <u>niyagú</u> naʔ néʔtho <u>ihswáʔ</u> naʔ gó·ʔ dogę́s gotgaʔdéʔ neʔ haųgwéʔtaʔ
(LG05).

gwas	nę	ni-yag-ų-h'		naʔ	neʔtho	ihswaʔ	naʔ	go·ʔ
INTS	LOC	PRT-3FI.A-be.an.amount-stv		ASRT	LOC	QNT	ASRT	MOD
very	here	thus they amount to		it's	there	a lot	but	

dogę́s	go-atgaʔd-eʔ		neʔ	ha-ųgweʔt-aʔ
MOD	3FI.P-be.plentiful-STV		NOM	3M.SG.P-kinsmen-NSF
for sure	they are plentiful		the	his folks

There were a lot [of people] there but many of them were his folks.

The particle functions as an entity expression:

(197) Na·yeʔ neʔ <u>ihswaʔ</u> waʔegwathwaʔ tshaʔ nųweh niwagadæheʔ (H622.13-14).[76]

nayeʔ	neʔ	ihswaʔ	waʔ-e-gwathw-aʔ	tshaʔ	nųwe
ASRT	NOM	QNT	FACT-3FI.A-visit-PNC	SUB	LOC
it's	the	many	they visited	that	place

ni-wag-ad-Ræhe-ʔ
PRT-1SG.P-SRF-standing.tree-STV
I have a standing tree
Many [persons] have paid a visit where I have a standing tree.

Nę gwaʔ 'little bit, less'

The particle cluster functions as a quantifier when it occurs with the extent classifier, and as a degree particle without it.

(198) Nę gwáʔ nigę́ nhehonenų́h … (HW07)

nę gwaʔ	nigę	n-he-hon-e-nųh
QNT	EXT	PRT-TRNS-3M.NSG.P-walk-STV
little bit	extent	thus they have gone

They have gone a short distance…

Ó·dyaʔk 'some'

The particle modifies entity expressions (199). It also occurs anaphorically or cataphorically as an entity expression in its own right, without further specifying the modified entity as in (200).

(199) Onę waʔhų́ʔnųyę́ʔ nayeʔ díʔ <u>neʔ hadiksaʔshųʔá</u> ó·dyaʔk gęs dehodi·hwahæ·ʔsę̨k
hęnéheʔ a·hųdé·yoʔ (CTL27.4-5).

onę	waʔ-hų-ę́ʔnų·yę-ʔ'	nayeʔ	diʔ	neʔ	hadi-ksaʔ + shųʔá	odyaʔk
TMP	FACT-3M.PL.A-play-PNC	ASRT	LNK	NOM	3M.PL.A-child = PL	QNT
then	they played	it's	moreover	the	children	some

---

[76] Vowel length as marked by Hewitt; he did not mark stress in this excerpt.

gęs	de-hodi-Rihwahæʔ-shę·-k	hęn-eR-heʔ	aa-hų-ade·yo-ʔ
REP	DL-3M.NSG.P-quarrel-DST-HAB	3M.PL.A-want-HAB	OPT-3M.PL.A-fight-PNC
repeatedly	they quarrel	they want	for them to fight

When they played, moreover, some of the children repeatedly quarreled, [and] they wanted to fight.

(200) a. <u>Odyáʔk</u> oʔ hodiʔse·hdayę́dų̧ʔ, neʔ automobile... (LG11)

odyaʔk	oʔ	hodi-ʔse-hd-a-yęd-ų-ʔ		neʔ	automobile
QNT	ADD	3M.NSG.P-vehicle-JN-have-DST-STV		NOM	NOUN
some	also	they have vehicles		the	automobile

Also, some of them had cars...

b. Odiyoʔdéʔ o·hęʔsę́·k <u>odyáʔk</u>, áhyaʔk gadéʔ jyadák, nigahwisdagé ęyų̧tgwenyáʔ neʔ jyę́dada, <u>odyáʔk</u> dé·gę·ʔ (LG11).

odi-yoʔde-ʔ	o·hęʔsę·k	odyaʔk	ahyaʔk	gadeʔ	jyadak
3FZ.NSG.P-work-STV	TMP	QNT	NUM	CNJ	NUM
they work	daily	some	six	or	seven

ni-ga-hwisd-a-ge-h'		ę-yų-at-gweny-aʔ		neʔ
PRT-3N/Z.SG.A-money-JN-amount.to-STV		FUT-3FI.A-SRF-be.able-PNC		NOM
how many dollars		they earned/won		the

s-y-ęd-a-d-'ah		odyaʔk	de·gę·ʔ
REP-3N/Z.SG.A-day-JN-be.one-STV		QNT	NUMBER
one day		some	eight

The women work every day; some earn six and seven dollars a day and some [earn] eight.

<u>(o)sthwiha</u> 'little bit'

The particle modifies situation expressions and other particles. It can precede or follow the modified expression.

(201) a. ...honathwisdų̧ní <u>sthwíhah</u> (LG03).

hon-at-hwisd-ų̧ni-h'	sthwiha
3M.NSG.P-SRF-money-make-STV	QNT
they are earning money	a little bit

...they are earning a little bit of money

b. Dahcyeit diʔ na·yeʔ tshaʔ nwaʔcyeæʔ tshaʔ waʔdejyadekhaʔ osthwihah (H683.1).[77]

d-a-hs-yei-t-Ø	diʔ	nayeʔ	tshaʔ	n-waʔ-hs-yeR-aʔ
CIS-FACT-2SG.A-be.right-CS-PNC	LNK	ASRT	SUB	PRT-FACT-2SG.A-do-PNC
you caused it to be right	moreover	it's	that	thus you did it

---

[77] Vowel length as marked by Hewitt; he did not mark stress in this excerpt.

tsha?	wa?-de-jy-ade-kh-a?	osthwi = há
SUB	FACT-DL-2DU-SRF-take.apart-PNC	QNT = DIM
that	you two separated	little bit

You made it right by what you did, separating [from one another] by a small [distance].

c. Ónę díʔ osthwíhah nęh hagwah haʔdęswadáʔshęʔ (H771.1).[78]

onę	di?	osthwi = há	nęgę	hagwa	ha?-d-ę-swa-da?-shę-?'
TMP	LNK	QNT = DIM	DEM	DIR	TRNS-DL-FUT-2PL-stand.up-DSTR-PNC
then	moreover	little bit	this	direction	you all will stand up there

Furthermore, you all will stand a little bit aside over there [literally, a little bit in this direction there you all will stand up]

7.12.5 Degree Expressions

Degree terms characterize scalable properties of entities or situations. Degree terms occur as particles or, less frequently, as verb forms that usually precede but may also follow (207) the entity or situation expression. Typically, the modifier and modified parts of the expression occur adjacently, but as (206) shows, they need not do so. Particles used in degree expressions are:

Table 7.9 Degree particles

Degree Particles	Gloss
dę́ʔgih	*very much, exceedingly*
heyóheʔ[79]	*exceedingly, to the highest degree* [Hewitt]; *more* [6N]
jík/swáʔjik	*excessively, too much*
nę gwaʔ	*little bit, less*
sę́hgeh	*barely, hardly, only just*
tgę́ʔih	*more* [ON]
thóha	*almost, practically, nearly, just about, soon, to be about to*
waʔjikʔá /gwajikʔá	*almost not; barely, nearly*

(202) ... [dę́ʔgí hyá deʔawętgádeʔ] tsháʔ gų́nheʔ (H170.3).[80]

dę?gi	hya	de?-aw-ętgad-e?	tsha?	g-ųnhe-?
DGR	NEG	NEG-3N/Z.SG.P-pleasant-STV	SUB	1SG.A-be.alive-STV
very much	not	it isn't pleasant		my life

...my life is not at all pleasant [literally, my life is very much not pleasant].

(203) ...onę heʔ neʔ Oha·æʔ waʔhoshwaʔ [węhsægaʔwih heyohéʔ] (H658.3-4).[81]

onę	he?	ne?	Ohaæ?	wa?-ho-shw-a?	w-ęhsR-a-ga?w-ih
TMP	REP	NOM	NAME	FACT-3M.SG.P-smell-PNC	3N/Z.SG.A-odor-JN-delicious-STV
then	again	the	Ohaæ?	he smelled it	it's a delicious odor

---

[78] Stress and vowel length as marked by Hewitt.

[79] The particle is used by Hewitt to indicate a high degree of a state or action. He glosses the particle 'utmost, exceedingly'. Contemporary 6N speakers, use it as a comparative marker, where ON speakers use *tgę́ʔih* 'more'. *Tgę́ʔih* does not occur in Hewitt's writings.

[80] Stress as marked by Hewitt; he did not mark vowel length in this excerpt.

[81] Stress and vowel length as marked by Hewitt.

heyohe?
DGR
exceedingly
…again Oháæ? smelled an exceedingly delicious odor.

(204) a. Ayé̜æ? yágę? yá sdę? de?ha·gé̜ [jík dedyó?ga·s] (HW07).

ayę·æ?	yagę?	hya	sdę?	de?-ha-gę-h'
SIM	HRSY	NEG	INDF	NEG-3M.SG.A-see-STV
it seems	they say	not	something	he doesn't see it

jik	de-d-yo-a?gaR-as
DGR	DL-CIS-3N/Z.SG.P-be.dark-HAB
too much	it is dark there

It seems, they say, he can't see anything [because] it's too dark there.

b. …dyu̜gwadé?gwę ne? akhwa·jí·yæ? nayé? gaihu̜·nyáha? [swá?jik deyode·yé̜?tha·t] … (CTL76.7-8)

d-yu̜gw-ade?gw-ęh	ne?	ak-hwajiR-a?	naye?	ga-Rihw-u̜ny-aha?
CIS-1PL.P-flee-STV	NOM	1SG.P-family-NSF	ASRT	3N/Z.SG.A-matter-make-HAB
we fled here	the	my family	it's	the reason

swa?jik	de-yo-ade·yę?tha·t-Ø
DGR	DL-3N/Z.SG.P-dangerous-STV
too much	it is dangerous

…my family and I fled here because it was too dangerous…

In (205) the extent classifier that occurs in the first clause is required because the modified expression is a motion verb which allows for the expression of intermittent stages. The interpolated clause with the same particle cluster, *nę gwa? oyę̜det* 'it is barely noticeable', lacks the extent classifier; here the degree term modifies a stative only verb with the gradable property of "being noticeable".

(205) [Nę̜ gwá? nigę̜ nhehonenú̜h] nę wa?hyatdogá? [nę gwá? oyę̜dét] nęgę̜ tsha? nú̜· dewadawę·yé̜?tha? ne? nęgę̜ nwa?gaya?dó?dę? (HW07).

nę gwa?	nigę̜	n-he-hon-e-nu̜h		onę̜	wa?-hy-atdog-a?
DGR	EXT	PRT-TRNS-3M.NSG.P-walk-STV		TMP	FACT-3M.DU.A-notice-PNC
little bit	extent	thus they have gone		now	they two noticed

nę gwa?	o-yędeR-t-Ø		nęgę̜	tsha?	nu̜·	de-w-ad-awę̜ye-?t-ha?
DGR	3N/Z.SG.P-know-CS-STV		DEM	SUB	LOC	DL-3FZ.SG.A-SRF-stir-CS-HAB
little bit	it is noticeable		this	that	place	she frequents [the place]

ne?	nęgę̜	n-wa?-ga-ya?d-o?dę-?
NOM	DEM	PRT-FACT-3FZ.SG.A-body-kind.of-STV
the	this	thus kind of being

They've gone just a little [way], when they notice it – it's just barely noticeable – that this is the place she frequents, this, like, animal.

(206) ...[sęhge thaʔgeyoʔ neʔ gá·yoʔ] [dęʔseʔ <u>waʔjikʔa</u> iʔ deʔwageyoh] (H668.15).[82]

sęhge	th-aʔ-g-e-Ryo-ʔ		neʔ	ga-Ryo-ʔ	dęʔseʔ	waʔjikʔá	iʔ
DGR	CON-FACT-1SG.A-EP-kill-PNC		NOM	NPF-animal-NSF	CNJ	DGR	PRON
barely	I killed it		the	animal	and	nearly	I/we

deʔ-wag-e-Ryo-ʔ
NEG-1SG.P-EP-kill-STV
I wasn't killed
...I barely killed the animal and it nearly killed me.

(207) a. [Tgaæhgwitgéʔs <u>thohá</u>] nę waʔhųhdę·dyaʔ (HW07).

t-ga-Ræhgw-itgęʔ-s		thoha	onę	waʔ-hų-ahdędy-aʔ
CIS-3N/Z.SG.A-sun-become.visible-HAB		DGR	TMP	FACT-3M.PL.A-depart-PNC
the sun rises		almost	now	they departed

The sun is nearly up when they depart.

b. Naʔ óhniʔ <u>thohá</u> ęhųwadiyenáʔ (NC02).

naʔ	ohniʔ	thoha	ę-hųwadi-yena-ʔ'
ASRT	ADD	DGR	FUT-3NSG > 3M.SG-catch-PNC
it's	also	almost	they will catch him

Also, they were about to catch him.

<u>Verb forms used in degree expressions:</u>

Degree Verb Forms	*gloss*
aųgóhdih / ęgóhdih[83]	*it goes beyond*
nigęhę·ʔ[84]	*unusually; exceedingly*

(208) [<u>Aųgohdíh</u> waʔshne·gá·ęʔ].

a-ųgohd-ih	waʔ-s-hneg-a-R-ęʔ
3N/Z.SG.P-go.beyond-STV	FACT-2SG.A-liquid-JN-put.in-PNC
it has gone beyond	you put water into it

You put too much water into it.

(209) [<u>Nigęhęʔ</u> neʔ ganowęʔ], hyá híhyaʔ thakgwenyaʔ neʔ iʔ agųyaʔdawęhæt (H616.15-16).[85]

ni-ga-i-hę·-ʔ		neʔ	ga-nowę-ʔ	hya	hihyaʔ
PRT-3N/Z.SG.A-be.the.only-DST-STV		NOM	3N/Z.SG.A-difficult-STV	NEG	MOD
it's unusually so		the	it's difficult	not	indeed

---

[82] Vowel length as marked by Hewitt; he did not mark stress in this excerpt.

[83] A form of the verb *-ųgohd-* 'go beyond'.

[84] A derived form of the verb *-i- / -yaʔdi-* v.s. 'be, exist, make up the total, be the only'.

[85] Stress as marked by Hewitt; he did not mark vowel length in this excerpt.

th-aa-k-gweny-aʔ   neʔ   iʔ   aa-gu̜-yaʔd-awȩhæ·t-Ø
CON-OPT-1SG.A-can.do-PNC   NOM   PRON   OPT-1SG > 2SG-body-move.across-PNC
I can't do it   the   I/we   I should move you across
It's unusually difficult, [so] as for me I won't be able to carry you across [literally: it is unique in difficulty].

7.12.6 Comparisons

Comparisons involve the expression of similarities or differences among two or more situations or entities. These may occur as similarity or difference of <u>degree</u> (*more, less*) of a scalable property such as *size, distance, weight,* or *age, etc.*; or as similarity or difference of <u>identity</u> of a nonscalable property *(same* or *different)*. The distinctions yield the following categories:

	Scalable property		Non-scalable property	
Entity Situation	more	less	same	different

Comparison expressions consist of the two or more entities or situations being compared – the compared element and the element used as the standard of comparison – and the property that is used for the comparison. An English example of a scalar comparison is *Jack is taller than Jill,* where *Jack* is the compared element *Jill* is the standard of comparison, and *tall* is the property in terms of which they are compared. An example of a non-scalar comparison is *Today, Jack made the same mistake he made yesterday* vs. *Today, Jack made a different mistake from the one he made yesterday.* Here the issue is the identity of the two mistakes Jack made, so the compared elements are the *mistakes.*

Onondaga speakers use a number of different approaches to express both types of comparison. The most explicit of these involves the following five elements:

> i. The compared element
> ii. A marker of comparison (more or less; same or different)
> iii. An expression that describes the property used for the comparison
> iv. A form of the manner classifier which refers anaphorically to the comparison property
> v. A standard of comparison.

The order of the five elements is not fixed, nor is the presence of all of the elements – except (ii) and (iii) – obligatory as long as the information is retrievable from context.

448 Syntactic Constructions

<u>Scalar comparisons</u>: *more* or *less*

Comparison markers used in scalar comparisons are:

Table 7.10 Scalar comparison markers

Comparison Markers	Gloss
heyóhe?[86]	*more* [6N]
tgé?i[87]	*more* [ON]
nę gwa?	*little bit; less*
-asthw-	*be less; be smaller*

In example (210) the comparison is made in the argument clause (marked off in square brackets):

(210) Thohgé ó·nę wa?hnigę? [ne? gwa?yę?ahgó·na osthwiha tgę?ih gaya?dowanę tsha? niyot ne? dehni·jyáęh][88] (JM03).

Main clause		(i)	
thohge onę	wa?-hni-gę-?	ne?	gwa?yę?ah = gona
TEMP	FACT-3M.DU.A-see-PNC	NOM	NOUN = AUG
then	they saw	the	big rabbit

(ii)		(iii)	(iv)	
o-asthw-i = há	tgę?ih	ga-ya?d-owanę-h	tsha?	ni-yo-hd-Ø
3N/Z.SG.P-little-STV = DIM	DGR	3FZ.SG.A-body-big-STV	SUB	PRT-3N/Z.SG.P-how.it.is-STV
little bit	more	she is big	that	how it is

(v)	
ne?	de-hni-jyaę-h
NOM	DL-3M.DU.A-both-STV
the	it's both of them

Then they two saw [that] the big rabbit was a little bit bigger than the two of them [literally, then they saw the big rabbit is a little bit bigger than how it is [with] the two of them].

The manner classifier *tsha? níyot* is not an obligatory part of the comparison expression and is frequently omitted. For example:

(211) ... tho nų tgę?í ihswa? dagatgwé·nya?, ne? thóhge (LG14).

	tho	nų	tgę?ih	ihswa?	d-a-g-at-gweny-a?		ne?	thohge
	LOC	LOC	DGR	AMT	CIS-FACT-1.SG.A-SRF-can.do-PNC		NOM	TMP
	there	place	more	a lot	I earned it		the	then

...I earned more [money] in that place [than I did] later.[89]

---

[86] The particle is used by Hewitt to indicate a high degree of a state or action. He glosses the particle 'utmost, exceedingly'. Contemporary 6N speakers, use it as a comparative marker, where ON speakers use *tgę?ih* 'more'. The particle *tgę?ih* does not occur in Hewitt's writings.

[87] The particle is probably derived from the base .tgę?- + cislocative 'persist, get more so'.

[88] Accent is marked intermittently in this transcription.

Of the participants, the compared participant is nearly always present (but see example 218); the participant used as a standard of comparison is often omitted as long as it is recoverable from the context. The excerpt in (212) refers, by implication, to earlier times that are being compared to the present:

(212) ...ayéę? gęs na? tgę?í honada?gaidé? ne? thóhge nigaháwi?,... (LG20)

ayeę? gęs na?	tgę?ih	hon-ada?gaid-e?	ne?	thohge	ni-ga-hawi-?
SIM CST ASRT	DGR	3M.NSG.P-healthy-STV	NOM	TMP	PRT-3N/Z.SG.A-carry-PRP
seems like	more	they are healthy	the	then	the time it is

...it seems like they were healthier in those times...

Example (213) is an excerpt from a passage in which the gradual approach of a thunderstorm is at issue. The particle *nę* 'now' supplies the spatio-temporal framework that functions as the compared element in the example:

(213) Gwas yágę? si· nigę́ nę tgę?í otcí?ge·? (HW07).

gwas yagę?	si·	nigę	nę	tgę?ih	o-atci?ge·-?
INTS HRSY	LOC	EXT	TMP	DGR	3N/Z.SG.P-be.cloudy-STV
really they say	far	extent	now	more	it is cloudy

They say [that] by now it's really getting cloudier over there.

The comparison may span two clauses. In (214) the standard of comparison (where grandmother lives) is stated in the first clause, and the compared entity (where my son lives), is stated in the second clause. The property used for the comparison (far distance) is stated in both clauses:

(214) Tsha? dyagonųhsayę́? khsodahá í·nųh; na? gó·? ne? hehawáh tsha? thana·gé·? tgę?i í·nųh (elicited HW).

tsha?	d-yago-nųhs-a-yę-?	k-hsodaha	inų	na?	go·?
SUB	CIS-3FI.P-house-JN-have-STV	1SG.A-grandmother	LOC	ASRT	CTR
where	she has a house	my grandmother	far	it's	however

ne?	he-hawah	tsha?	t-ha-nage·-?	tgę?i	inų
NOM	1SG > 3.M.SG-parent.*child*	SUB	CIS-3M.SG.A-live-STV	DGR	LOC
the	my son	where	he lives there	more	far

My grandmother's house is far away; but where my son lives is further.

In (215) the meaning of the marker of comparison (i.e., *more* in this case) is absorbed into the meaning of verb form, *aųdahaæ·gwá?* 'he would prefer it':

(215) ...na? di? hya? ne?, ųgwatboss wa?hęhę́·?, ne? agwegí ne? ųgwehųwé thayagoyo?dęhá? na? aųdahaæ·gwá? tsha? niyót ne? gų?shę·níh.... (LG14)

na?	di?	hya?	ne?	ųgwa-at-boss	wa?-ha-ihę·-?'
ASRT	LINK	MOD	NOM	1PL.P-SRF-boss	FACT-3M.SG.A-say-PNC
it's	so	indeed	the	our boss	he said

---

[89] Note that while this looks superficially as though the speaker is comparing apples with oranges, 'that place' refers to where she was trained at an earlier time, which she is comparing to a later time.

neʔ	agwegih	neʔ	ųgweh = ųwe	th-aa-yago-yoʔd-ęh-aʔ
NOM	QNT	NOM	person:POSS = AUTH	CON-OPT-3FI.P-work-INCH-PNC
the	all	the	Indian	they would work

naʔ	aųda-ha-Rægw-aʔ		tshaʔ	niyot	neʔ	gų-aʔshę·nih
ASRT	OPT:CIS-3M.SG.A-choose-PNC		SUB	MAN	NOM	3FZ.PL.A-white.person
thats.it	he would prefer it		that	how it is	the	white women

…our boss said he would prefer having only Indians rather than white women work [for him]…

Comparisons with *nę gwaʔ* 'little bit, less' is extremely rare in the corpus, indicating, perhaps, a preference for wording comparisons in terms of the *more*-equation. An example is (216) where the marker occurs in a verbless clause, a clause that, in addition, lacks the standard of comparison:

(216) Onę héʔ naʔ néʔ, ųkhigá·yaʔks, heʔ oʔ naʔ néʔ tshaʔ hadihnegahnho·dų́ʔ, [hya gó·ʔ naʔ hya naʔ dewęʔnyaʔé <u>nę gwáʔ</u> niyų́h] (LG19).

onę heʔ	naʔ	neʔ	ųkhi-gá·yaʔk-s	heʔ		oʔ	naʔ	neʔ
TMP REP	ASRT	NOM	3 > 1NSG-pay-HAB	REP		ADD	ASRT	NOM
also	it's	the	they pay us	repeatedly		also	it's	the

tshaʔ	hadi-hneg-a-hnhodų-ʔ'		hya go·ʔ naʔ
SUB	3M.PL.A-water-JN-close.a.door-STV		NEG CTR ASRT
where	they have dammed water = dam		but it's not

hya	naʔ	de-w-ę-ʔny-a-ʔe-h'		nę gwaʔ	niyų
NEG	ASRT	DL-3N/Z.SG.A-SRF-hand-JN-hit-STV		QNT	AMT
not	it's	hundred		little bit	amount

Also, we get payments for where they built the dam, but it is less than a hundred [dollars].

A different *less than* comparison scheme is used with kinship expressions as shown in (217). The comparison differs grammatically from the others in that it involves a verb form – *gosthwih* 'she is younger' – that combines the functions of the comparison marker (i.e. *less*) (ii) and the marker of the property used as a comparison (i.e. *young*) (iii). Note that the element being compared (i) is a subset of the element that functions as the standard of comparison (v). Example (217b) shows that *gósthwih* can be further inflected for the superlative degree by means of the translocative prepronominal prefix.

(217) a. Thohge onę nęgę dehniksaʔa naʔ neʔ agųgwe <u>gosthwih</u> waʔdyųhsęthwaʔ… (H613.12).[90]

thohge onę	nęgę	de-hni-ksaʔa		naʔ	neʔ	ag-ųgweh
TMP	DEM	DL-3M.DU.A-child		ASRT	NOM	3FI.A-person:SUFF
thereafter	this	two children		it's	the	female

---

[90] Hewitt did not mark stress or vowel length in this excerpt.

go-asthw-ih   waʔ-d-yų-ahsęthw-aʔ
3FI.P-be.less-STV   FACT-DL-3FI.A-cry-PNC
she is younger   she began to cry

Then the younger of these two children, the female, began to cry...

b. thohgé ónę neʔ hesga·gų́·daʔ <u>heyagósthwih</u> khehá·wah onę waʔe·jyę́haʔ...
  (CTL168.1-2)

thohge onę   neʔ   he-s-ga-gųd-aʔ   he-yago-asthw-ih
TMP   NOM   TRNS-REP-3N/Z.SG.A-be.last-STV   TRNS-3FI.P-be.less-STV
thereafter   the   it is last   she is the youngest

khe-hawah   onę   waʔ-e-jyę-h-aʔ
1SG > 3-*child*.parent   TMP   FACT-3FI.A-dip.water-DSLC-PNC
my daughter   then   she went to dip water

Then the last one, my youngest daughter, went to dip water...

<u>Non-scalar comparisons</u>: *same* or *different*

In expressions of equality or difference, two or more entities or situations are described as being the same or different from each other. The form of the most explicit way to describe non-scalar comparison includes the same five elements involved in scalar comparisons.

In the Iroquoian languages, equality or sameness is often expressed with a base that consists of a verb root that is prefixed with a combination of the coincident and the dualic prepronominal prefixes. Examples of just a few of these bases in Onondaga are *.a-* + coincident and dualic 'be the same size'; *.ahdędyųgw-* + coincident and dualic 'leave at the same time'; *.de-* + coincident, dualic, and cislocative 'be on the same level, be equal'; *.ęh- / .ęʔ- / .yaʔdawęh- / .węh-* + coincident and dualic v.a. 'happen the same way'; *.yeR- / .yR-* + coincident and dualic 'do the same thing; do the same way'. Two verb forms *tshaʔdéyot* and *tshaʔgá·dah* can occur as more general markers of sameness in expressions of non-scalar comparison. Table 7.11 lists comparison markers of sameness and difference.

Table 7.11 Non-scalar comparison markers

Comparison Markers	Gloss
tshaʔdéyot[91]	*it's the same (situation)*
tshaʔgá·dah[92]	*it's the same (entity)*
gadó·gęh[93]	*be the same (entity or situation)*
hya tho deʔoʔ[94]	*be different (situation)*
ó·yaʔ[95]	*be different (entity or situation)*

---

[91] A form of the verb *.t-/-hd-* plus coincident and dualic prepronominal prefix.

[92] A form of the verb *.d-/.yaʔdad-* + coincident prepronominal prefix and factual mode. [This is one of a small number of verbs in the factual mode that inflects for the stative aspect].

[93] A form of the verb *-dogę-* 'be a certain one; be the same.'

[94] A particle cluster composed of the negative *hya*, the manner particle *tho*, and the additive particle *oʔ* 'also' prefixed with the negative prepronominal prefix *deʔ-*.

[95] The root *-oya-* has verbal as well as nominal characteristics. It is used like a verb in comparison expressions.

Expressions of equality:

Tsha?dé·yot 'it's the same' (situation):

Example (218) follows a discussion about how, before the introduction of diseases by Europeans, native people had been a lot healthier. The example compares the present state of native people's health to that of Europeans. In (218) element (i) – the entity being compared (native people's health) – is missing, because it is retrievable from the preceding context:

(218) Nẹgẹ́ o? nigahawí? gwas <u>tsha?dé·yot</u> tsha? niyót hụ?shẹní... (LG20)

Introduction				(ii)
nẹgẹ	o?	ni-ga-hawi-?	gwas	tsha?-de-yo-ht-Ø
DEM	ADD	PRT-3N/Z.SG.A-carry-PRP	INTNS	COIN-DL-3N/Z.SG.P-how.it.is-STV
this	also	the time it is	really	it is the same [situation]

(iv)		(v)
tsha?	niyot	hụ-a?shẹnih
SUB	MAN	3M.PL.A-white.person
that	how it is	white people

Also, at this time it's the same [situation for Indians] as it is [with] white people ...

Tsha?gá·dah 'it's the same' (entity):

The excerpt in (219), instructs all the chiefs to sing the same song. The words of the song follow in the text (but are omitted here):

(219) Thohgé ó·nẹ ne? hodiyanéshụ? onẹ́ gagwégih ẹhụ·dé·nó·dẹ? nayé? tsha?gá·dah
　　　 (CTL626.6-7).

thohge	onẹ	ne?	hodi-yane = shụ?	onẹ	ga-gweg-ih
TMP		NOM	3M.NSG.P-good = PL	TMP	3N/Z.SG.A-all-STV
then		the	chiefs	then	it is all

ẹ-hụ-ad-Rẹn-od-ẹ?		naye?	tsh-a?-ga-d-ah
FUT-3M.PL.A-SRF-song-raise-PNC		ASRT	COIN-FACT-3N/Z.SG.A-be.the.same.one-STV
they will sing a song		it's	it's the same one

Then as to the chiefs, they will all sing the same song.

Gadó·gẹh 'it's the same' (situation or entity):

In (220) we understand from an earlier passage that there had been flooding in the past. In the argument clause of the excerpt, the present situation is compared to that earlier one:

(220) ...tsha? hagatho·yẹ·ní ha?shẹní [tsha? gadogẹ́ niyót gahno·dụ́?] (LG04).

tsha?	hag-atho·y-ẹni-h'	ha-?shẹni	tsha?	ga-dogẹ-h
SUB	3M.SG > 1SG-tell-BEN-STV	3M.SG.A-white.man	SUB	3N/Z.SG.A-certain.one-STV
that	he told me	white man	that	the same

ni-yo-hd-Ø	ga-hnodu̧-ʔ
PRT-3N/Z.SG.P-how.it.is-STV	3N/Z.SG.A-flood-STV
how it is	it is flooding

...what a white man told me was that it's still flooding.

(221) ...dogá·ʔ niyų́ waʔwa·dǽ·sdaʔ neʔ waʔgi·hwanų́·dų̧ʔ gadó·gȩh... (CTL19.5-6)

doga·ʔ	niyų	waʔ-w-adǽ·sd-a-ʔ		neʔ
QNT	AMT	FACT-3N/Z.SG.A-number.of.times-PNC		NOM
few	amount	it's a number of times		the

waʔ-g-Rihwanų̧dų̧-ʔ	ga-dogȩ-h
FACT-1SG.A-ask.a.question-PNC	3N/Z.SG.A-certain.one-STV
I asked a question	it's the same

I asked her the same question a few times...

Situations can be compared in a <u>relative-correlative construction</u> (section 7.5.3). Example (222) introduces a discussion about how, when a person dies, a lawyer reads the will to the assembled family:

(222) Naʔ néʔ naʔ <u>tho niyót nȩgȩ́hah, tshaʔ niyót</u> neʔ hų̧ʔshȩ·ní... (LG18)

naʔ	neʔ	naʔ	tho	niyot	nȩgȩ = há	tshaʔ	niyot	neʔ
ASRT	NOM	ASRT	MAN	MAN	DEM = DIM	SUB	MAN	NOM
it's	the	it's	how	it is so	this one	that	it is so	the

hų-aʔshȩ·nih
3M.PL.A-white.person
white people

That is the way it is [with us], it's the same as with white people [literally, the way it is [with us] it's how it is with white people...]

<u>Non-scalar expressions of difference:</u>

Hya tho deʔoʔ 'it's different' (situation)

In (223) the talk is about changes in women's fashion. In the example the speaker uses all five of the comparison-expression elements:

(223) Naʔ óʔ neʔ ų̧nisʔí tshaʔ nigų̧dineʔnoʔdȩʔsgwáʔ neʔ odiksdȩʔshų̧ʔáh, hya tho deʔóʔ
   tshaʔ ų̧hgȩʔ niyót nȩgȩ́ ų̧hgȩʔ (LG21).

Introduction		(i)		(iii)			
naʔ	oʔ	neʔ	ų̧nisʔih	tshaʔ	ni-gų̧di-neʔn-oʔdȩ-ʔs-gwaʔ		neʔ
ASRT	ADD	NOM	TMP	SUB	PART-3FZ.PL.A-clothes-kind-STV-HBPST		NOM
it's	also	the	time past	that	the kind of clothes they used to have		the

	(ii)	(iv)	(v)
odi-ksdȩʔ + shų̧ʔá	hya tho deʔ-o	tshaʔ ų̧hgȩʔ niyot	nȩgȩ ų̧hgȩʔ
FZ.NSG-P-old.person-PL	NEG MAN NEG-ADD	SUB TMP MAN	DEM TMP
old ladies	it's different	the way it is now	at this time

A long time ago the kind of clothes the old ladies wore was different from the way it is now.

<u>*ó·yaʔ*</u> 'it's different' (situation or entity)

In both of the examples with *ó·yaʔ* all but the compared element and the marker of comparison are omitted. In example (224) *ó·yaʔ* modifies a situation expression.

(224) …naʔ gó·ʔ jyestháʔ neʔ oshwęʔgá·ʔ oyáʔ sayųtnųhsų́·nyaʔ (LG17).

naʔ	go·ʔ	s-ye-st-haʔ	neʔ	o-shwęʔgaR-ʔ	(y)-oya-ʔ
ASRT	CTR	REP-3FI.A-use-HAB	NOM	NPF-lumber-NSF	3N/Z.SG.A-different-STV
it's	however	she uses	the	lumber	it is different

s-a-yų-at-nųhs-ųny-aʔ
REP-FACT-3FI.A-SRF-house-make-PNC
she built herself another house
…but she uses the lumber to build herself a different house.

The excerpt (225) is from a story that tells about a man who wants to give away his dog, but the dog keeps returning to its original home. Eventually, he takes him to a different settlement. In this example *ó·yaʔ* modifies the internally headed relative clause *dyená·ge·ʔ* 'settlement'.

(225)… nhwaʔhéʔ oyáʔ dyenagé·ʔ tho nų́ nhwaʔhoyaʔdę́hawaʔ (HW05).

n-h-waʔ-h-e-ʔ	(y)-oyaʔ	d-ye-nage-ʔ
PRT-TRNS-FACT-3M.SG.A-walk-PNC	3N/Z.SG.A-different-STV	CIS-3FI.A-live-STV
he went there	it is different	settlement

tho nų	n-h-waʔ-ho-yaʔd-ęhaw-aʔ
LOC LOC	PRT-TRNS-FACT-3M.SG > 3M.SG-body-take-PNC
to that place	he took him there

…he went to a different settlement, [and] that's where he took [the dog].

Appendix 1: Three Stories

The Old House (1949)
told by Lucenda George to Fred Lukoff[1]

(1) Tcigeksáʔah, ganedagę̨hyadáʔ dyagwanagé·hgwaʔ.

tci-ge-ksaʔah	ga-ned-a-gę̨hyad-aʔ	d-yagwa-nage·-h-gwaʔ
COIN-1SG.A-little.child	3N/Z.SG.A-hill-JN-elevate-STV	CIS-1EX.PL.A-live-HAB-HBPST
when I was a little child	it is on the top of a hill	we used to live there

When I was a little girl, we used to live up on the hill.

(2) Dę̨ʔseʔ onę̨ waʔdyagodų̨hwęjyós neʔ gnohaʔgę̨hǽ·ʔ neʔ ganadagų̨wá hagwá aų̨sayagwanagé·k.

dę̨ʔseʔ	onę̨	waʔ-d-yago-adų̨hwęjyo-s-Ø	neʔ	g-nohaʔ = gę̨hæʔ	neʔ
CONJ	TMP	FACT-DL-3FI.P-want-BEN-PNC	NOM	1SG.A-mother-DEC	NOM
and	then	she wanted	the	my late mother	the

ga-nad-agų̨wa	hagwa	aų̨sa-yagwa-nage·-Ø-k-Ø'
NPF-town-LOC	DIR	OPT + REP-1EX.PL.A-live-STV-CONT-PNC
in the village	towards	we should be living back there

And my late mother wanted for us to live back down in the village.

(3) Nę̨ hyáʔ naʔ neʔ kʔnihaʔgę̨hǽ·ʔ waʔhę̨hę́·ʔ ę̨ganų̨hsagę̨isdík diʔ hyaʔ nę́·gę̨, tho séʔ hę̨djidwadyę́·ʔ ganadagų́·wah.

nę̨	hyaʔ	naʔ	neʔ	k-ʔnihaʔ = gę̨hæʔ	waʔ-ha-ihę̨·-ʔ'
TMP	MOD	ASRT	NOM	1SG.A-father = DEC	FACT-3M.SG.A-say-PNC
then	indeed	it's	the	my late father	he said

ę̨-ga-nų̨hs-a-gę̨isd-i-k-Ø	diʔ	hyaʔ	nę̨gę̨	tho
FUT-3N/Z.SG.A-house-JN-move-STV-CONT-PNC	LINK	MOD	DEM	LOC
the house will be moved	so	indeed	this	there

---

[1] The late Lucenda George, a speaker of the Onondaga dialect, told this story to the late linguist Fred Lukoff. It is one of a set of stories that was recorded by Lukoff in 1948 and 1950, probably at Onondaga Nation, Nedrow, NY. Originals are located in the American Philosophical Society collection. Transcription, morpheme segmentation and translation by Hanni Woodbury.

se?	h-ę-s-dw-ad-yę-?'		ga-nad-agųwa
MOD	TRNS-FUT-REP-1IN.PL.A-SRF-place-PNC		NPF-town-LOC
actually	we will stay put back there		in the town

Then my late father said, "so the house will be moved and we will stay put in the town."

(4) Wa?hohninų? di? hyá?, ųhwę́·jya?, degní é·git tsha? niyų́h, nęgę́ hę́·gweh.

wa?-ho-hninų-?		di?	hya?	Ø-ųhwęjy-a?	degni	egit	tsha?	niyų
FACT-3M.SG > 3M.SG-buy-PNC		LINK	MOD	NPF-land-NSF	NUM	NOUN	SUB	AMT
he bought it from him		so	indeed	land	two	acre	that	so much

nęgę	hR-ųgweh
DEM	3M.SG.A-person:SUFF
this	man

So he bought a piece of land from this man, two acres, that's how much.

(5) Onę, wa?hųwędǽ·? ne? k?niha?gęhǽ·? tsha? nihonatga?dé? thogę́ tho nwa?hęné?.

onę	wa?-hųwę-idęR-a?		ne?	k-?niha? = gęhæ?	tsha?
TMP	FACT-3 > 3M.SG-help.out-PNC		NOM	1SG.A-father = DEC	SUB
then	they helped him out		the	my late father	that

ni-hon-atga?d-e?		thogę	tho	n-h-wa?-hęn-e-?´
PRT-3M.NSG.P-be.many-STV		DEM	LOC	PRT-TRNS-FACT-3M.PL.A-walk-PNC
there were many of them		that	there	they went there

Then a lot of [men] went there to help my late father.

(6) Na? ó? ne?, gohsadę́s o? wa?odiyo?dęhá?, tsha? ó? niga·gaęhé? tsha? nędwé?.

na?	o?	ne?	gohsadęs	o?	wa?-odi-yo?d-ęh-a?		tsha?	o?
ASRT	ADD	NOM	NOUN	ADD	FACT-3FZ.NSG.P-work-INCH-PNC		SUB	ADD
it's	also	the	horse	also	they worked		that	also

ni-ga-gaęhe-?		tsha?	n-ę-d-w-e-?´
PRT-3N/Z.SG.A-steep-STV		SUB	PRT-FUT-CIS-3N/Z.SG.A-walk-PNC
it is steep		that	thus it will come from there

There were horses also working, [as] it's steep where [the house] is going to come from.

(7) Ashę́? gahęwagųwashų́? nųdaganųhsí?se·?, gahnegó? o? thogę́ha né?tho, gęhyųhówanęh, wa?hųsgų·nyá? o? na?, tho nų́ wa?tgayahyá?k thogę́hah.

ashę?	ga-hę·w-agųwa = shų?	n-ųda-ga-nųhs-i?se·-?
LOC	NPF-valley-LOC = PL	PART-CIS:FACT-3N/Z.SG.A-house-drag-PRP
in the middle	through the valley	the house dragged

ga-hneg-o-?		o?	thogę = há	ne?tho	ga-ihyųhw-owanę-'h
3N/Z.SG.A-water-be.in.water-STV		ADD	DEM = DIM	LOC	3N/Z.SG.A-creek-be.large-STV
there's water in it		also	that specifically	there	large creek

wa?-hų-asgw-ųny-a?		o?	na?	tho	nų́	wa?-t-ga-yahya?k-Ø
FACT-3M.PL.A-bridge-make-PNC		ADD	ASRT	LOC	LOC	FACT-DL-3N/Z.SG.A-cross.over-PNC
they built a bridge		also	it's	there	place	it crosses over

thogę = há
DEM = DIM
that specifically
Also the house got dragged through the middle of the valley and where there's water, a creek, they also built a bridge for [the house] to cross over.

(8) Hya deʔwagęnųhdų́ʔ naʔ onę dó· nwaʔųnísheʔ, nęgę́ tho nihoná·dyę́ʔ.

hya	deʔ-wag-ęnųhdų-ʔ	naʔ	onę	do·	nwaʔųnísheʔ	nęgę	tho
NEG	NEG-1SG.P-know-STV	ASRT	TMP	INTR	TMP	DEM	LOC
not	I don't know	it's	then	how	length of time	this	there

ni-hon-ad-yę-ʔ
PRT-3M.NSG.P-SRF-place-STV
they set it down
I don't know how long it took for them to set it down.

(9) Dyę gwáʔ go·ʔ nę waʔhadiyųdá·k tshaʔ nų́.

dyę	gwaʔ	go·ʔ	nę	naʔ	waʔ-hadi-ųdaR-k	tshaʔ nų
INDF	RSTR	CTR	TMP	ASRT	FACT-3M.PL.A-put.in-PNC	SUB LOC
eventually	however	then	it's		they put it in it	at the place

Eventually however they put it in place.

(10) Ųhgęʔ niganųhsayędáhgwaʔ, neʔ waʔonųhsadegáʔ gwas nę nwaʔųnísheʔ.

ųhgęʔ	ni-ga-nųhs-a-yęd-ah-gwaʔ	ne?	waʔ-o-nųhs-adeg-a?
TMP	PRT-3N/Z.SG.A-house-JN-place-HAB-HBPST	NOM	FACT-3N/Z.SG.P-house-burn-PNC
soon after	the house was placed	the	house burned

gwas	nę	nwaʔųnísheʔ
INTNS	TMP	TMP
really	then	length time

A short while after they placed the house, it burned down.

(11) Naʔ tshaʔ jík waʔoʔdaihęháʔ ihswáʔ hyaʔ ų́· ohgáæʔ ų́thwih.

naʔ	tshaʔ	jik	waʔ-o-aʔdaih-ęh-aʔ	ihswaʔ	hyaʔ	ų·	o-ahgaR-aʔ
ASRT	SUB	DGR	FACT-3N/Z.SG.P-hot-INCH-PNC	QNT	MOD	MOD	NPF-chip-NSF
it's	that	too much	it get's hot	a lot	indeed	maybe	woodchips

Ø-ųthw-ih
3N/Z.SG.A-burn-STV
it is burning
[I guess, the chimney] got too hot, maybe because it burned woodchips.

(12) Naʔ thogę́ waʔonųhsadegáʔ oʔ hyaʔ gó·ʔ sayenųhsų́nyáʔ neʔ [a]ktciʔáh, naʔ ųhgęʔ tho dyená·ge·ʔ.

naʔ	thogę	waʔ-o-nųhs-adeg-aʔ		oʔ	hyaʔ	go·ʔ
ASRT	DEM	FACT-3N/Z.SG.P-house-burn-PNC		ADD	MOD	CTR
it's	that	house burned		also	indeed	however

s-a-ye-nųhs-ųny-aʔ		neʔ	ak-tciʔah		naʔ
REP-FACT-3FI.A-house-make-PNC		NOM	3FZ.SG > 1SG-older.sibling		ASRT
she built another house		the	my older sister		it's

ųhgę?	tho	d-ye-nage··?
TMP	LOC	CIS-3FI.A-live-STV
at this time	there	she lives there

After that house burned, however, my older sister built another house, [and] it's where she lives at this time.

(13) Ųnís?i nęgę́ tho nidya·wę́?ih, tcigeksa?á ni?áh.

ųnis?ih	nęgę	tho	ni-d-yaw-ę?-ih	tci-ge-ksa?ah
TMP	DEM	MAN	PRT-CIS-3N/Z.SG.P-happen-STV	COIN-1SG.A-small.child
time past	this	how	how it happened	when I was a little girl

ne?	i? = á
NOM	PRON = DIM
thc	I, myself

This happened a long time ago when I was a little girl.

Father Goes on a Trip (1972)
Told by Harry Webster to Hanni Woodbury[2]

(1) Na? di? nę́·gę, tsha? nigagae?dę́h.

na?	di?	nęgę	tsha?	ni-ga-gaR-o?dę-h'
ASRT	LNK	DEM	SUB	PRT-3N/Z.SG.A-story-be.a.kind-STV
it's	so	this	that	the kind of story it is

So this is the story:

(2) Na? nęgę́ ne? í? ne? Thahsogwę́ niwakhsęno?dę́h, tsha? niha·yę·no?dę́hna? ne? k?nihá tcigeksa?áh.

na?	nęgę	ne?	i?	ne?	Thahsó·gwęh	ni-wak-hsęn-o?dę-h'	tsha?
ASRT	DEM	NOM	PRN	NOM	NAME	PRT-1SG.P-name-kind-STV	SUB
it's	this	the	I/we	the	Thahsó·gwęh	that's the name I have	that

ni-ha-Wyęn-o?dę-hna?	ne?	k-?niha	tci-ge-ksa? = áh
PRT-3M.SG.A-task/way-kind-STV.PST	NOM	1.SG.A-father	COIN-1.SG.A-child = DIM
that's the ways he used to have	the	my father	when I was a little child

It's about me, Thahsó·gwę, that's my name, it's about the ways of my father when I was a little child.

(3) Na? nęgę́ gęs tsha? niyót tsha? ne? tciyagwaksa?shų?á ųgwa·di·hwayęní gęs gayo?dę́hsæ·?, ne? agwaksa?shų?áh.

na?	nęgę	gęs	tsha?	niyot	tsha?	ne?	tci-yagwa-ksa?-shų?a
ASRT	DEM	CST	SUB	MAN	SUB	NOM	COIN-1EX.PL.A-child-PL
it's	this	usually	that	how it is	that	the	when we children

---

[2] The late Harry Webster, a speaker of the Onondaga Nation dialect, first told me this story in 1972. At times, during the translation session, he remarked on alternative ways of expressing certain passages in the story. Some of these are provided in the footnotes for interested readers.

ų̀gw-ad-Rihw-yę-ni-h'		gęs	ga-yoʔdę-hsR-aʔ	neʔ	agwa-ksaʔ-shų̀ʔa
1PL.P-SRF-matter-have-BEN-STV		CST	NPF-work-NOM-NSF	NOM	1EX.PL-child-PL
we have responsibility		usually	work	the	we children

So normally, how it was when we were children, we had responsibilities, work, we children.

(4) Naʔ gę́s neʔ shų̀gwa·jyapshæwíh, kʔnihagęhǽʔ – shų̀gwa·jyapshæwíh – you could say, *work,* gayoʔdę́hsæ·ʔ.

naʔ	gęs	neʔ	shų̀gwa-jyap-hsR-awi-h'	k-ʔniha = gęhæʔ
ASRT	CST	NOM	3M.SG > 1PL-job-NOM-give-STV	1SG.A-father = DEC
it's	usually	the	he gave us a job	my late father

shų̀gwa-jyap-hsR-awi-h'	...	ga-yoʔdę-hsR-aʔ
3M.SG > 1PL-job-NOM-give-STV		3N/Z.SG.A-work-NOM-NSF
he gave us a job		work

My late father usually gave us a job to do – you could say gayoʔdę́hsæ·ʔ *'work'.*

(5) Tshaʔ nwaʔonishéʔ hohdędyų́h waʔdya·gwadade·yęnhá·hgwęʔ.[3]

tshaʔ	nwaʔonisheʔ	ho-ahdędyų-h	waʔ-d-yagw-adade-Wyęnhahgw-ęʔ
SUB	TMP	3M.SG.P-depart-STV	FACT-DL-1EX.PL.A-REF-keep.busy-PNC
that	length of time	he has departed	we kept each other busy

While he was gone, we kept busy.

(6) Naʔ díʔ gęs neʔ nę· hohdę́·dyų̀h, oihwí·yoʔ gęs tshaʔ oyę́·det neʔ nę· ų̀gwaihwayé·idih, wádęʔ shų̀gwahnháʔih.

naʔ	diʔ	gęs	neʔ (o)nę	ho-ahdędyų-h	o-Rihw-iyo-ʔ
ASRT	LNK	CST	NOM TMP	3M.SG.P-depart-STV	3N/Z.SG.P-matter-good-STV
it's	moreover	usually	when	he has departed	truly

gęs	tshaʔ	o-yędeR-t-Ø	neʔ (o)nę	ų̀gwa-Rihw-a-yei-d-ih
CST	SUB	3N/Z.SG.P-know-CS-STV	NOM TMP	1PL.P-matter-JN-complete-CS-STV
usually	that	it is noticeable	then	we have finished it

wadęʔ	shų̀gwa-hnhaʔ-ih
INTR	3M.SG > 1PL-hire-STVE
what	he hired us

So when he's gone, truly it is usually obvious when were done with our tasks.

(7) Naʔ gę́s neʔ nę· ų̀gwę·nų́hdųʔ, tshaʔ niga·hawíʔ dę́theʔ, ęshá·yųʔ.

naʔ	gęs	neʔ nę	ų̀gw-ęnų̀hdų-ʔ	tshaʔ	ni-ga-hawi-ʔ
ASRT	REP	NOM TMP	1PL.P-know-STV	SUB	PRT-3N/Z.SG.A-carry-STV
it's	usually	that's when	we know	that	it is time

d-ę-t-h-e-ʔ	ę-s-ha-yų-ʔ
DL-FUT-CIS-3M.SG.A-come-PNC	FUT-REP-3M.SG.A-arrive-PNC
he will come back	he will arrive home

That's when we know it's time for him to get back home.

---

[3] This sentence was added during the translation session.

(8) Tho gę́s, heyų̇·gwadnųhdų́ʔdi, tshaʔ dyotʔęhægahę́·daʔ.

tho	gęs	he-yųgw-adnųhdų́ʔd-i	tshaʔ	d-yo-at-ʔęhR-a-gahęd-aʔ
LOC	CST	TRNS-1PL.P-wait-STV	SUB	CIS-3N/FZ.SG.P-fence-JN-make.a.hole-STV
there	usually	we're waiting there	that	at the gate

Usually, we're waiting [for him] at the gate.

(9) Naʔ dyoíhwaʔ tshaʔ[4] ųgwa·haéʔ dęthéʔ tshaʔ ųgwaihwayé·idih, neʔ ųgwayoʔdę́hsæ·ʔ.

naʔ	d-yo-Rihw-aʔ		tshaʔ	ųgwa-Rhae-ʔ	d-ę-t-h-e-ʔ
ASRT	CIS-3N/Z.SG.P-matter-NSF		SUB	1PL.P-expect-STV	DL-FUT-CIS-3M.SG.A-walk-PNC
it's	the reason		that	we expect it	he will come back

tshaʔ	ųgwa-Rihw-a-yei-d-ih		neʔ	ųgwa-yoʔdę-hsR-aʔ
SUB	1PL.P-matter-JN-complete-CS-STV		NOM	1PL.P-work-NOM-NSF
that	we have finished it		the	our work

The reason we expect him to come back home is that we have finished our work.

(10) Naʔ ganyáhaʔ tho heyųgwadnųhdų́ʔdí gaʔęhǽkdaʔ.

naʔ	ganyahaʔ	tho	he-yųgw-adnųhdų́ʔd-i	ga-ʔęhR-akd-aʔ
ASRT	RSN	LOC	TRNS-1PL.P-wait-STV	3N/Z.SG.A-fence-near-STV
it's	the reason	there	we're waiting there	it's near the fence

It's the reason we're waiting near the fence.

Harry Webster comments in English: "Now, we come down and open the gate for him when he comes in, because we are glad we have accomplished what he told us, therefore we're not afraid when he comes home—[chuckles] aah, let's see now…"

(11) Naʔ gayędéthaʔ, tshaʔ agwaksaʔdiyóʔsgwaʔ, tshaʔ nwaʔonísheʔ hohdę́·dyų.

naʔ	ga-yędeR-t-haʔ		tshaʔ	agwa-ksaʔd-iyo-ʔs-gwaʔ		tshaʔ
ASRT	3N/Z.SG.A-know-CS-HAB		SUB	1EX.PL.A-child-good-PL-HBPST		SUB
it's	it shows		that	we were good children		that

nwaʔonisheʔ	ho-ahdędyų-h
TMP	3M.SG.P-depart-STV
length of time	he has departed

It shows that we were good children while he was gone.

(12) Naʔ ganyáhaʔ tho na·yóhdik, tshaʔ niyót tshaʔ deshųgwagáhæ·ʔ, neʔ gaęhyáʔge hę́ʔdę·ʔ.

naʔ	ganyahaʔ	tho	naa-yo-hd-i-k-Ø			tshaʔ	niyot
ASRT	RSN	MAN	PRT-OPT-3N/Z.SG.A-how.it.is-STV-CNT-PNC			SUB	MAN
it's	the reason	thus	how it should be			that	how it is

tshaʔ	de-shųgwa-gahR-aʔ		neʔ	ga-Ręhy-aʔ-ge	ha-iʔdę·-ʔ
SUB	DL-3M.SG > 1PL-watch-STV		NOM	3N/Z.SG.A-sky-NSF-LOC	3M.SG.A-reside-STV
that	he's watching us		the	in the sky	he lives there

The reason it should be this way is that he's watching us, the one who lives in the sky.

---

[4] *tshaʔ* was added during the translation session.

(13) Oʔniguhgetsgwát tshaʔ sgę́·nų̨ʔ, dę̨ʔseʔ wadæ·ʔshwi·yóh neʔ eksaʔdiyóʔs godwę·ná·hgwih.

o-ʔniguhR-getsgw-at-Ø	tshaʔ	sgęnų̨ʔ	dę̨ʔseʔ	w-adæ·ʔshw-iyo-h
3N/Z.SG.A-spirit-raise.up-CS-PNC	SUB	NOUN	CNJ	3N/Z.SG.A-luck-good-STV
it encourages	that	peace(ful)	and	it's good luck

neʔ	e-ksaʔd-iyo-ʔs	go-ad-węn-aR-hgw-ih
NOM	3FI.A-child-good-STV.PL	3FI.P-SRF-voice-be.in-INST-STV
the	they are good children	one is obedient

It encourages peace and good luck for good and obedient children.

(14) Ų̨gwaháeʔ gwaʔ thó neʔ nę̨· dęthéʔ neʔ shagwáʔni,[5] gaęhyáʔge hę́ʔdę̨·ʔ.

ų̨gwa-Rhae-ʔ	gwaʔ	tho	neʔ	nę̨	d-ę̨-t-h-e-ʔ	neʔ
1PL.P-expect-STV	RSTR	LOC	TMP	PRES	DL-FUT-CIS-3M.SG.A-walk-PNC	NOM
we expect it	just	there	the	right here	he will come back home	the

shagwa-ʔnih	ga-Rę̨hy-aʔ = ge	ha-iʔdę̨-ʔ
3M.SG < 1PL-father	3N/Z.SG.A-sky-NSF = LOC	3M.SG.A-reside-STV
our father	in the sky	he lives there

We expect that there and then he will return, our father who lives in the sky.

Harry Webster explains the import of the story in English: *It has a twofold meaning: If the children are obedient, and Dad goes away and we expect him to come back, we're glad, sitting down by the fence to open the gate when he comes. Why? Because we have accomplished what he told us and when we're ready in that same light, the Almighty God in Heaven, we're ready when he comes, because we know we've been good kids, see?*

The Long-Legged Deer (1993)
Read by Nora Carrier to Hanni Woodbury[6]

(Title) *Dehaʔnų̨dés Osgę̨nų̨dų́ʔ*

de-ha-ʔnų̨d-es-Ø	osgę̨nų̨dų̨ʔ
DL-3M.SG.A-leg-long-STV	NOUN
he has long legs	deer

The Deer with Long Legs.

(1) Ų̨nísʔih ahsų́ tciyohnegiyó neʔ gahnegáę·nų̨ʔ, waʔhahnegihǽʔ náʔ neʔ osgę̨nų̨dų́ʔ.

ų̨nisʔih	ahsų	tci-yo-hneg-iyo-h'		neʔ	ga-hneg-aR-ų-nyų-ʔ
TMP	TMP	COIN-3N/Z.SG.P-water-good-STV		NOM	3N/Z.SG.A-water-be.in-DST-DST-STV
long time	still	when there's good water		the	water in various places

---

[5] Note the use of the interactive prefix, showing the referent is the father in the sky, not the birth father.

[6] The late Nora Carrier of Niagara Falls, NY, is the author of this story which she read to me from her own manuscript in the fall of 1993. Ms. Carrier was a speaker of the Six Nations dialect.

wa?-ha-hnegihR-a?   na? ne? osgęnụdụ?
FACT-3M.SG.A-drink-PNC ASRT NOM NOUN
he drank   it's the deer
A long time ago, the waters everywhere were still clear, that's [when] a deer drank [some] water.

(2) Gaę nyó? di? hahne·gíha?, wa?hadátgę?, tsha? ohnégo?.

gaę nyo? di? ha-hnegiR-ha?   wa?-h-adat-gę-?   tsha?
INDF   LNK 3M.SG.A-drink-HAB FACT-3M.SG.A-REP-see-PNC SUB
some time so he's drinking   he saw himself   that

o-hneg-o-?
3N/Z.SG.P-water-immerse-STV
in the water
And he sees his reflection in the water as he's drinking.

(3) "Ó· nigeksa?gó·nah, o· niyoyá·ne·?, ne? agná?ga·?."

o·   ni-ge-ksa?gona-h   o·   ni-yo-yane·-?   ne? ag-na?gaR-a?
EXCL PRT-1.SG.A-handsome-STV EXCL PRT-3N/Z.SG.P-good-STV NOM 1SG.P.antler-NSF
Oh how handsome I am   oh how good it is   the my antlers
 "Oh, how handsome I am; oh, how good my antlers are."

(4) Gwas wa?thadnụ?wáę·dụ?, tsha? nihe·he?áh.

gwas wa?-t-h-ad-nụ?waR-ędụ-?   tsha? ni-h-eR-he?=á
INTS FACT-DL-3M.SG.A-SRF-head-shake-PNC SUB PRT-3M.SG.A-think-HAB=DIM
very shakes his head   that   how proud he is
He really shook his head, with pride.

(5) Wa?hatgathwá? ne? ha?nụdí?geh.

wa?-h-atgathw-a?   ne? ha-?nụd-i?=ge
FACT-3M.SG.A-look.at-PNC NOM 3M.SG.A-leg-NSF=LOC
he looked at it   the his leg(s)
He looked at his legs.

(6) Nę́· gwa? na?deha?nụ́·da?s.

nę gwa? na?-de-ha-?nụd-a-?s
PRES RSTR PRT-DL-3M.SG.A-leg-be.a.size-PL
little bit the size of his legs
His legs are skinny.

(7) Deha?nụdés óhni?.

de-ha-?nụd-es-Ø   ohni?
DL-3M.SG.A-leg-long-STV ADD
his legs are long   also
Also, his legs are long too.

(8) "Yá ni?a de?gnų́hwe?s."
yah	ni? = á	de?-g-nųhwe?-s
NEG	PRON = DIM	NEG-1.SG.A-like-HAB
not	I personally	I don't like it

"As for me, I don't like them."

(9) Gwas nę dogę́s dehadatgáhæ·?, dehniya?dagé hyadó·wæts, wa?hųwadí·gę?.
gwas	nę	dogę́s	de-h-adat-gahR-a?	de-hni-ya?d-a-ge-h'
INTS	PRES	MOD	DL-3M.SG.A-REF-watch-STV	DL-3M.DU.A-body-JN-amount.to-STV
really	this here	truly	he's looking at himself	two person

hy-adowæt-s	wa?-hųwadi-gę-?
3M.DU.A-hunt-HAB	FACT-3NSG > 3M.SG-see-PNC
hunters	they saw him

For sure, [as] he's looking at himself two hunters see him.

(10) "Hejyé·na," wa?hęhę́·? ne? hoshęhgó·na.
he-s-yena-h	wa?-ha-ihę·-?'	ne?	ho-ashę-h = gona
TRNS-2SG.IMP-catch-IMP	FACT-3M.SG.A-say-PNC	NOM	3M.SG.P-fat-STV = AUG
catch it!	he said it	the	he's really fat

"[Go] catch it," says the fat one.

(11) Wa?thaæhdát ne? hoya?dagéhde?.
wa?-t-h-aæhdat-Ø	ne?	ho-ya?d-a-gehd-e?
FACT-DL-3M.SG.A-run-PNC	NOM	3M.SG.P-body-JN-carry.on.one's.back-STV
he ran	the	hunter

The hunter ran.

(12) Gwás nę́h dahatgahægétsgwa?, ne? osgęnųdú?.
gwas	onę	d-a-h-at-gahR-a-getsgw-a?	ne?	osgęnųdų?
INTS	TMP	CIS-FACT-3M.SG.A-eye-JN-raise.up-PNC	NOM	NOUN
just then	he looks up		the	deer

Just then the deer looks up

(13) Wa?hųwadigę́? dahnidákhe?, ne? hyadó·wæts.
wa?-hųwadi-gę-?	d-a-hni-dakhe-?	ne?	hy-adowæt-s
FACT-3M.SG > 3M.NSG-see-PNC	CIS-FACT-3M.DU.A-run-PNC	NOM	3M.DU.A-hunt-HAB
he saw them	they ran [towards him]	the	they two hunt

He's seeing the two hunters run towards him.

(14) Wa?hade?nyę́·dę? da·háæhdat, dagayená? ne? honá?ga·?, tsha? ohųdų́·nyų?.
wa?-h-ade?nyędę-?	d-aa-h-aæhdat-Ø	d-a-ga-yena-?'	ne?
FACT-3M.SG.A-try-PNC	CIS-OPT-3M.SG.A-run-PNC	CIS-FACT-3N/Z.SG.A-catch-PNC	NOM
he tried	he should run	it's catching it	the

ho-na?gaR-a?	tsha?	o-hųd-ų-nyų-?
3M.SG.P-antler-NSF	SUB	3N/Z.SG.P-shrub-DST-DST-STV
his antlers	that	it's in the shrubs

He tries to run, [but] his antlers got caught in the shrubs.

(15) Ó·nę waʔthatnųʔwáę·dųk, hyá go·ʔ deʔawét ųdawatgaʔtcyáʔ neʔ ųsahadodáihcyaʔ.

onę	waʔ-t-h-at-nųʔwaR-ędų-k		hya	go·ʔ	deʔ-awet
TMP	FACT-DL-3M.SG.A-SRF-head-shake-PNC		NEG	CTR	NEG-MOD
then	he shook his head		not	however	impossible

ųųda-w-at-gaʔtcy-aʔ	neʔ	ųųsa-h-ad-odaihcy-aʔ
OPT:CIS-3N/Z.SG.A-SRF-take.apart-PNC	NOM	OPT:REP-3M.SG.A-SRF-untangle-PNC
it should come apart	the	he should extricate himself

Then he shook his head, but it wasn't possible for it to come apart, for him to extricate himself.

(16) Naʔ óhniʔ thóha ęhųwadiyenáʔ.

naʔ	ohniʔ	thohah	ę-hųwadi-yena-ʔ'
ASRT	ADD	DGR	FUT-3NSG > 3M.SG-catch-PNC
it's	also	almost	they will catch him

And they were about to catch him.

(17) Dahadadehsʔáhdaʔ, waʔtháhjyaęʔ, haʔnųdiʔgé hé·ʔtgę hwaʔthęnaʔsgwáhgwaʔ.

d-a-h-adade-hsʔ-ahd-aʔ	waʔ-t-h-ahjyaR-ęʔ	ha-ʔnųd-iʔ = ge
CIS-FACT-3M.SG.A-REF-take.all-CS-PNC	FACT-DL-3M.SG.A-push-PNC	3M.SG.A-leg-NSF = LOC
he did his best	he pushed	his leg(s)

heʔtgę	h-waʔ-t-h-ęnaʔsgwahgw-aʔ
LOC	TRNS-FACT-DL-3M.SG.A-jump.up-PNC
up	he jumped up

He pushed with his legs as hard as he could [and] jumped up.

(18) Onę, waʔhagwé·nyaʔ, sahadnųʔwá·gwaihcyaʔ.

onę	waʔ-ha-gweny-aʔ	s-a-h-ad-nųʔwaR-a-gwaihcy-aʔ
TMP	FACT-3M.SG.A-can.do-PNC	REP-FACT-3M.SG.A-SRF-head-JN-straighten-PNC
then	he could do it	he straighten out his head again

Then he was able to straighten up his head again.

(19) Osnó·weʔ waʔhadékhwaʔ.

o-snowe-ʔ	waʔ-h-adekhw-aʔ
3N/Z.SG.P-fast-STV	FACT-3M.SG.A-escape-PNC
it is fast	he escaped

Quickly, he escaped.

(20) Waʔtháæhdat, tshaʔ nigę waʔhatshęhdaʔ.

waʔ-t-h-aæhdat-Ø	tshaʔ	nigę	waʔ-h-atshęhd-aʔ
FACT-DL-3M.SG.A-run-PNC	SUB	EXT	FACT-3M.SG.A-get.exhausted-PNC
he ran	that	extent	he got exhausted

He ran until he was exhausted.

(21) Oné, waʔthadáʔnhaʔ, ganyadá·kdaʔ, tshaʔ nú· ęshahné·gihæʔ.

onę	waʔ-t-ha-daʔ-nhaʔ	ga-nyadaR-akd-aʔ	tshaʔ	nų
TMP	FACT-DL-3M.SG.A-stop-PNC	3N/Z.SG.A-lake-near-PNC	SUB	LOC
then	he stopped	near the lake	that	place

ę-s-ha-hnegihR-aʔ
FUT-REP-3M.SG.A-drink-PNC
he will drink again

Then he stopped near the lake, at the place where he could drink again.

(22) Sahadatgęʔé, hya deʔshonaʔgáe·daʔ.

s-a-h-adat-gę-ʔ = ʔé	hya	deʔ-s-ho-naʔgaR-od-aʔ
REP-FACT-3M.SG.A-REF-see-PNC = REP	NEG	NEG-REP-3M.SG.P-antlers-have-STV
he saw himself again	not	he didn't have antlers

He saw himself again [and] he didn't have antlers anymore.

(23) "O· ya naʔ stęʔ, dętgųdodyágaʔ náʔ, neʔ agnáʔga·ʔ."

o·	hya	naʔ	stęʔ	d-ę-t-gų-adodyag-aʔ	naʔ	neʔ
EXC	NEG	ASRT	INDF	DL-FUT-CIS-3FZ.PL.A-grow-PNC	ASRT	NOM
oh	not	it's	something	they will grow again	it's	the

ag-naʔgaR-aʔ
1SG.P-antlers-NSF
my antlers

"Oh, that's nothing, my antlers will grow again."

(24) Naʔ gó·ʔ waʔhonaʔdúhas, tshaʔ neʔ haʔnųdíʔge, gwás tgahwísheʔ, naʔ óhniʔ gwas nithatʔnųdí·yoʔs.

naʔ	go·ʔ	waʔ-ho-naʔdų-has-Ø	tshaʔ	neʔ	ha-ʔnųd-iʔ = ge	gwas
ASRT	CTR	FACT-3M.SG.P-show-BEN-PNC	SUB	NOM	3M.SG.A-leg-NSF = LOC	INTS
it's	however	it showed him	that	the	his legs	very

t-ga-hwishe-ʔ	naʔ	ohniʔ	gwas	ni-t-h-at-ʔnųd-iyo-ʔs
CIS-3N/Z.SG.A-strong-STV	ASRT	ADD	INTS	PRT-CIS-3M.SG.A-SRF-legs-good-PL
it is strongest	it's	also	very	his legs are fine

But this is what shows him that his legs are really the strongest [part of him], and also that he has really fine legs.

Appendix 2: Alphabetical List of Particles

Form	Frequent Speaker Glosses
agwé·gih	*all*
áhgwih	*don't [do it]*
ahsé·de	*yesterday*
ahsę́·nų / tshaʔdewahsę́·nų	*in the middle, half way between*
áhsę	*three*
áhsų, hya áhsų	*still, yet, not yet*
ahsų́he	*at night*
áhyaʔk	*six*
ákdaʔ / akdáʔa	*elsewhere, away; near close by, next to*
akdų́·dyeʔ	*close by [along]*
anųk / nųk	*for example*
asdé (hagwá)[1]	*outdoors*
aųgóhdih / ęgóhdih	*too much, overly*
há·dye(ʔ)	*never mind, let it go; even though*
awét	*about, like, it's possible, possibly, it seems*
awetʔáh	*it's make-believe*
awę·há·dyeʔ/há·dye(k)	*never mind, let it go*
awę́ʔge	*on the surface of water*
ayę́·æʔ/ayeęʔ/ayę́·ʔ/ayǽ·ʔ	*could be, it seems like, it's like*
dá·jya	*quickly*
dah / dá·ne	*so, subsequently*
daʔjíhwaʔ/ daʔjihwaʔáh	*immediately, a short while, right away*
dé·gę̨ʔ	*eight*
degáęh / degáęʔ / gá·ę̱ʔ	*intervals of time; often, rarely*
dégni	*two*
dejyáęh[2]	*both*
dę́ʔgih	*more, exceedingly, too much*
dę́ʔseʔ / dę́hseʔ	*and*
diʔ	*so, moreover, and so, besides* [linked topic in discourse]
do· / doh	*how; what if*
do·ga·ʔ / dó·gaʔ / do ga(·)ʔ	*both*

---

[1] Parentheses () enclose segments that are optionally pronounced; slashes (/) separate pronunciations by different speakers or accepted alternants.

[2] Hewitt spells this particle dedjyáų̈h.

Form	Frequent Speaker Glosses
doga?áh	*a few, several*
dó·gęs / dógę /dogę́h	*for sure, it's true, truly*
dyawę́?ih	*continually*
dyę́(ha?) gwa? /ędyę́ha?/dyę́	*perhaps, maybe; about; in case; if*
dyótgųt	*continually, all the time, constantly, always*
ę·	*I think (Hewitt)*
e·?/e?/he?/heh	*yet again, in turn, do again, repeated event*
ę(?)	*ah, eh*
ędiyó?ge	*daytime, by day*
ęh/ah/a·	*ah, eh*
ęk	*maybe*
ęyó?ga·k	*tonight*
gá·jyah	*come here!*
ga(·)? / ga? gwa? / gaę gwa?	*about, approximately; some/ any, several*
gadę́? / gadé? / ga·dę?	*or, alternatively; maybe*
gae / gaę + classifier	*when; where; how; which*
gáe? / gá·e?	*less [time / amount / space]*
gae?geh [> gae? + geh]	*hurry up!*
gahe·?	*'teens' marker*
ganę́h [> gaę nę]	*where*
ganų́k hagwa	*on the inner side*
ga(ę)nyó?/ ga·nyó	*whatever; whenever; wherever*
gátga?	*somewhere; anywhere*
gayé·ih	*four*
ga(·)?	*about, approximately; some, any, several*
ga? gwa?	*just about*
ga? gwa? nų	*some place; in the vicinity*
ga?t / doga?t / do ga?t	*if; whether; how; perhaps.*
gęhjíhwęh	*probably; apparently*
gęs	*customarily; usually*
gę́?jik	*eventually; in a while*
gi?	*well!*
gí?shę	*perhaps; alternatively; instead*
gó(·)? / na? gó(·)?	*but, however; actually*
gųdá·dye? / ogų́dá·dye?	*at once, right away*
gųdáhgwih / gųda?	*always, continually*
gų́·da? [>tga·gų́·da?]	*necessarily; it has to be; it's a must*
gwahsų́·de?	*last night*
gwas (ų)wé	*very much; a regular X; the real way*
gwas / ágwas	*just so; very, really, exactly, exceedingly*
gwas nę	*several*
gwas né?tho	*that's right!*
gwas o?	*even, because*
gwas tsha? niyų́	*every*
gwas ga? gwa?gó·na	*it's no use*
gwa? / gę́ gwa?	*just; only, merely; by a narrow margin*

Form	Frequent Speaker Glosses
há·dye(k)/awę·há·dyeʔ	*never mind, let it go*
há·gęh	*be an amount in space*
hagwá(di) / ęhagwa	*direction* [directional classifier]
háhsaʔ	*right away; as soon as; until.*
hányoʔ	*Alright! Get going! Come on! Get with it!*
hátsgwih	*well! OK*
haųʔ / haųʔ giʔ sáʔ	*let's go; come on*
haʔ diʔ	*come on! get going!*
haʔdé·yųh	*everything*
haʔgų́·wa	*under, below; down deep, on the ocean floor*
hęę́ / hę́·	*yes*
hehdáʔge	*low; down, on the ground, downstairs*
hehdaʔgehá	*very low*
hesgęháh	*be the last one; the last time*
heyóheʔ	*more, exceedingly*
héʔtgę	*up above*
hó· ʔé·	*Oh my!*
hot / ot	*what; why*
hų / ų	*probably, presumably*
hwę́·dų / wę́·dų³	*when; whenever*
hwiks	*five*
hya / híya/ ya	*not*
(h)yá gęk	*it shouldn't be*
hyá·eʔ	*meanwhile; for a while*
hyaʔ / hí·hyaʔ	*indeed, verily, truly*
í·nų	*far; over there*
igę́h⁴	*it is so; it is*
íhswaʔ	*a lot*
is / nis⁵	*you; you all*
iʔ / niʔ⁶	*I; we*
íʔgeh	*toward me; to me*
jíhwaʔ⁷	*extremely*
jík / swáʔjik	*excessively; very; too*
jyá·dak	*seven*
khę	*marks clause as question*
náyeʔ / naʔ⁸	*it's; that's it*

[3] *hwędų* and *ahsų* can take over the function of *hya* with negative verbs.

[4] Inflected form of the base -i-/-yaʔdi- 'be, exist, make up the total of'.

[5] The alternant *nis* may consists of neʔ + is.

[6] The alternant *niʔ* may consists of neʔ + iʔ

[7] 6N dialect. Note that -jihw-/-sjihw- is a verbal suffix with the meaning 'at once, suddenly, intensely'.

[8] As late as 1912 the assertion particle *nayeʔ* is attested as distributionally distinct from *naʔ* with different but related meanings. *Nayeʔ* occurred utterance-initially, *naʔ* preceding a nominal expression utterance-internally. In the League text (Woodbury et. al, 1992) *nayeʔ* is identified as DEC (declarative particle) and *naʔ* as CONTR (contrastive particle). At some time after 1912, with only very

Form	Frequent Speaker Glosses
naʔ dyóihwaʔ	*it's the reason why*
naʔ gányaʔ, naʔ ga·nyáhaʔ	*it's the reason why*
naʔ hí·hyaʔ	*that's right*
naʔ néʔ [non-initially]	*focus: this is what; this (other) one*
nę gwaʔ	*little bit*
nę néʔ	*this (other)* [contrastive]
nę́·gę	*this* [proximal demonstrative]
nę́·gęha	*this specific one; this only; this little one*
nęgę́ (ų́hgęʔ) ędá·deʔ	*today*
nęgę́ ų́hgęʔ / nęgyų́hgęʔ	*at this time; right now*
nę	presentational particle
neʔ	*the; it* [nominal particle]
neʔ thóhge	*at that time*
néʔtho / tho	*there;* [distance neutral locative deictic].
néʔtho / tho[9]	*thus; how; that's how [it is]* [manner particle]
ní·waʔ	*its size*
ní·yot	*how it is* [manner classifier]
nigę́	*extent of time / space / amount; until* [extent classifier]
nigęhę́·ʔ	*exceedingly*
nigeʔ / nigęʔ	*instead; could be*
niyawę́haʔ / niyá·wę	*thank you; goodbye*
niyohų	*little bit*
n(i)yų́h	*[how] much; amount* [amount classifier]
niʔá	*I, exclusively; I alone*
nų́·we / nų́	*place* [locative classifier]
(n)wa·hóʔdęʔ / (n)wadęʔ	*what; what kind*
nyóh / nyóʔ	*so be it*
ó·dyaʔk	*some*
o·hę́ʔsę·k	*daily*
ó·nę	*now, then, when* [proximal temporal deictic]
ó·wæs	*for sure*
odyaʔkshų́ʔa	*some (pl)*
óhniʔ / óʔ	*also, (that) too, likewise*
oihwí·yoʔ	*surely, really, the truth, for sure*
onę́ go·ʔ / onę go·ʔ hyá·eʔ	*good-bye*
onę...neʔ (o)nę...	*when...then...*
osthwihá / sthwihá[10]	*a little bit; just barely,*
oʔga·sʔáh	*[in the] evening*
saʔ[11]	*OK; tag*

few exceptions (usually in clause-final position), the two have merged, retaining their related – but now only distributionally identifiable – meanings, both occurring as *naʔ*. In this work *naʔ*, has uniformly been marked ASRT (assertion particle).

[9] followed by a verb inflected with the partitive prepronominal prefix.

[10] Derived from -sthw- v.s. *be less, be smaller.*

[11] Seneca *saʔ* is a diminutive particle (Seneca Dictionary #1511)

Form	Frequent Speaker Glosses
sa? se? khę	*you realize, don't you*
sdahǽ?ih	*eventually; finally*
sdę?	*something; anything*
se?	*actually; in fact*
se? khę	*you know?* [tag]
sgádah	*one*
sgę́·nų?áh	*slowly; peacefully*
sgęhá·dih	*other side*
shę́hgeh	*barely; hardly; only just*
sígę/sí	*over there; yonder; distal deictic*
sí nigáę	*once in a while*
sų́·	*who*
sų́·ga? / sų ga·? / sų	*someone; anyone*
swadyé·ęh (gęs)	*sometimes; ...at a time; once in a while*
tcihahsa?	*at first*
tcihę?gę́hjik / nęgę́ tcihę?gę́hjik	*this morning*
tgę́?i	*more* [comparative particle]
tho go·? hya?	*of course*
tho gwa? tho niyót	*it's the same way; it's the way (that...)*
tho nęshų?	*this area; this vicinity*
tho sgęháh / dosgęháh [Hewitt]	*nearer; nearby; a short distance*
thó·gę	*that one, that thing* [distal demonstrative]
thogę́ha	*that specific one; that only*
thó·nę / tho	*here* [proximal locative deictic]
thóha	*almost, nearly, just about; soon*
thohge nų nigahá·wi?	*at that time*
thóhge	*then; later* [distal temporal deictic]
tsha?	*that, what, which, as, how* [subordinating particle]
tsha? gá·yę?	*the one that* [relativizer]
tsha? ųníshe? / tsha? nwa?ųníshe?	*at the time that, while*
tshe? gwa?	*already*
ų́·gye	*indoors*
ų́·weh / ųwé	*typically, really, exactly; only*
ų́hdeh	*extremely; exaggeratedly*
ų́hgę? / ų́hgęh	*next (in turn), at present, presently*
ųnís?ih / nwa?ųníshe?	*long time (ago), at the time that*
washę́h	*ten*
wá?dę·h	*nine*
wa?jik?á /gwajik?á	*nearly, almost;*
wé / wéso? (Hewitt)[12]	*a lot, many times*
yágę?	*it is said; so they say* [hearsay particle]

---

[12] cf. Mohawk é·so? *much*

References

Abbott, Clifford. 1981. Here and There in Oneida. *International Journal of American Linguistics* 47. 50–57.

Abbott, Clifford. 1984. Two Feminine Genders in Oneida. *Anthropological Linguistics* 26. 125–37.

Abbott, Clifford. 2000. *Oneida.* (Languages of the World/Materials 301). München: Lincom Europa.

Abbott, Clifford. 2006. *Oneida Teaching Grammar.* (http://uwgb.edu Oneida/ Grammar.html).

Abbott, Clifford (ed.), with Christjohn, Amos & Hinton, Maria. 1996. *An Oneida Dictionary: Ukwehu·wehneha Tekawęnate?nyése.* Oneida, WI: Oneida Tribe of Indians of Wisconsin.

Abrams, Percy. 2006. *Onondaga Pronominal Prefixes.* Buffalo: State University of New York at Buffalo. (Doctoral Dissertation.)

Baker, Mark C. 1996. *The Polysynthesis Parameter.* Oxford: Oxford University Press.

Barrie, Michael. 2015. *A Grammar of Onondaga.* (Languages of the World/Materials 503). München: Lincom GmbH.

Blau, Harold & Campisi, Jack & Tooker, Elisabeth. 1978. Onondaga. In Trigger, Bruce G. (ed.), *Handbook of North American Indians,* vol. 17, *Northeast,* 491–499. Washington: Smithsonian Institution.

Barbeau, Marius. (1915). *Classification of Iroquoian Radicals with Subjective Pronominal Prefixes.* (Canada Department of Mines, Geological Survey. Memoir 46). Ottawa: Government Printing Bureau.

Boas, Franz. (1909). Notes on the Iroquois Language. In Boas, Franz (ed.), *Putnam Anniversary Volume: Anthropological Essays Presented to F. W. Putnam,* 427–60. New York: Stechert.

Boersma, Paul & Weenink, David. (2015). *Praat: Doing Phonetics by Computer* (Computer program Version 6.0.08).

Bradley, James. Forthcoming. *Onondaga and Empire: An Iroquoian People in an Imperial Era, 1650 to 1701.*

Chafe, Wallace. 1967. *Seneca Morphology and Dictionary.* (Smithsonian Contributions to Anthropology, 4). Washington, D.C.: Smithsonian Press.

Chafe, Wallace. 1970. *A Semantically Based Sketch of Onondaga.* (Indiana University Publications in Anthropology and Linguistics. Memoir 25. Supplement to the International Journal of American Linguistics 36.2.) Chicago: University of Chicago Press.

Chafe, Wallace. 1977a. Accent and Related Phenomena in the Five Nations Iroquois languages. In Hyman, L.M. (ed.), *Studies in Stress and Accent*, 169–81. (Southern California Occasional Papers in Linguistics 4).

Chafe, Wallace. 1977b. The Evolution of Third Person Verb Agreement in the Iroquoian Languages. In Li, Charles N. (ed.), *Mechanisms of Syntactic Change*, 493–524. Austin: University of Texas Press.

Chafe, Wallace. 1980. Consequential Verbs in the Northern Iroquoian Languages and Elsewhere. In Klar, Kathryn & Langdon, Margaret & Silver, Shirley (eds.), *American Indian and Indoeuropean Studies: Papers in Honor of Madison S. Beeler*, 43–49. The Hague: Mouton.

Chafe, Wallace. 1994. *Discourse, Consciousness, and Time*. Chicago: The University of Chicago Press.

Chafe, Wallace. 1996. Sketch of Seneca, an Iroquoian Language. In Goddard, Ives (ed.), *Handbook of North American Indians*, vol. 1, *Languages*, 551– 579. Washington: Smithsonian Institution.

Chafe, Wallace. 2012a. Are Adjectives Universal? The Case of Northern Iroquoian. *Linguistic Typology* 16. 1–39.

Chafe, Wallace. 2012b. The Seneca Amplification Construction. *Linguistic Discovery* 10. 27–41.

Chafe, Wallace. 2015. *A Grammar of the Seneca Language*. (University of California Publications in Linguistics, vol. 149). Oakland: University of California Press.

Chafe, Wallace & Foster, Michael. 1981. Prehistoric Divergences and Recontacts between Cayuga and the Other Northern Iroquoian Languages. *International Journal of American Linguistics* 47. 121–142.

Diessel, Holger. 1999. *Demonstratives: Form, Function, and Grammaticalization*. (Typological Studies in Language 42). Amsterdam: John Benjamins.

Dixon, R. M. W. 2010–2012. *Basic Linguistic Theory* (3 volumes). Oxford: Oxford University Press.

Dyck, Carrie. 1997. Accent and Lengthening in Cayuga (Iroquoian). *Canadian Journal of Linguistics* 42. 285–322. (=MS 12/14/2002. Cayuga accent: a synchronic analysis.)

Foster, Michael K. 1982. Alternating Weak and Strong Syllables in Cayuga Words. *International Journal of American Linguistics* 48. 59–72.

Froman, Frances & Keye, Alfred & Keye, Lottie & Dyck, Carrie. 2002. *English-Cayuga Cayuga-English Dictionary*. Toronto: University of Toronto Press.

Grimm, Cory. 1997. *The Phonetic Realization of Pitch Accent in the Ontario Dialect of Oneida*. Buffalo: University at Buffalo. (MA Thesis.)

Goldenweiser, Alexander. 1912. *Kanyhsyyníkeha?*. Archives of the Canadian Museum of Civilization, Ms. 1252.5. Toronto.

Hale, Horatio. 1883. *Iroquois Book of Rites*. Brinton Library of Aboriginal American Literature 2. Philadelphia: D. G. Brinton. (Reprinted 1963 with an introduction by William Fenton. Toronto: University of Toronto Press.)

Hale, Kenneth. 1983. Warlpiri and the Grammar of Non-Configurational Languages. *Natural Language and Linguistic Theory* 1. 5–47.

Hayes, Bruce. 1955. *Metrical Stress Theory, Principles and Case Studies*. Chicago: University of Chicago Press.

Heckewelder, J. 1820. *A Narrative of the Mission of the United Brethren among the Delaware and Mohegan Indians from Its Commencement in the Year 1740 to the Close of the Year 1808*. (Reprinted by Arno Press 1971. Philadelphia: Arno.)

Hewitt, John Napoleon Brinton. 1903. Iroquoian Cosmology (Part 1). *Annual Report for the Bureau of American Ethnology for the Years* 1899–1900, vol. 21. 127–339.

Hewitt, John Napoleon Brinton. 1928. Iroquoian Cosmology (Part 2), *Annual Report for the Bureau of American Ethnology for the Years* 1925–1926, vol. 43. 449–819.

Horsford, Eben Norton (ed.). 1887. *Zeisberger's Indian Dictionary*. Cambridge: John Wilson and Son.

Koenig, Jean-Pierre & Michelson, Karin. 2009. *The Structure of Nominal Expressions in Oneida*. (Paper presented at the 2009 Annual Meeting of the Society for the Study of Indigenous Languages of the Americas, San Francisco, CA.)

Koenig, Jean-Pierre & Michelson, Karin. 2010a. *The Semantics of Pronominal Affixes in Iroquoian*.

Koenig, Jean-Pierre & Michelson, Karin. 2010b. Argument Structure of Oneida Kinship Terms. *International Journal of American Linguistics* 76. 169–205.

Koenig, Jean-Pierre & Michelson, Karin. 2010c. *How to Quantify over Entities in Iroquoian (Oneida)*. (Paper presented at the 2010 Annual Meeting of the Society for the Study of Indigenous Languages of the Americas, Baltimore, Maryland.)

Koenig, Jean-Pierre & Michelson, Karin. 2011. *Issues in the Syntax, Morphology, and Semantics of Oneida (Iroquoian)*. (Course notes for a course taught at the 2011 Summer Institute of Linguistics.)

Koenig, Jean-Pierre & Michelson, Karin. 2012. The (Non)universality of Syntactic Selection and Functional Application. In Christopher Piñón (ed.), *Empirical Studies in Syntax and Semantics*, vol. 9, 185–205. Paris: Centre National de la Recherche Scientifique.

Koenig, Jean-Pierre & Michelson, Karin. 2013. *Counting Nouns is Not Always the Right Question: The Relative Frequencies of Nouns, Pronouns, and Verbs in Discourse*. (Paper presented at the international workshop on the relative frequencies of nouns, pronouns, and verbs in discourse. Max Planck Institute for Evolutionary Anthropology. Leipzig, Germany.)

Koenig, Jean-Pierre & Michelson, Karin. 2014. Deconstructing Syntax. In Müller, Stefan (ed.), *Proceedings of the 21st International Conference on Head-Driven Phrase Structure Grammar*, CSLI Publications, 114–134. (http://csli-publications. stanford.edu/ HPSG/2014). Buffalo: University at Buffalo.

Koenig, Jean-Pierre & Michelson, Karin. 2015a. Invariance in Argument Realization: The Case of Iroquoian. *Language* 91. 1–47.

Koenig, Jean-Pierre & Michelson, Karin. 1915. Morphological Complexity à la Oneida. In Baerman, Matthew & Brown, Dunstand & Corbett, Greville (eds.), *Understanding and Measuring Morphological Complexity*, 69–92. Oxford: Oxford University Press.

Koenig, Jean-Pierre & Michelson, Karin. 2016. *Two Kinds of Lexical Categories in Oneida*. (Manuscript)

Lehnert-LeHouillier, Heike. 2006. *An Acoustic Analysis of the Separation of Pitch and Stress in Onondaga*. (Paper presented at the 31st Meeting of the Berkeley Linguistics Society, Berkeley, CA.)

Liberman, Mark. 1975. *The Intonational System of English*. Cambridge: Massachusetts Institute of Technology. (Doctoral Dissertation.)

Liberman, Mark & Prince, Alan. 1977. On Stress and Linguistic Rhythm. *Linguistic Inquiry* 8. 249–336.

Lounsbury, Floyd Glenn. 1953. *Oneida Verb Morphology.* (Yale University Publications in Anthropology 48.) New Haven: Yale University Press.

Lounsbury, Floyd Glenn. 1964. The Structural Analysis of Kinship Semantics. In Lunt, H. G. (ed.), *Proceeding of the Ninth International Congress of Linguists,* 1073–1089.

Lounsbury, Floyd Glenn 1978. Iroquoian Languages. In Trigger, Bruce G. (ed.), *Handbook of North American Indians,* vol. 15, *Languages,* 334–343. Washington: Smithsonian Institution.

Melinger, Alissa. 2002. Foot Structure and Accent in Seneca. *International Journal of American Linguistics* 68. 287–315.

Michelson, Karin. 1981. Stress, Epenthesis, and Syllable Structure in Mohawk. In Clemens, G.N. (ed.), *Harvard Studies in Phonology* II, 311–353. Bloomington: Indiana University Linguistics Club.

Michelson, Karin. 1983. *A Comparative Study of Accent in the Five Nations Iroquoian Languages.* Cambridge: Harvard University. (Doctoral Dissertation.)

Michelson, Karin. 1986. Ghost r's in Onondaga: An Autosegmental Analysis of *r-stems. In Wetzels, Leo & Sezer, Engin (eds.), *Studies in Compensatory Lengthening,* 147–166. (Language Sciences 23). Dordrecht: Foris Publications.

Michelson, Karin. 1988. *A Comparative Study of Lake-Iroquoian Accent.* Dordrecht: Kluwer Academic Publishers.

Michelson, Karin. 1989. Invisibility: Vowels without a Timing Slot in Mohawk. In Gertz, Donna & Michelson, Karin (eds.), *Theoretical Perspectives on Native American Languages,* 38–69. New York: SUNY Press.

Michelson, Karin. 1991. Semantic Features of Agent and Patient Core Case Marking in Oneida. In Van Valin, Robert (ed.), *Buffalo Papers in Linguistics,* 91–101. Buffalo: Department of Linguistics. SUNY Buffalo.

Michelson, Karin. 1995. *Aspect Inflections of Oneida Manner-of-Motion Verbs.* (Manuscript)

Michelson, Karin. 2011. *Oneida Noun Incorporation.* (Paper presented at the XIth Iroquoian Linguistic Workshop.)

Michelson, Karin & Doxtator, Mercy. 2002. *Oneida-English/English-Oneida Dictionary.* Toronto: University of Toronto Press.

Michelson, Karin & Kennedy, Norma & Doxtator, Mercy. 2016. *Glimpses of Oneida Life.* University of Toronto Press.

Mithun, Marianne. 1980. Northern Iroquoian Dating Strategy. In Bonvillaine, Nancy (ed.), *Studies in Iroquoian Culture* (Occasional Publications in Northeastern Anthropology No.6), 131–146.

Mithun, Marianne.1984. On the Nature of Noun Incorporation. *Language* 60. 847–894.

Mithun, Marianne. 1987. Is Basic Word Order Universal? In Tomlin, Russel (ed.), Coherence and Grounding in Discourse. *Typological Studies in Language* 11. 281–328. Amsterdam: John Benjamins.

Mithun, Marianne. 1991. Active/Agentive Case Marking and its Motivations. *Language* 67. 510–546.

Mithun, Marianne. 1992. *Status of Adjectives in Iroquoian Languages.* (Paper presented at the 1992 Conference on Iroquoian Research.)

Mithun, Marianne. 1999. *The Languages of Native North America.* Cambridge: Cambridge University Press.

Mithun, Marianne. 2000. Noun and Verb in Iroquoian Languages. In Comrie, Bernard & Vogel, Petra (eds.), *An Anthology of Word Classes,* 379–420. Berlin: Mouton de Gruyter.

Mithun, Marianne, 2001. Lexical Forces Shaping the Evolution of Grammar. In Brinton, Laurel J. (ed.), *Historical Linguistics 1999,* 241–252. Amsterdam: John Benjamins.

Mithun, Marianne, 2002. Understanding and Explaining Applicatives. In Andronis, Mary & Ball, Christopher & Elston, Heidi & Neuvel, Sylvain (eds.), *Functionalism and Formalism in Linguistic Theory,* 73–98. (Proceedings of the Thirty-Seventh Meeting of the Chicago Linguistic Society). Chicago: Chicago Linguistic Society.

Mithun, Marianne. 2010a. The Search for Regularity in Irregularity: Defectiveness and Its Implications for Our Knowledge of Words. In Baerman, Mathew & Corbett, Greville & Brown, Dunstan (eds.), *Defective Paradigms: Missing Forms and What They Tell Us,* 125–149. Oxford: British Academy and Oxford University Press.

Mithun, Marianne. 2010b. The Fluidity of Recursion and Its Implications. In van der Hulst, Harry (ed.), *Recursion and Human Language,* 17–41. Berlin: Mouton de Gruyter.

Mithun, Marianne. (2016). Modality and Mood in Iroquoian. In Nuyts, Jan & van der Auwera, Johan (eds.), *Oxford Handbook of Modality and Mood,* 223–257. Oxford: Oxford University Press.

Mithun, Marianne & Corbett, Greville. 1999. The Effect of Noun Incorporation on Argument Structure. In Mereu, Lunella (ed.). *Current Issues in Linguistic Theory,* 49–72. Amsterdam: John Benjamins.

Mithun, Marianne & Woodbury, Hanni (eds.). 1980. *Northern Iroquoian Texts.* (International Journal of American Linguistics, Native American Texts Series. Monograph 4). Chicago: University of Chicago Press.

Morgan, Lewis Henry. 1871. *Systems of Consanguinity and Affinity of the Human Family.* Washington: Smithsonian Institution.

Nichols, Johanna. 1986. Head-Marking and Dependent-Marking Grammar. *Language* 62. 56–119.

Pierrehumbert, Janet. 1979. The Perception of Fundamental Frequency Declination. *Journal of the Acoustic Society of America* 79. 363–369.

Prince, Alan. 1983. Relating to the Grid. *Linguistic Inquiry* 14. 19–100.

Rudes, Blair A. 1999. Tuscarora-English/English-Tuscarora Dictionary. Toronto: University of Toronto Press.

Shea, John Gilmary (ed.). 1860. *A French-Onondaga Dictionary, from a Manuscript of the Seventeenth Century.* New York: Cramoisy Press.

Woodbury, Hanni. 1975. *Noun Incorporation in Onondaga.* New Haven: Yale University. (Doctoral dissertation.)

Woodbury, Hanni. 1981. The Loss of a Phoneme. *International Journal of American Linguistics* 47. 103–120.

Woodbury, Hanni. 1993 *Dislocatives, Purposives, and Modals: Where's the Action?* (Paper presented at the 1993 Conference on Iroquoian Research).

Woodbury, Hanni. 2003. *Onondaga-English/English-Onondaga Dictionary.* Toronto: University of Toronto Press.

Woodbury, Hanni (ed.), with Henry, Reg & Webster, Harry. 1992. *Concerning the League: The Iroquois League Tradition as Dictated in Onondaga by John Arthur Gibson.* (Algonquian and Iroquoian Linguistics Memoir 9). Winnipeg: University of Manitoba Department of Linguistics.

Woodbury, Hanni & Webster, Harry. 1980a. The Snowsnake: How to Make It. In Mithun, M. & Woodbury, Hanni (eds.), *Northern Iroquoian Texts*, 134–138. (International Journal of American Linguistics, Native American Texts Series Monograph 4). Chicago: University of Chicago Press.

Woodbury, Hanni, & Webster, Harry. 1980b. The Snowsnake Game: How to Play It. In Mithun, M., & Woodbury, Hanni (eds.), *Northern Iroquoian Texts*, 139–142. (International Journal of American Linguistics, Native American Texts Series Monograph 4). Chicago: University of Chicago Press.

Woodbury, Hanni, & Harry Webster. 1980c. The Dog. In Mithun, M., & Woodbury, Hanni (eds.), *Northern Iroquoian Texts*, 158–160. (International Journal of American Linguistics, Native American Texts Series Monograph 4). Chicago: University of Chicago Press.

Zeisberger, David, 1887 [1760]. *Zeisberger's Indian Dictionary; English, German, Iroquois – The Onondaga and Algonquin – The Delaware.* Cambridge: John Wilson & Son.

Zeisberger, David. 1887a. *Vocabularies.* From the Collection of Manuscripts Presented by Judge Lane to Harvard University, Nos. 1 and 2. Printed for the Alcove of American Native Languages in Wellesley College Library, by E. N. Horsford. Cambridge: John Wilson & Son.

Zeisberger, David. 1887–1888. Essay of an Onondaga Grammar, or a Short Introduction to Learn the Onondaga al. Maqua Tongue. *Pennsylvania Magazine of History and Biography* 11. 442–453; 12.65–75; 233–239; 325–340.

Stories by Onondaga Speakers cited in the text examples:

Stories by Nora Carrier: NC01 The Chicken Coop; NC02 The Longlegged Deer.
Stories by Lucenda George: LG01 *Locusts*; LG 02 *Clifford's Garden*; LG 03 *Wintertime*; LG 04 *The Dam*; LG 05 *The Funeral Yesterday*; LG 06 *Gypsies*; LG 07 *Missionary*; LG 08 *About Dorothy*; LG 09 *Murder*; LG 10 *Running a Taxi*; LG 11 *Old and New Times*; LG 12 *Hottest Summer*; LG13 *Work in the Gear Factory*; LG14 *Work in the Knitting Mill*; LG15 *Job Opportunities*; LG16 *The Old House*; LG17 *The Onondaga-Oneida Couple*; LG18 *Dead Feast*; LG19 *Onondaga Nation Property*; LG20 *Smallpox*; LG21 *Indian Clothes*; LG22 *Falling into the Water Barrell*; LG23 *Riding a Horse*; LG24 *Our Pets*.
Story by Pat Johnson: PJ01 *Onondaga Lake*.
Story by Jay Meacham: JM03 *Gwaʔyęʔashųʔá 'Rabbits'*.
Stories by Harry Webster: HW01 *About Harry and Lotte*; HW02 *Father Goes on a Trip*; HW03 *How to Make a Snowsnake*; HW04 *How to Play the Snowsnake Game*; HW05 *The Dog*; HW06 *Tall Corn*; HW07 *Thahsó·gwęh's Story*.

Index